Arthur John Maclean

Grammar of the Dialects of Vernacular Synac

as Spoken by the Eastern Syrians of Kurdistan

Arthur John Maclean

Grammar of the Dialects of Vernacular Synac
as Spoken by the Eastern Syrians of Kurdistan

ISBN/EAN: 9783337245702

Printed in Europe, USA, Canada, Australia, Japan

Cover: Foto ©Paul-Georg Meister /pixelio.de

More available books at **www.hansebooks.com**

GRAMMAR

OF THE DIALECTS OF

VERNACULAR SYRIAC.

London: C. J. CLAY AND SONS,
CAMBRIDGE UNIVERSITY PRESS WAREHOUSE,
AVE MARIA LANE.
GLASGOW: 263, ARGYLE STREET.

LEIPZIG: F. A. BROCKHAUS.
NEW YORK: MACMILLAN AND CO.

GRAMMAR

OF THE DIALECTS OF

VERNACULAR SYRIAC

AS SPOKEN BY THE EASTERN SYRIANS OF
KURDISTAN, NORTH-WEST PERSIA, AND
THE PLAIN OF MOSUL

WITH NOTICES OF THE VERNACULAR OF THE JEWS OF
AZERBAIJAN AND OF ZAKHU NEAR MOSUL

BY

ARTHUR JOHN MACLEAN, M.A., F.R.G.S.,

DEAN OF ARGYLL AND THE ISLES,
SOMETIME HEAD OF THE ARCHBISHOP OF CANTERBURY'S MISSION TO THE EASTERN SYRIANS.

CAMBRIDGE:
AT THE UNIVERSITY PRESS.
1895

Cambridge:

PRINTED BY J. AND C. F. CLAY,
AT THE UNIVERSITY PRESS.

CONTENTS.

SECTION			PAGE
—	Introduction		ix
1.	THE LETTERS.	Consonants	2
2.		Final letters	4
3.		Aspirated letters	4
4.		Notes on the pronunciation of letters	5
5.		Vowels	7
6.		Modification of vowel sounds	10
7.		Diphthongs	11
8.	ACCENT		13
9.	SIGNS		15
10.	PRONOUNS.	Personal	16
11.		Affix forms	18
12.		Demonstrative	20
13.		Interrogative	22
14.		Relative	23
15.		Indefinite	24
16.	SUBSTANTIVES.	States	26
17.		Gender	34
18.		Number	39
19.		Irregular and double plurals	49
20.		With pronominal affixes	54
21.	ADJECTIVES.	Gender	57
22.		Number	59
23.		Position	59
24.		Comparison	61
25.		Miscellaneous notes	61
26.		Cardinal Numerals	64
27.		Ordinal Numerals	67
28.		Various notes on Numerals	69

SECTION			PAGE
29.	VERBS.	Substantive Verb .	74
30.		Conjugations . . .	79
31.		First Conjugation . .	80
32.		Formation of tenses . .	84
33.		Verb used negatively .	88
34.		Passive	89
35.		Second Conjugation, first division	90
36.		,, second division	92
37.		,, third division . . .	94
38.		*Regular Variations.* Verbs with initial letter weak	95
39.		Verbs with middle letter weak .	97
40.		,, .	98
41.		,,	99
42.		Verbs with final letter weak	99
43		,,	103
44		,,	103
45		Causative Verbs . .	106
46.		Irregular Verbs, 1 Conj. .	117
47.		,, 2 Conj. . . .	131
48.		Verbal noun and past participle with affixes	134
49.		Present participle and imperative ,,	134
50.		Preterite ,, .	135
51.		*Use of the tenses.* Tenses derived from present part.	140
52.		Second present . .	143
53.		Imperfect	143
54.		Preterite	143
55.		Perfect	144
56.		Pluperfect .	145
57.		Verbal noun	145
58.		Participles .	146
59.		Imperative .	147
60.		Conditional Sentences .	148
61.		Temporal clauses . . .	148
62.		Absolute hypothetical clauses	150
63.		Impersonal verbs . .	150
64.		Direct object of the verb .	153
65.		Agreement .	154
66.		Oratio obliqua	155
67.	ADVERBS	.	156

CONTENTS.

SECTION			PAGE
68.	PREPOSITIONS.	Simple	169
69.		Compound	175
70.		With affixes	179
71.		After verbs, etc.	182
72.	CONJUNCTIONS		185
73.	INTERJECTIONS		189
74.	POSITION OF WORDS. EMPHASIS. QUESTIONS		192
75.	IDIOMATIC PHRASES		195
76.	DERIVATION.	Nouns of action	215
77.		Agents	223
78.		Abstracts	236
79.		Diminutives	239
80.		Negatives	241
81.		Adjectives	241
82.		Foreign terminations	247
83.		Verbs	251
84.	RULES FOR ASPIRATION		278
85.	VOWELS AND CONSONANTS. *Relation of N.S. to O.S. and of the dialects to one another.* Vowel subtracted		280
86.		Vowel added	281
87.		Pthakha and Zqapa	283
88.		Zlama for Pthakha or Zqapa	286
89.		Rwasa	290
90.		Sound of Rwasa	292
91.		Sound of Pthakha and Zqapa	292
92.		Metathesis	292
93.		Repetition	298
94.		Aspirate added	298
95.		Aspirate removed	300
96.		Alap prosthetic	308
97.		Béith and Pé	309
98.		Gamal silent	310
99.		Gamal and Jamal	311
100.		Jamal	311
101.		Sound of aspirated Gamal	313
102.		Gamal and Zain	313
103.		Dalath silent	313
104.		Dalath and Tau	314
105.		Dalath and Ṭéith	315
106.		Dalath and Béith or Zain	316

SECTION		PAGE
107.	Hé and Khéith	316
108.	Hé silent	317
109.	Wau inserted; Wau and Yudh	319
110.	Zain and Simkath or Ṣadhé, etc.	321
111.	Khéith	322
112.	Yudh and Alap; Yudh inserted or omitted	323
113.	Chap	324
114.	Liquids interchanged; Lamadh silent	327
115.	Mim silent	331
116.	Nun silent	331
117.	Sound of Nun (*a*) final, (*b*) before Béith and Pé	332
118.	ʻE	332
119.	Qop and Kap or Chap	333
120.	Qop and Gamal or Kléith	334
121.	Resh silent, and Resh pronounced as Dalath	334
122.	Shin silent	335
123.	Tau and Ṭéith	335
124.	Tau and Shin or Simkath; Dalath and Zain	338
125.	Sound of Tau	338
126.	Tau silent	339

APPENDIX.

I.	VERNACULAR OF THE AZERBAIJAN JEWS	340
II.	PROVERBS	345

INTRODUCTION.

THE object of the present grammar is to make known the various dialects of the Eastern Syrians (Nestorians or Chaldeans) who inhabit the mountains of Kurdistan, and the plains of Azerbaijan in North-west Persia, and of Mosul in Eastern Turkey. Their country is approximately comprised between 36° and 38° 30′, N. latitude, and 42° and 46°, E. longitude, and lies between Mosul and the Sea of Van, and between the Sea of Urmi (Urmia, Urumi, Urumia) and the Bohtan Su or Eastern Tigris. They live partly in Turkey and partly in Persia; but they are more definitely divided by religion than by political areas, into two portions, the larger of which consists of the adherents of the Patriarch Mar Shimun, the Catholicos of the East, who usually call themselves Syrians, but are better known in Europe by their nickname of Nestorians; and the smaller of which consists of the Roman Catholick Uniats who are usually known as Chaldeans. The former portion live chiefly in the mountains of Kurdistan in Turkey, and the high plains of Azerbaijan in Persia, the latter chiefly in the plain of Mosul in Turkey, though several of them are also found in Persia.

The region defined above was not the original home of the Eastern Syrians. They are all that remains of the Christian Church of the Persian Empire which, claiming to be founded in the first century, had its head-quarters on the Tigris at Seleucia-Ctesiphon, the twin capital of Persia, and thence sent out its missions over the whole of Central Asia. They were driven northwards by successive persecutions, of which the most terrible was that which they suffered at the hands of Tamerlane; and they are now reduced to a mere shadow, numbering probably not more than a hundred thousand souls, whereas at one time they were computed to be more numerous than all the other Christian bodies put together.

Their vernacular has, as far as is known, been until late years an unwritten language. They have long used, and still most commonly use, the classical Syriac (which they call *The Old Language*) in writing as well as for their religious services; indeed only those who have studied in the European missionary schools are able to write the vernacular, which they call *The New Language* or *The Language of Speaking*. In this grammar the terms 'Old' and 'New' Syriac are retained for convenience although they are somewhat of a misnomer, since, as will be seen in the sequel, the vernacular is not probably derived from the classical Syriac, and many forms in the latter are more developed than those which correspond to them in the former. In writing the classical Syriac the Eastern Syrians naturally employ their own character, which is that used in this book, and which resembles the old Estrangéla more than the Western Syrian or Jacobite character. There are also a few differences in pronunciation between the Eastern and Western Syrians in reading the classical language, the former for example saying $â$ where the latter say $ô$; and there are several differences in the grammatical forms. All the quotations from classical Syriac in this book are written in the Eastern Syrian manner.

The first attempt known to the present writer to reduce the vernacular to writing was made in the plain of Mosul in the seventeenth century, when some vernacular poems were written down on the baldest phonetic principles; but the writer shews many inconsistencies, and spells the same word in many different ways. In the last century the liturgical Gospels were written in the vernacular, also phonetically, and without much consistency[1].

But the first serious and scientific attempt to reduce any of these dialects to writing was made in the year 1836 by an American Presbyterian missionary at Urmi, the Rev. Dr Perkins, who translated the Bible into the Urmi vernacular; and this translation was published in 1852 by the American Bible Society in two large quarto volumes in parallel columns with the Pshiṭṭa[2]. The spelling of the

---

[1] The present writer is indebted for the loan of both these manuscripts to the American Presbyterian Missionaries at Urmi.

[2] A new edition of the Bible in the Urmi vernacular in one handsome volume has

classical Syriac, which the people were accustomed to see written, was necessarily taken for all words and forms common to it and the vernacular, and other forms and words were spelt analogously, or else according to the sound. It is a matter for some regret, however, that this work was published at a time when the genesis of the vernacular had been very little investigated, and consequently many misleading spellings were adopted, as for instance the final Alap in the third person singular of the preterite, where the final Hé gives exactly the same sound, and makes the tense intelligible etymologically. In 1856 Mr Stoddard, a colleague of Dr Perkins, published in the fifth volume of the American Oriental Society's journal a grammar of the Urmi dialect[1], which is chiefly useful for its list of the verbs used in that plain; and since then various educational and theological works both in classical and vernacular Syriac have issued from the printing presses of the three missions working among the Eastern Syrians,—all of which have their head-quarters at Urmi, the only large town in the country of the non-Uniat Syrians—the American Presbyterian, the French Roman Catholick (Lazarist), and the Archbishop of Canterbury's Mission. The vernacular works of the first of these follow the lead of Dr Perkins, though his spelling has been very slightly modified; those of the second are largely influenced by the dialect of the plain of Salámas, where many Uniats are found; while those of the third mission, which is of more recent origin, adopt a somewhat more etymological spelling than the others, and aim, while written in the Urmi dialect, at being intelligible to the neighbouring mountaineers of Kurdistan as well as the people of the Azerbaijan plains. This spelling is adopted in this grammar, and reasons for its use are given below.

The writer must express his particular obligations to the very useful *Grammatik der Neusyrischen Sprache* of Professor Nöldeke. This book, which was published in 1868, analyses the dialect of Urmi very fully; but being based on the Mission publications which had appeared before that date, it is necessarily almost entirely confined to that dialect. It has been particularly valuable in suggesting

---

been published by the same Society in 1893. A smaller type is used, and the Pshiṭta is omitted; while references and maps are added.

[1] The present writer has verified orally most of Mr Stoddard's variant grammatical forms. A few are given here on Mr Stoddard's authority, which the writer has not been able to find in use. These are marked 'St.' or 'Stod.'

etymologies; and while a search among other dialects has disproved a few of these, by far the greater number have been fully confirmed.

It will be seen by what has been said that while the Urmi dialect is well known, the others have not been brought to light. The Gospels have indeed been printed by the American Presbyterian Mission at Urmi in the Alqosh dialect, that of the plain of Mosul, but a very limited number of copies was issued, and it is now quite unobtainable; indeed it may be doubted if any were ever seen in Europe. Dr Socin also, in his *Neuaramäischen Dialekte von Urmi bis Mosul*, has given us a few specimens (chiefly in Roman character) of the Jilu, Salámas, Alqosh[1], and Zakhu[2] dialects, besides several of that of Urmi. But no grammar has been written of these other dialects; and those of the great Ashiret, or semi-independent tribes of Kurdistan, and several others, have been entirely untouched. The present writer has therefore set himself during a five years' sojourn among the Eastern Syrians, when engaged on the Archbishop of Canterbury's mission to them, to collect the materials for the present grammar[3]. The number of variations both in the vocabulary and in the grammatical forms used is extraordinarily great, and almost every village has its own way of speaking. It will be found that in this book a large number of variant forms have been added even in the Urmi dialect; but it is perhaps necessary to remind European readers that this is the speech of only a small proportion of the people. It has been chosen by the different Missions as their basis for writing the vernacular, but this choice has given it an exaggerated importance. It is therefore the object of this work to compare the other dialects, that is, those of nine-tenths of the Eastern Syrian people, with that of Urmi, which is already known. It is clear that a comparison of dialects will throw much light on etymology, and that one dialect will often supply a missing link which will remove a difficulty in the speech of another.

Classes of dialects. The variation of the dialects is geographical;

---

[1] Professor Sachau's sketch of this dialect, mentioned below, came to hand as the last sheets of this book were passing through the press; a few forms are taken from it.

[2] This is the vernacular of the Jews of that place. The writer, though he has visited Zakhu, has had no opportunities of taking notes of the Jews' language, and is therefore entirely indebted to Dr Socin for the examples of it in this volume.

[3] The Aramaic dialect of the Western Syrians (Jacobites) of Jebel Tur is not given in this book.

there are practically no differences of class among the people, and all in the same place have more or less the same tongue. An examination of the peculiarities of speech in different districts would lead us to divide the language into four main divisions, the two first of which may be called the non-aspirating, and the two last the aspirating dialects, the difference being in the hardening or softening of the letters Tau and Dalath. It is possible that these four classes represent four separate migrations from the plains of Mesopotamia and Assyria. The first two groups of dialects, which are spoken at the North-eastern and Northern extremities of the country, would thus represent the earlier migrations.

We thus have:—

I. *The Urmi group* (U.); the dialect of the great plain of Urmi, in Azerbaijan, to the west of the sea of that name; the dialect of the smaller plain of Solduz to the south of the sea, which is almost the same, though in a few of its Syrian villages Syriac has given place to Azerbaijani Turkish; the dialect of the north part of the plain of Urmi, noted here as 'Sp.,' i.e. Sipurghan, which is somewhat affected by the Salámas dialect (Group II.), as is also that of the small plain of Gavílan between the two.

II. *The Northern group.* This group is especially noticeable for dropping Tau.

a. (Sal.) Plain of Salámas, in Persia, to the north-west of the Sea of Urmi.

b. (Q.) Qudshanis, in Turkey, the village of the Patriarch Mar Shimun, gives its name to the dialect of the neighbouring district, which is a little south of the Sea of Van.

c. (Gaw.) The plain of Gawar, in Turkey, a high table-land to the west of the Perso-Turkish frontier. This plain and the district round Qudshanis are called 'Rayat' or *Subject*, being entirely under the direct government of the Turks.

d. (J.) The dialect of Jilu is practically the same. This very mountainous district lies a little to the west of Gawar, and geographically belongs to Group III., being Ashiret; but philologically it belongs to Group II. Its people are very different in appearance and character from most of the other Syrians, being of a more Jewish cast.

III. *The Ashiret group.* K. in the following pages denotes the dialects of the Ashiret or Tribal (semi-independent) districts of Central Kurdistan, which consist of inaccessible mountains and valleys lying between Van and Mosul. Over these districts the Turks exercise little more than a nominal sway, and the soldiers seldom penetrate it. Of these districts we have:—

a. (Ti.) Upper Ṭiari, to the north-west of the group; this is by far the largest Ashiret district.

b. (Tkh.) Tkhuma, a large valley east of Ṭiari, south-west of Jilu.

c. Ṭal, Baz, Diz, Walṭu, smaller Ashiret districts, north and east of Tkhuma.

d. (Ash.) Ashitha, in Lower Ṭiari, to the south-west of the group. This is the principal village in the Ashiret districts, and its dialect differs very greatly from that of Upper Ṭiari, and approaches rather those of the fourth group.

e. (MB.) Mar Bishu; (Sh.) Shamsdin. These are districts in Turkey close to the Persian frontier, south-west of Gawar, and are inhabited by colonies from Ṭiari. Their dialects are closely related to that of Tiari, but are somewhat influenced by the first, or Urmi, group. This is still more the case with the dialects of Tergawar, Mergawar, and Bradust, three neighbouring upland plains on the Persian side of the frontier. The village of Anhar in the plain of Urmi, near Tergawar, is also a colony from Ṭiari, and retains several Ṭiari peculiarities of language, grafted on the Urmi speech. These districts are separated from the rest of this group by Gawar and Jilu.

IV. *The Southern group.* *a.* (Al.) The Alqosh dialect, spoken in the villages of the plain of Mosul. In the town of Mosul itself vernacular Syriac almost entirely gives place to Arabic. This dialect receives its name from the village of Alqosh, about thirty miles north of Mosul, where is the famous monastery of Raban Hurmizd. The language of the other villages, Telkief, Teleskof, and the rest, differ in small particulars from that of Alqosh itself.

b. (Bo.) The Bohtan dialect, spoken in Bohtan, in Western Kurdistan, a district lying on the Eastern branch of the Upper Tigris.

c. (Z.) The Zakhu dialect, spoken by the Jews of that place, which is about sixty miles north of Mosul. It greatly resembles that of Alqosh.

With regard to foreign words, Groups I. and II. are chiefly affected by Persian and Azerbaijani Turkish; Group III. by Kurdish and Arabic; Group IV. by Arabic.

Origin of the Vernacular. It would appear that the dialects, though sufficiently different to make it difficult for a man to understand one of a distant district, are yet sufficiently alike to argue a common origin. This origin, however, we can hardly seek in the written or classical language. It would be a mistake to look on the spoken Syriac as a new creation, springing from the ruins of the written tongue; the former may indeed in a sense be called *The New Language*, as it has greatly developed its grammatical structure in an analytical manner, and has dropped many of the old synthetic forms, but much or most of it was doubtless in use side by side with the written classical Syriac for centuries. It retains in many cases forms less developed than corresponding forms in the written language; thus in § 32 we see that in the formation of the first person plural of the first present tense, the spoken Syriac retains the Khéith which is dropped in the classical. The contractions in the tenses of the vernacular shew independence of the written language (§§ 31, 32). Many words are found in the former which are not used in the latter, but which are found in the Chaldee and other older Aramaic dialects. So too, some of the compounds which are survivals of the construct state (§ 16, ii. *g*) and some of the few remaining agents of the old form (§ 77, 2) are formed from verbs not found even in the latest classical Syriac, though used now; this would shew that these verbs were in use in speaking, though not in writing, before those now almost obsolete constructions and formations were given up. The form of the past participle of the second conjugation, *mpu'la*, and of the verbal noun of the same, *mpa'uli* or *mpa'ulé*, can hardly have been derived from the very different forms which correspond to them in the classical language; and the same may be said of the method in which the prepositions take pronominal affixes.

The style of spelling adopted. European Orientalists have sometimes expressed surprise that the missionaries who reduced the language to writing did not adopt the Roman alphabet. Had their only object been to make the language known in Europe, they might have done so; but as their aim was to enable the Eastern Syrians themselves to read and write their own language, they had no option but to use the character to which the people themselves were accustomed. They already wrote classical Syriac, which contained a very large number of the words used in the spoken tongue, and therefore it was absolutely necessary to employ the alphabet which was in common use. Many difficulties however present themselves. Are words to be spelt on exact phonetic principles? And if so, what dialect is to be chosen? How is a man of one district to understand a book printed in the dialect of another? It is impossible to print the books in every dialect, and one must aim at spelling so as to make the books intelligible to the greatest number of readers possible. The Archbishop of Canterbury's Mission Press at Urmi has therefore laid before itself the following principles: (1) The Vernacular must be treated as a historical language, not as one invented in the present generation; in other words etymology must be considered. (2) The spelling of classical Syriac is taken as a basis. Thus when Old Syriac spelling gives the vernacular sound, it is adopted, although some other perhaps simpler spelling also gives the sound. (3) When some districts follow Old Syriac and some depart from it, the words are spelt in preference according to the former (see e.g. § 87, *c* to *m*). (4) But when all, or nearly all, the dialects differ from Old Syriac, the vernacular sound is followed. (5) Words not generally understood except in one dialect—and especially foreign words, which are often used in one district only,—are used as sparingly as possible. (6) The mark *talqana* (lit. *the destroyer*), which denotes a silent or fallen letter, is retained to a considerable extent[1], both because a letter thus marked may be sounded in some dialects though it has fallen in others, and also because a Syriac word thus marked may often be made intelligible to those who do not use it by the fact of its resemblance (to the eye) to the corresponding word in the classical

---

[1] On the other hand it is not used with an initial vowelless Alap or Yudh. In the later, but not the earlier East Syrian manuscripts, it is found with the very few words which begin with a vowelless Alap. In the vernacular, however, similar words are very numerous, and it is a great gain to be able to dispense with the mark. As Alap and Yudh without a vowel have no sound it seems needless to write a sign which denotes that the sound is taken away. In some cases (§ 29, Note 2) it would be a distinct error to write it, as the Yudh contributes to the diphthongal sound.

language, which all who can read and write understand to some extent. (7) The same remark applies to etymological spelling. A word thus spelt is easily recognized, even if not used in speaking; and moreover it is found that a word spelt etymologically is frequently capable of more than one pronunciation, and therefore suits the speech of several dialects.

There is of course no royal road to the end desired, of making the books intelligible to all the Eastern Syrians, and the method here advocated will not give the exact colloquial language of any one dialect; but it aims rather at producing a literary style which will make communication between the various districts easier.

Arrangement of this book. This grammar is primarily intended for the use of those who wish to learn vernacular Syriac practically, and therefore, while the classical language is constantly referred to for illustration, a knowledge of it is not assumed. Those who wish to learn only one dialect may do so by omitting all variant forms marked with letters denoting other dialects. The discussion of derived nouns and verbs, and of alphabetical peculiarities of the vernacular as compared with classical Syriac, is postponed to the end of the book, in order that the reader may have some knowledge of the language before he reaches them; and the accidence and syntax are placed together instead of being separated, as this has been found in several grammars of modern languages to be of practical advantage in rendering their acquisition easier. A large number of idiomatic phrases arranged in alphabetical order will be found in the book; and over one hundred proverbs, which may be of general interest, have been added in the Appendix.

The author is indebted to Miss Payne Smith and to Mr Norman McLean, Fellow of Christ's College, Cambridge, for reading the proofs of this work, and for making various suggestions.

NOTE. No dictionary of the vernacular has been published, but a vocabulary of verbs used in several districts, with meanings in English, has been compiled by the present writer and may be had from the English Mission Press at Urmi, or from the Secretary of the Archbishop of Canterbury's Mission (7, Dean's Yard, Westminster), price 5s.

ABBREVIATIONS.

N.S.	'New Syriac,' the vernacular.
O.S.	'Old Syriac,' the classical language.
Turk.	Azerbaijani Turkish.
Osm. Turk.	Osmanli Turkish.
Kurd.	Kurdish.
Gk.	Greek.
Pers.	Persian.
Chald.	Chaldee.
Arab.	Arabic.
Heb.	Hebrew.
pron.	pronounced.
Nöld.	Nöldeke's *Grammatik der Neusyrischen Sprache* (Leipzig, Weigel, 1868).
Nöld. O.S.G.	Nöldeke's *Syrische Grammatik* [the Classical language] (Leipzig, Weigel, 1880).
St. or Stod.	Stoddard's *Modern Syriac Grammar* (American Oriental Society, Volume v. 1856).
Socin	Socin's *Neuaramäischen Dialekte von Urmi bis Mosul* (Tübingen, 1882).
Sachau	Sachau's *Skizze des Fellichi-Dialekts von Mosul* (Berlin, 1895).

The usual grammatical abbreviations are used.

Abbreviations for dialects.

Al.	Alqosh.	Q.	Qudshanis.
Ash.	Ashitha.	Sal.	Salámas.
Az.	Azerbaijan Jews.	Sh.	Shamsdin.
Bo.	Bohtan.	Sp.	Sipurghan.
Gaw.	Gawar.	Tkh.	Tkhuma.
J.	Jilu.	Ti.	Tiari.
K.	Kurdistan (Ashiret districts only).	U.	Urmi.
		Z.	Zakhu Jews.
MB.	Mar Bishu.		

One of these abbreviations after a grammatical form indicates that the form is used in the district for which the abbreviation stands; but not necessarily that it is confined to that district.

When no abbreviation follows any particular form, it is to be read as being used in a large number of dialects.

The letters O.S. *after* a Syriac word denote that the word is used both in O.S. and N.S., though in the case of verbs ending in a guttural it is to be understood that the vocalization of the last syllable is different, see p. 286; but the letters O.S. *before* a Syriac word denote that it is used in O.S. and not in N.S.

Transliteration of Syriac words. When to indicate the pronunciation or for any other reason, Syriac words are transliterated into Roman letters, we read:—

á, ā as in *far*; ă as in *pat*.
é, éi as a in *fate*; ei as in *height*; ĕ as in *pet*.
í as in French *île*; ĭ as in *pit*.
o as in *pole*; oi, oy as in *hoiden, boy*.
ú, ū as in *flute*; ŭ as in *but*.

The Syriac Qop is represented by *q*, Téith by *ṭ*, and Sadhé by *ṣ*, except in abbreviations.

GRAMMAR OF VERNACULAR SYRIAC.

GRAMMAR OF VERNACULAR SYRIAC.

THE LETTERS.

§ 1. *Consonants*¹ ܐܳܬܘܳܬܳܐ.

Not joined to preceding letter.	Joined to preceding letter.	Estrangela.	Name of letter.	Value in English.
ܐ (ܐ final)	ܐ ܐ (ܐ final)	ܐ	ܐܳܠܰܦ Alap	See § 4.
ܒ	ܒ	ܒ	ܒܶܝܬ Béith	b; (aspirated, w. See § 7).
ܓ	ܓ	ܓ	ܓܳܡܰܠ Gamal	g; (asp. gh guttural).
ܕ	ܕ	ܕ	ܕܳܠܰܬ Dalath	d; (asp. as *th* in *then*).
ܗ	ܗ	ܗ	ܗܶܐ Hé or Hi	h
ܘ	ܘ	ܘ	ܘܰܘ Wau	w
ܙ	ܙ	ܙ	ܙܰܝܢ Zain	z
ܚ	ܚ	ܚ	ܚܶܝܬ Khéith	kh guttural.

CONSONANTS.

ܛ	ܛ	Ṭéith	t, very hard. § 4.
ܝ	ܝ	Yudh	i or y
ܟ	ܟ (ܟ final)	ܟ (ܟ final)	Kap	k; (asp. kh guttural).
ܠ	ܠ	ܠ	Lamadh	l
ܡ	ܡ (ܡ final)	ܡ (ܡ final)	Mim	m
ܢ	ܢ (ܢ final)	ܢ (ܢ final)	Nun	n
ܣ	ܣ	ܣ	Simkath	s
ܥ	ܥ	ܥ	ʿE	See § 4.
ܦ	ܦ	ܦ	Pé or Pi	p; (asp. §§ 3, 7).
ܨ	ܨ	ܨ	Ṣadhé	ṣ, sometimes rather sharp.
ܩ	ܩ	ܩ	Qop	q, very hard. § 4.
ܪ	ܪ	ܪ	Resh	r
ܫ	ܫ	ܫ	Shin	sh
ܬ	ܬ	ܬ	Tau	t; (asp. as *th* in *thin*).

[1] For grammatical terms, the O.S. names, with their O.S. plurals are usually retained in N.S. Vowels not being counted as letters there are not separate Syriac words for *consonants* and *letters*.

These letters should be written by beginning at the right hand bottom corner, and most of them in several separate strokes.

The Estrangéla letters are now as a rule only used for headings of chapters, titles of books, and the like. There are no capitals, and the Estrangéla letters are not used for this purpose, but rather correspond to our black letter.

Of these consonants all may be affixed to the preceding letter; and all also to the following letter except ܙ, ܕ, ܗ, ܘ (usually), ܩ, ܨ, ܪ, ܬ (ܬ). In manuscripts ܡ followed by ܠ is not joined on; but this rule is not now generally observed. In some of the older manuscripts ܡ is not joined on to ܘ, ܚ, and other letters. Estrangéla letters follow the same rule in joining on as the others, but ܡ is never joined to the letter following.

Alap is written ܐ except (1) after ܠ when it is written ܠܐ whether final or not; (2) when final, when it is written ܐ. But after ܕ and ܪ it is written ܐ even though final.

§ 2. *Final letters.* For ܐ see above. Final Kap, Mim, and Nun take the forms ܟ or ܟ, ܡ or ܡ, ܢ or ܢ. These letters when standing alone are usually written double, as ܡܡ, ܢܢ, ܟܟ; though the final disjoined forms may stand alone; the others never.

When ܒ, ܓ, ܚ, ܛ (ܛ), ܟ, ܠ, ܡ, ܣ, ܦ, ܨ, ܫ are final, whether joined to the preceding letter or not, a small stroke is added: thus ܒ, ܦ. Yudh final after ܗ is generally written > in manuscripts. ܠ followed by ܐ at the end of a word is generally written ܠܐ if the ܠ be attached to the preceding letter; if not attached, it is written ܠܐ or ܠܐ.

§ 3. *Aspirated letters.* The letters ܒܓܕܟܦܬ have a dot below them when aspirated, and a dot above them when not aspirated.

But these dots are not written when they would interfere with vowel signs[1].

ܦ aspirated is written ܦ̇; a dot is never placed above this letter. It is only aspirated in Syriac words (in most districts) when forming a diphthong (see § 7), whether in the vernacular or in the classical language in its Eastern form, which thus differs from Western or Jacobite Syriac. In words from Persian, Arabic, etc., there are a few exceptions in the speech of the better educated, and ܦ then is *ph*; but in general *f* of a foreign language becomes *p* in Syriac. In Al. and Z. it is often aspirated even in Syriac words, especially at the beginning. Thus ܦܓܼ *to abound* has ܦ.

The letters which are capable of aspiration are called by the East Syrians ܒܓܕܟܦܬ, *bagh-dakh-path*. An aspirated letter is called ܪܟܝܟܐ (see § 95 d) and aspiration ܪܘܟܟܐ, or softening; an unaspirated letter is ܩܫܝܐ, and non-aspiration ܩܘܫܝܐ or hardening.

In U. Sp. Q. Sal. J. Gaw. etc. ܕ and ܬ are never aspirated. The vernacular is more simple than the classical language in the matter of aspiration; if a letter is aspirated in the normal form of the word, it is aspirated throughout all its grammatical changes in the vernacular. See § 84 for Bar Zu'bi's rules; §§ 94, 95, for differences between O.S. and N.S. in this respect.

§ 4. *Notes on the pronunciation of the letters.*

(1) ܐ is not pronounced. It is used chiefly as a peg to hang a vowel on, or as a quiescent final letter.

(2) ܥ in many words modifies the vowel sound which is connected with it. See § 6. But a vowelless ܥ at the beginning of

---

[1] In fully vocalized writing if one of these letters in the middle of a word has not a dot below it when there is a vacant space beneath, we understand it to be hard; and so if there is no dot above and the space above is vacant, we understand it to be soft. Thus ܓܒܐ has ܒ; ܟܬܒܐ has ܟ. When in this book ܬ and ܕ are written with a dot beneath, it is of course only meant that they are aspirated in K. Al. etc.

a word ordinarily adds nothing to the sound. One or two words like ܥܢܳܢܳܐ *cloud* gave a half vowel to ܠ. So ܒܕܶܝܢ *Eden*; sometimes ܐܬܬܥܡܶܕ *he was baptized*, ܥܡܳܕܳܐ *baptism*. In Al. Z. initial vowelless ܠ usually has a half vowel. Thus ܠܥܒܳܕܳܐ *act*, ܪܶܗܛܶܬ *I ran* have half vowels, though elsewhere they are pronounced *wadha* (*wada*), *riq li*. ܠ and ܐ are not passed over in the middle of a word after a vowelless consonant; a break in the breath must be made. Thus ܐܰܪܥܳܐ *earth* is pronounced *ăr-'ā* not *ărā*.

(3) ܥ and ܛ are pronounced low down in the mouth and throat respectively; they have a very hard sound and necessarily modify the accompanying vowel (see § 6). ܛ is pronounced by putting the middle, not the tip, of the tongue against the roof of the mouth.

(4) ܚ and ܟ aspirated have the same sound[1]; it is somewhat harsher than the Scottish and North German *ch*; in some districts it is a very harsh aspirate indeed. The ܓ is a soft aspirate, pronounced lower down the throat, something like the German *g* in *tag*.

(5) ܡ before ܒ is pronounced ܡܒ, as ܐܰܡܒܰܪ *store room* (*ămbar*).

(6) A mark ~ under or above ܓ or ܟ make them = *j* (in *jay*) and *ch* (in *church*) respectively. These letters are then called Jamel and Chap. The same mark with ܘ or ܙ makes them = *j* in French *jamais*. The name of this mark is ܡܰܓܠܝܳܢܳܐ U. *majliyána* or *wearing away* (ܟ̇ K.).

(7) A letter repeated must be pronounced twice, not as in English as a single letter. This is a matter of considerable importance. Thus we have ܡܬܰܡܡܶܝܢ K. *I complete* (§ 36), pronounced *mtă-m'min*, not *mtămin*.

---

[1] But see § 107.

(8) In other words all letters must be pronounced in full, and none left half pronounced as is so often done in English. Thus in ܒܶܣܕܳܪܐ *firewood*, the ܣ must be finished before the ܕ is begun.

(9) Care must be taken to pronounce letters not marked with talqana (§ 9), especially ܗ, which though feeble when without a vowel, is still sounded; thus ܙܳܗܡܬܐ *trouble* is not *zāmǎt* but *zāh'mǎt*. § 6 (1).

(10) Initial ܘ if it has no vowel has no sound.

(11) In most words ܨ and ܣ have the same sound. If any difference is made, ܨ is somewhat more sibilant. It is not *ts*.

(12) ܗ final is silent. See § 108.

§ 5. *Vowels* ܘܳܩܶܐ.

The vowels are marked by dots placed above or below the consonants, as shown by the following table.

⁻ Pthakha, ܦܬܳܚܐ = *a* in *fut*; sometimes *e* in *pet*.

⁼ Zqapa, ܙܩܳܦܐ = *a* in *psalm*.

⁻̤ Zlami zogi, ܙܠܳܡܐ ܙܳܓܝ or Zlama zoga ܙܠܳܡܐ ܙܳܓܐ = *i* in *fit*.

⁻· Zlami pshuqi, ܙܠܳܡܐ ܦܫܺܝܩܐ or Zlami yarikhi ܙܠܳܡܐ ܝܰܪܺܝܟܐ (also Zlama pshuqa, yarikha) (1) as *ee* in *feet*, *i* in French *si*, (2) as *a* in *fate* or often somewhat shorter.

ܘ̣ Khwaṣa, ܚܒܳܨܐ = *ee* in *feet*, *i* in French *si*.

ܘ̇ Rwaṣa, ܪܒܳܨܐ = *u* in *rule*; in a few words like *oo* in *wool*, e.g. ܕܘܢܝܐ *world* (Turk.) [so ܟܠ *all*; see below]. In Sh. and M.B. more like a French *u* in all words.

ܘ̊ Rwakha, ܪܘܳܚܐ = *u* in *rule*, slightly inclining to *o*, especially in Al. Z.

Half vowels.

ܔ Half Pthakha, a very short vowel: very rarely written in N.S.

ܔ Half Zlama, a very short Zlama.

These are usually written between consonants in manuscripts, but in printing they are necessarily put under one of them; e.g. ܡܲܕܝܼܢܚܵܐ *west* O.S. and N.S. ܡܲܥܡܕܵܢܵܐ O.S., K. *Baptist* (= ܡܲܥܡܕܵܢܵܐ U.). Half Pthakha is also called ܡܲܪܗܛܵܢܵܐ *mar-h'ṭana* or *making to run*; half Zlama is ܡܗܲܓܝܵܢܵܐ *m'hagyana* or *spelling*. The former must not be confused with talqana (§ 9). An O.S. half vowel is frequently replaced by a whole vowel in N.S. See § 86.

Of these vowels Khwaṣa can only be used with ܘ, Rwaṣa and Rwakha with ܘ. The others can be used with any letter, provided it be not final.

Notes. (1) The form Zqapa is preferred by the Eastern, Zqopho by the Western Syrians.

(2) There is much variation in different districts in the pronunciation of long Zlama. In Urmi the first pronunciation is usual, except in a few words such as ܠܵܐ *not* (if indeed this is the proper method of spelling this word; see § 67): ܐܚܹܪܢܵܐ *other* (rarely with the first pronunciation): ܗܹܐ *yes* (sometimes: but ܐܹ *yes* always has the first pronunciation); ܬܪܹܝܢ *two* (O.S. ܬܪܹܝܢ); and in the names of the letters ܚܹܝܬ, ܚܹܐ, ܒܹܝܬ, but the sound is rather a short one; and ܠܹܐ where the sound is long. On the other hand both in K. and U. the letters ܚܹܝܬ, ܗܹܐ, ܒܹܝܬ, ܓܵܡܲܠ usually (but not always) have the first sound. In K. Al. the second pronunciation is more common except in plurals in ܐܹ̈ and in the pronominal affix ܗܿ; but in Ṭiari these plurals also often have the second sound, as ܡܲܠܟܹ̈ܐ, and in Al. both these plurals and ܗܿ often have the second sound.

In many cases the variation of pronunciation shows that long Zlama should be written, as etymology also would suggest. Thus the 3rd pl. present of ܓܠܐ verbs, as ܓܳܠܶܝܢ *they reveal* (O.S. ܓܳܠܶܝܢ) is pronounced *galé* in K. Al., *gali* in U.; in the K. form of the 3rd pers. pl. possessive pronoun with nouns, as ܟܬܳܒܗܘܢ *their book*, the first sound prevails in Tkh., the second in Ti. The K. imperfect ܗܘܘ ܗܘܰܘ *they were* (O.S. ܗܘܘ ܗܘܰܘ) is *wé-wa*, § 29. ܪܺܝܚܐ *smell*, has the first sound in U., the second in K. ܙܶܠ *go*, is pronounced *zé, zi, sé* or *si*. ܡܳܪܶܗ *lord of* (§ 16) is *mari* in U., *maré* in K. The K. forms ܐܚܪܢܐ m., ܐܚܪܬܐ f., are *khréna* and *khréta* (= *other*).

(3) No vowel can be placed on the final letter of a word, except ܝ, ܘ, ܘ; hence the use of the Alap in which nearly all purely Syriac nouns now end.

(4) ܝ final must be distinguished from ܐ and ܗ. It is marked, in U., by the breath being made to pass sharply over the tongue as the vowel *i* is being pronounced. The distinction is hardly marked in K. Al. Z. etc. ܝ has the sound of short *i* in ܐܝܬ *there is*; in the fem. past part. of 1st conj. as ܩܕܝܡܐ *finished*; and usually in the preterite 1st conj. as ܩܕܝܡ ܠܝ *I finished*; but not when the object is expressed by affixes. See § 50. Also in ܒܝܕܡܗ *husband's brother*, but not in ܒܝܕܡܬܐ *husband's sister*.

(5) ܘ often does duty both as a vowel and as a consonant. Thus ܕܝܰܢ *di-yan*, *of us*. This is not the case with ܘ; if Rwaṣa or Rwakha or a diphthongal Wau is followed by the sound of Wau consonantal, ܘ must be repeated. Thus ܓܰܘܰܢ *in us*, is *gá-wan*, not *gó-wan*. ܝ initial is pronounced *i* not *yi*.

(6) A few words are always written without vowels; as ܡܢ (*min*) *from*; ܡܢ (*man*) *who*; ܟܠ (*kul*) *all*; ܗܘ (*ū* or *ow* as in *cow*)

he or *that*; ܗܺܝ (*ā* as in *fate* or *ei*) *she* or *that*; and so their derivatives, as ܟܽܠܢܳܝܳܐ *universal*, ܗܺܝ ܟܽܠܳܗ̇ *then*, ܟܽܠܶܗ *all of it*. But ܡܶܢ with affixes receives Zlama zoga, as in O.S., as ܡܶܢܶܗ *from him*.

(7) The letters ܕ *of*, ܘ *and*, ܒ *in, with*, ܠ *to*, and combinations of them, are prefixed to words without vowels, except in Al. where they have Zlama zoga before a vowelless letter. But they do not quite coalesce with the word following. Thus there is a distinction between ܕܪܰܢܓ *late* (*drang*) and ܕܪܰܢܓ *of colour* (*d'rang*), though the former word is sometimes pronounced, especially by children, like the latter. Between a preposition and a demonstrative pronoun an inserted ܕ coalesces with the latter as ܥܰܠ ܕܗܳܐ *on this*, § 70 (12); and so often ܒ, ܠ before demonstrative pronouns, and sometimes ܕ when = *of*. In O.S. these particles receive Pthakha before a vowelless letter. ܘ is pronounced *u* when = *and*. ܐ with a vowel, preceded by these particles, does not in N.S. usually throw back the vowel to the particle, as always in the Western and sometimes in the Eastern form of O.S.

(8) Before ܐ Zlama is always the long one.

§ 6. *Modification of vowel sounds by certain consonants.*

(1) Before a silent letter a short vowel is lengthened; this applies to a letter with talqana (§ 9) as well as to a vowelless ܠ or ܐ, as ܩܰܕܡܳܝܳܐ *first* (*qā-maya*); ܚܰܕ *one* (*khā*), usually; ܦܰܐܬܳܐ *face* (*pátha*), ܒܺܝ ܘܰܕܗܳܐ *doing* (*bî-wadha*). For exceptions see § 37 b. So also Pthakha before ܗ as in ܙܳܐܚܡܰܬ *trouble* (*záh'mŭt*).

(2) The vowel sounds are slightly modified when in the same syllable with ܓ, ܚ, ܟ, ܥ, ܩ, and sometimes with ܡܨ. Pthakha, Zlama zoga, and often Zqapa are then sounded nearly like *u* in *but*, as ܚܰܡܫܳܐ *five* (*khŭmshu*), ܚܛܶܐ *wheat* (*khŭṭi*), but not in ܚܛܳܐ *to sin* (*khāṭi*); ܩܰܡܨܳܐ *locust* (*qŭmṣa*). There are however many exceptions,

especially with ܝ. Almost always in Al., and often in K., ܣ does not modify the vowel, but is pronounced like ܐ. In other districts this modification is the only way of distinguishing ܣ and ܐ. ܐܬܪܐ *country*, is pronounced '*ăthra* (U. '*ătra*), as if written with ܣ; and so ܐܘܨܪܐ *store room* (*ămbar*).

The long vowels ܘ, ܝ, after ܓ, ܣ, ܒ, are necessarily somewhat modified. If these letters are properly pronounced, far back in the mouth and throat, the proper vowel sound follows naturally. Thus ܬܐܢܐ *fig* and ܛܝܢܐ *mud* have quite distinct vowel sounds; and so also ܐܝܕܐ *hand* and ܥܐܕܐ *feast*, even if the Zlama of the latter have the first sound. (In Tkh. it has the second sound.)

Note that the preterite (§ 32. 4) of the first conjugation is always pronounced with the *ĭ* sound even with these letters in it. This is an additional reason for spelling it with ܝ (though the sound is usually short) and not with Zlama. Thus ܩܡܠܗ is *qĭmli*; if we wrote it ܩܡܠܗ it would be *qŭmli*.

The word ܨܗܝܘܢ *Sion* is usually pronounced *Seihyun* (sound the *h*).

§ 7. *Diphthongs* ܘܳܐܬ̈ܐ ܡܫܝ̈ܢܝܐ.

ܰܝ as *a* in *fate*, as ܩܝܡܐ *one who rises*; or *ei* in *height* as in ܣܘܪܝܝܐ *Syrian*, where the ܝ does duty first in the diphthong and then as a consonant. If the ܝ has no vowel the first sound is more common. Some words are pronounced both ways, as ܩܕܡܐ *gain, interest*. The following are irregular: ܛܒ *good* (U. *spoi-i*, K. *spei*, rather drawn out), ܡܪܐ U. *bitter* (*moira*), ܩܪܐ U. *cold* (*qoira*), but not the kindred words ܚܡܐ U. *hot* (*kheima*), ܕܩܠ *thinned out*, as trees (*deila*). In K. Al. and O.S. these are ܡܕܝܬܐ, ܡܕܝܬܐ, ܕܠܝܬܐ, ܫܡܝܥܬܐ.

The diphthong ܰܝ has the same sound. But in U. ܒܚܕܢܐ *wishing*, ܝܕܝܥܢܐ *knowing*, ܙܘܕܥܒܐ *fearing*, have the sound of *oi*; in K. Sal. etc. of *ei*.

ܒܳܘ, ܘܳ, ܦܳܘ, as *o* in *pole*. But ܘܳܗܘ is pronounced *wá*; and in the names of the letters ܘܳ, ܘܳܐ the diphthong has the sound of *ow* in *cow*.

ܒܺܘ, ܦܺܘ, generally as *o* in *pole*, rarely as the following diphthong. [In the name ܝܳܦܬ *Japhet*, ܦ has a feeble sound, *Yópht*.]

ܘܶ (rare), somewhat like *ow* in *cow*, as pronounced by the uneducated in London, as ܘܶܢ *tinder*.

ܝܺ and ܰܝ, generally as *a* in *fate*, sometimes as *ei* in *height*. ܥܝܢܐ *eye, fountain*, has the first sound in K. the second in U. Distinguish ܫܡܝܐ *heaven* (first sound) and ܫܡܕܢܐ *hearing* (second). Exceptions: ܐܝܟ as (*akh*), ܡܕܝܟ as (*makh*, but in Al. *mékh*): ܠܝܬ *there is not* (*lit*) and its variant ܠܝܬܝܢ (*lítin*). [In K. Al. we have ܠܝܬ which in Ti. is *láth*, in Tkh. *líth*, in Al. *léth*.] ܗܝܟܠܐ *temple* (*hékla*).

ܒܽܘ, ܘܽ, ܦܽܘ, ܒܺܝ, ܦܺܝ, either as *u* in *tune* or *u* in *rule*. At the end of a word these are not properly diphthongs, but the consonant has a feeble, half-whistling sound. Thus ܝܬܒ *to sit* is not *yátiv* nor yet *yátu* (*u* as in French), but between the two, and ends with a soft whistle.

In ܘܽ, ܘܽ (followed by a consonant) the ܘ and ܘ give no additional force to the Rwaṣa. In ܝܺ Yudh gives no additional force to the Zlama, except at the end of a word in U.

ܘܿ at the end of a word gives Yudh a very short sound; but ܘܗܝ is *it* only.

Note. The combination ܘܿ has always been distasteful to the Eastern Syrians. Hence when the Western Syrians used this diphthong, the Easterns put Zqapa for Pthakha. Hence we have ܝܵܘܡܵܐ *day*, O.S., Ti. Al. not ܝܘܿܡܵܐ (pron. in U. Q. Tkh. etc., ܝܘܿܡܵܐ). So in quadriliterals ܡܵܘܕܹܐ *to confess*, not ܡܘܿܕܹܐ.

This applies also to a great extent when the Wau has a vowel, not only in O.S. but also (especially in K.) in N.S.; thus, where in U. they say ܡܲܘܬܸܒ݂ *to join*, in K. they say ܡܲܘܬܸܒ݂.

§ 8. *Accent* ܢܸܒ݂ܪܵܐ.

In speaking the accent is almost invariably placed on the penultimate, even in foreign words.

Exceptions. (1) ܡܲܠܦܵܢܵܐ *teacher*, ܐܵܚܘܿܢܝ *my brother*, and the like, when used vocatively, are accented on the first.

(2) Words with the 3rd pl. pronominal affix ܗܘܿܢ‍ are often accented on the last especially in U. There was originally another syllable here, which is still used in K. See § 11. Cf. ܐܸܕ݂ܝ *now* (= ܐܸܕ݂ܝܵܐ) which is oxytone.

(3) Adverbs in ܐܝܬ݂ are also usually oxytone. But they are rare (§ 67).

(4) ܒܸܠܚܘܿܕ݂ *especially* (pers.), ܒܨܲܦܪܵܐ *in the morning*, ܒܝܲܠܚܘܿܕ݂ (ܗ‍ Sal.) *in short*, and ܫܲܡܵܫܵܐ *deacon*, are accented on the first. But the plural ܫܲܡܵܫܹܐ is accented regularly, and in K. often the singular. ܡܸܚܕܵܐ *immediately*, is accented on both first and last, ܡܸܢܕܝ U. *always*, on the first. Also the following are accented on the first and pronounced as one word: ܓܘܕ݂ܒܵܐ *last year*, ܚܲܕ݂ ܟܲܒ Ti. Al.

upwards, ܠܥܝܠ ܬܚܕ Ti. Al. *downwards,* ܒܪܡܫܐ U. *in the evening,* ܚܕܐ ܓܪܢ *one qran* (7d.), ܚܕ ܬܘܡܢ *one tumân* (6s.), ܡܪܝ ܫܡܥܘܢ *Mar Shimun* (but not the names of the other bishops), ܐܗܐ ܓܒܐ *this side,* ܗܘ ܓܒܐ *that side;* and so ܡܢܫܠܝܐ *suddenly.*

(5) When the 2nd pl. pronominal affix ܐܘܟܘܢ, or the plural imperative affix ܡܘܢ are added, the accent is often on the antepenultimate.

(6) Generally when any affix is added to a word, whether written as part of the word or not, it counts as part of the word in determining the accent. Thus ܒܕ ܡܚܠܡ *he will heal,* is accented on ܚ, but ܒܕ ܡܚܠܡ ܠܗ *he will heal him,* on ܠ.

(7) The verb ܗܘܐ, ܗܘܘ *was,* similarly counts as part of the word. Thus in ܒܕ ܦܪܩ ܗܘܐ *he would finish,* the accent is on the ܪ.

(8) In ܩܡܬܐ *first* (adv.), the accent is often on the first, and the first Zqapa is very feeble, especially in U. Thus *qâm'ta.* So in abstracts in ܥܡܘܬܐ the ܘ often falls or is feeble, and the Zqapa before ܬ is accented, especially in U.

(9) ܓܕܐ ܕܩܘܡܬܐ *Easter* U., ܓܕܐ ܕܘܠܕܐ *Christmas* U., are each pronounced as one word, with the accent on ܕ.

(10) All plurals in Sal. Q. Gaw., which correspond to U. plurals in ܐܢܐ, and K. plurals in ܐܢܐ, are oxytone, the last syllable having fallen. Thus we only distinguish ܕܦܢܐ *sides* (*dipnâ*) from ܕܦܢܐ *side* (*dípna*) by the accent. See § 18. Note 3.

(11) The numerals in § 28 (1) are accented on the first, as ܬܪܘܝܗܘܢ *both of them,* also the days of the week, § 28 (5).

§ 9. Signs. N.S. ܣܝܵܡܹ̈ܐ, or Al. ܣܝܵܡܹ̈ܐ.

Talqana. A line above a letter ‾ denotes that it is silent. This mark is called *talqana*, ܛܲܠܩܵܢܵܐ (or '◌̄'), i.e. the destroyer: and a letter thus marked is called *tliqta*, ܛܠܝܼܩܬܵܐ (or '◌̄').

Sign of the plural. Two large dots above a word denote the plural in nouns, adjectives, and participles used adjectivally. They are called *Siami*, ܣܝܵܡܹ̈ܐ, or 'positions.' By preference they are put over ܪ and ܘ if these letters occur in the word, whether they already have a vowel or not. But they may be put over any letter. They are not written slanting over ܠ as by the Western Syrians. When written over ܪ one of them counts as the dot of the letter itself, as ܪ̈. They are not now used with verbs.

Various. A large dot is put over ܗ in the 3rd fem. pronominal affix (§ 11); and in ܗܘ, ܗܝ (§ 10); over ܡ̇ *who* and under ܡ̣ *from.* See § 5 (6). ܠܐ is written without a dot.

The large dots which marked the tenses and persons of the old verb have disappeared with those tenses.

The stops usually used are—: ؛ comma; . semi-colon or full stop; ⁕ full stop, especially at the end of a paragraph. This, or a star, often divides verses of psalms and anthems. The Syrians use their stops very loosely. The first of the above stops is more used than the comma in English. It is often called ܢܦܩܬܵ ܫܵܐ *drawing of breath.* In manuscripts a distinction is often made between the two ways of writing these two dots, according as they slant to the right or to the left.

For a fuller discussion of vowels and consonants in particular words see §§ 85—126 incl.

PRONOUNS.

ܚܠܦܫܡܗ̈ܐ

§ 10. *Personal Pronouns* ܚܠܦܫܡܗ̈ܐ ܠܦܪ̈ܨܘܦܐ.

The forms most commonly used are those written first.

Sing. 3 m. ܗܘ *he*, or ܗܘܘܢ U. (*ow-wun*), or ܗܘܝܘܢ U., or ܐܓ̰ܗܘܢ U., or ܗܘܘܐ Z., or ܐܗܘ K. Al. In all but the last ܗ is silent.

f. ܗܝ *she*, or ܗܝܢ U. (*ey-in*), or ܐܗܝ Al. Tkh., or ܐܢܢ Z., or ܐܗܝ Ti. In the first two and last ܗ is silent.

2 m. ܐܢܬ *thou*, or ܐܢܬܗ Tkh., or ܐܢܬܝܢ U. K. (ܬ in Ṭal), or ܐܗܬ Al. Ti. Z., or ܐܗܝܕ Z., or ܐܗܬ Z., or ܐܗܬܗ Ti. Tkh., or ܐܢܬܝ Gaw.

f. ܐܢܬܝ *thou*, or ܐܢܬܗܝ Tkh., or ܐܢܬܝܢ U. K. (ܬ in Ṭal), or ܐܗܬܝ Al. Ti., or ܐܗܬܗܝ Ti. Tkh., or ܐܢܬܝ Gaw.

1 m. and f. ܐܢܐ *I*.

Plur. 3 m. and f. ܐܢܝ *they* U. K. Al. Z., or ܐܢ K. Sal. Al., or ܐܢܝ Al. (*âné*), or ܐܢܗܝ Al. (*ânhé*).

2 m. and f. ܐܚܬܘܢ *you* U. K., or ܐܚܬܘ K. Al., or ܐܚܬܘܟܘܢ U., or ܐܚܢܬܘܢ Al., or ܐܚܬܘܚ Sal., or ܐܚܬܘܟܘܢ U.

1 m. and f. ܐܚܢܢ *we* U., or ܐܚܢܝ U. K. Al., or ܐܚܢܢܝ U.

ܗܘ and ܗܝ as personal pronouns are pronounced *ow* (as in *cow*) and *ei* (as in *height*) respectively. In reading O.S. the Eastern Syrians read them *how*, *hei* unless the ܗ has talqana.

All these pronouns are abbreviated when used with verbs. See §§ 29 *sqq*.

Of these ܗܘܿ, ܗܝܼ, ܐܲܢ̄ܬܘܿܢ, ܐܲܢ̄ܬܹܝܢ are O.S. forms. In O.S. ܐܸܢܵܐ the short gives place to a long vowel (§§ 87, 88) and we get ܐܵܢܵܐ. The form ܐܵܚܢ should perhaps be written ܐܲܚܢ giving in U. K. the first sound to Zlama, in Al. the second. All the forms for *they* seem to be derived from the *feminine* ܗܸܢܹܝ (whence ܐܝܼܢܗܝ by metathesis), which has ousted the masculine. The reverse usually happens, as we see in the verb forms, but other instances of the feminine surviving and not the masculine will be seen in the following sections. For O.S. ܚܢܲܢ we have ܐܲܚܢܲܢ with ܐ prosthetic.

Most of the variants are due (*a*) to a love of aspiration in Tkhuma, (*b*) to a desire to emphasize by adding ܡ. [Qu. = O.S. ܕܝܼܡ ?]. (*c*) from a confusion with the affix forms of §11, as ܐܲܚܢܲܢܝܢ, ܐܲܚܬܘܿܟ݂ܘܿܢ, ܐܲܚܬܘܿܟ݂ܘܿܢ (which has a double confusion with ܐܲܚܢܲܢ). Perhaps ܐܲܚܬܘܿܢ is itself formed by confusion with the affix of the 2 pers., in which case we should write ܐܲܟ݂ܬܘܿܢ. Possibly also ܐܲܚܢܬܘܿܢ may be a reminiscence of the termination of ܗܘܝܼܬܘܿܢ *ye are* or *become* = ܗܘܝܼܬ ܐܲܢ̄ܬܘܿܢ. (*d*) ܐܲܚܬܘܿܓ̰ is in accordance with the usual Salamas usage of putting ܓ̰ for ܡ final. (*e*) ܐܲܚܬܘܿ and perhaps ܐܲܚܢ are formed by a common dropping of ܡ final, § 116.

The personal pronouns of the first and second persons are not used objectively; affix forms are substituted, §§ 48—50. But rarely in Al. we have such instances as the following: St John xv. 24, ܣܢܹܐ ܠܗܘܿܢ ܗܸܡ ܐܵܢܵܐ ܗܸܡ ܠܒܵܒܝ *they hated both me and my Father*. The 3 pers. pronoun is used objectively after prepositions in U., and also in K. Al. directly after verbs, as ܚܙܹܐ ܠܝ ܗܘܿ K. Al., *I saw him*. When used after prepositions ܕ must be inserted except sometimes after ܠ. Thus ܩܵܐ ܕܗܘܿ *for him* = ܩܵܐ ܕܝܼܘܗܝ or ܩܵܐ ܕܝܹܗ.

The 2 pers. plural is only used of more persons than one.

§ 11. *Affix forms.* ܢܩܦ̈ܐ ܡܬ̈ܬܣܠܚܢܐ.

Sing. 3 m. ܘܗܝ U. Q. Sal. Gaw. J., or ܗ K. Al. Z. (and elsewhere more rarely with nouns, but always in the preterite of verbs).

3 f. ܗܿ or ܗ̇ (as above).

2 m. ܘܟ. The ܟ is frequently silent in J., especially with verbs.

2 f. ܟܝ or ܟܝ Ti. MB.

1 m. and f. ܝ.

Plur. 3. ܗܝ U. Sal. Q. Ash. Al. (and K. J. after preps.) m. f., or ܗܝ K. J. Al. Tal. (nouns), or ܗܘ MB. Sh. (and Z. after ܠ) m. f., or ܗܘ m. f. U. (after ܠ), or (rare) ܗܘ Al. m., ܗܝ Al. f. (also for masc.), or ܗܘܝ Bo. m.; ܗܝ Bo. f.

2 m. f. ܘܟܘ or ܟܘ Ti. or ܘܟܘ Ti. or ܟܘ Al. Z. Also rarely in Ti. ܟܘ (§ 70).

1 m. f. ܢܝ or ܡܝ or ܢܝ K. U. Z. (nouns only except in Ti.).

Notes. (1) *Origin of the affixes.* We may compare the O.S. forms.

a. With masc. sing. nouns and all feminines, sing. and pl. in ܐܬܐ [' Singular affixes'].

S. 3 m. ܗ, f. ܗ̇, 2 m. ܟ, f. ܟܝ, 1 m. and f. ܝ (no vowel).

Pl. 3 m. ܗܘ, f. ܗܝ, 2 m. ܟܘ, f. ܟܝ, 1 m. and f. ܢܝ.

b. With masc. pl. nouns [' Plural affixes'].

S. 3 m. ܘܗܝ (Western ܘܗܝ), f. ܗ, 2 m. ܟܝ, f. ܟܝ, 1 m. and f. ܝ.

Pl. 3 m. ـܝܗܘܿܢ, f. ـܝܗܝܢ, 2 m. ـܝܟܘܿܢ, f. ـܝܟܝܢ, 1 m. and f. ـܝܢ.

From the 'Singular affixes' we have the N.S. forms ـܗ, ـܗ̇, ܗܘܿܢ, ܗܝܢ, ܗܘ̈ܢ, ܗܘܿ, ܟܘܿ, ـܢ.

From the 'Plural affixes' we have ܘܗܝ (= O.S. ـܘܗܝ), ـܘܗ̇ (= O.S. ـܝܗ̇, ܘ for ܝ, cf. § 109), ܘܟ݂ (= O.S. ـܝܟ, ܘ for ܝ, and the ܟ softened, cf. § 94), ـܝܟ݂ and ـܝܟ݂ܝ (= O.S. ـܝܟܝ ܝ dropped, ܟ softened), ـܝܗܘܿܢ, ـܝܗܝܢ. Hence also ـܝܗܝ and ـܗܝ (for which reason the accent in words containing the latter is irregular, § 8). ـܝܟ݂ܘܿ and ـܝܘܟ݂ܘܿܢ (= O.S. ـܝܟܘܿܢ). Hence also ـܘܟ݂ܘܿܢ with ܘ for ܝ, and ܟ softened. ـܝܢ and ـܝܢܝ are O.S. ـܝܢ.

It is doubtful if N.S. ܝ is from the O.S. Singular affix ܝ or the Plural ـܝ. If the former it is one of the many instances in which N.S. agrees with Chaldee rather than with O.S.

The old form ـܟܘܿܢ is found in Ti. in one or two prepositions: as ܕܝܼܟ݂ܘܿ *of you* (pl.), § 70.

(2) These affix forms are used with nouns (to denote possessive pronouns), prepositions, in the preterite of verbs, and for objective pronouns to verbs.

(3) When they are emphatic after nouns and prepositions these forms are separated therefrom and ܕ (*of*) is inserted. Thus ܟܬ݂ܵܒܵܐ ܕܝܼܝ my *book*. For the additional ܝ see § 70. But in Al. this method of expression is common when no emphasis is intended. In the same way in O.S. the Apocalypse differs from the Pshiṭta by having the detached forms when there is no emphasis.

For greater emphasis another ܕ is often added: ܟܬ݂ܵܒܵܐ ܕܕܝܼܝ my *book*.

(4) No distinction is made in N.S. between the forms used with singular and those with plural nouns.

(5) In the form ܝܗܘܢ. the first Zlama sound is used in Tkhuma, the second (but very short) in Ṭiari. This and the similar form ܝܗܘܢ are instances of the feminine surviving to the exclusion of the masculine. Cf. §§ 10, 32. For the accent see § 8 (2).

(6) For two other forms for 3 pers. pl. see § 20 (12).

(7) For ܘܿܝ, in Salamas ܘܿܓ is often substituted.

(8) The objective pronouns *me, thee*, etc. are expressed by ܐܸܠܝܼ, ܐܸܠܘܼܟ݂ etc., or in U. also by ܩܵܬܝܼ, ܩܵܬܘܼܟ݂ etc.; or by attaching the affixes to verbs as in §§ 48 sqq. Cf. also § 10 above.

(9) *Mine, thine*, etc. are expressed by ܕܝܼܝܼ ܕܝܼܘܼܟ݂ etc., see § 70 (5); as ܗܵܘ ܟܬ݂ܵܒ݂ܵܐ ܕܝܼܝܼ ܝܠܹܗ *that book is mine*. These may be used absolutely, as ܡܚܘܼܒܹܐ ܠܹܗ ܠܕܝܼܗ U. K. = ܚܒ݂ܹܐ ܠܹܗ ܠܐܵܢܝ ܕܝܼܗ Al. *he loved his own.*

My own etc. is usually expressed by ܕܝܼܠܝܼ (ܕܝܼܠܝܼ Ti.)

§ 12. *Demonstrative Pronouns.* ܫܘܼܠܵܦܹ̈ܐ ܡܚܵܘܝܵܢܹ̈ܐ.

(1) Sing. m. ܐܵܗܵܐ *this*, or ܐܘܿܐ U. K., or ܐܘܿܐ Al. Z., or ܐܵܗ Sal. U. Sp., or ܗܵܕܵܐ MB., or ܗܵܕܵܐܗܵܐ MB., or ܐܵܕܵܐ Sh., or ܐܵܕܵܗܵܐ Sh., or ܐܵܕܵܐ Al. (ܕ݂), or ܐܵܕܝ Al., or ܐܵܬܝ Gaw. (the last three also = *that*), or ܐܵܕ Al. (cf. U. ܐܵܕܠܸܠܝܵܐ *to-night* = ܐܵܕܠܸܠܝܵܐ K. § 67), or ܗܵܕܠܸܠܝܵܐ J. (both Zlamas second sound), or ܗܵܐ ܗܘܿ Z.

f. ܐܵܗܵܐ *this*, or ܐܵܝܵܐ K. U. (*é-ya*), or ܐܝܼܵܐ Al. (*eiya*), or ܐܵܗ Sal. U., or ܐܵܕܵܐ etc., as above, or ܗܵܐ ܗܝ Z.

Plur. m. and f. ܐܵܢܝܼ U. Ti., or ܐܵܢܵܐ Tkh. Ash., or ܐܵܢܵܐ Al. K. (not Ash.), or ܐܵܢܝ Al., or ܗܵܢܵܐ MB., or ܗܵܢܵܐ MB. [Stoddard gives ܐܵܢܵܗܘܼ U. ܐܵܢܵܗܵܐ, and ܐܵܢܵܗܵܢܵܐ, but these are at any rate very rare.]

The singular ܗܳܕ݂ܶܐ is also used in ܒܦܘܬ ܗܳܕ݂ܶܐ *about this = therefore* (see § 67). Sometimes ܐܳܗܳܐ = *he, she, it*: ܐܳܢܶܐ = *they*, and so the others.

(2) Sing. m. ܗܿܘ *that*, i.e. *ille*, [pronounced ō when a dem. pronoun, and so all its derivatives, as ܠܗܿܘ ܓܰܒܳܐ *on that side*, ܒܗܿܘ ܨܰܦܪܳܐ *in the morning*], or ܗܿܘܘܿܢ U. (*ow-wun*), or ܗܿܘܐܳܗܳܐ U. (*o-waha*), or ܐܿܘܗܳܐ Ash., or ܗܿܘܘܿܗܳܐ (*o-woha*) U. Ti., or ܗܿܘܗܳܐ Tkh. (*o-ha*), or ܗܿܘܗ Sal., or ܗܳܕ݂ܘ MB., or ܗܳܕ݂ܘܗܳܐ MB., or ܐܳܕ݂ܘ Sh., or ܐܳܕ݂ܘܗܳܢܳܐ Sh., or ܗܿܘܗܳܐ U. (the longer the distance pointed out, the longer the penultimate is drawn out).

f. ܗܿܝ *that* [pron. ā as in *fate*: sometimes in Ash. etc. *ei* as in *height*], or ܗܿܝܝܼܢ U. (*eiyin*), or ܗܿܝܝܶܗܳܐ U. *ei-yéha*, or ܗܿܝܗ Sal., or ܐܝܼܗ Tkh. MB., ܐܝܼܗܳܐ Tkh. MB.

Plur. m. and f. ܐܳܢܝܼ *those*, or ܐܳܢܶܐ Al. (*a-né*), or ܐܳܢ K. Al. Sal., or ܐܳܝܢܝܼܗܳܐ U.[1] Bo., or ܐܳܝܢܝܼܗ Tkh., or ܐܳܝܢܝܼܗܳܐ Tkh., or ܐܝܼܢܝܼܗܳܐ U.[1], or ܐܝܼܢܝܼܗ U.[1]

(3) Sing. m. ܐܳܗܘ, f. ܐܳܗܝ *that*, i.e. *iste* K. (not Ash.). Elsewhere the above forms are used in this sense.

All these pronouns precede their nouns in N.S., as ܐܳܗܳܐ ܐܢܳܫܳܐ *this man* = O.S. ܓܰܒܪܳܐ ܗܳܢܳܐ (usually).

When used with prepositions these pronouns cannot be omitted as sometimes in O.S. Thus ܠܰܝܠܶܝܢ ܕܟܳܦܪܺܝܢ ܒܶܗ O.S. = ܠܐܳܢܝܼ ܕܟܳܦܪܝܼ ܒܝܼܗ N.S. *to those who deny him.*

Of the pronouns in the first series some seem to be derived from O.S. ܗܳܢܳܐ: we thus have ܐܳܗܳܢܳܐ (by metathesis) and ܗܳܢܳܐ, singular for plural; then by dropping ܗ, ܐܳܗܳܐ or ܐܳܗ, whence ܐܳܘܢ, ܐܳܘܐ, ܐܳܢܶܐ,

[1] Village of Anhar.

ܐܢܝ. (ܘ and ܘ for ܗܝ, § 109.) The forms with ܕ, m. and f., seem to come from the O.S. feminine ܗܘܕܝ or ܗܘܕܝ. Stoddard conjectures that ܐܢܝ is from ܗܢܝܢ.

The pronouns in the second series are the same as the personal pronouns, with extra syllables added for emphasis, and ܗܐ *behold* attached as often in other cases, § 73.

§ 13. *Interrogative Pronouns.* ܫܡܗ̈ܢܐ ܫܘܘ̈ܠܢܐ.

ܡܢܝ *who?*, or ܡܢܝ Sal. Gaw., or ܡܢܝ Al. (not Ash.) = O.S. ܡܢ (usually written ܡܢ). ܡܢ is also used in N.S. [Qu. ܡܢ ܐܦ = ܡܢܝ fem. for masc.?]

Whose? is expressed by ܕܡܢܝ etc.; and so the other cases.

ܡܘܕܝ *what?* U. Ash. (perhaps = O.S. ܡܐ ܕܝ, or for ܡܐ ܐܕܝ), or ܡܘܕ (before a noun), or ܡܐ U. Ti., or ܡܐ K. Al., rare in Ash. U. (so O.S.), or ܡܘܕܝ Sh. Ti. (not Ash.), or ܡܝ Al., or ܡܕܪܐ K. Al., or ܡܘܕܗ Ti. (for ܗܘ ܡܘܕ?).

ܐܝܢܝ *which?* U. Ash., with or without a noun (O.S. ܐܝܢܐ), or ܐܝܢܝ K. Sh. (the O.S. fem. ܐܝܕܐ, now used for both genders), or ܐܝܢܐ U., or ܐܝܕ, or ܐܝܡܐ Al. Z. (Mim for Nun), or ܐܝܡ Q. U.—(all sing. and pl.). Qu. ܐܝܢܝ, ܐܝܢܝ for ܐܦ ܐܝܢܐ : ܐܝܕܐ ܐܦ? cf. ܡܢܝ.

ܟܡܐ *how much*, or ܐܟܡܐ Al.; also an adverb, see § 67, and equivalent to *many* in ܐܢܝ ܟܡܐ ܫܢ̈ܐ *these many years* (τοσαῦτα ἔτη, St Luke xv. 29).

Notes. (1) ܡܘ is not used with a noun following.

(2) It is frequently used in U. at the end of a sentence as an interjection; as: ܟܐܒܐ ܡܥܕܢܝ ܓܒܝ : ܡܘ? *I have a stomach ache,*

what (*shall I do?*) And often in expostulation, thus: ܠܹܐ ܝܠܹܗ ܡܲܕܪܵܐ ܚܒܝܼܒܵܐ. ܡܘܿܢ؟ *It is not dear. What* (*do you say?*) Cf. the use of ܩܵܐ ܡܘܿܢ؟ *why?* in expostulation, at the beginning of a sentence.

(3) ܐܲܝܢܝܼ ܡ̈ܢܲܝܗܝ *which of them?* is contracted in U. to ܐܝܼܡ̈ܢܲܝܗܝ (accented on the first), in Bo. to ܐܝܼܡܢܲܝܗܝ.

(4) ܡܘܿܕܝܼ is used elliptically thus: ܡܘܿܕܝܼ ܕܫܸܡܥܘܿܢ ܝܠܹܗ *what* (*relation*) *of Simon is he?*

(5) ܡܵܐ is thus used: ܡܵܐ ܠܘܼܟ݂ ܥܲܡܲܢ؟ *what hast thou to do with us?* St Luke iv. 34. ܡܵܐ ܠܘܼܟ݂ ܠܡܲܡܠܘܼܠܹܐ *what hast thou to do with speaking?* ܡܵܐ ܗܘܹܐ ܠܝܼ ܐܵܗܵܐ *of what use is this to me?* (for ܗܘܹܐ see under ܗܘܵܐ in § 46). ܡܵܐ ܟܒܸܥ *what wilt thou? or what is the matter with thee?* Judg. i. 14. So for other persons. In Al. ܡܵܐ = ܡܸܕܸܡ ܕ *that which*; thus ܠܡܵܐ ܕܐܵܡܪܝܼ ܗܘܵܘ *to what they said.* ܝܲܬܝܼܪ ܡܸܢܡܵܐ ܕܝܠܹܗ ܦܩܝܼܕܵܐ *more than that which is commanded,* St Luke iii. 13; also ܡܢ ܒܵܬܲܪ ܡܵܐ ܕܩܵܛܹܠ *after he kills,* St Luke xii. 5. In U. ܡܵܐ ܠܘܼܟ݂ = *what is it?* as a reply when a person is called, is rather more polite than ܡܘܿܕܝܼ, rather less polite than ܒܠܵܐ (§ 73).

§ 14. *Relative Pronouns.* ܚܠܵܦܫܡܵܗܹ̈ܐ ܕܝܲܚܝܼܕܵܝܹ̈ܐ.

ܕ *who, which.* ܐܲܝܢܝܼ ܕ, or ܗܿܘ ܕ (chiefly in Al.) *he* (*she, they*) *who, that which.* Thus St Luke ii. 44. ܠܟܠܵܐ ܗܿܘ ܕܟܹܐ ܝܕܝܼܥ ܗܘܵܐ ܠܗܘܿܢ Al. = ܠܟܠܵܐ ܗܿܘ ܕܟܹܐ ܝܕܝܼܥ ܗܘܵܐ ܠܗܘܿܢ U. *with any one who knew them.* So ܡܵܐ ܕ *that which* in Al. (§ 13, note 5, above) = ܡܸܕܸܡ ܕ U.; ܐܲܝܡܵܐ ܕ *he who*, Z.

ܟܡܵܐ ܕ, or ܟܠ ܡܸܢܕܝܼ ܕ, or ܡܵܟܘܠܵܐ Al. *everything that,* see § 67.

Whom, which, as the direct object of a verb can be expressed by the simple relative, or by the relative and by an objective pronominal affix added to the verb (§ 48), as ܓܒܪܵܐ ܕܒܸܬ ܚܵܙܹܬ ܠܹܗ *the man whom you will see.* For the other cases we use the simple relative with the pronominal affixes of § 11 added to the noun or preposition, though the preposition and affix are sometimes omitted. Thus ܓܒܪܵܐ ܕܟܬܵܒܘܼܗ ܝܼܠܹܗ *the man whose book it is.* So ܓܒܪܵܐ ܕܝܗܒܸܠܝ ܠܹܗ ܟܬܵܒܵܐ ܩܵܐܕܹܗ *the man to whom I gave the book.* ܗܵܘ ܝܘܡܵܐ ܕܐܬܹܝܬ ܠܘܼܟ *the day on which you came* (sc. ܒܝܘܡܹܗ). So also ܕܘܼܟܬܵܐ ܕܚܙܹܐ ܠܝ ܠܵܗ (or ܒܝܵܗ) *the place where I saw him.*

When a relative is implied in English it is usually expressed in Syriac, though the substantive verb is often omitted. Thus: ܥܹܕ̈ܬܵܐ ܕܓܵܘ ܡܵܬ̈ܘܵܬܵܐ *the churches in the villages (which are in the villages).* But ܒܲܪ ܢܵܫܵܐ ܠܸܒܘܼܗ ܟܘܡܵܐ *a malicious man (whose heart is black),* because the relative clause is treated as an adjective. So ܡܕܝܼܢ݇ܬܵܐ ܫܡܘܼܗ̇ ܐܘܼܪܡܝ *a city named Urmi.* But we might say ܕܫܡܘܼܗ̇. So ܚܘܼܒܘܼܟ ܕܥܲܠܲܢ *your love to us.* The O.S. usage is similar. But note that ܢܸܚܙܘܢ ܡܢ ܥܲܡܡ̈ܐ O.S. = ܕܝܼ ܚܙܘܝ ܐ̄ܢܝ ܕܡܢ ܥܲܡ̈ܡܹܐ N.S. *they of the peoples will see,* Rev. xi. 9. So ܠܕܒܐܘܪܫܠܡ O.S. = ܠܐ̄ܢܝ ܕܒܐܘܪܫܠܡ N.S. *to those who are in Jerusalem.*

§ 15. *Indefinite Pronouns.*

The indefinite *ever* is expressed by the adjective ܟܠ *all, every* (*kul*). Thus ܟܠ ܡܲܢ ܕ *whoever,* or ܟܠ ܕ (so O.S.), or ܟܠ ܢܵܫܵܐ ܕ; ܟܠ ܕ *whatever* (so O.S.), or ܟܠ ܡܸܢܕܝܼ ܕ (O.S. ܟܠ ܡܵܐ ܕ or ܟܠ ܡܸܕܸܡ ܕ); ܟܠ ܐܵܕܵܢܵܐ ܕ *whenever, as soon as,* and so on. ܟܠ ܕܗܘܵܐ

= *any you please.* ܟܠ is often shortened to ܟܘ in Al. K. and sometimes becomes ܟܘܕ.

ܟܠ ܐ̈ܢܵܫܵܐ or ܐ̈ܢܵܫܵܐ alone = *each one*: ܗܲܒ݂ܠܘܿܗܝ ܐ̈ܢܵܫܵܐ ܚܲܕ ܟܬ݂ܵܒ݂ܵܐ *give each one a book.*

The indefinite *one* (French *on*), *any one, some one,* may often be rendered by ܚܲܕ ܐ̈ܢܵܫܵܐ *a man.* *No one* is ܗܝܼܟ݂ ܐ̈ܢܵܫܵܐ U. or ܟܘ ܐ̈ܢܵܫܵܐ K. *Nothing* is ܗܝܼܟ݂ ܡܸܢܕܝܼ U., or ܟܘ ܡܸܢܕܝܼ K., or ܟܘ ܡܸܕܸܡ Ti. But if a verb follows, ܠܹܐ or ܠܵܐ *not* must be prefixed, as ܟܘ ܐ̈ܢܵܫܵܐ ܠܵܐ ܐܼܬ݂ܹܐ ܠܹܗ *no one came.* The ܗܝܼܟ݂ and ܟܘ are often omitted when a verb follows. *None of them* is usually ܐ̈ܢܵܫܵܐ ܡܸܢܵܝܗܘܿܢ followed by ܠܹܐ or ܠܵܐ.

Some is ܚܲܕܟܡܵܐ (which preserves the Pthakha sound); but see § 28 (4, 9). *Some of them* is ܚܲܕܟܡܵܐ ܡܸܢܵܝܗܘܿܢ or ܐ̈ܢܵܫܵܐ ܡܸܢܵܝܗܘܿܢ. *Some* may also be rendered by ܡܸܢ: as ܐܟ݂ܘܿܠ ܡܸܢ ܕܐܵܗܵܐ *eat some of this*; also by ܚܲܕܟܹ̈ܐ, § 28 (9). *Some* may also be omitted in N.S.: ܚܙܹܐ ܠܝ ܐ̈ܢܵܫܵܐ *I saw some men.* Or it may be expressed by ܐܝܼܬ, thus: ܐܝܼܬ ܗ݈ܘܵܐ ܕܢܦܸܠܠܗܘܿܢ *some fell*; ܐܝܼܬ ܗ݈ܘܵܐ ܕܣܟ݂ܸܠܬܵܐ ܡܚܝܼܠܗ ܗ݈ܘܵܐ *some one had blundered.*

One another is expressed thus: ܚܲܕ ܩܵܐ ܕܗܘܿ ܐ̱ܚܹܪ̈ܢܵܐ U. = ܚܲܕ ܟܵܠܵܐ ܕܗܘܿ ܐ̱ܚܹܪ̈ܢܵܐ K (Al. ܟܠܵܐ or ܟܵܐ) *one another, one to another*; or with ܠ for ܩܵܐ (O.S. ܚܲܕ ܠܚܲܕ).—ܚܲܕ ܒܵܬ݂ܲܪ ܕܗܘܿ ܐ̱ܚܹܪ̈ܢܵܐ U. (ܐ̱ܚܹܪ̈ܢܵܐ, ܒܵܬ݂ܲܪ K. Al.) *one after the other* = O.S. ܚܲܕ ܒܵܬ݂ܲܪ ܚܲܕ.—So ܐܸܩܠ̈ܵܬ݂ܵܐ ܡܲܚܘܸܝܠܗܘܿܢ ܠܗܘܿܢ ܚܲܕ ܒܗܘܿ ܕܚܲܕ ܕܗܘܿ ܐ̱ܚܹܪ̈ܢܵܐ *one another's feet*:—ܐ̱ܚܹܪ̈ܢܵܐ U. (ܐ̱ܚܹܪ̈ܢܵܐ, ܚܙܸܝܠܗܘܿܢ K. Al.) *they looked at one another.* These may also be expressed as frequently by ܠܚܕܵܕ݂ܹܐ U., or ܐܚܕܵܕ݂ܹ̈ܐ K., or

ܣܰܕܳܪܳܐ K., or ܡܣܰܕܪܳܐ K., or ܣܰܕܪܳܐ Al. Thus ܚܕܳܢܶܐ ܡܚܰܕܢܶܗ O.S. ܘܡܶܚܕܳܐ ܣܰܕܪܳܐ K.) = ܣܰܕܪܳܐ ܕܚܰܕܕܳܕܶܐ U. (ܕܚܰܕܕܳܕܶܐ *and bear ye one another's burdens*, Gal. vi. 2. Or as the direct object, ܡܚܰܕܶܗ ܡܚܰܕܕܶܐ U.) ܩܛܠܘ ܠܚܕܕܳܕܶܐ K. (ܩܛܠܘ ܠܣܰܕܪܳܐ *they killed one another*. So O.S. ܠܣܰܕܪܳܐ.

SUBSTANTIVES.

ܫܡܳܗ̈ܶܐ.

§ 16. There are no cases, but there are a few traces of the old 'states'. It is customary in grammars of Classical Syriac to treat the *absolute state* as the normal form, representing the simple state of the noun, as *king*, and to derive thence the *construct state* as representing *king of*, and the *definite state* as representing *the king*, though in O.S. the last is by far the most common and is often used for the first, and, with the help of ܕ *of*, for the second. But the East Syrians look on the definite state as the normal one and call it ܫܡܳܐ *the noun*, while the other states are called ܠܚܘܕܳܡܳܐ *abbreviations*. The absolute state is ܠܚܘܕܳܡܳܐ ܓܘܡܕܳܢܳܐ, the construct state ܠܚܘܕܳܡܳܐ ܕܡܶܠܘܡܳܐ.

In the vernacular the definite state alone is used normally, the other two being confined to certain words and phrases.

(i) The *Absolute state* remains in a few words.

a. In the present participles, as ܩܳܕܶܫ m. ܩܕܫܳܐ f.; ܩܕܫܝ Pl. O.S. becomes ܩܳܕܫ; in the past participles, as ܩܕܝܫ m. ܩܕܝܫܳܐ f. ܩܕܝܫܝ pl. (see §§ 31, 50) used in the preterite. For ܡܚܝ, etc. see § 46.

b. The numerals ܥܶܣܪܝ *twenty* (= ܥܶܣܪܝܢ) and the like, § 26.

c. ܐܘܪܳܐ *manger* f. = O.S. ܐܘܪܝܳܐ which has no abs. or const. state (Bar Hebraeus); ܪܰܚܝܳܐ U. *mill* f. (ܪܰܚܝ K.) O.S. ܪܚܝܳܐ, ܟܶܣܦܳܐ; ܕܘܽܟܬܳܐ

place f. of which the definite state ܕܘܟܬܐ is also used; ܚܘܝ K. *serpent* (also ܚܘܘܝ U. K.) m. = O.S. ܚܶܘܝܳܐ; ܟܠ *all* (the O.S. alternative ܟܠܐ is not now used); ܟܠ ܝܘܡ *daily* (iu Z. ܝܘܡ is used by itself); ܡܳܐ or ܡܐܐ f. *a hundred*; ܡܬܘܕ *again* (in U. ܬ is silent) = O.S. ܬܘܒ; ܡܝ ܣܘܣܝܐ *horse* m. = O.S. ܣܘܣܝܐ; ܣܟܝܢܐ *knife* f. (O.S. ܣܟ) of which the definite ܣܟܝܢܐ is also used; ܥܩܪܬܐ U. O.S. f. *a barren woman*, and a few other feminines. In Al. we have also ܐܡܝܢ *faithful*.

d. Some in ܘ or ܘ̈, as ܥܡܝܩ *deep*, ܒܠܝܘܗܝ or ܒܠܝܘܗܝ f. *affliction*, O.S. ܐܘܠܨܢܐ; ܥܡܩܐ *deep*, lit. *depth*, O.S. ܥܘܡܩܐ; ܚܒܝܘ or ܚܒܝܘ f. *affliction*, O.S. ܐܒܝܘܬܐ; ܦܕܡܘ *understanding* (rare), see ܡܦܕܡܘ § 83 (6); ܕܩܦܣܘ *by chance*, § 67 (Arabic root); ܢܓܝ *pain* f. (foreign). These seem to be the absolute state of nouns whose definite state would end in ܘܬܐ. Diminutives in ܘ, as ܕܚܘ *little father*, are not of this class, § 79: nor are the Turkish words in § 82 (8).

e. The phrase ܠܥܠܡ ܥܠܡܝܢ ܗܘ *for ever and ever*, and its imitation ܗܘ ܐܚܪܝ ܐܚܪܝܢ *id.*

(ii) The *Construct state* remains in several phrases.

a. Phrases with ܒܝ[1] or ܒܝ. In O.S. ܒܝ is the constr. st. of ܒܝܬܐ *house* m. We have ܒܝ ܡܪܝ ܫܡܥܘܢ *the household of Mar Shimun* (so any name); also with ܒܝ.

ܒܝ ܕܪܐ *threshing floor* f. from ܐܕܪܐ O.S.

ܒܝ ܡܥܪܒܐ Ti. (*house of setting*) *the west.*

ܒܝ ܕܝܘܬܐ *ink* f. = O.S. ܕܝܘܬܐ.

[1] In some of these the prefix may be a form of the preposition *between*. Nöld. O.S.G. §§ 156, 252.

ܒܝ ܘܕܢܚܐ Ti. (house of the rising) *the east.*

ܒܝ ܒܝܢܓܐ K. (In U. Sh. ܒܝܢܓܐ as O.S.) *the palate.* See ܚܢܟܐ below.

ܒܝ ܢܝܣܢܐ U. Tkh. (house of the Aprils) *the spring* m. In Ti. ܪܒܝܥܝ. (Tkh. ܕܒܝܥܝ ܒܝ m. and ܕܗܘܐ m. K.).

ܒܝ ܣܕܝܐ or ܒܣܕܝܐ O.S. *pillow.* Now almost always in the forms ܗܩܕܝܢܝ U. K. (not Ti.) by metathesis, or ܗܩܕܐ or ܕܣܡܕܝܟܐ Sal. (ܒ as ܦ). Cf. ܣܕܕܢܐ below.

ܒܝ ܗܘܪܐ U. See below e.

ܒܝ ܓܢܐ or ܓܢܐ or ܣܓܢܐ (house of the eyes) *eyebrows.*

ܒܝ ܥܠܠ K. *upper room.* In Al. ܒܠܓܐ.

ܣܦܠܟܐ (in U. ܒ as ܦ) or ܒܣܦܠܟܐ *in the middle.* Also with ܬ-.

ܒܝ ܪܡܫܡܐ[1] U. m., ܒܝ ܪܡܫܐ[1] K. m. (house of the evenings) *evening.*

ܒܝ ܪܫܐ Ti. f.; rarely ܒܝ ܪܫܐ (house of the head) m. *pillow.*

ܒܝ ܗܟܡܐ K. f. *a hem* at the top of trowsers in which a string (ܗܟܡܐ) runs. This when gathered up supports them.

ܒܝ ܓܒܝܢܐ = O.S. and N.S. ܓܒܝܢܐ § 92, *eyebrow* or *brow* of a hill.

ܒܝ ܓܘܣܐ *refuge* O.S. (not colloquial).

ܒܝ ܕܢܚܐ O.S. or ܒܝ ܕܢܚܐ or ܕܢܚܐ O.S. (house of the shining forth) *Epiphany* (ܥܡܕܐ ܢܓܗܐ U.)

ܒܝ ܝܠܕܐ O.S. or ܒܝ (house of the Nativity) *Christmas* (ܒܓܕܐ ܘܟܘܕܐ U.). The former also is used for any birthday.

---

[1] Zlama has the second sound; in the prefix of the other phrases, the first.

ܒܹܝܬ ܢܲܗܪ̈ܝܢ O.S. or ܒܹܝܬ݂ (house of the rivers) *Mesopotamia.*

ܒܹܝܬ ܩܒܘܼܪ̈ܐ m. or ܒܹܝܬ ܩܒܘܼܪ̈ܘܵܬܼܐ or ܒܹܝܬ ܩܒܘܼܪ̈ܐ *graveyard.*

b. Phrases with ܒܲܪ *son of* (ܒܹܪ Al. Z.). This word is used, but not very colloquially, with any name, as ܒܲܪ ܝܲܥܩܘܿܒ *son of James.* So ܒܲܪ ܬܘܠܡܲܝ *Bartholomew,* and other Biblical names; and colloquially to denote age, as ܒܲܪ ܬܠܵܬܼ ܫܸܢܹ̈ܐ *three years old* (for the fem. see below, *d*). We must distinguish ܒܲܪ ܫܸܢ̄ܬܵܐ *one year old* and ܒܲܪ ܚܕܵܐ ܫܸܢ̄ܬܵܐ *contemporary.* So also:

ܒܲܪ ܐܸܓܵܪܵܐ Ti. (son of a roof) *a lunatic* = ܒܲܪ ܐܸܓܵܪܵܐ O.S. *a devil.*

ܒܲܪ ܐܲܬܼܪܵܐ ܕ *fellow countryman of.*

ܒܲܪ ܙܘܼܓܵܐ (son of a pair) *companion,* rare.

ܒܲܪ ܙܲܪܥܵܐ (son of seed) *seed.* ܙܲܪܥܵܐ is used = *descendant.*

ܒܲܪܚܸܡܵܘܵܐ (rare) or ܒܲܪܚܸܡܵܐ *wife's brother* (= O.S. ܒܲܪ ܚܡܵܘ̈ܗܝ *son of parents in law*). So ܒܲܪܚܸܡܬܵܐ *wife's sister* (Pthakha like Zqapa)[1].

ܒܲܪ ܟܝܵܢܵܐ ܕ (son of the nature of) = ὁμοούσιος (not colloquial). So O.S.

ܒܲܪܢܵܫܵܐ (son of man) *man*; so O.S. Al. ܒܹܪ ܕܢܵܫܵܐ. Ash. ܒܹܪ ܐܢܵܫܵܐ.

ܒܲܪ ܨܸܕܪܵܐ (son of chest) *a shirt front.*

ܒܲܪ ܩܕܵܠܵܐ K. (son of neck) *a collar.* In U. simply ܩܕܵܠܵܐ.

ܒܲܪ ܩܸܡܬܵܐ *an ally* (rare).

[1] These do not mean *brother's wife* or *sister's husband* which are expressed by ܟܲܠܬܵܐ (lit. *bride*) and ܚܲܬܼܢܵܐ (lit. *bridegroom*) respectively. These do not only mean a man's own wife, or a woman's own husband, but the wife or husband of almost any near relation.

ܒܰܪ ܫܡܶܗ ܕ (son of the name of) *namesake of.* In K. a man speaks of or to his namesake as ܒܰܪ ܫܡܝ and does not use his name.

c. The plural of ܒܰܪ, ܒܢܶܐ, is thus used : ܒܢܰܝ ܡܕܝܼܢܬܳܐ *a citizen* or *citizens* ; ܒܢܰܝ ܐܘܿܪܡܝ *an Urmian* or *Urmians.* In the singular we should perhaps understand ܒܢܰܝ ܡܶܢ ܒܰܪ *one of the sons of.* In K. adjectives are used in this sense. See § 81 (1).

d. ܒܰܪܐ is used of age : ܒܰܪܐ ܒܶܗ ܝܰܪܚܳܐ *one month old* f. (O.S. ܒܰܪܚ).

e. ܒܰܪܬ is used for ܒܰܪ in the following feminines :

ܒܰܪܬ ܐܝܕܐ (daughter of the hand) *glove.*

ܒܰܪܬ ܒܰܪܕܐ (or ܒܰܪܕܐ) (hail) *quartz* = Ash. ܒܰܪܕܐ ܒܰܪܕܡܐ.

ܒܰܪܬ ܕܰܒܳܐ (wooden bolt) *a bolt-socket.* Also ܕܒܰܒܳܐ ܚܳܡܐ in K.

ܒܰܪܬ ܝܰܘܡܐ *halo round the sun.* (ܝܰܘܡܐ *day* often is used for *the sun*). In Ash. ܒܰܪ ܝܰܩܕܐ or ܒܰܪܕܐ.

ܒܰܪܬ ܗܰܪܡܐ Tkh. *halo round the moon*; also a child's disease, supposed to come at new moon. In U. the latter is ܒܰܪ ܗܰܪܡܐ. In Ash. ܣܶܒܰܪܕܐ.

ܒܰܪܬ ܨܶܒܥܐ (finger) *thimble.*

ܒܰܪܬ ܩܳܠܐ (voice) *echo.*

ܒܰܪܬ ܫܡܫܐ *halo round the sun.*

f. ܡܳܪܝ, the irregular const. st. of ܡܳܪܐ *lord* (not, according to East Syrian grammarians, of ܡܳܪܝܐ which is only applied to Jehovah and said by them to contain the sacred name ܝܰܗ *Jah,* being a compound word) is prefixed to almost any noun to form an adjective, as

ܡܵܪܹܐ ܛܝܼܡܵܐ *lord of price = dear.* ܡܵܪܹܐ ܡܝܼܵܐ *lord of water = watery.* ܡܵܪܹܐ ܕܹܢܵܐ *lord of debt = creditor.* ܡܵܪܹܐ ܕܘܼܚܠܵܐ *lord of fear = dangerous* (as a road). But ܡܵܪܹܐ may be left out, as ܐܵܗܵܐ ܛܝܼܡܵܢܵܐ *this is dear*; and especially in phrases like ܚܲܡܬܵܐ ܠܹܗ *it is in the sun*, ܚܸܡܵܐ ܠܹܗ *it is hot* (lit. heat), ܩܲܪܬܵܐ ܠܹܗ *it is cold* (lit. coldness), ܣܘܼܓܵܐ ܠܹܗ *it is dark* (lit. darkness), ܦܲܘܚܵܐ ܠܹܗ *it is windy* (lit. wind). ܡܵܪܹܐ is also used in O.S. (but rarely in this sense) with a feminine ܡܵܪܲܬ. This is not used in N.S., the masculine serving both genders. In O.S. ܒܥܸܠ is used in the same way. (So Heb. בַּעַל).

g. So the following; but those marked with an asterisk are ecclesiastical or literary and not commonly used.

ܐܵܟܸܠ ܚܲܒܪܹܗ m. (K. بی) *late snow* in the spring, lit. eater of its companion.

ܐܵܟܸܠ ܩܲܪܨܵܐ m. *the Devil* (eater of accusation) O.S. Cf. Gk. διάβολος. Not used in pl., but we have ܫܹܐܕܹ̈ܐ = *devils*.

ܐܲܟ݂ܠܵܐ ܕܪܲܡܫܵܐ m. f. *supper* (evening meal).

ܟܲܠܟܵܐ ܣܘܼܡܵܐ f. *bat*.

ܨܲܝܵܕ ܢܘܼܢܹ̈ܐ m. Ti. *a cormorant* (fish snatcher). See below ܨ.

ܓܢܸܚܠܝܼ ܦܸܪܬܵܐ *a beetle*, perh. = ܨ݇ = ܡܓܲܢܚܠܹܐ ܦ݇ = *wallowers in dung*.

ܠܸܒ ܠܸܒ U. *my very self* (soul of my soul).

ܠܒܸܠ ܫܸܡܫܵܐ m. Tkh. *sunset, the west.*

ܓܲܪܡܹܐ ܦܝܼܠܵܐ m. *ivory* (elephant's bone) O.S. In Ash. ܓܲܪܡܵܗ ܦܝܼܠܵܐ (so pronounced), also ܘܲܙܢܵܐ m.

ܕܸܚܠܲܬ ܐܲܠܵܗܵܐ * f. *piety* (fear of God) O.S.

ܒ̈ܓܵܐ ܓ̈ܓܵܐ (for ܒ̈ܓܵܐ) *a malignant fairy* supposed to haunt pregnant women.

ܘܨܕܵܐ ܟܵܕܘܿܪ (or ܨܘܿܕܲܪ) *spider* (web spinner).

ܘܕܢܚ ܝܘܿܡܵܐ Tkh. *sunrise, the east.*

ܣܵܒ݂ܵܐ ܕܩܢܵܐ m. *an old man* (white beard), a term of respect. In Ash. ܓܗܟܵܐ.

ܣܵܒ݂ܬܵܐ ܚܘܿܪܬܵܐ f. *an old woman* (white locks), a term of respect.

ܣܵܒ݂ܵܐ ܦܨܝܼܚܵܐ *innocent* (white faced), not common.

ܢܵܕܸܡ ܠܚܡܵܐ m. Sal. *a baker.*

ܚܘܒ ܦܨܚܵܐ m. f. *guilty* (black faced), not common.

ܠܚܡܵܐ ܕܐܦ̈ܐ* O.S. *shewbread.* Also ܠܚܡܵܐ ܕܩܵܕܘܿܡܵܐ.

ܠܚܡܵܐ ܕܚܡܢܵܐ *a herb* (bishop's bread), pron. *lakhmi.* See ܡܪܚܡܵܐ ܠܚܡܵܐ below.

ܚܙܝܼ ܒܘܿܙܵܐ Ti. *lizard* (goat sucker). In U. ܚܙܝܼ ܒܕܘܿܡܵܐ f. (with ܟ like ܘ), or ܚܙܝܼܒܘܿܙܵܐ f., or ܡܚܓܘܿܙܵܐ¹ f.

ܡܢܫܝܼܕ ܡܕܢܵܐ (for ܡܢܫܝܼܕ) *clout* (dish washer). In Ash. ܡܢܫܟܠܢܵܐ.

ܡܠܟܵܐ ܥܒ݂ܕܵܐ* *participle* f. (verb of noun) O.S.

ܡܣܒ ܕܐܦ̈ܐ* *hypocrisy* (taking in face) O.S.

ܡܚܝܟܵܐ ܠܚܡܵܐ U. *the larynx* (that which makes bread descend). In K. ܘܢܩܵܐ m.

ܢܵܛܪ ܚܘܕܪܵܐ m. *bishop's successor* (keeper of the seat). In Ash. ܢܚܝܼܕܵܐ. Also, esp. in K. ܢܘܝܼܪܵܐ, lit. *a Nazarite.*

ܢܣܒ ܕܐܦ̈ܐ* *hypocrite* (taker in face) O.S.

¹ Village of Ardishai, in the plain of Urmi.

ܣܝܳܡ ܐܝܕܐ m. f. *ordination, confirmation, consecration* (of bishops and churches), *blessing* (lit. laying on of hands) O.S.

ܥܒܝܕ ܒܐܝܕܐ* *made with hands* O.S.

ܓܘܠܐ ܕܚܘܛܐ f. *spider* (web spinner).

ܐܦܝ ܡܝܐ f. Sal. *surface of water.*

ܩܦܣܐ* m. *abbreviation* (in grammar) O.S.

ܦܪܫܐ ܠܠܝܐ *butterfly, moth* (night flier). Also *a bat,* in which case ܕܓܠܕܐ (*of skin*) may be added. In K. ܓܕܐ ܦܪܚ.

ܩܪܛ ܟܡܟܐ Ti. *a small basket* (spoon holder ?).

ܩܕܘܫ ܩܘܕܫܐ m. *holy of holies* (the sanctuary of a church) O.S.

ܩܪܛ ܛܦܪܘܗܝ *a churl* (nail biter).

ܩܫܐ ܩܕܠܐ* *stiff-necked* (hard of neck) O.S.

ܩܫܬܗ ܕܡܪܝ *rainbow* (bows of our Lord), pron. *qishti*; or perhaps we should write ܩܫܬܗ, ܕ being omitted. The full form ܩܫܬܗ ܕܡܪܝ is also used as in O.S.

ܪܫ *upon* (head of). Especially in K.

ܪܫ ܥܝܢܝ *on my eyes be it* (sign of obedience), or *welcome!*

ܪܩܕ ܕܘܢܒܐ lit. *a wagtail*: term of contempt for a Mussulman.

ܫܠܐ ܢܘܢܐ U. *cormorant* (fish snatcher).

ܫܒܪܐ ܩܘܡܩܡܐ (or ܩܘܡܩܡܗ) *a herb* (pot breaker).

ܫܡܝܐ U. m., or ܫܡܝܘܣܐ Tkh. f., or ܫܡܫܟܐ Ti. Ash. Sh., or ܫܡܫܟܐ Q. (which in Ti. = *the gums*) = ܚܟܐ ܒܝܫ O.S. *palate*; lit. *heavens of the palate,* Ps. xxii. 15. Cf. O.S. ܚܟܐ ܓܦܐ *a ceiling,* and ܚܟܐ ܦܘܡܐ *the palate.*

ܟܘܡܣܬܐ U. *crown of the head,* perhaps ܟܘܡܬܐ ܕܡܘܚܐ *heavens of the brain* (Nöld. § 61). In K. ܟܘܡܬܐ with plural irregular; see § 19.

ܫܡܫܬ ܣܗܪܐ *moonlight,* pron. *shimshi.* (In Tkh. ܩܡ). See ܒܪܥܕ ܚܕ.

ܢܣܒ ܦܬܐ m. K. *hypocrite* (taker of face).

ܩܕܚܐ ܓܦܐ (or ܩܕܚܐ) Ti. (*a bird*).

ܬܪܥ ܒܕܩܐ * m. *sanctuary door* O.S.

h. In K. all present participles may be used in construction, thus:—

ܩܛܠ ܓܒܪܐ *a man killer;* fem. ܩܛܠܬ ܓܒܪܐ; ܡܚܐ ܛܠܝܐ *a striker of boys;* fem. ܡܚܝܬ ܛܠܝܐ.

i. Several proper names in O.S. and N.S. like ܣܒܪܥܝܣܘܥ, ܚܕܒܫܒܐ, ܕܒܝܥܣܘܥ, ܒܓܕܝܥܣܘܥ, ܥܒܕܝܥܣܘܥ, retain the construct state, though in the second and fourth the vowel has been thrown back; they literally mean, Mercy, Hope, Uncle, Servant, of Jesus; and Day of our Lord.

§ 17. *Gender* ܓܢܣܐ.

There are two genders, masculine and feminine. It is difficult to give rules for determining the gender of a particular noun, but generally:—

a. Nouns ending in ܬܐ are feminine; the converse however is by no means the case.

Exception: if ܬ be part of the root. The following are masculine: ܦܣܝܬܐ *a gelding* (Tau radical?); ܒܝܬܐ *a house,* so O.S.; ܟܘܡܬܐ *a fist* (Tau radical?); ܡܘܬܐ *death,* so O.S. (ܬ K.). Bar Hebraeus adds to masculines ܙܝܬܐ *olive tree,* ܬܘܬܐ *mulberry,* ܚܣܬܐ *hole in the ground,* ܟܢܣܐ *cassock;* but the first two are usually feminine in

N.S., and the last two are obsolete. ܩܶܫܬܳܐ *bow*, ܕܽܘܥܬܳܐ *sweat*, and ܢܺܝܫܳܐ K. *conversation*, are feminine in N.S. although the ܐ is radical.

b. The names of letters of the alphabet are feminine.

c. Most birds are feminine; we even have ܢܺܝܫܳܐ ܚܰܒܺܝܕܳܐ U. *a beautiful drake*.

d. Nouns denoting sex follow the gender appropriate thereto.

e. Nouns in ܰ ܐ are feminine, as ܥܝܳܕܳܐ *custom*.

f. Several foreign feminines end in ܰ ܐ [cf. § 21 (5)] as ܚܰܢ *lady*, ܢܺܫܺܐ (a woman's name), ܢܳܙܺܐ *coquetry*, ܚܰܕܨܺܐ (name of a village near Urmi), ܕܽܘܡܝܳܐ *world* (Sal. ܕܺܢܝܳܐ).

Genders often differ according to district, especially in the case of foreign words, to which genders seem to be given quite arbitrarily; as e.g. words from Turkish, a language which has no genders. The gender of Syriac words is usually, but not always, the same as in O.S.

Examples :—

ܐܘܪܝܳܐ *manger*, fem. N.S. In O.S. ܐܘܪܝܳܐ masc.

ܚܫܳܡܺܝܬܳܐ *supper*, is common in N.S. (f. in U.), by etymology should be masculine.

ܒܶܪܳܐ or ܒܺܪܳܐ *well*, masc. N.S. fem. O.S.

ܟܺܣܳܐ *pocket*, masc. K. (second Zlama sound) fem. U. (first Zlama).

ܥܳܘܕܳܐ *ditch*, masc. O.S. fem. N.S.

ܙܰܝܬܳܐ *olive*, see above.

ܚܽܘܒܳܐ *love*, fem. in Sal. Elsewhere masc. as O.S.

ܛܰܝܪܳܐ *bird*, masc. (rarely fem.) N.S. fem. O.S.

ܝܰܡܳܐ *sea*, fem. N.S. = ܝܰܡܳܐ O.S. masc.

ܟܺܐܦܳܐ *stone*, common N.S. fem. O.S.

ܓܶܢܳܪܳܐ *harp*, masc. O.S. fem. N.S.

ܠܺܠܝܳܐ *night*, fem. N.S. = ܠܺܠܝܳܐ O.S. masc.

ܡܳܐܐ *hundred*, fem. O.S. and N.S. but ܡܳܐܐ masc. in Al. See § 26.

ܡܰܕܢܚܳܐ *east*, common U. fem. K. In O.S. usually masc., sometimes fem.

ܡܶܛܪܳܐ *rain*, masc. O.S. fem. N.S.

ܢܽܘܢܳܐ *fish*, masc. O.S. fem. N.S.

ܢܽܘܪܳܐ *fire*, masc. N.S. fem. O.S.

ܣܝܳܡܺܝܕܳܐ or ܣܝܳܡ ܐܺܝܕܳܐ *ordination*, masc. O.S., U.; fem. (usually) K.[1] and (sometimes) O.S.

ܥܶܕܳܢܳܐ *time*, fem. N.S. = ܥܶܕܳܢܳܐ O.S. masc.

ܥܢܳܢܳܐ *cloud*, masc. O.S. fem. N.S. (not used in O.S. by Western Syrians?).

ܩܰܒܪܳܐ *grave*, masc. O.S. fem. N.S.

ܩܪܰܢ *qran* (7d.), masc. K. fem. U.

ܫܡܰܝܳܐ *heaven*, fem. sing. in N.S.; in O.S. masc. and fem. sing. and masc. plur.

ܫܶܡܫܳܐ *sun*, masc. in O.S. and N.S. usually, but sometimes fem. in N.S. and rarely in O.S.

ܫܪܳܓܳܐ or ܫܪܳܓܳܐ *lamp*, fem. N.S. = ܫܪܳܓܳܐ O.S. masc.

ܬܽܘܬܳܐ or ܬܽܘܬܳܐ *mulberry*, see above.

Some are common as ܗܘܳܐ *air*, ܚܰܝܘܳܐ *a beast*.

The rule for forming a feminine from a masculine is to change the termination into ܬܳܐ, as ܣܽܘܣܳܐ *horse*, ܣܽܘܣܬܳܐ *mare*; ܣܽܘܣܳܐ

---

[1] By attraction, because the second noun is feminine. So colloquially a grammatical error is often made with the substantive verb: as ܗܰܘ ܝܰܘܡܳܐ ܐܺܝܬܰܘܗ̱ܝ (ܫܰܒܬܳܐ), *that day is Saturday*.

Syrian, ܣܘܪܝܬܐ *a Syrian woman.* If necessary a vowel is added for euphony, as ܟܠܒܐ *dog*, ܟܠܝܒܬܐ *bitch*, or ܟܠܒܬܐ; ܡܠܟܐ *king*, ܡܠܝܟܬܐ or ܡܠܟܬܐ *queen*; ܬܘܪܐ *bull*, ܬܘܝܪܬܐ *cow* (*ta-wirta*, not *tô-irta*).

Some feminines end in ܝܬܐ, as those formed from masculines in ܝܐ preceded by a consonant; thus ܣܢܝܐ, f. ܣܢܝܬܐ both *a bush*; ܟܒܒܝܐ, ܟܒܒܝܬܐ *roast meat, cutlet*; they then usually lose their euphonic vowel. But the O.S. ܚܘܝܐ, in N.S. ܚܘܐ or ܚܘܘܐ *serpent*, makes fem. ܚܘܝܬܐ (or 'ܚܘܘ) in N.S.. So also the following; but the forms marked with an asterisk are themselves feminine.

ܐܠܗܐ *god*	fem.	ܐܠܗܝܬܐ	or ܐܠܗܬܐ
ܐܪܝܐ *lion*	...	ܐܪܝܬܐ	
ܓܣܐ *buttock* (O.S. *side*)...		ܓܣܝܬܐ	
ܓܦܐ *cave*	...	ܓܦܝܬܐ	*a small cave*
ܕܐܒܐ *wolf*	...	ܕܐܒܝܬܐ	or ܕܐܒܬܐ
ܕܒܐ* *bear*	...	ܕܒܝܬܐ	
ܕܒܘܪܐ *gadfly*		ܕܒܘܪܝܬܐ	or ܕܒܘܪܬܐ
ܙܢܝܐ *fornicator*	...	ܙܢܝܬܐ	
ܡܠܐܟܐ *angel*	...	ܡܠܐܟܝܬܐ	
ܢܡܪܐ *tiger*	...	ܢܡܪܝܬܐ	
ܣܘܠܛܢ *Sultan, captain* ...		ܣܘܠܛܢܝܬܐ	(also used for the raisin).
ܣܛܢܐ *Satan, devil*	...	ܣܛܢܝܬܐ	or ܣܛܢܬܐ
ܥܙܐ *goat**	...	ܥܙܝܬܐ	
ܥܩܒܐ *heel**	...	ܥܩܒܝܬܐ	*id.*
ܥܪܒܐ *sheep*	...	ܥܪܒܝܬܐ	(In K. both have ܦ)

ܦܠܢ (O.S. ܦܠܢ) or ܦܠܢܟܣ *So and So*, fem. ܦܠܢܝܬܐ (O.S. 'ܦ)

ܦܳܥܠܳܐ *workman* fem. ܦܳܥܰܠܬܳܐ

ܐܶܡܪܳܐ *lamb* (ܒ Ti.) ... ܐܶܡܰܪܬܳܐ U. or ܐܶܡܪܬܳܐ K.

ܓܘܦܳܐ *porch* ... ܓܘܦܬܳܐ Ti. *id.*

ܓܰܝܳܪܳܐ *adulterer* ... ܓܰܝܳܪܬܳܐ also as masc.

ܐܘܙܳܐ *goose or gander* ... ܐܘܙܬܳܐ

ܪܳܥܝܳܐ *shepherd* ... ܪܳܥܝܬܳܐ

ܫܶܡܫܳܐ *sun* ... ܫܶܡܫܳܢܬܳܐ *a ray of the sun* or ܫܶܡܫܳܢܝܬܳܐ

ܬܘܠܥܳܐ *worm* ... ܬܘܠܥܬܳܐ Tkh. or ܬܘܠܰܥܬܳܐ Tkh. (ܒ U.).

ܬܥܠܳܐ *fox* ... ܬܥܰܠܬܳܐ (ܒ Tkh.)

So also ܐܳܢܳܐ ܒܝܕܰܥܢܬܳܐ Al. *sycomore* (= ܐܳܢܳܐ ܒܝܕܰܥܢܬܳܐ Tkh. or ܐܳܢܳܐ ܦܚܝܪܬܳܐ U.). And so the words with double plurals in § 19.

The following do not take an euphonic vowel:—ܚܰܢܦܳܐ *heathen*, f. ܚܰܢܦܬܳܐ; ܣܳܗܕܳܐ *martyr*, f. ܣܳܗܕܬܳܐ.

ܚܰܒܪܳܐ U., O.S. *companion* (Al. K. ܚܒܝ) makes ܚܰܒܰܪܬܳܐ K., O.S. U. or ܚܰܒܘܰܪܬܳܐ U. (Pthakha like Zqapa) or ܚܰܒܰܪܬܳܐ Al.; ܒܪܳܢܳܐ *son* (Al. often ܒ) makes ܒܪܰܬܳܐ (Al. ܒܪܬܳܐ); ܒܰܥܠܳܐ *landlord* ܒܰܥܠܬܳܐ; ܒܰܥܡܳܐ (pron. *î*) *husband's brother* ܒܰܥܡܬܳܐ (*î*); ܚܡܳܬܳܐ U. (ܚܡܬܳܐ K.) *paternal uncle*, ܚܡܬܳܐ or ܚܡ, O.S.; ܫܰܠܳܦܬܳܐ U. (ܫܰܠܬܳܐ K., O.S) *maternal uncle*, ܫܰܠܬܳܐ; ܚܰܡܝܳܢܳܐ *father in law* ܚܰܡܝܳܢܬܳܐ; ܐܰܪܡܠܳܐ or ܐܰܪܡܠܬܳܐ *widower* ܐܰܪܡܰܠܬܳܐ; ܟܘܕܶܢܳܐ K., O.S. or ܟܘܕܳܢܳܐ U. *mule*, ܟܘܕܶܢܬܳܐ U. or K., O.S.; ܪܘܡܳܐ *height*, ܪܘܡܬܳܐ *hill*; ܡܰܬܠܳܐ *allegory* ܡܰܬܠܬܳܐ *maxim*.

When the noun does not admit the idea of sex the feminine usually denotes the diminutive of the masculine; but in Tiari, where feminine forms are much used, there is often no difference in meaning.

Feminines are often expressed by a different word, as ܓܲܒܪܵܐ *man*, ܒܲܟ̰ܬܵܐ *woman* or *wife* (ܓܲܒܪܵܐ in U = *husband*, in K. as O.S. = *man*). In K. the form ܐܸܢܬܵܐ for *woman* is also used (§ 19).

The proper names ܪܘܼܚܵܐ ܕܩܘܼܕܫܵܐ *Holy Ghost*, ܡܸܠܬܵܐ (or ܡܹܐܡܪܵܐ) *the Word* are usually masc. in N.S.

§ 18. *Number* ܡܸܢܝܵܢܵܐ.

There are two numbers in N.S.; singular and plural. As in O.S., there is no dual, the only relics being ܬܪܹܝܢ *two* for O.S. ܬܪܹܝܢ, ܬܲܪܬܹܝܢ (or ܬܪܸܬ) *two*, f. K. for O.S. ܬܲܪܬܹܝܢ, and ܡܸܨܪܹܝܢ *Egypt*.

The Plural is formed in the following ways. ܵܐ or ܹܐ of the singular is changed into:

1. ܹ̈ܐ, ܡܲܠܟܵܐ *king*, ܡܲܠܟܹ̈ܐ m.
2. Or ܵܘܵܬܵܐ, ܠܸܒܵܐ *heart*, ܠܸܒܘܵܬܵܐ m.
2ª. Or ܘܵܬܵܐ, ܐܲܚܘܼܢܵܐ *brother*, ܐܲܚܘܿܢܘܵܬܵܐ m.
3. Or ܵܬܵܐ, ܓܢܵܒܵܐ *side*, ܓܢܵܒܵܬܵܐ f.
4. Or ܵܢܹ̈ܐ, ܛܘܿܒܵܐ *noble*, ܛܘܿܒܵܢܹ̈ܐ m.
5. Or ܹ̈ܐ, the last consonant being doubled and taking Zqapa, ܥܩܵܐ *frog*, ܥܩܵܩܹ̈ܐ f.
6. ܬܵܐ of sing. becomes ܝ̈ܵܬܐ as ܝܲܠܢܬܵܐ *kerchief*, ܝܲܠܢܝܵܬܵܐ f.
7. Or ܘܵܬܵܐ, ܣܸܦܬܵܐ *lip*, ܣܸܦܘܵܬܵܐ f.
8. Or ܵܗܵܬܵܐ, ܒܲܟ̰ܬܵܐ *woman*, ܒܲܟ̰ܗܵܬܵܐ f.
9. Or ܵܬܵܐ, ܕܵܪܬܵܐ *courtyard*, ܕܵܪܵܬܵܐ f.,

or ܘܬܵܐ becomes ܘܵܬܵܐ: ܒܥܘܼܬܵܐ *request*, ܒܥܘܵܬܵܐ f.

Notes. (i) If the noun has not the termination ܐܵ or ܐ these endings are added on.

(ii) The mark Siami *must* always be placed over a plural substantive or adjective.

(iii) The above endings apply to U. Sh. MB., but in U. ܢ is hard, in Sh. MB. soft. For K. Al. in all the forms with ܢܐ we must substitute Zqapa for Zlama and write ܢܵܐ. In Sal. Q. Gaw. J. the ܢ is silent, or becomes a feeble ܘܗ. We thus have ܕܩܸܢܬܵܐ K. Al. ܕܩܸܢܬܵܐ Sal. Q. Gaw. J. (oxytone).

(iv) In these forms also in U. the ܢ is often silent in speaking, but the vowel is preserved: thus ܣܘܼܣܵܘܵܬܐ is often pronounced *susawa-i (horses).* [This word must be distinguished from ܣܘܼܣܵܘܵܬܐ *mares.*] The word ܡܵܬܼܘܵܬܐ *villages,* is often pronounced *mawa-i.* See § 26.

(v) Of these plurals the first and sixth are by far the most common. Generally speaking all regularly formed derivatives (§§ 76—82) take these forms. But the plural cannot be determined by the gender. Many masculines take the ܢ in the plural, many feminines make the plural without it.

(vi) Dissyllables in ܵܐ either drop the dot of Khwaṣa and take a euphonic vowel under the first consonant, as ܒܪܝܼܬܵܐ *creation* or *a creature,* ܒܪܝܵܬܐ *creatures* (or ܵ, ܵ); or retain Khwaṣa, and make the plural ܐܹ, as ܢܒܝܼܬܵܐ *prophetess,* pl. ܢܒܝܵܬܐ (or ܵ, ܵ). Polysyllables in ܵܐ (which in Q. Sal. Gaw. J. are of the form ܚܘܿܡܒܵܐ) in the plural usually retain the dot of ܘ in U. MB. Sh. Sal. Q. Gaw. J. and drop it in K. Al.; as ܚܘܿܡܒܵܐ *hat:* pl. ܚܘܿܡܒܵܬܐ, ܚܘܿܡܒܵܬܐ or ܚܘܿܡܒܵܬܐ (oxytone). The O.S. usage is as K. Al.

(vii) Nouns in ܒܝ ܳ take the first plural, but drop the dot under the second ܒ, as ܕܒ݂ f. *plan, advice*, pl. ܕܶܒ̈ܐ. § 67 (3).

(viii) Nouns in ܘܳ or ܘ (§ 16) make their plural in ܘܶܐ̈, rarely ܘ̈, but ܶܘ̈ܳܬܐ in Sal. Q. Gaw.

(ix) Nouns in ܝܘܼܬܐ follow this model: ܢܒ݂ܝܘܼܬܐ *prophecy*, pl. ܢܒ݂ܝܘܳܬܐ̈ (ܝ̈). The corresponding forms in Q. Sal. Gaw. J. are ܢܒ݂ܝܘܳܬܐ sing. ܢܒ݂ܝܘܳܬܳܐ̈.

(x) Other nouns in ܘܳܐ (the Sal. Q. Gaw. form of ܘܼܬܐ) make their plural in ܘܳܬܳܐ̈, as ܒܳܥܘܳܬܳܐ̈ *requests*.

(xi) In Al. we find a few plurals in ܶܐ̈ ܳ in Arabic words, as ܛܝܦܐ̈ *people*, pl. ܛܝܦܶܐ.

(xii) Many nouns have more than one plural. See the following lists.

(xiii) Many foreign nouns ending in a closed syllable with short Zlama lengthen the vowel in the plural; as ܪܝܫ *head man of a village*, pl. ܪ̈ܝܫܶܐ or ܪ̈ܝܫܶܐ. Sometimes a final letter in foreign words is hardened in the plural, as ܡܢܣ K. *lodging place on a journey*, pl. ܡܢ̈ܣܶܐ.

Lists of the Regular Plurals.

1. The usual form. Note (a) ܚܕ ܘܚܕܐ *companion*, ܙܕܘܙܕܐ *seed*, ܚܡܝܢܐ *wife's brother*; (b) ܒܝܕܐ *glove* (also 3), ܕܕܐ ܕܕܐ *bolt socket*, ܕܕܐ ܕܕܐ *echo*; (c) ܕܝܢܐ ܣܳܒ݂ܐ *old man*, ܣܒ݂ܬܐ *old woman*, ܢܒ݂ܝܕ ܚܘܕܒܝ *bishop's successor*, ܚܨܠܐ U. *palate*, all of

which take the first plural irregularly[1]; also (*d*) some in ܬܳܐ; viz. ܐܶܣܬܳܐ *gelding*, ܙܰܝܬܳܐ *olive*, ܡܘܼܫܬܳܐ *fist*, ܡܰܘܬܳܐ *death*, ܗܰܦܬܳܐ *a hafta* (= 8 lbs. avoirdupois), ܕܶܥܬܳܐ *resin*, *sweat*[2] (in Tkh. ܕܺܥܬܳܐ with 3d pl.), ܩܶܫܬܳܐ *bow* (but it usually takes 8th pl. as O.S.), ܬܘܼܬܬܳܐ *mulberry* or ܬܘܼܬܳܐ (also 6). See § 17. (*e*) ܓܰܒܪܳܐ *man*, makes ܓܰܒܪ̈ܶܐ for O.S. ܓܰܒܪ̈ܶܐ (in Al. 2).

2. In Ti. this is very common, especially for proper names, as ܕܶܢܚ̈ܘܳܬܳܐ *men named Dinkha*. In K. MB. all the letters take this plural as ܘܳܘ̈ܘܳܬܳܐ (ܬ MB., soft ܬ) *Waus*, elsewhere 1st pl.

ܐܳܓ̰ܳܐ m. *master*, in K. Sal. See § 19.

ܐܶܓܳܪܳܐ m. *roof*, O.S. ܐܶܓܳܪܳܐ.

ܐܘܼܪܝܳܐ f. *manger*, O.S. ܐܘܼܪܝܳܐ.

ܐܶܪܚܝܳܐ f. *mill*, also the game '*sacks on the mill*', O.S. ܪܚܝܳܐ; K. ܐܶ.

ܐܰܪܝܳܐ m. *lion* O.S. Also 1.

ܐܰܬܪܳܐ m. *country* O.S.

ܒܳܒܳܐ m. *father*, foreign.

ܒܳܪܳܐ f. *ditch*. Also 1.

ܓ̰ܳܕܳܐ m. *path*, foreign.

ܓ̰ܺܕܳܐ f. *spear*, foreign. Also 3.

ܓ̰ܘܿܠ *pool* f., also 1, foreign.

ܓܶܫܪܳܐ (Eastern O.S. ܓܶ) m. *bridge* Ti. In U. 1.

ܚܰܒܪܳܐ m. *companion* O.S. In Al. 1 (ܚܺ).

ܚܶܘܝܳܐ or ܚܘܼܘܝܳܐ *serpent*. Rarely 3. O.S. ܚܶܘܝܳܐ.

ܚܘܼܠܡܳܐ m. K. *servant*, § 115 *b*.

[1] The second noun only being altered. Most of the compounds in § 16 have no plural or have plural like the singular. See also § 19.

[2] For the latter ܕ is pronounced ܛ.

ܚܝܠܐ m. *strength, host* O.S.

ܚܢ m. *a khan, nobleman,* foreign.

ܚܨܐ m. *back, girdle, belt* (with first pl. = *loins*), O.S. ܚܨܐ.

ܚܬܢܐ m. (O.S. 'ܚܬܢ) *bridegroom, sister's (daughter's) husband.* Also 1. See page 29, note.

ܟܘܬܐ f. *recess in wall.* Also 3. (O.S. ܟܘܬܒܐ, pl. ܟܘܐ̈.)

ܠܒܐ m. *heart* O.S.

ܠܠܝܐ f. *night,* O.S. ܠܠܝܐ.

ܡܘܒܠܐ m. *barn.* Also 1 and 3.

ܥܡܐ m. K. *paternal uncle.* (In U. ܥܡܘܡܐ and ܥܡܘܡܐ̈ 1.)

ܡܪܐ m. *lord, possessor* O.S.

ܢܗܪܐ m. *river* O.S.

ܣܘܣܝܐ m. *horse,* O.S. ܣܘܣܝܐ.

ܥܐܕܐ m. *festival*; rarely 4. O.S.

ܥܕܐ f. *island,* in Sal. See § 19. Turk.

ܥܡܐ m. K. *paternal uncle,* not O.S.?

ܥܣܟܪ f. *army,* foreign.

ܩܒܪܐ *grave,* f. N.S. m. O.S. Also 1.

ܢܘܟܪ m. U. *servant,* foreign.

ܬܫܪܝܢ m. (or ܬܫܪܝܢ), O.S. ܬܫܪܝܢ, *October* or *November.* With first plural, ܬܫܪܝ̈ܢܐ or 'ܬܫܪ̈ܐ, = *autumn.*

2ª. Days of the week, from Sun. to Thurs. incl., in Ti. Also 1 and 4.

ܪܡܫܐ m. K. *evening.* See 4 and § 19.

ܓܗܠ *youth* (abstract), foreign. In pl. *youthful follies.*

ܐܵܡܵܐ K. m. *maternal uncle* O.S.

ܚܵܬܵܐ f. *sister* (O.S., but pl. in O.S. ܐܲܚܘܵܬܵܐ).

ܡܵܬܵܐ f. *village* (rare in O.S. See note iv above, and § 26, note 5). In Q. ܡܵܬܼܵܐ.

ܦܵܬܼܵܐ f. *face* (O.S., but rare in sing.; O.S. pl. ܐܲܦܹ̈ܐ).

ܢܲܥܡܵܐ f. *grace*, Arab.

3. ܐܵܘܵܢܵܐ f. *state, condition*, foreign.

ܐܘܿܪܚܵܐ f. *road* O.S. (= ܡܲܓܪܵܐ K.)

ܐܝܼܕܵܐ f. *hand*, also 1. (In O.S. first pl., also ܐܝܼܕܹ̈ܐ; and ܐܝܼܕܵܘܵܬܵܐ *handles*.)

ܐܸܩܒܵܐ f. *heel*, Turk.; or ܥܸܩܒܵܐ.

ܐܸܠܟܵܐ f. *plough handle*, foreign.

ܐܲܗܠܵܐ f. *crescent* (rare) O.S.

ܐܲܩܠܵܐ f. *foot.* Also 1.

ܐܲܪܥܵܐ f. *earth* O.S.

ܐܲܟܣܵܐ f. *testicle* O.S.

ܐܸܕܪܵܐ f. *threshing floor*, O.S. ܐܸܕܪܵܐ.

ܓܘܼܡܵܐ f. *earthen bowl.* Also 1.

ܓܘܼܕܵܐ m. *flock*, O.S. ܓ.

ܐܟܲܦܵܐ f. *glove.* Also 1. See page 42, note 1, and § 19.

ܟܝܼܣܵܐ f. U., m. K. *pocket.*

ܓܝܼܕܵܐ See 2.

ܥܕܵܢܵܐ f. *time*, in Al. Elsewhere 1.

ܠܒܘܼܫܵܐ f. *garment.* Also 1.

ܓܘܼܒܵܐ *pit.* Also 1 (f. N.S. m. O.S.).

ܓܘܼܕܵܐ f. *long cloak.*

ܓܘܼܠܵܐ f. *cannon ball.*

ܓܘܼܡܠܵܐ m. *camel.* Also 1 (O.S. ܓܲܡܠܵܐ).

ܓܘܼܣܛܵܐ f. *tail coat.* Also 1.

ܓܸܠܵܐ m. *grass.* Also 1 and 5. In O.S. *stubble.*

ܓܵܢܵܐ, ܓܵܢ Ti., f. *soul, self*, Pers. See § 20 (5).

ܕܸܒܵܐ f. *bear.* Also 1. O.S.

ܕܸܓܵܐ m. *hawk.* Also 1.

ܕܲܝܪܵܐ m. *monastery* O.S.

ܕܲܦܢܵܐ f. *side*, O.S. ܕ.

ܕܘܼܕܵܐ f. *wound.*

ܗܵܘܵܐ m. f. *air.* Also 1.

ܗܲܝܟܠܵܐ m. *temple.* Also 1. O.S. [Used also for any one of the divisions of a church, esp. for the nave.]

ܙܘܼܪܢܵܐ m. *chanter* (as of bagpipes).

ܚܹܘܵܐ See 2.

ܚܲܪܓܵܐ f. *large cog.* Also 1.

ܚܵܠܘܿܙܵܐ m. U. *maternal uncle.*

ܡܚܲܛܬܵܐ f. *needle.* Also 1. (O.S. ܡܚܲܛܵܐ; Ti. ܡܚܲܛܬܵܐ 1.)

ܚܲܡܪܵܐ m. *wine.* Also 1 and 4 (as O.S.).

ܚܲܩܠܵܐ f. *field, column* (of a book). Also 4. O.S.

ܚܸܙܒܵܐ f. K. *small spear.*

ܛܸܦܪܵܐ f. *nail, claw.* See § 19. O.S.

ܝܘܿܡܵܐ Ti. Al. Z. (or ܝܘܡ U. Tkh.) m. *day* (in K.; also 1. K. Al. Z.; in U. Al. Z. 4). O.S.

ܝܘܿܢܵܐ m. *dove.* Also 1. O.S.

ܝܸܡܵܐ f. *mother* (O.S. ܐܸܡܵܐ: pl. in O.S. ܐܸܡܗܵܬܵܐ and ܐܸܡܗܵܬܹܐ).

ܝܲܡܵܐ *sea* N.S. f., O.S. ܝܲܡܵܐ m.

ܟܘܼܝܵܐ See 2.

ܟܘܿܟܵܐ f. *a house in a vineyard.*

ܕܘܝܬܵܐ f. *inkstand,* foreign.

ܟܘܼܪܵܐ f. *bellows, kiln* O.S.

ܟܝܼܟܵܐ *girl.* See § 19.

ܟܲܪܣܵܐ (ܟܸ Ti., ܟ Al. Z.) f. *belly, womb*; O.S. ܟܲܪܣܵܐ.

ܠܘܿܬܟܵܐ f. *boat.* Also 1.

ܡܘܿܗܪܵܐ f. *seal.* Also 1. See § 19.

ܡܘܿܫܟܵܐ See 2.

ܡܸܫܒܵܐ f. *a wood.* Also 1.

ܡܲܫܚܵܢܵܐ f. *grindstone* O.S.

ܢܘܿܒܵܐ m. *turn* (= *vices*).

ܣܘܼܢܓܵܐ m. *bayonet.*

ܥܸܛܵܐ f. *thigh.* Also 5.

ܦܲܪܣܵܐ m. *hoof.*

ܡܲܥܒܪܵܐ m. *ford.* Also 1.

ܓܵܙܲܪܬܵܐ f. *island,* in K. See 2 and § 19. Turk.

ܥܸܕܵܢܬܵܐ f. *time,* O.S. ܥ.

ܥܘܿܡܵܐ f. *skirt, petticoat,* pron. nearly *oyma* in U.

ܥܲܛܡܵܐ f. *thigh,* O.S. ܥ.

ܥܢܵܢܵܐ m. *cloud, sponge.* Also 1; m. O.S., f. N.S. See § 17.

ܥܲܝܢܵܐ f. *fountain* O.S. (with 1 = *eyes*).

ܥܲܡܘܿܙܵܐ m. U. *paternal uncle.*

ܥܲܪܣܵܐ f. *bier.* Also 1. In O.S. ܥܲܪܣܵܐ = *a bed.*

ܦܲܣܬܵܐ m. *sole of foot or boot.* Also 1.

ܨܸܒܥܵܐ f. (ܒ as ܦ) *finger,* O.S. ܨܸܒܥܵܐ.

ܨܘܼܕܪܵܐ f. *shirt.*

ܩܲܕܵܐ f. *calamity,* in K. (In U. 1.)

ܩܲܪܢܵܐ f. *horn.* Also 4. O.S. ܪ.

ܩܲܠܥܵܐ f. *castle,* foreign.

ܪܘܼܚܵܐ f. *spirit* O.S. Also 1, K.

ܪܘܼܡܚܵܐ f. *spear* O.S. Also 1.

ܪܘܼܦܬܵܐ m. *shoulder.* Also 4. O.S. ܪܲܦܬܵܐ = N.S. ܪܘܼܦܫܬܵܐ *shovel.*

ܫܡܲܝܵܐ, see § 19.

ܫܲܡܥܵܐ f. *wax.*

ܫܸܡܫܵܐ m. *sun.* Also 1. O.S.

ܫܵܩܵܐ m. *leg.* Also 1, 4.

ܫܪܵܓ݂ܬܵܐ f. *lamp,* O.S. ܫܪܵܓ݂ܵܐ m.

ܬܘܼܦܵܐ f. *wheel.* Also 5.

ܬܘܼܪܢܵܐ f. *bag.*

ܬܲܣܬܵܐ f. *metal basin,* or ܬܲܣ. O.S. ܛܲܣܬܵܐ. Also 1.

ܬܘܼܣܡܵܐ f. *strap.*

4. Days of the week, esp. in U. See 2ⁿ.

ܒܵܓ̰ܟ̰ܵܐ f. *garden,* Turk.

ܒܘܼܣܬܵܢܵܐ or ܒܣ' m. *melon field.* Also 1. (In Al. *a garden.*)

ܒܪܲܡܫܹܐ m. U. *evening.* See also 2ⁿ and § 19.

ܓܒܵܐ m. *side,* O.S. ܓܒ; Ti. ܓܸܒ.

ܓܲܒ݂ܪܵܐ m. *husband;* in K. as O.S. *a man.* Also 1. See § 19. ܓܸܒ Ash.

ܓܘܼܕܵܐ m. *wall.*

ܓܘܼܠܦܵܐ m. *fin, wing.* See § 19. (O.S. ܓܸܠܦܹ̈ܐ pl. only.)

ܓܘܼܡܵܐ m. *sheepfold.*

ܓܘܼܪܵܐ m. *nobleman* (with 1, *great*).

ܕܘܼܟܬܵܐ f. *place* O.S.

ܕܘܼܪܵܐ m. K. *the gums* (of the mouth) pl. same meaning. (In U. ܒܸܣܪܵܐ ܕܟܵܟܹ̈ܐ.)

ܕܝܼܘܵܐ m. *devil* O.S.

ܕܘܼܟܵܢܵܐ m. *shop,* foreign.

ܕܪܵܥܢܵܐ m. U. *arm,* K. ܕܪܵܥܵܐ (which in U. is a *yard*), O.S. ܕܪܵܥܵܐ.

ܚܲܒ݂ܪܵܐ m. *word,* Arab. Also 1.

ܚܸܙܘܵܐ m. *vision* O.S.

ܚܲܩܠܵܐ f. *field.* See 3. O.S.

ܛܘܼܪܵܐ m. *mountain* O.S.

ܝܘܼܡܵܐ or ܝܵܘܡܵܐ. See 3.

ܟ̰ܲܕܪܵܐ m. *tent,* Turk. Also 1.

ܡܲܚܲܠܹܐ or ܡܚܲܠܵܐ m. *lane, quarter* of a city, foreign.

ܡܘܼܩܵܐ m. *keyhole.* Also 1.

§ 18] REGULAR PLURALS.

ܟܰܪܡܳܐ m. *vineyard* O.S.

ܨܰܦܪܳܐ ܕܝܰܘܡܳܐ f. *morning* U. § 8 (4).

ܡܰܘܠܝ f. *landed property*.

ܡܰܘܬܳܐ m. *death*. Also 1. O.S.

ܡܺܝܠܳܐ m. *mile*. Also 1.

ܡܶܕܶܡ m. *thing*, in U. See § 19.

ܓܰܒܳܐ m. *side*, foreign.

ܙܶܒܠܳܐ f. *dunghill*.

ܣܶܦܳܐ m. *seashore*.

ܒܙܕܐ See 2.

ܫܩܳܩܳܐ m. *street*.

ܩܰܠܳܐ m. *stable*, foreign.

ܦܘܡܳܐ m. *mouth, edge* of a sword. Also 1. O.S.

5. ܬܕܳܐ m. *breast* O.S.

ܒܘܪܟܳܐ f. *knee*, O.S. 'ܒܘ.

ܠܶܠܳܐ See 3.

ܩܛܳܐ m. *buttock*. Also 1. O.S.

ܝܰܪܩܳܐ K. *vegetables*, pl. only.

ܕܘܕܳܐ See 3.

ܘܰܪܳܐ m. *stripe*.

ܓܶܦܳܐ m. *eyelash*, O.S. ܗܠܟܒܐ.

ܢܩܕܳܐ m. *dot*.

ܦܠܩܳܐ m. *crack*.

ܒܰܙܳܐ See 3.

ܦܶܕܥܳܐ U., ܦܶܕܢܳܐ K. m. *branch*.

ܢܳܓܳܐ m. *cheek*. See § 19.

ܣܶܕܢܳܐ See 3.

ܕܘܩܢܳܐ See 3.

ܪܶܫܳܐ m. *chief* (with 1, *head*) O.S.

ܬܘܦܳܐ m. *footprint, stead*. Also 1, 5.

ܚܘܡܳܐ m. *wall* (of a town).

ܢܦܳܐ m. *thong of a whip*. Also 1.

ܫܶܡܳܐ m. *name*. O.S. ܫܡܶܐ (pl. in O.S. ܫܡܳܗܶܐ). See § 19.

ܥܶܩܳܐ See 3.

ܗܣܘܡܳܐ Al. *border, frontier*. O.S.

ܓܶܟܳܐ m. *morsel*. Also 1.

ܬܰܪܥܳܐ m. *door*. Also 1. O.S.

ܢܘܩܒܳܐ (ܕ) Al. m. *hole*. [In U.K. ܒܥܡܶܐ *eye of a needle* (1st. pl.), O.S. *hole*. ܒܥܡܶܐ = *female*.]

ܗܠܳܐ m. *box on the ear*. Also 1.

ܩܘܡܳܐ m. *snout*. Also 1.

ܢܘܩܳܐ m. *nostril* (with 1, *holes in a beehive*).

ܦܶܠܓܳܐ m. *half*, O.S. ܓ. Also 1. See § 27.

ܩܶܦܳܐ f. *frog*.

ܦܰܪܕܳܐ m. *crumb*.

ܣܘܦܳܐ m. *thumb*.

ܫܘܒܒܘܬܐ *neighbourhood*, pl. only.
ܢܨܒܬܐ f. *handle*.
ܟܘܬܐ See 4.

ܟܢܦܐ m. *skirt, border, lower flap of coat*, O.S. 'ܟ. Also 1.
ܨܟܬܐ K. m. *a slap*. Also 1.
ܟܘܬܐ See 3.

6. The usual plural of nouns in ܬܐ. Note ܣܓܕܬܐ, ܣܓܝܢܬܐ, § 29 (9).

7. ܣܦܬܐ f. *lip* O.S., also 9 rarely. ܡܕܝܢܬܐ *village*, see 2ª.

8. ܬܚܬܝܬܐ f. *bottom*.
ܒܟܬܐ f. *woman*. See § 19.
ܕܗܢܬܐ f. *company, band*. Also 1.
ܕܘܥܬܐ Tkh. f. *sweat*, see 1.

ܒܠܕܬܐ f. *girl* (rare).
ܥܪܘܒܬܐ f. *Friday* O.S.
ܩܫܬܐ f. *bow* O.S. Also 1, 6. (The ܬ is radical.) See § 17.

9. Almost all words in ܘܬܐ may take both this and the sixth plural, but ܐܓܪܬܐ *letter*, and ܒܥܘܬܐ *request*, take the ninth only. For ܨܠܘܬܐ *prayer*, see § 19. ܡܚܘܬܐ *plague* makes ܡܚܘܬܐ.

ܩܘܪܒܢܐ f. *the Holy Loaf* O.S.
ܒܘܪܟܬܐ f. *blessing* O.S.
ܒܝܫܬܐ f. *evil* O.S.
ܒܬܘܠܬܐ f. *virgin* O.S. Also 6.
ܟܘܪܬܐ f. *ball*.
ܕܪܬܐ f. *courtyard* O.S.
ܫܡܫܬܐ f. *maiden, young woman*.
ܛܒܬܐ f. *benefit, good* O.S.
ܚܡܠܬܐ f. *burden*.
ܠܘܛܬܐ f. *curse* O.S.
ܣܦܬܐ See 7.

ܥܕܬܐ f. *church* (the society) O.S. In O.S. also the building.
ܚܕܬܐ f. *a rival wife*.
ܩܡܘܪܬܐ f. *apron*.
ܦܪܚܬܐ f. *lamb* K., O.S.
ܥܡܘܪܬܐ f. K. *conversation*, O.S. m.
ܩܪܬܐ f. *cold* (In pl. Pthakha has the sound of Zqapa) O.S. The pl. = *cold weather*.
ܫܒܬܐ f. *week, Saturday* O.S. (ܬ is radical).

§ 19. (i) *Irregular Plurals*.

Singular. ܣܓ̈ܝ̈ܐ.   ܗ̈ܝܟܢܬ̈ܐ ܟܠ ܚܕܢܬ̈ܐ.

Plural. ܗܝܟܢ̈ܬܐ.

ܐܓ݂ܐ m. *master, landlord*. Turk.   ܐܓ̈ܠܪ U. (Turk. pl.); K. Sal., 2.

ܐܘܣܬܐ U. or ܗܘܣܬܐ K. MB. m. *master workman*. Cf. Al. ܐܘܣܬܝ (or ܝ̈) *Sir* (also used with other pronom. affixes).   ܐܘܣܬܘܬܐ U., or ܐܘܣܬ̈ܐ U., or ܗܘܣܬ̈ܐ MB., or ܗܘܣܬܘܬܐ MB., or ܐܘܣܬܘܬܐ U., or ܗܘܣܬܘܬܐ K.

ܐܚܘܢܐ m. *brother*.   ܐܚ̈ܐ Al. Elsewhere 2ª.

ܓܘܚܐ m. *hole* O.S.   ܓܘܚ̈ܐ. Also 1.

ܓܢܕܪ m. Ti. *upper room*. § 16.   ܓܢܕܪ̈ܐ.

ܓܕܡܫܐ m. U. *evening*.   ܓܕܡܫ̈ܐ. Also 4.

ܒܝܬܐ K. U., O.S. or ܒܝܬ Q. Sal. Gaw. J., m. *house*.   ܒܬܐ, or ܒ̈ܬܘܬܐ U. (rarely *bâwâ-i*), or ܒܬ̈ܐ Sal. etc., or ܒܬ̈ܐ.

[In the singular it usually means a room with an oven in the floor for baking bread. In this sense ܕܣܬܘܐ *of winter* is sometimes added. ܒܬܐ (which is also the O.S. plural) is a collection of buildings in a courtyard, the English *house*, but also *houses*. The ܬ is radical.]

ܒܟܬܐ (also ܒܓܐ K.), f. *woman*.   ܒܢܬ K. Al., or ܒܢ̈ܐ K., or ܒܢܟ̈ܐ Ti. Al. But in U. K. Sal. Q. Gaw., 8.

ܒܚܬܐ f. *egg* O.S.   ܒܚ̈ܐ.

ܒܪ m. *son* (const. st.) O.S.   ܒܢ̈ܐ.

ܒܪ ܐܬܪܐ m. *fellow countryman*.   ܒܢ̈ܝ ܐܬܪܐ. (Also *natives* as O.S.)

ܒܪܢܫܐ m. *man, human being* (§ 16 ii. *b*) O.S.   ܒܢܝܢܫ̈ܐ.

[But the other compounds of ܒܪ, § 16 ii. *b*, usually take the first plural, the second noun only being altered.]

S. GR.

Singular.	*Plural.*
ܒܪܘܢܐ m. (Al. ܒ) *son.*	ܒܢܘܢ̈ܐ ; rarely 1 (Al. ܒ, not Z.).
ܒܪܬܐ f. U.[1] K., or ܒܪܬܐ Q., or ܒܪܬܐ Al. (O.S. ܒ) *daughter, girl.*	ܒܢܬ̈ܐ U., ܒܢ̈ܬܐ K. O.S., ܒܢ̈ܬܐ Q. Sal. Gaw., or ܒܢܬ̈ܐ U.
ܒܪܬܐ ܕܐܝܕܐ f. *glove.*	ܒܪ̈ܬܐ Ash. Elsewhere 1, 3.
ܓܒܪܐ m. *husband, man,* p. 46.	ܓܒܪ̈ܐ. Usually 1.
ܓܘܠܦܐ m. *fin, wing.*	ܓܘܠܦ̈ܢܐ. See also 4.
ܓܙܪܬܐ f. *island* (rare in U.) O.S.	ܓܙܪ̈ܬܐ (ܬ K., O.S.). Also 6.
ܓܙܬܐ f. *fleece.*	ܓܙ̈ܐ.
ܕܡܥܬܐ f. *tear* (not Ash.). O.S. ܕܡܥܬܐ.	ܕܡܥ̈ܐ.
ܙܡܝܢܬܐ f. Al. K. *banquet.*	ܙܡܝܢ̈ܬܐ Al.
ܙܠܘ f. *leech.*	ܙܠܘ̈ܬܐ.
ܚܛܝܬܐ f. *sin* O.S.	ܚܛܗ̈ܐ Al. (as O.S.). Also 6 as elsewhere always.
ܚܠܦܫܡܐ m. *pronoun* O.S.	ܚܠܦܫܡ̈ܗܐ (not colloquial).
ܛܦܪܐ f. O.S., or ܛܦܪܬܐ, or ܛܦܘܪܬܐ *nail, claw.*	ܛܦܪ̈ܬܐ U. (ܬ K.), or ܛܦܪ̈ܬܐ U. (ܬ Sal.), or ܛܦܪ̈ܐ.

(The first form usually used for a human nail.)

ܟܘܪܣܝ f. *seat, chair* (O.S. ܟܘܪܣܝܐ).	ܟܘܪ̈ܣܝܬܐ K. as O.S. Elsewhere 1.
ܟܚܬܐ f. *daughter, girl* (*old maid* K.).	ܟܚ̈ܬܐ U. (ܬ K.), or 3 in Tkh. Sal.
ܟܠܬܐ O.S. (or ܟ Ti.) *bride,* or ܟܠܐ Gaw., or ܟܠܐ Gaw., or ܟܠܘ U. (Zqapa sound), or ܟܠܘ Ti.	ܟܠ̈ܠܬܐ K. as O.S. (U. ܬ), or ܟ Ti. (Zqapa sound in all.)
ܡܟܝܟܘ U. f. (ܡ Sal.), or ܡܟܝܟܘܬܐ U. *bladder.*	Makes plural from the latter (No. 6).

[1] Used of any unmarried woman.

Singular.	*Plural.*
ܡܕܝܼܢ݇ܬܵܐ f. *city* O.S.	ܡܕܝܼ̈ܢܵܬܹܐ U. (ܵ K. ܲ Sal. Q. Gaw.).
ܡܘܼܗܪ f. *seal.*	ܡܘܼܗܪ̈ܘܵܬܹܐ. Also 1, 3.
ܡܘܼܡܬܵܐ f. U., O.S., or ܡܘܼܡܵܬܹܐ K. O.S. *oath* (ܡܘܼܬܵܐ Ash.).	ܡܘ̈ܡܵܬܹܐ U. (ܵ K., O.S.).
ܣܘܼܬܹܐ f. U. K. (ܘ like ܝ), or ܣܝܘܼܬܵܐ Al. *hair.*	ܣܝܼ̈ܘܹܐ K. Al. as O.S. In U. 6.
ܡܸܠܬܵܐ f. *verb* O.S.	ܡܸ̈ܠܹܐ, or ܡܸ̈ܠܵܬܹܐ (not colloquial).
ܡܸܠܬܵܐ ܫܡܵܗܵܐ m. *participle* O.S.	ܡܸܠܬܵܐ ܫܡܵܗ̈ܐ (not colloquial).
ܡܸܢܕܝܼ U. Tkh. Ash. Al., or ܡܸܕܸܡ (ܕ) Ti. (O.S. ܡܸܕܸܡ) m. *thing.*	ܡܸܢܕܝܵ̈ܢܹܐ K. Al.; in U. 4; ܡܸܕܝܵ̈ܢܹܐ Ti.; ܡܸܢܕܝܵ̈ܢܹܐ Ash.
ܦܝܼܠܓܘ f. *concubine.*	ܦܝܼܠܓܘܵܘ̈ܐ, rarely ܦܝܼܠܓܘܵܬܹ̈ܐ.
ܢܵܣܹܒ ܒܐܦܹ̈ܐ m. *hypocrite* O.S.	ܢܵܣ̈ܒܲܝ ܒܐܦܹ̈ܐ (not colloquial).
ܢܵܬܹܐ f. *ear*, or ܢܵܘܝܼܬܵܐ Q. Sal. Gaw. (Also *handle* in K.)	ܢܵܬܼܝܵܬܹ̈ܐ K. Al. (ܹ U.), or ܢܵܘܝܵܬܹ̈ܐ Q. Sal. Gaw., or ܢܝܵܬܹ̈ܐ Ash., or ܢܵܬܼܘܵܬܹ̈ܐ Al.
ܣܲܟܼܘ f. U. *platform* or ܣܲܟܼܘܵܬܵܐ.	ܣܲܟܼܘܵܬܹ̈ܐ, or ܣܲܟܼܘܵܬܹ̈ܐ.
ܣܸܟܬܵܐ f. *peg* O.S.	ܣܸ̈ܟܹܐ.
ܐܲܕܵܐ f. *island* (rare in K.) Turk.	ܐܲܕܵܠܵܪ̈ܐ U. (Turk. pl.). In K. 3, in Sal. 2.
ܥܲܡܵܐ m. Tkh. Al. *people* O.S.	ܥܲܡܡܹ̈ܐ, as O.S.
ܥܩܲܪܬܵܐ Al. f. *barren woman.*	ܥܩܵܪܵܬܹ̈ܐ.
ܨܠܘܼܬܹܐ f. *prayer* O.S., or ܨܠܘܼܬܵܐ Q. Sal. Gaw.	ܨܲܠܘܵܬܹ̈ܐ U. (ܵ K. Al. O.S.). Also 6 U., or ܨܠܘܵܬܵܐ Sal. Q. Gaw., or ܨܲܠܘܵܬܵܐ Sal. J.
ܨܵܨܵܐ m. *cheek.*	ܨܵܨܵܢܹ̈ܐ. Also 4.
ܦܸܣܩܵܐ m. *a fraction* O.S.	ܦܸܣܩܵܢܹ̈ܐ.

Singular.	Plural.
ܒܢܬܐ f. *kernel*, also *a quarter of a walnut*, or ܒܢܬܐ K.	ܒܢܬܐ as O.S., or ܒܢܬܐ.
ܣܕܐ m. *tortoise*.	ܣܕܢܐ.
ܩܫܬ ܕܡܪܝ *rainbow* § 16 ii. *g*.	ܩܫܬ ܕܡܪܝ (rare).
ܕܦܩܐ *a throb* of the heart.	ܕܦܩܢܐ.
ܫܡܐ m. *noun* O.S.	ܫܡܗܐ (not colloquial).

(The corresponding N.S. ܫܡܐ *name*, takes the fourth plural.)

ܫܡܝܐ f. *heaven* O.S. (now sing.).	ܫܡܝ. Also 1; and in Ash. Al. 3.
ܩܡܚܢܝ f. K. *crown of the head*, § 16 ii. *g*.	ܩܡܚܢܝ Tkh., ܩܡܚܢܝ Ti.; ܩܡܚܢܝ Ash.
ܫܢܬܐ f. *year* (ܫ Al. as O.S.).	ܫܢܝ.
ܬܘܪܬܐ f. *cow* (O.S. ܬܘܪܬܐ).	ܬܘܪܬܐ Ti. Elsewhere 6.

The abbreviated diminutives of § 79 as a rule have no plural (but see ܓܠܝܠܐ, ܗܟܐ, ܘܠܐ above); and so many words whose sense excludes a plural. ܕܘܟܐ *place*, has no plural in U. (in K. 6) but borrows that of ܕܘܟܐ (4).

Note that ܨܒܬܐ is *a pair of tongs* (m.), ܨܒܬܐ is *several pairs*; and that ܥܠܡܐ *world*, is often used in a plural or collective sense (*men, people*); as ܥܠܡܐ ܕܒܝܬܐ *the people of the house*. Some have no singular, as ܡܝܐ *water* (Al. ܡܝܐ as O S.) ܚܝܐ *life* O.S., ܪܚܡܐ *mercy* O.S., ܐܒܗܬܐ *parents* O.S. (from O.S. sing. ܐܒ *father*), ܐܒܗܬܐ (ܐ K., O.S.) *spiritual parents*, ܣܓܕܬܐ *environs*, ܘܗܘܢ = *money* O.S. (but ܗܘܢ m. a rare word = *a piece of money*), ܫܒܒܘܬܐ *neighbourhood*.

(ii) *Double Plurals*.

Many nouns denoting collections of units (e.g. corn) have two

§ 19] DOUBLE PLURALS.

plurals, one to denote the whole species, the other individual units. Thus ܣܥܳܪ̈ܶܐ = barley, ܣܥܳܪ̈ܝܳܬܐ = barley corns. So we have:—

Singular.	Plural.
ܟܠܡܬܐ white cherry.	ܟܠܡܐ rarely 6.
ܓܪܒܐ stocking, or ܓܪܒܬܐ K.	ܓܪܒܐ and 6 (odd stockings).
ܓܪܡܐ dried pea.	ܓܪܡܐ and 6.
ܕܓܘܚܐ grain.	ܕܓܐ (in numbering; e.g. ܡܐܐ ܕܓܐ a hundred things) and 6.
ܘܕܟܐ yellow-beard.	ܘܕܟܐ and 6.
ܚܛܬܐ wheat, O.S. ܚܛܐ.	ܚܛܐ, as O.S. and 6.
ܣܡܘܕܟܐ bead, O.S. ܣܡܘܕ̈ܐ.	ܣܡܕܐ (O.S. ܣܘܡ̈) rarely 6.
ܫܓܗܡܢܐ pea.	ܫܓܗܡܐ rarely 6.
ܚܨܡܐ top boot, or ܚܨܡܐ K.	ܚܨܡܐ also 6 (odd boots).
ܓܗܡܢܐ precious stone.	ܓܗܡܐ O.S., also 6.
ܓܕܦܕܐ a shot (of a gun).	ܓܕܦܐ also 6.
ܓܪܡܒܬܐ raisin.	ܓܪܡܒܐ also 6.
ܚܥܡܒܐ eyeglass.	ܚܥܡܐ also 6.
ܟܬܠܬܡܗܐ roasted pea.	ܟܬܠܬܡܐ also 6.
ܡܥܢܐ bean.	ܡܥܐ also 6.
ܡܓܪܡܒܬܐ apricot.	ܡܓܪܡܒܐ also 6.
ܗܓܡܢܐ a shot (of a gun).	ܗܓܡܐ also 6.
ܣܥܕܢܐ barleycorn, or ܣܥܕܕܐ Ash., or ܣܥܕܡܒܗ Ash.; O.S. ܣܥܕܢܐ.	ܣܥܕܐ, O.S. ܣܥܕܕܐ also 6.
ܒܕܒܓܐ U. (ܒ K.) grape (O.S. ܒܕܒܓܐ). In Ash. ܡܕܓܐ.	ܒܓܕܐ U. (ܒ K., O.S.), also 6.

Singular.	Plural.
ܩܘܕܚܠܐ lock of hair.	ܩܘܕܚܠܐ (a complete set), also 6 (odd locks).
ܩܢܕܝܢܐ chestnut (ܕ).	ܩܢܕܝܢܐ also 6.
ܢܘܠܬܐ shoe (sa-wilta).	ܢܘܠܐ (a pair), also 6 (odd shoes), or ܢܘܘܠܟܐ J.
ܣܬܘܠܐ (or ܡ ?) half a moustache.	ܣܬܘܠܐ K., or ܣܬܘܠܟܐ U. the whole moustache (also 6 ?).
ܚܒܨܢܐ lily O.S.	ܚܒܨܢܐ as O.S. (also 6 ?).
ܓܕ ܠܓܐ turnip.	ܓܕ ܠܓܐ (also 6 ?).
ܗܘܡܚܬܐ trowser leg.	ܗܘܡܚܬܐ or ܗܘܡܚܬܢܐ pair of trowsers, also in K. ܗܘܡܚܬܐ in this sense, (also 6 ?).
ܚܘܕܒܐ bead.	ܚܘܕܒܐ also 6.

§ 20. *Substantives with pronominal affixes.*

For a table of the affixes see § 11.

If the noun ends in ܐ܊ or ܐ this ending is dropped and replaced by the affix, thus, ܡܠܟܐ *king*, ܡܠܟܝ *my king*, ܣܘܣܐ *horse*, ܣܘܣܘܟ *thy horse*, ܒܢܘܢܐ *sons*, ܒܢܘܢܝܗܘܢ *their sons*. The same affixes are added to singular as to plural nouns. Thus ܡܠܟܝ *my king* and ܡܠܟܝ *my kings* are only distinguished by Siami. If the noun has not the above endings, the affixes are added on, as ܕܝܓܡܝ *enemy*, ܕܝܓܡܢ *our enemy*. Those compounds in § 16 which take the first plural (§§ 18, 19, pp. 42, 49) add the affix to the second noun. Cf. O.S. ܪܚܡܬ ܐܢܫܘܬܟ *thy philanthropy*.

Notes. (1) Words in ܝ܊ drop the dot of Khwaṣa. Thus ܡܕܥܢ *our meaning*, from ܡܕܥܝ (another form of ܡܕܥܐ).

(2) Words in ܘܼܝ or ܘܼ drop the ܝ and take ܘ; as ܢܟܝܘܼܘܼܗܝ *his affliction*, from ܢܟܝܘܼܝ.

(3) Words in ܝ have ܝ both as a vowel and as a consonant: as ܡܸܢܕܝܼܝܘܿܟ݂ܘܿܢ *your* (pl.) *thing, mindiyôkhon*; and so in words like ܫܘܝܼܝܘܼܗܝ from ܫܘܝܼܬܵܐ Sal. Q. Gaw. J. (= ܫܘܝܼ K. U.) *bed* (*shwi-yu*).

(4) ܚܲܕ ܕܘܼܣܬܝ = *a friend of mine*, ܚܲܕ ܒܵܓ݂ܝ *a garden of mine.*

(5) *Self* is expressed by ܓܵܢܵܐ. Thus ܓܵܢܝ *myself*, ܓܵܢܘܼܟ݂ *thyself* etc. In Ti. ܓܝܵܢܝ etc., or ܓܝܵܢܝ ܕܝܼܕܝ *my own self*, cf. ܓܵܢܝ ܓܼ § 16. For *ourselves* we may have either ܓܵܢܲܢ or ܓܵܢܵܬܲܢ, but the latter may also mean *our souls*. *My own* is expressed by ܕܓܵܢܝ, and so for the other persons; as ܟܬܵܒ݂ܵܐ ܕܓܵܢܘܼܟ݂ *your own book*. The preposition ܒ is often prefixed: as ܐܵܢܵܐ ܒܓܵܢܝ ܐܵܬܹܐ ܠܝ *I myself came.* Note that ܓܵܢܵܐ is feminine, and we therefore have ܡܣܘܼܪܩܬܵܐ ܠܹܗ ܓܵܢܘܼܗܝ = *he emptied himself*, Phil. ii. 7, where the participle is feminine: lit. *his self was emptied by him.*

(6) The O.S. ܢܲܦ݂ܫܵܐ *soul* is thus used: ܒܢܲܦ݂ܫܝ *alone*, lit. *by myself* [contrast ܒܓܵܢܝ = *myself*]. So for the other persons. Thus ܐܵܬܹܐ ܠܗܘܿܢ ܒܢܲܦ݂ܫܝܗܘܿܢ *they came alone.* In Al. and often in K. we have ܠܚܘܿܕܝ or ܒܠܚܘܿܕܝ (O.S. ܢ) for *alone*. The O.S. ܒܢܲܦ݂ܫ or ܩܢܘܿܡܝ = N.S. ܓܵܢܝ.

(7) ܒܣܵܐ *enough*, takes affixes like a noun; as ܒܣܘܼܟ݂ *enough for you.* So ܠܵܙܹܡ *necessary*, esp. in K., as ܠܵܙܹܡܝ *necessary for me*; then Zlama is lengthened, but not in ܠܵܙܸܡܘܿܟ݂ܘܿܢ *necessary for you* (pl.).

(8) ܠܵܪܵܟ݂ܵܐ *here* takes affixes; ܗܲܠ ܠܵܪܟ݂ܝ *up to this point on my body* (pointing).

(9) The affixes are often redundant, especially in Al. though not so often as in O.S., as ܒܪܘܿܢܹܗ ܕܐܲܠܵܗܵܐ *the Son of him, of God.*

(10) When there is an epithet, the affix is attached to the substantive, as ܒܵܒܘܼܗܝ ܒܝܼܫܵܐ *his wicked father.*

(11) ܡܵܪܝܵܐ *Lord* (of God only) and ܐܵܓ̰ܵܐ *master, landlord*, are not used with affixes. For the latter ܐܵܓ̰ܝܵܐ is used. For the former ܡܵܪܵܐ is not now used (though it is used when = *owner*), but the O.S. ܡܵܪܝ lit. *my Lord,* ܡܵܪܬܝ lit. *my Lady,* are retained as titles of bishops and saints, as ܡܵܪܝ ܫܸܡܥܘܿܢ *Mar Shimun,* ܡܵܪܬܝ ܡܲܪܝܲܡ *St Mary.* For ܡܵܪܲܢ see (14) below.

(12) In Lower Ṭiari they say for *their king* ܡܲܠܟܲܢܵܐ, in Bas ܡܲܠܟܲܢܹܗ. So for all nouns.

(13) From ܪܹܝܫ *head man* we have ܪܹܝܫܲܢ as in § 18, note xiii, and so similar words; and the same hardening of final letters takes place.

(14) The words ܪܲܒܝ lit. *my great one* (now usually pronounced with Zqapa), ܪܲܒܲܢ *our great one* (with Pthakha sound) are now treated as any other substantives, and mean *master* and *monk* respectively. They take the first plural, and affixes are added on, but the second Pthakha of ܪܲܒܲܢ is then strengthened to Zqapa. Thus ܪܲܒܵܢܲܢ *our master.* But in Al. this is ܪܲܒܲܢ; so ܪܲܒܘܼܟ݂ܘܿܢ Al. *your* (pl.) *master.* ܪܲܒܝ is also used before ܩܲܫܵܐ (the usual vernacular for ܩܲܫܝܼܫܵܐ § 81, *b*) both in speaking to a priest and in speaking of him. For ܪܲܒܬܵܐ see § 25 (7).

ܡܵܪܲܢ *our Lord,* is even more used as a name for Christ than with us: e.g. it is constantly used vocatively; but it has not quite come to be an independent substantive, and does not take affixes.

(15) Demonstrative pronouns and these affixes may be used with the same substantive. Thus ܐܳܗܳܐ ܥܳܠܡܘܽܟ݂ *this thy world*, O.S. ܗܳܢܳܐ ܥܳܠܡܳܟ݂.

ADJECTIVES.

ܫܡܳܗ̈ܶܐ ܡܫܘܳܕ̈ܝܶܐ

§ 21. Adjectives are very much more frequent in O.S. than in Hebrew, and more so in N.S. than O.S.; see § 81 for their formation. The periphrasis ܪܘܼܚܳܐ ܕܩܘܼܕܫܳܐ *Holy Spirit*, though used as a proper name, is not in accordance with common N.S. usage, which would say ܪܘܼܚܳܐ ܩܲܕܝܼܫܬܳܐ when not speaking of the Holy Ghost. So ܠܲܚܡܳܐ ܕܣܘܼܢܩܳܢܲܢ *bread of our need* (*our necessary bread*), though used in the Lord's prayer as a well known expression, is not what would naturally now be said.

Feminine of Adjectives and Participles.

General Rule. Change ܵܐ of the masculine to ܬܳܐ, as ܛܳܒ݂ܳܐ m., ܛܳܒ݂ܬܳܐ f. *good.*

Notes. (1) Words of the form ܩܫܝܳܐ *hard*, make ܩܫܝܼܬܳܐ; ܓܠܝܳܐ *revealed* ܓܠܝܼܬܳܐ; ܫܡܝܼܥܳܐ *heard* ܫܡܝܼܥܬܳܐ.

(2) A few other adjectives make feminines in ܝܼܬܳܐ, as ܟܐܦܳܢܳܐ *stony*, ܬܪܲܝܳܢܳܐ *second* (not colloquial), ܙܥܘܿܪܳܝܳܐ *small*, Al., ܒܘܼܪܟܳܢܳܐ *blessed* (as a title). We have also ܟܐܦܳܢܬܳܐ.

(3) ܐ̱ܚܪܹܢܳܐ U. makes ܐ̱ܚܪܹܬܳܐ *other*; ܐܚܪܹܢܳܐ K., O.S. ܐܚܪܹܬܳܐ (second Zlama U. K.); ܐ̱ܚܪܵܢܳܐ Al. Tkh. Z. ܐ̱ܚܪܵܬܳܐ; the ܪ is often silent (so also Sal.), and the Zlama sometimes long, with the first sound. [In Al. there is a fem. pl. as well as the usual masc. pl., viz. ܐ̱ܚܪ̈ܵܢܝܳܬܳܐ. See § 22.]

(4) The present participle, being in the absolute state, makes its feminine in ܐ܂, not ܐܵ; as ܦܵܕ݂ܫܵܐ, ܦܵܕ݂ܫܵܐ *finishing*, § 31. So the absolute state of the past participle, as ܟ݁ܒ݂ܝܼܒ݂ܵܐ, ܟ݁ܒ݂ܝܼܒ݂ܬ݁ܵܐ *left*, § 50. So ܡܘܼܫܚܸܠ, ܠܐ݇ܚܪܹܐ; ܡܵܟ݂ܘܼܕ݂ܡܹܐ ܡܵܟ݂ܘܼܕ݂ܡܵܐ U., or ܡܵܟ݂ܘܼܕ݂ܡܵܢܵܐ K.; ܡܘܼܫܚܸܠ, ܡܘܼܫܚܸܠܵܐ U., or ܡܘܼܫܚܠܵܢܵܐ K. For ܠܐ verbs see § 44.

(5) The feminine of a few foreign adjectives is formed by changing ܐ܂ to ܐ܁, as ܝܵܘܸܬ݂ܐ Ti. *beautiful* (in U. a subst. = *a young man*); ܘܸܣܛܵܐ *energetic, bold*, ܘܸܕ݂ܕ݂ܵܐ *yellow*, ܟܵܘܡܵܐ *blind*, ܟܲܕ݂ܵܐ *deaf*, ܠܲܠܐ *dumb*, ܚܸܕ݂ܕ݂ܵܐ *bold, generous*; so ܩܘܼܚܒܵܐ *hunchbacked*. Thus we have ܝܵܘܸܬ݁ܵܐ, ܘܸܣܛܵܐ etc. So ܩܘܼܠܵܐ *male slave* (coolie), ܩܘܼܠܐ *female slave*, § 17*f*. [We must distinguish ܚܸܕ݂ܕ݂ܘܼܬ݂ܐ in the sense of *boldness*, a foreign word, from the same in the sense of *education*, an O.S. word, root ܕ݂ܕ݂ܐ.]

(6) Foreign adjectives are generally not inflected. We say ܒܵܟ݂ܬܵܐ ܚܸܠܝܹܐ *a dear woman*, not ܚܸܠܝܬܐ ܒܵܟ݂ܬܵܐ. But we may say ܚܸܠܝܬܐ by itself for *a dear one* (f.).

(7) Some others also are not inflected; as ܥܸܡܩܵܐ *deep* (properly a subst. Cf. N.S. ܥܸܡܩܘܼܬ݂ܵܐ, O.S. ܥܸܡܩܬ݂ܐ), ܩܘܼܪܒܵܐ *near* (so O.S.), ܩܸܣܛܵܐ *far* or *absent* (O.S. ܪܵܘܣܵܐ). So usually ܫܪܵܝܵܐ K. *true* (in U. ܫܪܝܪܐ) § 123; in Al. it is inflected. For ܕ݂ܵܐ see § 25 (7). Foreign adjectives may often be known by not ending in ܐ; but some do so end, as ܚܵܐܬܵܐ *new*, Turk., ܒܸܕ݂ܕ݂ܵܐ *bad*, Arab., ܒܲܚܵܐ *big*, ܡܲܝܠܵܐ *blue*, which are not inflected to make feminines. See § 22.

(8) If necessary a euphonic vowel is added in the feminine; as ܡܲܟ݂ܘܼܕ݂ܩܵܐ *saved*, ܡܲܟ݂ܘܼܕ݂ܩܬܐ U. Ti. (ܫ Tkh.); ܡܚܘܼܒܟ݂ܐ *compound*, ܡܚܘܼܒܟ݂ܬܐ; ܡܦܘܼܪܫܵܐ *absolute*, ܡܦܘܼܪܫܬܐ.

[§§ 21, 22, 23]   PLURALS OF ADJECTIVES AND PARTICIPLES.

(9) ܚܰܕܬܳܐ *new* (*khâtha*) makes fem. ܚܰܕܬܳܐ K., ܚܰܕܬܳܐ U. (Pthakha sound). The O.S. fem. ܚܕܰܬܳܐ is now used as a substantive = *the New Testament* (p. 48). In Q. the masculine is ܚܰܕܶܬ.

(10) The U. forms of adjectives from ܥܥ verbs, like ܩܰܪܺܝܪ *cold*, *drop* ܝ; thus ܩܰܕܚܳܐ. So ܕܰܩܺܝܩ, ܕܰܥܢܳܐ *small*; ܫܰܚܶܕ, ܫܰܚܢܳܐ *hot*, ܡܰܪܺܝܪ, ܡܰܕܚܳܐ *bitter*, ܕܰܠܺܝܠ, ܕܰܠܳܐ *thinned out* (as trees), ܓܰܠܺܝܠ, ܓܕܳܐ *wet*. So also ܩܰܢܺܝܢ, ܩܰܢܳܐ *cool*. In K. Al. we have ܩܰܕܺܝܕ, ܩܰܕܺܝܕܳܐ, and so on, as O.S.; and ܩܰܡܺܝܢ, ܩܰܡܺܝܢܳܐ. See § 81 (5).

(11) ܚܰܠܺܝܡ Al. *sweet* [elsewhere ܚܰܠܳܐ] drops ܝ: ܚܰܠܳܘܡܳܐ.

§ 22. *Plurals of Adjectives and Participles*.

Both masculines and feminines are alike in the plural, which is of the first form; thus ܢܶܫܶܐ ܛܳܒ̈ܳܬܳܐ (ܐ̈ K.) *good women*. But the adjectives mentioned in § 22 (7) are not inflected; foreign adjectives are usually not inflected, though we may say ܚܡܺܝܒܐ *dear*, from ܚܡܺܝܒ. Those however which end in ܐ݇ as ܚܰܕܬܳܐ *new*, do often take the first plural, though they do not take ܐ݇ in the fem. sing. Siami is written on plural adjectives, not on participles unless used as epithets.

The present participle of both conjugations follows the following models: ܩܳܕܶܫ: ܩܳܕܫܺܝܢ (O.S. ܩܳܕܫܺܝܢ); ܡܰܠܶܠ: ܡܰܠܠܺܝܢ (O.S. ܡܰܠܠܺܝܢ). The past participle, absolute state, is similar in K.: ܩܺܝܫ: ܩܺܝܫܺܝܢ (O.S. ܝ); ܡܰܠܺܝܠ, ܡܰܠܺܝܠܺܝܢ (O.S. ܡܰܠܺܝܠܺܝܢ). For the U. anomalous plural see § 50.

§ 23. *Position of Adjectives*. The Syriac adjective when used as an epithet comes after its substantive, as ܒܰܝܬܳܐ ܓܰܐܝܳܐ *a large house*.

Exceptions. (1) ܛܵܒ݂ *good* usually; and rarely other monosyllables.

(2) Numerals: ܚܲܕ ܓ݂ܲܒ݂ܪܵܐ *one man.* (In O.S. often after the noun.)

(3) Titles, as ܡܘܼܝܩܪܵܐ ܩܲܫܵܐ ܡܘܼܫܹܐ *the Reverend Priest Moses*; ܛܘܼܒ݂ܵܢܵܐ ܦܵܘܠܘܿܣ *Blessed Paul.* [But ܝܘܿܚܲܢܵܢ ܫܠܝܼܚܵܐ *the Apostle John.* A few names are seldom used except with a title added: as ܥܹܠܝ ܟܵܗܢܵܐ *Eli the priest,* ܕܵܘܝܼܕ ܡܲܠܟܵܐ *David the King,* ܝܘܿܚܲܢܵܢ ܡܲܥܡܕܵܢܵܐ *John the Baptist.*]

(4) The words ܪܵܒܵܐ *many*[1], § 25 (7); ܦܠܵܢ *a certain* (when an adjective this is both m. and f., ܦܠܵܢܝܼܬ݂ is a substantive only = *So and So,* f. § 17); ܟܠ *all*; ܚܲܕܟܡܵܐ[2] *a few,* ܗܸܡ U. = ܚܘܿ K. *no, any,* ܙܵܘܕܵܐ *more*[1] (usually: also a substantive); ܚܲܕܟܲܡܵܐ[2] *some,* and compounds of ܚܲܕ § 28 (9); ܗܵܕܲܟ݂ܵܐ or ܗܵܕܵܐ or ܐܘܼܣܟܵܐ *such,* when thus used:—ܚܲܕ ܗܵܕܲܟ݂ܵܐ ܓ݂ܲܒ݂ܪܵܐ *such a man* (also without ܚܲܕ).

(5) Occasionally when the adjective is emphatic.

(6) All adjective pronouns. Thus O.S. ܓܲܒ݂ܪܵܐ ܗܵܢܵܐ = N.S. ܐܵܗܵܐ ܓ݂ܲܒ݂ܪܵܐ *this man.*

(7) The words ܡܢܝܼܚܵܐ U., O.S. = ܕܢܝܼܚܵܐ K. = ܢܝܼܚܵܐ K. *the late* (sometimes); as ܡܢܝܼܚܵܐ ܫܲܡܵܫܵܐ ܥܘܼܒ݂ܕܝܼܫܘܿܥ *the late Deacon Audishu.* So ܕܟ݂ܝܼܪܵܐ ܠܛܵܒ݂ܬܵܐ ܫܠܹܝܡܘܿܢ *Solomon of blessed memory,* lit. *remembered for good.*

When the adjective is a predicate it comes between the subject and the substantive verb if affirmative; but it follows a negative verb: as ܗܵܘ ܓ݂ܲܒ݂ܪܵܐ ܣܘܼܪܵܝܵܐ ܝܠܹܗ *that man is a Syrian*; but ܠܹܐ ܝܠܹܗ ܣܘܼܪܵܝܵܐ *he is not a Syrian.*

[1] These rarely follow the noun. [2] Pthakha sound.

§ 24. *Comparison.* Comparatives are thus formed: ܟ̰ܐܩܒ ܡܢ (ܒܝܫ K. Al.) *better*: ܡܢܝ ܟ̰ܐܩܒ ܒܝܫ, or more rarely, ܟ̰ܐܩܒ ܡܢܝ *better than me*, ܡܝ̈ܐ ܙܘܕ ܒܝܫ *more watery*. A comparative with a verb is expressed by ܡܢ ܕ. Thus ܗܘ ܟ̰ܐܩܒ ܡܢ ܡܗ ܕܗܝܫܒܬ *he is better than you think*, ܒܝܫ ܕܘܩ̈ ܠܟ̰ܐ ܡܢ ܕܐܙܠܢ *I would rather go than stay here.*

More as a substantive is expressed by ܘܙܘܕܐ or ܙܘܕܐ ܒܝܫ (this also means *especially*) or, especially in K., by ܙܘܕ or ܒܝܫ alone.

A Syriac adjective has not only a positive, but also a comparative and a superlative sense, as seen in the examples given above and below; and it also expresses the idea of *too*. Thus ܟ̰ܐܩܒ may mean *good*, *better*, *best*, or *too good*, according to the context. The last sense may be expressed, though not commonly, by ܟ̰ܐܩܒ ܡܢ ܕܘܠܐ, lit. *better than is right.*

Superlatives may be expressed thus: ܐܢܫܐ ܟ̰ܐܩܒ ܡܢ ܟܠܗܘܢ, or ܡܢ ܟܠ, or ܟ̰ܐܩܒ ܒܝܫ etc., *the best man*, lit., *a man better than all of them*; or by the simple adjective, as ܐܝܢܐ ܟ̰ܐܩܒ ܐܝܠܗ? *which is best?*; or by prefixing ܟܕ *very*, or a similar particle to the adjective.

§ 25. *Miscellaneous notes on Adjectives.*

(1) Adjectives are frequently used as substantives, as ܗܘ ܒܝܫܐ *that evil one*; and occasionally participles, as ܟܬܝܒܬܐ U. *a writing.*

(2) ܟܠ standing alone means *every*, ܟܠ ܕܐܢܐ *whenever*, lit. *every time*, ܟܠ ܐܢܫܐ *each man*; see § 15. With pronominal affixes it denotes *the whole* or *all*, as ܟܠܗ ܒܝܬܐ *the whole house, all the house*, ܟܠܗܘܢ ܒܬܐ *all the houses.* So ܟܠܢ *we all, all of us*, ܟܠܗ ܒܝܬܐ ܐܗܐ (or ܕܐܗܐ) *all this house*, ܟܠܗܘܢ ܥܡܒܬܐ ܕܠܟܐ *all the*

broken-hearted = O.S. ܟܠ ܕܲܓ̣ܒ݂ܝܼܕ݂ܵܐ. [ܟܠ always takes the affixes ܗ܊, ܗ܊ for 3 pers. sing., and almost always ܘܗ܊ for 3 pers. pl.] We have also ܟܠܵܘܬܲܢ *all of us* (*kuluntan*), by a false analogy; cf. ܟܠܵܘܬܲܢ in § 28. So for the other persons. ܟܠ is never used without affixes, as sometimes in O.S., before a plural or collective noun, e.g. ܟܠ ܒܸܪܝ̈ܬ݂ܵܐ O.S. *all the creatures*; in N.S. we must put ܟܠܗܘܢ. We may put the personal pronouns absolutely, thus: ܐܸܢܝ ܟܠܗܘܢ *all of them*. For ܗܘ, ܗܘܐ in Al. Z. K., see § 15.

(3) *Articles*. As a rule the definite article is not expressed in Syriac. But if necessary for distinctness, the demonstrative pronouns ܗܘ, ܗܝ, ܐܢܝ are used. So in O.S. ܗܘ ܡܸܠܬ݂ܐ ܕܲܐܠܵܗܵܐ *the Word of God*, Rev. xix. 13. For the indefinite article the Syrians use ܚܲܕ݂ m., ܚܕ݂ܵܐ f. *one* (U. f. often ܚܵܕ݂ܵܐ; in Ti. and J. ܘ is often silent), see § 26; but they often omit it. In O.S. it is omitted unless emphatic and = *a certain*, as ܚܲܕ݂ ܓܲܒ݂ܪܵܐ *a certain man*, St John iii. 1; ܚܕ݂ܵܐ ܐܲܪܡܲܠܬܵܐ *a certain widow*, St Luke xxi. 2. In N.S. ܚܲܕ݂ renders *a certain* in this sense; but when it means *a particular person* we must say ܚܲܕ݂ ܦܠܲܢ (O.S. ܚܲܕ݂ ܦܠܲܢ).

Very rarely ܡܸܕܸܡ after a noun is an indef. article, as ܟܬ݂ܵܒ݂ܵܐ ܡܸܕܸܡ *a book* (some sort of a book) § 93. In O.S. ܐܢܫ̈ܝܼܢ ܡܸܕܸܡ = *a few men*, Nöld. § 125.

(4) *Adjectives* are often formed, as in O.S., by repeating nouns; as ܓܵܘܢܹܐ ܓܵܘܢܹܐ *particoloured*, lit. *colours colours*; ܦܸܬ݂ܠܵܐ ܦܸܬ݂ܠܵܐ *zigzag*, lit. *twists twists*; ܐܵܕ݂ܫܹܐ ܐܵܕ݂ܫܹܐ *various*, lit. *kinds kinds*, O.S. ܘܒܢ ܘܒܢ. This last may also be expressed by ܡܸܬ݂ܦܲܠܓܹܐ U., or ܡܸܬ݂ܦܲܠܓܹܐ K., (O.S. ܡܚܲܬܟܹܐ), St Mark i. 34. We may also repeat adjectives, as ܙܥܘܪ̈ܬ݂ܐ ܙܥܘܪ̈ܬ݂ܐ *in small pieces*. Cf. § 28 (4) for distributive

numerals; and § 67 (7) for adverbs thus repeated. So also ܕܡܵܕ݂ ܚܘܼܩܵܐ high, low = uneven, up and down.

(5) *Blessed is* = ܛܘܼܒ݂ ܠ if followed by a noun. If pronouns follow we have the forms ܛܘܼܒ݂ܸܗ or ܛܘܼܒ݂ܠܸܗ U. *blessed is he*. So for the other affixes; the 3 pl. is ܛܘܼܒ݂ܠܗܘܿܢ K. Al.; or ܛܘܼܒ݂ܠܗܘܿܢ U. In O.S. ܛܘܼܒ݂ܘܗܝ ܠܓܒ݂ܪܵܐ *blessed is the man*, ܛܘܼܒ݂ܝܟ *blessed art thou*. We have also in N.S. ܛܘܼܒ݂ ܠܸܗ etc.

(6) Compound adjectives are frequently formed by a noun and participle, as ܐ݇ܢܵܫܵܐ ܥܛܝܼܦ݂ ܩܸܫܬܵܐ *a bow-legged man*; these are indeclinable. See § 14.

(7) ܪܵܒܵܐ *many*, in U. Q. Sal. Gaw. and sometimes K. is indeclinable and precedes the noun. In K. Al. it is usually ܪܵܒܵܐ (in Al. also, as O.S. = *great*), which may follow the noun, and takes the first plural. As a subst. = *much* it is used with Zqapa almost everywhere. We have ܪܵܒܵܐ ܥܲܡ ܚܲܕ݇ܬܵܐ Al. = ܚܲܕ݇ܬܵܐ ܕܪܵܒܵܐ ܠܘܼܡܵܐ U. = ܪܵܒܵܐ ܚܲܕ݇ܬܵܐ O.S. In U. K. ܪܵܒܵܐ ܡܸܢܲܝܗܘܿܢ = *many of them*. ܪܵܒܵܐ is also colloquially used in U. ܪܵܒܵܐ in Q. (first Zlama). In Al. ܓ̰ܲܒ݁ܵܐ = *many*, but ܓ̰ܲܒ݁ܵܐ = ܠܵܘ݂ܐ U. K. *great*. For the adverb see § 67.

(8) *The same* is expressed if not emphatic by a simple demonstrative pronoun, but if emphatic by ܗܲܘ ܕܹܝܢ m., ܗܲܝ ܕܹܝܢ f., lit. *just that*; pl. ܐܲܢܝ ܕܹܝܢ. O.S. ܗܘ ܗܘ or ܗܘ ܓܸܪ ܗܘ. So ܕܹܝܢ ܕܘܼܟܵܐ *at the same place*, ܕܹܝܢ ܐܲܝܟܵܐ *at the same place where*, ܕܹܝܢ ܒܥܸܕܵܢ *at the same time that* etc. So also ܕܹܝܢ ܓܸܒ݂ ܗܲܘ U. *the very same*.

§ 26. *Numerals.* ܡܶܢܝܳܢܶܐ ܐܶܡܢܶܐ.

No.	In letters.	Masculine.	Feminine.
1	ܐ	ܚܰܕ	ܚܕܳܐ (usually ܚܰܕ in U.). In Ti. J. ܚ often silent.
2	ܒ	ܬܪܶܝ	ܬܰܪܬܶܝ K., rarely ܬܰܪܬܶܝ K., ܬܰܪܬܶܝ Al.
3	ܓ	ܬܠܳܬܳܐ K. Al., ܬܠܳܬܳܐ U., ܬܠܳܬܶܐ Z.	ܬܠܳܬ K., ܬܠܳܬ U., ܬܠܳܬ Q.
4	ܕ	ܐܰܪܒܥܳܐ	ܐܰܪܒܰܥ U. (ܕ). ܐܰܪܒܰܥ K. Al. (*arbé* or *arbi*).
5	ܗ	ܚܰܡܫܳܐ	ܚܰܡܶܫ K.
6	ܘ	ܐܶܫܬܳܐ	ܐܶܫ K.
7	ܙ	ܫܰܒܥܳܐ (*shōwa* U.K., but *shō'a* Ti. Z.).	ܫܒܰܥ Ti. Ash. Sh., Tkh. (both ܒ).
8	ܚ	ܬܡܳܢܝܳܐ	ܬܡܳܢܶܐ K., ܬܡܳܢܶܐ Sh.
9	ܛ	ܬܶܫܥܳܐ[1] Ti. Sh., ܬܶܫܥܳܐ[1] (ܬܶܫܥ) U. Sal. Tkh., ܬܫܰܥ Al., ܐܶܫܬܰܥ Ash.	ܬܫܰܥ Ti., ܬܫܰܥ Tkh., Sh., ܬܫܰܥ Al.
10	ܝ	ܥܶܣܪܳܐ	ܥܣܰܪ K.

[In U. Z. the masculines and feminines are alike unless otherwise marked: also in the following numbers there is only one form for both. In Sal. Q. Gaw. J. the feminine forms are used, but in Sal. often with masculine nouns.]

---

[1] The pronunciation of these differs in the modification or non-modification of the Zlama sound, § 6.

No.	In letters.	
11	ܝܐ	ܚܵܕܸܥܣܲܪ (*khâdessar*); ܚܲܕܥܣܲܪ Q. Sal.
12	ܝܒ	ܬܪܸܥܣܲܪ; ܬܪܹܥܣܲܪ Q. ܬܪܹܝܥܣܲܪ Sal.
13	ܝܓ	ܬܠܵܬܥܣܲܪ. In these numbers to 19 incl. Pthakha is like Zqapa in U., not K.
14	ܝܕ	ܐܲܪܒܥܣܲܪ (ܒ).
15	ܝܗ	ܚܲܡܫܥܣܲܪ.
16	ܝܘ	ܐܸܫܬܥܣܲܪ.
17	ܝܙ	ܫܒܲܥܣܲܪ U. Tkh. (*shô-wâsar*); ܐܸܫܒܲܥܣܲܪ (ܒ݂) Ti. Tkh. Sh. Ash.
18	ܝܚ	ܬܡܵܢܥܣܲܪ; ܬܡܵܢܝܥܣܲܪ Ti. Ash.
19	ܝܛ	ܐܸܬܫܲܥܣܲܪ Ti. Sh. Ash. ܝܸܬܫܲܥܣܲܪ U. Tkh. ܬܸܫܲܥܣܲܪ Al.
20	ܟ	ܥܸܣܪܝ.
21	ܟܐ	ܥܸܣܪܝ ܘܚܲܕ K. MB. ܥܸܣܪܝ ܚܲܕ U. ܚܲܕ ܘܥܸܣܪܝ Al. [f. ܚܕܵܐ].
30	ܠ	ܬܠܵܬܝ K. MB. Sh. ܬܠܵܝܝ (*tlayi*) U. J. ܬܠܲܝܝ Q.
40	ܡ	ܐܲܪܒܝ; ܐܸܪܒܝ Sal.
50	ܢ	ܚܲܡܫܝ.
60	ܣ	ܐܸܫܬܝ.
70	ܥ	ܫܲܒܥܝ (usually *shô-wi*, but *shő'i* Ti. Z.).
80	ܦ	ܬܡܵܢܝ U. Tkh. Ash. ܬܡܵܢܹܐ Ti. Ash. (second Zlama sound).
90	ܨ	ܐܸܬܫܥܝ Ti. Ash. Sal. ܝܸܬܫܥܝ U. Tkh. Sh. ܬܸܫܥܝ Al.
100	ܩ	ܐܸܡܵܐ, rarely ܡܵܐ.

No.	In letters.	
101	ܩܐ	ܐܡܐ ܘܚܕ (*ĭmokhâ*, accent on first and last); ܚܕ ܘܐܡܐ Al. (ܚܕܐ f.).
200	ܪ	ܬܪܝ ܡܐܐ (*trĭma*); ܬܪܝ ܐܡܐ Al. Ash.
300	ܫ	ܬܠܬ ܡܐܐ U. ܬܠܬ ܡܐܐ Q. ܬܠܬ ܐܡܐ K. ܬܠܬܐ ܐܡܐ Al. [ܐܡܐ made masculine. So for the rest in Al., but the K. forms are also used there].
400	ܬ	ܐܪܒܥܡܐܐ (ܒ Pthakha sound) U. Q. ܐܪܒܥ ܐܡܐ K.: ܐܪܒܥ ܐܡܐ Ash.
500	ܢ̇	ܚܡܫܡܐܐ U. ܚܡܫܡܐܐ Q. ܚܡܫ ܐܡܐ K.
600	ܣ̇	ܐܫܬܡܐܐ U. ܐܫܬܡܐܐ Q. ܐܫܬ ܐܡܐ K. Sh.
700	ܥ̇	ܫܒܥܡܐܐ U. (*shō-wŭma*). ܐܫܒܥܡܐܐ Q. Sh. ܐܫܒܥ ܐܡܐ Ti. Al. ܐܫܒܥ ܐܡܐ Tkh.
800	ܦ̇	ܬܡܢܡܐܐ U. ܬܡܢܐ ܡܐܐ Q. ܬܡܢܐ ܐܡܐ K.
900	ܨ̇	ܬܫܥܡܐܐ U. ܬܫܥܐܡܐܐ Tkh. ܐܬܫܥܡܐܐ Ti. ܐܬܫܥܡܐܐ Sh. ܐܬܫܥܐܡܐܐ Ti. ܬܫܥܡܐܐ Al. [ܫ Pthakha sound].
1000	ܐ̱	ܐܠܦܐ; ܐܠܦܐ Sal.
10,000	ܝ̱	ܪܒܘ or ܪܒܘܬܐ (both rare).

Notes. (1) In ܬܠܬܐ and its compounds the first ܬ is usually pronounced ܛ. See § 123.

(2) ܚܕ is pronounced *khé* in Sal. Q. Gaw. J., § 91; and we even hear ܚܕ ܝܠܗ *it is one*, pronounced *khéli* for ܚܕ ܝܠܗ *khâ-ili*, § 29.

(3) For numbers higher than 110 ܐܡܐ comes first in Al. as elsewhere. The Zqapa everywhere makes a diphthong with the following ܘ; so in ܐܠܦܐ which is a masculine substantive taking the first plural.

(4) ܐܸܡܵܐ is a fem. substantive (but apparently masc. in Al.; see above) making plural ܐܸܡ̈ܘܵܬܹܐ when not used, as in the table, for 200, 300 etc. The form ܡܐܵܐ is used in forming the numbers 200 etc., and in the phrase ܒܫܠܵܡܵܐ ܡܐܵܐ ܫܠܵܡ̈ܐ *in peace, a hundred peaces*, sc. *you have come* (*you are very welcome*).

(5) The O.S. definite state ܡܐܬܐ, whose plural is ܡܐܘ̈ܬܐ (or ܡܐ), appears in ܡܵܬܵܐ *village* (rare in O.S. but so spelt), i.e. *a hundred houses.* This accounts for the colloquial pronunciation in U. of the plural, where both Taus drop, *mâ-wâi.* (The usual O.S. word is ܩܪܝܬܐ, not used in N.S.)

(6) The other numbers form plurals regularly, as ܫܒ̈ܥܐ *sevens*, ܬܫܥ̈ܝܐ *nineties.* Thus *three times five* can be expressed by ܬܠܬܐ ܚܡܫ̈ܐ or by ܬܠܬ ܟܪ̈ܘܬܐ ܚܡܫܐ. [Distinguish ܚܡܫ̈ܐ and ܚܡܫܝܢ of which the pronunciation is different, § 5 (4).]

(7) For 10,000 ܥܣܪܐ ܐܠܦ̈ܐ is commonly used. If ܪܒܘ is used the plural is ܪܒ̈ܘܢ or ܪܒ̈ܘܬܐ. But this is not colloquial. After ܪܒܘ etc. a ܕ is placed before a noun: not after ܐܡܐ, ܐܠܦܐ or their plurals when a plural noun follows, as ܐܡܐ ܓܒܪ̈ܐ *a hundred men;* but we may say ܬܪܝܢ ܐܠܦ̈ܐ ܕܥܡܡܐ *two thousand of the people.*

(8) In putting letters for numbers the dots and strokes for 500 etc. are often omitted. 1889 is written ܐܦܦܛ, and the year is called ܐܦܦܛ *appaṭ.* So for other years.

§ 27. *Ordinals* are expressed by prefixing ܕ to the cardinals, as ܕܚܡܫܐ *fifth.* This was also common in O.S. They may stand without a substantive, thus: ܗܘ ܕܬܪܝܢ (ܗܘ ܕܬܪܝܢ O.S.) *the second one.* The O.S. ordinals are used for fractions up to tenths. Thus:

ܦܠܓܐ (fem. ܚܕܝܢܝ) *half* (or ܦܠܓܐ). ܫܒܝܥܝܐ *seventh*.

ܬܠܝܬܝܐ *third*. ܬܡܝܢܝܐ *eighth*.

ܪܒܝܥܝܐ *fourth*. ܬܫܝܥܝܐ *ninth*.

ܚܡܝܫܝܐ *fifth*. ܥܣܝܪܝܐ *tenth*.

ܫܬܝܬܝܐ *sixth*.

These are not common in the colloquial speech.

Higher fractions are expressed by ܕ, as also are the above. Thus:

$\frac{2}{3}$ = ܬܠܝܬܝܐ ܗܕܟ or ܬܠܬܐ ܕܗܕܒ (ܗ K.).

$\frac{5}{12}$ = ܕܬܪܥܣܪ ܚܡܫܐ.

The O.S. ܩܕܡܝܐ *first*, becomes ܩܕܡܝܐ (rarely ܩܕܡ) in N.S.

Fractions may also be expressed by ܡܢ (so O.S.), as ܚܕ ܡܢ ܬܪܝ *one-half*. The other O.S. fractional forms such as ܬܘܠܬܐ *a third*, are now almost if not quite obsolete. But ܚܘܡܫܐ is used for *decimals*. ܡܥܣܪܐ *tithes* (so O.S.) is used colloquially.

ܦܠܓܐ (O.S. ܦܠܓܐ) is a substantive taking the first and fifth plurals. Before substantives it takes affixes, and also usually when standing by itself. In U. no difference is made between the genders, and ܦܠܓܗ is used for both; while in K. a difference is made. Thus:—

ܦܠܓܗ ܕܠܚܡܐ *half the bread*; U. ܦܠܓܗ ܕܠܚܡܐ = ܦܠܓܗ ܕܠܚܡܐ K. *half an hour*; U. ܗܕܒ ܦܠܓܗ = ܗܕܒ ܘܦܠܓܗ K. masc. = 2½; U. ܫܥܐ ܦܠܓܗ = ܫܥܐ ܘܦܠܓܗ K. *an hour and a half*; ܓܢܝ ܗܠܟ U. ܦܠܓܗ = ܓܢܝ ܗܠܟ ܘܦܠܓܗ 3½ *years*; and so on. After nouns ending in ܐ, ܘ is inserted in U. as well as K.: and makes a diphthong. Thus ܗܦܬܐ ܘܦܠܓܗ *haptopelgi* (in K. ܦ) = *a hafta and a half* [1 hafta = 4 lbs. avoirdupois approximately]. ܦܠܓܐ = *by halves*, § 67; ܦܠܓܗ ܡܝܬ = *half dead*; ܪܘܒܥ = *a quarter*.

§ 28. *Various notes on Numerals.*

(1) *Both of them, all three of them*, etc., are expressed thus:—

2. ܗܕܳܦ̈ܘܗܝ U. Tkh. Al. ܗܕܳܘ̈ܦܝܗܝ U. (both ܗ K.). ܗܕܳܦܘܗܝ K. Al. ܗܕܳܦ̈ܘܗܝ Ash. Al. ܗܕܦܘܗܝ Ti. ܗܕ̈ܡܦܘܗܝ Al. ܗܕܦܘܗܝ Sal. Sp. Al. ܗܕܦܘܗܝ Ash. (fem.). ܗܕܳܦܳܘܬܗܝܢ MB.

3. ܗܳܟܠܳܬܦܝܗܝ U. Q. Sal. ܗܟܠܘܗܝ Sal. ܗܟܠܘܗܝ U. ܗܟܠܦܝܗܝ K. (ܗ Al. Ash.). ܗܟܠܟܕܝ U. ܗܟܠܳܘܬܗܝܢ MB. [ܢ = ܠ, see § 123.]

4. ܐܪܒܥܳܘܗܝ U. ܐܪܒܥܬܝܗܝ K. (Al. ܗ). ܐܪܒܥܳܘܬܗܝܢ MB. ܐܪܒܥܦܝܗܝ Ash.

5. ܚܡܫܳܘܗܝ U. ܚܡܫܬܝܗܝ K. (Al. ܗ). ܚܡܫܳܘܬܗܝܢ MB. ܚܡܫܦܝܗܝ Ash.

6. ܐܫܬܳܘܗܝ U. ܐܫܬܝܗܝ K. (Al. ܗ). ܐܫܬܳܘܬܗܝܢ MB. ܐܫܬܦܝܗܝ Ash.

7. ܫܒܥܳܘܗܝ (*shô-wunté*) U., or ܫܒܥܬܝܗܝ K. (ܗ Al.) ܫܒܥܳܘܬܗܝܢ MB. ܫܒܥܦܝܗܝ Ash.

8. ܬܡܢܳܘܗܝ U. ܬܡܢܝܗܝ K. (Al. ܗ). ܬܡܢܳܘܬܗܝܢ MB. ܬܡܢܦܝܗܝ Ash.

9. ܬܫܥܳܘܗܝ U. ܬܫܥܝܗܝ Tkh. (½ Ti.). ܬܫܥܳܘܬܗܝܢ MB. ܬܫܥܳܘܗܝ Al. ܬܫܥܝܗܝ Al. ܬܫܥܝܗܝ Ash.

10. ܥܣܪܳܘܗܝ U. ܥܣܪܝܗܝ K. (ܗ Al.). ܥܣܪܦܝܗܝ Ash.

We also have, though rarely, for *all eleven of them*, in U. ܚܕܥܣܪܳܘܗܝ, in Sal. Q. ܚܕܥܣܪܳܘܗܝ, in Ti. ܚܕܥܣܪܦܝܗܝ, and so for the other numbers to 19 inclusive.

For ܒܠܘܕܝܗܘܢ see § 25 (2).

The other plural affixes may be used with any of the above; thus: ܥܣܪܘܬܢ *all ten of us*, ܫܬܐܘܬܘܟܘܢ *all six of you*.

With nouns we have ܬܪܘܝܗܘܢ ܝܘܡܢ̈ܐ *both days*, (but with ܒ before ܐܢܝ or ܐܢܐ, as ܬ' ܒܐܢܝ ܝܘ' *both of those days*).

(2) *Once, twice, thrice* etc. are expressed by the substantive ܓܐܪܐ *time*. In the singular ܗ is often silent; in the plural ܓܐܪ̈ܐ it sometimes has a ܝ sound, but often is like ܐ (*gâ-yi* or *gâ-i*). Plural in Al. ܓܐܪܗܬܐ. Thus ܚܕܐ ܓܐܪܐ *once* (U. ܚܕܟܐ). ܬܪܝ ܓܐܪ̈ܐ U. (ܬܪܘܝܗܝ K.) *twice*. ܟܠ ܬܪܘܝܗܝ ܫܢ̈ܝܐ ܚܕܐ ܓܐܪܐ K. (U. ܬܪܝ .. ܚܕܟܐ) *once every two years*.

The following may be used instead of ܓܐܪܐ: ܣܦܪ f. U. *journey*, ܒܪܬ K. *load*, ܐܩܠܐ f. *foot*, ܢܦܐ f. K. *breath*, ܦܫܬܐ m. K., O.S. *span*. All take the first plural in this sense. But ܐܩܠܐ is only used when motion is implied: as ܐܬܐ ܠܗ ܬܪܝ (ܬܪܘܝܗܝ) ܐܩܠ̈ܬܐ *he came twice*. Not so ܣܦܪ, which is constantly used thus: ܐܗܐ ܣܦܪ *this time*, ܗܘܝ ܣܦܪ *that time, then*, § 67.

(3) *Twofold, threefold* etc., are ܚܕ ܒܬܪܝ, ܚܕ ܒܬܠܬܐ etc. Also without ܒ, and with ܒܠ, as ܚܕ ܚܡܫܐ ܒܠ .. *fivefold more than*.

(4) *Distributives* are expressed by repeating the numeral, as ܚܡܫܐ ܚܡܫܐ *five each*: ܚܕ ܚܕ *one each*, or *one at a time*, which we may also render ܚܕ ܒܚܕ. Notice ܓܒܪܐ ܡܢ ܒܝܬܐ ܘܒܝܬܐ ܐܙܠ ܠܗ *a man went from each house* (not ܓܒܪܐ ܒܝܬܐ as Stoddard. St. also gives ܛܠܝܐ ܩܠܡܐ ܐܝܬ ܠܗ for *each boy has a pen*, but it means *the boy has a pen*).

Sometimes may be rendered by ܫܬܳܐ ܫܬܳܐ ܒܫܬܳܐ, or by ܒܫܕܚܕ ܒܚܕ, or by ܚܕܳܐ ܚܕܳܐ.

(5) *Days of the week.* The words ܝܘܡܳܐ ܕ (ܝܘܡܐ) *day of*, are often prefixed to the following, but they are as frequently used alone.

Sunday ܚܕܒܫܒܐ khôshîba, U. Tkh. (Ti. ݇ with Zqapa sound, and khéshâba in Upper Ṭiari). ܒܚܕܒܫܒܐ Al. Sh. MB. Sal. (khiûshâba). O.S. ܚܕܒܫܒ. (In K. ܚܕܒܫܒܐ is a common name for a man, especially given to one born on a Sunday.)

Monday ܬܪܝܢܒܫܒܐ U. ܕܬܪܝܢܒܫܒܐ trûshîba, Tkh. Ash. (Ti. MB. Al. ݇ as above). ܬܪܝܢܒܫܒܐ Upper Ti. O.S. ܬܪܝܢ ܒܫܒܐ.

Tuesday ܬܠܬܒܫܒܐ (tlôshîba or tlâshîba) U. ܬܠܬܒܫܒܐ Tkh. Ash. (Ti. Al. ݇). ܬܠܬܒܫܒܐ MB. Sh. O.S. ܬܠܬܐ ܒܫܒܐ.

Wednesday ܐܪܒܒܫܒܐ U. Tkh. Ash. (Ti. Al. ݇) ܐܪܒܥܒܫܒܐ MB. Sh. O.S. ܐܪܒܥܐ ܒܫܒܐ.

Thursday ܚܡܫܒܫܒܐ U. Tkh. Ash. (Ti. Al. ݇) ܚܡܫܒܫܒܐ MB. Sh. O.S. ܚܡܫܐ ܒܫܒܐ.

Friday ܥܪܘܒܬܐ. So O.S.

Saturday ܫܒܬܐ, so O.S.; or ܫܒܬܐ Sal.

In part of U. Thursday is called ܒܙܪܐ i.e. *market day*, though it is not now the usual day for going to market.

(6) *Per cent.* Example: 20 *per cent.* ܚܡܫܐ ܒܫܬܐ (*five in six*, i.e. 100 produces 120); but 17 *per cent.* ܚܕܥܣܪ ܒܡܐܐ. Note ܒܥܣܪܐ ܚܕ *one part in every ten*.

(7) The numeral ܚܕ prefixed to another makes the second a *quasi*-substantive, as ܚܕ ܓܒ̈ܪܐ ܐܣܪܐ *ten men*. The verb of which this is the subject is plural. In Al. ܚܕ is used to intensify ܚܨܕ, as ܚܨܕ ܟܡܐ (or ܟܒ) *how much more precious* = ܟܡܐ ܚܨܕ ܚܕ ܕܩܢܝܠ U.

(8) Notice the following constructions: ܐܝܟ ܚܕ ܠܘܬܐ ܠܐ ܐܝܟ ܚܕ ܦܠܓܐ ܕܣܥܝܒ ܠܒ *not so great as I thought*, ܕܣܥܝܒ ܠܒ (or better ܕܣܥܓܕܒ) *not half as great as I thought*.

(9) Compounds of ܚܕ, mostly accented on that syllable.

ܚܕ ܓܕܐ Z. *for a while* = ܓܕܐ K. = ܣܥܬܐ ܚܕ K.

ܚܕ ܘܕܐ *a slight*....This and all the following take a noun without ܕ.

ܚܕ ܛܘܕܐ *a certain amount of*.

ܚܕ ܕܕܢܐ U. *several, a good deal of* = ܚܕ ܕܕܟܐ K.

ܚܕܘܐ U. K. *few, a little*, Pthakha sound (dim. ܚܕܓܘܦܢܗ) = ܚܕ ܐܕܐ Ti. (dim. ܚܕ ܚܦܢܗ Ti.) = ܚܕ ܐܕܐ U. = ܚܕ ܡܕܪܡ Ti. = ܚܕ ܢܓܐ K. (in Jilu *khénawa*) = ܚܕܐ Az. Al. = ܚܕ ܓܕܐ Ash., see § 67.

ܚܕܚܕܐ *some* (*khákma*) = ܚܕ ܕܡܐ Ti.

The above precede the noun, but ܚܕ ܐܘܕܐ *such and such* (almost *khá'cha*) follows it (= ܚܕ ܐܘܕܐ?). It usually refers to numbers and is the complement of ܦܠܢ *so and so, a certain*. It is often doubled, as ܠܕܕܠܐ ܚܕ ܐܘܕܐ ܚܕ ܐܘܕܐ *such and such a verse*. So ܚܕ ܐܘܕܐ *one such as this*, ܐܘܕܐ ܗܟܒ *twice as much*, etc., or with ܐܘܕܐ or ܐܘܣܚܐ for ܐܘܕܐ; a subst. or adj. often follows immediately.

(10) For reckoning sums of money, weights, etc., which are just under a round number, subtraction is very commonly employed. Thus 1 *gran* 19 *shahis* is usually ܬܪܹܝܢ ܩܪܵܢ̈ܐ ܚܲܕ ܫܵܗܝܼ ܒܨܘܼܪܵܐ *two grans, one shahi less.* In compound sums the noun following the numeral is usually made singular.

(11) For the *twelve Apostles* the noun ܬܪܸܥܣܲܪ̈ܬܵܐ is sometimes used as in O.S. In O.S. we also have ܥܸܣܲܪ̈ܬܵܐ *a tenth,* not in N.S.

(12) *Months,* in the Syrian order:

October ܬܸܫܪܝܼܢ ܩܲܕܡܵܝܵܐ (ܬܼ) (O.S. ܬܸܫܪܝܼ ܩܕܡܵܝܵܐ). See page 43.

November ܬܸܫܪܝܼܢ ܐܲܚܪܵܝܵܐ (O.S. ܬܸܫܪܝܼ ܐܚܪܵܝܵܐ).

December ܟܵܢܘܿܢ ܩܲܕܡܵܝܵܐ (O.S. ܟܼ).

January ܟܵܢܘܿܢ ܐܲܚܪܵܝܵܐ (O.S. ܫ).

[ܟܵܢܘܿܢܹ̈ܐ = Dec. and Jan.]

February ܫܒܵܛ (O.S. ܫܒܵܛ).

March ܐܵܕܵܪ O.S.

April ܢܝܼܣܵܢ O.S.

May ܐܝܵܪ U. ܐܝܼܪ K., O.S.

June ܚܘܼܙܝܼܪܵܢ O.S.

July ܬܲܡܘܼܙ O.S.

August ܛܲܒܵܚ Kurd. (O.S. ܐܵܒ).

September ܐܝܼܠܘܿܢ, rarely ܐܝܼܠܘܿܠ as O.S. (Nun from Kurdish.)

(13) *The clock.* ܣܵܥܲܬ ܟܡܵܐ ܝܼܠܵܗ̇ ؟ *what o'clock is it?,* ܣܵܥܲܬ ܚܲܕ *one o'clock,* ܣܵܥܲܬ ܫܲܒܥܵܐ *seven o'clock,* ܬܪܸܥܣܲܪ ܣܵܥܵܬ̈ܐ *twelve hours,* ܛܲܗܪܵܐ (ܥܲܪܘܼܒܬܵܐ Ti. Al.) *noon,* ܦܲܠܓܹܗ ܕܠܸܠܝܵܐ U. (ܦܲܠܓܵܗ̇ K.) *midnight,* ܣܵܥܲܬ ܫܲܒܥܵܐ ܦܲܠܓܹܗ U. (ܦܲܠܓܵܗ̇ K.) *half past seven,* ܚܲܡܫܵܐ ܕܩܝܼܩܹ̈ܐ ܦܝܼܫܝܼ ܠܹܗ ܩܵܐ ܣܵܥܲܬ ܫܲܒܥܵܐ *five minutes to seven* (lit. *five minutes remain for seven o'clock*), ܚܲܡܫܵܐ ܕܩܝܼܩܹ̈ܐ ܥܒܝܼܪܹ̈ܐ ܠܹܗ ܡ̣ܢ ܣܵܥܲܬ ܫܲܒܥܵܐ *five minutes past seven* (lit. *five minutes are past from seven o'clock*).

(14) Measures are often rendered thus: ܐܘܼܪܚܵܐ ܐܘܼܪܟܹܗ ܬܪܹܝܢ ܦܲܪ̈ܣܲܟܹܐ ܗܘܼܝܵܐ ܠܹܗ *a road two farsakhs* (7 miles) *long* (lit. *its length*); or we might say ܐܲܪܝܼܟܵܐ *long,* here.

VERBS.

ܡܸܠܹ̈ܐ or ܡܸܠܹ̈ܐ

§ 29. *The Substantive Verb.* ܡܸܠܬ݂ܵܐ ܕܐܝܼܬ݂ܘܼܬ݂ܵܐ.

The forms without distinctive letters are used almost universally.

Present tense. He is, etc.

Sing. 3 m. ܝܼܠܹܗ : ܝܼܠܹܗܝ U.

f. ܝܼܠܵܗ̇ : ܝܼܠܵܗ̇ܝ U.

2 m. ܝܼܘܸܬ (ܬ݂ Tkh.) : ܝܼܘܸܬܝ U. (ܬ݂ Tkh.) : ܝܼܘܸܬܢܵܐ (ܬ݂) Tkh.

f. ܝܼܘܵܬܝ (ܬ݂ Tkh.) : ܝܼܘܵܬܝ U. (ܬ݂ Tkh.) : ܝܼܘܵܬܢܵܐ (ܬ݂) Tkh.

1 m. ܝܼܘܸܢ : ܝܼܘܸܢܵܐ K. : ܗܘܸܢܵܐ K. : ܗܘܹܐ ܐܢܵܐ K.

f. ܝܼܘܲܢ : ܝܼܘܲܢܵܐ K. : ܗܘܲܢܵܐ Ash.

Plur. 3 m. f. ܝܼܢܵܐ U. Q. Sal. Sp. : ܝܼܢܝ Tkh. : ܝܼܠܗܘܢ Tkh. Ti. J. Al. Ash. : ܝܼܠܗܘܿܢ Al. : ܝܼܠܗܘܢ ܝܢ J.

2 m. f. ܝܼܘܬܘܿܢ. U. K. (ܬ݂ Tkh.) : ܝܼܬܘܿܢ Ti. : ܗܘܝܬܘܿܢ Bo. : ܗܘܘܬܘܿܢ Al.; or with pronoun, ܐܲܚܬܘܿܢ ܐܝܼܬܘܿܢ Ti.

1 m. f. ܝܼܘܲܚ (*îwŭkh*) : ܝܼܘܵܚܢ (*î-wâkhn*) U. : ܝܼܘܲܚܝ Tkh. (*ŭ*) : ܝܼܘܚ Ti. Al. Ash. : ܝܼܘܚܢ Ti.

Imperfect. He was, etc.

Sing. 3 m. ܝܼܗ݇ܘܵܐ U. Q. Sal.[1] : ܗ݇ܘܵܐ ܗܘܸܐ K. Al. Sh. MB.

f. ܝܼܗ݇ܘܵܐ U. Q. Sal.[1] : ܗ݇ܘܵܐ ܗ݇ܘܵܐ K. Al. Sh. MB.

[1] Usually spelt by error in the printed books ܗ݇ܘܵܐ. Thus ܒܦܪܵܩܹ̈ܐ ܗ݇ܘܵܐ : ܦܪܝܼܩܹ̈ܐ ܗ݇ܘܵܐ. It is never thus pronounced, and should be ܒܦܪܵܩܹ̈ܐ ܝܗ݇ܘܵܐ *biprâqé wâ*, and ܦܪܝܼܩܹ̈ܐ ܝܗ݇ܘܵܐ *priqé wâ*. See Note 2 below.

2 m. ܝܼܘܸܬ ܗ̄ܘܵܐ (ܬ Tkh.): ܗܘܝܼܬ ܗ̄ܘܵܐ Ash.

f. ܝܼܘܸܬܝ ܗ̄ܘܵܐ (ܬ Tkh.): ܗܘܸܬܝ ܗ̄ܘܵܐ Ash.

1 m. ܝܼܘܸܢ ܗ̄ܘܵܐ: ܗܘܸܝܢ ܗ̄ܘܵܐ Ash.

f. ܝܼܘܲܢ ܗ̄ܘܵܐ: ܗܘܲܢ ܗ̄ܘܵܐ Ash.

Plur. 3 m. f. ܝܼܗ̄ܘܵܘ (*ī-wā* nearly) U. Q. Sal.: ܗܘܸܝ ܗ̄ܘܵܘ (Zlama second sound) K.: ܗ̄ܘܵܘ ܗ̄ܘܵܘ Al.

2 m. f. ܝܼܘܬܘܿܢ ܗ̄ܘܵܐ (ܬ Tkh.): ܝܼܬܘܿܢ ܗ̄ܘܵܐ K. (ܬ Tkh.): ܗܘܝܬܘܿܢ ܗ̄ܘܵܐ Ash.

1 m. f. ܝܼܘܲܚ ܗ̄ܘܵܐ: ܝܼܘܸܚ ܗ̄ܘܵܐ Ti. Ash. Al.

Notes. (1) For the terminations of these forms see on the regular verb, § 32 (1). The ܘ is clearly part of ܗܘܵܐ *to be*, as seen by the variations (see under ܠܐ verbs, § 42, also § 46); the ܝ has been thought to be a corruption of ܐܝܼܬ *there is* (whose ܬ often falls, see below); and sometimes the verb is written ܐܝܼܬܠܹܗ etc., but this somewhat interferes with the ܝ becoming diphthongal as in Note 2. The third person seems to be for ܐܝܼܬ ܠܹܗ: ܐܝܼܬ ܠܵܗ̇: ܐܝܼܬ ܠܗܘܿܢ. The forms ܝܼܠܵܐ, ܝܼܢܝ are perhaps for ܐܝܼܬ ܗܵܘܸܢ: ܐܝܼܬ ܗܵܝܢ. Cf. Az. ܝܼܬܠܘܟ *thou art*: ܝܼܠܹܗ *he is*: ܝܼܠܵܗ̇ *she is*: ܝܼܠܗܘܿܢ *they are*, see Appendix 1.

(2) The point under the Yudh is omitted if a vowel sound precedes, with or without ܐ, but not after ܘ. The ܝ is not then silent, but forms a diphthong with the preceding vowel. Thus ܕܘܿܣܬ ܝܘܸܢ *I am a friend* (*dôst îwin*), but ܐܵܢܹܐ ܝܘܸܢ *I am* (*ânéwin*). But the accent remains as if the two words did not coalesce. After ܟܡܵܐ the point is retained; also, in U. in ܝܼܬܘܿܢ (but not in K.) as ܦܝܵܫܵܐ ܝܼܬܘܿܢ *pyâshîtûn*,

ye are remaining, U. (*pyâshétun* K.). In Al. Z. Bo. Sal. the point is frequently omitted even after a consonant.

(3) If the preceding word ends in a silent consonant, the point is usually retained, as ܝܘܰܚ ܚܰܕ݂ *we are one*: but see § 26 (2).

(4) Note that in Ashitha the Yudh appears in the present, but not, except in 1 pl., in the imperfect.

(5) In poetry, or for emphasis, we may have ܬܐܘܡܐ ܘܰܐܢ (*and twin*); and conversely we may omit the Khwaṣa after a consonant in similar cases. But this is uncommon except in Al. Z. Bo. Sal.

(6) As the terminations of ܘܰܢ etc. contain the personal pronouns, it is unnecessary, except for emphasis or distinction, to repeat these.

(7) The following examples explain the usage:— ܐܢܐ ܘܰܢ *I am*, ܐܢܬ ܝܘܰܬ ܐܢܬܝ ܝܘܰܬܝ *thou* (f.) *art*, ܐܚܢܢ ܝܘܰܚ *we are*, ܗܘ ܝܠܗ ܗܝ ܝܠܗ̇ *he is*, *she is*, ܗܘ ܗܘܐ *he was*, ܗܝ ܗܘܬ *she was*, ܐܢܝ ܗܘܘ *they were*. The ܝ of the 3rd pers. imperfect is never omitted except in the K. and Al. forms.

(8) The first and second persons singular, with the pronouns added, are often contracted to *àninwâ, ànànwâ, àtitwâ, àtatwâ*.

(9) The ܗܘܐ is almost the only relic of the old past tense. [Stoddard also gives ܕܟܺܝܒ݂ܰܕ. See § 68, under ܒܗܐ.]

(10) The other tenses of the substantive verb are formed regularly from ܗܘܐ *to be*, see §§ 42, 46, but the imperative is not very much used in the sense *to be* (use rather the first present) and the second present never. This verb also means *to become*, to be made, to be born*, and in the last sense is also used in the passive ܦܝܫ ܗܘܐ, see § 34. The preterite ܗܘܐ ܠܗ is much used for *he was* as an alter-

native to ܗܘܵܝܵܐ. ܗܵܘܹܐ ܕ = *to belong to*, as ܐܵܗܵܐ ܕܡܲܢܝܼ ܝܼܠܹܗ؟ *To whom does this belong?* ܗܵܘܹܐ also means *to be possible*, § 63 (5): ܒܸܕ ܗܵܘܹܐ *it will do*, or *it is possible*. ܠܵܐ ܗܵܘܹܐ or ܠܵܐ ܗܵܘܝܵܐ *it is impossible*. Cf. the use of this verb with verbal nouns, to denote possibility, § 34. So more rarely ܠܵܐ ܝܼܠܹܗ ܒܲܗܘܵܝܵܐ *it is impossible*.

(11) *There is, there are* = ܐܝܼܬ [ܝܼܬ U. etc., often ܝܼܬ Q. Also in Al. ܐܝܼܬܵܐ (ܝܼܬ)] pronounced with short ĭ. When ܠ follows, ܬ becomes hard. The negative is ܠܲܝܬ (ܠܹܝܬ K. Al.; for pronunciation see page 12). In reading O.S. this is usually pronounced *lét* (ܠܹܝܬ). Variants are ܐܝܼܬܝܼܢ, ܠܲܝܬܝܼܢ *îtîn, lîtîn*. The imperfect is ܐܝܼܬ ܗ݇ܘܵܐ, the future ܒܸܕ ܗܵܘܹܐ and so on.

These forms do not take the pronominal affixes, as in O.S., and cannot express *he is, thou art*, etc.; but see Note 1 above.

(12) *He has*, when expressing possession, is ܐܝܼܬ ܠܹܗ (O.S. ܐܝܬ). Past ܐܝܼܬ ܗ݇ܘܵܐ ܠܹܗ. Future ܒܸܕ ܗܵܘܹܐ ܠܹܗ. Sometimes, especially in Al., we have ܐܝܼܬܹܗ etc. If the pronoun is emphatic it is put absolutely: as ܐܵܢܵܐ ܐܝܼܬ ܠܝܼ I *have*. So *you have me* is ܐܵܢܵܐ ܐܝܼܬ ܠܘܼܟ݂ܘܿܢ.

(13) But when mere *holding* is intended we cannot use this form, and must say ܗܵܘܹܐ ܠܸܓܹܒ݂ *to be with* or *at*. Thus *I have your book* must be ܟܬ݂ܵܒ݂ܘܼܟ݂ ܠܸܓܹܒ݂ܝ ܝܼܠܹܗ.

(14) ܐܝܼܬ, ܠܲܝܬ may also be used thus:— ܐܸܟܵܐ ܝܼܠܹܗ ܬܐܘܿܡܵܐ؟ ܠܲܝܬ ܠܵܟܵܐ *Where is Thomas? He is not here.* But ܠܹܐ ܝܼܠܹܗ ܠܵܟܵܐ is equally good.

(15) On the other hand the substantive verb is used where we might expect ܐܝܼܬ: as ܦܘܼܚܵܐ ܝܼܠܹܗ (*there is wind*), *it is windy*, § 16 ii. *f*.

(16) *Here he is* and the like are expressed differently in different districts.

U. ܕܘܝܠܗ: ܕܘܝܠܵܗ̇: ܕܘܝܘܗ: ܕܘܝܘܼܟ̣: ܕܘܝܘܼܢ: ܕܘܝܘܼܢܝ: ܕܘܝܢܵܐ: ܕܘܝܘܿܟ̣ܘܿܢ: ܕܘܝܘܼܚ (ܚ usually silent).

Tkh. ܗܘܠܗ: ܗܘܠܵܗ̇: ܗܘܘܗ: ܗܘܘܼܟ̣: ܗܘܘܼܢ: ܗܘܘܼܢܝ: ܗܘܠܗܘ (or ܗܘܘܼ): ܗܘܘܿܟ̣ܘܿܢ: ܗܘܘܼܚ (ܚ silent).

Ash. ܗܘܠܗ: ܗܘܠܵܗ̇: ܗܘܘܗ (or ܗܘܕܘܼ): ܗܘܘܼܟ̣ (or ܗܘܓ̣ܕܝ): ܗܘܘܼܢ: ܗܘܘܼܢܝ: ܗܘܠܗܘ: ܗܘܓ̣ܟ̣ܘܿܢ (*sic*): ܗܘܘܼܚ (ܚ silent).

Ti. ܗܘܠܗ: ܗܘܠܵܗ̇: ܗܘܕܘܼ: ܗܘܓ̣ܕܝ: ܗܘܒ̣: ܗܘܠܗܘ: ܗܘܓ̣ܟ̣ܘܿ: ܗܘܠܝ.

Al. ܗܘܠܗ: ܗܘܠܵܗ̇: ܗܘܕܘܼ: ܗܘܓ̣ܕܝ: ܗܘܒ̣: ܗܘܠܗܘ: ܗܘܓ̣ܕܟ̣ܘܿܢ: ܗܘܠܝ.

Q. ܗܘܠܗ: ܗܘܠܵܗ̇: ܗܘܘܐ (m. f.): ܗܘܢܐ: ܗܘܢܝܗܘ (or ܗܘܝ with second Zlama sound): ܗܘܟ̣ܘܿܢ: ܗܘܢܐ.

(17) *There he is* and the like are expressed thus (3 pers. only):—

U. ܗܠܗ: ܗܠܵܗ̇: ܗܢܵܐ.

Ti. ܗܠܗ: ܗܠܵܗ̇: ܗܠܗܘ.

Ash. ܗܠܗܘ: ܗܠܵܗ̇ܘ: ܗܠܗܘܿ.

Al. ܗܠܗ: ܗܠܵܗ̇: ܗܠܗܘ.

The Ash. forms are distinguished from those of (16) by lengthening the first syllable; and in the other districts also the accent is a strong one.

In Al. ܗܠܗ is also an interjection = ܗܐ *behold*!

(18) ܐܝܠܗ ܠܗ or ܐܝܠܗ ܠܗ in K. Al. = *he can* [sometimes also

ܐܝܬܘܗܝ, rarely ܐܝܬ ܠܗ as above (12)] or *he has*, as ܠܒܝܗ ܓܝܪ ܐܠܗܐ *God can*, ܠܝ ܓܝܪ ܠܝܬ or ܠܝܬ ܠܝ *I cannot*, ܠܝܬ ܗܘܐ ܠܢ *we could not*. So ܠܐ ܗܘܐ ܬܘܡ *thou wilt not be able*. The verbal noun with ܠ usually follows, as ܠܡܐܙܠ ܠܝܬ ܠܝ *I cannot go*.

(19) For *it is I*, we have ܐܢܐ ܐܝܬܝ; and so the other persons. For *is it you?* (pl.), we have commonly ܐܝܬܝܟܘܢ? *ánitun* U., *ánétun* K.

(20) *I may* (i.e. *I am allowed*), is expressed by U. ܠܝ ܐܝܬ (or ܕܡܦܣ U. K. or ܕܡܣܝܒ, ܕܡܦܣܝܒ) *I have permission*, e.g. ܠܝܬ ܠܗ ܐܢܫ ܕܢܥܘܠ U. *no one may enter*; or sometimes by the verb ܡܨܐ *to be able*.

(21) The substantive verb is used for emphasis: as ܠܐ ܡܛܠ ܠܐ ܗܘܐ ܕܠܐ ܐܬܐ; ܕܫܘܐ ܐܢܬ *not that thou art worthy*; *it was not that he did not come*.

(22) It is frequently omitted in relative clauses, § 14.

(23) For ܗܘܐ used for the substantive verb, see § 34.

§ 30. *Conjugations.*

The method of denoting conjugations by names derived from ܦܥܠ *to work*, and of denoting classes of verbs by the same root[1], is not used in East Syrian grammars; instead they use the terms ܦܥܠ (= ܡܙܕܟܝܢ) P'al and ܐܬܦܥܠ Ethp'el) *simple*;

---

[1] For convenience this simple method is used in this Grammar. Thus ܦ denotes the first radical, ܥ the second, ܠ the third; verbs whose first radical is ܐ are ܐܦ, those whose second is ܘ are ܥܘ, and so on. Verbs whose second and third radicals are the same are ܥܥ.

Pa'el, and ܐܬܦܥܠ Ethpa'al) *compound*; ܝܬܝܪ ܡܪܟܒܬܐ ܒ (= ܐܦܥܠ Aph'el, and ܐܬܬܦܥܠ Ettaph'al) *more compound*; ܝܬܝܪ ܡܪܟܒܬܐ ܓ (= ܫܦܥܠ Shaph'el, and ܐܫܬܦܥܠ Eshtaph'al). They distinguish the active and passive in each division by adding respectively the names ܡܬܥܒܕܢܝܬܐ, ܥܒܘܕܝܬܐ.

In the vernacular there are two conjugations: the first chiefly taken from the Pshitta active (P'al), the second from the other active conjugations. We seldom have all four active conjugations surviving in any one word, but we find ܚܠܦ *to be changed*, P'al: ܡܫܚܠܦ K. *to change* tr., Pa'el: ܡܚܠܦ *to interchange*, Aph'el: ܡܫܚܠܦ *to change* tr., Shaph'el. The distinguishing mark of the first conjugation is the softening of the second radical, of the second conjugation the preformative Mim, and, in triliterals, the hardening of the second radical. But there are many exceptions, see §§ 94, 95.

The passive conjugations have disappeared, with one or two exceptions. Thus we have in Al. ܡܫܬܡܠܐ *to be fulfilled*, root ܡܠܐ, Eshtaph'al; in U. ܡܫܬܒܗܪ, in Ti. ܡܫܬܒܗܪ *to be proud* = O.S. ܡܫܬܒܗܪ, root ܒܗܪ, Eshtaph'al. Perhaps also some verbs are contracted from passive conjugations as ܬܥܪ *to wake* intr. = ܐܬܬܥܝܪ O.S., for which see § 83 D. *c*.

The Regular Verb.

§ 31. *First Conjugation.* ܦܪܩ *to finish*, intr.

The old past and future tenses and the infinitive have disappeared. In O.S. we find participles frequently taking the place of the old past and future, and now they have done so entirely. The following parts of the old verb alone remain and are the foundation of the whole conjugation.

Present participle. Sing. ܦܪܩ m., ܦܪܩܐ f. Plur. ܦܪܩܝ m. f. (O.S. ܝܢ m.)

Past participle (absolute state). Sing. ܦܪܝܩ m., ܦܪܝܩܬܐ f. Plur. ܦܪܝܩܝ m. f. K. Al. J. Sal. (O.S. ܝ̈ m.), see § 50.

(*Definite state*). Sing. ܦܪܝܩܐ m., ܦܪܝܩܬܐ f. (ĭ). Plur. ܦܪܝܩܐ m. f.

Imperative. Sing. ܦܪܘܩ m., ܦܪܘܩܝ f. Plur. ܦܪܘܩܘܢ (usually ܦܪܘܩܘ O.S.).

Verbal noun. ܦܪܩܐ.

[The letters ܗܚܥܪ when final do not in N.S. cause the preceding letter to take Pthakha in the present participle as in O.S.]

The Tenses. ܙܒܢ̈ܐ

First present (*he finishes*). The forms without distinctive letters are used almost universally. For use of the tenses see §§ 51—59.

Sing. 3 m. ܦܪܩ : ܦܪܩܝ U. J.

f. ܦܪܩܐ : ܦܪܩܐܝ U. J.

2 m. ܦܪܩܝܬ (ܬ݂ Tkh.): ܦܪܩܬ U.[1]: ܦܪܩܝܬܘܢ U. Tkh. (ܬ݂): ܦܪܩܝܬܐ (ܬ݂) Tkh.: ܦܪܩܬܐ MB. Q.

f. ܦܪܩܬܝ (ܬ݂ Tkh.): ܦܪܩܬܝ U. Tkh. (ܬ݂): ܦܪܩܬܝܐ (ܬ݂) Tkh.: ܦܪܩܬܝܐ MB. Q.

1 m. ܦܪܩܢ : ܦܪܩܢܐܢܐ U. Ti.[2] (not Ash.): ܦܪܩܘܢܐ J.[3]: ܦܪܩܢ[1] U.

f. ܦܪܩܢ : ܦܪܩܐ ܐܢܐ U. Ti.[2] (not Ash.).

Plur. 3 m. f. ܦܪܩܝ : ܦܪܩܝܝ U. J.

2 m. f. ܦܪܩܝܬܘܢ (ܘܢ Sal. Sp.): ܦܪܩܝܬܘ Ti.[2] J. Z.[2] (ܬ݂ Tkh.): ܦܪܩܘܬܘܢ Al.[2] or ܦܪܩܬܘܢ Al.[2]

[1] Village of Digalah, in the plain of Urmi. [2] Paradigm form.

[3] This variation is common in many districts in verbs ܠܐ, as ܟܠܝ ܐܢܐ.

1 m. f. فَدْصِپ (párqákh) : فَدْصِپ (párqákhn) U.:
(ă) Tkh., and esp. U.: فَدْصِپ Ti. Al. Sh. Ash.: فَدْصِپ
Ti. Sh.: فَدْصِپ Al.: فَدْصِپ Q.

Future. جِه فَجِص *he will finish* : جِج فَجِص Al. K.: حفَجِص Al. Z. Sal. (even in ܒ and ܩ verbs) and sometimes U. K. [In Ash. there is no prefix except ܒ before ܐ or ܘ, as دِنْجِہ (d' áthi) *he will come*. So often in Ti. Z. Az. In Ti. Ash. ܩܵܐܡ *he arises*, ܢܵܚܸܬ *he descends*, prefixed to the verb as above makes the future, the proper personal affix being employed. فَجِص is a verb not used in those districts. For the Ṭal future see § 46 under ܢܬܠ.] Conjugate like the First present.

Conditional. جِه فَجِص هَوَا *he would finish*, etc., 3rd plur. هَوَو جِه فَجِص (see Future). Or thus, contracted, in MB. Sal. Q. جِه فَجِطَا : جِه هَوَا فَذَطَا : جِه فَذِطِيَا : جِه فَذْطَا : فَذِينَا (pár-qáná, but accented on the short a).

Habitual and historic present. جِ فَجِص *he finishes*, U. MB. Sp. and rarely Sal. : بِ فَجِص Tkh. Q. Sal.: حفَجِص Al. Z. (and often Sal. with ܒ and ܩ verbs): فَجِص Ti. Ash. For ܟ see § 119.

Habitual imperfect. جِ فَجِص هَوَا *he used to finish*, as above. Also contracted in MB. Sal. Q. like the Conditional.

Preterite (rarely used except in Al.). ܦܪܸܩ U. Z. (rarely Sal.) *he finished* [ܦܪܸܩ (Pthakha sound) = ܦܘܩ Sal., and Al. rarely = ܟܒܪ Al. = O.S. ܩܕܸܡ *he was before*, often used adverbially]. Not used in Ti. Ash.

Second present. ܝܠܹܗ ܦܩܕܹܬܐ *he is finishing*, or ܝܠܹܗ فَذْطِ. See the substantive verb, § 29. The ܝ is much omitted in K., and before labials in U. It is almost always omitted in Ash. except before ܐ or ܝ and often even then. Note ܒܦܪܵܩܵܐ ܝܠܹܗ U. but ܒܦܪܵܩܵܐ ܝܠܹܗ K. § 29, note 2.

Imperfect. Put ܒܦܪܵܩܵܐ or ܦܪܵܩܵܐ before the imperfect of § 29 (*he was finishing*). The second and first persons are often contracted to: 2. ܒܦܪܵܩܵܝܬ݂ m. f.; 1. ܒܦܪܵܩܵܢܐ m. f.; Pl. 1. ܒܦܪܵܩܵܚܢܐ m. f. In Q. these have the force of the Second present tense. Or they are half contracted: 2. ܒܦܪܵܩܵܝܬ݂ ܗܘܵܐ m. f.: 1. ܒܦܪܵܩܵܢ ܗܘܵܐ m. f.: Plur. 1. ܒܦܪܵܩܵܚܢ ܗܘܵܐ m. f. The 2. plur. is not contracted.

Preterite (*he finished*):

Sing. 3 m. ܦܪܝܼܩ ܠܹܗ or ܦܪܝܼܩ K.[1] (rarely).
  f. ܦܪܝܼܩ ܠܵܗ̇.
2 m. ܦܪܝܼܩ ܠܘܼܟ݂.
  f. ܦܪܝܼܩ ܠܵܟ݂ܝ or with ܠܵܟ݂ܝ Ti. MB.
1 m. f. ܦܪܝܼܩ ܠܝܼ.

Plur. 3 m. f. ܦܪܝܼܩ ܠܗܘܿܢ U., or with ܠܗܘܿܢ MB., or with ܠܗܘܿܢ K. Al. J. Sp. Z.
2 m. f. ܦܪܝܼܩ ܠܵܘܟ݂ܘܿܢ or with ܠܵܟ݂ܘܿܢ Ti., or ܠܵܘܟ݂ܘܿܢ Al. Z.
1 m. f. ܦܪܝܼܩ ܠܲܢ or with ܠܲܢܝ Ti.

[The pronunciation of the Khwaṣa is like short *i*, except in K. Al. with ܠܵܐ verbs, and sometimes with others; see page 86.]

Second preterite. ܦܪܝܼܩ ܗܘܵܐ ܠܹܗ *he finished,* or *he was on the point of finishing* (rare in U., common in K. Al. Z.[1]).

Perfect. ܦܪܝܼܩܵܐ ܝܠܹܗ *he has finished*: ܦܪܝܼܩܬܵܐ ܝܠܵܗ̇ f. Plur. ܦܪܝܼܩܹܐ ܝܢܵܐ (ܝܢܵܗܝ) etc., as § 29.

Pluperfect. The above ܦܪܝܼܩܵܐ with the imperfect of § 29 (*he had finished*). Or contracted in the first and second persons: 2.

[1] Paradigm form.

ܦܪܝܩܬܐ m., ܦܪܝܩܬܬܐ f.: 1. ܦܪܝܩܢܐ m., ܦܪܝܩܬܢܐ f. Plur. 1. ܦܪܝܩܢܢܐ [the Zlama has nearly the second sound]. In Q. these have the force of the perfect. Or they may be half contracted, as ܦܪܝܩܬ ܗܘܐ. The 2nd plur. is not contracted.

Imperative. Sing. 2 m. ܦܪܘܩ *finish*; f. ܦܪܘܩܝ. Plur. 2 m. f. ܦܪܘܩܘܢ (so O.S., but usually ܦܪܘܩܘ) or ܦܪܘܩܘ K. J. Al. Z.: ܦܪܘܩܘܢ Sal.

Infinitive. ܠܦܪܩܐ *to finish.*

§ 32. *Formation of the tenses.*

(1) *First present.* This is formed by joining the present participle in its various inflections to the personal pronouns, and by abbreviating them. [A present was formed in O.S. in the same way, and both the simple and the contracted forms were used. It was as follows (cf. the N.S. forms on page 81):

Sg. 3 m. ܦܪܩ or ܦܪܩ ܗܘ	Pl. 3 m. ܦܪܩܝܢ or ܦܪܩܝܢ ܗܢܘܢ
f. ܦܪܩܐ or ܦܪܩܐ ܗܝ	f. ܦܪ̈ܩܢ or ܦܪ̈ܩܢ ܗܢܝܢ
2 m. ܦܪܩܬ or ܦܪܩ ܐܢܬ	2 m. ܦܪܩܝܢ ܐܢܬܘܢ or ܦܪܩܝܬܘܢ
f. ܦܪܩܬܝ or ܦܪܩܐ ܐܢܬܝ	f. ܦܪ̈ܩܢ ܐܢܬܝܢ or ܦܪ̈ܩܬܝܢ
1 m. ܦܪܩܢܐ or ܦܪܩ ܐܢܐ	1 m. ܦܪܩܝܢ ܚܢܢ or ܦܪܩܝܢܢ
f. ܦܪܩܢܐ or ܦܪܩܐ ܐܢܐ	f. ܦܪ̈ܩܢ ܚܢܢ or ܦܪ̈ܩܢܢ]

The N.S. contractions are not all the same as in O.S. Thus we have N.S. ܦܪܩܝܬ = O.S. ܦܪܩܬ, Zlama for Pthakha as very frequently, § 88 *d*. The contractions of 1 pl. are noteworthy, as preserving the ܚ of ܚܢܢ which the O.S. does not do. Probably ܦܪ̈ܩܚ and ܦܪ̈ܩܚܢ are from the feminine ܦܪ̈ܩܢ ܚܢܢ. [So in Digalah, in the Urmi plain, we have one, perhaps two, fem. forms for masculine in the singular; see also § 50.] The other feminine plurals drop out. The syllable ܝܒ (or ܝܕ) is added for emphasis and is an O.S. particle = *indeed*, § 67. The Q. forms like ܩܕܝܫܐ are contractions = ܩܕܝܫܐ ܗܘܐ the past for the present, as we see also in the imperfect contracted forms, and in the pluperfect which has the force of a perfect. The O.S. abbreviations like ܫܦܝܪܬ *thou art beautiful*, are not found in N.S.

(2) *Second present*. The substantive verb is added to the verbal noun with ܒ which takes Zlama, not Pthakha as it would in O.S., § 88 *i*. The ܘ of the substantive verb makes a diphthong with the preceding vowel sound. Thus ܒܦܪܩܠܗ = *he is in the act of finishing*, (biprâqéli accented on *â*).

(3) The *imperfect* similarly follows from the past of the substantive verb.

(4) The *preterite* is formed from the past participle, absolute state, by the addition of ܠ and the pronominal affixes. The past participle, as in O.S., has both an active and a passive sense; in the N.S. preterite the latter appears. Thus ܩܕܝܡ ܠܝ *it is finished by me = I finished*, ܫܒܝܩ ܠܝ ܗܘ ܓܒܪܐ *that man was left by me = I left that man*. When the object, as it would be in English, (which is really the subject), is feminine, we should expect the participle to agree with it, and so when it is plural; and this is usually or very often the case, see § 50: as ܫܒܝܩܐ ܠܝ ܒܪܬܝ *he left my daughter* (*my daughter was left by him*): but the inverted sense has become so much attached to this form that this is not necessary. When the verb ends in ܠ, ܒ, or ܢ the preposition ܠ is omitted, as ܫܩܠܗ *he took*, ܐܡܪܘܝ *thou saidst*. In J. it is usually omitted in all verbs; in O.S. it is not omitted. The pronunciation is usually with short *i*, even in words containing ܒ, ܠ, etc. (p. 11); but in K. Al. ܠܗ verbs

are pronounced with Khwaṣa, and in a phonetically spelt MS. of the Alqosh dialect, 200 years old, other verbs are written so as to be pronounced with long *i*. Even now in some parts of K. there is a tendency to do so, especially in verbs with medial ܐ. When the object is included in the verb, as in § 50, Khwaṣa is universally retained.

That this is the origin of this tense is seen also (*a*) from the way in which the (English) object is expressed when a pronoun, see § 50: the personal pronouns are inserted, not the usual objective affixes, as ܩܛܝܠܬ݂ ܠܶܗ *he killed thee* (*thou wast killed by him*).—(*b*) by the use of these forms in O.S. instead of the past tense. Thus ܛܳܒ݂ܳܐ ܕܰܒ݂ܛܺܝܠ ܠܶܗ ܥܰܠ ܚܰܝܰܝܢ *the good* (*God*) *who hath taken care for our lives* (Collect at Nocturns). So ܫܰܝܢܳܟ ܫܪܺܝܳܐ ܒܥܰܡܳܟ ܕܰܓ݂ܒ݂ܺܝܳܐ ܠܶܟ *make thy peace to dwell in thy people whom thou hast chosen* (Anthems at the end of Baptismal Service): ܟܽܠ ܕܠܳܐ ܢܣܺܝܒ݂ܳܐ ܠܶܗ ܡܰܥܡܽܘܕܺܝܬ݂ܳܐ ܢܶܐܙܰܠ *let any who has not received baptism depart* (Expulsion of Catechumens in the Liturgy). See also St Luke xxiii. 15, 41, 2 Cor. v. 10 Pshiṭta, and Rev. xvii. 7 etc.—(*c*) by the use of the second preterite, especially in K., as ܩܛܝܠ ܗܘܳܐ ܠܶܗ (see above).—(*d*) by the use of the participle alone in K. Al., in either an active or a passive sense, as ܓܰܒ݂ܪܳܐ ܫܒ݂ܝܩ *the man was left*, more rarely *the man left*: ܬܰܘܪܳܐ ܫܪܺܐ *the bull has got loose*: ܗܿܝ ܒܰܟ݂ܬܳܐ ܩܛܝܠܬܳܐ ܬܰܡܳܐ *that woman was killed there*: ܐܳܢܝ ܓܰܒ݂ܪ̈ܶܐ ܦܝܫ ܠܗܘܢ ܢܘܒܠܐ ܠܬܰܡܳܐ ܘܩܛܝܠܝ (not ܩܛܝܠܐ) *those men were taken there and killed.* So very frequently in O.S. both actively and passively, as ܫܰܝܢܳܐ ܫܪܳܐ ܒܶܗ *peace dwelt in it* (Martyrs' Anthem, Tues. morn.): ܠܳܐ ܡܨܺܝܳܐ ܝܰܡܳܐ *the sea could not* (id.): ܐܰܚܺܝ ܐܳܕܳܡ ܕܰܐܒ݂ܺܝܕ ܗܘܳܐ *he quickened Adam who had perished,* (id. Tues. even.) ܘܰܥܠܰܝܗܽܘܢ ܣܺܝܡ ܡܰܕܒ݂ܚܳܐ *and above them was placed an altar* (id.): ܡܰܘܬܳܐ ܕܰܐܚܺܝܕ ܗܘܳܐ ܠܰܢ ܒܚܰܛܳܗ̈ܰܝܢ *death which held us in our sins* (First Fri. even., First anthem) [notice here the objective ܠܰܢ

in the N.S. manner when the pronominal affixes are not inserted in the verb, § 50]: ܡܲܢܘ ܡܨܸܐ ܦܵܪܸܥ ܛܲܝܒܘܼܬܵܐ؟ *who can repay the grace?* (id.): ܐܝܼܟ ܕܟܬܝܼܒ *as it is written* (the Nicene Creed): ܘܡܸܢ ܫܲܩܝܼܠ ܟܵܗܢܵܐ ܩܲܪܢܵܐ ܕܡܸܫܚܵܐ ܡܢ ܐܝܼܕܹ̈ܐ ܗܵܘ ܕܐܠܒܝܫ ܠܹܗ *and then let the priest take the horn of oil from the hands of him that holds it* (Baptismal rubric): notice the ܠܹܗ as above. So Rev. xix. 9, and elsewhere frequently. In O.S. this use of the participle in an active sense appears to be confined to certain verbs.

(5) The *perfect* and *pluperfect* use the definite state of the past participle with the substantive verb.

(6) *Imperative.* The O.S. forms are used, except the fem. pl. The more common O.S. form ܦܘܼܪܘܩܘ m. pl. gives way to the variant, less common in O.S., ܦܘܼܪܘܩܘܿܢ, for the termination of which the Eastern copies of Bar Hebraeus' grammar (chap. IX. § 4) and Bar Zu'bi give Rwaṣa, not Rwakha. We must notice that in N.S. all except ܠܐ verbs (§ 42) and a few ܦܐ verbs in Ẓ. (§ 38) make the imperative in ܘ; thus ܐܡܘܿܪ N.S. = ܐܸܡܲܪ O.S. *say.* This leads to a simplification in grammar. [So ܪܵܗܸܛ *to run,* = O.S. irregular verb ܪܗܛ, is in N.S. quite regular. Imper. ܪܗܘܿܛ = O.S. ܪܗܘܿܛ or ܪܗܸܛ. This verb is not used in Ti.]

(7) The other persons of the imperative are expressed by the first present tense; see § 51 (10).

(8) *Subsidiary tenses* may be formed by ܗܵܘܹܐ, as ܒܸܕ ܗܵܘܹܐ ܒܦܵܪܘܿܩܵܐ *he will be finishing* (rare): ܒܸܕ ܗܵܘܹܐ ܦܪܝܼܩܵܐ *he will have finished* (not common): ܒܸܕ ܗܵܘܹܐ ܗܘܵܐ ܦܪܝܼܩܵܐ *he would have finished* (common). So ܐܸܢ ܗܵܘܹܐ ܦܪܝܼܩܵܐ (common) *if he shall have finished*, §§ 60—62.

(9) The personal pronouns may always be prefixed to the tenses,

or may follow them for emphasis. So in O.S. ܐܢܐ ܐܙܠ ܐܢܐ *I go* = N.S. ܐܢܐ ܐܙܠܢ (§ 46) Gen. xv. 2.

(10) The *Conditional* is like O.S., with the addition of ܒܸܬ. Thus Ps. cxxiv. 3, ܒܠܥܝܢ ܗܘܘ ܠܢ O.S. = ܒܸܬ ܒܠܥܝܢ ܗܘܘ ܠܢ *they would have swallowed us up.*

§ 33. *The verb used negatively.*

Not is expressed by ܠܹܐ or ܠܵܐ (see § 67). It will be observed that ܒܸܬ (almost always) and ܟܸܐ (except Al.) are omitted with the negative, but not ܩܲܡ.

First present. ܠܹܐ ܦܵܪܹܩ *he does not finish.*

ܠܵܐ ܦܵܪܹܩ *let him not finish,* and so in subjoined clauses.

Future. ܠܹܐ ܦܵܪܹܩ : ܠܵܐ ܒܸܬ ܦܵܪܹܩ Ti.[1] (rarely U.) : ܠܵܐ ܟܦܵܪܹܩ[1] Al. *he will not finish.*

Conditional. ܠܹܐ ܦܵܪܹܩ ܗ̄ܘܵܐ or ܠܹܐ ܦܵܪܩܵܐ MB. Q., or (in subjoined clause) ܠܵܐ ܦܵܪܹܩ ܗ̄ܘܵܐ *he would (should) not finish* Always in Al. ܠܵܐ ܟܦܵܪܹܩ ܗ̄ܘܵܐ[1].

Habitual present. ܠܹܐ ܦܵܪܹܩ : ܠܵܐ ܟܦܵܪܹܩ Al.[1] *he does not finish.*

Habitual imperfect. ܠܹܐ ܦܵܪܹܩ ܗ̄ܘܵܐ : ܠܹܐ ܦܵܪܩܵܐ : ܠܵܐ ܟܦܵܪܹܩ ܗ̄ܘܵܐ Al.[1] *he used not to finish.*

Preterite. ܠܵܐ ܩܲܡ ܦܵܪܹܩ *he did not finish.* For variations of the particle see p. 82.

Second present. ܠܹܐ ܝܼܠܹܗ ܒܦܪܵܩܵܐ (ܠܵܐ Al.[1], rare) *he is not finishing.*

Imperfect. ܠܹܐ ܝܼܘܵܐ ܒܦܪܵܩܵܐ U. ܠܵܐ ܗܘܹܐ ܗ̄ܘܵܐ ܒܦܪܵܩܵܐ Tkh. Al.[1] etc. (ܠܹܐ Ti.[1]) *he was not finishing.*

[1] Paradigm form.

Preterite. ܠܵܐ ܦܪܝܼܩ ܠܹܗ *he did not finish,* ܠܵܐ ܦܪܝܼܩ K. (rare).

Second preterite. ܠܵܐ ܦܪܝܼܩ ܗ݇ܘܵܐ ܠܹܗ *he did not finish.*

Perfect. ܠܹܐ ܝܠܹܗ ܦܪܝܼܩܵܐ (ܠܵܐ Al.) *he has not finished.*

Pluperfect. ܠܹܐ ܝܗ݇ܘܵܐ ܦܪܝܼܩܵܐ U., ܠܵܐ ܗ݇ܘܹܐ ܗ݇ܘܵܐ ܦܪܝܼܩܵܐ Tkh. (ܠܹܐ Ti.) *he had not finished.*

Imperative. ܠܵܐ ܦܪܘܿܩ or ܠܵܐ ܦܪܝܼܩܸܬ *do not finish* (see § 59).

The above table applies equally to the second conjugation.

§ 34. *The passive* of transitive verbs of both conjugations is formed by the addition of the past participle to the various tenses of ܦܝܼܫ *to remain,* for the conjugation of which see § 39.

Examples: ܦܝܼܫ ܠܹܗ ܫܩܝܼܠܵܐ *he was taken:* ܦܵܐܫܵܐ ܝܠܵܗ ܫܒܝܼܩܬܵܐ *she is being left.*

More rarely it is expressed by ܐܵܬܹܐ *to come*; thus, ܐܬܹܐ ܠܹܗ ܠܩܛܵܠܵܐ *he came to killing* = *he was killed.*

Often the passive is expressed merely by the past participle, alone in K., or with the substantive verb both in K. and U. Thus ܩܛܝܼܠܵܐ ܝܠܹܗ = *he was killed,* or *he has killed.* In O.S. also this construction often replaces a passive verb; thus, ܢܸܗܘܸܐ ܫܡܝܼܥܬܵܐ ܨܠܘܿܬܲܢ *may our prayer be heard.* ܦܝܼܫ and ܗ݇ܘܹܐ may rarely be used in the past part., ܐܝܼܬ ܦܝܼܫܵܐ ܕܟܝܼܪܬܵܐ ܕܟܪܵܢܵܐ *there is made reference* = *reference is made*: ܐܝܼܬ ܗ݇ܘܵܐ ܗܘܝܵܐ ܫܘܼܚܠܵܦܵܐ *a change was made.* The verb ܦܝܼܫ is not much used in Ti. for the passive, and hardly at all in Tkh. Ash. For the past tense passive they will say ܐ̇ܢܝ ܓܲܒܪܹ̈ܐ ܚܙܝܼ *those men were seen*: ܗ̇ܝ ܚܙܝܼܬܵܐ *she was seen* (p. 86) [for the verb, see § 42]. For other tenses a periphrasis is generally made with the active voice.

قْدِم is also used with past participles in the sense of *to be* or *remain* or *become*, as قْمد قيٰبَا مِن حِبْثَا *be avoiding evil*; and, especially in K. Z., for the simple substantive verb.

Possibility is often expressed by أَهَي K. or أَوَهِ U., as أَهَي ܠܝ ܠܡܦܩܕ K. *if it can be subtracted.* So ܠܡܦܩܕ ܠܐ ܗܘܐ (or ܗܘܐ § 46) U. *it cannot be subtracted*, § 29 (10, 18).

§ 35. *Second Conjugation. First division.* Zqapa verbs.

مخَذِس *to save*, or *finish* tr. (= O.S. مخَذِس but in another sense). For the Mim see below.

Present participle. Sing. مخَذِس m., مخَذَثا f.; Pl. مخَذسِ m. f. Al. Z. K. MB. Sh.; or مخَذِس etc. U. Sp., or مخَذِس etc. Sal. Q. Gaw. J. (Zlama either sound) = O.S. Sing. مخَذِس m., مخَذَثا f.; Pl. مخَذسِ m., مخَذثا f.

Past participle (abs. state). Sing. مخُذس m., مخُذثا f.; Pl. (K. etc.) مخُذسِ. [In U. etc. Mim silent.] = O.S. Sing. مخَذِس m., مخَذثا f.; Pl. مخَذسِ m., مخَذثا f. See § 50.

(*Def. state.*) Sing. مخُذثا m., مخُذسا Ti. U., or مخُذسا Sp. Tkh. Sal. f.; Pl. مخُذسا m. f. = O.S. Sing. مخَذثا m., مخَذسا f.; Pl. مخَذسا m., مخَذسا f. [In U. etc. Mim silent.]

Imperative. Sing. ڤُذِس m., ڤُذِس f.; Pl. ڤُذمه or ڤُذمه U. In Sal. Q. Gaw. we have ڤُذِس, ڤُذِس, ڤُذمه (ܝ Sal.). In K. MB. we have مخَذِس, مخَذِس, مخَذمه (or مخَذمه). In O.S. ڤَذِس, ڤَذِس, ڤَذمه (or ڤَذمه), ڤَذسِ (or ڤَذسِ).

Verbal noun. مخَذوثا : مخَذوثا Sal. Q. Gaw., or مخَذومه Sal. [In U. etc. Mim silent.]

Notes. (1) The tenses follow as in the first conjugation. Thus the preterite is ܡܦܘܪܩ ܠܗ *he saved.* The infinitive is ܠܡܦܪܘܩܐ K., ܠܡܦܪܘܩܐ U. and often Al., ܠܡܦܘܪܩܐ Sal. Q. Gaw. ܒ is not prefixed to the verbal noun in the second present and imperfect; but see § 37, note 6. Future in Al. Z., ܒܡܦܪܩ.

(2) This and the next division correspond to the O.S. Pa'el. But the Pthakha on the first radical is strengthened to Zqapa, perhaps by way of compensating for a Dagesh, as the East Syrians dislike doubling a letter. See also § 87 *c*.

(3) The N.S. past participle differs from the O.S. by the insertion of ܘ. See § 89.

(4) The verbal noun also is quite unlike O.S.; though it has its counterpart in other Aramaic dialects (Nöld. § 101).

(5) The Mim prefixed to this conjugation is silent in U. Sal. Sp. Q. Gaw. and usually J. In Al. the form ܒܡ ܡܦܪܩ (= ܒܡܦܪܩ) is pronounced as one word, with one Mim. The Mim is never prefixed to verbs beginning with ܡܡ; thus ܡܪܡܪ *to growl,* not ܡܡܪܡܪ; so ܡܫܡܫ *to smell* (O.S. ܡܫ). Causatives, whether triliteral or quadriliteral, and all verbs from Aph'el, have Mim already, and do not take a second: as ܡܚܒ *to love* (root ܚܒܒ, cf. ܚܘܒܐ *love,* O.S. and N.S.): ܡܩܛܠ *to cause to be killed.* The same is the case with ܠܒܠ U. = ܡܒܠ K. = ܢܒܠ K. = ܢܘܒܠ Al. = O.S. ܡܘܒܠ (root ܝܒܠ) *to carry,* where the ܠ and ܢ take the place of ܡܡ, § 45. In the verb ܡܝܩܪ *to honour,* the ܡܡ is always retained in U. etc. though not in the cognate ܡܝܩܪ *to weight.* Perhaps we have here the influence of ܡܝܩܪܐ *reverend* (O.S. ܡܝܩܪܐ). It is also retained in ܡܗܝܡܢܐ *faithful* (O.S. ܡܗܝܡܢܐ), ܡܪܚܡܢܐ *merciful.*

The Mim in the imperative in K. is an instance of false analogy.

(6) If a verb is conjugated according to both conjugations, it is usually intransitive in the first, and transitive in the second, as ܦܠܛ *to go out*, ܡܦܠܛ *to put out*. We may often distinguish them by the second radical being soft in the first, hard in the second conjugation: as ܙܒܢ *to buy* (1), ܡܙܒܢ *to sell* (2); but there are exceptions, see §§ 94, 95.

(7) Frequently a verb follows the first conjugation in K., the second in U., as ܦܩܕ K. *to command* = ܡܦܩܕ U.

(8) The imperfect and pluperfect are often contracted as in the first conjugation, as ܡܦܪܘܩܝܢ ܗܘܐ = ܡܦܪܘܩܐ ܝܘܢ ܗܘܐ *I was saving.*

(9) We may take as an instance of the difference between the two conjugations ܒܪܝܟܐ *blessed*, a first conjugation form (but the other parts of the verb are not used) and ܡܒܘܪܟܐ *blessed*, from ܡܒܪܟ 2 conj. *to bless.* The latter has reference to an agent, the former merely to a state of blessedness. A man visiting another on a feast day says ܥܐܕܘܟ ܗܘܐ ܒܪܝܟܐ *may your feast be blessed*; but ܐܬܐ ܠܝ ܠܡܒܪܘܟܐ ܥܐܕܘܟ *I have come (came) to bless your feast.*

(10) Many verbs express an English copula and adjective, or a passive, as ܡܩܪܪ U. *to be cold* (as a person): ܥܡܕ *to be baptized* (cf. ܡܥܡܕ *to baptize*): ܫܡܠ Al. *to be fulfilled.*

§ 36. *Second Conjugation. Second division.* Pthakha verbs. ܡܚܠܠ *to wash* (so O.S.).

Present participle. Sing. ܡܚܠܠ m., ܡܚܠܠܐ f.; Pl. ܡܚܠܠܝ m. f. K. MB. Sh. Al. Z., (so O.S. but pl. ܝܢ m.) or ܡܚܠܠ, ܡܚܠܠܐ, ܡܚܠܠܝ U., or ܡܚܠܠ, ܡܚܠܠܐ, ܡܚܠܠܝ Q. Sal. Gaw. J.

Past participle (abs. state). ܡܚܘܠܠ, ܡܚܘܠܠܐ, ܡܚܘܠܠܝ K. etc., or ܡܚܘܠܠ, ܡܚܘܠܠܐ [for Pl. see § 50] U. Q. Sal. Gaw. J.

[§ 36] SECOND CONJUGATION. SECOND DIVISION.

ܡܣܘܠܸܟܼܕ, K.: ܡܣܘܠܸܟܼܕ (ܓ̰ ܡܣܘܠܸܟܼܕ) ܬܝ.), ܡܣܘܠܸܟܼܕ, ܡܣܘܠܸܟܼܕ (Def. state.)
ܡܣܘܠܸܟܼܕ (ܓ̰ Sal. Sp.), ܡܣܘܠܸܟܼܕ U. etc. = O.S. ܡܢܝܠܸܟܼܕ etc.

Imperative. Sing. ܢܲܝܠܸܟܼܕ m., ܢܲܝܠܸܟܼܕ f.; Pl. ܢܲܝܠܸܟܼܕܘܢ (or ܢܲܝܠܸܟܼܕܡܗ ?)
m. f. U., or ܢܲܝܠܸܟܼܕ, ܢܲܝܠܸܟܼܕ, ܢܲܝܠܸܟܼܕܡܗ (ܓ̰ Sal.) Q. Sal. Gaw. J., or
(or ܡܢܲܝܠܸܟܼܕܡܗ) K. MB. = O.S. ܢܲܝܠܸܟܼܕ, ܡܢܲܝܠܸܟܼܕ, ܡܢܲܝܠܸܟܼܕ
ܡܢܲܝܠܸܟܼܕ, ܡܢܲܝܠܸܟܼܕ (or ܡܢܲܝܠܸܟܼܕܡܗ) (or ܢܲܝܠܸܟܼܬܘܢ) (or ܢܲܝܠܸܟܼܬ).

Verbal noun. ܡܢܲܝܠܘܟܼܕ K. etc. (Mim silent U.), ܡܣܘܠܘܟܼܕ Sal.
Q. Gaw., or ܡܝܠܘܟܼܕ Sal.

The tenses follow as before: the *First present* is given in full.

	K. MB. Sh. Al. Z.	U. Sp.	Q. Sal. Gaw. J.
S. 3 m.	ܡܢܲܝܠܸܟܼܕ	ܡܢܲܝܠܸܟܼܕ	ܡܢܲܝܠܸܟܼܕ
f.	ܡܢܲܝܠܸܟܼܕܐ	ܡܢܲܝܠܸܟܼܕܐ	ܡܢܲܝܠܸܟܼܕܐ
2 m.	ܡܢܲܝܠܸܟܼܕܸܬ	ܡܢܲܝܠܸܟܼܕܸܬ	ܡܢܲܝܠܸܟܼܕܸܬ
f.	ܡܢܲܝܠܸܟܼܕܲܬܝ	ܡܢܲܝܠܸܟܼܕܲܬܝ	ܡܢܲܝܠܸܟܼܕܲܬܝ
1 m.	ܡܢܲܝܠܸܟܼܕܢ	ܡܢܲܝܠܸܟܼܕܢ	ܡܢܲܝܠܸܟܼܕܢ
f.	ܡܢܲܝܠܸܟܼܕܢ	ܡܢܲܝܠܸܟܼܕܢ	ܡܢܲܝܠܸܟܼܕܢ
Pl. 3 m. f.	ܡܢܲܝܠܸܟܼܕܝ	ܡܢܲܝܠܸܟܼܕܝ	ܡܢܲܝܠܸܟܼܕܝ
2 m. f.	ܡܢܲܝܠܸܟܼܕܐܘܢ	ܡܢܲܝܠܸܟܼܕܐܘܢ	ܡܢܲܝܠܸܟܼܕܐܘܢ
1 m. f.	ܡܢܲܝܠܸܟܼܕܣ	ܡܢܲܝܠܸܟܼܕܣ	ܡܢܲܝܠܸܟܼܕܣ

For variations in the terminations see page 81.

Thus are conjugated all triliterals of the second conjugation with Pthakha, among which are many causatives, as ܡܲܚܙܸܕ *to raise*, from ܙܸܕ (but ܚܸܕܸܪ *to lift*, from ܕܸܪ is of the first division). In the K. forms the half vowel often drops altogether, as ܡܒܸܣ *I love* = ܡܲܒܸܣ U. The first Zlama in the Q. Sal. Gaw. J. forms is often lengthened to long Zlama. It is usual to write the verbal noun of this division with Rwasa, of the first division with Rwakha.

§ 37. *Second Conjugation. Third division.* Quadriliterals. ܡܛܟܣ ܕܒܥܕ̈ܐ ܐܗܘ̈ܐ.

ܡܩܛܶܠ *to cause to be killed* (so O.S.).

	U. Sp. MB. Sh.	Sal. Q. Gaw. J.	K. Al. Z.
Pres. part. S. m.	ܡܩܛܶܠ	ܡܩܛܶܠ	ܡܩܛܶܠ
f.	ܡܩܛܠܐ	ܡܩܛܠܐ	ܡܩܛܠܐ
Pl. m. f.	ܡܩܛܠܝ	ܡܩܛܠܝ	ܡܩܛܠܝ
Past part. (abs. state) S. m.	ܡܘܩܛܶܠ	ܡܘܩܛܶܠ	ܡܘܩܛܶܠ
f.	ܡܘܩܛܠܐ	ܡܘܩܛܠܐ	ܡܘܩܛܠܐ
Pl. m. f.	see § 50.	ܡܘܩܛܠܝ	ܡܘܩܛܠܝ
(*Def. state*) S. m.	ܡܘܩܛܠܐ	ܡܘܩܛܠܐ	ܡܘܩܛܠܐ
f.	ܡܘܩܛܠܬܐ[1]	ܡܘܩܛܠܬܐ[1]	ܡܘܩܛܠܬܐ[1]
Pl. m. f.	ܡܘܩܛܠܐ	ܡܘܩܛܠܐ	ܡܘܩܛܠܐ
Imp. S. m.	ܡܩܛܶܠ	ܡܩܛܶܠ	ܡܩܛܶܠ
f.	ܡܩܛܠܝ	ܡܩܛܠܝ	ܡܩܛܠܝ
Pl. m. f.	ܡܩܛܠܘܢ	ܡܩܛܠܘܢ[2]	ܡܩܛܠܘܢ
Verbal noun	ܡܩܛܘܠܐ	ܡܘܩܛܘܠܐ[3]	ܡܩܛܘܠܐ

The tenses follow as before.

Notes. (1) Quadriliterals, not causatives or beginning with ܡ, are of the form ܡܚܡܠܐ *to reconcile*, but follow the above.

(2) All quadriliterals have Pthakha on the first radical unless

[1] ܠܐ Sp. Sal., ܠܐ Ti.   [2] ܣ Sal.   [3] Or ܡܚܕ Sal.

the second radical be ‍ܘ, when Zqapa is substituted, as ܡܚܵܣܸܒ݂ *to beseech*, § 7, but this makes no difference in the conjugation. In these verbs in the past participle etc. one Wau may be omitted: as ܡܚܘܼܒܹܐ ܠܹܗ.

(3) For first conjugation quadriliterals see § 46.

(4) Some verbs have more than four letters; these follow the above conjugation.

(5) In K. Al. when the second letter is ܗ or a weak consonant, the euphonic vowel which it would take is dropped, as ܡܲܕܸܘܕܘܼܢ Al. *prepare ye*. So with ܡܕܲܝܡܸܢ *to believe*, ܡܲܥܓ݂ܸܕ *to cause to enter*, in K. and ܡܲܟ݂ܠܸܨ *to discipline*, in all districts; e.g. ܡܲܥܓ݂ܸܕ (mô-rin) *I cause to enter*, ܡܲܚܘܼܠܨܵܐ *punished*. This is the case especially with causatives of ܦ, ܩ verbs, as ܡܲܐܟ݂ܸܠ *to feed*, ܡܲܦܸܐ *to have baked*. Yet we have ܡܲܘܕܝܵܐ Al. *she informs*, from ܡܲܘܕܸܥ (= ܡܲܝܕܸܥ K. U., causative of ܝܵܕܸܥ *to know*).

(6) In the tenses ܒ is sometimes added to the verbal noun in Al. as ܟܕ ܡܩܲܛܘܼܠܗ݇ܘܵܐ *he was causing to be killed*.

§ 38. *Regular Variations from the above verbs.*

The variations are due as in O.S. to certain weak letters being in the root; but ܦ verbs now present no irregularities, nor yet those which in N.S. have the second and third radicals the same.

{ Verbs ܦ . ܡܸܟ݂ܠ ܐܲܠܩܸܛܸܗ ܕܹܐ
{ Verbs ܩ . ܡܸܟ݂ܠ ܡܲܘܕܸܥܸܗ ܕܹܐ

These verbs may be taken together. The variations are due to ܐ becoming ܝ, and in some cases to a metathesis taking place. We must notice that in N.S. ܐ and ܝ can, but in O.S. (except in a few words like ܐܡܪ̈ܐ) cannot, stand at the beginning of a word without a vowel. When vowelless they have no sound.

ܐܡܕ or ܐܡܗܕ to bind.　　ܢܓܝ to be long.

Verbal noun with ܒ. ܓܗܡܕܐ U. Q. Sal. Gaw. ܓܒܗܕܐ Ti. MB. Sh. Al. Ash.　　ܓܕܢܓܐ U. Ash. (also ܕܢܓܐ Ash.) MB. Sh. : ܓܒܕܓܐ Al.

Pret. ܐܡܒܝܕܗ (i U. i K.) ܐܡܗܒܕܗ Al. and sometimes Tkh.　　ܠܗ ܡܕܝܥ ܠܗ Al. Tkh.

Imp. ܐܡܗܗܕ : ܐܡܗܗܕ Al. (Pl. in Al. : ܐܡܗܕܘܢ or ܐܡܗܕܘ). The Sing. in Z. in some verbs has no Wau, as : ܐܡܕ say.　　ܒܕܗܘܢ : ܢܕܗܘܢ Al.

Past part. ܐܡܒܝܕܐ : ܐܡܗܒܝܕܐ Al. Tkh.　　ܡܕܒܓܐ : ܒܕܒܓܐ Al. Tkh.

But a few verbs only have one form of verbal noun. ܐܙܠ (but see § 46) to go, ܐܟܠ to eat, ܐܡܪ to say (in Al. and sometimes in K. to speak or tell), ܐܬܐ to come (see § 46), ܢܓܝܕ to know (see § 46), ܓܝܪ to curdle Sp., only make ܓܝܘܟܠܐ, ܓܒܝܕܗܐ etc.

In some there is a metathesis in the First present tense, as ܠܟܝ or ܡܠܟܝ I learn (§ 46). In Sp. this arrangement even extends to verbs ܩܕ as ܡܟܡܕܝ (médî) = ܢܡܕܩܝ they are baptized.

Many of these verbs have ܐ in one district, ܗ in another : as ܡܓܕ (or ܩܒܝ) U. = ܐܦܝ MB. as O.S. to bake, ܢܓܒ U. K., O.S. = ܐܓܒ Al. to sit (ܠ N.S., ܠ O.S.).

The only second conjugation verbs ܐܩ or ܩܕ are ܡܕܡܝ to be

peaceful or *tame* K., *entrust* Al.: ܡܰܕܩܶܕ *to reverence* (retaining ܡܕ always), and a few quadriliterals, as ܡܰܕܟܶܟ U. (ܟ݂ K.) *to be numb*, ܡܰܕܘܶܡ *to be cheap*, ܡܰܕܘܺܝܠ *to be a widow or widower*, *to tumble over*, ܡܰܕܕܶܥ Sp. (= ܡܰܕܘܶܥ K.) *to be muddy or broken*, ܡܰܕܚܶܕ *to be shy*, ܡܰܕܝܶܩ *to be heavy*. These are regular.

Verbs ܩܳܡ and ܣܳܟ of the first conjugation may in the Future colloquially drop Zqapa in U. (not K.), as ܠܳ ܐܬܶܐ *we will not come*, ܠܳ ܥܳܡܶܕ *he will not dwell*, ܠܳ ܐܳܙܠܺܝܢ *they will not go*; but not ܠܳ ܡܰܕܶܒ etc., where too many consonants intervene between the vowels. So ܐܳܡܶܕ Al. Z. = ܚܳܡܶܕ Sal. = ܐܳܡܶܕ ܓܐ *he says*.

§ 39. *Verbs* ܩܳܡ *or* ܣܓܶܕ.

The O.S. verbs ܩܳܡ (o non-consonantal) and ܣܓܶܕ correspond to this class, as the present participles are of the form ܩܳܝܶܡ from ܩܳܡ (ܩܳܡ) *to rise up*, ܓܳܙܶܝ from ܓܳܙ (ܣܓܶܕ) *to bow*. These classes are called by the Eastern Syrians respectively ܡܶܟܠܰܕ ܘܡܶܒܩܰܦ ܙܢܰܥ and ܡܶܟܠܰܕ ܩܳܥܢܶܦ ܙܢܰܥ. We must however notice that O.S. ܣܳܟܺܝܦ = N.S. ܚܒܺܝܩ *bowed*.

Example. ܦܳܐܶܫ *to remain* (so O.S.; ܦܳܫ is the past tense).

Pres. part. Sing. ܦܳܐܶܫ (in U. Zlama usually feeble) or ܦܳܝܶܫ K. m.; ܦܳܝܫܳܐ f.; Pl. ܦܳܝܫܺܝܢ m. f.

Past part. (abs. state). Sing. ܦܺܝܫ m., ܦܺܝܫܳܐ f.; Pl. (K.) ܦܺܝܫܺܝܢ m. f. (Def. state.) Sing. ܦܺܝܫܳܐ m., ܦܺܝܫܬܳܐ f.; Pl. ܦܺܝܫܶܐ m. f.

Imperative. ܩܽܘܡ (Rwasa in O.S. ܩܳܡ verbs: but Rwakha in O.S. ܣܓܶܕ verbs as ܚܦܽܘܩ).

The *First present* thus is: فَجَحٖ: فَجَحٖ: فَجَرٖ: فَجَرٖ (فَجِرٖ) فَجِرٖ: فَجَعٖ: فَجَحِهٖ: فَجَسٖ. فَجَرٖ: فَجِرٖ: فَجِرٖ.

In the second present ܒ is commonly omitted in this verb, which is used to form the passive voice of other verbs, § 34.

In Z. in some verbs the Alap remains in the preterite, as ܕܐܝܕܒ (*d'îrî*) *I returned*, from ܕܐܪ.

Several verbs whose second radical is silent are conjugated similarly. Such are: ܕܟܠ *to look intently* (so O.S. ܕܟܠ, Barbahlul): ܐܓܪ Al. *to hire* (O.S. ܐܓܪ. So ܐܓܝܪܐ Al. *a hired servant*): ܢܓܗ K. *to dawn*, see § 46 (O.S. ܢܓܗ): ܣܗܕ (as O.S.), or ܣܗܕ K. *to bear witness*: ܣܗܕ (also ܣܗܕ) Al. Bo. *to understand* = ܒܝܢ K., O.S. (= ܡܚܟܡ U. p. 102): ܕܟܠ *awake, find out about, feel pain* (O.S. ܕܟܠ *to feel*): ܢܟܠ *to light a fire* (O.S. ܢܟܠ): ܢܟܠ *to shake* (O.S. ܢܟܠ. In N.S. ܢܟܠ *to disturb*, is also used). See also § 40.

Second conjugation verbs ܝܕ, or ܝܕ, as ܡܚܓܙ Al. *to borrow* (= ܡܚܕܝ U. So ܕܡܐ *debt*, Pers.): ܡܚܣܝܕ *to help*, Pers., (so ܣܗܕ *help*) are regular. So also ܡܚܓܙ K. *to pour in grease* (= ܣܗܕ U. § 46 = ܓܕܙ O.S.); ܡܚܙܥ K. (= ܡܚܙܥ U.) = ܗܪ! Chald. *to defile* (putting milk in lenten food gives the idea) [hence ܘܣܗܙܐ *a summer pasturage* for making butter etc.].

We may notice ܫܝܦ Ti. *to bathe* (= ܢܝܦ U. Tkh.) which retains both Pe's. This is an ܝܕ verb, while the corresponding O.S. is ܣܟ, ܢܣܟ; but ܣܦܩܐ = *washing and rubbing down in the bath* O.S. [In U. this verb is used of women only, ܢܣܒ being used of men.] So some others, § 81 (5).

§ 40. *Verbs with middle* ܝ.

These are like the preceding, or else are regular. But in the preterite ܕ is nearly always silent. Thus ܢܲܟ݂ܕܸܒ U. = ܢܲܟ݂ܕܸܒ Al. K. *they bear*, from ܟܵܕܹܒ *to bear*; Pret. ܟ݁ܕܝܼܒ *I bore*. The noun denoting the agent [§ 77] is ܟ݁ܲܟ݂ܕܢܵܐ U. ܟ݁ܲܟ݂ܕܵܢܵܐ K. *one who carries or bears*. The action is ܟ݁ܲܟ݂ܕܵܢܵܐ U. ܟ݁ܲܟ݂ܕܵܢܵܐ K. *bearing*. So ܟܲܟ݂ܕܵܢܵܐ U., or more commonly ܟܲܟ݂ܕܵܢܵܐ U. K. *bearing*.

The verb ܟܵܕܹܒ and perhaps others in § 39 may also be conjugated thus.

§ 41. *Verbs* ܥܒ *and* ܝܒ.

In the First present tense, ܘ and ܝ, if they have no vowel, form a diphthong with Zqapa, as ܢܵܓ݂ܝܼܒ *I leave (shó-qin)*.

In the first conjugation imperative, the ܘ is usually, ܝ sometimes, dropped. Thus from ܢܘܙ *to leap*, ܢܘܙ U. K., but ܢܘܘܙ sometimes in U.; ܫܒܘܩ *leave*, is *shúq* usually in K., *shwúq* usually in U.: ܓ݂ܝܼܙ *to pass or to enter*, does not drop ܝ: ܓ݂ܝܼܓ݂ *to do*, never except in Al.

Verbs ܥܒ of the second conjugation have Pthakha in U. Q. etc. Zqapa in K., as ܡܲܩܘܸܡ U., ܡܲܩܘܸܡ K. *to happen*, § 87 c. (For ܡܲܩܘܲܡܬܵܐ K., ܡܲܩܘܲܡܬܵܐ U., see § 63.) These verbs are like ܡܲܢܒܸܠ, but in K. do not take even a half-vowel; thus ܡܙܵܘܸܓ݂ *thou joinest* (*mzógit*) K.

For ܪܘܙ *to be drunk*, and ܩܛܘܡ *to spread* (always Zqapa), see ܠ verbs, § 42; for ܢܓ݂ܝܼܕ *to bubble up*, ܣܓ݂ܝܼܕ *to be satisfied*, ܨܓ݂ܝܼܕ *to dye* (all ܝ), see ܠ verbs, § 44.

§ 42. *Verbs* ܠ. ܡܸܬ݂ ܓ݁ܲܠܝܵܢ ܥܘܼܒܕܵܐ.

First Conjugation. ܓܵܠܹܐ *to reveal*.

Present participle. Sing. ܟܵܠܸܒ m., ܟܵܠܒܵܐ f.; Pl. ܟܵܠܒܹܐ m. f. (= O.S. ܟܵܠܒܝܼܢ). In U. Sp. Sal. with first, in J. K. Al. Z. MB. Sh. with second Zlama sound. (So below wherever Lamadh has long Zlama.)

Past participle (abs. state). Sing. ܟܠܝܼܒ m., ܟܠܝܼܒܵܐ f.; Pl. (K.) ܟܠܝܼܒܹܐ m. f. (see § 50). = O.S. Sing. ܟܠܝܼܒ m., ܟܠܝܼܒܵܐ f.; Pl. ܟܠܝܼܒܹܐ m., ܟܠܝܼܒܵܢ f.

(Def. state.) Sing. ܟܠܝܼܒܵܐ U. K., or ܟܠܝܼܒܬܵܐ Ti. MB., or ܟܠܝܼܒܬܵܐ Tkh. m., ܟܠܝܼܒܬܵܐ f.; Pl. ܟܠܝܼܒܹܐ, ܟܠܝܼܒܹܐ or ܟܠܝܼܒܹܐ. = O.S. Sing. ܟܠܝܼܒܵܐ m., ܟܠܝܼܒܬܵܐ f.; Pl. ܟܠܝܼܒܹܐ m., ܟܠܝܼܒܵܬܵܐ f.

Imperative. Sing. ܟܠܘܿܒ m., ܟܠܘܿܒ f.; Pl. ܟܠܘܿܒܘܢ m. f., K. MB. Sh. as O.S. (but O.S. f. ܟܠܘܿܒܝܼ is wanting). In U. Q. Sal., Sing. ܟܠܘܿܒ m. f.; Pl. ܟܠܘܿܒܡܘܢ m. f. (ܓ Sal.).

Verbal noun. ܟܠܵܒܬܵܐ, or ܟܠܵܒܵܐ U. Sal. Q. Gaw.

From these the tenses follow as before. We may notice:

The first present.

S. 3 m. ܟܵܠܸܒ or ܟܵܠܒܝܼܒ U. J.

    f. ܟܵܠܒܵܐ or ܟܵܠܒܵܒܝܼ U. J.

  2 m. ܟܵܠܒܸܬ (ܒ Tkh.), ܟܵܠܒܝܼܬ U. Tkh. (ܒ), ܟܵܠܒܘܢܸܬ Tkh. (the long Zlama of Tau has the first sound) or ܟܵܠܒܸܬ Q. MB.

    f. ܟܵܠܒܵܬܝ (ܒ Tkh.), ܟܵܠܒܝܼܬܝ U. Tkh. (ܒ), ܟܵܠܒܘܢܸܬܝ Tkh., ܟܵܠܒܵܬܝ Q. MB. or ܟܵܠܒܵܬܝ Al.

  1 m. ܟܵܠܸܒ or ܟܵܠܸܒܢܵܐ U. Ti. Sh. (common).

    f. ܟܵܠܒܵܢ or ܟܵܠܒܵܢܵܐ U. Ti. (common), or ܟܵܠܒܵܐ Al.

Pl. 3 m. f. ܟܵܠܒܝܼ, ܟܵܠܒܝܼܒ U. J.

[§ 42] VERBS WITH WEAK FINAL LETTER. 101

2 m. f. ܓܲܠܝܬܘܿܢ (ܸ Sal.), or ܓܲܠܝܬܘܿܢ Ti. (ܹ Tkh.), or ܓܲܠܠܝܬܘܿܢ Al.

1 m. f. ܓܲܠܹܢ : ܓܲܠܣܼܝܢ U.: ܓܲܠܝܼܢ Ti. Al. Sh. Ash.: ܓܲܠܣܼܝܢ Ti. Sh.: ܓܲܠܣܼܝܢ U. Tkh.: ܓܲܠܝܼܢܲܢ Q.: ܓܲܠܠܘܼܢ Al.

[The O.S. contracted forms are given for comparison: Sing. ܓܠܵܐ : ܓܠܵܬ݂ : ܓܠܲܬ݂ : ܓܠܲܝܬ݂ : ܓܠܲܝܬܝ : ܓܠܹܝܬ݂ ; Pl. ܓܠܵܘ : ܓܠܲܝܬܘܿܢ : ܓܠܲܝ̈ܝ : ܓܠܲܝܬܸܢ : ܓܠܲܝܬܹܝܢ : ܓܠܲܝܢ.]

Second present. ܒܸܓ݁ܲܠܹܐ ܠܹܗ *he is revealing* etc.; or in Sal. ܒܸܓ݁ܲܠܹܐ ܠܹܗ etc.; in Gaw., Sing. ܒܸܓ݁ܲܠܠܹܐ : ܒܸܓ݁ܲܠܠܵܗ̇ : ܒܸܓ݁ܲܠܠܘܼܟ݂ ; Pl. ܒܸܓ݁ܲܠܠܲܢ (or ܒܸܓ݁ܲܠܠܲܟ݂ܘܢ) : ܒܸܓ݁ܲܠܠܘܼܗܝ : ܒܸܓ݁ܲܠܠܘܼܢ : ܒܸܓ݁ܲܠܠܗܹܝܢ : ܒܸܓ݁ܲܠܠܗܘܿܢ.

Infinitive. ܠܓ݂ܲܠܘܼܝܹܐ ; or often ܠܓ݂ܲܠܘܼܝ U. Q. Sal. Gaw.

Second Conjugation. First division.

ܡܲܟ݂ܣܹܐ *to hide.*

Present participle. Sing. ܡܲܟ݂ܣܹܐ m., ܡܲܟ݂ܣܝܵܐ f.; Pl. ܡܲܟ݂ܣܹܝܢ K. MB. Sh. Al. Z. In U. Mim is silent. In Q. Sal. Gaw. J. ܡܲܟ݂ܣܹܐ etc. [For the Zlama under Shin see above § 42.] O.S. ܡܟܲܣܹܐ : ܡܟܲܣܝܵܐ : ܡܟܲܣܹܝܢ.

Past part. (abs. state). Sing. ܡܟ݂ܘܼܣܹܐ m., ܡܟ݂ܘܼܣܝܵܐ f. (Mim silent as above); Pl. ܡܟ݂ܘܼܣܹܝܢ (for U. see § 50). = O.S. ܡܟܲܣܲܝ : ܡܟܲܣܝܵܐ : ܡܟܲܣܹܝܢ : ܡܟܲܣܲܝܵܐ.

(*Def. state.*) Sing. ܡܟ݂ܘܼܣܝܵܐ m., ܡܟ݂ܘܼܣܲܝܬܵܐ U. Ti., or ܡܟ݂ܘܼܣܸܬܵܐ Sp.

Tkh. Sal.; Pl. ܡܚܟܡܬܗ (Mim silent in U. etc.). Also in Al. as O.S. ܡܚܟܬܢܐ : ܡܚܟܬܢܐ.

Imperative. Sing. ܡܚܟܒ m. f., Pl. ܡܚܟܡܘܢ U.; or ܡܚܟܒ, ܡܚܟܡܘ Sal. Q. Gaw. (ܘ Sal.); or Sing. ܡܚܟܒ m., ܡܚܟܒ f., Pl. ܡܚܟܬܗ K. Sh. MB. In O.S. ܟܬܒ : ܟܬܒ : ܟܬܒܘ : ܟܬܒܝܢ.

Verbal noun. ܡܚܟܘܦܐ K. MB. ܡܚܟܘܦܐ sometimes Ti.: ܡܚܟܘܦܐ U., ܡܚܟܘܦܐ Sal. Gaw. Q., or ܡܚܟܘܦܐ Sal.

The tenses follow as before.

Second Conjugation. Second division. The only verbs conjugated thus are ܡܦܠܓ U. *to divide* (for which see below), and the causatives like ܡܚܒܪ § 46. They are like ܡܚܟܒ but take an euphonic vowel whenever ܡܢܒܠ does so. For ܡܕܪܐ *to throw*, see § 46.

Second Conjugation. Third division.

ܡܚܟܘܡܕ *to understand* (not common in K.). For the Zlama of Mim, see ܡܠܠ . Several are paradigm forms only.

Present participle. Sing. ܡܚܟܘܡܕ m., ܡܚܟܘܡܕܐ f., Pl. ܡܚܟܘܡܕܝ m. f. K. Al.; or ܡܚܟܘܡܕܝ : ܡܚܟܘܡܕܢܐ : ܡܚܟܘܡܕܝ U. MB. Sh. (but Mim silent U.); or ܡܚܟܘܡܕܝ : ܡܚܟܘܡܕܢܐ : ܡܚܟܘܡܕܝ Q. Sal. Gaw. J.

Past participle (abs. state). Sing. ܡܚܟܘܡܕ m., ܡܚܟܘܡܕܐ f., Pl. ܡܚܟܘܡܕܝ m. f. K.; or Sing. ܡܚܟܘܡܕ m., ܡܚܟܘܡܕܢܐ f. U. Sal. Q. Gaw. (for pl. see § 50), so MB. Sh. with Mim sounded.

(*Def. state.*) Sing. ܡܚܟܘܡܕܐ m., ܡܚܟܘܡܕܢܐ (ܡܚܟܘܡܕܢܐ Ti.) f.,

Pl. ܡܟܘܕܡܝܢ m. f. K.; or ܡܟܘܕܡܝܢ: ܡܟܘܕܡܝܢ (ܡܟܘܕܡܢܐ Sp. Sal.) ܡܟܘܕܡܝܢ U. etc.

Imperative. Sing. ܩܕܡܝ m. f., Pl. ܩܕܡܘܡ m. f. U.; or ܩܕܡܝ: ܩܕܡܘܡ (ܓ Sal.) Q. Gaw. Sal.; or Sing. ܡܩܕܡܝ m., ܡܩܕܡܐ f., Pl. ܡܩܕܡܘ m. f. K. MB. Sh.

Verbal noun. ܡܩܕܡܘܡܐ K. MB., or ܡܩܕܡܘܬܐ Ti. sometimes, or ܡܩܕܡܘܡܐ U., or ܡܩܕܡܘܡܐ (ܡܟܘܕܡܘܡܐ (or ܩܕ') Sal., or ܡܩܕܡܘܡܐ Gaw. The tenses follow as before: for the euphonic vowel see § 37 (5).

Some verbs with a silent final letter are conjugated like ܠܐ verbs (but see § 46 ad init.). Such are: ܚܡܝ *to be extinguished* (O.S. ܚܡܕ): ܡܘܟ *to mix* (also ܡܘܓ as O.S.): ܢܬܒ U. *to knock, attack, butt* (in Al. Tkh. as O.S. ܢܬܒ. In K. also ܢܛܒ): ܤܝܟ or ܤܝܟ *to make a fence, see* § 46: ܩܓܝ K. (= ܩܦܝ U., hard Kap) *to lose savour* (O.S. ܩܓܕ): ܦܠܟ K. U., also ܦܠܝܓ Al., as O.S. *to divide,* §§ 46, 98 (cf. ܦܠܓܐ *midlent* = O.S. ܦܠܓܐ *the division*, and ܦܠܓܐ *half* = O.S. ܦܠܓܐ: ܦܠܓܐ Tkh. *a wave* = πέλαγος ?): ܕܓܝ K. *to be like*, Arab.

So in the second conjugation ܡܦܠܟ U. = ܡܦܠܝܓ Al. = ܡܦܠܟ K. *to divide*: ܡܚܢܕ K. *to call to prayer*, Arab.: ܡܚܨܓ Al. *to liken* (O.S. ܚܓܕ) = ܡܚܨܓ K. (Arab.): ܡܢܟܘܓ U. *to pant.*

§ 43. Verbs ܠܗ (ܓܢܣܐ ܕܦܬܚ ܒܐܠܦܐ) of the first conjugation are usually written with only one ܘ in the imperative, as ܠܒܗ from ܠܒܗ *to snatch.*

§ 44. Verbs ܠܐ. ܓܢܣܐ ܕܡܬܓܡܠܢܗܝ ܒܝܘܕ.

These verbs are in most places, in many of their forms, conjugated as if ܥ was absent, and like ܠܐ verbs. In others, as in O.S., they are conjugated as if ܥ was a strong consonant.

First Conjugation. ܫܳܡܶܥ *to hear* (= O.S. ܫܡܰܥ). In U. etc., pronounced ܫܶܡܶܥ, see § 46.

Present participle. Sing. ܫܳܡܶܥ m., ܫܳܡܥܳܐ f. U. Sh. as O.S., or ܫܳܡܥܳܝܳܐ f. K., Pl. ܫܳܡܥܝ m. f. (in Tkh. pron. *shâmé*, as if ܫܳܡܶܝ, a ܠܐ verb); O.S. ܫܳܡܥܺܝܢ.

Past participle (abs. state). Sing. ܫܡܺܝܥ m., ܫܶܡܥܬܳܐ f. U., or ܫܡܝܥܬܳܐ f. Ti. Ash., ܫܡܺܝܥܳܐ Al. Z. as O.S.; Pl. ܫܡܺܝܥܶܐ Ti. (as if ܠܐ), see § 50.

(*Def. state.*) Sing. ܫܶܡܥܬܳܐ m. U. Tkh., or ܫܡܝܥܬܳܐ Al., or ܫܡܺܝܥܳܐ Ti. Z. Al. as O.S.: ܫܡܺܝܥܬܳܐ f. as O.S. [pron. *shmi'ta* Ti.]; Pl. ܫܶܡܥܶܐ, ܫܡܝܥܶܐ, or ܫܡܺܝܥܶܐ as O.S.

Imperative. Sing. ܫܡܥܝ m. f., Pl. ܫܶܡܥܡܘܢ m. f. U. Q. Sal. Gaw. (as if ܠܐ) [in Sal. ܦ]; or Sing. ܫܡܥܝ m., ܫܡܰܥܶܐ f., Pl. ܫܡܰܥܘ m. f. K. MB.; or Sing. ܫܡܘܿܥ m., ܫܡܘܿܥܝ f., Pl. ܫܶܡܥܘ m. f. Al. Ash. In O.S. ܫܡܰܥ : ܫܡܰܥܝ : ܫܡܰܥܘ : ܫܡܰܥܶܝܢ.

Verbal noun. ܫܡܳܥܬܳܐ : ܫܡܳܥܳܐ Al. Ash.: also ܫܡܳܥܳܐ U. Q. Sal. Gaw.

From these come the tenses; we notice especially:

The first present. In U. Sh. ܫܳܡܶܥ : ܫܳܡܥܳܐ : ܫܳܡܥܶܢ : ܫܳܡܥܳܢ : ܫܳܡܥܶܬ : ܫܳܡܥܰܬ : ܫܳܡܥܝ : ܫܳܡܥܝܬܘܢ : ܫܳܡܥܰܚ. In K. the feminines are ܫܳܡܥܳܝܳܐ : ܫܳܡܥܝܳܢ : ܫܳܡܥܝܰܬ. In Al. the 2 pl. is ܫܳܡܥܘܬܘܢ, and in Tkh. is pronounced *shâmétun*, as if a ܠܐ verb. For variations in the terminations see § 31.

§ 44]   VERBS WITH WEAK FINAL LETTER.

The second present. ܓܲܡܚܲܕܸܢ ܡܲܕ݂ܸܢ : but in Sal. ܡܲܕܸܢ ܓܲܡܚܲܕܸܢ ; in Gaw. and also Sal. ܓܲܡܚܲܕܸܢ etc., as in ܠܐ verbs, p. 101.

Second Conjugation. ܡܚܲܡܸܕ or ܡܚܲܡܸܕ *to assemble.*

Pres. participle. Sing. ܡܚܲܡܸܕ m., ܡܚܲܡܸܕ݂ܵܐ or ܡܚܲܡܸܕܬܵܐ f., Pl. ܡܚܲܡܸܕ U. MB. Sh. (but in U. Mim is silent); so Sal. Q. Gaw. J. but with ܐ; or Sing. ܡܚܲܡܸܕ m., ܡܚܲܡܸܕ݂ܵܐ f., Pl. ܡܚܲܡܸܕ m. f. K. (in Tkh. pron. *mjámé*, as if ܠܐ); and so Ash. but with ܐ.

Past participle (abs. state). Sing. ܡܚܘܲܡܸܕ m.: ܡܚܘܲܡܸܕܬܵܐ U., or ܡܚܘܲܡܲܕܬܵܐ K. f.; Pl. ܡܚܘܲܡܕܝ K. (for U., see § 50).

(*Def. state.*) Sing. ܡܚܘܲܡܸܕܬܵܐ K., or ܡܚܘܲܡܸܕܬܵܐ U. MB. Sal. Q. m.; ܡܚܘܲܡܸܕܬܐ K., or ܡܚܘܲܡܸܕܬܢܐ U. Ti. f.; Pl. ܡܚܘܲܡܕܝ or ܡܚܘܲܡܕܹܐ.

Imperative. Sing. ܚܲܡܸܕ m. f.; Pl. ܚܲܡܸܕܘܿܢ m. f. U. So Q. Gaw. Sal. with ܐ (ܢ Sal.). In K. ܡܚܲܡܸܕ m., ܡܚܲܡܸܕܸܢ f.; Pl. ܡܚܲܡܸܕܸܢ m. f. So Ash. MB. Sh. with ܐ.

Verbal noun. ܡܚܲܡܕܘܿܡܲܕ K.: ܡܚܲܡܕܘܿܡܲܕܐ MB. Sh. Ash.: ܡܚܲܡܕܘܿܡܲܕܐ U.: ܡܚܲܡܘܿܡܲܕܐ Q. Sal. (or 'ܚܲܡܸܕ' Sal.): ܡܚܲܡܕܘܿܡܲܕܐ Gaw. The tenses follow as before.

The verbs ܢܵܓܸܕ *to bubble up,* ܣܵܓܸܕ *to be satisfied,* ܨܵܓܸܕ *to dye* (which in U. have a Pthakha sound, see § 46), are pronounced differently in U. and K. in the First present. Thus ܣܵܓܸܓ *I am satisfied,* is *sá-win* K., *só'in* U. But ܣܲܓܸܕܐ U. *she is satisfied,* is *só'a*, and also ܣܲܓܸܕܐ K. is *só'ya*. Past part. ܣܓܝܓܵܐ *su'ya*, etc.

For verbs with more than one weak letter, see § 46.

S. GR.

§ 45. *Causative verbs.*

(*a*) These verbs are derived from Aph'el, and are formed by prefixing ܡ to the root (Gaw. Q. Sal. J. ܡܹ or ܡܲ), as ܩܲܛܸܠ to *kill*, ܡܩܲܛܸܠ to *have killed*. Almost all first conjugation verbs form causatives in N.S.; and they are frequently used where in English the original verb would be used, when the sense is that a person does a thing by the hand of another, as, *St Paul wrote an epistle by the hand of a scribe*, ܦܵܘܠܳܘܣ ܟܬܝܼܒ݂ܵܐ ܐܰܝܟ ܒܝܲܕ ܟܳܬܘܿܒ݂ܵܐ ܡܲܟܬܸܒ݂ (or ܟܬܸܒ݂ ܦܵܘܠܳܘܣ).

The meaning must be noted: thus, ܢܫܸܦ to *dry up* intr., ܡܲܢܫܸܦ to *cause to dry up*; but ܛܚܸܢ to *grind* tr., ܡܲܛܚܸܢ to *have ground*. In the first case the object of the causative is the subject of the original; in the second case the object of both verbs is the same. But there are some exceptions, as ܕܟ݂ܸܪ to *remember*, ܡܲܕܟܸܪ to *cause to remember, remind*, see below, *h*.

Some causatives are triliteral owing to a weak letter having dropped. These are noted below. But notice that verbs ܝ, which in O.S. drop ܝ in Aph'el, retain it in the N.S. causative.

(*b*) *Causatives of* ܦ *and* ܝ *verbs*. These are very irregular. In O.S. these verbs usually insert ܘ in the Aph'el, and a few of them are now so formed in Al., as noted in the following list.

ܐܙܸܠ to *go*, O.S.—ܛܥܸܢ U. to *carry*, (ܠ J.) or ܡܲܛܥܸܢ K. or ܢܲܩܸܠ K. Z. (ܠ J.) or ܢܲܩܸܠ Al.; no preformative Mim (O.S. ܐܰܘܒܸܠ, *root* ܝܒܠ, cf. O.S. ܝܰܒܠܳܐ *a caravan, herd*), § 46.

ܐܟ݂ܸܠ to *eat*, O.S.—ܡܲܐܟܸܠ (O.S. ܐܰܘܟܸܠ) to *feed*.

ܐܚܸܕ or ܚܡܸܣ to *shut*—ܡܲܚܡܸܣ §§ 46, 113.

ܐܡܸܪ to *say*, O.S.—none, § 46.

CAUSATIVES.

ܣܠܩ *to go up*—ܡܣܩ, or ܣܘܩ Al. (O.S. P'al ܣܠܩ, Aph. ܐܣܩ), § 46.

ܐܣܪ *to bind*, O.S.—ܡܣܪ, or ܐܘܣܪ Al. § 46.

ܒܪܕ *to be cold*—ܡܒܪܕ §§ 46, 92.

ܪܩ or ܪܩ *to spit*—ܡܪܩ § 46.

ܐܬܐ *to come*, O.S.—ܡܬܐ (ܒ) K. or ܡܬܐ U. or ܡܬܐ (also ܡܬܐ) Sal. Q. Gaw. or ܡܬܐ Al. (ܒ), (O.S. ܐܬܐ) *to bring*.

ܡܪ *to hazard, be bold*—none.

ܝܠܕ *to beget, lay (eggs)*—ܡܝܠܕ § 92. See p. 114.

ܝܕܥ *to know*, O.S.—ܡܝܕܥ (ܡ Ash.) or ܡܘܕܥ Al. § 46 (O.S. ܐܘܕܥ) *to inform*.

ܝܗܒ *to give*—none, § 46.

ܡܘܟ Ti. *to borrow*, O.S.—ܡܘܟ Ti. *to lend* (O.S. ܐܘܟ).

ܐܒܠ *to mourn*—ܡܐܒܠ U. or ܡܒܠ § 46.

ܠܝ *to hasten* intr.—ܡܠܝ *to hasten* tr. and intr. Kurd.

ܝܠܦ *to learn*, O.S.—ܡܝܠܦ, ܡܠܦ Al. (O.S. ܐܠܦ) *to teach*, § 46.

ܐܠܝ K. *to afflict* (O.S. ܐܠܝ)—ܡܠܝ U. K. *to afflict*.

ܝܡܐ (as O.S.) or ܐܡܝ or ܡܝ *to swear*—ܡܝܡܐ K. or ܡܝܡܐ Sh. (ܡ Sal. Q.) or ܡܝܡ U. or ܡܘܡ Al. U. O.S. *to swear* tr., § 46.

ܐܦܐ, or ܐܦܐ as O.S. *to bake*—ܡܐܦܐ U. or ܡܦܐ U. or ܡܦܐ K. or ܡܘܦܐ Al. or ܡܦܐ Sal. Q. Gaw. § 46.

ܝܩܕ *to burn* intr. O.S.—ܡܝܩܕ or ܡܩܕ Al. O.S. *to burn* tr.

ܝܩܪ K. Al. *to weight, affirm*, O.S.—ܡܝܩܪ (O.S. ܐܘܩܪ).

ܢܵܓܹܐ *to be long* (O.S. ܢܓܝܼܕ)—ܡܲܢܓܹܐ, or ܡܲܢܓܹܐ Al. Z. (O.S. ܐܘܿܢܓܹܐ).

ܝܵܪܹܩ or ܝܵܪܹܩ *to be green* (cf. ܐܝܵܪܹܩ)—ܡܲܝܪܹܩ (O.S. ܐܘܿܪܹܩ *to make pale or green*), § 46.

ܢܵܓܹܚ *to inherit* O.S.—ܡܲܢܓܹܚ (O.S. ܐܘܿܢܓܹܚ).

ܝܵܬܹܒ (ܝ, O.S. ܝ) or (ܝ) ܐܝܵܬܹܒ *to sit*—ܡܲܬܹܒ U. K. *to place*, or ܡܘܿܬܹܒ Al. O.S. (both ܝ), or rarely ܡܲܝܬܹܒ *to cause to sit*, § 46.

[In Sal. Q. Gaw. J. the causatives all have Zlama on the first, and so in the lists which follow.]

(c) *Causatives of* ܝܠ or ܠ *verbs.* As a rule these are regular, except that ܝ is changed into ܘ. But the following are exceptions.

ܕܵܐܹܢ *to judge*, O.S. ܕܵܐܹܢ—(none). (ܡܲܕܹܢ is another verb, see below g).

ܕܵܐܹܪ *to turn* intr.—ܡܲܕܪܹܪ or ܡܲܕܝܪܹܪ Al. § 46.

ܕܵܐܹܙ *to increase* intr.—ܡܲܕܘܹܙ (rare) or ܡܲܕܝܘܹܙ, foreign.

ܚܵܡܹܡ *to be warm*, O.S. ܚܵܡܹܡ or ܫܵܚܹܢ—ܡܲܚܹܢ or ܡܲܚܣܹܢ.

ܚܵܝܹܐ *to live*, O.S.—ܡܲܚܹܐ.

ܟܵܕܹܒ or ܟܵܬܹܒ *to be worth*—ܡܲܟܹܒ § 46

ܟܵܠܹܐ *to come to an end* (as a fight), *to press down*—ܡܲܟܹܠܹܐ.

ܟܵܦܹܪ *to hazard*—(none), § 46.

ܟܵܡܹܪ *to be black*, O.S. ܟܵܡܹܪ—ܡܲܟܡܹܪ.

ܟܵܪܹܟ *to bow* intr., O.S. ܟܵܪܹܟ—ܡܲܟܪܹܟ U. (ܟ K.).

ܟܵܪܹܐ U. *to pay*, O.S. ܟܹܐ (= ܚܬܵܒ *to collect?*)—ܡܲܟܪܹܐ.

ܠܵܫ *to knead*, O.S. ܠܵܫ—ܡܲܠܹܫ or ܡܲܠܝܫ.

ܡܵܐܹܐ *to melt* intr. (by rubbing)—ܡܲܡܝܹܐ or ܡܲܡܝܹܐ (Heb. and Chald. root מוג).

§ 45] CAUSATIVES.

ܡܷܨܝ to suck, O.S. ܡܰܨܷܝ—ܡܨܝ to suckle, suck up.

ܡܷܨܕܶܗ to die, O.S. ܡܨܕܶܗ—ܡܰܨܕܶܗ or ܡܰܨܕܶܗ.

ܢܷܝܫ to rest intr., die, O.S. ܢܷܫ—ܡܰܢܷܫ or ܡܷܢܷܫ to rest tr. and intr.

ܡܨܰܕ to ordain, O.S. ܡܨܰܕ—ܡܰܨܨܰܕ.

ܩܷܝܫ to cool intr., O.S. ܩܷܫ to blow—ܡܰܩܷܝܫ or ܡܰܩܷܝܫ.

ܩܷܝܩ U. to lose savour (= ܩܷܓ K. p. 103), O.S. ܡܰܩܷܝ—ܩܓܝ U.

ܩܷܕܝ to remain, O.S. ܩܰܕ—ܡܰܩܷܕ or ܡܰܩܷܕ.

ܨܷܕ to hunt, fish, O.S. ܨܶܕ—ܡܰܨܷܕ.

ܨܷܪ to rise, O.S. ܨܶܪ—ܡܰܨܷܪ U. Tkh. (ܨܰ Ti.).

ܛܷܡܝ to wink, U. to bruise, cut—ܡܰܛܷܝ. Root ܛܡܝ.

ܛܷܪܕ to dig (so Heb.)—ܡܰܛܷܪܕ.

ܛܷܪܕ or ܛܶܕ to be cold, O.S. ܡܰܛܷܕ—ܛܷܕ.

ܛܷܝܡ to hit, knock—ܡܰܛܷܝܡ or ܡܰܛܷܡܝ.

ܕܷܪܕ to darn—ܡܰܕܷܪܕ. Root ܕܘܕ?

ܕܷܡ to be high—ܡܰܕܷܡ to lift, or ܡܰܕܕܘܡ Al. In O.S. Aph. ܐܰܕܷܡ.

ܚܷܡ to be in love—ܡܰܚܷܡ. Heb. and Arab. root.

(d) The causatives of verbs with middle ܝ have sometimes ܝ silent, the vowel being thrown back to the preceding letter; as ܡܰܝܕܷܠ to have carried, or to load, from ܝܰܕܷܠ to carry. Or we may say ܡܰܝܕܷܠ, but this is less common.

(e) Also verbs which have a silent letter for their second radical, throw back their vowel in the causatives; as ܕܰܟ to wake intr., ܡܰܕܟ to wake tr.

(f) Those first conjugation quadriliterals which insert ܘ after

ܠ or ܗ (§ 46) drop it in the causative. In the case of ܗ that letter is sometimes sounded in the causative, sometimes not; thus:

ܟ݁ܕܶܢ *to desire,* ܡܰܟ݂ܶܕ݂ܢ *to cause to be desired.*

ܨܰܗܝܶ *to thirst,* ܡܰܨܗܶܐ U. Tkh. or ܡܰܨܶܐ Ti. *to make thirsty.*

(*g*) Several causatives have no originals in N.S.

ܡܰܚܕ݂ܶܡ *to bear a bastard,* cf. N.S. ܚܕ݂ܺܡܳܐ *a bastard.*

ܡܰܚܬܶܐ *to appear.* O.S. ܐܰܚܬܝ *to perceive.*

ܡܰܓ݂ܠܶܐ U. or ܡܓ݂ܺܝܠ K. or ܡܰܓܠܶܒ *to blossom,* see § 115. Cf. O.S. ܥܰܡܘܢܳܐ *green.*

ܡܓ݂ܰܕܶܟ or ܡܰܓ݂ܕܶܟ K. *to search.* O.S. ܓܰܒ and ܓܰܐ *id.*

ܡܰܓ݂ܕ݂ܶܡ *to fine,* Arab. Cf. N.S. ܓ݂ܺܕ݂ܺܡܳܐ *a fine.*

ܡܰܓ݂ܕܶܒ *to borrow.* Cf. N.S. ܓ݂ܶܒܳܐ *a debt,* Pers. In Al. ܡܓ݂ܰܕܶܒ.

ܡܰܓ݂ܕ݁ܶܠ *to drive a shuttle.* O.S. ܓܘܠܕ *thread,* (from ܓܰܕ *to enter*?).

ܡܓ݂ܰܕ݁ܶܕ Al. *to prepare,* § 106. But we have ܐܰܗܕ݁ܶܐ K., ܡܰܗܘܶܕ K. and ܡܰܕ݁ܘܕ U. K., all *to prepare.*

ܡܓ݂ܰܕ݁ܶܡ Al. *to neglect,* O.S.

ܡܓ݂ܰܗܶܝ Ti. Al. *to vomit.* O.S. ܗܦ݁ܝ *to turn,* Aph. *to overturn*; O.S. ܗܦ݁ܺܓܬܳܐ *vomit.*

ܡܰܘܕ݂ܶܐ *to confess.* So O.S. In Sal. ܡܰܓ݂ܕ݂ܺܝ.

ܡܰܘܡܶܕ U. *to mew.* Arab.

ܡܰܚܶܒ *to love,* (O.S. ܒ), see § 95 *e.*

ܡܰܣܠܶܕ *to make presents.* Cf. N.S. ܒܠܶܕ݂ܡܳܐ *a present,* Arab.

ܡܰܓ݁ܓ݂ܶܦ or ܡܓ݂ܰܓܶܦ *to blister, prick up the ears.* Arab. Cf. § 113 *i*. (See also below.)

CAUSATIVES.

ܡܟܵܕܸܡܸܟ݂ *to be lazy.* Arab.

ܡܟܵܕܸܡܸܟ *K. to give or take interest.* Cf. O.S. ܟܸܣܦ̇ܵ *money.*

ܡܟܵܕܸܙܘ *to preach, say the litany.* O.S. ܟܪܙ and ܐܸܟܪܸܙ.

ܡܟܲܕܸܕ *to plaister,* § 113 *i.*

ܡܟܲܝܸܕ *to justify,* § 119.

ܡܟܲܠܘܹܒ݂ *to pant.* Cf. ܡܟܲܠܒܸܣ *to snuff about* (as a dog); perh. formed from O.S. ܟܲܠܒܵܢܵ *panting.*

ܡܟܲܠܕܸܒ݂ *to mimic.*

ܡܟܲܡܸܕ *K.* or ܡܟܲܡܸܗܸܕ *U. to linger.* In Al. ܡܟܲܡܸܕ is *to seal,* as N.S. ܟܬܲܡܵܐ *a seal.* In Chald. the Paʻel is *to hasten.*

ܡܟܲܝܸܣ *to smell.* O.S. ܟܣ.

ܡܟܲܚܸܠ *to make blue* or *green,* foreign. Cf. N.S. ܟܚܹܠܵܐ *blue* or *green.*

ܡܟܲܪܸܙ *to comment on;* in Z. *to light a candle.* ܡܟܲܪܸܙ Tkh. *to light a candle.* O.S. ܐܲܟܪܸܙ *to illumine.*

ܡܟܲܬܸܬ *to fester.* Cf. N.S. ܟܸܬܠܵܐ *matter,* (perhaps root ܢܸܬ *to ooze, distil*).

ܡܟܲܚܸܡ *to rebuke.* = O.S. ܡܟܲܚܸܡ (ܟܚܡ), [Nun inserted by false analogy?], but in N.S. the Kap is soft.

ܡܟܲܝܸܬ *to leak,* perhaps O.S. ܢܬܠ *to ooze.* See above.

ܡܟܲܬܸܪ *to prosper tr., thank,* Arab. Cf. N.S. ܟܬܵܪܵܐ *thanks.*

ܡܟܲܡܸܝܸܕ *to mock.* O.S. ܟܲܡܝܸܕ *to beg.* N.S. meaning from Arabic.

ܡܟܲܡܟܸܡ *to be* or *make poor,* as O.S. Also caus. of ܟܡܸܟ݂ *to be hushed.*

ܡܟܲܠܕܸܒ݂ *to despise, reject.* So O.S.

ܡܓ̱ܪܸܒ U. or ܡܓ̱ܪܸܒ K. (ܒ like ܘ) to *prove, affirm*, Arab. Cf. N.S. ܓ̱ܪܒܐ = *proof*, which retains the ܒ sound.

ܡܓ̱ܥܸܣ to *cry out*. O.S. ܙܓܥܦܐ.

ܡܓ̱ܕܸܠ K. to *ask for*, Arab.

ܡܓ̱ܕܸܪ to *put in order*. Cf. N.S. ܓ̱ܕܪܐ *order*, Kurd.

ܡܓ̱ܝܼܚ to *preach the Gospel*.

ܡܓ̱ܝܸܣ U. or ܡܓ̱ܝܸܣ K. to *find*, § 113 *j*. (Conjugate like ܡܩܕܸܫ.)

ܡܓ̱ܥܸܓ̱ to *give a pledge, flood*, (see ܡܓ̱ܝܓ̱). O.S. Chald. to *pledge*.

Also many causatives have no original except in one particular district.

(*h*) Many causatives differ from their originals in meaning, or else undergo a development of meaning; but most of them may also be used in a simple causative sense.

ܒܝܼܬ K. Al. to *spend the night* (O.S. ܒܬ), *be stale*. ܡܒܝܸܬ to *fast, be stale, keep over till next day* U. Cf. N.S. ܒܝܼܬ *stale* U.

ܒܪܹܐ to *create*, O.S. ܡܒܪܸܐ to *beget* K., *bear* K.

ܒܪܸܩ to *flash* (lightning) [so O.S.], to *have a sudden pain*. ܡܒܪܸܩ to *polish, be bright*, as O.S.

ܓ̱ܕܸܠ to *weave, tie, wrestle* K., O.S. ܡܓ̱ܕܸܠ to *freeze* (for § 92).

ܓ̱ܙܸܪ to *circumcise, to cut down wood* K. ܡܓ̱ܙܸܪ to *inform against*. Cf. O.S. ܓ̱ܙܪ to *cut, give sentence*, ܓ̱ܙܪܕܝܼܢܐ *a penalty*.

ܒܠܹܐ to *wear out* intr. ܡܒܠܹܐ to *write Majliyana* (~), p. 6.

ܓ̱ܕܸܕ to *draw* (O.S. ܓ̱ܕܕ). ܡܓ̱ܕܸܕ to *prolong, draw out*.

ܕܒܸܩ to *hold, catch* [so O.S.], *take, hire, correspond to*, etc. ܡܕܒܸܩ to *compare, let out on hire*.

ܕܵܒܹܚ Al. *to subdue.* ܡܲܕܒܹܚ Al. *to make, mend.*

ܕܵܟ݂ܹܪ *to remember* O.S. ܡܲܕܟ݂ܹܪ *to remind* (ܒ like ܠ).

ܕܵܡܹܐ *to be like* O.S. ܡܲܕܡܹܐ *to compare.*

ܕܵܡܹܟ݂ *to lie down, sleep, die* O.S. ܡܲܕܡܹܟ݂ *to put to bed* (children).

ܗܵܘܹܐ *to be, become* O.S. ܡܲܗܘܹܐ *to beget* K., *bear* K.

ܙܵܒܹܛ K. *to subdue*, (so N.S. ܙܒܝܛ *subject*). ܡܲܙܒܹܛ or ܡܲܙܒܹܚ Al. *to subdue, to confiscate.*

ܙܵܪܹܓ̰ *to scratch*, also *to be squeezed out* (juice), *to be overripe.* ܡܲܙܪܹܓ̰ *to scratch.* Also *to glitter*, as snow (= ܡܲܙܪܹܩ).

ܙܵܪܹܩ *to rise*, as the sun (O.S. ܙܪܚ; cf. O.S. ܙܪܝܩܐ *scattered*). ܡܲܙܪܹܩ K. *to glitter* as snow, (in U. ܡܲܙܪܹܓ̰).

ܚܵܒܹܪ *to find out*, Arab. ܡܲܚܒܹܪ *to announce, inform, warn.*

ܚܵܕܹܪ *to revolve, travel* O.S. ܡܲܚܕܹܪ *to overturn, pass* (at table), *translate.*

ܚܵܘܹܐ Al. Tkh. *to keep, gather together.* ܡܲܚܘܹܐ Al. *to shew*, (O.S. ܚܘܝ).

ܚܵܘܹܪ *to be white* O.S. ܡܲܚܘܹܪ *to tin saucepans, whitewash.*

ܚܵܙܹܐ *to see* O.S., in K. Al. *to find.* ܡܲܚܙܹܐ *to shew.*

ܚܵܬܹܡ K. *to grow perfect.* ܡܲܚܬܹܡ U. K. *to affirm, make firm.*

ܚܵܠܹܐ *to be sweet* O.S. ܡܲܚܠܹܐ *to forgive, cause to be desired.*

ܚܵܡܹܠ *to be patient* as Arab.; *stand* Al., *chat* K. (O.S. *to collect, keep in*). ܡܲܚܡܹܠ *to postpone, keep waiting.*

ܚܵܒܹܐ K. *to be content with*, cf. ܗܵܘܹܐ § 46. ܡܲܚܒܹܐ U. K. *to miss* a person.

ܚܵܦܹܐ *to sit*, as a hen (O.S. *to cover*): *to fall in*, as a roof, as O.S. ܡܲܚܦܹܐ *to overturn*, (= O.S. ܗܦܟ݂).

ܚܵܪܹܒ *to go bad, deteriorate* O.S. ܡܲܚܪܹܒ *to spoil, injure.*

ܢܕܪ K. *to be under a vow, be prohibited, repay for loss.* ܡܢܕܪ *to excommunicate*, as O.S. Aph., *to curse* Al., *to lay under a vow* K.

ܒܥܐ *to ask for*, (also in marriage) Arab. ܡܒܥܐ *to give in marriage* (a daughter).

ܛܥܢ *to carry* O.S. ܡܛܥܢ *to load* an animal.

ܬܕܐ *to whip up* a horse O.S., *plough, row* a boat. ܡܬܕܐ *to canter* a horse, tr.

ܝܠܕ K. U. or ܝܠܕ Al. O.S., *to bear, lay eggs.* ܡܝܠܕ *to beget* U.

ܝܠܦ *to learn* O.S. ܡܝܠܦ *to teach, instigate*, p. 107.

ܟܬܒ *to write* (as a scribe) O.S. ܡܟܬܒ *to dictate, write* (as an author).

ܠܒܫ *to put on* O.S.; *to fight* Ti. Al. ܡܠܒܫ *to clothe*, (both ܒ).

ܠܒܡ *to fit* O.S. ܡܠܒܡ *to compose* songs, books, etc.

ܡܛܐ *to arrive*, also *to be ripe* or *grown up, to catch up, to be sent*, all as O.S.; and *to wrestle* K. ܡܡܛܐ *to send, to cause a thing to happen to a person.*

ܡܟܝ *to be meek*, O.S. ܡܟܝ, § 81 (5). ܡܡܟܝ *to humiliate.*

ܡܠܐ *to fill* O.S., *suffice, load* a gun. ܡܡܠܐ *to make shift with.*

ܡܪܕ *to rub* (or ܡܪܕ). ܡܡܪܕ *to fix.*

ܢܚ *to rest, die* O.S.; *to go out*, as a lamp; *be ruined*, as a church. ܡܢܝܚ or ܡܢܚ *to rest*, tr. and intr. The causative is the usual word in U. for *to rest.*

ܢܓܕ *to gnaw* K., *hew*, O.S. ܡܢܓܕ *to rake*, cf. N.S. ܡܢܓܕ *a rake.*

ܢܦܠ *to fall* O.S. ܡܢܦܠ *to dethrone, turn out of office.*

ܢܥܨ *to drive* a nail, chisel as O.S., bump as Arab. ܡܢܥܨ *to tattoo, vaccinate.*

ܢܫܐ K., O.S. and ܡܢܫܐ U., both *to forget*, (not in causative sense).

ܩܨܡ *to ordain* O.S.   ܡܩܨܡ *to present for ordination*; (with ܠܟܠ) *to attend to*, § 71.

ܣܗܕ K. Al., O.S. and ܡܣܗܕ K., both *to testify*. In U. ܣܗܕܓ *&c.* ܣܗܕܘܬܐ.

ܣܬܠ *to fall in* (a well or roof); *fit stones together* K., O.S. ܡܣܬܠ *to repair tools.*

ܣܡܩ *to be red* O.S., *blush.*   ܡܣܡܩ *to toast* (bread), *shame.*

ܣܪܩ O.S. and ܡܣܪܩ *to comb.* The former also *to grow lean.*

ܥܡܠ U. *to do skilfully* (O.S. *to labour*). ܡܥܡܠ *to bargain, barter.*

ܥܡܪ *to dwell* O.S.   ܡܥܡܪ *to build*; and in U. *to people* (a country).

ܥܩܪ *to dig up, destroy* O.S.   ܡܥܩܪ Tkh. *to take root.*

ܥܪܩ *to flee* O.S.; *to run* K. Al.   ܡܥܪܩ *to pursue, allow to escape.*

ܦܫܛ *to stretch out* O.S., *go a long distance.*   ܡܦܫܛ *to see off on a journey, to stretch out* K., *let go* Ti. Al.

ܨܘܬ O.S. (rare in U.) and ܡܨܘܬ *to listen, obey, pay attention* (not in caus. sense).

ܩܒܠ K. *to receive, believe,* (= ܡܩܒܠ U.) as O.S. Pa'el. ܡܩܒܠ *to make acceptable.*

ܩܪܐ *to read, call, name, crow* O.S.   ܡܩܪܐ *to teach.* Cf. also ܩܠܡܐ ܡܩܪܝܢܐ *a legible hand,* lit. *pen.*

ܩܪܒ *to receive Holy Communion*; in K. Al. *to approach,* both as O.S.   ܡܩܪܒ *to offer, celebrate the Eucharist* K., *bring near* K. Al.

ܩܪܨ *to bite* as O.S. Pa'el (rare).   ܡܩܪܨ *to cut with scissors, keep back part of a price or debt.*

ܩܨܡ *to win a game* U., *cover* as O.S.   ܡܩܨܡ *to lose a game* U.

ܩܕܝ *to be angry, squeeze* K., *sweep* with a wooden rake (ܩܕܘܝ).
ܡܩܕܝ *to quarrel*.

ܪܙܡ K. (O.S. ܪܣ) and ܡܪܙܡ *to sprinkle*.

ܪܓܠ *to shiver* with cold or fear, Arab. ܡܪܓܠ *to shiver* with fever.

ܪܚܡ K. *to love* O.S. ܡܪܚܡ *to make friendly, to put an orphan lamb to another dam* K. Cf. ܡܪܚܡ *to have pity* (O.S. ܪܚܡ).

ܪܚܫ *to go*, (in First present, only in Al. in the sense *to wander*) [O.S. *to creep*]. ܡܪܚܫ *to have a miscarriage*.

ܪܦܝ *to be slack, loose*. ܡܪܦܝ *to grant a divorce* U. (ܡܪܦܝ U. or ܡܪܦܝ K. *to throw, divorce*). In O.S. Pa. Aph. *to loose*.

ܫܡܛ *to run fast* U., *run to and fro* K., *wrench* K., *stray*. ܡܫܡܛ *to dip* a red hot iron in water, or yarn in paste (O.S. Aph. *to water*).

ܫܩܠ *to take* O.S., *charge, force to pay, subtract*. ܡܫܩܠ *to overlay with metals, interweave*, p. 119.

ܫܪܐ *to loose, lodge* intr., *be profaned, forgive, dismiss, break* a command or fast, O.S. ܡܫܪܐ *to entertain, pitch tents*.

ܫܪܒ *to suck the whole* of an egg, *flash; slip off peel* K. ܡܫܪܒ *to whistle*, as O.S. Aph.

ܫܬܐ *to drink* O.S., *be irrigated, smoke* tobacco K. ܡܫܬܐ *to dip* a red hot iron, or *stretch* yarn after dipping on poles, or the warp, in weaving (see ܡܫܡܛ above), *to irrigate*. So ܫܬܝܐ = *dipped yarn*.

ܗܘܐ *to be delirious* Al.; *to be pleasant* Ti. (= ܗܘܐ U.). ܡܗܘܐ Ti. or ܡܗܘܐ U. *to do as one likes*, § 46¹.

(i) *Irregular Causatives; and Causatives from Second Conjugation verbs*. See also above *b* to *f* incl. and *h*.

---

¹ Many of these O.S. verbs are not found in Aph'el in O.S.; and many have not the N.S. meaning in O.S. Aph'el.

ܕܵܓܹܡ *to cover*, O.S.; also ܡܕܲܓܸܡ K. Al. Caus. ܡܓܲܕܸܡ or ܡܕܲܓܸܡ
to cover, shut a door.

ܡܕܲܪܡܸܢ K., O.S. *to believe* = ܡܕܲܪܡܸܢ U. Caus. ܡܕܲܪܡܸܢ U.

ܡܓ̰ܝܼܕ or ܡܓ̰ܝܼܘܕ *to play.* Caus. ܡܓ̰ܲܝܸܕ, see § 47.

ܡܕܲܚܸܫ K. Al. and ܡܕܲܚܸܫ K. *to swell.* O.S. ܟܒܬ.

ܡܚܲܝܸܕ *to wonder*, Arab. ܡܚܲܝܸܕ *to astonish.* ܚܝܼܕ is used in
K. Al. as an impersonal verb = *to be pleased to do a thing.*

ܡܕܲܟܕܸܡ *to understand.* Caus. ܡܕܲܟܕܸܡ, which is also the causative of ܩܵܛܹܥ *to cut*, § 83 (6); also very rarely ܡܕܲܟܕܸܡ. [In K.
Al. Bo.) ܩܲܝܸܕ (ܩܵܪܸܡ) is substituted for ܡܕܲܟܕܸܡ, pp. 98, 102.]

ܚܲܡܸܠ *to bathe, wash* O.S. Caus. ܡܚܲܡܸܣ or ܡܚܲܡܸܠ.

(j) When a verb has no causative the same sense may sometimes be rendered by ܥܵܒܹܕ *to make*, ܝܵܗܹܒ *to give*, ܡܲܠܸܦ *to teach* or *incite*; as ܡܲܪܚܸܡ ܠܕܝܼܡܘܼܗ̇ U. *he caused him to be loved*; ܥܒܼܸܕ ܠܹܗ
ܗܵܘܸܐ ܡܲܪܚܸܡ ܠܬܐܘܡܐ *he made Thomas love*; ܗܵܘܸܐ ܕܠܵܐ ܥܵܒܸܕ ܠܹܗ
ܡܵܝܸܬ U. K. *he would have caused him not to die* = ܥܵܒܸܕ ܠܹܗ [ܗܵܘܸܐ]
ܡܵܝܸܬ U.); = Al. (ܐܕܝܼܒ Al., St John xi. 37 ܗܵܘܸܐ ܕܠܵܐ ܕܝܸܒ ܡܵܐܸܬ
ܥܒܸܕ ܠܛܠܝܘ̈ܗܝ ܕܝܘܲܡܕܘܼܢ *make the boys sing* (O.S.).

§ 46. *Irregular Verbs.* ܡܹܟܠܵܐ ܠܵܐ ܬܲܩܢܹܐ
First Conjugation.

The following verbs have a Pthakha sound in U. Sal. Q. Gaw. and
most of them in Ash.; but a Zqapa sound in Ti. Tkh. etc. The fem.
of the pres. part. of those which are ܠܲܕ or ܠܵܕ are either with or
without ܝ, as ܝܵܕܠܵܐ or ܝܵܕܠܵܢ *she sleeps.*

ܚܵܘܸܕ *to make a hole* O.S.   ܢܵܦܸܠ *to fall down*, as a new wall

ܒܵܠܸܥ *to swallow* O.S.   (not ܢܵܦܸܠ *to indent*).

ܠܓܡܕ *to assemble* intr., Arab.

ܓܕܕ *to shave, shear* O.S.

ܦܠܕ *to crack*, (in O.S. *to draw out water*), meaning from Arab.

ܙܪܕ *to sow* O.S.

ܚܡܕ *to be leavened* O.S.

ܛܒܥ *to sink* intr. U. K. (not used in Ash.), *to print* Al. [O.S. ܛܒܥ *to impress, sink*.]

ܕܡܟ *to sleep*. In O.S. *to be young*.

ܝܕܥ, see ܝܕܥ below.

ܝܕܥ *to know* O.S. (see below).

ܠܚܡ *to lap* (Ash. Zqapa), § 92. Chald. לַךְ.

ܚܘܝܕ *to mix*. O.S. and Al.

ܟܐܒ *to be ill* or *in pain* (not used in Ash.)[1]. O.S. Peal, Pa. and Aph. *to be ill*.

ܢܒܥ *to well forth* O.S.

ܢܓܚ U. *to butt, attack* (O.S., Al. Tkh. ܢܓܚ).

ܣܒܥ *to be satisfied* O.S.

ܣܡܝ *to be blind* O.S., *go out* (fire).

ܦܟܗ *to lose savour* O.S. p. 103.

ܦܠܓ *divide* (U. rare in 1 conj.); O.S., Al. ܦܠܓ.

ܦܣܥ *to step, step aside* K., O.S., *leave* K., *leave off* K.

ܦܩܥ *to explode* O.S.

ܦܪܥ *to pay* O.S.

ܦܫܪ *to be lukewarm* (not used in Ash.), cf. O.S. ܦܫܝܪ *tepid*.

ܨܒܥ *to dye, dip* O.S.

ܨܪܦ *to be refined*, as metals O.S. Also *to sting* with Zqapa sound.

ܩܘܡ (or ܩܡܡ?) *to be firm, hard*. O.S. ܩܡܡ and ܩܘܡ.

ܩܛܥ *to cut, decide* O.S.

ܩܡܕ *to scorch* (Ash. Zqapa).

ܪܟܟ U. *to be tired*. (Sp. ܪܟܝ). O.S. ܪܟܟ *to make soft*, Pa. id.

ܫܡܥ *to hear, listen, obey* O.S.

ܫܩܠ. See p. 116.

ܬܒܥ *to adhere, be a follower of* Arab.

ܬܪܥ *to make an opening* O.S.

---

[1] In N.S. ܟܡܐܒܐ = *in pain*, ܟܐܒܢܐ = *ill*.

§ 46] IRREGULAR VERBS. 119

Note. In the following verbs only the irregular parts are written. Some of these verbs are really anomalous, and some have two weak radicals.

ܐܙܠ *to go*, O.S., in many districts uses for some of its tenses ܕܒܩ, which in O.S. is *to creep*. *First present*: ܐܙܠ : ܐܙܠܟ : ܐܙܠܟܐ etc. The 2 pl. in Al. is ܐܙܠܟܬܘܢ.—In Al. ܕܒܩ : ܕܒܩܬ etc. = *to move about* (= ܫܓܫ U. K.).—Or ܐܙܠ : ܐܙܠܟ : ܐܙܠܟܗ : ܐܙܠܟܒ : ܐܙܠܒ m. f.: ܐܙܠܟܘܢ : ܐܙܠܟܕܦ : ܐܙܠܟܒ (Pthakha sound) Bo. *Verbal noun with* ܕ : ܕܕܒܩܐ U. Sh. ܕܕܫܬܐ Ti. Al.: ܕܕܫܬܐ U. (rare) Sh.: ܕܕܫܬܐ U. (rare) ܕܐܙܠ K. Sal. and sometimes U. The *infinitive* is ܠܕܫܬܐ U. Sh. ܠܐܙܠ K. U. ܠܕܫܬܐ Ti. *Preterite*: ܕܒܩ ܠܗ U. ܐܙܠܗ K. J. *Past participle*: ܕܒܝܩ U. ܐܙܝܠ K. *Second preterite* in Al. ܐܙܐ ܠܗ or ܐܙܗ ܠܗ (for ܐܙܝܠ ܠܗ). *Imperative*: ܕܣܐ : ܕܣܐܡܘܢ U. (common); or ܙܠ : ܙܠܡܘܢ (§ Sal.) U. (common) J. Sal. Q. Gaw. (the Zlama has either sound); or ܙܠ : ܙܠܕ : ܙܠܗ K. MB. Sh. Al. Z.; often with a pronoun, ܙܠ ܠܘܟ etc. In all these ܒ = ܠ usually. The O.S. is ܙܠ : ܙܠܕ : ܙܠܗ : ܙܠܬܘܢ. *The Agent is* ܐܙܠܢܐ U. K. but ܒܐܙܠܐ Ash. Al. *Noun of action*: ܕܫܬܐ or ܐܙܠܬܐ. *Causative*: ܠܒܠ, ܢܒܠ, ܠܒܠ, ܡܒܠ, ܡܒܝܠ, ܡܒܝܠ or ܢܘܒܠ § 45 b. [Distinguish ܠܒܠ *to carry, take*, ܢܒܠ *to take away*. Thus *he took the horses to Urmi* = ܢܒܠܗ ܣܘܣܘܬܐ ܠܐܘܪܡܝ, not ܠܒܠܗ.]

ܓܢܙ *to shut, cover*. So Heb. אָטַם and Chald. and Arab. *Pres. part*. ܓܢܙ or ܓܢܝܙ.

ܐܡܪ *to say*, in K. also *to speak, tell* (so Al. always), O.S. *Imperative*: ܐܡܪ Ti. Z. (O.S. ܐܡܪ), elsewhere ܐܡܘܪ.

أُهمذ *to go up*, O.S. هَلِم, an irregular verb with some forms from اُهمذ. In N.S. *Pres. part.* أُهمذ U. or أُهمذ U. Ti. Sal.: otherwise regular as § 38.

أُهمد *to bind* O.S. *Pres. part.* أُهمد U. K. or أُهمد U.

أُهذ *to be cold* (in U. of things only, in K. of persons also; the latter in U. is مَشْتِهد) makes some parts from قُذ in Ti., retaining ا: as *pret.* قِشلي (*q'ishli*), *past part.* قِشا (*q'isha*); not in Ash. or elsewhere. Perhaps from O.S. قذ *to be old*, or قذ *to freeze*, tr.; in N.S. قذ is *to be crisp* (snow), *to be white* (eyes).

أُها *to come* O.S. *First present:* أُها : أُهها etc. K. U.; or أَي : أَي etc. Q.; or أُها : أُجا : أُهها : أُجِها : نَي : أُجِن : أُها : أُهاوه : كِس أُها Sal.; or أَي : أَيِي : أَهي : أُيهِي : أُيهِ (or أَي) : أَي : أُيوه : أَيه Gaw. *Second present:* كَل جاها K. U. MB. Sh.: كَل جاها, or كَل جَها جاها Sal. Q.; or جاتها : جاتها etc. as لَكَل § 42, Gaw. *Preterite:* كَل أَها K. U., كَل أَها Q. Gaw. Sal., هَو كَل *id.,* كَل أَها Ti. Sal. (sic) § 124, كَل أَها Al. (sometimes Tkh.). *Past part.* أَها U.: أَها Tkh. Ash. Ti. أَها Ti. or أَها Ti. or أَها Ti.: أَها or أَها or أَها Q. Sal. Gaw. The fem. is أَها : أَها أَها or أَها. *Imperative:* أَها U. J.: أَهمو (Zlama second sound) U.; أَها (m. f.): أَها MB. Sh.; أَها : أَها Tkh.; أَها : أَها Amadia; أَها : أَهمو or أَهمو or أَهمو or أَهمو (also ـو) Q. Sal.; أَها : أَها Al. or أَها : أَها Al.[1] Ash.; أَها : أَهمو Gaw.; أَها : أَها Ti. (common), Tkh. (sometimes). The sing. أَها also in Sal. In Ti. we also have أَها أَهمو, with plural

---

[1] Used also for *let* before a first or third person imperative, for سَهم § 51 (10).

ܐܘ ܓܘܬܘ or ܓܕ ܓܠܓܘ or ܓܕ ܓܘ ܠܓܘ, the pronouns being taken in (Zlama second sound). Throughout the m. and f. sing. are the same. In O.S. we have ܐܕ : ܐܘ : ܐܘ : ܐܒܝ or ܐܒܝ (ܐ). *Causative:* ܡܓܕܐ *mé-yi* U., ܡܓܕܐ or ܡܓܟܐ Sal. Q. Gaw. ܡܓܕܐ K. (ܐ) ܡܓܕܝ Ti. ܡܓܕܐ Al. (ܐ), see § 47. In the forms with ܗ and ܓ (not ܕ as Nöld.) the sound is often between the two. It is remarkable that the ܙ should appear in Salamas, which as a rule shows no affinities with Ṭiari. For the interchange of ܙ and ܐ see § 124. It does not occur in the present participle.

ܓܕ (as O.S.) or ܓܕܐ *to wish.* The tenses are formed from ܓܕ but the first present has in some districts the lengthened form. Thus *First Present:* ܓܕ : ܓܕܐ etc. K. Al.; or ܓܕܐ : ܓܕܐ : ܓܕܝܗ : ܓܕܣ : ܓܕܝܣܗ : ܓܕܝܣ : ܓܕܡ : ܓܕܝܡ : ܓܕܡܗ U. Ash. (in U. *bâ-yi* etc.; in Ash. *bé-yi* etc.); or ܓܕ, ܓܕܐ etc. (ܓ like ܓ) Tkh.; or ܓܕ : ܓܕܐ : ܓܕܝܗ : ܓܕܡܗ : ܓܕܐ : ܓܕܡ : ܓܕܣ : ܓܕܓܗ ܓܕܣ Gaw. In Ti. Al. another form of the present is formed from the abs. state of the past participle:—ܓܕܓ : ܓܕܐ : ܓܕܝܓ : ܓܕܓܗ : ܓܕܝܡ : ܓܕܡ : ܓܕܒ : ܓܕܡܗ Ti. or ܓܕܡܗ Ti. (or ܓܕܗܡܗ Al.?): ܓܕܣ or ܓܕܣ Ti. or ܓܕܗܣ Al. (cf. § 50). *Verbal noun:* ܓܕܐ (pron. in U., not K. Sal. etc., *boya*, as with ܒܕܝ *to know* and ܒܕܝ *to fear*) or ܓܕܐ K. Al. *Pret.* ܓܕ ܠܝ (very rare in Ash. where ܗܘܐ ܓܕܝ is used instead). *Past part.* ܓܕܐ : ܓܕܝܓ. *Imperat.* ܓܕܝ : ܓܕܡܗܡ (ܝ Sal.) U. Q. Sal. Gaw. or ܓܕܝ : ܓܕܟ : ܓܕܟ K. MB. Sh. Al.; in Ash. Sing. ܓܕܗ m. ܓܕܟ f., Pl. ܓܕܗ, rather inclining to *bô*. *Agent:* ܓܕܢܐ U. K. ܓܕܢܐ Ash. Al. *Noun of action:* ܓܕܢܝܬܐ or ܓܕܣܢܝܬܐ U. ܓܕܣܢܝ K. *Causative:* ܡܓܕܓ, § 47.

From this verb comes the sign of the future: ܒܸܕ or ܓܸܕ or ܒ (§ 31). These = ܕ ܓܹܐ or ܕ ܓܹܐ *he wishes to...* or *it is desired that* = *he will...* It is unchanged throughout the tense. This is the exact counterpart of the English future and the modern Greek θὰ (= θέλω νὰ). A curious variation is found in Ṭal [Stoddard, p. 109]. Taking the verb ܙܵܡܹܪ *to sing*, we have[1]:

Sing. 3 m. ܓܸܕ ܕܙܵܡܹܪ   Pl. 3 m. f. ܓܸܕ ܕܙܵܡܪܝܼ

f. ܓܸܕܵܐ ܕܙܵܡܪܵܐ

2 m. ܓܸܕ ܕܙܵܡܪܹܬ   2 m. ܓܸܕܝܼܬܘܿܢ ܕܙܵܡܪܝܼܬܘܿܢ

f. ܓܸܕܵܬ ܕܙܵܡܪܵܬ   f. ܓܸܕܝܼܬܝܼܢ ܕܙܵܡܪܝܼܬܝܼܢ ?

1 m. ܓܸܢ ܕܙܵܡܪܸܢ   1 m. f. ܓܸܕܚ ܕܙܵܡܪܵܚ

f. ܓܸܢ ܕܙܵܡܪܵܢ

The feminine plural is noteworthy.

In this verb the first present is much used for the second (§ 51).

ܓܵܚܸܟ *to laugh*, O.S. ܓܵܚܹܟ. Verbal noun with ܒ: ܒܓܸܚܟܵܐ U. K., ܓܸܟܫܸܢܹܐ Al. (ܓܵܚܟܵܐ = O.S. ܓܘܿܚܟܵܐ). This verb has hard Kap throughout.

ܓܥܹܐ (as O.S.) or ܓܵܥܹܐ *to bleat, cry out* (in prayer), not common. Cf. Heb. גָּעָה and Chald. גְעָא *to bleat*; in O.S. *to cry out*. All from ܓܥܹܐ except *first present* ܓܵܥܹܐ: ܓܵܥܝܵܐ: ܓܵܥܝܹܐ etc. as ܓܥܹܐ: or ܓܵܥܹܐ: ܓܵܥܝܵܐ etc. (In Ti. ܓܵܥܹܐ as O.S.) But when ܠ has a vowel it usually throws it back to ܓ, though before ܐ final it is convenient to write it with a vowel, as in the causative ܡܲܓܥܹܐ.

ܓܵܝܹܙ or ܓܵܐܹܙ *to be tired*. Conjugate like ܓܵܥܹܐ. In Al. ܓܝܼܙܵܐ, in Ti. ܓܹܐܙ, in Heb. יָגַע, Arab. وجع. *Causative*: ܡܲܓܝܹܙ. The second present of this verb is very rarely used.

[1] This has not been orally verified.

§ 46] IRREGULAR VERBS.

ܕ݁ܒ݂ܰܪ to turn, return, be converted. Pres. part. ܕ݁ܳܒ݂ܰܪ : ܕ݁ܳܒ݂ܰܪܬ݁ܳܐ Al. Sh. or ܕ݁ܳܒ݂ܰܪ U. Verbal noun: ܕ݁ܒ݂ܳܪܳܐ or ܕ݁ܒ݂ܳܪܬ݁ܳܐ U. Sh. or ܕ݁ܒ݂ܳܪܳܐ Al. Agent: ܕ݁ܳܒ݂ܽܘܪܳܐ Sh. ܕ݁ܳܒ݂ܽܘܪܳܐ U. Sh. ܕ݁ܒ݂ܽܘܪܳܐ Al. Noun of action : ܕ݁ܒ݂ܳܪܬ݁ܳܐ or ܕ݁ܒ݂ܳܪܳܐ U. ܕ݁ܒ݂ܳܪܳܐ Al. Causative: ܡܰܕ݂ܒ݁ܰܪ : but in Al. ܡܰܕ݂ܒ݁ܪܰܝ. [For this verb ܦ݁ܠܰܚ is used in Ash. which in U. = to turn aside.] In O.S. ܕ݁ܰܝܰܪ is to inhabit but the N.S. meaning is from the Arabic.

ܕ݁ܳܗܶܢ to cement (O.S. ܕ݁ܳܗܶܢ to become greasy). Conjugate as if ܗ was absent. In K. ܡܰܕ݂ܗܶܢ. §§ 39, 108 c.

ܕ݁ܡܶܟ݂ to lie down, sleep O.S. Imp. pl. in K. Al. ܕ݁ܡܽܘܟ݂ܽܘܢ (ܕ݁ܰܡܕ݁ܶܟ݂ܽܘܢ).

ܗ݈ܘܳܐ to be, become, be born O.S. Second present: ܟ݁ܺܐܡܰܪ ܗ݈ܘܳܐ, but ܟ݁ܺܐܡܰܪ ܗ݈ܘܳܐ Sal. or ܒ݁ܗܳܘܶܐ ܟ݁ܺܐ Gaw., see § 42. Pret. ܗ݈ܘܳܐ ܟ݁ܶܐ. Past part. ܗܳܘܶܐ. Imp. ܗܘܺܝ. Agent (wanting). Noun of action: ܗܘܳܝܳܐ. In Al. Z. ܗ is pronounced, and the verb is regular, thus past part. ܗܳܘܶܐ ; but ܟ݁ܺܐ ܗ݈ܘܳܐ is contracted to ܟ݁ܺܗܘܳܐ. In this verb the forms ܠܰܝܬ݁ ܗ݈ܘܳܐ : ܟ݁ܺܐ ܗ݈ܘܳܐ etc. are very common; cf. p. 97.

ܗܢܳܐ to please O.S. Verbal noun: ܗܶܢܝܳܢܳܐ U. Th. ܗܶܢܝܳܢܳܐ Sp. Ti. Pret. ܟ݁ܶܐ ܗܢܳܐ or ܟ݁ܶܐ ܗܢܶܐ: ܟ݁ܶܐ ܗܳܢܶܐ Ti. Sh. Past part. ܗܶܢܝܳܐ or ܗܶܢܝܳܐ Ti. or ܗܳܢܝܳܐ Sh. Another form of the pres. part. is seen in the phrase ܢܶܗܢܶܐ ܠܳܟ݂ may it be pleasant to you (to a person about to drink or about to eat after drinking). In K. this verb is used impersonally: as ܟ݁ܺܐ ܗܳܢܶܐ ܠܺܝ I shall be pleased, ܗ݈ܘܳܐ ܟ݁ܶܐ ܠܺܝ I was pleased. Otherwise it is rare.

ܘܕ݂ܶܝܕ݂ to fear (see § 83, D. c) has two impersonal forms: ܟ݁ܽܠ ܘܕ݂ܶܝܠܳܟ݂ ܠܽܘܡ Ti. U.: and in Ti. (pron. ܘ = ܗ) ܟ݁ܽܠ ܘܕ݂ܶܝܕ݂ ܠܽܘܡ let it not *frighten you: do not fear.* The same with ܕܚܠ = *you are afraid.* Cf. Az. ܙܕܝܕܘܟܐ *fear* subst. (= N.S. ܙܕܘܚܬܐ). These perhaps point to a derived verb (1st conj.) ܙܕܝܕܠ. The fem. pres. part. of ܙܕܝܕ is ܙܕܚܬܐ only.

ܙܥܘܪ *to grow small* (pron. ܙ = ܨ), O.S. ܙܥܪ. Cf. ܙܥܘܪܐ N.S., O.S. *small* with ܙ = ܨ exc. Al. Z. Conjugate as if ܥ were absent.

ܚܝܐ *to live* O.S. *First present:* ܚܝܐ : ܚܝܬܐ : ܚܝܝܢ etc. *Second present:* ܒܚܝܬܐ ܝܠܗ U. Tkh. Ash. ܒܚܝܝܬܐ ܝܠܗ Ti.: ܒܚܝܬܐ ܝܠܗ Al. ܒܚܝܢ ܝܠܗ Sal. ܒܚܝܬܐܠܗ Gaw. (see ܝܠܐ § 42). *Pret.* ܚܝܐܠܗ U. Tkh. ܚܝܐ ܠܗ Ti. *Past part.* ܚܝܐ : ܚܝܬܐ Ash. *Imp.* ܚܝ : ܚܝܡܘܢ U.; or ܚܝܝ : ܚܝܐܡܘܢ (ܘ Sal.) U. Sal.; or ܚܝ : ܚܝ : ܚܝܘ K.; or ܚܘ Sing. m. ܚܝ f. ܚܝܘ pl. m. f. Ash. (In O.S. ܚܝܝ : ܚܝܝ : ܚܝܘ : ܚܝܝܝܢ). *Agent:* ܚܝܝܬܐ U. K. ܚܝܝܬܐ Ash. Al. *Noun of action:* ܚܝܬܐ U. Tkh. or ܚܝܝܬܐ U. Ti. *Causative:* ܡܚܝܐ.

ܛܝܒ *to be worth* (O.S. *to be well with* (impers.), *to be glad*, cf. O.S., N.S. ܛܒܐ *good*). *First present:* ܛܝܒ or ܛܐܒ (pron. in Sal. *ṭâ-ūkh* see § 90): ܛܒܐ : ܛܝܒܐ : ܛܒܝܢ etc. Sal. Q. Gaw. Tkh. Sh.; or ܛܒܐ : ܛܒܬܐ etc. U. Ti. Al. *Verbal noun with* ܒ. ܒܛܒܐ K. Sh. or ܒܛܝܒܬܐ Al. *Pret.* ܛܝܒ ܠܗ (pron. in Sal. *ṭiūgh-li*) or ܛܒܐ ܠܗ Ash. *Past part.* ܛܝܒܐ : ܛܝܒܬܐ (pron. in Sal. *ṭiūkhta*). *Imp.* ܛܘܒ (*ṭūkh* Sal.). *Causative:* ܡܛܝܒ (*máṭūkh* Sal.). This verb is not much used in U.; ܩܪܘܒ *to touch* or ܡܛܝܐ *to bring* is substituted.

ܛܠܒ K. *to seek*, in Al. *to err* as O.S. The vowel is sometimes thrown back from the ܥ, as ܛܠܒܬܐ or ܛܥܠܬܐ; ܛܠܒܐ or ܛܥܠܐ. In U. ܡܛܠܒܘܐ, see § 47.

§ 46]   IRREGULAR VERBS.   125

ܛܥܡ *to taste* O.S. Sometimes in U. by metathesis ܡܛܥ, causative ܡܛܥܡ (the former with Pthakha sound), p. 118.

ܓܪܓ *to hazard, be bold* (origin?). *Pres. part.* ܓܪܓ : ܓܪܓܐ. *Verbal noun with* ܕ: ܓܪܓܐ. *Pret.* ܓܪܓ or ܓܪܓܗ U. *Past part.* ܓܪܝܓܐ. *Imp.* ܓܪܘܓ. *Agent:* ܓܪܓܢܐ (this in K. = *a friend*, cf. ܓܪܓܘܡܐ *a joke* K. Sh.) or ܓܪܓܢܐ Q. Sal. *Causative* (none). For this verb in Ti. Ash. ܓܗܓܕ is substituted.

ܓܟܪ Al. *to hire.* O.S. ܓܟܪ. Conjugate like ܓܪܓ.

ܝܕܥ *to know* O.S. *First present:* ܝܕܥ : ܝܕܥܐ etc. [In U. Ash. the first has a Pthakha sound; in U. pron. ܕ = ܠ, in Sh. = ܠ] or ܒܝܕܝ : ܒܝܕܥܐ etc. Tkh. Al.; or ܝܕܥ (yei): ܝܕܥܐ : ܝܕܥܗ : ܝܕܥܟ : ܝܕܥܟܘܢ : ܝܕܥܘ Sal.; or ܝܕܥ : ܝܕܥܢܐ : ܝܕܥܢ : ܝܕܥܬܘܢ : ܝܕܥܘܗܘܢ : ܝܕܥ : ܝܕܥܒ (or ܝܕܥܟ) : ܝܕܥܟܘܢ : ܝܕܥܗܘܢ : ܝܕܥܘܗܘܢ : ܝܕܥܣ Gaw. *Second present:* ܟܕ ܒܕܘܝܐ (bi-doi-ya U. bi-dei-ya Sal. bi-dhei-ya K.) or ܒܕܝܗ Sal. or ܒܕܥܕܗ Gaw. (see § 44); or ܒܕܝܕ Ash. *Pret.* ܓܝܕܥ U. Ti. Ash. etc. ܒܕܝܕ Al. Tkh. *Past part.:* ܡܝܕܥܐ : ܡܝܕܥܬܐ; but in Al. Tkh. ܡܝܕܥ : ܡܝܕܥܬܐ Ti. sometimes. *Imp.* ܡܝܕܥ Tkh. Sh. U. Sal. Q. Gaw. (conjugate like ܓܓܕ § 44); or ܡܘܕܥ : ܡܘܕܥܕ : ܡܘܕܥܗ Ti.; and so Ash. but pl. ܒܝܕܥܘ; or ܒܝܕܥ Al; or ܒܘܕܥ Ti. (O.S. ܕܥ cf. ܓܗܠ from ܓܗܠ—ܕ hard). *Agent:* ܡܝܕܥܢܐ (ܕ = ܠ U.) ܒܘܕܥܢܐ (ܕ soft) Ash. For ܒܘܕܥ K., or ܒܘܕܥܗ U. (ܕ = ܠ), see § 77 (2). *Noun of action:* ܡܝܕܥܬܐ, or ܒ Al. (O.S. ܡܝܕܥܬܐ). *Causative:* ܡܝܕܥ (ܕ Ash.), ܡܝܕܥ Sal. Q. Gaw., ܡܗܘܕܥ Al., p. 107.

In Sh. Ti. (but not Ash.), Auhar village (in U.), the First present is often ܓܹܒ݂ܹܐ: ܓܹܒ݂ܵܐ: ܓܹܒ݂ܹܐ: ܓܹܒ݂ܵܐ: ܓܹܒ: ܓܹܒ݂: ܓܹܒ, ܓܹܒ݂ܹܗ or ܓܹܒ݂ܹܗ: ܓܹܒܣ or ܓܸܒܣ. Perhaps these are for ܡܓ݂ܝܒ etc. abs. state of past part., as in ܕܓ݂ܝܼܚ, ܕܓ݂ܝܼܚ, and ܒ = ܓܹܒ݂. For the interjections ܡܵܦܹܓ݂ ܡܵܕ݂ܹܓ݂ and the like see § 73.

ܝܵܗ݇ܒܸܠ *to give*, O.S. ܝܵܗ݇ܒ, the ܠ being an addition, appearing in only some forms. *First present:* ܝܵܗ݇ܒܸܠ: ܝܵܗ݇ܒܵܐ: ܝܵܗ݇ܒܹܐ etc.; in O.S. ܝܵܗ݇ܒ: ܝܵܗ݇ܒܵܐ (ܟ̇) etc. *Second present:* ܟܝܵܗ݇ܒ̇ ܡܠܸܟ U. Sh. ܟܝܵܗ݇ܒܸܢ ܡܠܸܟ K. Z. ܟܝܵܗ݇ܒܸܠܵܟ ܡܠܸܟ Al. *Preterite:* ܝܗܸܒ݂ܠܹܗ U. [with f. object ܝܗܸܒ݂ܵܐ ܠܹܗ and so with objective pronouns, § 50] ܝܗ݇ܒ ܠܹܗ Sal. (*yūgh-li*), ܝܘܼܗܒܸܕ݂ ܠܹܗ K. J. Z. ܝܘܼܗܒܸܕ݂ܠܹܗ Al. (ܟ). *Past part.* ܗܘܼܝܒܵܐ: ܗܘܼܝܒܸܠܬܵܐ U.; ܗܝܼܒ݂: ܗܝܼܒ݂ܬܵܐ K. Sh.; ܗܘܼܡܒ: ܗܘܼܡܒܬܵܐ Gaw.; ܗܘܼܒ݂: ܗܘܼܒܸܠܬܵܐ Al.; ܗܘܼܒܵܐ: ܗܘܼܒ݂ܬܵܐ (*yūkhta*) or ܗܘܼܒ݂ (*hukhta*) Sal.; in O.S. ܗܝܼܒ, ܗܝܼܒܬܵܐ. *Imp.* ܗܵܒܸܠ: Pl. ܗܵܒܠܘܼܢ U. or ܗܵܒܠܡܘܼܢ Sp. Q. (ܗ Sal.) or ܗܵܒܸܠ K. (O.S. ܝܵܗ݇ܒ). *Agent:* ܝܵܗ݇ܒܵܐ but in Ash. ܝܵܗ݇ܒܸܠܵܐ. *Noun of action:* ܝܵܗ݇ܒܸܠܬܵܐ U. Ti. or ܝܵܗ݇ܒܹܠܬܵܐ Tkh. or ܗܝܼܒܸܠܬܵܐ Al. or ܗܝܼܒ݂ܬܵܐ Ash. [The masc. verbal noun ܝܵܗ݇ܒ is much used in this verb by itself.] *Causative* (none).

ܝܵܐܹܐ *to curdle*, Sp. etc. only. *First present:* ܝܵܐܹܐ (*yei-yi*): ܝܵܐܝܵܐ: ܝܵܐܝܹܐ etc. *Second present:* ܟܝܵܐܹܐ ܡܠܸܟ. *Pret.* ܝܐܹܠܹܗ. *Past part.* ܝܐܵܐ. *Imp.* ܝܐܝܼ: ܝܐܘܿܢ. *Agent:* ܝܵܐܝܵܐ. *Noun of action:* ܝܐܵܬܵܐ (*yéta*). [Origin?]

ܝܵܠܸܠ *to lament*, O.S. ܐܲܝܠܸܠ, the West Syrian ܐܲܝܠܸܠ. Not used in K. MB. Sh. *Verbal noun:* ܝܼܠܬܵܐ. *Pret.* ܝܠܸܠ ܠܹܗ or ܝܠܸܠ ܠܹܗ. *Past part.* ܝܠܝܼܠ: ܝܠܝܼܠܬܵܐ. *Imp.* ܝܠܝܼܠ: ܝܠܝܼܠܘܼܢ U.; or ܝܠܸܠ: ܝܠܸܠܡܘܼܢ Sal. *Agent:* ܝܠܵܠܵܢܵܐ U. ܝܠܵܠܵܢܬܵܐ Sal. *Noun of action:* ܝܠܵܠܬܵܐ U. ܝܠܵܠܬܵܐ Sal. *Causative:* ܡܲܝܠܸܠ U. or ܡܲܝܠܸܠ.

ܝܵܠܹܦ to learn O.S. *Pres. part.* ܝܵܠܸܦ : ܝܵܠܦܵܐ, or ܝܵܠܸܦ : ܝܵܠܦܵܐ.
Causative: ܡܲܠܸܦ : in Al. ܡܘܵܠܸܦ : = O.S. ܡܲܠܸܦ.

ܝܡܵܐ to swear O.S. *Pres. part.* ܝܵܡܹܐ : ܝܵܡܝܵܐ U. K. or ܡܵܐܹܐ : ܡܵܝܵܐ U. or ܐܵܡܹܐ ܐܵܡܝܵܐ MB. Sh. *Second present:* ܒܝܡܵܝܵܐ ܝܠܹܗ U. or ܒܡܵܝܵܐ U. K. Sh. MB. *Pret.* ܝܡܹܐ ܠܹܗ U. Ti. Ash. ܝܡܹܐ ܠܹܗ Al. Tkh. *Past part.* ܝܡܝܵܐ : ܝܡܝܬܵܐ K. U. or ܐܝܡܝܵܐ : ܐܝܡܝܬܵܐ Sh. or ܡܝܵܐ : ܡܝܬܵܐ U. [Al. ܝܡܝܬܵܐ?] *Imp.* ܝܡܝ or ܡܝ U. *Agent:* ܝܡܵܝܵܢܵܐ U. K. ܐܡܵܝܵܢܵܐ MB. Sh. ܝܡܵܝܵܐ Al. Ash. *Noun of action:* ܝܡܵܝܬܵܐ U. K. or ܝܡܵܝܬܵܐ Al. or ܡܵܝܬܵܐ U. Sh. Ti. *Causative:* ܡܝܡܹܐ K. ܡܐܡܹܐ Sh. ܡܐܡܹܐ Sal. Q. ܡܘܡܹܐ Al. (also U. sometimes), ܡܲܡܹܐ U.

ܝܦܵܐ to bake (O.S. ܐܦܵܐ, West Syrian ܐܦܵܐ). *Pres. part.* ܝܵܦܹܐ : ܝܵܦܝܵܐ U. K. or ܦܹܐ : ܦܝܵܐ U. or ܐܵܦܹܐ : ܐܵܦܝܵܐ MB. Sh. *Second present:* ܒܝܦܵܝܵܐ ܝܠܹܗ U. : ܒܐܦܵܝܵܐ ܝܠܹܗ MB. K. Sh. *Pret.* ܝܦܹܐ ܠܹܗ (ܐܦܹܐ ܠܹܗ) or ܝܦܹܐ ܠܹܗ Al. Tkh. *Past part.* ܝܦܝܵܐ (ܐܦܝܵܐ) : ܐܝܦܝܵܐ Sh. Tkh. *Imp.* ܦܝ : ܦܝܡܘܢ U.; ܝܦܝ : ܝܦܝܡܘܢ (ܘ Sal.) U. Q. Sal.; ܝܦܝ : ܝܦܘ : ܝܦܘܢ K. *Agent:* ܝܦܵܝܵܢܵܐ U. Sal. K. ܐܦܵܝܵܢܵܐ MB. Sh. ܝܦܵܝܵܐ Ash. Al. *Noun of action:* ܝܦܵܝܬܵܐ or ܦܵܝܬܵܐ U. *Causative:* ܡܦܹܐ U. or ܡܐܦܹܐ U. ܡܝܦܹܐ K. ܡܝܦܹܐ Sal. Q. Gaw. ܡܘܦܹܐ Al.

ܝܪܵܩ to be green Al. Tkh. (O.S. ܝܘܪܵܩܵܐ = *green*). *Pres. part.* ܝܵܪܸܩ Al. ܐܵܪܸܩ Tkh. [For ܐܵܪܸܩ *to spit* see below.] *Caus.* ܡܲܪܝܸܩ, p. 108.

ܝܬܸܒ to sit (ܝ̇, O.S. ܝ̣). *Pres. part.* ܝܵܬܸܒ : ܝܵܬܒܵܐ U. K. or ܐܵܬܸܒ : ܐܵܬܒܵܐ Al.; O.S. ܝܵܬܸܒ : ܝܵܬܒܵܐ (ܝ̣). *Second present:* ܒܝܬܵܒܵܐ ܝܠܹܗ U. or ܒܬܵܒܵܐ ܝܠܹܗ K. *Pret.* ܝܬܝܒ ܠܹܗ (*tiughli* Sal.) or ܝܬܝܒ ܠܹܗ Al. Tkh. *Past part.* ܝܬܝܒܵܐ or ܝܬܝܒܵܐ Tkh. Al. *Imp.* Sing. ܬܘܒ

ܗܿܘܒ (O.S. ܝܗܒ etc.), in Sal. pron. *tūkh*, in U. *tū* or *tū-i*, the last *i* very short; Plur. ܗܿܘܒܢ or ܗܿܘܒܘܢ U. or ܗܿܘܒܝܗܘ U. or ܗܿܘܒܝܗܘܢ Sal. In Ti. they say for sing. ܗܿܘܒ ܗܒܘܚܐ, for plural ܗܿܘܒܘܢ ܗܒܘܚܐ. *Noun of action:* ܗܒܒܐ K. ܗܒܒܐ U. *Causative:* ܡܗܒܒ U. K. ܡܗܒܒ Sal. Q. Gaw. ܡܗܒܒ Al. as O.S. (all ܐ); also ܡܗܒܒ, p. 108. This verb is constantly used where we should use another verb: as, to sit in a carriage (to drive): to sit in a boat (to go by boat): to sit on a horse (to ride).

ܓܕܠ or ܓܕܠ *to be smooth*, see ܓܕܠ. In Ti. ܓܕܠ = ܓܕܠ *to be tired.* See also § 113 *i*.

ܟܠܗ or ܟܠܗ *to burn* as a flame, [cf. ܟܠܗ N.S. *a flame* (Al. ܟܠܗ), perhaps = Chald. and Heb. לַהֵב *a flame;* cf. O.S. ܟܠܗ *to burn* or O.S. ܟܠܗ id.] *First present:* ܟܠܗ : ܟܠܗ : ܟܠܗ etc. Ti. Tkh. Al. or ܟܠܗ : ܟܠܗ : ܟܠܗ etc. U. Ash. Tkh.; or ܟܠܗ : ܟܠܗ : ܟܠܗ : ܟܠܗ : ܟܠܗ : ܟܠܗ (or ܟܠܗ): ܟܠܗ Gaw. *Second present:* ܟܠܗ ܟܠܗ U. ܟܠܗ ܟܠܗ K. Al. ܟܠܗ ܟܠܗ Sal. Sp. ܟܠܗ ܟܠܗ Gaw. (or ܟܠܗ ܟܠܗ). *Preterite:* ܟܠܗ ܟܠܗ U. Sh. ܟܠܗ ܟܠܗ K. Al. *Past part.* ܟܠܗ : ܟܠܗ U. Sh., or ܟܠܗ : ܟܠܗ K. Al. *Imp.* ܟܠܗ U. ܟܠܗ K. *Agent:* ܟܠܗ U. ܟܠܗ K. ܟܠܗ Ash. Al. *Noun of action:* ܟܠܗ U. ܟܠܗ K. *Causative:* ܟܠܗ U. Sh. ܟܠܗ Sal. Q. Gaw. ܟܠܗ K. Al.

ܡܚܕ or ܡܚܕ *to churn*, O.S. ܡܚܕ. See ܡܚܕ; but the verbal noun is ܡܚܕ (= ܡܚܕܐ) or ܡܚܕܐ U.

ܡܨܐ *to be able* O.S. *First present:* ܡܨܐ : ܡܨܐ etc. U. Sh. Ash.; or ܡܨܐ : ܡܨܐ etc. U.; or ܡܨܐ : ܡܨܐ : ܡܨܐ etc. Tkh.; or

§ 46] IRREGULAR VERBS. 129

ܡܲܨܹܐ : ܡܲܨܝܵܐ : ܡܲܨܝܼܗܿ etc. Ti. In U. with ܓ: ܟ݂ܵܨܹܝ : ܟ݂ܵܨܝܵܐ; and the Tkh. form (perhaps also that in Ti.) seems to be = ܒ݂ ܡܵܨܝܼ = ܓ݂ ܒ݂ ܡܵܨܝܼ ; the latter is also in use in U. etc. For ܠܵܐ see below. In Ti. (not Ash.) the past part. abs. state gives another form; ܡܨܝܵܐ :

ܡܨܝܹܗܿ : ܡܨܝܵܐ : ܡܨܝܼܐܿܗ (or ܡܨܝܼܐ): ܡܨܹܐ : ܡܨܝܼ ܡܵܨܹܐ : ܡܵܨܝܵܐ ܡܵܨܝܼ (Zlama second sound), cf. ܬܵܓ݂ܹܐ above and § 50. These forms are also common elsewhere when ܠܵܐ is prefixed: but in U. etc. Zlama has the first sound in the plural; and the first pers. pl. is ܠܵܐ ܡܵܨܝܼܢ or ܠܵܐ ܡܵܨܹܢ. Similar forms are common in O.S., cf. § 32 (4). *Verbal noun*: ܡܨܵܝܵܐ; also ܡܨܵܝܬܵܐ U. The second present of this verb is not common, the habitual present being used instead. *Pret.* ܠܐ ܡܨܹܐ: also in U. ܠܐ ܡܝܼܨܝܼ which is properly the pret. of ܡܵܨܹܐ *to suck the breast.* But the habitual imperfect is generally substituted. For ܓ݂ ܗܘܵܐ = ܡܵܨܝܵܐ see § 29 (18).

ܢܓܲܗ K. *to dawn*, a defective verb, O.S. ܢܓܲܗ (= ܘܕܲܡ U.). The following forms are used. *Pres. part.* f. ܢܓܲܗܵܐ Ti. ܢܵܓ݂ܗܵܐ Tkh. Ash. *Verbal noun*: ܢܵܓ݂ܗܵܐ. *Pret.* ܓ݂ ܢܓܲܗ ܢܓܸܗܠܹܗ Ti. *Noun of action*: ܢܓܲܗܬܵܐ Ti. ܢܵܓ݂ܗܬܵܐ Tkh. Ash.; much used with ܠܲܝܠܹܐ or ܠܲܝܠܹܐ as ܠܲܝܠܹܐ ܕܢܵܓ݂ܗܬܵܐ *morning twilight.*

ܢܓ݂ܗ (rare) or ܢܓ݂ܵܗܵܐ *to groan*, O.S. ܢܗܵܡ and ܓ݂ܢܲܚ. See ܠܓ݂ܗ.

ܢܩܸܦ Al. *to go out* O.S. (= ܦܠܸܝܕ U. K.). *Imp.* ܩܦܘܿܦ as O.S.

ܣܝܸܒ *to be old* (so O.S., pret. ܣܐܸܒ). *Pres. part.* ܣܵܐܸܒ : ܣܵܝܒܵܐ or ܣܵܝܹܒ, ܣܵܐܸܒ݂.

ܣܝܵܓ or ܣܝܵܓ K. (O.S. ܣܝܵܓ; cf. ܣܵܝܵܓ Al. *an avenue*, ܣܝܵܓܬܵܐ O.S. *a hedge*) = ܡܣܲܝܸܓ U. *to fence, hedge.* See ܫܘܪ.

S. GR. 17

ܓܚܕ to curdle (with a thin sound, ܚ = ܐ); to rain or snow, U. K. (with broad sound of first vowel); to hold, Al., O.S. or hold together (cf. N.S. ܡܓܚܕ to patch. The fundamental sense seems to be to hold together). Pres. part. ܓܚܕ U. K. Sh., or in U. ܕܚܓ, but the latter only in the sense to rain, snow.

ܣܓܕ (ܗ) K. to be old. O.S. ܣܓܕ (ܗ), cf. ܣܓܝ. Verbal noun: ܕܩܢܬܐ or ܕܩܢܐ.

ܨܗܐ as O.S. or ܨܗܐ to thirst. See ܟܐܕ.

ܩܝܡ to rise up: stand, so O.S. ܩܡ (in the latter sense in U. usually with ܒܓܠ ܕܫܠܩܗ). Imp. ܩܘܡ: ܩܘܡܟ: ܩܘܡܘܢ (ܝ Sal.); but in Al. ܩܡ remains. ܠܡܗ, ܠܓ, ܠܡܗܢ are very commonly added. Causative: ܡܩܝܡ U. Tkh. ܡܩܘܡ Ti. ܡܩܝܡ Sal.

ܨܗܐ Al. as O.S. or ܨܗܐ U. K. to be set on edge: also in K. to be blunt. See ܟܐܕ.

ܪܩܕ to spit (so O.S. ܪܩ). Pres. part. ܪܩܕ: ܪܩܕܐ U. Tkh. Ash. or ܐܪܩܕ: ܐܪܩܕܐ U. Ti. Sh. Second present: ܡܟ ܪܩܕܐ U. Ti. Sh. or ܡܟ ܪܩܕܢܐ K. Ash. See ܪܩܕ to be green, above.

ܪܩܐ Ti., O.S., ܪܩܐ Tkh. to look (O.S. to lie in wait for). See ܟܐܕ.

ܕܝܢ see ܐܘܠ.

ܪܟܒ¹ to ride U. Z. (in K. in another sense); so O.S. but with ܒ soft. First present: ܪܟܒ: ܪܟܒܐ: ܪܟܒܝ etc. or ܪܟܕ: ܪܟܕܐ etc. U. In U. they also say ܪܟܒ ܐܘܠ (not K.). In K. for to ride they say ܬܒ ܒܓܠ ܣܘܣܝܐ to sit on a horse.

ܪܥܐ as O.S. or ܕܥܝ to pasture, intr. See ܟܠ. We must dis-

¹ Hence ܪܟܒܐ Al. or ܪܟܒܢܐ Al. or ܡܪܟܒܢܐ K. a ship (= ܐܠܦ U.).

tinguish the causative ܡܓܲܕܸܓ to pasture tr., from ܓܵܕܸܓ to be ill, which also in U. etc. has a Pthakha sound.

ܓܕܹܐ as O.S. or ܓܲܕܸܕ to plaister. See ܓܠܲܕ. In Sal. Q. Gaw. the First present is ܓܵܕܸܕ: ܓܵܕܕܵܐ: ܓܵܕܝܵܐ: ܓܵܕܝܼܚ: ܓܵܕܹܡ: ܓܵܕܘܼ: ܓܵܕܸܗ. ܓܵܕܕܹܗ (ܒ Sal.): ܓܕܹܣ.

ܓܗܹܐ Ti. Al. or ܓܗܹܐ U. to be pleasant (delirious Al.). See ܓܠܹܐ. In O.S. Pa'el to delay, be late, repent. Chald. to be desert.

§ 47. *Irregular Verbs of the second conjugation.*

Verbs with five or more radicals are like ܡܓܲܒܸܕ. Cf. § 83 c.

ܡܓܲܕܸܓ to cause to be desired, caus. of ܓܵܕܸܒ or ܓܕܹܐ. Past part. ܡܓܘܓܕܵܐ U. ܡܓܘܓܕܵܐ K. So all causatives of this form.

ܡܓܲܒܸܕ to bring (caus. of ܐܸܬܹܐ) = O.S. ܡܓܒܹܐ. First present: ܡܓܲܒܸܕ: ܡܓܲܒܝܵܐ etc. Ti. or usually ܡܓܲܒܹܐ: ܡܓܲܒܝܵܐ Ti. or ܡܓܲܒܹܐ: ܡܓܲܒܝܵܐ Tkh. Ash. Sh. (the Pthakha of fem. is short); or ܡܓܲܒܹܐ: ܡܓܲܒܝܵܐ Al. or ܡܓܲܒܹܐ (mé-yi, so throughout): ܡܓܲܒܹܐ: ܡܓܲܒܝܵܐ: ܡܓܲܒܹܝܚ: ܡܓܲܒܝܵܗ̇: ܡܓܲܒܘܼܗ̇: ܡܓܲܒܝܵܗܘܼܢ U.; or ܡܓܲܒܹܐ (also ܡܓܒܹܐ) Sal. Q.; or ܡܓܲܒ: ܡܣܓܲܒ: ܡܣܓܲܒܘܼܗ: ܡܓܲܒܘܼ: ܡܓܲܒܝܵܐ: ܡܓܲܒܝܚ: ܡܓܲܒܝܵܐ: ܡܓܲܒܝܐ Gaw. Verbal noun: ܡܓܒܘܼܝܹܐ K. Sh. MB. ܡܓܲܒܘܼ U. ܡܓܲܒܘܼܝܹܐ Sal. ܡܓܲܒܘܼܝܹܐ Gaw. Preterite: ܡܓܘܼܒܹܐ ܠܹܗ Tkh. Ash. MB. Sh. ܡܓܘܼܒܹܐ ܠܹܗ Ti. ܡܓܘܼܒܝܹܐ ܠܹܗ U. [with fem. object ܡܓܘܼܒܝܵܐ ܠܹܗ, and so with objective pronouns, § 50] ܡܓܘܼܒܹܐ ܠܹܗ Sal. Gaw. Past part. ܡܓܘܼܒܝܵܐ, ܡܓܘܼܒܝܵܢܵܐ K. (Ti. f. ܡܓܘܼܒܝܼܬܵܐ); ܡܓܘܼܒܝܵܐ, ܡܓܘܼܒܝܼܬܵܐ (mū-yita) U.; so Sal. with fem. ܡܓܘܼܒܝܼܬܵܐ. Imp. ܡܓܲܒܝ K. ܡܓܲܒܝ Ti.; but in U. ܡܓܲܒܹܐ (pl. ܡܓܲܒܝܘܼܢ), in Gaw. ܡܓܲܒܹܐ (pl. ܡܓܲܒܝܘܼܢ). Agent: ܡܓܲܒܝܵܢܵܐ, but usually ܡܚܰܕܬܰܢ Ti. ܡܚܰܕܬܳܢܳܐ Tkh. Ash. ܡܚܰܕܬܳܢܳܐ U. ܡܚܰܕܬܳܢܳܐ Sal. Q. Gaw. *Noun of action:* ܡܚܰܕܢܺܝ K.: ܡܚܰܕܢܳܐ (*mé-yéta*) U.

ܡܚܰܕܶܕ or ܡܚܰܕܘܕ. *Present part.* ܡܚܰܕܕܳܐ : ܡܚܰܕܕܳܢܳܐ U.; or ܡܚܰܕܶܕ : ܡܚܰܕܕܳܢܳܐ K. or ܡܚܰܕܘܕ : ܡܚܰܕܘܕܳܢܳܐ U., and so sometimes Ash., but with Mim sounded. *Verbal noun:* ܡܚܰܕܘܕܳܐ U. K. ܡܚܰܕܘܕܳܐ Al. *Preterite:* ܡܚܰܕܘܕܗ Ash. U. (Mim silent throughout, U.): ܡܚܰܕܘܕܗ K. Al. (also Ash.). *Past part.* ܡܚܰܕܘܕܳܐ m., with varying feminine: ܡܚܰܕܘܕܬܳܐ Ash. U. ܡܚܰܕܘܕܬܳܐ Sp. ܡܚܰܕܕܬܳܐ Ti. *Imp.* ܚܰܕܶܕ. *Agent:* ܡܚܰܕܕܳܢܳܐ. *Noun of action:* ܚܰܕܳܕܳܐ U. (first conj. form?) or ܡܚܰܕܘܕܳܐ Ash. U. ܡܚܰܕܕܳܐ Tkh. ܡܚܰܕܕܳܐ Ti. *Causative* in U. ܡܚܰܕܶܕ as if from a first conj. form. This verb is probably the O.S. ܚܕܰܕ *to walk about for relaxation*, also *to wander*. The following quotation from Malpana Khamis (cir. A.D. 1300) seems to justify this derivation[1]: ܒܓܰܢܬܳܟ ܐܚܘܢ ܗܐ ܡܚܰܕܕܺܝܢ: ܚܰܕ݁ܬܳܐ ܥܡ ܒܶܢ ܕܘܢܒܠܗ: ܘܥܳܡܪܺܝܢ ܕܟܺܝ ܡܥܓܶܒܝܢ: ܘܳܠܳܐ ܡܢܦܘܩܝܢ ܕܗܡ ܐܘܟܠܝܢ. *In thy garden, O our brother, lo they play, the gazelles with the young harts, and dwell and are quite at ease; and though without life they eat and drink.* [He is speaking of the crumbs which fall on a board, which he compares to a garden.]

[ܡܚܰܕܕ or] ܡܚܰܕܶܕ *to seek* U. Sal. Gaw. [For K. Al., O.S. see ܚܕܰܕ § 46.] *Pres. part.* ܡܚܰܕܕܳܐ : ܡܚܰܕܕܬܳܐ (*tó-ya*) U.; ܡܚܰܕܕ : ܡܚܰܕܕܬܳܐ (or ܡܚܰܕܕܳܐ) Sal.; ܡܚܰܕܕ : ܡܚܰܕܕܬܳܐ Gaw. *Verbal noun:* ܡܚܰܕܘܕܳܐ U. or ܡܚܰܕܘܕ U. or ܡܚܰܕܘܕܳܐ Sal. or ܡܚܰܕܘܕ Sal. *Pret.* ܡܚܰܕܘܕܗ. *Past part.* ܡܚܰܕܘܕܳܐ m. ܡܚܰܕܘܕܬܳܐ f. U. or ܡܚܰܕܘܕܬܳܐ Sp.; or ܡܚܰܕܘܕܳܐ m. ܡܚܰܕܘܕܬܳܐ Sal. Gaw. *Imp.*

---

[1] For this quotation the writer is indebted to Qasha Oshana Saru.

§ 47]   IRREGULAR VERBS.

ܓܕܡܒ : ܓܕܡܐܓܡܘ ܓܕܡܒ U. or ܓܕܡܒ : ܓܕܡܐܓܡܘܗܝ Sal. or ܓܕܡܒ :
ܓܕܡܒ Gaw. *Agent:* ܡܓܕܟܢܐ or ܡܓܕܡܢܐ U. or ܡܓܝܕܡܢܐ Sal.
or ܡܓܕܢܐ Gaw. *Noun of action:* ܡܓܕܟܢܐ or ܡܓܕܢܐ Gaw.

ܡܨܝܕ *to revile,* O.S. ܝܨܕ. Some forms are as if from ܡܨܘܕ.
Pres. part. ܡܨܝܕ : ܡܨܝܕܐ ; or ܡܨܝܕ : ܡܨܝܕܐ Sal.; or ܡܨܝܟܕ :
ܡܨܝܟܕܐ Gaw. *Verbal noun:* ܡܨܝܕܐ or ܡܨܝܟܕܐ Gaw. *Pret.*
ܡܨܝܘܕܗ Ash. U. ܡܨܝܘܕܘܗ K. ܡܨܝܝܕܗ in Amadia. *Past
part.* ܡܨܝܘܕܐ K. U. ܡܨܝܘܕܐ U.; both have fem. ܡܨܝܘܕܬܐ (ܗ̄).
Agent: ܡܨܝܕܕܐ K. U. or ܡܨܝܘܕܢܐ U. *Noun of action:* ܡܨܕܢܐ
(first conj. form?) U. ܡܨܝܕܢܐ K. ܡܨܝܘܕܢܐ U. Ash. In U. &c.
Mim silent throughout.

ܡܕܩܪ U. or ܡܕܩܪܐ K. *to throw, divorce.* This verb follows the
first, not the second division of the second conjugation and takes no
euphonic vowel. The *past part.* is ܡܕܘܩܪ rarely in K., usually in
U: ܡܕܘܩܪܐ K. See p. 116.

ܡܓܐܝܓܘܕ Ti. (not Ash.) or ܡܓܕܪܘܕ U., see § 30, *to be proud.*
Conjugate like ܡܨܝܕ, prefixing ܡܓ Ti. ܡܓ U.

ܡܓܐܡܕܐ Al. *to be fulfilled,* see § 30. Like ܡܕܩܪܐ, prefixing
ܡܓ.

ܡܓܪ (ܠ) *to place* (see ܢܓܕ § 46); like ܡܕܩܪܐ, not ܡܨܝܕ. In
U. sometimes ܓ drops, as ܡܓܪܟܝ *they place,* ܓܪ ܡܓܕܗ *he placed.*

ܡܕܘܠܕ *to have worms.* Conjugate as if ܠ were absent (cf. O.S.
ܬܘܠܕܐ N.S. ܬܘܠܕܐ *a worm*).

VERBS WITH OBJECTIVE AFFIXES.

§ 48. *Verbal noun and past participle.* These often take the affixes of § 11 in U. Q. Sal. Gaw. etc. But in K. these forms are not much used, the object being rather expressed by adding ܒܹܗ : ܒܗܘܿܝ etc. after the verb in Ti.: ܓܵܒܹܗ etc. in Tkh.: ܓܵܠܹܗ etc. in Ash., also U. (§ 70).

After most of these affixes the substantive verb will require Khwaṣa, as they end in a consonantal sound. Such combinations as ܡܚܘܼܠܨܘܼܢܘܟ݂ ܝܘܸܬ are by their meaning excluded. *Thou hast saved thyself* must be expressed by ܡܚܘܼܠܨܵܐ ܝܘܸܬ ܠܓܵܢܘܟ݂. In the third pers. sing. the forms ܘܗܝ -, ܘܗ̇ - are used in U.; in the third pers. pl. ܝܗܘܢ-. In K. ܗ- ܗ̇- are preferred for the singular.

Examples. ܡܲܚܠܨܘܼܢܹܝ ܠܝܼ U. *they are saving me.* ܡܚܘܼܠܨܘܼܟܘܿܢ ܝܘܸܢ *I have saved you* (rare), ܓܠܝܼܘܗܝ ܝܠܹܗ *he is revealing it.*

But the past participle is not much used with affixes; the forms in § 50 are preferred, the preterite being used instead of the perfect.

§ 49. The *present participle* (and derived tenses) and *imperative* take the same affixes with ܠ. They are then accented on the penult (except 2 pl. and Condit.), the affix being counted as part of the word (§ 8). The ܠ is omitted generally in Al. Z. and often in Gavilan and elsewhere; everywhere after the first pers. sing.; and in verbs ending in ܠ (usually), ܢ, ܪ, after the 3 sing. first present (and similar tenses) and 2 sing. imperative. The 3 sing. affix forms are ܗ-, ܗ̇ only; the 3 pl. are ܗܘܿܢ- U. ܗܘܿܢ- MB. ܝܗܘܢ- K. Al. Sp.

We cannot usually write ܒܹܐ ܡܲܚܠܨܹܢܝ for *I will save myself* or similar constructions, but must use ܓܵܢܝ as in § 48. Yet in Al., in the third person at any rate, such a construction is allowable. Thus

St Matt. xiv. 15 ܘܲܓܒܸܢ ܠܗܘܿܢ ܡܸܐܟܘܿܠܬܵܐ *let them buy themselves food* (ܠܐܲܟܠܘܿܣ U. K.). In U. K. we may use this construction in the Imperative thus: ܘܓܒܸܢ ܠܘܼܟ *buy for thyself*; cf. ܠܒܵܬ݂ܪܹܗ ܗܘ *backwards*, lit. *behind himself*, § 67. The O.S. usage is the same as Al. [Note that the O.S. affixes to the Imperative are not found in N.S. The disappearance of the old past and future tenses leads to a great simplification in affixes. On the other hand N.S. has affixes for *them* where O.S. has to use the separate pronouns.]

Examples. ܒܸܕ ܡܲܦܸܨܕܝܼܗ *I will save him* [in Jilu, where the variant ܠܹܗ is used (§ 31), this will be ܒܸܕ ܡܲܦܸܨܕ ܠܹܗ]; ܠܲܢ ܡܲܦܸܨܕܸܢ ܗܘܹܗ ܠܘܼܟ U. ܠܝܼ ܗܘܹܗ ܡܲܦܸܨܕܸܢ ܠܝܼ Tkh. *thou savedst us*; ܒܕܸܪ ܡܲܦܸܨܕܝܼܗܘܢ U. *you* (pl.) *saved them*; ܐܝܼܒܹܗ ܗܘ U. *he is in the habit of saying it*; ܘܡܲܚܕܘܼܗ U. or ܘܡܲܚܕܘܿܠܘܢ K. *sing them* (sing. imp.), ܘܡܲܚܕܘܼ ܠܘܿܗܘܢ U. (ܠܝܗܝ K.) *sing them* (pl.); ܚܡܘܿܡܝ or ܬܚܡܘܿܡܘܢ ܠܝ U. or ܚܡܘܿܡܘܢ ܒܐܠܟܡܘܡܝ *heal me* Sal. = (ܠ before ܠ for ܠܝ); ܝܵܕܥܸܢܹܗ Gaw. *I know him*, § 46.

Note. The affixes in this section are often added even when the object, a substantive, is also expressed. Cf. § 20 (9).

§ 50. *Preterite.* As the preterite is inverted, so that ܠܝܼ ܫܒܝܼܩ means *he was left by me* and so *I left him*, § 32 (4), we must express the English objective pronoun by the subjective forms ܐܸܢܵܐ: ܐܸܢܬ: ܠܹܗ etc., abbreviating them in exactly the same way as in the formation of the First present tense, and placing them between the participle and the ܠ. We thus get, remembering that the fem. of ܫܒܝܼܩ is ܫܒܝܼܩܬܵܐ, the pl. ܫܒܝܼܩܝܼ, and that the third person requires no subject-pronoun:

ܫܒܝܼܩ ܠܹܗ *he left him*, lit. *he was left by him*.

ܫܒܝܼܩܬܵܐ ܠܹܗ *he left her*, lit. *she was left by him*.

ܟܒܝܫܗ ܠܗ for ܟܒܝܫ ܐܢܹܟ ܠܗ *he left thee* (m.).

ܟܒܝܫܗܝ¹ ܠܗ for ܟܒܝܫܐ ܐܢܹܟܝ ܠܗ *he left thee* (f.).

ܟܒܝܫܘܗܝ for ܟܒܝܫ ܐܢܐ ܠܗ *he left me* (m.).

ܟܒܝܫܘܗܝ¹ (Pthakha sound) for ܟܒܝܫܐ ܐܢܐ ܠܗ *he left me* (f.).

ܟܒܝܫܒܝ ܠܗ for ܟܒܝܫܝ ܠܗ *he left them*, K. Al. Z. Sal. J. (U. below).

ܟܒܝܫܘܟܘܢ ܠܗ (or ܘܟܘܢ K.) for ܟܒܝܫܝ ܐܢܐܟܘܢ ܠܗ *he left you*.

ܟܒܝܫܣܝܢ ܠܗ for ܟܒܝܫܝ ܣܢܝ ܠܗ Ti. Al. Sh. Ash. or

ܟܒܝܫܣܝܢ ܠܗ for ܟܒܝܫܝ ܣܢܝ ܠܗ (f. for m.) U. Tkh. } *he left us*.

So for *she left him* ܟܒܝܫ ܠܗ̇; *she left her* ܟܒܝܫܐ ܠܗ̇; and similarly for all persons and both numbers. But we cannot say ܟܒܝܫܗܝ ܠܘܚ for *thou hast left thyself* (§ 48), but must say ܟܒܝܫܐ ܠܘܚ ܘܗܝ lit. *thy self has been left by thee* [ܢܦܫ is feminine].

It will be noticed that for *he left the woman* we should say ܟܒܝܫ ܠܗ ܒܟܬܐ; for *he left the men* we should say ܟܒܝܫ ܠܗ ܐܢܫܐ K. etc., and this is the usual construction. But ܟܒܝܫ ܠܗ ܠܟܬܐ (ܠܐܢܫܐ) is also used, § 31 (4). If the object precedes the verb, we must almost always use the former construction.

In O.S. also the absolute state of the past part. is used with the pronouns, but the contractions are not the same as in N.S.; they are those given in § 32 (1). Thus ܟܒܝܫ: ܟܒܝܫܐ: ܟܒܝܫܗ: ܟܒܝܫܗܝ: ܟܒܝܫܢܝ etc.

In the above forms (except 2 pl.) the accent is on the syllable immediately preceding ܠ, the whole being treated as one word.

---

¹ In the village of Digalah these are frequently used for the masculine, cf. § 31 (First present tense).

There is an important variation in U.: ܫܒܝܩܝܘܗܝ ܠܗ with a strong accent (*shwiqéli*), for ܫܒܝܩܝ ܠܗ. This seems to be due to a false analogy, the affix form of § 11 being added on. Nöldeke (§ 104) suggests that this is ܫܒܝܩܐ ܠܗ, the definite state for the absolute, giving Zlama its second sound. But in U. this second sound is rare, and only occurs in a few words like ܬܪܝܢ *two*, ܐܚܪܢܐ *other* etc.; never in the plurals. Indeed this plural ending in most districts has the first Zlama sound. And the strong accent would point to the affix form ܝܘܗܝ which itself has this strong accent, § 8 (2).

Except in the third person, sing. and pl., these forms are not much used in U. in colloquial conversation.

In all districts for *he left him* we can treat ܫܒܝܩ ܠܗ as an active verb and add on pronouns: thus—ܫܒܝܩ ܠܗ ܠܗ esp. Al., or ܫܒܝܩ ܠܗ ܠܗ K.; so ܐܡܝܪܗ ܠܗ *he told him* K. This, though not very grammatical, is an expedient to avoid the ambiguity of ܫܒܝܩ ܠܗ meaning *he left* as well as *he left him*. In U. this is carried a step further, and we can add on ܐܠܗ, ܐܠܗ̇: ܐܠܘܟ etc. to all persons and both numbers. Thus ܫܒܝܩ ܠܘܟܘܢ ܐܠܝ *you* (pl.) *left me*. More rarely we may express the same thing with ܩܕܡ, as ܩܕܡ ܫܒܝܩܘܟܘܢ ܠܝ. This method is also much in use in Al.

Second Conjugation.

ܡܚܘܡܝܪ ܠܗ *he healed him.*

ܡܚܘܡܪܐ ܠܗ *he healed her.*

ܡܚܘܡܝܪܟ ܠܗ *he healed thee* (m.).

ܡܚܘܡܪܟܝ ܠܗ *he healed thee* (f.).

ܡܚܘܡܝܪܢܗ *he healed me* (m.).

ܡܚܘܡܪܢܗ *he healed me* (f.), (second Mim with Pthakha sound).

ܠܗ ܡܚܘܡܗܒ J. K. Al. Z. Sal. ⎫
ܠܗ ܡܚܘܡܗܕܘܢ U.   ⎬ he healed them.
ܠܗ ܡܚܘܡܗܕܝܘܢ he healed you (Nun often omitted in K.).
ܠܗ ܡܚܘܡܗܦܢ U. Tkh.   ⎫
ܠܗ ܡܚܘܡܗܒܢ Ti. Al. Sh. Ash. ⎬ he healed us.

Verbs ܠܐ : *first conjugation.*

	O.S., Al. Z. K.	U.
he revealed him	ܠܗ ܓܠܠܗ¹	ܠܗ ܓܠܠܗ
he revealed her	ܠܗ ܓܠܠܗ̇ (O.S. ܠܐ)	ܠܗ ܓܠܠܗ̇
he revealed thee m.	ܠܗ ܓܠܠܘܟ¹	ܠܗ ܓܠܠܘܟ
he revealed thee f.	ܠܗ ܓܠܠܟܝ (O.S. ܠܐ)	ܠܗ ܓܠܠܟܝ
he revealed me m.	ܓܠܠܢܝ¹ (O.S. ܠܗ ܓܠܠܢܝ)	ܓܠܝܠܗ
he revealed me f.	ܓܠܠܢܝ² (O.S. ܠܗ ܓܠܠܢܝ)	ܓܠܢܝ²
he revealed them	ܠܗ ܓܠܠ¹ (O.S. ܠܗ ܓܠܠܗܘܢ)	ܠܗ ܓܠܠܢܗܘܢ
he revealed you	ܠܗ ܓܠܠܟܘܢ¹ (or without ܢ)	ܠܗ ܓܠܠܟܘܢ
he revealed us	ܠܗ ܓܠܠܢ¹ or ܠܗ ܓܠܢ (O.S. ܠܗ ܓܠܠܢܝ)	ܠܗ ܓܠܠܢ

In the second person forms ܟ in Tkh.

Verbs ܠܐ : *second conjugation.*

ܠܗ ܡܛܘܫܗ he hid him.   ܠܗ ܡܛܘܫܗ K. Al. Z. (ܡܛܘܫܗ U.).
ܠܗ ܡܛܘܫܗ̇
ܠܗ ܡܛܘܫܗܟ K. Al. Z. (ܡܛܘܫܗ U.).   ܠܗ ܡܛܘܫܗܘܢ K. Al. Z., or without ܢ (ܡܛܘܫܗ U.).
ܠܗ ܡܛܘܫܟܝ

¹ Second Zlama sound.   ² Pthakha sound.

§ 50] VERBS WITH OBJECTIVE AFFIXES. 139

ܡܚܝܘܒܝܗܝ K. Al. Z. (ܡܚܝܘܒܝܢ ܠܗ ܡܚܝܘܒܣ or ܡܚܝܘܒܢ) K. U.). (ܡܚܝܘܒܢ U.).

ܡܚܝܘܒܢܗܝ Pthakha sound.

So Pthakha verbs (§ 42), e.g. ܡܚܝܕ : ܡܚܕܝܢܝ U. *he quickened me*. And so quadriliterals, e.g. ܡܟܘܕܥ ܠܗ ܡܟܘܕܥܢ K. (ܡܟܘܕܥܢ U.) *he understood us*.

Verbs ܠܕ are similar: thus ܫܡܥ ܠܗ *he heard him*, ܫܡܥܠܗ ܠܗ U. ܫܡܥܠܗ Ti. Ash. ܫܡܥܗ ܠܗ Al. Z. *he heard her*, ܫܡܥܟ ܠܗ Tkh. or ܫܡܥܝܟ Ash. or ܫܡܥܝܟ ܠܗ U. *he heard thee* m. etc.

And in the second conjugation: in U. with ܘ, as ܡܟܘܡܣܢ ܠܗ *he assembled us*, ܡܟܘܡܣܢܘܢ ܠܗ *he assembled them*. But in K. Al. without ܘ, as ܡܕܬܡܕ, as ܡܟܘܡܕ ܠܗ : ܡܟܘܡܕܗ ܠܗ : ܡܟܘܡܕܝ : ܡܟܘܡܕܟ ܠܗ : ܡܟܘܡܕܟܝ ܠܗ : ܡܟܘܡܕܟܘܢ ܠܗ (Pthakha sound): ܡܟܘܡܕܒ ܠܗ (or 'ܡܟܕܒ'): ܡܟܘܡܕܗܢ ܠܗ (or without ܘ, also 'ܡܟܕܣ'): ܡܟܘܡܕܣ ܠܗ or ܡܟܘܡܣ ܠܗ.

Note. (1) The indirect object may often be represented by the affixes. Thus from ܡܟܬܒ *to ask* (a question) which takes ܡܢ after it (§ 71) we have ܡܟܬܒܬܗ ܠܝ *I asked her*. So ܕܒܝܗܒܘܢܟܘܢ ܝܘܗ *I am giving you* (pl.).

(2) The second preterite takes affixes like the first. Thus ܩܕܝܒܗ ܗܘܐ ܠܗ *he nearly cut it* (f.) *off*.

(3) A very common Upper Tiari usage is ܩܛܝܠܬ ܠܝ ܠܗ or ܩܛܝܠܐ ܠܝ ܠܗ *I have killed him*. ܩܛܝܠܬ ܠܝ ܠܗ̇ or ܩܛܝܠܬܐ ܠܝ ܠܗ̇ *I have killed her*. ܩܛܝܠܬ ܠܝ ܠܗܘܢ or ܩܛܝܠܐ ܠܝ ܠܗܘܢ *I have killed them*.

And so for all persons and both numbers, of both subject and object.

Use of the Tenses.

§ 51. *Tenses derived from the present participle.*

(1) The *first present* is rarely used, as it is in O.S., as an ordinary present in a simple sentence: and when thus used in the translation of the Bible into the Urmi dialect it is an archaism; as in St Matt. iii. 2 ܘܐܵܡܸܪ: ܬܘܼܒܘܼ *and he saith Repent.* This is not colloquial [see below (3)] except in the verb ܒܵܥܹܐ *to wish,* which is thus used, as ܒܵܥܹܢ ܐܵܙܹܠ *I wish to go* (ܕ omitted).

(2) The same with ܗ̄ܘܵܐ, as an ordinary past, is likewise archaic, e.g. St Matt. iii. 1 ܘܡܲܟܪܸܙܘܼ ܗ̄ܘܵܐ ܒܡܲܕܒܪܵܐ ܕܝܼܗܘܼܕ *and he preached in the wilderness of Judæa.*

(3) The *habitual present,* with ܟܹܐ, ܟܝ, or ܟ́ (see p. 82, also § 119) prefixed, or in Ti. and Ash. without prefix, is very common. Thus ܟܹܐ ܦܵܝܹܫ = *he finishes* (as a habit), but ܒܦܵܝܫܵܐ ܝܼܠܹܗ *he is finishing* (now). But in Al. this tense is constantly used for the second present. After a negative the prefix disappears except in Al., § 33. This tense is also frequently used as a historic present, in narration. In a few verbs it is also used as a simple present; as ܟܹܐ ܒܵܥܹܐ *he wishes,* ܟܹܐ ܝܵܕܹܥ *he knows,* ܟܹܐ ܡܵܨܹܐ *he can.* Cf. ܟܹܐ ܗܵܘܹܐ or ܟܹܐ ܗܵܘܝܵܐ *it may be = perhaps.*

(4) With ܗ̄ܘܵܐ this tense becomes a habitual imperfect: as ܟܹܐ ܐܵܙܹܠ ܗ̄ܘܵܐ *I used to go.*

(5) The *future* (with ܒܸܕ U. K. or ܒܕ Al. K. [esp. before ܐ, ܝ] or ܒ Al. Z. Sal. or ܒ [before ܐ, ܝ] Ash. or without prefix in Ash. and often Ti. Z. and more rarely elsewhere; the negative without prefix except in Al. where ܟ́ is used as ܠܵܐ ܟܩܵܛܠܸܢ *I will not kill,* and except sometimes in U. and Ti. where we have ܠܵܐ ܒܸܕ ܩܵܛܠܸܢ) cor-

responds to a common usage in later ecclesiastical Syriac, where the present participle replaces the old future, as ܠܐ ܟܳܦܪܺܝܢܰܢ ܒܡܫܺܝܚܳܐ *we will not deny Christ* (Martyrs' Anthem, Tues. even.) = ܠܐ ܟܳܦܪܺܝܢ ܒܡܫܺܝܚܳܐ N.S. or ܠܐ ܡܟܰܦܪܺܝܢ Al. Cf. below (10). So Rev. xvii. 7 etc. O.S.

ܒܸܕ is not prefixed to questions of the form ܐܳܙܠܸܢ *shall I go?* i.e. *do you wish me to go?* ܩܳܝܡܸܢ *shall I get up?* Another future may (more rarely) be formed by ܗܘܳܐ ܡܥܰܬܕܳܐ U. K. or ܗܘܳܐ ܡܥܰܬܸܕ Al. *to be about* (lit. *ready*), as ܗܘܳܐ ܡܥܰܬܕܳܐ ܠܸܗ ܠܡܳܛܝܳܐ (or ܠܡܳܛܝܳܐ) *he is about to come.*

(6) The same with ܗܘܳܐ is a conditional, or is the equivalent to the future in *oratio obliqua*, as ܒܸܕ ܐܳܬܹܐ ܗܘܳܐ ܐܸܢ... *he would come if...* (§ 60), ܐܡܝܪܳܐ ܕܒܸܕ ܐܳܬܹܐ ܗܘܳܐ *he said he would come*, but see § 66.

(7) The form of the preterite with ܟܹܐ, as ܟܹܐ ܦܪܸܩ *he finished* (for variations see p. 82) is much used in Al., rarely elsewhere except with objective affixes (and then not very often, see § 50), and never in Ti. Ash. With a negative the prefix is retained.

[*Note.* The prefixes ܟܹܐ : ܒܸܕ : ܒܸ : ܟܸ etc. are not necessarily repeated when two verbs are joined by ܘ : as ܒܸܕ ܐܳܬܝܼ ܘܐܳܙܠܝܼ *they will come and go.* But we may say ܘܒܸܕ ܐܳܙܠܝܼ here.]

(8) The First present is constantly used in relative and subjoined clauses where no time is expressed, after certain conjunctions, or after such verbs as ܒܥܳܝܳܐ *to wish*, ܡܦܰܩܹܕ (ܦܰܩܹܕ) *to command*, ܡܨܹܐ *can*, ܠܵܙܸܡ *must*, ܠܘܵܙܸܡ *must*, ܘܳܠܹܐ *ought*; ܕ being usually prefixed, but often omitted after ܠܵܙܸܡ : ܒܥܹܐ : ܡܨܹܐ and always after ܐܸܢ *if.* Thus ܟܸ ܡܨܹܐ ܕܐܳܬܹܐ *he can come*, ܠܵܙܸܡ ܐܳܬܹܐ ܗ̇ܘ *he must*

come, ܟܘܡ ܕܐܬܐ *id.*, ܐܢܐ ܕܚܙܝܢܗ *when I see him*, ܐܢ ܒܥܝܐ ܠܘܟ *if you please* (sing.), ܦܩܝܕ ܕܐܬܐ (ܦܩܘܕ K.) *bid him come*, ܟܠ ܐܢܫܐ ܕܩܪܐ *everyone who reads.* Rarely this construction is used with ܡܫܪܐ *to begin*, see § 57. This tense has not a potential force; for *I may go*, see § 29 (20).

In O.S. we have the same usage. Thus: ܡܐ ܕܕܐܢܐ ܠܢ ܟܐܢܘܬܟ *when thy justice judges us*, ܒܝܘܡܐ ܕܕܢܚܐ ܪܒܘܬܟ *in the day when thy Majesty shines forth.*

(9) In these cases if a past precedes, ܗܘܐ must ordinarily be added, especially in U. where the sequence of tenses is more closely followed than elsewhere; as ܒܗ ܡܨܝܐ ܗܘܐ ܕܐܬܐ ܗܘܐ *he could come*, ܡܦܩܘܕܐ ܠܗ ܕܐܬܐ ܗܘܐ *he bade him come.* But in Al. it is very often omitted; as ܪܡܙܘ ܠܗܘܢ ܠܚܒܪ̈ܐ ܕܝܠܗܘܢ....ܕܐܬܝ ܡܥܕܪܝ ܠܗܘܢ *they beckoned to their companions to come and help them*, St Luke v. 7 [ܠܟܡܘ ܠܗܘܢ ܠܚܒܪ̈ܘܬܗܘܢ... ܕܐܬܝ ܗܘܘ ܘܡܥܕܪܝܢ ܗܘܘ ܠܗܘܢ U.], and so sometimes in K.

(10) This present is used for an imperative of the first and third person, as ܐܬܐ *let him come.* This is common in O.S. though the old future is the usual substitute for these persons of the imperative, the imperative itself having only the second person. Thus in the service books we have constantly such rubrical directions as ܐܡܪ *let him say* (N.S. ܐܡܝܪ): ܥܢܝܢ *let them answer* (N.S. ܡܥܢܝܢ U. ܡܥܢܝܢ K. ܥܢܝ Al.), ܨܠܒ *let him make the sign of the cross* and so on. In N.S. ܫܘܩ ܕ (lit. *suffer*, imp. of O.S. ܫܒܘܩ) [or without ܕ] or ܫܘܩܘܢ ܕ (ܫܘܩܕ Al.), which are not changed even if more than one person is addressed, are often prefixed, as ܫܘܩ ܕܐܬܐ (or ܫܘܩ ܐܬܐ) *let him come.* So we have sometimes ܐܬܘܢ *come* in Al., see ܐܬܐ § 46. This tense is also

used in the second person to denote a prohibition (= O.S. ܠܐ with the future) and also to denote a positive command weakly or politely expressed, as ܐܡܪܬ ܠܗ *pray tell it.* For the difference between ܠܐ ܐܡܪܬ and ܠܐ ܥܒܕ see § 59.

(11) This tense is used with ܐܚܠܐ ܕ U. *would that* = ܟܘܒܐ ܕ U. K. or ܣܘܦ ܕ Tkh. or ܣܘܦܟ Ti. (hard Kap) or ܟܡܐ Al. (O.S. ܠܘܝ or ܐܝܟܐܘܦ); as (*a*) ܐܚܠܐ ܕܐܬܐ ܗܘܐ *would that he would come*; (*b*) ܐܚܠܐ ܕܗܘܐ ܗܘܐ ܐܬܝܐ *would that he had come.*

(12) For its use in protasis and apodosis see § 60; for the rendering of the English participle see § 58.

§ 52. *Second present.* This denotes an act going on at the present time, as ܒܫܠܡܐ ܝܘܢ *I am finishing*; but it may be a single and not a continuous act, as ܒܐܡܪܐ ܝܘܢ *I say.* In some verbs a present act denotes also a habit, as ܒܥܡܪܐ ܝܠܗ *he dwells.* Occasionally this tense denotes a future, as ܒܐܬܝܐ ܝܘܢ *I am coming*, i.e. not only *I am on my way* but *I will come.* This tense is not much used in Al. where the habitual present replaces it, § 51 (3).

It is frequently used where the English has *will* = *is willing*; as ܠܐ ܝܠܗ ܒܐܙܠܐ *he will not go* (is not willing to go); so ܠܐ ܝܠܗ ܒܝܗܒܐ ܩܐ ܬܪܝ ܩܪܢܐ *he will not sell* (lit. *give*) [*it*] *for two grans.*

§ 53. *The imperfect* denotes (*a*) an act formerly in progress, (*b*) a former wish or intention; but not a habit. Thus ܒܐܙܠܐ ܝܘܢ ܗܘܐ *I was in the act of going* or *I was just about to start*: but not *I used to go* (ܟܐ ܐܙܠܢ ܗܘܐ).

§ 54. *The preterite* properly denotes an action done at a particular past time. But it is frequently used loosely for a perfect or pluperfect; as ܒܫܝܢܐ ܐܬܐ ܠܘܟ *you have come in peace* (*are welcome*),

ܒܵܬ݂ܲܪ ܕܐܵܬ݂ܹܐ ܠܹܗ *after he had come.* So often in dependent sentences.

It is used prospectively for an immediate future. A man seeing another at a distance about to arrive will say ܐܵܬ݂ܹܐ ܠܹܗ *he has come,* i.e. *he is coming, he is in sight.* So the Turkish preterite *galdi* is used, cf. Modern Greek ἔφθασε. A sick man, or one in peril, says ܡܝܼܬ݂ ܠܝܼ *I am dying.* [With this compare the habit a servant has of saying ܗܘܹܐ ܒܝܼܠܹܗ *it is ready,* when anything is ordered, meaning that he will set about getting it ready.] When a man asks for information and understands the answer, he says ܝܼܕܝܼܥ ܠܝܼ *I knew = I comprehend.*

The preterite very frequently denotes pure hypothesis, § 62.

§ 55. *The perfect* is not so much used in U. as the preterite which often replaces it (§ 54). It is used both actively and passively; thus ܓܠܹܐܠܹܗ ܝܼܠܹܗ = *he has revealed* or *it is revealed.* In K. it is very common as rendering the passive.

In several cases the perfect denotes a present result. Thus: ܟܠܝܼܐ ܝܼܠܹܗ *he has come to a standstill = he is standing,* ܕܡܝܼܟ݂ܵܐ ܝܼܠܹܗ *he has laid himself down = he is in bed* [ܕܡܘܼܟ݂ܵܐ ܝܼܠܹܗ = *he is getting into bed*]. Similarly we have ܟܦܝܼܢܵܐ ܝܼܠܹܗ *he is hungry,* ܨܗܝܵܐ ܝܼܠܹܗ *he is thirsty,* ܕܡܝܼܟ݂ܵܐ ܝܼܠܹܗ *he is asleep,* ܨܝܼܡܵܐ ܝܼܠܹܗ *he is fasting,* ܦܫܝܼܡܵܢܵܐ ܝܼܠܹܗ *he is sorry,* ܦܝܼܫܵܐ ܝܼܠܹܗ *he remains*[1], ܡܚܝܵܐ ܝܼܠܹܗ *he is tired,* ܕܥܝܼܬ݂ܵܐ ܝܼܠܹܗ Ti. *he is perspiring* [elsewhere the second present], ܪܟ݂ܝܼܒ݂ܵܐ ܝܼܠܹܗ *he is riding* U. only (see § 46), ܫܬܝܼܩܵܐ ܝܼܠܹܗ or ܫܠܝܵܐ ܝܼܠܹܗ *he is silent.* We see the same thing in many cases where the past participles have become simple adjectives: as ܒܣܝܼܡܵܐ ܝܼܠܹܗ *it is sweet,* from ܒܣܵܡܵܐ *to be* or *become sweet.* We may compare the Greek perfects ἐγρήγορα, οἶδα, ὄλωλα, etc.

[1] So ܦܝܼܫܵܐ ܦܝܼܫܬ݂ܵܐ *the remainder* (also ܫܪܵܟ݂ܵܐ as O.S.).

§ 56. *The pluperfect* denotes an action finished at some past time, but it is often replaced by the preterite, § 54.

As the perfect often denotes a present result, the pluperfect denotes a past result, as ܕܡܟ݂ܒ݂ܵܐ ܝܗ݇ܘܵܐ *he had laid himself down* = *he was in bed.* The ܝܗ݇ܘܵܐ is sometimes omitted in a subjoined clause, as ܚܙܼܝܠܗܘܿܢ ܠܝܼ ܕܩܝܼܡܹܐ U. *I saw them standing* [not very common colloquially] § 58 (1); cf. O.S. ܘܚܙܼܝܬ ܠܫܡܲܝܵܐ ܕܦܬܝܼܚܝܼܢ *and I saw heaven opened*, Rev. xix. 11.

§ 57. *Verbal noun.*

(1) This does not usually represent the English infinitive after *can, must, command* and the like, see § 51 (8); but occasionally it does so, and after ܡܫܲܪܝܵܐ *to begin*, ܕܪܵܝܵܐ ܐܝܼܕܵܐ *to begin* (lit. *pour hand*), it is almost always so used, usually with ܠ, more rarely with ܒ; as ܡܫܘܼܪܹܐ ܠܝܼ ܠܡܵܡܪܵܐ *I began to say* (or ܒܡܵܡܪܵܐ). But in Al. we have the other construction here: thus St Luke iii. 23 ܡܫܘܼܪܹܐ ܠܗ ܕܗܵܘܹܐ [ܝܗ݇ܘܵܐ] *he began to be.* So very rarely in U.

(2) With ܡܘܿܣܸܦ *to increase*, it is employed as the equivalent of the O.S. construction with ܐܘܿܣܸܦ:—ܡܘܿܣܸܦ ܠܗ ܓܠܵܝܵܐ *he revealed yet again.* But this is not colloquial.

(3) It is used simply as a substantive, § 76 (1). In this case it may govern an object directly, [which often precedes it, especially if it is of the first conjugation]; or more rarely, as any other substantive, with ܕ; thus ܥܕܵܢܵܐ ܕܠܲܚܡܵܐ ܐܟ݂ܵܠܵܐ *dinner time* (*time of eating bread*). It would be possible to say ܥܕܵܢܵܐ ܕܐܟ݂ܵܠܵܐ ܕܠܲܚܡܵܐ (or ܕܐܟ݂ܵܠܵܐ ܠܲܚܡܵܐ), especially in Al., but in U. K. ܐܟ݂ܵܠܬܵܐ would naturally be substituted, § 76 (3). So ܥܒ݂ܵܪܵܐ ܠܗ ܡܢ ܡܩܲܛܠܵܢܘܼܬܵܐ ܕܝܲܠܕܹܐ *he stopped having the children killed* (or ܝܲܠܕܹܐ ܡܩܲܛܠܵܢܘܼܬܵܐ). Instead of the verbal noun we have a finite verb in the following:—ܡܢ ܕܵܟ݂ܵܐ ܕܐܵܙܹܠ ܓܲܒ݂ܪܹܐ ܐܵܘܟ݂ܝܼ *instead of those men going.* In ܠܐ verbs the form ܡܚܵܠܵܐ

is preferred to ܠܩܪܵܝܵܐ when it is used as a simple substantive not followed by ܕ and another noun (U. Q. Sal. Gaw.). Thus ܐܬܹܐ ܠܝ ܩܵܐ ܩܪܵܝܵܐ *I came to read* (*for reading*), i.e. *to learn*, at school: but we should have ܩܪܵܝܵܐ ܕܟܬܵܒܹ̈ܐ *reading books:* in U. more often ܩܪܵܝܬܵܐ here.

(4) It is used participially (in the first conjugation with ܒ), the particles ܗܵܕ ܗܵܕ *just*, ܟܕ (esp. K.) or ܟܡܕ Al. *whilst*, ܗܵܠܐ *yet* or ܗܹܫ K. Al. *now* and the like being often prefixed; or with the conjunction ܕ, the substantive verb being omitted. It is often repeated for emphasis or intensity. Thus: ܚܙܹܐܠܝ ܠܵܗ̇ ܒܹܐܬܵܝܵܐ *I saw her coming* (or ܕܒܹܐܬܵܝܵܐ), ܟܕ ܡܩܲܛܠܘܼܝܹܐ *whilst causing to be killed*, ܗܵܠܐ ܠܵܐ ܒܹܐܬܵܝܵܐ *while not yet coming*, ܣܚܪܵܗ ܒܡܵܬܘܵܬܹ̈ܐ ܒܙܘܡܵܪܵܐ ܒܙܘܡܵܪܵܐ *he went round the villages perpetually singing.* The ܒ is sometimes omitted from the verbal noun, as ܒܕܪܵܐ ܕܡܘܼܚܵܐ ܕܨܦܵܪܵܐ *daybreak.*

(5) It is added on to all the tenses, especially in K., for emphasis or intensity; as ܣܓܵܐ ܣܓܹܐ ܠܹܗ *it greatly increased* (not ܣܓܝܼܐܵܐ as often printed); ܡܲܠܗܘܼܝܹܐ ܡܲܠܗܘܼܝܹܐ ܝܠܹܗ *he is hasting greatly.*

(6) It expresses, with ܠ, the English infinitive except as noted above (1); it even expresses a purpose, though this may also be expressed by the present with ܩܵܐ ܕ *in order that*, or its variants, § 72. Also occasionally with ܠ it is an ordinary substantive, as above (3); thus ܡܢ ܠܫܩܵܠܵܐ (or ܡܢ ܕܫܩܠ) *from taking*, ܡܢ ܠܡܟܲܒܫܢܘܼܝܹܐ *from subduing:* so also ܡܢ ܫܩܵܠܵܐ ܘܝܗܵܒܵܐ *from taking and giving.* Cf. ܠܐ ܫܘܝܼܢ ܠܡܣܢܘܗܝ ܠܫܩܵܠܵܐ *I am not worthy to bear his shoes*, Matt. iii. 11.

§ 58. *Rendering of the English participle, used absolutely.*

(1) *Present participle.* This is not rendered by the Syriac present participle except in the rare cases when the latter is 'in

construction' as in § 16. Even in O.S. the participial use of the present participle not 'in construction' is not very common; though we have ܕܚܵܙܹܐ ܕܗܘܹܝܬ ܚܙܝܐ *that thou mayest be seeing*, Rev. iii. 18, N.S. ܗܵܕ ܕܗܘܹܝܬ ܚܵܙܝܵܐ; so ܗܵܟ݂ܢܵܐ ܗܘܵܝܬܘܿܢ ܥܵܒ݂ܕܝܼܢ *thus be ye doing*, 1 Cor. xi. 25 = ܗܵܕܟ݂ܵܐ ܗܘܵܝܬܘܿܢ ܥܒ݂ܵܕܵܐ N.S. The English present participle, standing absolutely, is rendered either (*a*) by a conjunction or relative and finite verb, as ܐܝܼܡܲܢ ܕܚܵܙܹܐ ܕܐܵܬܹܐ *when he sees him coming*, St John x. 12 (O.S. similar); or (*b*) by the verbal noun as in § 57 (4). We must however distinguish the English noun of action and participle which are of the same form; thus *he saw me coming* (part.) ܚܙܹܝܠܹܗ ܕܐܵܬܝܵܐ; but *he saw my coming* (noun) ܚܙܹܐܠܹܗ ܠܹܗ ܐܵܬܵܝܬܝ. But in the case of an intransitive verb we may use the past participle, though only in the following construction: ܚܙܹܐܠܝ ܠܵܗ ܕܝܼ ܟܠܝܼܬܵܐ *I saw her standing* (or ܕܟܠܝܼܬܵܐ).

(2) *Past participle, active.* This is rendered by a separate clause, as *having seen the affair, he told me* = ܒܵܬ݂ܪ ܕܚܙܹܐܠܹܗ ܗܵܘ ܡܸܠܬܵܐ ܡܘܼܕܥܹܐ ܠܹܗ ܠܝܼ. And very rarely with a transitive verb past part. ܚܙܹܐܠܗܘܿܢ ܠܝܼ ܫܩܝܼܠܹܐ ܛܥܘܿܢܹܐ *I saw them having taken (loaded with) burdens.*

(3) *Past participle, passive.* This is rendered by the past participle in Syriac. The particles of § 57 (4) may be prefixed.

§ 59. *The Imperative* has only the second person, and the other persons are expressed by the first present; the second person is also thus expressed when a prohibition, or a weak or polite positive command is intended, § 51 (10). A prohibition, 2 pers., may be also expressed by the imperative with ܠܵܐ, unlike O.S. This denotes the prohibition of a single action, while the first present with ܠܵܐ denotes that of a continued action. Thus a man seeing a boy running would shout to him ܠܵܐ ܟܠܝ *do not stop*; but sending a boy on a message in haste he would say ܠܵܐ ܟܵܠܹܝܬ. But this is not a hard and fast rule.

The Syriac imperative is much more used than the English, and does not denote any incivility; it is often used by an inferior to a superior. A man speaking to a servant or inferior would always use the Imperative where in English he might say *Will you?*

§ 60. *Conditional clauses. Protasis and apodosis.*

(1) A probable hypothesis, neither implying affirmation nor negation. *If he comes I shall see him* = ܐܢ ܐܬܐ: ܒܕ ܚܙܝܢܗ (ܐܢ is sometimes omitted); or ܐܢ ܐܬܐ ܠܗ: ܒܕ ܚܙܝܢܗ; or rarely ܐܢ ܐܗܐ ܗܘܝܐ ܗܟܢ ܒܚܕܘܬܐ ܝܘܢ.—ܐܢ ܐܬܐ ܠܗ: ܚܕܐ ܠܝ *if this is so, I rejoice.* So *If he has come, I shall see him* = ܐܢ ܗܘܐ ܐܬܝܐ: ܒܕ ܚܙܝܢܗ; or ...ܐܢ ܐܬܐ ܠܗ.—*If he came, James saw him* (i.e. *I do not know how the fact lies*) = ܐܢ ܐܬܝܐ ܠܗ: ܝܥܩܘܒ ܚܙܝܘܗܝ ܠܗ.

(2) Pure hypothesis. *If he came* (or *If he were to come*) *I should see him* = ܐܢ ܐܬܐ ܗܘܐ: ܒܕ ܚܙܝ ܗܘܐ ܠܗ; or ܐܢ ܐܬܐ ܠܗ: ܒܕ ܚܙܝܢܗ as above. ܐܢ is sometimes omitted: as ܐܢ ܥܒܕܬ ܠܗܘܢ ܗܕܟܐ: ܛܒ. ܠܐ ܥܒܕܬ ܠܗܘܢ... *if you do thus, well; if not...* The preterite is also much used with ܐܦܢ *although;* the apodosis is then often introduced by a redundant ܐܠܐ *but* (cf. ἀλλά used similarly after ἐάν and εἴπερ, 1 Cor. iv. 15, viii. 5).

(3) Implying negation. *If he had come I should have seen him* = ܐܢ ܗܘܐ ܗܘܐ ܐܬܝܐ: ܒܕ ܚܙܝ ܗܘܐ ܠܗ; or for the apodosis ܒܕ ܗܘܝ ܗܘܐ ܚܙܝܘܗܝ; or more rarely for the protasis ܐܢ ܐܬܝܐ ܗܘܐ. So, ܐܢ ܗܘܐ ܗܘܐ ܠܟܐ: ܒܕ ܗܘܝ ܗܘܐ ܕܐܙܠܬܐ *if he had been here I should have gone;* ܐܢ ܗܘܐ ܗܘܐ ܐܬܝܐ: ܛܒ ܗܘܐ *if he had come it would be well.*

§ 61. *Temporal clauses* are ordinarily expressed as in English. But an English perfect after *when*, which is in effect a future perfect, may be expressed in four ways. Thus, *when the sun has set* (= *shall have set*) = ܐܝܡܲܢ ܕܫܸܡܫܵܐ ܗ̄ܘܹܐ ܛܒ̣ܝܼܥܵܐ or ܐܝܡܲܢ ܕܫܸܡܫܵܐ ܛܵܒ̣ܥܵܐ (loosely) or ܐܝܡܲܢ ܕܫܸܡܫܵܐ ܛܒ̣ܝܼܥܵܐ ܝܠܹܗ̇. A very common method, however, of rendering this is to replace the temporal clause by another; thus, ܫܸܡܫܵܐ ܛܵܒ̣ܥܵܐ: ܐܝܼܡܵܐ ܒܹܬ ܐܵܙܠܸܢ *let the sun set, then I will go.* After ܐܝܼܡܵܐ there is often an aposiopesis; as ܐܝܡܲܢ ܒܹܬ ܐܵܙܠܸܬ؟—ܐܵܬܹܐ: ܐܝܼܡܵܐ *When will you go?—I shall go when he comes.* With this we may compare the method of expressing *the day after to-morrow* and *the day before yesterday.* The translation of both is ܝܵܘܡܵܐ ܐ̱ܚܹܪ̈ܢܵܐ K. or ܝܘܿܡܵܐ ܐ̱ܚܹܪ̈ܢܵܐ U., lit. *the other day.* But a Syrian will generally be more exact, and say ܩܘܼܕܡܵܐ ܠܵܐ: ܝܘܿܡܵܐ ܐ̱ܚܹܪ̈ܢܵܐ U. [= ܬܸܡܵܠ ܠܵܐ: ܝܵܘܡܵܐ ܐ̱ܚܹܪ̈ܢܵܐ K.], which stands both for *not to-morrow but the next day,* and *not yesterday but the day before* (§ 67). So for *Monday week* we generally have ܐܵܗܵܐ ܬ݂ܪܲܒܫܲܒܵܐ ܠܵܐ: ܬ݂ܪܲܒܫܲܒܵܐ ܐ̱ܚܹܪ̈ܢܵܐ U. [K. similar] = *not this, but the other Monday.*

In Al. a temporal clause is sometimes replaced by the verbal noun, thus ܗܸܫ ܐܸܢܘܿܢ ܕܠܵܐ ܡܒܲܪܟܘܼܬܵܐ lit. *now they without blessing* = *before they were married,* St Matt. i. 18. This would not be possible in U.; they would usually say ܡ̣ܢ ܩܲܕܲܡ ܕܩܵܒܹܠ ܠܗܘܿܢ ܡܒܲܪܟܘܼܬܵܐ but they might say ܗܵܠܵܐ ܐܸܢܝ ܠܵܐ ܡܒܲܪܟܘܼܬܵܐ lit. *as yet they not blessed* [all ܒ].

The preterite is used in a temporal clause if there is uncertainty, as ܒܵܬܲܪ ܕܐܵܬܹܐ ܠܝ ܒܹܬ ܚܵܙܹܝܢܹܗ *after I have come* (if ever I do come) *I shall see him.* This is equivalent to ܐܸܢ ܐܵܬܹܐ ܠܝ, § 60. So also if no particular time is referred to and a general case or hypothesis is intended.

An English temporal clause is often rendered by the noun of action, as ܒܕܥܵܪܬܝ *when I returned, return, was returning,* ܒܵܬܲܪ ܕܥܵܪܬܝ *after I have (had) returned,* ܗܲܠ ܐܵܬܝܼܬܝ *till I come (came).* The noun of action is thus more used than the English noun. But the finite verb might readily be used in Syriac in these cases.

When is replaced by a periphrasis in cases such as the following: ܐܝܟ ܕܗܘ ܥܕܢܐ ܕܠܟܐ ܗܘܝܬ ܗܘܐ *as when you were here*, lit. *as that time that you were here.*

§ 62. *Absolute hypothetical clauses.*

(1) The preterite is much used to express a possibility where no protasis is attached, as ܒܠܟܐ ܕܡܝܬ ܠܝ *perhaps I might die* (or without ܕ). ܒܬ ܐܙܠܢ ܠܡܣܥܪܢܐ ܕܒܘܗܝ: ܕܝ ܒܠܟܐ ܐܬܐ ܠܗ *I will go and visit him in case by chance he has come.*

(2) The conditional is used as in English where *would* = *were about to.* ܐܝܟ ܕܝܠܗ ܒܬ ܐܙܠ ܗܘܐ *as if he were about to go* (*would go*).

(3) The preterite is also used to denote pure hypothesis in the following: ܛܒ ܝܘܬܪ ܕܠܐ ܢܕܪܬ ܗܘܐ ܡܢ ܕܢܕܪܬ ܘܠܐ ܦܪܥܬ ܠܗ *It is better that thou shouldest not have vowed than that thou shouldest vow and not pay,* cf. Eccles. v. 5.

§ 63. *Impersonal verbs.*

(1) These are generally in the feminine, but sometimes, especially in Al., in the masculine. [The O.S. rule is similar.] Thus ܐܝܟ ܕܝܠܗ ܟܬܝܒܐ and ܐܝܟ ܕܝܠܗ ܟܬܝܒܬܐ both express *as it is written.* So ܒܝܫܐ and ܒܝܫܬܐ both express the abstract idea of *evil* (subst.), though the latter is more common. It is interesting to note that the East Syrians take the ܒܝܫܐ of the Lord's prayer personally as *the Evil one,* and paraphrase it frequently in their service-books *the Evil one and his hosts* ܒܝܫܐ ܘܡܫܪܝܬܗ.

Examples of masculines: ܦܪܝܫ ܠܝ, the preterite, *it is finished by me* = *I finished,* ܐܒܝܕ ܠܗ ܠܟܠܒܐ (or ܠܝ) *it lost on me* = *I have*

§ 63] IMPERSONAL VERBS. 151

lost my head (also fem.), ܢܶܒܣܰܡ ܠܳܟ݂ *may it be pleasant to you*, see § 75 and ܗܘܳܐ ܒܺܝ § 46.

Examples of feminines: ܒܶܗ ܨܳܒ݂ܬ݂ ܢܰܦ݂ܫܝ ܕܺܝܠܝ *In him I am well pleased*, lit. *in him it pleased me*, St Matt. iii. 17. So ܨܒ݂ܺܝ . ܠܝ ܠܳܟ݂ *if you please*, ܨܒ݂ܺܝ ܢܰܦ݂ܫܳܟ݂ *bravo!* § 73.

(2) Some verbs which in English are impersonal may take a subject in Syriac. Thus ܡܶܛܪܳܐ ܡܳܚܶܕ݂ or simply ܡܳܚܶܕ݂ ܡܶܛܪܳܐ *it rains*. So we have ܬܰܠܓܳܐ ܡܳܚܶܕ݂ ܠܳܗ݇ *it snows*; ܡܳܚܶܕ݂ ܒܰܪܕ݂ܳܐ *it hails*, ܩܳܫܬܳܐ ܕܚܰܡܫܳܢܳܐ ܡܳܚܶܕ݂ *it blows*, ܠܳܗ݇ (K. ܡܰܚܕܳܐ) *it thunders*, ܕܳܐܶܩ ܚܰܡܫܳܢܳܐ ܡܳܚܶܕ݂ *it lightens*, ܡܳܚܶܕ݂ (or ܡܶܛܪܳܐ) *it rains*, lit. *the world is raining*, ܕܰܘܕ݂ܳܐ . ܚܰܡܫܳܢܳܐ ܡܶܛܪܳܐ *it is stormy*.

(3) ܠܳܙܶܡ (Turk.) *must*, generally stands without ܡܶܛܪܳܐ, ܠܘܳܡ (Arab.) *must* and ܘܳܠܶܐ (Arab.) *ought*, generally with it. They are thus conjugated:— ܕܺܐܙܰܠ ܠܳܙܶܡ *I must go*, ܠܳܙܶܡ ܠܘܳܡ ܕܺܐܙܰܠ *id.* In Al. we have ܓ݁ ܠܘܳܡ = ܡܳܠܶܡ. After ܘܳܠܶܐ we may insert a pronoun, as ܘܳܠܶܐ ܠܳܟ݂ ܕܬܺܐܙܰܠ U. (ܘܳܠܶܐ K. Al.) *you ought*. These words may be used with a negative, especially ܠܘܳܡ, as ܠܳܐ ܠܳܙܶܡ ܠܳܐ *it is not necessary*; this must be distinguished from ܠܳܐ ܣܢܺܝܩ ܗܘܳܐ *he was not obliged*, which is a personal verb; the latter implies that nothing was lacking. ܠܘܳܡ and ܠܳܙܶܡ may be used as simple adjectives and may occasionally take the first plural. ܠܳܐ ܠܳܙܡܺܝܢ *they are not necessary* (or ܠܳܙܶܡ: or the singular of either). For the lengthening of the vowel in the plural see § 18 (xiii). For ܠܘܳܡ with affixes see § 20 (7). ܘܳܠܶܐ implies moral obligation; and if this is not the idea of *ought* we must render by ܠܘܳܡ or ܠܳܙܶܡ.

Thus ܟܒܝܟ ܕܗܘܝ ܗܘܘ ܠܟܐ *they ought to be here*, i.e. I should have expected it. Also in referring to a past event they often are used for ܘܒܝܟ, as ܟܒܝܟ ܕܗܘܝܬ ܗܘܐ ܐܙܠܐ *you ought to have gone.* ܠܘܡ is used both in U. and K.: ܟܒܝܟ in U. only.

(4) For *it is I* and the like see § 29 (19); for ܐܝܬ, ܠܝܬ, § 29 (11).

(5) We may notice ܒܠܟܐ ܗܘܝܐ *it may be* = *perhaps* [or *it is possible* which is also rendered by ܒܠܟܐ ܗܘܐ § 29 (10)] and ܡܨܛܘܦܐ *it may happen* = *perhaps*; the ܡܨ is usually dropped, even in K. If this is used as a verb in U. it is ܡܨܛܘܦܐ; in K. ܡܛܘܦܐ, see §§ 36, 87 *c*.

(6) In Al. and sometimes K. ܚܒܝܒ is used impersonally for ܒܥܐ *to wish*, which in Al. usually = *to love*. Thus ܚܒܝܒ ܗܘܐ ܠܝ *I wished.* Also *to be pleased*; as ܐܢ ܚܒܝܒ ܠܗ ܒܗ ܠܐܠܗܐ Al. *if it pleases him* (God) *in him* (Christ) = *if he will have him*, St Matt. xxvii. 43; ܠܐܠܗܐ ܚܒܝܒ ܠܗ ܒܝ Al. *In thee I am* (lit. *was*) *well pleased*, St Luke iii. 22.

(7) ܚܣ ܠܝ or ܚܣ ܡܢܝ = *far be it from me*, usually followed by ܕ and the first present. Thus ܚܣ ܠܢ ܕܢܟܦܘܪ O.S. = ܚܣ ܠܢ ܕܟܦܪܚ N.S. *far be it from us to deny.* Also standing by itself ܚܣ ܠܐܠܗܐ or ܚܣ ܡܢ ܐܠܗܐ = *God forbid!*

(8) For ܚܡܝܡܐ ܠܗ *it is warm* (lit. *warmth*) and the like, see § 16 *f*. ܩܪܝܪܐ ܠܗ would not be impersonal, but would refer to some particular thing, as e.g. water, being cold.

(9) ܗܘܐ before its subject has a quasi-impersonal use in the following: ܗܘܐ ܠܗ ܠܒܐ ܠ *he had the heart* (or *intention*) *to* =

ܐܝܼܬ݂ ܗ̇ܘܵܐ; so ܗ̇ܘܵܐ ܗ̇ܘܹܐ ܠܗܘܿܢ ، ܡܸܠܬ݂ܵܐ *they had word,* ܡܘܿܕܝܼ ܗ̇ܘܹܐ ܗ̇ܘܹܐ ܠܹܗ? *what has come over him?*

§ 64. *The direct object of the verb.*

(1) This is generally expressed by the simple substantive, but ܠ may be inserted, especially if the object precede the verb, § 74; or in U. ܩܵܬ; as ܠܡܵܢܝܼ ܡܚܹܐ ܠܹܗ? (also ܩܵܬ ܡܵܢܝܼ U.) *whom did he strike?* If the object is a pronoun the affixes with ܠ or ܩܵܬ must be used; but ܠ with a pronominal affix cannot ordinarily stand in U. K. apart from its verb, and in this case ܐܝܼܠܹܗ, ܐܝܼܠܵܗ̇ etc. must be used. For exceptions in particular cases see §§ 10, 50 and § 70 (3).

(2) Many verbs take two objects without prepositions, as ܥܒܵܕ݂ܵܐ *to make,* ܡܠܵܝܵܐ *to fill* (of the thing filled, and that with which it is filled, but the latter may also be expressed by prefixing ܡܸܢ), ܙܪܵܥܵܐ *to sow* (of the place sown and the seed). So some causatives whose originals are transitive, as ܡܲܠܒܘܼܫܹܐ *to clothe* (a person with a dress), ܡܲܠܘܿܦܹܐ *to teach,* ܡܲܩܪܘܼܝܹܐ *to teach.* ܒܩܵܪܵܐ *to ask,* does not take two direct objects, but ܡܸܢ is placed before the person asked, § 71.

(3) A second noun is often placed in apposition to the object; as ܝܗܝܼܒ݂ܠܹܗ ܚܲܕ݂ ܬܘܼܡܵܢ ܕܲܝܢܵܐ *he gave a tuman as a debt = he lent a tuman.* So ܫܩܵܠܵܐ ... ܕܲܝܢܵܐ *to borrow (take as a debt),* ܝܗܵܒ݂ܵܐ ܦܸܫܟܹܫ *to give as a present* etc.; ܠܘܼܒ݂ܠܹܗ ܠܒܢܲܝ̈ ܐܝܼܣܪܵܝܹܠ ܫܒ݂ܝܼܵܐ *he led the children of Israel captive,* ܡܚܝܼ ܟܬ݂ܵܒ݂ܵܐ ܒܨܲܡܵܐ *print the book.* So many of the idioms in § 75. For the passive also we have: ܦܝܼܫ ܠܲܢ ܡܚܝܼܬ݂ܵܐ ܚܬܵܡܵܐ *we were sealed.* ܙܘܼ̈ܙܹܐ ܦܝܼܫ ܠܗܘܿܢ ، ܝܗܝܼܒ݂ܹܐ ܕܲܝܢܵܐ *the money was lent.*

(4) For the passives of causatives cf. § 45 *a.* Thus ܦܝܵܫܵܐ ܡܲܩܛܘܼܠܹܐ = *to be caused to be killed,* not *to be caused to kill.*

(5) The English direct object sometimes becomes indirect in Syriac and *vice versâ*, see § 71; § 50, note 1.

(6) The verbs ܡܨܠܐ *to pray*, ܡܕܡܟ *to lie*, frequently take cognate accusatives, as ܡܨܘܠܐ ܠܗ ܨܠܘܬܐ *he prayed*, ܡܕܡܟܠܗ ܕܡܟܐ ܗܘ *he is lying*.

(7) A singular object is sometimes used for a plural one as in the following:—ܪܫܐ ܗܘܘ ܟܦܘ *they bowed their heads* (*the head*), (but ܪܫܝܗܘܢ might be used here); ܓܒ ܡܕܩܒ ܐܝܕܐ ܡܢܝ *they will give up my cause* (*cast hand from me*, § 75).

(8) The object of a noun of action in ܬܐ may be often expressed by ܠ as well as ܕ; as ܣܓܕܬܐ ܠܒܪܝܬܐ *the worship of a creature*, where ܕ might cause confusion and give the sense *a creature's worship*. So ܣܓܕܬܐ ܕܝܠܘܟ *the worship of thee*; or without ܠ, ܝܗܒܠܟ ܣܓܕܬܐ *giving thee worship*. But ܩܨܬܗ ܕܥܒܕܐ *the end of the affair*.

(9) When the object is expressed pleonastically by a pronoun as well as by a noun, ܠ cannot be prefixed to the latter as in O.S. Thus ܐܢܫܐ ܗܘܘ ܡܠܦ *teach the men* (not ܠܐܢܫܐ). But we can say simply ܡܠܦ ܠܐܢܫܐ. The first is the commoner method.

§ 65. *Agreement*.

(1) In general verbs agree with their subjects in person, gender and number; but nouns of multitude, as ܟܢܫܐ *a crowd*, may take either a singular or plural verb.

(2) Two or more nouns coupled by ܘ *and*, always, and by ܐܘ *or*, generally, take a plural verb.

(3) When the genders differ the masculine verb is used.

(4) When the persons differ the first is preferred to the second and the third, and the second to the third.

(5) When the numbers differ the plural is used, as *you and the women have come* = ܐܲܢ̱ܬ ܘܢܸܫܹ̈ܐ ܐܬܹܐܠܹܗ ܝܘܲܚ.

(6) *Agreement of pronouns with one another in person.* Here N.S. differs from O.S. in which the third person often refers to the second; in N.S. the same person is used throughout. Thus ܐܲܢ̱ܬ ܡܥܲܕܪܵܢܵܐ ܕܩܲܕܝܼܫܵܝܟ O.S. = ܐܲܢ̱ܬ ܡܥܲܕܪܵܢܵܐ ܕܩܲܕܝܼܫܲܝܗܘܿܢ N.S. *thou helper of thy saints*; ܐܲܢ̱ܬ ܗܘܿ or ܐܲܢ̱ܬܘܿ O.S. = ܐܲܢ̱ܬ ܝܘܲܬ N.S. (also in O.S. ܐܲܢ̱ܬ ܐܲܢ̱ܬ) *thou art*; ܐܸܢܵܐ ܗܘܿ O.S. = ܐܵܢܵܐ ܝܘܸܢ N.S. *I am*; ܐܲܢ̱ܬܘܿܢ ܐܸܢܘܿܢ O.S. = ܐܲܚܬܘܿܢ ܝܘܲܬܘܿܢ N.S. *ye are.*

(7) The verb agrees with the interrogative pronoun in a case like ܐܲܝܢܝܼ ܡܸܢܵܘܟܼܘܿܢ ܐܬܹܐ ܠܹܗ *which of you came?*

§ 66. *Oratio obliqua.*

(1) This may be used in N.S., and if so the sequence of tenses must usually be observed, especially in U., § 51 (9): ܒܵܐܡܵܪܵܐ ܝܠܹܗ ܕܐܬܹܐ ܝܠܹܗ *he says he has come,* ܐܡܝܼܪܹܗ ܕܐܬܹܐ ܝܘܵܐ *he said he had come.*

(2) More frequently oratio recta is substituted. Thus ܐܡܝܼܪܹܗ: ܒܸܬ ܐܬܹܝܢ *he said, I will come.* So in O.S. In indirect questions oratio obliqua is more common. ܡܲܫܘܼܐܸܠܹܗ ܐܸܢ ܒܸܬ ܐܬܹܝ ܗܘܵܘ *he asked if they would come* is more usual than ܡܲܫܘܼܐܸܠܹܗ: ܒܸܬ ܐܬܹܝܬܘܿܢ *he asked: Will you come?*

(3) The use of ܬܲܡܵܐ *there,* ܠܵܟܵܐ *here* etc., is in these cases often very confusing. Thus ܐܡܝܼܪܹܗ: ܒܸܬ ܐܵܙܠܸܢ ܬܲܡܵܐ *he said: I will go there = he said he would come here.*

(4) Before the oratio recta ܕ is often inserted: as, *I said ye are gods* = ܐܡܝܼܪܝ ܕܐܲܠܵܗܹ̈ܐ ܝܘܲܬܘܿܢ St John x. 34. The same thing is common in O.S. ܐܸܡܪܹܬ ܕܐܲܠܵܗܹ̈ܐ ܐܲܢ̱ܬܘܿܢ.

ADVERBS.

ܒܶܠܓܶܕܶܐ

§ 67. [The following list includes several adverbial expressions which cannot strictly be called adverbs.]

ܐܕܺܝܐ U. *now*, or ܐܕܺܝܘܗ Ti. MB. or ܐܕܺܝ MB. or ܐܕܺܝ U. (oxytone), or ܕܺܝ U. or ܕܺܝܢܐ K. or ܐܗܐ Al. or ܐܕܺܝܗܐ K. (= ܐܕܺܝ ܗܐ, § 12, = ܗܐ ܗܘܐ) or ܕܺܝܢܐ K. (= ܐܕܺܝܢܐ? Nöld.) or ܕܝܘܢܐ Al. or ܠܗܕܐ Al. (= ܠܗܐ). So ܗܠ ܐܕܺܝ *so far*, ܡܢ ܩܕܡ ܐܕܺܝ *ago, already*.

ܐܕܝܘܡ *to-day* U. K. Z. or ܐܘܕܝܘܡ Gaw. Sal. or ܝܘܡܢܐ ܐܕܝܘܡ (ܝܘܡܢ ܗܘܐ, f. for m.) or ܐܠܝܘܡ Tkh. = O.S. ܝܘܡܢܐ.

ܐܕܠܠܝܐ U. *to-night* (ܠ = ܒ) or ܒܕܠܠܝܐ K. (= ܗܕܺܝ ܠܠܝܐ) or ܒܗ ܠܠܝܐ or ܠܠܝܐ ܕܗܐ. In N.S. ܠܠܝܐ is fem., see § 17. In Z. ܠܠܝܐ, ܒܕܠܠܝܐ being used absolutely for ܠܠܝܐ.

ܐܗܫܥܬܐ U. *this time, now*, or ܐܗܐ ܥܕܢܐ K. or ܐܗܐ ܗܕܬܐ U. or ܐܺܝ ܗܕܬܐ Ti. or ܐܓܕܕܐ K. (= ܗܘܐ + ܓܕܐ, § 28. 2).

ܐܘܣܓܝ U. *so, so much, so many* (considered rather colloquial), thus, ܐܘܣܓܝ ܠܘܗܐ ܕ *so great that*. In K. ܐܣܓܘܬܐ (see ܐܣܓܝ) or ܗܕܟ Kurd. (not ܗܕܟܐ as Stod. Nöld. ?).

ܐܘܡܚܕܐ or 'ܘܐ U. *topsy-turvy* (rare); also *endways*, = ܘܟܗܬܐ.

ܐܘܦ, *also, even*: or ܐܦ K. as O.S., in Al. ܗܡ (see below); hence ܐܘܦ ܒܝܓ K. or usually ܐܦ ܒܝܓ *not one* [in U. ܒܝܓ ܗܘܐ]. ܐܘܦ ܟܠ U. ܐܦ ܟܠ K. *not even*.

§ 67]   ADVERBS.   157

ܐܸܣܓ̰ܝ U. *only*, or ܐܸܣܓܘܼܢܹܗ Sal. or ܐܸܣܓܘܼܗ Sal. Baz Al. In Al. ܘܿܚܸܕ is used, coming after the word qualified.

ܐܸܒܝܼܕ *at last*, Z.

ܐܸܒܝܼܕܢܵܐ U. ܐܸܣܝܼܕܢܵܐ K. as O.S. *again, after this*. In Z. ܐܸܒܝܼܕ (*khîn*) and ܐܸܒܝܼܕܹܝܢ = *then*. See § 21 (3).

ܐܸܫܝܼܕܢܹܐ or ܐܸܒܝܼܕܹܝܢ or ܐܸܒܝܼܕ (as O.S.) *finally*.

ܐܸܟܵܐ U. K. Z. as O.S. *where*, or ܐܸܟܵܐ Q. Sal. Gaw. and U. sometimes (first Zlama). When followed by ܗܘ, ܐܝܠܹܗ, ܐܝܢܵܐ, or ܫܟܝܼܒܹܐ it is often shortened to ܟܵܐ as ܟܵܐ ܝܠܹܗ ؟ *where is he?* (also in a dependent clause). Also with ܠ (ܠܐܸܟܵܐ etc.) = *whither*, with ܡܶܢ = *whence or which way*.

ܐܸܒܝ ܟܠܵܚܸܕ *usually, mostly, on the whole*.

ܐܸܝܡܵܓ̰ܝ *when?* or ܐܸܡܘܿܕ Ti. (O.S. ܐܸܡܓ̰ܝ), or ܐܸܡܣܹܒ ܐܸܕܵܢܵܐ, or ܐܸܡܚܕܵܢܵܐ U. or ܐܸܣܝܼܕ ܐܸܕܵܢܵܐ K. or ܐܸܣܓ̰ܝ ܐܸܕܵܢܵܐ K. So ܟܡܵܐ ܐܸܝܡܵܓ̰ܝ *how long?*

ܐܸܒܝܼܢ U. K. *then* = εἶτα. In O.S. ܐܸܒܝܼܢ and so rarely K., according to the rule by which Greek τ = ܛ, while θ = ܬ.

ܐܸܟܵܐ K. Q. *here*, or Sal. ܐܸܓܵܐ, or ܐܸܓܘܼܢܹܗ Tkh. (in U. ܟܠܲܟܵܐ see p. 164) = O.S. ܗܿܘ or usually ܗܿܘܓܵܐ. So Chald. הָכָא.

ܟܠܲܟܕܸ U, *especially*, Arab. Pers. (proparoxytone), or ܚܒܸ ܘܿܗܝ U.: ܚܒܸ ܘܿܓܸ K.

ܐܸܟܟܵܕ U. (accented on first and last) *immediately*, Turk. Pers. (= *hand over hand*) = ܐܸܒܝܼܕ ܐܸܒܝܼܕ K. as O.S. or ܐܸܒܝܼܕ ܓܒܸܕ K.; also ܕܸܒ̰ܨܵܥܬܐ U. Pers. (lit. *in the hour*); or ܘܫܵܥܬܐ MB. or ܚܸܒܝܼܟܹܝܗ Tkh. or ܓܸܣܠܟܹܝܗ Ti. or ܡܝܼܓ̰ܟܠܲܕܹܝܗ Al. Arab.; or ܕܸܚܡܝܼܢܸܕ.

ܠܟܝܣܐ U. *down*, or ܒܝܠܟܝܣܐ Sal. or ܠܟܝܣܐ Al. (O.S. ܠܟܣܐ). Also ܠܟܝܠܟܝܣܐ, whether motion downwards is meant or not, and ܕܠܟܝܣܐ. So ܡܢ ܠܕ *from beneath* (all ܐ).

ܐܢܟܣ U. *only just, scarcely*, Turk. Kurd. In K. ܗܕܝ or ܗܕܝ ܗܕ.

ܐܕܝܟܐ ܒܗܐ *hereabouts*.

ܓܝ ܓܐ *doubtless*, Pers. Also ܓܝ ܕܠܓ (hard Kap).

ܐܕܝܟܐ ܒܗܘ *thereabouts*.

ܗܘܣ U. or ܒܝܕ K. MB. Gaw. Al. Z. *more*, Pers.; sign of the comparative; occasionally used to qualify verbs: as ܗܘܣ ܣܒܕ ܓܐ ܒܙܕ *love will increase more*. But in this case it would be more usual to use ܗܘܣ ܘܒܪ, p. 161.

ܩܬܟ U. Q. *therefore*, or ܗܘܗ ܒܗ ܕܠܗ or ܗܘܗ ܒܗ ܕܟܕ or ܗܘܗ ܒܗ ܕܠܗ ܐܗ U. K. or ܐܗ ܒܗ ܗܘܗ U. or ܗܘܗ ܕܟ ܕܠܗ U. K. or ܐܗ ܗܘܪ Sal. or ܐܗ ܗܕ Sal. or ܐܗ ܗܕܟ U. or ܐܗ ܗܘܗ U.; or ܡܕܗܘܟ K. or ܗܘܟ Ti. or ܗܘܟ ܠܟܕ K. See ܗܘܟ p. 160, and for the prepositions § 68.

ܒܘܓܢܝ K. *the year before last* (perhaps for ܒܢܝ *at the seasons*, i.e. lit. *at an indefinite time*, § 88 *g*). In U. ܐܬܟ ܐܣܕܟܐ lit. *the other year*, cf. ܐܣܕܟܐ ܩܡܕ *below*. In Al. ܐܠܟܐ (cf. ܐܠܟܐ *three?*). These also mean *the year after next*.

ܒܘܓܢܝ U. K. *last year, next year* (perhaps for ܘܓܢܝ ܕܐ *at those seasons*, i.e. *at a definite time*), in Sal. pron. *bazūghni*. Also ܗܕܒܝܕܗ (ܕܐܗܡܐ) ܟܢܟܐ. In Al. ܓܕܗܝܡ, in Ti. ܟܗܡܝܓ = O.S. ܒܐܗܩܕܝ or Chald. אשתקד, (for ܟܢܟܐ ܩܕܡܢܟܐ?).

[In Ti. they say ܗܘܗ ܠܗ ܒܘܓܢܝ for *three years ago* = U. ܗܠܟܐ ܟܢܝ ܡܢ ܐܕܡܪ ܐܕܢܝ; and ܐܗ ܒܘܓܢܝ ܒܘܓܢܝ for *four years ago*.]

ܒܦܲܠܓܹܗ *in the midst* (pron. ܒ = ܦ U.) or ܒܒܦܲܠܓܹܗ § 16 (ii) *a*.

ܒܪܲܡܫܵܐ U. *in the evening*, or ܒܪܲܡܫܵܐ K. with second Zlama sound in both forms [both are also substantives, § 16, with plural as §§ 18, 19], or ܒܪܲܡܫܵܐ Q.

ܒܲܠܟܵܐ U. *perhaps*, Pers. or ܒܲܠܟܝ K. Al., Turk. Kurd. or ܟܹܐ ܗܵܘܹܐ ܕ or ܗܵܘܹܐ ܕ [even in the middle of a clause; as ܐܸܢ ܟܠܗܘܢ ܗܵܘܹܐ ܕܡܲܢܫܝ ܠܘܟ *if perchance all forget you*], εἰ τύχοι = ܡܛܘܟܵܐ p. 152.

ܒܡܫܝܚܵܐ lit. *by Christ*, and ܗܐ ܒܐܲܠܵܗܐ lit. *yes, by God*, Ti. are little stronger than *indeed*, esp. in K. So the negative:—ܠܐ ܒܐܲܠܵܗܐ ܠܐ U. or ܠܐ ܒܐܲܠܠܐ ܠܐ Ti. or ܠܐ ܒܐܲܠܵܗ ܠܐ Tkh.

ܒܢܲܦܫܘܗܝ U. Q. *alone* (*by himself*), or ܒܢܲܦܫܗ K. Z. or ܠܚܘܕܝܗ Ti. Al. or ܒܠܚܘܕܝܗ Al. [so O.S. but with pl. affixes]. So for the other persons, § 20 (6).

ܒܣ U. *then* (causal), *therefore* Pers. Kurd. or ܗܫܡܵܐ Ti. ܗܫܡܵܐ Sh. or ܐܕܠܵܐ K. or ܒܕܝܢ Al. (not so emphatic as ܒܣ ܕܗܵܪܵܐ). For ܘܒܣ Al. see ܐܣܝܒ above. ܒܣ is used somewhat redundantly in such a phrase as the following ܐܸܢ ܐܵܗܵܐ ܡܣܢܝܩܐ ܠܘܡ ܒܝܠܗ : ܒܣ ܗܘ ܡܣܢܝܩܐ ܕܟܐ ܒܘܫ ܠܘܡ ܒܝܠܗ *If this thing is necessary, that thing is much more so.*

ܒܟܒܟ U. *together, equally*, or ܒܟܒܟ K., Pers. Turk.

ܒܸܬ : ܒܹܕ : ܒ sign of the future, §§ 31, 46 s.v. ܒܵܥܐ.

ܒܩܲܣܕ *by chance*, also *probably* (? St.) Arab. (not common).

ܒܬܲܨܵܕܘܦ *by chance*, from ܬܨܵܕܦ *to happen, to meet* (Arab. word).

ܒܬܪ ܗܵܕܟܼ U. *hereafter*, or ܒܬܪ ܗܵܕܟܼܵܐ U. ܒܬܪ ܗܵܕܟܼ Al. ܒܬܪ ܗܵܕܟܼ Al.

ܠܥܶܠ ܚܰܕ Ti. Al. *upwards* [or ܚܰܕ?] proparoxytone, or ܒܕܶ ܠܟܶܠ Ti.

ܠܬܰܚܬ ܚܰܕ Ti. Al. *downwards*, proparoxytone.

ܓܳܗܶܐ ܓܳܗܶܐ or ܓܳܗܶܐ ܓܰܕܰܓܰܕ or ܓܳܗܶܐ ܢܓܶܕ ܢܓܶܕ *sometimes, occasionally*, § 28 (4).

ܠܓܰܘ *within*, see p. 168, also ܡܶܢ ܠܓܰܘ *from within*: with ܠ *to the inside*.

ܒܰܠܕܰܓ or ܓܰܠ *quickly, soon, early*. In the first sense chiefly U. = ܡܠܗܰܟ K. or ܘܰܟܶܬ Ti. which also = *certainly*. ܡܶܢ ܒܰܠܕܰܓ = *a long time ago* = ܡܶܢ ܘܓܶܕ Al.

ܕܶ ܕܶ Z. *hither and thither* = ܐܰܟܐ U. ܐܠܟܶܐ ܠܟܶܐ ܠܗܰܘ ܠܟܶܕ

ܕܐܶܟܝ *how* or ܕܶܐܝ when by itself (= ܕܰܐܝܒܰ?) or ܕܐܶܓܗܰܐ: ܕܶܐܝ Ti. See § 73 or ܡܳܓܶܒ K. (= ܡܳܕ ܚܕܽܘܒ?) rare.

ܕܽܘܗܽܘܢ Z. *still, again*.

ܕܰܝܶܨ U. K. *always*, or ܕܰܝܡܰܢ, ܕܰܝܡܰܢ K., Kurd. Arab.; or ܗܳܡܶܨ U. Pers. (ܡ Az.) or ܚܰܠ ܘܓܶܕ Al. (O.S.) or (ܚܠܘܒ) or ܚܰܠ ܚܕܶܢܰܐ U. K.

ܗܳܕܶܡ *in vain*, Arab. Pers. or ܗܳܕܶܦ K. See ܣܳܘܕܶܒ.

ܗܳܕܝ K. *slowly, gently* (Zlama second sound) Kurd. = ܢܝܫܰܐ U. as O.S., see p. 166 (whence ܢܝܫܳܢܶܟ *very slowly*); or ܗܰܡܓܽܘܕ U. Pers. or ܓܰܗܡܶܪ K. or ܚܓܶܪ Ti.

ܗܳܕܝ *so, thus*, or ܗܳܕܶܐ or ܗܳܕܝ. These seem to be the O.S. ܗܳܕܶܐ or ܗܳܕܶܐ, the fem. of ܗܳܕ *this*. The ܕ (which is soft, not hard as in Nöld. § 85) is a common Aramaic addition. So ܗܳܕܶܓ *thus, so, such* (ܓ = ܟ) U. K. Z. or in Ṭal ܗܳܕܶܓ (ܓ sound) or ܗܳܕܶܐ Al. (= ܗܳܕܶܐ ܗܳܕ?) or ܐܽܕܶܓ U. So also ܗܳܕܶܐ ܢܶܓ or ܗܳܕܶܓ ܢܶܓ *so much*. See also § 23.

§ 67]   ADVERBS.   161

ܗܘܡܨܕܐ *at first* (rare). Qy. past part. of ܡܕܡܨ U. (= ܡܕܡܨ K.) *to believe?*

ܗܢ ܟܠܗ U. K. Q. *then*, or ܗܢ ܟܠܗ Al. or ܟܓܕ ܕܗܢ ܟܠܗ Ti. or ܗܢ ܒܕܘܢ or ܗܢ ܗܦܕ or ܗܢ ܒܡܠܟ. Also with ܡܕ. So in Ti. we have ܩܕܡ ܕܗܢ ܟܠܗ *before that* = ܩܕܡ ܕܗܢ ܒܕܘܢ U.

ܗܘ U. *not at all, never* (with a negative), as ܗܘ ܠܐ ܝܕܥ U. (= ܗܕ K.) *I will never allow* (see under ܫܒܩ). So ܗܘ ܟܠܗ U. = ܓܒ ܟܠܗ K. Z. Q. *never*, ܗܘ (Turk.) and ܓܒ (Kurd.) being also adjectives = *no* or *any*.

ܗܠܐ U. *yet*, Arab. Turk. or ܗܠܐ ܐܕܟܝ Sal. (see ܐܕܟܝ) or ܗܕ or ܗܕ K. Al. (also *now*: O.S. ܗܕ or ܗܕܐ) or ܚܕܝ Al. Arab.

ܗܠܟܕ or ܐܠܟܕ *certainly, of course*, Arab. Also ܗܠܟܕ or ܐܠܟܕ.

ܗܡ in Al. *also*, Pers. In U. K. as conjunction, repeated, *both... and*.

ܗܕ *just, certainly*, Pers.; with negative *never*, esp. in K., as ܗܕ ܒܗ ܐܙܠ *I will certainly go*, ܗܕ ܠܐ ܐܬܐ *he shall never come*. ܗܕ ܗܟܕ *just thus*, ܗܕ ܗܘ *just that* = *the same*, § 25 (8). Nöldeke gives ܗܕ ܠܐ ܟܠ Pers. Turk. *never*.

ܝ U. or ܝܗ K. Z. or ܝܗ Z. *also*, Kurd. This follows the word qualified. Often used with ܫܒܩ or ܐܦ, thus ܐܢܐ ܐܦ ܝ *I also*.

ܙܘܕܐ *more*, or ܙܘܕܐ ܕܡܣ (ܚܒ) or ܕܡܣ ܘܡܕܙ Ti. (from N.S. ܙܘܕ *to increase*, an Arabic word), or ܚܕܝܕ Al. These are also used as substantives = *more*.

ܗܣܘܬ K. *certainly, on that account*.

S. GR.   21

ܣܓ݂ܕܐ Al. *together*, or ܓܼܣܓ݂ܕܐ K. or ܓܣܓ݂ܕܐ Al. or ܠܓܼܣܓ݂ܕܐ K. or ܡܓܣܓ݂ܕܐ K. or ܡܚܘܣܓ݂ Sal. U.; or from the Persian we have ܒܚܘܕ݂ܟܐ U. (or ܕ or ܡ), pron. in Sal. *ukhdali* etc. See § 15.

ܢܲܓ݂ܕܵܐ *rather, somewhat, a little*. See § 28 (9) for variations. Also ܚܝܼܐ Al. K. ܚܒܪ K. (below), ܢܲܩܸܣ K. Al. ܚܘܡܨܝ Al. ܚܡܕܐ Ti. So ܢܲܓ݂ܕܵܐ ܦܵܫܐ *almost*, lit. *a little remains* (e.g. ܚܘܡܪܐ ܦܵܫܐ ܢܲܓ݂ܕܵܐ *almost black*); in K. ܦܵܫܐ ܢܲܓ݂ܕܼܓ݂ܕ݂. Also expressed thus: ܢܲܓ݂ܕܵܐ ܩܸܕ ܠܗ ܕܠܐ ܕܐܬܐ ܠܝ *I nearly did not come*. So ܕܢܫܥ ܡܠܗ ܩܝܢܗ ܕܚܐ *he is far from thinking.*

ܣܲܚܕܸܒ U. *in vain* or *gratis*, Kurd. or ܦܠܟ Al. K., Kurd. (Nöld. St. give ܦܠܟ Pers.) or ܡܲܓܵܢ U. (*gratis*); see ܐܘܚܐ.

ܒܝܠܲܢܝܼ U. *in short*, or ܣܘܟܲܢܝ Sal., Arab. (both proparoxytone).

ܢܲܕܒܝܼܐ or ܢܲܕܒܝܢܐ *upside down* K. *inside out* U. or ܐܕ݂ܩܐ U. Ti. (both senses) or ܩܘܡܪܐ ܩܘܡܨܢܗ (= ܩܘܡܪܐ ܣܚܵܢܐ) *edge, edge lowermost*). The form ܣܚܵܢܐ *lower*, is seen in ܕܓܵܐ ܕܓܸܢܗ (below) and in ܥܘܡܪܐ ܣܚܵܢܐ lit. *lower church*, the name of a church in Ti. in the Zab valley; it is another form of ܚܣܵܢܐ K., O.S.; cf. the verb ܫܚܢ *to be abased*, Al. and also ܠܟܸܣܠ above.

ܢܘܡܐ ܡܢ ܝܘܡܐ K. (U. ܗ݅) *from day to day.*

ܣܲܚܕܝܐ U. *the day before yesterday* or *the day after to-morrow*, or ܚܘܡܐ ܣܓ݂ܕܐ Ti. or ܢܲܕܓܐ ܚܘܡܐ Tkh. § 61. So ܓܸܕܢܲܓ݂ܕܐ *the week before last (after next).*

ܒܟܲܠܟܸܕ K. entirely, quite, very, or ܒܟܲܠܟܸܕܝ K., Kurd.; or ܓܼܓ U. Turk. (so ܓܼܓ ܕܸܕ *extremely*) or ܗܸܕ ܓܼܓ U. (*very emphatic*) or ܢܓܼܓ Al. Arab. or ܟܵܡܣܘ U. (also an adj. = *clean*); or ܟܵܡܨܐ (also an adj.

= *entire*). For emphasis ܟ̈ܡ is often put by itself at the end of a sentence. See ܕܘܟܐ p. 167.

ܡܥܢܐ *that is*, Arab.

ܡܚܩܩ K. *certainly*, or ܡܚܩܝܩ U., Arab.

ܟܐ U. MB. Sp. Sal. or ܓܐ Q. Tkh. Sal. or ܟ́ Al. Z. Sal. sign of the habitual present, § 31. Origin, Chald. קָא = γε, § 119?

ܟܡ *a little, somewhat*, Tkh. or ܟܝܡ Ti. (contrast ܟ̈ܡ above), or ܟܡ U., Kurd. See ܒܕܟܐ.

ܟܠܝܘܡ *daily*, so O.S.; also ܟܠܝܘܡܐ Ti. and ܟܠܝܘܡܐ : ܟܘܡ ܝܘܡ Al.

ܟܡܐ *how much, how*, so O.S.; or ܕܟܡܐ Al. or ܡܕܟܡܐ Al. or ܡܕܝܡ ܟܡܐ Al. Thus: ܟܡܐ ܛܒܐ *how good* = O.S. ܡܐ ܛܒ. ܟܡܐ ܓܘܪܐ ܝܠܗ *how great he is!* ܟܡܐ ܐܢܫܐ ܓܘܪܐ ܝܠܗ *how great a man he is!*

ܠܐ *not*, as O.S., or ܠܐ (not Al.) prefixed to certain parts of the verb only, § 33 [thus ܠܐ ܝܠܗ ܛܒܐ ܘܠܐ ܒܝܫܐ *it is neither good nor bad*]. ܠܐ ... ܠܐ = *neither...nor;* a third ܠܐ then is often used with the verb, pleonastically. ܠܐ has the second Zlama sound and perhaps should be ܠܐ ܗܘܝ = ܠܝ? Cf. O.S. ܠܘ (West Syrian ܠܘ) = ܠܐ ܗܘ? Nöld. conjectures ܠܐ ܐܝܬ = ܠܐ. Or perhaps this is the origin of it: ܠܐ + the substantive verb (ܠܐ ܝܘܢ etc.) takes the pronunciation *lé-win;* and then by false analogy ܠܝ or ܠܐ is placed before the present tense. ܠܐ is thus used with ܡܝܕܝ in Ti. ܡܘܕܝ ܒܥܝܬ? ܡܝܕܝ ܠܐ— *What do you want? Nothing.*

ܠܐܗ ܓܒܐ *on this side, this way*, or ܠܐܗܐ ܓܒܬܐ Ti. (fem. form of

ܓܒܐ = O.S. ܓܒܐ *side*), rarely without ܠ; also with ܡܢ. See ܕܝ ܕܝ p. 160.

ܠܟܐ *here*, U. (see ܐܟܐ) *hither*, U. K. (the ܠ coalesces) or ܠܟܐ ܗܘ K. or ܠܓܕܘܗܝ MB. or ܠܓܕܘܗܝ K. or ܠܓܐܟܐ Ti. So ܠܟܘܓܐ K. *towards this way* = ܓܒܐ ܠܗܐ ܟܐ U. Also ܡܟܐ U. K. *this way, hence*, and similarly the rest (ܡܟܪܝ Sal.).

ܠܓܘܕ U. Ti. *outside* (ܕ) Kurd. or ܠܓܘܕܗ K. or ܠܓܕܝ (or ܠܓܕܣ ?) Al. or ܠܓܕܝ Al. (so ܓܕܝܐ U. K. Al. *outer*) or ܠܓܕ Al.

ܠܟܬܪ ܗܘ *backwards, behind* (ܗ K.), or with the other affixes, also ܠܟܬܪ K. or ܠܟܬܪܗ or ܠܟܬܪܣ (common). Sometimes without ܠ; often with ܡܢ. Also with ܠ = *towards the rear*.

ܠܓܒܐ ܗܘ U. *on that side, that way, over there*, rarely without ܠ; also with ܡܢ; or ܗܘܕܟ Ti. It also means *abroad* (= ܠܗܘܕܗ much used in this sense).

ܠܗܘܦܢܝܬܐ K. MB. (or with Dalath, § 69. 2 *b*) *in that direction*. So ܡܗܘܦܢܝܬܐ *from that direction*.

ܠܟܕܘܙܐ K. MB. or ܣܓܝ ܟܕܘܙܐ *for a little time*, § 28 (9), or ܗܘ ܠܟܕܘܙܐ (rare with Lamadh).

ܠܩܕܡܣ *forwards*, or ܠܩܕܡܐ or ܠܩܕܡܘܗܝ or with the other affixes.

ܡܢܐܕܝܠܟܬܪܗ U. *henceforward* (lit. *from now to after it*); or ܡܢܐܕܝܢ ܠܟܬܪܗ U. (ܡܢ coalesces) or ܡܢܐܕܝܢ ܠܟܬܪܗ or ܡܢܐܕܝܠܟܬܪܗ U. or ܡܢܐܕܝܢ ܠܟܬܪ K. or ܡܢܐܘܓܐ ܠܟܬܪ MB. or simply ܡܢܐܕܝܢ (see above ܐܕܝܢ). So also ܡܢ ܗܘ ܠܟܬܪܗ *after that, thereafter*.

§ 67] ADVERBS.

מְגַד U. Ti. *indeed*, or מְגִידְ Sal., Arab. Kurd.; often with ܢ sound as Kurd. [used both in question and answer, thus: ... ? מְגַד Q. *Indeed?* Ans. *Yes, really*]; or מְדֻמִּימִ K. or דֻמִי U. or דֻמִי Sal. [these are the imperatives of the verb מְדֻמִּימִ, מְדֻמִּימִ *to believe*, § 83 D,] or שְׁגַדלְמַד, (also adj. = *certain*).

מְדֻוׂרְשָׁא U. (*môrisha*, proparoxytone) *in the morning*, lit. *from that head*, or מֶז דֻמ or מְגַדדְּנֻמֶז Ti.; or שְׁדֻמִדָ K. or שְׁדֻמִדָ U. (lit. *the anticipation*, from מַחֻדֶר), טִי קֻדְ Al., O.S., or חֶנֻדְבִ Z. or חֶנֻדְבִ Z. or מֻחֻנ Z. These also (exc. the Ti. and Al. forms) mean *to-morrow* (but not *yesterday*), cf. Scottish *the morn, the morn's morn*, German *morgen*. See בֻמְדֻמַ below.

מְלִילַד Ti. *in early morning*, lit. *from the night*. So מְלִילַנְפַד Ti. *very early* (from the little nights) or דְּלַלְנַפֶד Ti. MB. Tergawar or מְגַדלַד K. lit. *from the watch* (גְּדֻל K. *to change*, Arab.). [Also בְּבִהַפְנֻלַ U. or דְּמַגְדַנְשַׁל דְּמַכַּנְדַךַ Ti. חֶנַכַּדַךַ דְּלַךַ לַלַךַ U.]

מֵן לְנַזַה *secretly*.

מְגַדדֻך K. *yet* (not temporal), *again*, usually מְגַדדֻך (ד silent in U.) or מְגַדדֻך Al. or מְגַדדֻכַדְבִ Ti.; lit. *from the head*;—also לַךַ לַ לַ לְבַדַךַ U. (לְבַדַךַ K. Al. or לְבַדַךַ Tkh. Al. Z.) or דַהֻדְבִ לַךַ לַ U. (דְּהַגְדַךַ K.) [also ... לַךַ];—also מְבַלִגַךַ U. Ti. or מֻדְבַלִגַךַ Sal. or מְגַדַךַ or מְגַדַךַדְבִ Ti. *Once again* is שְׁגַד לַךַ לַ לְבַדַךַ U. (K. similar).

מְחַנְלַ U. *for example*, or מְחַנְלַד K.

נַלִמְחַל U. *suddenly*, or שְׁגַדַךַ מֵן Al. or בַ לַךַ לַ K. [Qy.

= ܐܳܕܳܐ ܗܿܘ *at that time?*], or ܫܰܩܠܳܟ̣ܶܒ;—also ܡܶܓ̇ܕܳܘܠܳܕܶܒ or ܡܶܓ̇ܶܠܳܕܶܒ
Al. rarely U. or ܡܳܘܡܳܕܶܒ Sal. These = O.S. ܡܢ ܗܳܕ̇ܶܐ.

ܟܶܒ added on to the verb to strengthen it, § 31. In O.S. it = *indeed* (also ܟܺܝ).

ܟ̇ܶܡܫܳܐ O.S. *quietly, by degrees*, often repeated; also ܟ̇ܡܫܳܐ ܟ̇ܡܫܳܐ.

ܚܰܓܳܘܓ ܟ̇ܘܟ *probably* (ܟ̇ܘܟ = *trust*, N.S.).

ܠܳܥܳܠܳܕ U. Q. Sal. Gaw. *up, upwards*, or ܠܓܶܠ K. or ܠܓܰܠ MB. (all these also with ܒ, ܠ or ܡܢ), or ܠܥܶܠ Al. as O.S.; ܠܥܶܠ Z. *upwards* (second Zlama).

ܦܰܠܓ̇ܳܐ *by halves*, § 27.

ܩܳܡܳܕܠܠܳܐ ܕܩܳܡܳܕܠܳܐ *gradually*, § 77 (2).

ܩܰܕܺܝ *well*, not Ti., (pronunciation, § 7) [also an adj. = *good*]; in Ti. ܒܰܟ̇ܝܪܳܐ (elsewhere adj. = *beautiful*); in Al. ܩܕܰܘܐ. Perhaps ܩܰܕܺܝ is from ܩܕܺܐ *to be clear*: ܩܕܳܐ *pure*. For the termination see p. 168.

ܩܰܠܟ U. Sh. *why* or ܩܰܠ ܟܰܠ ܡܳܗ U. or ܩܰܠܟ ܩܰܠ ܡܳܕܗ Tkh. ܩܰܠܟ Ti. or ܡܳܘܕܺܝ ܩܰܠܟ Ash. Q. or ܩܰܠ ܡܳܕܗ Al. or ܩܰܡܝ Al. or ܡܳܘܕܰܐ Al. or ܡܳܗ Ti. (= ܠܡܳܗ?). For ܡܳܘܕܺܝ etc. see § 13.

ܩܳܕܰܡ U. Z. Sal. ܩܳܡܘܢ Sal. Al. ܩܰܡ Al. sign of the past, § 31.

ܩܰܕܡܳܝܳܐ *first*, or ܩܰܕܡܰܝܳܐ U. or ܩܰܕܡܳܝܳܐ Al. § 27.

ܩܳܘܡܳܐ U. *yesterday, to-morrow*, § 61, from ܩܰܕܶܡ *to anticipate*. Or ܩܡܰܠ K. Al. Z.: rare in U. (O.S. ܩܰܡܶܠ or ܩܰܡܶܠ). If a distinction is necessary ܕܚܰܒܶܕܳܐ *that is past*, ܕܐܳܬܶܐ *that is coming*, must be added. So ܩܰܕ ܒܳܐ ܕܐܳܬܶܐ *next week*, ܩܰܕ ܒܳܐ ܕܚܰܒܶܕܳܐ *last week*. See above, ܩܰܕܡܳܐ.

ܡܘܕܟ݂ O.S. *near, nearly*, e.g. ܟܕ݂ ܬܠܬܐ ܫܢܐ ܡܘܕܟ݂ *nearly three years*.

ܚܡܐ K. *at all*, or ܦܘ Tkh. or ܦܘ K. or ܦܘ Ti. ܦܝܕ Al., Kurd. Usually with a negative, = *never, not at all*. Often repeated, esp. in Ti.: ܦܘ ܘܦܘ *certainly not, nothing at all*, or ܦܘ ܘܚܡܐ.

ܕܕ݂ *very* [see § 25 (7) for the adjective], or ܕ݂ܘܕ݂ U. or ܕܕ݂ Q. Gaw. (first Zlama); or ܓ݂ܬܝܕ Al., Arab.

ܕܕ݂ ܟܠܐ *often*, see above. ܘܕ݂ ܘܕ݂ܘ ܬܘܒ *oftener*.

ܕܥܫ *easily, comfortably*, also an adj. = *comfortable*, and subst. = *ease*, Pers.

ܪܚܩܐ *afar*, also with ܡܢ; Al. and O.S. ܕ݂ܘܪܚܩܐ.

ܕ݂ܓܼ݂ ܕ݂ܓ݂ܒ݂ܢܫ *head downwards*, U. or ܕ݂ܓ݂ ܣܡܟܐ K. rarely ܕ݂ܓ݂ ܐܣܟܪܐ K. (see above ܟܘܡܨ ܟܘܡܓ݂ܢܫ under ܒܕܢܝܗ); or ܡܓ݂ܝܣܟܕ݂ Al. from ܢܨܝ O.S. Al. *to descend*, which is also ܢܨܝ N.S.

ܥܕ݂ܝܠܐ *endways*.

ܨܩܝܟ݂ *in a shuffling or gliding manner*, § 83 A (2).

ܐܡܕܝ Ti. or ܐܡܨ U. K. *there* (O.S. ܐܡܨ = ܐܡܨ). Also ܐܡܓ݂ܘܡܿ U. ܐܡܨܘܡܿ U. K. ܐܡܨܘܡܿ K. ܐܡܓ݂ܘܡܕ Tkh. MB. ܐܡܓ݂ܘܡܿܘ Al. ܐܡܨ Sp. Sal. Also with ܠ = *thither*, with ܡܢ = *thence or that way*.

Notes. (1) The old adverbs in ܐܝܬ are not now used colloquially, except only ܡܘܕܟ K. Al. *in Syriac* (the language), ܥܪܒܝܬ Al. *in Arabic*, ܟܘܪܕܟ K. Al. *in Kurdish*, ܐܘܕܟ U. *in Turkish*, ܦܪܣܟܐ U. *in Persian*; which appear to stand for ܡܘܕܝܐ etc. These are used also as substantives. [When the old adverbs are used, as in theological discussions, they are oxytone.]

(2) Adjectives, especially those most commonly in use and those which do not change in the feminine, are very often used as adverbs; in U. K. chiefly in the masculine, in Al. in both genders. Thus ܗܕܘܡܝܐ ܗܕܘܡܝܐ ܓܐܡܪܢܐ ܡܘ ܀ U. K. *Verily, verily, I say* = ܕܐܡܪܚ ܗܕܘܡܝܚܐ ܗܕܘܡܝܚܐ Al.; ܩܡܬ ܟܐ ܩܠܘܠܐܝܬ K. Al. *she rose quickly*, ܡܕܚܒܐ ܣܩܘܒܐ *they were badly ill*, St Mark i. 32 = ܒܝܫܐܝܬ ܟܒܝܒܝܢ O.S.

(3) There are a large number of adverbs, adjectives, and substantives in ܝܒ, some of which Nöldeke suggests (§ 54) may come from the old ܝܐܝܬ, dropping ܐ. They may also be the abstract termination ܘܬܐ of which the ܘ falls in colloquial speech in U., § 78. Or it may be the Kurdish ending though in some cases added on to words which are not Kurdish. Examples: ܗܿܣܢܒܝ U. or ܗܣܢܒܝ K. *easy*, the latter Kurdish, ܒܘܫܒܝ *excessive, abundant*, from ܒܘܫ (above), ܡܕܢܒܝ Kurd. *meaning*, more commonly ܡܕܢܬܐ, ܫܘܟܒܝ *bad*, Turk. Pers. ܐܡܝܩܒܝ *sure, certain*, ܟܢܒܝ *tame*, ܗܘܕܡܒܝ *deep blue*, ܨܒܝ *advice*, ܐܒܒܝ *colony*, Kurd. ܗܕܪܢܒܝ *easy*, ܓܪܕܘܒܝ *coffee-coloured*, ܗܘܒܝ *rude, wild*, ܕܕܒܝ *silk*, ܩܠܒܝ *tin*, Turk. Kurd.; and see the above list.

(4) *Too* is usually expressed by the simple adjective, see § 24.

(5) For numeral adverbs see § 28 (2).

(6) *At least, at any rate*, is expressed by ܚܕܐ ܠܐ ܗܘܝܐ ܒ U. or ܚܕܐ ܠܐ ܕܗܘ ܒ K. or ܥܠ ܕܗܘܝܐ U. K. Thus ܚܕܐ ܠܐ ܗܘܝܐ ܒ ܐܢܐ ܐܙܠܟ *I, at any rate, will go*. Prefixed to numerals *at least* may be rendered by ܡܢ ܒܨܘܪܐ ܠܐ *not less than*.

(7) Adverbs are frequently repeated for emphasis: e.g. ܚܒܝܫܐ ܚܒܝܫܐ *slowly*, ܝܠܕܝ ܝܠܕܝ U. *quickly*, ܩܠܘܠܐܝܬ ܩܠܘܠܐܝܬ K. id. So in

O.S.: e.g. ܒܝܫ ܒܝܫ *very evilly;* and so in Turk. etc. From ܕܪܘ *equal, straight,* we have ܕܪܘܐ ܕܪܘ *on exactly equal terms,* used, e.g. of a bill cashed without commission. Cf. § 69 (1).

(8) English adverbs may very frequently be rendered in N.S. by a substantive with ܒ, as ܒܫܪܝܪܘܬܐ *truly,* (so O.S. ܒܫܪܪܐ); ܒܥܣܩܘܬܐ *hardly, with difficulty;* rarely without ܒ. So the comparative ܒܝܫ ܒܥܓܠܘܬܐ (ܒܝܫ) *more hurriedly,* lit. *more in haste.*

(9) ܠܐ is sometimes redundant: thus ܡܘܢܥܠܗ ܠܝ ܕܠܐ ܐܙܠ *I prevented him from going;* ܠܐ ܡܫܩܠܒܝܬ ܠܟܪܣܛܝܢܐ܆ ܗܕܟ ܕܪܕܦܝܬܘܢ ܠܐ ܗܘܝ ܦܝܫܐ ܡܣܝܒܐ *do not persecute the Christians until they have been accused.*—ܗܝܟ, ܗܘ when accompanied by verbs take ܠܐ. Thus ܗܝܟ ܢܫܐ ܠܐ ܚܙܐ ܠܝ (ܗܘ) *I saw no man.* But they may stand without ܠܐ if there is no verb: as ܡܘܕܝ ܥܒܕܠܘܟ ܠܘܟ؟ ܗܝܟ ܡܕܡ *What did you do? Nothing.*

PREPOSITIONS.

ܦܬܓܡܐ ܦܫܝܛܐ

§ 68. *Simple prepositions.*

ܐܝܟ O.S. or ܡܐܟ (*âkh, mâkh,* rarely *ă; ékh, mékh* Al.) or ܡܐܝܟ Al. (*mĭkh*) or ܟ' Al. as Heb.; = *according to, like,* as ܐܝܟ ܕܝܝ *like me,* ܐܝܟ ܢܡܘܣܐ ܕܝܢ *according to our law;* or *about:* ܐܝܟ ܫܥܬܐ ܚܕܐ *about one o'clock.*

ܒ O.S. or ܒܝ Sal. (see ܒܝܕ); = *at:* ܬܐ ܒܫܥܬܐ ܚܡܫܐ *come at five o'clock:* ܡܘܙܒܢܠܗ ܒܬܪܝ ܩܪ̈ܢܐ *he sold it at two qrans;* it denotes a measure, or time when: ܚܕܐ ܒܐܗܐ *one of this measure,*

ܗܕ ܗܕܫܢܐ ܫܢܬܐ *this year* [we may omit the preposition; as ܗܕܒܫܒܐ ܗܘ *come on Monday*]; =*in*: ܒܫܪܪܐܝܬ *in truth*, ܒܥܩܐ *in sorrow* (see ܥܩܐ); or *with*: ܒܗܕܘܡܘܬܐ *with difficulty*, ܒܕܡܥܐ *with many tears* (see ܒܕ); or *of*: ܗܕܒ ܬܪܝܢ ܒܝܪܚܐ *the second of January* (or ܚܕܒ ܒܝܪܚܐ ܗܕܒ ܟܢܘܢ); in K. it is also the sign of the object in a particular case, § 50.

ܒܠܐ *without*, Kurd. Pers.

ܒܠܐ, ܒܠܝ see ܓܠܐ.

ܒܘܬ U. or ܒܓܘ Sal. Az. *for, concerning, about, for the sake of, on account of, because of*: ܡܪܢ ܡܝܬ ܒܘܬ ܕܝܢ *Our Lord died for us*, ܒܘܬ ܪܕܘܦܝܐ *on account of the persecution*, ܒܘܬ ܡܘܕܝ ? *what about?* This preposition probably is ܒ ܘܬܐ, lit. *in the matter of*. Stod. gives two rare forms ܒܘܬ ܕܡܝܪܝ U. *with regard to what I said*, i.e. ܒܘܬܗ = ܒܕܡܥܘܕ K. Cf. § 72, ܒ ܘܬܗ, which is also used as a preposition in the phrase ܒܕܥܝ ܕܟܬܒ or ܒܕܥܝ ܐܢܐ *I believe, in my opinion* (pron. *bad-libi* or *bid-libi*); also ܒܕܥܝ (*bad-di* or *bid-di*). Rarely also with a substantive ܒܕܥܝ ܕܢܫܐ *bad-nâsha, in man's opinion*, [cf. ܗܘ ܒܝܕ ܢܦܠܗ ܕܓܒܪܐ *the cause of a man's falling*.]

ܒܝܕ (ܒ = ܠܐ) not common in K. = O.S. = ܒܝܕ ܒ. Also ܒ (see ܒ) and ܒܝ. It means *by* (of the agent): ܟܠ ܡܕܡ ܒܝܕ ܐܠܗܐ ܐܬܒܪܝ ܠܗ *everything was created by God*. But the full form is often used, especially when attention is called to the hand: ܐܓܪܬܐ ܡܛܝ ܠܗ ܒܝܕ ܬܐܘܡܐ *the letter arrived by the hand of Thomas*, ܟܠ ܡܕܡ ܒܝܕ ܕܐܠܗܐ ܝܠܗ *everything is in the hand (power) of God*, ܒܝܕ ܒܪܐ ܐܬܒܪܝ *created by the Son*.

ܒܹܝܠ (= ܒܹܝܬ݂ ܠ : O.S. ܒܹܝܬ݂) *between, among:* ܒܹܝܠܵܝܗܘܿܢ *between them,* or *among them;* or *including,* or *notwithstanding, in spite of:* ܒܹܝܠ ܠܵܝܼ ܝܼܘܲܚ ܥܸܣܪܵܐ ܢܵܫܹ̈ܐ *including myself we are ten men.* So ܒܹܝܠ ܟܠ *in general,* or *all included,* or *in spite of all.* When in English we have *between...and,* we may repeat ܒܹܝܠ or insert ܠ or simply say ܘ: as ܒܹܝܠܲܢ ܘܒܹܝܠܵܘܟ݂ܘܿܢ *between us and you,* or ܒܹܝܠ ܝܼܫܘܿܥ ܘܫܸܡܥܘܿܢ ; ܒܹܝܠܲܢ ܘܠܵܘܟ݂ܘܿܢ *between Joshua and Simon;* ܒܹܝܠܝܼ ܠܓ݂ܵܢܝܼ *between me and myself,* i.e. *alone.* So O.S. ܒܹܝܬ݂ ܪ̈ܗܘܿܡܵܝܹܐ ܠܦܵܪ̈ܣܵܝܹܐ *between Romans and Persians,* ܒܹܝܬ݂ ܠܵܟ݂ ܠܐܸܡܵܟ݂ ܘܠܐܲܚܘܼܟ݂ *between you and your mother and your brother,* cf. Nöld. O.S.G. § 251. Also O.S. with ܘ for ܠ *id.* But the O.S. ܒܹܝܬ݂ ܦܲܓ݂ܪܵܐ ܠܢܲܦ̮ܫܵܐ *both body and soul* will not stand in N.S.

ܒܹܝܢ (Arab.) or ܒܹܝܢܝ or ܒܹܝܢܵܬ݂ all Al. for ܒܹܝܠ (O.S. ܒܹܝܢܝ or ܒܹܝܢܵܬ݂). Hence ܒܹܝܢܹܗ ܠܓ݂ܵܢܹܗ *between him and himself,* i.e. *alone,* as above.

ܒܠܵܐ (not common) or ܕܠܵܐ (common) as O.S., or ܠܵܐ ܒ݂ Sal.; = *without,* cf. O.S. ܡܢ ܒܠܥܕ *id.*

ܒܵܬ݂ܲܪ K. Sh. MB. as O.S. or ܒܵܬ݂ܲܪ U. Q. Sal. Gaw.; or ܡܢ ܒ݂ or ܡܒ݂; = *after:* ܒܵܬ݂ܲܪ ܬܪܹܝܢ ܝܵܘܡܵܬ݂ܵܐ *after two days;* or *behind:* ܒܵܬ݂ܲܪ ܕܗܵܘ ܛܘܼܪܵܐ *behind that mountain;* or *in* (*after*), ܒܵܬ݂ܲܪ ܬܠܵܬ݂ ܫܵܥܹ̈ܐ *in three hours.*

ܓܵܘ O.S., U. Sp. or ܓܘܿ K. Sal. Sp. (sometimes) or ܒܓ݂ܘܿ K. J. or ܒܓ݂ܵܘ Al.; = *in, in the midst of* (of place only, U. K.: ܒ usually renders *in,* otherwise, though that is also used of place): ܓܵܘ ܐܘܼܪܡܝܼ *in Urmi.* In Al. ܓܵܘ is *by means of* (= ܒܝܲܕ U.), and ܒܓ݂ܵܘ is *in,* or *amongst,* or is the sign of the indirect object (= ܠ, U. K.), as: ܩܵܡܘܼ ܥܒ݂ܝܼܕܘܼܟ݂ ܠܗܵܘܟ݂ ܗܵܕܟ݂ܵܐ ܒܓ݂ܵܘܲܢ؟ Al. *why didst thou do thus to us?*

St Luke ii. 48 (= ܐܰܟ݂ܝܼ U. K.).—In U. K. J. ܓܰܘ, ܓܰܘܶܗ are occasionally used of motion = *into*, though ܓܰܘ is also thus used: ܥܒ݂ܝܼܪܠܹܗ ܓܰܘ ܡܕܝܼܢ݇ܬܵܐ *he entered into the city.*—ܡܶܢ ܓܰܘ or ܡܓܰܘ or ܡܶܢ ܓܵܘ or ܡܓܵܘ *through*, ܗܰܠ ܓܰܘ *up to the inside of*, ܩܵܐ ܓܰܘ *for the inside of* (ܛܠܵܒ݂ ܓܵܘ K.), ܠܓܰܘ *towards the inside of*, etc.

ܕ as O.S. or ܕܝܼ Sal. = *of* (also a relative pronoun and conjunction); sometimes also ܕܝܼܕ in Z. before nouns, see § 70 (5). This preposition is frequently omitted; as ܚܕ݂ܵܐ ܐܘܼܪܚܵܐ ܡܡܲܠܠܘܼܬ݂ܵܐ *a manner of speech;* ܚܕ݂ܵܐ ܛܥܵܢܵܐ ܣܥܵܪܹ̈ܐ *a load of barley;* ܥܹܐܕ݂ܵܐ ܨܠܝܼܒ݂ܵܐ *the festival of the Cross* (Sept. 13, old style): ܚܕ݂ܵܐ ܥܲܝܢܘܼܗܝ U. *one of his eyes.* Perhaps also in some compound words in § 16, ii. *g*, as ܩܫܬܐ ܡܸܛܪܵܐ (or ܩܫܬܡܛܪ ?) *rainbow.* But ܕ is inserted in dates, as ܒܫܢܬ݂ܵܐ ܕܡܐܐ *in the year* 100 (O.S. ܒܫܢܲܬ݂ ܡܐܐ).

ܗܲܠ U. K. Q. or ܗܲܕ Al. Q. Z. or ܗܘܲܠ Al. Sal. [perhaps this is the emphatic ܗܵܐ, § 73, with ܠ], also ܗܲܠܟܹܡ U. K., cf. ܟܹܡ, ܠܟܹܡ below; = *up to, until;* ܗܲܠ ܐܵܟ݂ܵܐ *so far (up to there),* ܗܲܠ ܐܝܼܡܲܢ *how long? (until when?);* used of duration of time, ܗܲܠ ܬܠܵܬ݂ܵܐ ܫܸܢܹ̈ܐ *for three years,* which may also be expressed without any preposition. Cf. ܗܵܐ ܡܶܢ § 69 (3).

ܛܠܵܒ݂ K. Q. or ܬܠܵܒ݂ J. or ܛܠܲܒ݂ Al. or ܬܵܐ Al. J. Z. or ܬ in Bo. Ti. with affixes, § 70 (10) = O.S. ܡܶܛܠ or ܡܶܛܽܠ of the West Syrians; = *for*. It has the meanings of ܩܵܐ (below), except the sign of the object.

ܟܹܡ, see ܠܟܹܡ, rarely used by itself, except in Ash. Z.

ܠ O.S. *to, for:* ܐܬܝܬ ܠܒܝܬ ܘܢ *I came to Van.* [It is sometimes omitted in this sense: as ܒܥܝܢܐ ܐܙܠ ܠܫܘܩܐ U. *I will go to market.* So Z.] ܗܒܝܗܝ ܠܫܡܥܘܢ *give it to Simon,* ܟܠܢ ܚܝܒܝܢ ܠܗ̇ܕܐ *we all ought;* in dates, ܠܫܢܬ ܕܚܡܫܝܢ ܕ... ܐ.ܕ. 50: ܫܢܬ ܡܐܬܝܢ ܕܝܘܢܝܐ *in the year 200 of the Greeks* = B.C. 111; sign of the object, direct or indirect (more frequently than in O.S.), as ܠܡܢ ܡܚܐ؟ *whom did he strike?* cf. also § 49; = *by* in the preterite ܓܡܝܪ ܠܝ *it is finished by me = I finished,* § 32 (4), and elsewhere in Al. K.; for its use with ܥܡ see above.

ܠ *towards,* ܠܐܪܥܐ *towards the earth,* often with ܓܒܐ *side* (= *direction*) added after the noun, as ܠܡܕܝܢܬܐ ܓܒܐ *towards the city,* or *in the direction of the city* (not necessarily of motion). [Origin? Perhaps = ܠܗܐ (cf. ܠܗܘ) or ܠܗܢܐ *to this.* Nöld. § 87.]

ܠܘܬ O.S., Al. only, *to.*

ܠܓܒܝ U. K. *to,* chiefly with pronouns: ܬܐ ܠܘܬܝ *come to me,* as ܠ is not used of motion with pronouns, § 70; = *with, at, at the house of* etc., French *chez:* ܟܬܒܟ ܠܘܬܝ ܐܝܬ *your book is with me, I have your book,* § 29 (13), ܠܘܬܢ ܐܬܪܐ *in our country,* ܒܐܬܪܢ ܩܘܝ ܠܘܬܢ *he stayed at our house.* Also *compared with,* as ܡܘܕܥ ܠܘܬ ܗܢܐ ܕܗܘ؟ *what is this compared with that?* This preposition is not used in Al.; instead we have ܒܝܕ or ܕ.— So ܠܘܬ *towards* (not common).— Also ܡܢ ܓܒ or ܡܢ ܓܒܝ or ܡܢ ܠܘܬ (common) *from the presence of, from near.*— Perhaps ܠܘܬ = ܕ ܠܓܒܐ *to the side of,* Nöld. § 87. It exactly corresponds to O.S. ܠܘܬ.

ܡܲܓܲܪ (ܠܐ) U. *except*, Pers.

ܡܢ O.S. (*mĭn*), also ܡ̄ esp. in K. J. Al. Az. (even before ܐ and ܝ) as in some words in O.S.; =*from*: ܡܢܘܟܼܘܢ *from you*; or *by*, after passive verbs: ܦܝܫ ܠܲܢ ܒܪܝܐ ܡܢ ܐܲܠܵܗܵܐ *we were created by God*; or *with*: ܐܲܠܵܗܵܐ ܡܢܘܟܼܘܢ *God be with you, goodbye*, ܐܬܹܐ ܠܹܗ ܡܢܢ *he came with us*; or *than*: ܪܲܒ݂ ܡܢ ܕܗܘ *better than he*; or *since*: ܡܢ ܕܗܘ ܙܲܒ݂ܢܵܐ *since that time*; or *by reason of* (so Gk. ἀπό): ܡܢ ܕܐܵܗܵܐ ܥܸܠܬ݂ܵܐ *for this reason*; or *via, by way of*: ܐܬܹܐ ܠܘܟܼ ܡܢ ܩܘܕܫܐܢܝܣ؟ *did you come by way of Qudshanis?* ܡܢ ܗܵܘܟܵܐ *that way*, ܗܵܪܟܵܐ *this way*, ܥܵܐܹܠ ܡܢ ܬܲܪܥܵܐ *he enters by the door* (see § 71): cf. ܡܚܝܼܠܗܘܢ ܡܢ ܓܢܒܘܗܝ *they wounded him in the thigh*; or *some of*: ܐܟܘܠ ܡܢ ܕܐܵܗܵܐ *eat some of this.*—ܡܢ may occasionally be omitted, as in ܦܲܠܓܵܐ ܚܛܗ̈ܝܗܘܢ *some of their faults.* It is rarely used before verbal phrases equivalent to nouns, as in O.S.: thus O.S. ܠܐ ܝܕܥܐ ܡܢ ܕܐܡܪܐ = N.S. ܠܐ ܝܕܥܢ ܡܢ ܕܐܡܪܢ.

ܥܠ O.S., U. K. Al. or ܥܝܠ Sal.; =*on*: ܥܠ ܦܐܬܐ ܕܝܡܐ *on the surface of the sea*, ܥܠ ܕܐܵܗܵܐ *hereupon*; or *about*, esp. in K.: ܥܠ ܬܠܝܬܝܘܬܐ ܩܕܝܫܬܐ *about the Holy Trinity*; or *against*, esp. in Al. ܐܬܐ ܠܗܘܢ ܥܠܢ *they came against us.* Also with ܡ̄: ܡܥܠ *across*, or *from over*, as ܡܫܘܕܐ ܠܗ ܡܥܠ ܢܗܪܐ *he threw it across the river.* Also in K. ܡܥܝܠ.—So ܡܥܠ ܒܣܪܐ or ܡܥܠ ܒܘܣܪܐ or ܡܥܠܢ ܒܣܪܐ (O.S. ܡܥܠܝ ܒܣܪܐ) *Carnival*; ܡܥܝܠ ܫܒܬܐ K. *Saturday evening* (our Friday evening).

ܥܡ O.S. (*ăm*), in Al. and often K. ܥܝܡ (*īm*), ܐ = ܥ, § 6 (2); = *with*, i.e. *together with*, rather more emphatic than ܡܢ.

ܨܘܿܒ݂ Al. (Arab. صوب *side*) = ܠܓ݂ܒ݂ܐ q. v. So ܡܨܘܿܒ݂ = ܡܓ݂ܒ݂ܐ.

ܩܵܐ U. Sal. = *for*: ܩܵܐ ܝܲܥܩܘܿܒ݂ *for James*, ܩܵܐ ܡܘܿܕܝ *what for? why?*; or *to*: ܝܗ݂ܒ݂ܠܝܼ ܠܵܗ̇ ܩܵܐ ܕܵܘܝܼܕ݂ *I gave it* (f.) *to David*; to express duration of time: ܩܵܐ ܬܪܹܝܢ ܝܘܿܡܵܬ݂ܹܐ *for two days*; or a stated time: ܬܵܐ ܗܵܪܟܵܐ ܗܘܝ ܩܵܐ ܦܠܓܵܐ ܕܝܘܡܵܐ *be here by noon*, see § 28 (13), ܗܵܕ݂ܪܵܐ ܗܵܘܹܐ ܩܵܐ ܥܸܣܪܵܐ ܝܲܪ̈ܚܹܐ *it will be ready in ten months.*—For the direct object see § 64. Nöldeke is in error in saying it is not used (Nöld. § 87).—In Sal. pron. *qé*.—Origin?

ܩܵܕܵܡ (O.S. ܩܕ݂ܵܡ) or ܡܢ ܩܵܕܵܡ (O.S. ܡܢ ܩܕ݂ܵܡ) or ܡܩܵܕܵܡ *before, in front of*: ܐܬ݂ܹܐ ܠܹܗ ܡܢ ܩܵܕܵܡ ܬܐܘܿܡܵܐ *he came before Thomas*, ܩܪܹܐ ܠܹܗ̇ ܩܵܕܵܡ ܕܝܵܢܹ̈ܐ *he called her before the law courts*; or to express *ago*: ܩܵܕܵܡ ܬܠܵܬ݂ ܫܢܹ̈ܐ *three years ago*, (or ܬܠܵܬ݂ ܫܢܹ̈ܐ ܡܢ ܩܵܕܵܡ ܐܕܝܵܐ); so also ܩܵܕܵܡ ܫܬܵܐ ܝܘܿܡܵܬ݂ܹ̈ܐ ܕܦܸܨܚܵܐ *six days before the passover*, St Joh. xii. 1 (not common); also *because of, from fear of*: ܠܐ ܡܵܨܹܢ ܦܵܬ݂ܚܸܢ ܥܲܝܢܵܬ݂ܝ ܡܢ ܩܵܕܵܡ ܪܹܫܝ *I cannot open my eyes because of my head(ache)*: so ܡܢ ܩܵܕܵܡ ܩܲܪܬܵܐ ܠܐ ܐܙܸܠܝ *I did not go from fear of the cold*. So the Greek ἀντί (Clyde's *Greek Syntax*, § 83, 2) and possibly ἐναντίον, Lu. xx. 26, are used for *because of*. Also ܠܩܵܕܵܡ *towards the front of*, ܗܲܠ ܩܵܕܵܡ *until the front of*.

ܒܪ O.S., K. sometimes U. or ܡܒܪ, = ܒܬܪ, ܡܒܬܪ.

ܬܚܘܿܬ U. or ܬܚܘܿܬܬ Sh. Sal. Tkh. or ܬܚܘܿܬ Sal. Ti. or ܬܚܘܿܬܬ Gaw. = O.S. ܬܚܘܿܬ or ܬܚܝܬ; = *under*, with ܠ and ܡܢ or ܡ̇ of motion to and from under.

§ 69. *Compound prepositions.*

(1) Most of the above prepositions may be repeated to express intensity. Thus ܒ ܓܲܘܵܐ U. or ܓܘ ܓܲܘܵܐ U. Sal. *along* (but in K. J.

ܐܙܠܝ ܒܪܘܟ ܢܗܪܐ ܢܗܪܐ *I went along the river*), or ܒܪܝܫܗ ܕܒ ܕ U. or ܒܪܝܫܗ ܕ Sh. [so ܒܪܝܫܗ ܕܡܘܫܐ = (*going*) *up hill*], ܒܬܪܗ ܒܬܪ U. *ever after*, ܒܝܢܬܗ ܒܝܢ *ever between*, ܠܘܬܗ ܠܘ U. *along*, ܡܢܬܗ ܡܢ *ever with*, ܥܠܬܗ ܥܠ *along*, ܥܡܬܗ ܥܡ *ever with*, ܩܕܡܬܗ ܩܕܡ *ever before*, ܬܚܘܬܗ ܬܚܘܬ U. *ever under*. So in O.S. ܥܡܗ ܥܡ ܝܫܘܥ *with Jesus*. But in the above N.S. instances only the feminine pronoun is used, though the noun be masculine; see below (2) *a*.

(2) *Compound prepositions with* ܕ.

a. Several simple prepositions take a pronominal affix and ܕ without change of meaning, esp. in K. Al.; this is common in O.S. e.g. ܥܡܗ ܕܚܬܢܐ *with the bridegroom* (Martyrs' Anthem, Tues. even.); ܥܠܝܗܘܢ ܕܟܘܪܣܘܬܐ *on the seats*, Rev. iv. 4; ܩܕܡܘܗܝ ܕܟܘܪܣܝܐ *before the throne*, Rev. iv. 5; cf. ܐܝܟ ܕܕܡܘܬܐ *in the likeness*, Rev. iv. 3. So also in N.S. we have ܓܘܗ ܕ K. = ܓܘ; ܒܘܗ ܕ = ܒܘܗ ܕ see *b* below; ܒܬܪܗ ܕ Ti. = ܒܬܪ; ܒܦܠܓܗ ܕ U. m. f. K. m. or ܒܦܠܓܗ ܕ K. f. or with ܒ prefixed, or ܒܦܠܓܗ ܕ Al. *in the midst of*, § 27; ܠܘܗ ܕ K. m. ܠܘܗ ܕ K. f. U. m. f. = ܠܘ; ܡܢܗ ܕ, sometimes pronounced *mĭnĭt* = ܡܢ; ܥܠܗ ܕ, sometimes pronounced *ĭlĭt* = ܥܠ, or ܥܠܗ ܕ Al. id. *ĭlĭt* [thus ܥܠܗ ܕܡܐ ܕܚܙܐ ܠܗܘܢ Al. *about what they saw*]; ܥܡܗ ܕ Z. and ܥܡܗ ܕ U. = ܥܡ; ܠܦܝܬܗ ܕ Tkh. Sh. = ܠܦܝ ܕ, below *b*; ܩܕܡܗ ܕ (*qâmit*) = ܩܕܡ; ܓܒܗ ܕ m. or ܓܒܗ ܕ f. K. Al. = ܓܒ. Perhaps others of the above have both m. and f. forms in some districts. For emphasis we have the preposition repeated, as in (1). Thus ܠܘܗ ܠܘܗ ܕܛܘܪܐ *in the mountain*, ܒܬܪܗ ܒܬܪܗ ܕܚܝܠܐ *after the army*; ܥܡܗܘܢ ܥܡܗܘܢ ܕܓܒܪܐ *with the men* (the plural affixes are not very common in this connexion).

b. ܐܪ̈ܘܚܬܐ ܕ or ܚܕܪܬܐ‐ ܕ U. *around*, also with ܠ and ܡܢ. Perhaps we should write ‐ܚܕܪܗ as above, *a*. This seems to be a corruption of ܐܪܒܥܐ ܓܢ̈ܒܐ ܕ *the four sides of*, cf. Az. ܐܪܒܥܐ ܟܢܢܒ *around* (Appendix I.). As a substantive ܐܪ̈ܘܚܬܐ = *surroundings, neighbourhood*.

ܒܝܢܬܐ ܕ, see ܒܝܢ, § 68.

ܒܐܪܬܐ ܕ U. *in the middle of*, Turk.

ܒܓܢܒܐ ܕ K. Sh. or ܒܓܢܒܐ ܕ U. *by the side of*, or without ܒ; also with ܠ or ܡܢ.

ܒܚܘܣ ܕ or ܚܘܣ ܕ Al. *about, concerning* (see *a*). Rarely with ܠ.

ܒܘܝܐ ܥܠܬܐ ܕ U. *on account of*.

ܒܘܝܐ ܫܘܕܐ ܕ U. or ܒܫܘܕܐ ܕ *for the sake of*.

ܕܪܒܪܒܠ ܕ (not Al.) *opposite*, or ܡܩܒܠ. So ܕܪܒܪܒܠ ܕ *against*, also in Al. *opposite* [hybrid words, the first syllable being Persian (در *in*, and بر) the second O.S. ܠܘܩܒܠ *against*, which with affixes is ܠܘܩܒܠܗ etc.? or else = O.S. ܒܠܘܩܒܠܗ, ܕܠܘܩܒܠܗ].

ܣܚܪܢܐ ܕ U. K. *around* (or ‐ܚܕܪܗ), or with ܠ. So ܣܚܪܢܐ *environs*. Cf. ܣܚܪ *to go round*, as O.S.

ܠܗܝ ܓܒܐ ܕ U. (or ܠܗܠܐ) or ܠܗܝ ܓܒܐ ܕ U. or ܠܗܘܢ ܣܛܪܐ ܕ MB. or ܠܗܝ ܓܒܐ ܕ or ܠܗܠܐ ܓܒܐ ܕ Ti. or ܠܗܘܢܐ ܓܒܐ ܕ Tkh. or ܠܗܠܐ ܣܛܪܐ ܕ or ܗܝܐ ܓܒ Sh. or ܠܗܠܐ ܓܒܐ ܕ Ti. or ܠܐܝ ܓܒ ܕ Al. *on this side of*.

ܠܓܒܐ ܕ Al. = ܠܓܒܗ, see § 68.

ܠܗܘ ܓܒܐ ܕ or ܠܗܘ ܟܢܪܐ ܕ U. or ܠܗܘ ܥܒܪܘܐ ܕ or ܠܗܘ ܗܢܕܐ ܕ or ܗܘܦܪܝܐ ܕ Ti. or ܒܟܘܪ ܕ Al. or ܠܗܘ ܟܪ ܕ Al. *on that side of.*

ܡܩܒܠ ܕ U. ܡܩܒܠ ܕ Al. *for the sake of, instead of,* Arab.

ܡܢ ܓܒܐ ܕ U. K. or ܡܓܒܐ ܕ or ܡܓܒܝ Sh. or ܡܢ ܓܒܐ ܕ Ti. *instead of,* lit. *from the side of.* We must distinguish ܡܢ ܓܒܐ ܕܐܘܪܡܝ *instead of Urmi,* from ܡܢ ܐܘܪܡܝ ܓܒܐ *from the neighbourhood of Urmi,* or *concerning Urmi.*

ܡܚܕܘܪܐ ܕ or ܡܚܕܘܪܬܐ ܕ (or ܒܪܗ-) *around,* cf. N.S. ܡܚܕܘܪܐ *the edge.*

ܬܘܟܡ ܕ Tkh. Sh. *in the midst of,* see *a,* above.

ܣܒܒ ܕ or ܒܣܒܒ ܕ or ܡܣܒܒ ܕ *by reason of, for the sake of,* rare in U. [sometimes without ܕ]. ܣܒܒ in K. = *cause,* Arab.

ܩܘܪܒܐ ܕ (also ܩܘܪܒܐ ܓܒ U. or ܩܘܪܒܐ ܠ) *near,* O.S.

(3) *Compound prepositions with* ܡܢ *following.*

ܩܘܡ ܩܕܡܝܬܐ ܡܢ (ܩܡ K.) *before.*

ܠܒܪ ܡܢ U. Ti. or ܠܒܪ ܡ̇ Tkh. *except, besides.* Before a phrase, Dalath is often added: thus ܠܒܪ ܡܢ ܕܦܥܠܐ *except in verbs.* Also all these take Dalath before a demonstrative pronoun, § 70 (12).

ܗܐ ܡܢ or ܗܐ ܡ̇ (*hăm*) *since,* cf. ܗܘܠ.

ܠܬܠܬܚܬܐ ܡܢ or ܬܠܬܚܬܐ ܡܢ or ܬܠ̇ Sal. or ܠܬܚܬܐ ܡܢ Al. *below.*

ܠܒܪܪ ܡܢ (ܕ) U. Ti. or ܠܒܪ ܡܢ Al. *outside.*

ܠܗܘ ܓܒܐ ܡܢ *the other side of,* see (2) above.

ܠܥܠܘܠ ܡܢ U. or ܥܠ̇ U. or ܠܥܠܠ ܡܢ K. or ܠܥܠ ܡܢ MB. *above.*

ܡܩܕܡ ܡܢ Al. *before.*

מִן כּוֹבַּת (ב usually silent) *except, beside.* Also בַּלְכַּד, § 72.

מִן כָּלְבַד (לְ) Al. *except, beside,* or מִן כָּלְבַד.

(4) These compound prepositions are sometimes reduplicated for emphasis, as מְדָוַר מְדָוַר ב *ever round.*

§ 70. *Prepositions with pronouns.*

(1) Of the proper prepositions, the following take the pronominal affixes simply: בְּד : בַּמֵּהּ Al.: בָּם Al. (בָּמִּי takes no affixes ?): תְּחוֹת U. Q. Sal. Gaw.: כָּל and כָּלֵהּ (but then o becomes consonantal: thus כָּלְוַן is *gá-wan*; the forms כָּלֵהּ, כָּלֹהּ take affixes like כָּל, e.g. כָּלְוֹהִי): ל (see below): מִן, בַּל : בַּד (בִּדַ): קֳדָם: בִּד: חַסוֹת U. And so all prepositions which end with the above. Thus we have מִנִּי : קֳדָמְסוֹן : חַסוֹתֵהּ U. etc. In Z. we have for *before him* also קֳדָמֵהּ and בֵּידֵהּ.

(2) בַּתֹּר K. MB. Sh. Al. drops Pthakha: as בַּתְרַן *after us.* So in O.S., but O.S. בַּתְרִי = N.S. בַּתְרִי, K. etc. *after me.*

(3) ל in U. K. does not take the affixes in the sense *to* (of motion); we say לְאוּרְמִי *to Urmi*, but כֶּסלִי *to me.* It takes affixes simply in the forms of § 49, in the formation of the preterite, and after אִית; otherwise with affixes it takes the form אֶל (אֶלֵהּ: אֶלָהּ etc.). Thus בַּק שַׁבֵק מִנַּן *he would leave us,* but שַׁבֵקלַן אֶל לֵהּ U. *he left us,* חָזֵינָא לָךְ *I see you.* But in Al. Z. the forms אֶלֵהּ, אֶלָהּ etc. may be used in all cases, and sometimes in K.; so also in U. in the phrases: מָא הֲוָה לֵהּ מֶרְחַמְתֵּהוֹן *he pitied them,* lit. *their pity came to him,* מָא הֲוָה לֵהּ *what has happened to him?*—ל does not take the forms הַוְ, הִיא, הִנּוֹן ֗, הַוָּא, הַוָּא ֗, הִם. We thus have לֵהּ,

ܕܗ݂ universally for 3 sing.; and ܠܓܒܘܗܝ K. J. Al. Sp. ܠܓܘܗ U. ܠܓܘܗ MB. Z. for 3 pl. The form ܠܓܒ is only used in Ti. In Ti. for the 2 pl. we have ܠܓܝܟܘܢ only. The parallel form ܬܠ makes either ܬܠܗ or ܬܠܘܗܝ, more often the former; the 3 pl. is ܬܠܝܗܘܢ or ܬܠܝܗܘܢ Al. K. In Ti. we have both ܬܠܟܘܢ and ܬܠܝܟܘܢ for 2 pl., ܬܠܒ for 1 pl.

(4) ܠܓܝܗ takes ܠ after it when affixes are added: as ܠܓܡܠܝ to me. In J. ܠܓܝܗ = ܠܓܕܝܗ U. ܠܓܝܗ ܕܠ to him. In Ash. Z. ܓܡܠܝ etc. without the first ܠ. The 3 pl. is ܠܓܝܗ ܠܒܝܗܘܢ, even in U.

(5) ܕ takes ܝ, e.g. ܕܝܢ of us = O.S. ܕܝܠܢ. The 3 pl. is ܕܝܢܝܗܘܢ U. or ܕܝܢܝܗܘܢ K. J. In Ti. (not Ash.) Z. and Sh. we have ܕܝܕܗ etc. i.e. ܕܝܕܝܗ Nöld. (2 pl. Ti. ܕܝܕܝܟܘܢ or ܕܝܕܟܘܢ; in all these the second ܕ is soft); in Ash. ܕܝܢ or ܕܝܢܗ. In Anhar (village in U.) and Sh. we have ܕܝܕܘܟܘܢ of you (pl.).—In Z. ܕܝܢܒ of us.

(6) ܒ also takes ܝ, as ܒܝ in me, U.; also in K. and in Al. ܒܗ, ܒܗ etc.; in Ti. Sh. MB. Ash. Z. ܒܓܗ, ܒܓܘܗܝ (?) or ܒܓܘܗܝ Ti. or ܒܓܘܗ MB., ܒܓ or ܒܓܒ, ܒܓܘܟܘܢ MB. Sh. or ܒܓܝܟܘܢ Ti. etc., and sometimes so in other parts of K.: where the forms ܒܗ etc. are used to denote the object, ܒܓܗ is used in the sense *in*; but see § 48.

(7) The following take ܕ with its ܝ before affixes: ܕܝ : ܕܝܢ: ܕܘܟܐ [ܐ and ܕ kept quite distinct; that is ܕܝܒ ܕܘܟܐ = ܕܕܝܒ ܕܘܟܗ, cf. (11) below]: ܕܝܓ : ܕܠܟ (so ܕܠܟ Sal.) : ܕܠܟ : ܠܗ : ܠ, ܓ݂ܝܠܕ, (but in Ti. and Al. ܓܝܢ takes affixes thus: ܓܘܗ ܓܘܗ ܠ *like him*, etc. as in O.S.); we thus have ܓ ܕܝܢ *without us*, and so on.

(8) ܩܘܼܡܬܼ K. with affixes regains ܬ: as ܩܘܼܡܬܹܗ. In Gaw. from ܩܡܘܼܬܼ we have ܩܡܘܼܬܘܼܗ, ܩܡܘܼܬܹܗ etc. In Sal. from ܩܘܼܡܬܼ or ܩܘܡܬܼ we have ܩܘܼܡܬܘܼܗܘܿܢ (or ܩܘܼܡ) etc.

(9) ܩܵܐ takes affixes in various ways. *For him* is ܩܵܬܘܼܗܝ U. or ܩܵܬܹܗ U. or ܩܵܬܹܗ MB. Sh. Q. or ܩܵܐ ܕܝܼܗ U. or ܩܵܐ ܕܝܼܘܼܗܝ U. or ܩܵܐ ܕܝܼܕܹܗ Sh. (rare). In ܩܵܬܝ *for me*, ܬ is often silent: *qâ-i*; so ܩܵܬܲܢ Sal. *for us*. The ܬ, which is hard, being in the U. forms, is perhaps for ܕ, so that ܩܵܬܹܗ = ܩܵܐ ܕܝܼܗ. The MB. form seems to be ܩܵܐ + ܠ.

(10) ܒܬܵܠܵܐ, ܗܬܵܠܵܐ, ܬܵܠܵܐ, ܗܬܵܐ take ܠ. Thus ܒܬܵܠܵܠܹܗ K. Q. ܬܵܠܹܗ Al. ܗܬܵܠܹܗ Z. For 2 pl. we also find ܬܵܠܵܟ݂ܘܿܢ Al. or ܬܵܠܵܟ݂ܘܿ: also ܒܬܵܠܵܠܟ݂ܘܿ Ti. (or ܒܬܵܠܵܠܵܟ݂ܘܿ). Another Al. and J. form is with ܬ, ܗܬܵܠܬܹܗ J. ܗܬܹܗ Al. etc. which perhaps = O.S. ܡܢ ܒܬܲܠܬܹܗ (Nöld. § 87). In Bohtan we have ܠܵܠܹܗ etc., which is either = ܒܬܵܠܹܗ, or is from ܠ, by reduplication. In Ti. (not Ash.) we have the same in the forms of § 50, note 3, and ܠܵܠܝ = *I myself* (*I for my part*). In J. ܗܬܵܠܝ *for me*, often has the second Tau silent.

(11) *Emphasis.* All prepositions except ܠܓܸܒ, ܠ, ܒ, take ܕ with its ܝ if the pronoun is emphatic. Even ܕ very commonly takes a second ܕ, as ܕܕܝܼܝ *of me*. When an emphatic pronoun follows ܠ, the forms ܐܠܹܗ etc. are used, especially in U. In Al. Z. the use of Dalath is common even where there is no emphasis.

(12) All prepositions take ܕ before the demonstrative pronouns ܗܘܿ: ܗܝܼ: ܐܵܢܝ: ܐܵܗܵܐ: ܐܵܕܵܐ etc., and ܐܵܢܝ; e.g. ܒܘܼܬܼ ܕܐܵܗܵܐ *about this*. But ܒ, ܠ, and in Al. ܬܵܐ usually (though not always) precede them without ܕ, thus ܬܵܐ ܗܘܿ ܢܵܫܵܐ Al. = ܒܬܵܠܵܐ ܕܗܘܿ ܢܵܫܵܐ K. (ܩܵܐ U.)

for that man. But in Al. ܠܓܲܐܕܝ *to this* (= ܠܵܗܐ or ܠܵܗܐܕܝ) would be preferred to ܠܐܕܝ. Also, especially in K. Al. ܡܸܢ does not take ܕ, though the full form ܡܶܢ requires it. Thus ܡܕܗܐ ܒܓܲܐܢܐ *from that time;* in U. they would say by preference ܡܶܢ ܕܗܐ ܒܓܲܐܢܐ. In O.S. this ܕ was not inserted: ܒܵܬܰܪ ܗܘ̇ O.S. = ܒܵܬܰܪ ܕܗܘ̇ N.S. In N.S. the ܕ coalesces with the demonstrative pronoun, and so do ܒ, ܠ usually. Thus ܕܗܘ̇ *dow* or *dō' ܒܗܐ̇ bāha,* rarely *b'āha,* ܠܐܢܝ *lēni,* rarely *l'ēni.*

(13) The personal pronouns of the third person are often used after prepositions (with ܕ as above) instead of the affix forms. Thus ܡܶܢ ܕܗܘ̇ = ܡܶܢܗ or ܡܶܢܗ *from him,* cf. § 10.

§ 71. *Prepositions idiomatically used after verbs, etc.*

ܒ is used as follows:

ܒ ܡܨܐ K. Al. *to be able,* § 29 (18).

ܒ ܓܲܚܟ (hard Kap) *to laugh at.*

ܒ ܕܦܸܕ *to touch.*

ܒ ܗܘܐ ܕܓܲܐܒܝ (ܦܝܕ) *to trust.*

ܒ ܚܵܙܐ *to look at* (this verb is rare in U.).

ܒ ܚܕܐ *to rejoice at.*

ܒ ܚܛܐ *to sin against.*

ܒ ܥܵܒܸܕ ܣܗܕܘܬܐ *to bear witness to.*

ܒ ܟܦܪ *to deny* (a person), *be offended at,* or *with* ܥܠ.

ܟܦܪܢܬܐ ܕܓܢܗ *self-denial.*

ܒ ܡܚܣܕ *to envy.*

ܒ ܡܟܠܨ U. = ܒ ܚܙܐ *above.*

ܒ ܡܙܓܠ *to lie against, to disappoint.*

ܒ ܡܗܘܡܢ *faithful to.*

ܒ ܡܗܘܡܢ (ܡܗܝܡܢ) *to believe.*

ܒ ܡܘܕܐ *to acknowledge* (a person or sin). So ὁμολογέω ἐν, Lu. xii. 8.

ܒ...ܡܫܠܟ *to exchange* (something) *for...*

ܡܟܪܙ ܕܗܝܡܢܘܬܐ *to preach the faith.*

§ 71] PREPOSITIONS.

ܡܒܲܣܹܕ ܒ *to mock.*   ܗܲܝܡܸܢ ܒ *to trust.*

ܡܲܚܙܹܐ ܒ *to wonder at.*   ܚܛܹܐ ܠܓܸܢܒ݂ ܒ *to sin against.*

ܡܸܬܟܲܫܸܦ ܒ *to beseech.*   ܩܪܹܐ ܒ *to call on, invoke.*

ܡܲܥܒܸܪ ܠܠܸܫܵܢܵܐ ܕ... *to translate into....*   ܕܘܿܒ ܒ *content with (of things),* ܡܸܢ *is more usual.*

ܟܐܹܐ ܒ *to rebuke.*   ܓܵܚܸܟ݂ (or ܚܢܸܓ) *to banter.*

ܢܟܸܦ ܒ *to be ashamed of.*   ܚܵܙܸܐ (ܕܠܹܗ Al.) *to meet, visit.*

ܦܪܸܫ ܚܲܕ...ܘܚܲܕ ... ܚܲܕ: — ܚܲܕ *to separate...from...*(also with ܡܸܢ).

ܒܵܬܲܪ or ܒܵܬܸܪ :—

ܐܵܙܹܠ ܒܵܬܲܪ *to follow.*   ܡܫܲܕܸܪ ܒܵܬܲܪ *to send for.*

ܡܲܚܕܸܡ ܒܵܬܲܪ *to look for, § 47.*   ܢܵܦܸܩ ܒܵܬܲܪ *to pursue.*

ܠܹܗ :—ܥܵܐܸܠ ܠܹܗ *to enter* (direct object not admissible), also with ܠ.

ܕ :—

ܝܵܗܸܒ݂ ܕܘܸܣܛܵܗ ܕ *to give leave of absence to.*

ܡܸܟܠܹܐ ܕ (or ܡܸܟܠܵܐ ܕ) *at a standstill for* (also with ܗܘܿܐ).

ܢܵܦܸܩ ܗܸܡܕܵܐ ܕ *to take revenge for* (with ܡܸܢ *of the person*).

ܠ :—

ܠܐܝܼܢ ܠܝܼ ܠܐܸܡܲܪ *I was tired of saying.*

ܡܦܲܠܓ ܠܐܸܕ ܢܩܸܕ *to divide into two parts.*

ܚܲܝܸܕ ܠ *to need* (must have ܠ).

ܕܐܸܒ݂ ܠ (U. only) *to ride on.*

ܡܢ :—

ܫܐܠ ܚܕܐ (ܚܕܡܐ) *to ask* (a thing) *of...*

ܟܡܬ ܙܗܪ (ܟܡܬ K.) *cautious of.*

ܕܚܠ ܡܢ ܘܕܝܕ *to fear* (as O.S. and so also* φοβέομαι ἀπό, *Lu. xii. 4).*

ܚܕܐ ܡܢ = ܚܠܕܬ ܡܢ.

ܝܕܥ ܚܢܢܐ *to thank.*

ܚܪܒ ܡܢ *to be angry with.*

ܡܫܐܠ ܡܢ *to ask* (a question) *of.*

ܡܣܒܪ ܡܢ *to long for.*

ܡܠܐ ܡܢ.. *to fill...with* (also without ܡܢ).

ܡܘܕܐ ܡܢ *to thank* (rare), *to prosper tr.* (in the latter sense usually without ܡܢ).

ܚܢܢܐ ܡܢ *thanks to.*

ܦܩܕ (or ܡܦܩܕ K.) *to command.*

ܢܕܘܒ ܡܢ *displeased with.*

ܢܫܩ ܡܢ *to kiss* (K. always, and U. sometimes, without ܡܢ).

ܣܒܪ ܘܗܒ ܡܢ *to trust in.*

ܥܒܪ ܡܢ *to pass by, cross, transgress,* or *to enter by* (a certain way).

ܦܪܩ ܡܢ *to finish tr., have done with.*

ܕܘܒ ܡܢ *satisfied with, content with, assenting to.* See above.

ܬܪܝܨ ܡܢ } *to cower before, run away from, be defeated by.*
ܐܪܩ ܡܢ }

ܥܠ :—

ܪܚܡ ܥܠ *to cast up against.*

ܪܚܡ ܗܘܦܩ ܥܠ *to aim a gun at.*

ܙܘܕ ܥܠ *rebellious against.*

ܘܠܨ ܥܠ U. *to oppress.*

ܫܘܪ ܥܠ *to look at* (also direct object).

ܩܡ ܥܠ *to stand to, to stand out for.*

ܡܚܝܪ ܥܠ *to look upon, look at.*

ܡܚܐ ܥܠ *to strike* (also direct object).

ܡܚܐ ܢܦܩܗ ܥܠ *to cause loss to.*

ܡܓܕܓܕ ܥܠ *to murmur against.*

ܡܩܝܼܡ ܦܵܬܵܐ ܥܲܠ *to pay attention to, set one's face towards.*

ܡܙܝܼܕ ܥܲܠ *to add to.*

ܣܵܗܸܕ (ܡܣܵܗܸܕ) ܥܲܠ K. Al. *to testify to.*

ܣܢܝܼܩ ܥܲܠ *to need.*

ܣܟܝܼܪ ܥܲܠ *to expect.*

ܥܒܝܼܪ ܥܲܠ *to transgress.*

ܫܟܝܼܠ ܥܲܠ *to complain against* or *about* (a thing or person).

ܚܫܸܕ ܥܲܠ *to suspect* (a thing).

ܫܡܝܼܥ ܥܲܠ *to hear*, in U. Also direct object.

ܫܩܝܼܠ ܡܲܠܟܘܼܬܼܵܐ ܥܲܠ *to conquer.*

ܢܩܝܼܦ ܥܲܠ *to adhere to*, U. (K. with ܠ).

ܩܕܵܡ :—

ܐܵܙܹܠ ܠܩܕܵܡ *to go out to meet* (a person arriving on a journey).

ܡܕܚܹܐ ܩܕܵܡ *to beat back, parry.*

ܢܝܼܠ (ܢܝܼܚ) ܩܕܵܡ *susceptible to.*

ܢܦܝܼܠ ܩܕܵܡ Z. *to go before.*

ܥܒܝܼܪ ܩܕܵܡ *to undertake.*

In many cases where in English a verb is used with an adverb or preposition, a single word is used in Syriac, as ܢܚܸܬ *to go* or *come down*, ܥܒܝܼܪ *to go in, come in, pass by*, ܐܣܝܼܩ *to go up, come up*, ܡܚܬܹܐ *to put away*, ܦܠܝܼܛ *to go out*, and so on.

§ 72. CONJUNCTIONS.

ܐܣܘܼܪܹ̈ܐ

ܐܸܓܲܪ *if*, not common, U. Ti., Pers.

ܐܘܿܦ U. K. or ܐܵܦ K. as O.S. *both*, § 67, followed by ܘ or ܘܐܘܿܦ (ܘܐܵܦ).

ܐܲܝܟ (as O.S.) or ܐܲܝܟ ܕ *as, according as.* Also ܕܐܲܝܟ (*dékh*) Al.

ܐܲܝܟ ܕ *in order that.*

ܐܝܟ ܕܐܢ *as if.*

ܐܝܟ ܟܡܐ ܕ = ܟܡܐ ܕ below. So ܐܝܟ ܟܡܐ ܙܒܢܐ ܕ *as often as* (cf. ܐܝܟ ܟܡܐ ܠܓܘܕܐ ܕ *as great as*).

ܐܡܬܝ ܕ = O.S. ܐܝܡܬܝ, § 67, *when*, or ܐܡܬܐ Ti.

ܐܝܢܐ *but, yet*, perh. = ܐܢ ܠܐ or ܐܠܐ? (Nöld. § 24.) For its redundant use see § 60.

ܐܠܐ *but*, O.S. = ἀλλά? or ܐܢ ܠܐ, Nöld. O.S.G. § 155.

ܐܠܐ ܐܢ *unless.*

ܐܢ O.S. *if* (see ܐܢ).

ܐܢ ܠܐ *unless* (see ܐܢ).

ܐܦܢ U. K., O.S. *although*, = ܐܦ ܐܢ. Often answered by ܐܝܢܐ *although...yet*, § 60. Very rarely ܐܘܦ ܐܢ.

ܒܪܡ *nevertheless.*

ܒܗܝ ܕ *in that, because.* O.S. ܒܕܚܙܐ = N.S. ܒܗܝ ܕܚܙܐ ܠܗ *in that he saw;* see § 68, s.v. ܒܗܝ.

ܒܠܝ *but, but yet* (not common).

ܒܬܪ ܕ or ܒܬܪ ܕ as O.S. (§ 68) *after that*, or with ܡܢ prefixed. In Al. ܒܬܪ ܡܢ ܕ § 13.

ܕ *that*, also *in order that*, O.S. (In O.S. also *because*, when standing alone; but not in N.S.)

ܕܐܝܟ ܕ *as*, much used in similes: as ܕܐܝܟ ܕܝܘܣܦ ܗܘܐ ܠܗ ܡܙܘܒܢܐ : ܗܕܟܐ ܐܦ ܡܪܢ ܗܘܐ *As Joseph was sold, so was our Lord.* For variations see § 67. Also *so that*, and *in order that.*

ܕܠܐ *lest*, U., O.S. or ܕܠܡܚܘܢ Al. (= ܕܠܐ ܡܢ ?)

ܗܕܟܐ ܕ or ܗܕܟܐ ܕ *so that*, § 67.

ܗܿܠ ܕ *until*, § 68; also *before*, ܒܸܕ ܐܵܬܹܐ ܗܿܠ ܕܥܵܒܸܕܢܵܗ̇ *he will come before I do it.*

ܗܵܡ...ܗܵܡ *both...and* (without ܘ), Pers., § 67.

ܘ O.S. *and.*

ܟܘܼܫܟܹܐ ܕ Tkh. or ܟܘܼܫܟܹܝ Ti. *would that.*

ܫܒܘܿܩ *let*, (imp. of ܫܒܲܩ O.S. *to suffer*), § 51 (10).

ܟܵܫܟܹܐ ܕ U. *would that.*

ܩܵܐ ܕ Q. K. or ܬܵܐ ܕ Al. *in order that.* But ܕ alone is more common. See ܩܵܐ ܕ.

ܝܵܢܲܕ *or* U., Turk.

ܝܲܢ *or*, perh. = O.S. ܐܲܢ̈, which in K. is used as an alternative. (In some parts of K. ܝܲܢ is not used.) Thus ܐܸܢ ܬܐܘܿܡܵܐ ܝܲܢ ܡܘܼܫܹܐ K. *either Thomas or Moses* (U. ܝܲܢ...ܝܲܢ). ܒܸܕ ܐܵܬܹܐ ܐܸܢ ܠܵܐ؟ K. *will he come or not?* ܝܲܢ sometimes means *at any rate*; thus: ܒܲܠܟܵܐ ܠܹܐ ܐܵܬܝܵܐ ܠܹܗ̇: ܝܲܢ ܠܵܐ ܚܙܹܐ ܠܝܼ ܠܵܗ̇ *perhaps she did not come; at any rate I did not see her.*

ܟܹܐ...ܟܹܐ *whether...or*, not common.

ܟܲܕ as O.S. or ܟܲܕ ܕ Al. (in U. ܕ = ܟܲܕ) *when, while.*

ܟܵܫܟܹܐ Al. *would that.*

ܟܘܼܢܟܹܐ ܕ *because*, Turk., also without ܕ.

ܟܡܵܐ ܕ O.S. *as much as, whenever, just as, in so far as.* So ܐܝܼܢ ܟܡܵܐ ܕܚܙܹܐ ܠܝܼ ܠܵܗ̇: ܟܡܲܕ ܙܵܘܕܵܐ *the more I saw her, the more...,* or without ܟܡܲܕ ܙܵܘܕܵܐ as O.S.; also answered by ܗܲܕܟ݂ܵܐ. ܗܿܠ ܟܡܵܐ ܕ or ܟܡܵܐ ܕ = *as long as,* ܟܡܵܐ ܥܲܓܠܵܐ ܕ = *as quickly as,* and so with many adjectives and adverbs.

ܠܵܐ ܗܵܘܹܐ ܕ *lest*, = ܠܵܐ ܗܘܹܐ ܕ.

ܠܸܛܘܿܠ *because*.

ܠܵܟܸܢ Turk. or ܐܸܠܵܐ ܡܸܢ U. *but*.

ܡܲܓܲܪ (ܟܹ) U. Ti. *unless*, Pers. (also with ܕ).

ܡܸܢ ܕ *since* (also ܡܸܢ ܕܒܵܬܲܪ); or *than*, see § 24.

ܣܲܒܲܒ ܕ *because*, or ܣܲܒ′ Al. Also without ܕ.

ܣܲܒܓܵܐ ܕ *although*, not common; or ܣܲܒܓܵܐ[1] or ܣܲܒܟܵܐ ܕ[1] Nöld. § 93.

ܩܵܐ ܕ U. Sal., often pron. *qat*, *in order that*, also in Sal. the simple *that*.

ܩܵܕܸܡ ܕ or ܡܸܢ ܩܵܕܸܡ ܕ or ܡܩܵܕܸܡ ܕ *before that*.

ܥܠܘܿܠ ܕ = ܠܥܸܠ above (also without ܕ). In Al. Ti. ܥܠܘܿܒ. Also *although*, *except*.

ܟܸܫܟܵܐ ܕ U. *would that*.

Notes. (1) Conjunctions are frequently omitted. Thus ܠܗܵܐ ܓܸܒܵܐ ܠܗܘܿ ܓܸܒܵܐ *to and fro*, ܬܪܹܝܢ ܬܠܵܬܵܐ ܝܘܿܡܵܬܹ̈ܐ K. *two or three days*, ܠܲܙܸܡ ܐܹܙܵܠ *I must go*, ܠܐ ܝܗܘܵܐ ܒܘܕ ܕܵܐܗܵܐ ܐܸܬܹܐ ܠܝ *it was not for this I came*, ܐܝܡܲܢ ܐܵܬܹܢ *when I come*, ܬܪܹܝܢ ܦܠܵܓܘܿ *two and a half*, ܫܵܥܵܐ ܦܠܵܓܘܿ U. *an hour and a half* (in K. ܫܵܥܵܐ ܘܦܠܵܓܘܿ § 27): ܣܵܦܪܹ̈ܐ ܦܪܝܼܫܹ̈ܐ *the Scribes and Pharisees*, ܢܘܿܪܘܿܝ ܣܘܿܝܹܕ *Norway and Sweden*, and so on. So we may write either ܘܫܪܵܟܵܐ or ܫܪܵܟܵܐ for *etcetera* (usually shortened to ܘܫܪ or ܫܪ). This is more used than in English and often ends each paragraph of a letter.

(2) ܘ is often inserted where it would be out of place in English. Thus ܘܗܘ ܘܠܐ ܗܘܵܐ ܡܸܢܝܼܢ ܕܟܬܒܘܿܢ ܝܘܼܢ ܟܘܿܢ ܟܘܿܫ (ܟܝܫ)

[1] These forms have not been verified orally.

I would rather my son died than he. So O.S. Rev. ix. 20 ܘܵܐܚܪܹܢܹܐ *and the rest of the men...did not repent.* On the other hand a common colloquialism is ܫܸܡܥܘܿܢ ܘܐܲܢܝܼ *Simon and they,* for ܫܸܡܥܘܿܢ ܘܐܲܢܝܼ.

(3) When a conjunction joins two nouns governed by the same preposition, the latter is usually repeated. ܒܹܝܬ ܕܡܘܿܫܹܐ ܘܕܦܝܼܪܵܐ *the house of Moses and Pira.*

§ 73. INTERJECTIONS.

ܐܵܗܹܐ ܡܹܐܕܹܡܕܵܢܹܐ

ܐܘ *why, pretty well,* rare.

ܐܘܿ *Oh!*

ܐܘܿ *O* (vocative), pron. long in K. (common), short in U. (rare); or *alas!* (long) O.S.

ܐܘܿ ܒܵܒܝܼ K. *O my father!*

ܐܘܿܗ, ܐܘܿܗܝ *alas!*

ܗܘܿܝ *hurrah!* rare.

ܐܘܿ ܠܝܼ ܒܵܒܝܼ K. *O my father!*

ܐܘܿ ܠܝܼ ܝܸܡܝܼ K. or ܐܘܿ ܕܐܲܝܼ Al. *O my mother!*

ܐܝܼܘܲܐ *well! to be sure,* Arab.

ܐܝܼܘܲܐܠܵܐ *Well!* (begins a sentence).

ܐܝܼ *O,* vocative, rare.

ܐܸܚܹܐ *wonderful!* rare.

ܐܲܗܘܿ *hallo there!* rare.

ܐܲܣܘܼ *alas!* rare.

ܐܲܦܩܸܕ (ܘ usually) or ܐܲܦܩܸܕ Sal. or ܐܲܝܼ K. or ܐܲܝܼ Ti. *bravo!*

ܐܲܨ *hush!* not common.

ܒܝܲܥܵܕܵܐ ܕܡܵܪܝܼ ܫܸܡܥܘܿܢ *by the habit of Mar Shimun* [when addressed to the Catholicos

ܕܡܸܫܟܘܿܝ ܡܓܝܼܢܹܐ also ܕܓܘܿܝ],an asseveration much used in K.

ܕܹܗ Pers. *bravo,* rare.

ܕܸܢܹܐ ܕܠܸܝܒ *I believe,* see § 68 s.v. ܒܗܵܐ.

ܒܲܠܝܼ U. ܒܲܠܝܼ Ti., Pers. *yes.*

ܒܢܵܐ *here I am* (polite answer when one is called).

ܕܵܐܟ݂ ܒܲܣ U. lit. *then how?* a strong assertion in reply to a negation. Or ܕܵܐܟ݂, ܕܝܼܟ݂ Ti.

ܒܣܝܼܡܘܼܬ݂ܘܼܟ݂ *your pleasure!* § 75.

ܒܲܣܡܵܐ ܟܹܝܦ݂ܘܼܟ݂ (ܟܹܦ̮ Ti. Sh.) *bravo!*

ܒܵܒ݂ܝܼܓ݂ܪܝܼܒ݂ܟ݂ܠܹܗ Ti. = French *mon Dieu!*

ܟ݂ܒ݂ܝܼܢ K. ܟ݂ܒ݂ܠܹܗ Al. Sh. *alas!* § 75.

ܒܣܝܼܡܬ݂ܵܐ ܟܹܝܦ݂ܘܼܟ݂ Ti. *bravo!*

ܒܲܣܡܵܐ ܟܹܝܦ݂ܘܼܟ݂ *bravo!*

ܒܵܐ almost = ܗܵܐ.

ܒܵܗܵܐ or ܒܹܐ *be off!* esp. K. In Sal. much used before an imperative to strengthen it.

ܒܵܠܡܸܢ̮ K. *I mean*, used to correct a statement previously made. Thus ܡܲܢܝܼ ܝܠܹܗ ܗܵܘ ܓܲܒ݂ܪܵܐ? Ans. ܓܝܼܘܲܪܓܝܼܣ، ܒܵܠܡܸܢ̮ ܕܵܘܝܼܕ݂. *Who is that man?* Ans. *George—no I mean David.*

ܕܘܼܩܲܗ ܠܹܗ (*dûq-ah*) or ܕܘܼܩܠܹܗ ܠܹܗ *catch hold!*

ܗܵܐ *behold!* often used at the end of a sentence to call attention, as ܕܪܹܐ ܠܝܼ ܒܹܥ̈ܐ ܗܵܐ *I have put on the eggs* (to boil); and often when the assertion is likely to be disputed. Also before a word emphasized, cf. ܗܵܐ ܗܡ, and ܗܵܠ = ܗܵܐ ܠ, §§ 68, 69. So also in O.S. (Uhlemann, § 86).

ܗܹܐ (Zlama has either sound) or ܗܵܐܐ K. *yes*, (= ܗܵܐ ܐܝܼܬ݂ܵܐ ?) or ܗܵܘܵܐ Z. (= ܗܵܘܝܵܐ ?). See ܐܝܼ.

ܗܵܐܕܵܐ *catch hold!* (= O.S. ܗܵܐ ܗܵܕܵܐ *behold this*).

ܗܲܝ *hullo!*

ܗܘ *O!*

ܗܹܝܫ ܦܝܼܫ *nonsense!* not common.

ܗܵܕܸܟ݂ Ti. *hold on! wait!*

ܗܸܝܠ *push on!*

ܗܸܝܢܵܢܵܐ U. or ܗܸܝܢܝܵܐ U. Tkh. *what do you call it?* (pronounce both Nuns).

ܘܵܐ *wonderful!* very common.

ܘܲܝ O.S. (*wei*) *woe!* or ܘܲܝܠܵܐ Al., O.S

ܘܲܝ ܠܝܼ ܒܵܒܵܐ K. *O my father!*

ܘܲܝ ܠܝܼ ܝܵܡܵܐ K. *O my mother!*

ܙܒܸܢܵܗ Al. *lo!* § 29 (17).

ܘܸܠܟ݂ ܗܘܼܕܝܼܟ݂ Ti. *out of the way!*

ܫܲܒ݂ܩܵܕܵܐ U. *out of the way!*

INTERJECTIONS.

ܗܶܕܡܰܗ ܒܸܬܕܳܘܝ true! (sc. ܗܶܕܡܰܗ ܒܸܠܝ is true) so ܣܸܬܕܳܘ ܕܦܠܢ what N. says is true.

ܣܳܘܬܳܘܝ your health, so ܣܳܘܬܳܘ. etc. or ܣܳܘܬܳܐ ܕܦܠܢ N.'s health.

ܣܘܫ tush! rare.

ܫܗܶ or ܫܗܶ ܚܕܝܒ, ܫܗܶ ܠܒܝ ܠܐ ܠܗ God forbid! so the other affixes, § 63 (7).

ܐܳ U. J. Al. O (vocative), common.

ܒܰܠ yes. This is used to deny a negative statement, or to answer an objection, and always means *you are wrong*: ܗܳܐ means *you are right*.

ܐܳ ܗܶܕܰܝ heyday!

ܐܳ ܕܳܟ U. alas! mon Dieu! Arab.

ܓܶܢܓܶܐ Kurd. bravo! esp. K.

ܚܳܟܘܝ Turk. as you please, lit. your pleasure. So with other affixes, or a name, ... ܚܳܟ ܕ.

ܠܳܐ no, O.S.

ܠܳܐ ܗܳܘܝܐ or ܠܐ ܠܗܘܐ God forbid!

ܕܰܘܢܐ or ܕܳܗ ܕܕܳܢܐ Ti. or ܕܳܗ Ti. or ܕܳܗܕܢܶܕ, or ܕܳܗܕܢܶܕ ܢܕܺܝܓ = ܕܰܘܢܐ what do I know? how can I tell? So the Hebrew מַדּוּעַ which = מַה יָדוּעַ = Gk. τί μαθών (Gesenius).

ܡܶܣܟܺܢܳܐ poor fellow!

ܡܳܕܳܐܢܳܐ Pers. bravo!

ܢܒܶܠ ܠܳܟܝ may it be pleasant to you! § 46, s.v. ܐܳܗܳܐ.

ܢܓܶܒ Arab. yes.

ܗܘܫ hush! Turk., rare.

ܢܰܟܣܳܘܕܳܐ K. Sh. well! = ܐܺܝܕ.

ܢܰܓܺܝܟܳܘܓܳܐ = ܐܳܗ, very common.

ܦܰܗ, ܦܰܗ pshaw! pah!

ܟܣܳܟ be off! § 46 s.v. ܐܙܶܠ.

ܓܶܕܺܝ K. alas! Pers.

عَلَب
ܨܟܳܘܣ } silence!

ܐܳܗܳܐ Tkh. = ܗܶܕܳܐ.

§ 74. Position of words in a sentence. Emphasis and Questions.

(1) In the position of words in the sentence N.S. very closely resembles English. The subject with any qualifying words comes first, then the verb, then the direct object with qualifying words, then the indirect object. But variations are commoner than in English.

(2) Adjectives used as epithets follow their substantives. For exceptions see § 23.

(3) Numerals precede substantives.

(4) So also demonstrative pronouns, and interrogative pronouns when used with substantives.

(5) The substantive verb when positive generally follows the predicate, as ܗܿܘ ܓܲܒܪܵܐ ܙܕܝܼܩܵܐ ܝܼܠܹܗ *that man is righteous.* But not after interrogative pronouns, as ܡܘܼܕܝܼ ܝܼܠܹܗ ܦܲܐܝܕܵܐ ؟ *what is the use?*: nor with negatives, as ܠܹܐ ܝܼܠܹܗ ܛܵܐܒ *it is not good*, and often not with demonstrative pronouns, especially when the predicate is definite, as ܐܵܗܵܐ ܝܼܠܹܗ ܟܬܵܒ݂ܘܼܟ݂ *this is your book* (here it would not be so usual for the verb to follow): nor sometimes in relative clauses, as ܗܿܘ ܓܲܒܪܵܐ ܕܝܼܠܹܗ ܠܬܲܡܵܐ *that man who is there.* The predicate is not necessarily an adjective or substantive, e.g. ܗܿܘ ܒܹܐ ܒܝܼܢ ܝܼܠܹܗ *he is without care.* If the predicate is long, the substantive verb may come after the first part of it; as ܗܿܘ ܝܲܢ ܓܲܒܪܵܐ ܝܼܠܹܗ ܕܩܲܡܘܼܗ݇ ܕܝܼܘܗܝ ܡܲܘܡܘܹܝܢ ܠܝܼ *that is a man about whom I spoke.*

(6) *Emphasis.* Very commonly the emphatic word is put first, and stands absolutely, and redundant affixes are added in the sentence which follows. This is especially the case in the imperative and in questions, and applies in all cases when attention is called to a particular word, whether it would be in italics in English, or not. Ex. ܙܲܢܓܵܐ ܡܚܝܼ ܠܹܗ *ring the bell*, lit. *the bell ring it.* So ܐܵܗܵܐ ܟܬܵܒ݂ܵܐ

ܕܡܢܝ ܝܠܗ؟ *whose is this book?* (shewing it). ܐܗܐ ܟܬܒܐ ܡܘܕܝ ܐܝܬ ܠܓܘܗ؟ *what is in this book?* (shewing it). ܐܢܐ ܠܝܬ ܠܝ ܟܬܒܐ I *have no book.* We could also say ܕܡܢܝ ܝܠܗ ܐܗܐ ܟܬܒܐ—ܡܢܝ ܘܟܐ ܠܝܬ ܠܝ ܟܬܒܐ—ܡܘܕܝ ܐܝܬ ܠܗ ܓܘ ܕܐܗܐ ܟܬܒܐ—, but these would not be so emphatic. So *I for my part, as for me,* and the like may be rendered by the simple pronoun standing as above (cf. modern Greek ἔγω· πρέπει νὰ λάβω I *must take*), or by ܡܢ ܦܬܐ ܕܝܠܝ etc. if they are very emphatic.

We must notice however that a noun standing absolutely before ܐܝܬ ܠܗ *he has,* if it is the subject in English, is not emphatic. Thus ܗܘ ܓܒܪܐ ܐܝܬ ܠܗ ܟܬܒܐ = *that man has a book,* simply. We could not say ܐܝܬ ܠܗܘ ܓܒܪܐ ܟܬ'. If the English object of *to have* is emphatic we must put it first, as ܟܬܒܐ ܐܝܬ ܠܝ *I have a book.* Note also that the subject of a preterite stands absolutely, § 32 (4), but it is not necessarily emphatic. Thus ܐܢܐ ܐܬܐ ܠܝ *I came,* ܗܘ ܓܒܪܐ ܐܬܐ ܠܗ *that man came.*

The subject, pronoun or noun, may be placed last for emphasis, as an alternative to the above construction, or when it cannot stand absolutely. Thus ܩܐ ܡܘܕܝ ܐܬܐ ܠܘܟ ܐܢܬ؟ *why did* you *come?* (not the other man). So even if there are no italics in English, but the subject is pointed out: ܩܡܠܗ ܒܠܒܐ ܕܗܘܐ ܚܕܐ ܒܟܬܐ *there stood a woman,* ܚܙܝ ܡܘܕܝ ܒܥܒܕܐ ܝܠܗ ܗܘ ܓܒܪܐ or else ܗܘ ܓܒܪܐ ܚܙܝ ܡܘܕܝ ... or ... ܚܙܝ ܗܘ ܓܒܪܐ ܡܘܕܝ ... all express *see what that man* (I point out, or I am speaking of) *is doing.*

(7) The object of a verbal noun used as in § 57 (3) usually precedes it.

(8) Short adverbs, as ܒܫܡ *very, quite,* ܪܒܐ *very,* etc. generally precede adjectives and adverbs; those which qualify verbs usually follow them, but there is no exact rule as to this. We must except

such a phrase as ܓܲܒ݂ܪܵܐ ܪܲܒܵܐ ܠܸܚܕܵܐ ܝܠܹܗ *he is a very great man*, ܪܲܒܵܐ ܠܸܚܕܵܐ being treated as one word, though we might equally well say ܚܲܕ݇ ܪܲܒܵܐ ܓܲܒ݂ܪܵܐ ܠܸܚܕܵܐ ܝܠܹܗ, cf. ܟܡܵܐ ܡܸܢܕܝܼ ܫܲܦܝܼܪ ܝܠܹܗ *how good a thing it is!*

(9) *Questions* take the same order as affirmative sentences, and often can only be distinguished from them by the inflection of the voice. But interrogative pronouns, with or without a noun or preposition, and interrogative adverbs are placed first, unless an emphatic word stands absolutely at the beginning of the clause, as described above. This absolute construction is especially common with interrogative pronouns and adverbs: as ܐܲܚܢܲܢ ܡܫܝܼܚܵܝܹ̈ܐ ܒܢܘܿܢܹ̈ܐ ܕܡܲܢܝܼ ܝܘܲܚ؟ *whose sons are we Christians?*

(10) After interrogative pronouns and adverbs the subject often follows the verb, e.g. ܡܘܿܢܝܼ ܐܡܝܼܪܗܘܿܢ ܐܵܢܝܼ ܓܲܒ݂ܪܹ̈ܐ؟ *what did those men say?* But not, of course, if the pronoun itself be the subject. In the same case the copula follows the pronoun or adverb. We cannot say ܡܘܿܢܝܼ ܦܘܼܪܩܵܢܵܐ ܝܠܹܗ؟ *what is salvation?* but ܡܘܿܢܝܼ ܝܠܹܗ ܦ̇ or ܦ̇ ܡܘܿܢܝܼ ܝܠܹܗ؟.

(11) Indirect questions follow the same lines; ܕ often redundantly introduces them, as ܡܫܘܼܝܠܹܗ ܕܒܗܵܬ݂ ܥܘܼܠܹܗ ܡܘܿܢܝܼ ܒܲܥܒ݂ܵܕ݂ܵܐ ܝܘܸܢ ܗܘܵܐ *he asked what I was doing in his affair.* But the oratio directa is often substituted, § 66.

(12) In questions the Syrians use ܝܲܢ ܠܵܐ (ܝܼܢ ܠܵܐ K.) *or not,* very much more than Europeans do. ܒܹܬ݂ ܐܵܙܠܲܬ݂ ܝܲܢ ܠܵܐ؟ *will you go or not?* is not meant to be rude or peremptory though at first sight it often appears to be so.

§ 75. IDIOMATIC PHRASES AND SALUTATIONS.
[See also §§ 71, 73.]

ܐܵܗܵܐ ܒܸܗ ܫܵܘܹܐ (or ܒܵܣܹܐ) *this will do.*

ܐܵܙܹܠ ܒܕܘܼܢܝܹܐ *to prosper,* intr.

ܐܵܙܹܠ ܒܕܘܼܢܝܹܐ ܒܓܵܘ *to bear with.*

ܐܵܙܹܠ ܠܩܘܼܪܡܵܐ ܕ U. (or ܠܩܘܼܪܡ U.) } *to go to meet* (a person
ܐܵܙܹܠ ܠܩܘܼܪܡܓܵܐ ܕ   } arriving from a journey).

ܐܵܙܹܠ ܒܪܸܟ݂ܫܵܐ U. *to go on horseback.*

ܐܵܙܹܠ ܠܣܸܕܪܵܐ *to take a walk.*

ܐܵܙܹܠ ܒܐܲܩܠܵܐ *to go on foot.*

ܐܸܒܕܘܼܟ݂ ܒܸܗ ܗܵܘܹܐ ؟ U. *Will you have time?* [Only as a question, or as a negative: ܠܹܐ ܗܵܘܹܐ ܠܝܼ ܐܸܒܕܘܼܟ݂.]

ܐܵܘ ܐܸܒܕܘܼܟ݂ ܠܵܐ ܢܵܒܸܕ݂ܵܐ ܠܵܐ ܢܵܗܹܐ U. *may you be friendless!* [Socin].

ܐܝܼܒܹܗ ܒܠܸܒܹܗ ܕ or ܐܝܼܒܹܗ ܠܹܗ ܠܸܒܵܐ ܕ *he intends to...*

ܐܝܼܒܹܗ ܠܹܗ ܗܸܕ݂ܒ݁ ܦ݁ܵܗܘܿܢܵܐ (ܗܸܕ݂ܒ݁ ܦ݁ܵܗܘܿܢܵܐ K.) *he is a hypocrite.*

ܐܵܓ݂ܸܕ ܓܘܼܡܕܵܐ U. (or ܓܘܼܡܕ K. or ܠܲܩܵܐ K.) *to threaten.*

ܐܵܓ݂ܸܕ ܠܲܩܵܐ (or ܟܹܡ or ܦܘܿܣܵܐ) *to take trouble.*

ܐܵܓ݂ܸܕ ܠܸܕ݂ܵܐ *to receive a pension.*

ܐܵܓ݂ܸܕ ܪܓ݂ܘܼܡܚܵܢܹܐ *to eat one's words.*

ܐܵܓ݂ܸܕ ܘܵܩܘܿܠ *to embezzle money.*

ܐܵܓ݂ܸܕ ܢܝܼܚܘܿܡ *to break a fast* (by eating animal food).

ܐܵܓ݂ܸܕ ܩܸܢܛܪ *to be bastinadoed.*

ܐܲܚܸܕ ܫܘܼܚܕܵܐ see § 16 (so ܐܲܚܸܕ ܫܘܼܚܕܹܗ).

ܐܲܚܸܕ ܕܩܲܚܫܹܐ *to take bribes.*

ܐܲܠܵܗܵܐ ܢܲܚܹܕ ܡܢܝܼܚܸܗ *requiescat in pace.*

ܐܲܠܵܗܵܐ ܢܲܚܠܸܡ ܚܘܼܦܹܗ *God strengthen you!* (said to a man working in a field).

ܐܲܠܵܗܵܐ ܠܵܐ ܢܸܚܸܕ *God forbid!*

ܐܲܠܵܗܵܐ ܡܲܘܪܸܒ ܠܘܼܟ *God increase you!* (said by a guest to a host).

ܐܲܠܵܗܵܐ (or ܡܲܚܕܘܼܦ) ܡܲܚܒܘܼܟ *Goodbye* (said to one departing).

ܐܸܢܵܐ ܒܲܠ ܢܝܼܕܵܐ *it is your affair* (so all persons).

ܒܨܲܦܪܵܐ ܕܡܲܚܕܸܢܫܵܐ *early morning.*

ܗܝܼܵܐ ܛܥܝܼܢܬܵܐ ܒܲܛܢܵܐ (also simply ܒܲܛܢܵܐ) *she is pregnant.*

ܐܸܡܥܵܘܗܝ ܓܝܸܕ ܒܲܠܹܗ *he is constipated.*

ܐܸܡܥܵܘܗܝ ܦܲܠܝܼܢܵܐ ܒܲܠܹܗ *his bowels are working.*

ܐܸܡܥܵܘܗܝ ܗܵܘܹܐ ܒܪܝܼܟܵܐ *may his foot be blessed* [said in U. of a new-born child, in K. of a stranger arriving just after a birth. In K. they say ܗܵܘܹܐ ܒܪܝܼܟܵܐ of a new-born male child].

ܐܸܡܥܵܘܗܝ ܚܠܝܼܦ ܒܲܠܹܗ *his diarrhœa is cured.*

ܐܸܡܠܲܩܘܗܝ ܡܣܝܼܡ ܠܹܗ ܘܡܸܬ *he died.*

ܐܸܡܥܵܘܗܝ ܒܲܠܹܗ ܕܒܝܼ ܦܨܝܼܚ *his foot was blistered.*

ܒܥܹܐ ܒܲܠܹܗ ܠܹܗ ܡܕܘܼܡܟܸܢܘܼܗܝ *he pitied them.*

ܒܹܝ ܒܥܹܐ *I am coming* [said by a man at a distance when called].

ܒܝܼ ܒܝܼܫ *displeased; unwell.*

ܒܗ݊ܝ ܦܸܠܵܐ ܐܸܒܹܐ ܗܵܘܝܵܐ *in that way it is possible.*

§ 75]   PHRASES.   197

ܒܝܬܝ ܣܬܪܐ ܝܠܗ K. *my house is destroyed* [said by a man on receiving bad news. The ܝܠܗ stands absolutely].

ܒܚܘܒܐ ܘܡܘ *I have come on a visit of friendship only* (not business). Also the reply to ܒܫܠܡܐ ܐܬܝܬ and then = *nothing*.

ܓܕܕܚܘܗ ܚܠܝܐ ܠܗ *he is tired out.*

(ܟܡܐ) ܚܒܝܬܐ ܕܐܙܐ ܠܘܟ or ܕܒܝܬܐ or ܚܒܝܬܐ ܚܕܐ ܒܝܬܐ or ܚܒܝܬܐ ܕܒܝܬܟ } *Welcome* (the answer to ܚܠܦܟ ܠܘܟ. Also the first two are said by a host to his guests. The other persons are also used).

ܒܗ ܡܚܢܐ ܠܘܟ؟ K. *will you have time?*

ܚܕ ܙܗܢܘܗܝ ܩܒܠܐ ܠܗ *he will not listen to reason.*

ܓܪܘܠܐ ܠܗܘܗ ܠܗ *he has bad diarrhœa.*

ܗܘܐ ܥܠ ܗܝܕܗ K. *he was pleased with himself.*

ܒܘܡܐ ܟܘܡܐ ܝܠܗ K. *I am a black owl* (said by a woman on hearing bad news).

ܐܚܕ ܡܘܗܝ ܟܘܕ *one whose hospitality none will accept.*

ܚܕܐ ܫܒܩ ܡ *to cease to support.*

ܚܕܐ ܕܕܚܩܐ *to sign* (a deed, etc.).

ܚܕܐ ܗܩܘܡ *to attack.*

ܚܕܐ ܦܩܗ *to take trouble.*

ܚܕܐ ܚܝܠܐ or ܦܕܘܘܡ U. (ܦܕܘܘܡ K.) *to mount guard.*

ܚܕܐ ܚܢܕ (or ܠܓܕܘܦܐ) *to step aside, keep out of.*

ܚܕܐ ܡ ܫܒܩ ܕ *to put up with.*

ܓܵܪܹܫ ܡܲܪܥܵܐ *to contract a disease.*

ܓܵܪܹܫ ܙܲܒ݂ܢܵܐ *to take time* [so ܓܪܸܫܠܹܗ ܠܹܗ ܬܠܵܬ݂ ܣܵܥܵܬ݂ܹ̈ܐ *it took three hours*].

ܓܵܪܹܫ ܩܸܢܐܵܐ *to be zealous.*

ܓܵܪܹܫ ܨܘܼܠܡܵܐ *to draw, to take a photograph.*

ܓܵܪܹܫ ܬܘܼܬܘܼܢ *to smoke tobacco* (so all words for pipes). In K. Z. ܬܢܵܢܵܐ is used for all kinds of smoking.

ܕܵܒܹܩ ܐܝܼܕܵܐ ܒ *to help.*

ܕܵܒܹܩ ܣܸܛܪܵܐ *to do line by line.*

ܕܵܒܹܩ ܟܸܪܝܼ *to hire.*

ܕܵܒܹܩ ܒܲܗܵܢܹܐ K. *to make excuses, find an excuse* (for fighting, etc.).

ܕܵܒܹܩ ܛܲܪܦܵܐ ܒ *to protect, side with.*

ܕܵܒܹܩ ܟܘܼܫܬܝܼ U. *to wrestle* [in K. simply ܓܵܠܹܫ].

ܕܵܒܹܩ ܟܲܝܠܵܐ *to measure.*

ܕܵܒܹܩ ܡܲܗܵܢܵܐ *to make an excuse.*

ܕܵܒܹܩ ܡܸܢ ܪܹܫܵܐ *to read from the beginning.*

ܕܵܒܹܩ ܡܲܪܲܚ *to bet.*

ܕܵܒܹܩ ܢܘܼܒܵܐ *to take one's turn.*

ܕܵܒܹܩ ܢܘܼܒܵܬ݂ܵܐ *to take turns.*

ܕܵܒܹܩ ܦܸܫܵܐ *to pay attention.*

ܕܵܒܹܩ ܢܟܲܠ *to cast up against,* § 71.

ܕܵܒܹܩ ܥܩܸܒ݂ܵܐ ܒ *to supplant.*

ܕܵܒܹܩ ܩܲܕܠܵܐ ܒ *to restrain.*

ܕܵܝܹܩ ܩܲܕܲܡܬܘܿܢܹܗ ܕ U. (ܩܲܕܲܡܬܹܗ ܕ K.) *to be in the way of.*

ܕܵܝܹܩ ܐܝܼܩܵܪܵܐ ܕ K. *to do honour to.*

ܕܵܝܹܩ ܩܲܪܵܘܘܼܠ U. (ܩܲܪܵܩܘܼܠ K.) *to mount guard.*

ܕܵܝܹܩ ܕܘܼܟܬܵܐ ܕ *to fill the place of.*

ܕܵܝܹܩ ܬܘܼܦܸܢܓ ܥܲܠ *to aim a gun at,* § 71.

ܕܘܼܟܬܵܐ ܟܒܝܼܫܬܵܐ ܝܼܠܵܗ̇ *there is no room.*

ܕܘܼܟܬܘܼܗܝ ܝܼܠܵܗ̇ } *it serves him right.*
ܕܘܼܟܬܘܼܗܝ ܡܘܼܬܲܟܝܼܠܬܘܼܗܝ ܝܼܠܵܗ̇ }

ܕܘܼܟܬܘܼܗܝ ܡܚܘܼܪܬܵܐ ܝܼܠܵܗ̇ *he is missed.*

ܕܸܡܹܗ ܡܪܘܼܚܸܫ ܠܹܗ *he heaved with emotion.*

ܕܸܡܘܼܗܝ ܩܲܪܝܼܪܵܐ *one who though handsome does not please.*

ܕܵܡܘܼܟ ܒܫܲܝܢܵܐ *Goodbye* (rare).

ܕܪܹܐ ܐܝܼܕܵܐ ܠ *to begin.*

ܕܪܹܐ ܟܘܼܫܵܓ *to slander.*

ܕܪܹܐ ܬܲܚܬ ܐܸܩܠܹܐ *to lay by the heels.*

ܕܪܹܐ ܬܲܚܬ ܬܢ̈ܵܐ *to delay, connive at.*

ܕܪܹܐ ܠܹܗ ܒܘܼܗܸܫܬܵܐ U. (ܗܲܦܣܵܐ K.) *to imprison.*

ܕܪܹܐ ܓܲܪܓܵܐ *to cast a net.*

ܕܪܹܐ ܙܘܼܙܹ̈ܐ ܥܲܠ *to subscribe money to.*

ܕܪܹܐ ܫܸܢܟܢܵܐ *to startle.*

ܕܪܹܐ ܚܲܢܕܲܩ *to make a moat.*

ܕܪܹܐ ܠܐܘܼܪܚܵܐ *to see off, start* (a person on the road).

ܕܪܹܐ ܠܦܸܓ݂ܵܐ ܕ *to importune.*

ܕܪܐ ܦܠܵܫܵܐ *to give battle.*

ܕܪܐ ܩܵܠܵܐ *to cry out.*

ܕܪܐ ܓܘܼܚܟܵܐ *to mock.*

ܫܠܵܡܵܐ (or ܥܠܵܡܵܐ) ܕܪܐ *to salute, send greetings.*

ܕܪܐ ܗܘܿܦܸܟ ܒܸܕ *to shoot.*

ܗܘܹܐ ܡܒܘܼܪܟܵܐ *may it be blessed* (said by a friend to another of anything new belonging to the latter).

ܗܘܿܝܘܼܗܝ ܠܵܐ ܦܵܗܸܡ *he does not understand.*

ܗܘܹܐ (or ܩܘܼܪܒܵܢܘܼܟ) ܫܠܵܡܘܼܟ *May I be your sacrifice!* (expression of politeness to a superior on presenting a petition, etc.).

ܗܘܹܐ ܒܣܝܼܡܵܐ *thank you* (so all persons).

ܘܗܘܿ ܒܵܥܹܐ ܓܘܼܚܟܵܐ ܡܸܢܹܗ *he is exaggerating.*

ܘܵܕܪ ܟܸܡ (also ܕܸܪ ܟܸܡ K.) *never mind.*

ܣܬܘܼܡܵܐ ܕܦܵܬܵܐ Tkh. *a cheek* (= ܢܲܥܹܐ).

ܫܲܓܸܫ ܥܘܼܠܵܐ *to injure a plan, intrigue.*

ܫܲܓܸܫ ܠܹܗ ܥܘܼܠܵܐ *to interfere in the matter.*

ܣܸܓܢܹܐ ܕܝܘܿܡܵܐ Tkh. *twilight, evening.* ܣܸܓܢܹܐ ܕܚܸܕܵܕܹܐ U. Tkh.:

ܣܸܓ ܡܸܢܕܝܼ ܡܕܸܪ *that is a different matter.*

ܣܸܓ ܗܵܘܹܐ ܡܕܸܪ *almost = I cannot exactly describe it or him.*

ܣܘܿܬܵܐ ܚܣܝܼܓܵܐ ܡܕܸܪ *a quarrel has arisen.*

ܣܘܿܡܵܐ ܕܚܒܝܼ K. *blue on my head!* (said by a woman on hearing bad news).

ܡܚܘܼܡܸܕ ܟܹܗ (also ܣܘܼܠܟܘܿܗܝ ܗܵܕܹܐ ܟܹܗ) *his face fell.*

ܫܡܥܝܒ ܠܝ ܒܒܝ ܠܝܐ *I was home sick, discontented.*

ܫܘܝܘܗܝ ܟܡܐ ܕܡܕܘܗܝ ܟܠܕܝܕܝܕܗ U.[1] *May I see you rolling in blood!*

ܫܘܝܘܗܝ ܩܕܐ ܫܬܕܘܗܝ ܐܚܢܐ U.[1] *Bad luck to you!*

ܫܘܝܘܗܝ ܠܡܗ ܕܒܘܗܝ ܠܐ ܨܝܚܗ U.[1] *May you not get what you wish!*

ܫܘܝܘܗܝ ܡܢܐ ܕܝܗܒܘܗܘܗܝ ܠܐ ܢܘܗ ܚܟܢܘܗܝ U.[1] *May you never see the khena of your wedding!* [khena, *a dye*].

ܫܝܠܐ ܩܕܡ ܕܢܬܐ ܕ *to please*, tr.

(ܒܘܝܕܗ) ܒܠܬܕܗ ܐܘܘܣ? K.) *have you any business for me?* [said by a visitor before taking leave, see ܟܗܝܡܘܚܘܗܝ].

ܫܝܠܝ ܟܕܝܗ *to strive.*

ܣܩܕܐ ܕܝܨܝܩܐ *a trestle.*

ܫܝܒ ܚܨܝܟܐ ܐܢܐ K. *my back is broken* (said by a man on hearing bad news).

ܣܕܒܬ ܠܝܐ ܝܬܒ *I do not feel well.*

ܣܓܚܢܗ ܕܠܢܗ (or ܐܗܕܢܐ or ܠܓܙܝ ܟܕܐ) *twilight, evening.*

ܟܠܝܬ ܡܣܠܕܢܗ *to say goodbye,* as an inferior to a superior.

ܢܓܠܬ ܒܓܠ ܡܙܠܘܚܘܣ (or ܢܓܠ) *to avow, take the responsibility of.*

ܠܩܕܐ ܠܝܐ ܝܬܒ *I was tired.*

ܡܕܝܕ ܠܒ *I understand* (said on receiving information).

ܟܘܓܠ ܚܘܘܢܐ *to sell for money.*

ܟܘܓܠ ܚܓܕܒ *to let out* (on hire).

---

[1] These four curses are from Socin.

ܝܵܗܹܒ݂ܠ ܠܸܒܵܐ ܠ *to comfort, give heart to, encourage.*

ܝܵܗܹܒ݂ܠ ܡܸܠܟ݂ܘܼܬܵܐ (or ܕܵܪܹܐ) *to advise.*

ܝܵܗܹܒ݂ܠ ܡܲܫܩ *to drill.*

ܝܵܗܹܒ݂ܠ ܣܵܗܕܘܼܬܵܐ ܒܘܼܬ݂ (or ܒ) U. *to testify to,* § 71.

ܝܵܗܹܒ݂ܠ ܦܵܬܵܐ ܩܵܐ *to support, take the side of.*

ܝܵܗܹܒ݂ܠ ܪܘܼܚܣܲܬ݂ ܒ *to give leave of absence to,* § 71.

ܝܵܗܹܒ݂ܠ ܫܠܵܡܵܐ ܠ (or ܩܵܐ) *to salute* (face to face).

ܝܵܗܹܒ݂ܠ ܐܲܬ݂ܘܼܒܹܗ *to comfort.*

ܝܵܠܸܦ ܟܹܐܟ ܩܲܪܝܵܐ *to learn fluently.*

ܝܲܒܡܘܼܪܵܐ ܝܠܹܗ *he is a slow coach* (a man, horse, etc.).

ܝܵܪܝܼܟ݂ ܚܲܝܘܼܟ݂ *long life to you!*

ܝܵܬܹܒ݂ ܒܕܘܼܟܵܐ ܕ *to succeed,* tr.

ܝܵܬܹܒ݂ ܥܲܠ ܣܘܼܣܝܵܐ K. *to ride.*

ܒܲܠܟܵܐ ܗܵܘܹܐ ܕ or ܒܲܠܟܵܐ ܗܵܘܝܵܐ ܕ *perhaps, it is possible that.*

ܟ݂ܘܼܠܘܼܟ݂ ܦܬܝܼܚܵܐ ܠܹܗ ܡܸܢܝܼ *you are angry with me.*

ܟܲܠܝܵܐ ܒܕܘܼܟܘܼܗ̇ܝ *to stand one's ground;* or *to stop short.*

ܟܲܠܝܵܐ ܥܲܠ ܚܒ݂ܘܼܪܘܼܗ̇ܝ *to stick to one's word,* esp. in bargaining [ܚܒ݂ܘܼܪܵܐ, *a word,* often = the price asked for a thing].

ܦܵܠܹܓ ܡܘܼܙܵܐ *to split hairs.*

ܟܡܵܐ ܚܫܸܒ݂ܠܹܗ? *how much did he charge?*

ܟܡܵܐ ܕܫܲܦܝܼܪܵܐ ܒܸܫ ܝܠܹܗ *he is very good.*

ܡܝܼܬܠܹܗ ܠܹܗ ܒܕܘܼܟܘܼܗ̇ܝ *he died where he stood.*

ܟܲܦܟܵܐ ܕܠܵܐ ܡܫܝܼܓ̣ܬܵܐ *an unwashed spoon* (one who interrupts a conversation).

ܟܬ̣ܵܒ̣ ܡܢ ܦܸܬ̣ܓ̣ܵܡܵܐ ܕ *to copy* (from a book, etc.).

ܠܹܐ ܗܵܘܹܐ U. or ܠܹܐ ܗܵܘܝܵܐ U. or ܠܹܐ ܫܵܟ̣ܢܵܐ (rare) or ܠܵܐ ܡܫܲܟ̣ܢܵܐ Al. *it is impossible* [contrast ܠܵܐ ܗܵܘܹܐ = *God forbid*, § 73.]

ܠܹܐ ܝ ܘܸܢ ܥܲܡܘܼܟ̣ (or ܥܲܡܘܿܟ̣ܘܿܢ) {*Mind your own business.* / *I am not speaking to you.*}

ܠܹܐ ܝܠܵܗ ܒܸܗܬܬ̣ܵܐ ؟ *For shame!*

ܠܹܐ ܝܠܹܗ ܡܲܚܙܘܼܝܵܐ *I cannot find it, or it is not in sight.*

ܠܹܐ ܡܵܛܹܐ ܚܲܝܠܝ ܗܵܠ *I cannot conceive.*

ܠܹܐ ܡܲܨܸܝܢ ܕܵܝܘܹܗ *I cannot stand him.*

ܠܹܐ ܡܵܛܝܵܐ ܒܟ̣ܝܼܣܝ or ܠܹܐ ܡܲܟ̣ܬܸܢܵܐ ܠܝ *I cannot afford to...*

ܠܵܐ ܦܘܼܪܨܲܬ̣ܵܐ ܠܝ Ti. Al. *I have not time.*

ܠܵܐ ܚܲܝܠܵܐ ܠܝ ܒܓܵܘܹܗ *I have no chance against him.*

ܠܸܒܵܐ ܒܡܲܚܵܝܵܐ ܝܠܹܗ *the heart is beating.*

ܠܸܒܘܿܗܝ ܒܟ̣ܪܵܝܵܐ ܝܠܹܗ *he has a stomach ache*; or, metaphorically, *he is unwilling to do it.*

ܠܸܒܘܿܗܝ ܣܘܼܪܵܐ *unmanly.*

ܠܸܒܘܿܗܝ ܚܠܝܼܨܵܐ ܝܠܹܗ *he is sad, homesick.*

ܠܸܒܘܿܗܝ ܡܚܸܠܹܗ ܠܹܗ *he pitied.*

ܠܸܒܘܿܗܝ ܡܲܠܒܸܫܘܼܝܹܐ ܝܠܹܗ *he will not allow it to be done.*

ܠܸܒܘܿܗܝ ܟܘܼܦ (hard Kap) *an impetuous man.*

ܠܸܒܘܿܗܝ ܒܟܹܝܦܹܗ *he was in an ecstasy.*

ܠܸܒܘܿܗܝ ܦܝܼܫ ܠܹܗ ܡܢ *he was not hearty with, he was displeased with.*

ܠܒܘܗܝ ܦܩܥ ܠܗ *he was much frightened.*

ܠܒܘܗܝ ܦܬܚ ܠܗ *he was pleased.*

ܠܒܘܗܝ ܩܫܝܐ U. *merciless.*

ܠܒܐ ܬܪܝ *to doubt.*

ܠܝܬ ܠܗ ܐܝܕܐ ܥܠ ܕܐܗܐ *he cannot interfere in this.*

ܠܝܬ ܠܗ ܚܒܪܐ *he has not heard* (news).

ܠܝܬ ܠܗ ܫܘܩܠܐ ܡܢ ܕܐܗܐ *it is not his business.* [So: ܪܥܘܝܐ ܟܬܒ ܠܗ ܕܩܫܝܫܐ ܠܐ ܗܘܐ ܠܗ ܫܘܩܠܐ ܡܢ ܡܪܥܝܬܐ *the bishop wrote suspending the priest from the parish.*]

ܡܕܪܝ ܐܕܝܘܡ *this day week,* or *this time to-morrow.*

ܡܚܫܡ ܦܬܐ ܕ *to condole with* (after a death), *to pay a visit of condolence to.*

ܡܫܩܬܐ ܠܒܗ ܕܝܘ *to charm, please.*

ܡܒܪܟ ܡܠܟܬܐ (or ܟܪܡܐ or ܒܝܬܐ etc.) *to congratulate* on receiving a present, buying a vineyard, building a new house, etc.

ܡܒܪܟ ܥܐܕܐ ܕ *to visit on a feast day.*

ܡܒܪܟܬܐ ܕܒܝܬܐ *a house-warming* (see above).

ܡܡܠܠ ܗܝܕܘܡܐܝܬ *to speak deliberately.*

ܡܓܚܟ ܫܦܘܬܐ *to smile.*

ܡܪܝܡ ܡܢܘ U. *to take away* (at table).

ܡܪܝܡ ܥܝܢ ܐܘܪܚܐ ܕ U. *to expect.*

ܡܪܝܡ ܥܝܢ ܪܓܠܘܗܝ U. *to be humble* (cf. Proverb 23).

ܡܕܝܢܚܐ ܦܬܚܠܗ (or ܦܬܚܗܐ) U. or ܡܕܝܢܚܐ ܦܬܚܗܘܐ
or ܡܕܝܢܚܐ ܦܪܐ ܠܗ } *the day broke.*

ܦܪܝܕ ܫܢܝܐ *to run away.*

ܡܘܢ ܫܥܐ ܝܠܗ؟ *what o'clock is it?*

ܡܘܢ ܥܘܠܐ ܐܝܬ ܠܘܟ؟ *Mind your own business.*

ܦܘܝܕ ܒܡܕܠܐ ܕ *to outbid.*

ܡܚܝܐ ܐܘܪܚܐ *to be a traveller, to travel.*

ܡܚܝܐ ܒܩܘܡܨܐ *to gather* (a dress).

ܡܚܝܐ ܛܒܥܐ *to print* (the thing printed is the direct object, § 64).

ܡܚܝܐ ܒܥܝܢܐ *to cast the evil eye on.*

ܡܚܝܐ ܓܪܘܡ *to entangle.*

ܡܚܝܐ ܒܪܟܐ *to kneel.*

ܡܚܝܐ ܩܪܨܐ ܐܘܪܚܐ *to backbite.*

ܡܚܝܐ ܠܘܓܡܐ *to hit out.*

ܡܚܝܐ ܠܘܡ *to dive.*

ܡܚܝܐ ܓܢܒܐ *to steal.*

ܡܚܝܐ ܒܐܪܥܐ *to resolve.*

ܡܚܝܐ ܕܪܒܐ *to wound* (direct object).

ܡܚܝܐ ܕܪܘܫ ܒ *to accuse.*

ܡܚܝܐ ܕܪܡܢܐ ܥܠ *to paint* (a door, etc.).

ܡܚܝܐ ܒܛܡܓܐ *to sign* (a paper); *to cheat in weighing.*

ܡܚܝܐ ܙܘܪܢܐ *to blow a trumpet;* or, metaphorically, *to waste one's breath.* [ܡܚܝܐ is used with all musical instruments.]

ܡܚܝܐ ܙܚܠ *to slide* (as boys at play).

ܡܚܝܐ ܙܪܪ ܠܗ (or ܠ) *to injure* (of a personal agent).

ܡܚܐ ܢܡܠܐ *to make an effort.*

ܡܚܐ ܢܬܡܕܐ ܒܝܕ *to cause loss to.*

ܡܚܐ ܢܣܝ ܕ *to take refuge in.*

ܡܚܐ ܟܘܕܢܐ *to assemble.*

ܡܚܐ ܓܠܒܐ U. *to make an effort, strive.*

ܡܚܐ ܦܩܗܠܐ *to slap.*

ܡܚܐ ܦܩܕ *to make a fence.*

ܡܚܐ ܚܕܬܐ *to be angry.*

ܡܚܐ ܚܕܕܐ (or ܚܕܕܕ) *to plough.*

ܡܚܐ ܟܕܘܟܝ (hard final Kap) *to snap the fingers.*

ܡܚܐ ܒܕܟܝܐ *to be appalled* (by bad news). [Striking the knees is a common action on hearing bad news.]

ܡܚܐ ܠܟܡܐ *to put on a bridle.*

ܡܚܐ ܠܦܪܨܘ ܕ *to throw in one's face, recriminate.*

ܡܚܐ ܠܬܚܬ *to undermine* (direct object).

ܡܚܐ ܚܠܠܐ *to reap well.*

ܡܚܐ ܚܘܬܡ *to seal* (direct object).

ܡܚܐ ܡܗܡܙܘ *to spur* (direct object).

ܡܚܐ ܡܬ (ܡܬ = *checkmate*) *to die.*

ܡܚܐ ܡܝܥܕܐ *to make a mark or note.*

ܡܚܐ ܢܥܠܐ *to shoe* (horses, etc.; direct object).

ܡܚܐ ܢܘܠ *to fall ill a second time.*

ܡܚܐ ܦܬܟ *to paint* (as an artist).

ܡܚܝܐ ܢܫܫܬܐ *to starch.*

ܡܚܝܐ ܣܒܘܢ *to soap.*

ܡܚܝܐ ܣܚܘܬܐ *to swim.*

ܡܚܝܐ ܣܟܬܐ *to mint, coin.*

ܡܚܝܐ ܥܓܘܪ *to play the organ.*

ܡܚܝܐ ܦܢܬܐ ܒ *to intercede for.*

ܡܚܝܐ ܦܝܢܕ (ܒ) *to engraft* (direct object).

ܡܚܝܐ ܦܠܟ *to inform against.*

ܡܚܝܐ ܦܠܟܠ K. *to fillip*, or *to snap the fingers.*

ܡܚܝܐ ܡܗܪܐ K. *to sign* (a letter).

ܡܚܝܐ ܢܘܪܓܐ *to fell with an axe* (with direct object of thing felled).

ܡܚܝܐ ܬܡܝܕ (see ܡܚܝܐ ܢܝܟ).

ܡܚܝܐ ܩܕܡܬܐ *to hit on the top of the head.*

ܡܚܝܐ ܒܠܟܒܕܘܪܐ *to besiege* (direct object).

ܡܚܝܐ ܕܪܡܢܐ = ܡܚܝܐ ܪܢܟ.

ܡܚܝܐ ܪܢܕܐ *to plane* (direct object) = ܡܪܢܕܝܢ K.

ܡܚܝܐ ܪܦܣܬܐ (in K. ܪܦܣ) *to kick out.*

ܡܚܝܐ ܬܡܓܐ *to imprint, take an impression.*

ܡܚܝܐ ܝܣܢܐ *to blight* (direct object).

ܡܚܝܐ ܚܢܕܐ *to flatter.*

ܡܚܝܐ ܢܩܫܐ *to draw* (a picture).

ܡܚܝܐ ܒܠܣܡ *to vaccinate.*

ܚܒܪ ܐܒܢܐ *to be ironical.*

ܚܒܪ ܐܢܟ *to measure (a field).*

[See also ܝܕܐ : ܒܨܢܐ : ܒܕܩܐ *and* § 63 (2).]

ܒܚܠܬ ܒܣܠܟܢܐ (cf.) ܒܣܠܒ ܠܝ *forgive me = goodbye.*

ܒܣܒܝ ܙܢܟܘܗܝ *to frown.*

ܒܣܙܒ ܒܚܕܐ ܕ *to calumniate.*

ܚܒܕ ܠܐܝܕܐ ܕ *to be received by.* [Also: *he laid hold of* (the book) = ܚܒܕ ܠܗ ܠܐܝܕܘܗܝ (ܟܬܒܐ).]

ܚܒܕ ܠܐܕܘܗ *to be driven to extremities.*

ܚܒܢܐ ܕܐܝܕܐ *dexterity.*

ܚܒܢܐ ܕܦܪܨܘܦܐ *modesty.*

ܚܒܝܠܐ ܚܣܒܝ ܐܢܐ K. *I am struck blue* (said by a woman on hearing bad news).

ܚܒܝܠܐ ܒܕ ܚܣܘܩܗ K. *sorrow on him!*

ܒܓܚܕ ܦܪܨܘܦܐ ܕ *to put to shame, convict.*

ܒܓܕܢܟ ܒܦܩܐ *to pout.*

ܒܓܕܓܕ ܠܗ ܦܪܨܘܦܐ ܕ *to insult.*

ܒܓܕܓܐ ܠܒܐ *to tickle the fancy.*

ܚܒܟ ܗܘܦܟܐ *to load a gun.*

ܒܓܚܕ ܠܒܐ ܕ *to displease.*

ܡܢ ܛܘܒܐ ܕܐܠܗܐ ܘܕܪܝܫܘܟܝ K. *from the bounty of God and of your head* (an expression of gratitude). So, *thanks to* N., ܡܢ ܛܘܒܐ ܕܦܠܢ U. K.

§ 75]   PHRASES.   209

مجبورﮪ (or ܡܢܘܗܝ) K. *of necessity.*

ܡܚܘܐ ܒܟ *I am speaking to you, I want to speak to you* (used to call a person's attention).

ܡܢܘܕܐ ܟܘܦܪܐ K. or ܡܚܡܝܕ ܟܘܦܪܐ U. *to say grace.*

ܡܚܓܕ ܓܒܕܗ *to rival, envy.*

ܡܚܠܝܢ ܗܟܘܡܐ = ܡܚܕܪ ܗܟܘܡܐ.

ܡܚܟܝܕ ܓܢܐ K. *to take leave of* one remaining: see ܩܘܕ ܓܢܐ.

ܡܚܓܠ ܘܡܓܘܡܢ *to take back a promise, prevaricate.*

ܡܚܠܣ ܙܠܐ *to open the bowels.*

ܡܩܠܝܕ ܫܠܝ *to acquit.*

ܡܩܠܝܕ ܠܓܪܗܐ *to detect, bring to light.*

ܡܩܠܝܕ ܚܘܡ *to juggle.*

ܡܚܕܘܗܝ ܥܠܡܐ *to break the peace.*

ܡܚܡܝܕ ܒܝܫ *to suffer.*

ܡܚܡܝܕ ܦܪܓܐ ܕ *to disappoint.*

ܡܚܣܘ ܦܪܓܐ ܕ *to importune.* (So: *importunity* = ܒܘܗܪܐ ܕܦܪܓܐ.)

ܡܚܕܪ ܫܢܐ ܕ *to defend.*

ܡܚܣܝܘ ܗܟܘܡܐ *to pout.*

ܡܚܕܝܥ ܓܢܐ *to be long suffering.*

ܡܚܕܝܥ ܥܘܠܐ ܕ *to remand* (as a judge).

ܡܚܪܩܐ ܒܝܕܐ (ܒܡ) *to give up, give in, renounce.*

ܡܚܝܟܕ ܒܝܕܐ *to beckon.*

ܡܚܢܕܐ ܡܢ ܒܝܬܐ *to break ground, begin at the beginning.*

...ܕ ܟܠܝܼܬܹܗ ܡܚܒ to *intend to*....

ܒܣܝܕܢܐ ܠܟܒܐ ܡܚܒ ܒܝ̈ ܡܚܒ to *compare one thing with another*.

ܒܠܐ ܓܐܦܐ ܡܚܒ to *shelve* (a matter).

ܕ ܡܕܠܐ ܒܠ ܥܘܠܐ ܡܚܒ to *make responsible for the matter*.

(ܚܒܝܐ see) ܡܚܒ ܥܘܩܐ.

ܠܡܬ݂ܝܘܗ̈ܝ ܒܣܘܕܐ *Light to your dead!* (said for ܠܘܗ̈ܝ ܥܠܘܗܝ on Good Friday and Easter Even).

ܠܘܗ̈ܝ ܢܒܝ (see ܢܘܗ § 46) said to a person about to drink or to eat after drinking: the answer to ܣܘܚܘܗ̈ܝ § 73.

ܠܐܘܪܚܐ ܢܦܝܩ to *start* (on a journey).

ܕ ܠܐܝܙܐ ܢܦܝܩ (or ܕ ܐܝܙܐ) to *happen to*. [So: *He laid hold of it* = ܠܐܝܕܘܗܝ. *He understood it* = ܒܗܘܫܗ ܢܦܝܩ (or ܕܒܪܘܗܝ or (ܠܗ̈).]

ܚܘܢܒܝ ܟܠܗ ܠܒܝܠܐ *bedridden*.

ܒܓܢܗ ܠܟܗ ܡܚܕܗ *he is homesick*.

ܠܟܗ ܒܓܢܗ ܡܗܘܕܗ *he is pleased, content: he feels at home*.

ܠܟܗ ܕܣܝܒܠܐ ܣܘܣܐ *the horse is hardened* (to heat, cold, etc.).

ܠܗ ܕܡܚܝ ܥܕܢܐ *the watch stopped*.

ܠܘܗ̈ܝ ܢܒܝ = (sic) ܠܘܗ̈ܝ ܗܘܬ ܥܕܢܐ.

? ܝܠܗ ܟܡܐ ܥܕܢܐ *What o'clock is it?*

ܬܕܝܙܢܐ ܗܘܐ ܣܘܩܕܡܘܗ̈ܝ *May your journey be blessed!* (said after, not before, a journey).

[§ 75]

ܒܐܕܘܢܝ ܗܘܝ ܒܕܝܟܐ *May your feast be blessed!* (esp. at Christmas and Easter).

ܥܒܕ ܐܕܘ ̈ *to celebrate the Eucharist.*

ܥܒܕ ܢܕܐ *to negotiate a cheque.*

ܥܒܕ ܠܡܢܕܚܕ *to condemn.*

ܥܒܕ ܚܢܗܐ ܬ § 71, *to sin against.*

ܥܒܕ ܕܝܢܐ *to go to law* [he went to law before the heathen = ܚܒܒܕ ܠܗ ܕܝܢܐ ܕܢܫܠܡܘܢܐ].

ܥܒܕ ܗܒ ܡܢ § 71, *to trust in.*

ܥܒܕ ܗܓܡ (or ܗܘܓ) *to attack.*

ܥܒܕ ܗܘܝ *to take pleasure in.*

ܥܒܕ ܘܕܕ ܠܡ (or ܠ) *to injure (of an impersonal agent).*

ܥܒܕ ܚܝܛܐ ܠ (or ܩܒܝܡܘܓܐ ܠܡ) *to benefit, treat well.*

ܥܒܕ ܚܕܡ ܠ *to pity.*

ܥܒܕ ܟܕܒܐ (or ܩܕܒ) *to deceive (rare in U.).*

ܥܒܕ ܡܘܕܫܡܐ *to dismiss (in peace), let go.*

ܥܒܕ ܡܘܣܘܓܐ *to be hospitable.*

ܥܒܕ ܡܠܟܘܡܐ *to reign.*

ܥܒܕ ܡܝܠܟܐ (or ܕܡܒ) *to take counsel or give advice.*

ܥܒܕ ܡܤܡ *to drill,* intr.

ܥܒܕ ܢܘܙ *to wheedle, coquet.*

ܥܒܕ ܗܘܡܐ (= ܓܠܘܕ K. or ܡܓܕܘܕ Al.) *to circumcise.*

ܥܒܕ ܗܘܕܟܡ ܢ *to exile, banish.*

ܥܒܵܕܵܐ ܣܲܦܲܪ *to travel.*

ܥܒܵܕܵܐ ܥܲܪܙ ܠ *to petition.*

ܥܒܵܕܵܐ ܥܲܪܙ ܡܢ ܕܝܼܢܵܐ ܕ *to prosecute; appeal against or from.*

ܥܒܵܕܵܐ ܦܲܝܘܲܢܕ *to engraft.*

ܥܒܵܕܵܐ ܩܲܕܲܓ݂ܲܢ (or ܩܲܕܲܓ݂ܵܐ K.) *to prohibit.*

ܥܒܵܕܵܐ ܓ݂ܝܼܒܲܬ *to backbite.*

ܥܒܵܕܵܐ ܓ݂ܝܼܪܲܬ *to be zealous.*

ܥܒܵܕܵܐ ܪܲܕ *to beat off.*

ܥܒܵܕܵܐ ܪܵܙܝܼ *to persuade.*

ܥܒܵܕܵܐ ܪܲܚܡܵܐ ܠ *to be merciful to.*

ܥܒܵܕܵܐ ܓܪܝܼ *to weep.*

ܥܒܵܕܵܢܵܐ ܕܡܲܟ Tkh. *a hypocrite.*

ܥܒܵܕ ܥܲܠ ܡܵܘܡܵܬܵܐ § 71, *to perjure oneself.*

ܥܲܝܢܘܼܗܝ ܕܫܸܢܬܵܐ ܝܠܹܗ *he is sleepy.*

ܥܲܝܢܘܼܗܝ ܠܵܐ ܚܵܘܪܝܼ *his eyes shall not be white* (a curse).

ܥܲܝܢܘܼܗܝ ܟܦܝܼܢܹܐ *avaricious.*

ܥܲܝܢܘܼܗܝ ܣܒܝܼܥܹܐ *generous.*

ܥܲܝܢܘܼܗܝ ܡܚܹܐ ܠܹܗ ܥܸܠܝܼ *he saw me; or he cast the evil eye on me.*

ܥܲܠ ܕܪܵܥܵܢܘܼܗܝ *in his arms.*

ܥܲܠ ܥܲܝܢܝܼ *on my eye be it* (said by a servant receiving a command: he puts his hand over his eye).

ܥܲܠ ܣܘܼܦܪܵܐ ܝܠܹܗ (or ܥܲܠ .. ܝܠܹܗ ܕܣܘܼܦܪܵܐ) *he is at table* (dinner, &c.).

ܢܛܠ ܡܕܠܘܗܝ ܝܠܗ (see ܢܛܝܢ, ܡܛܝܒ) *he is responsible.*

ܗܘܝܢ ܚܠܦܘܟ = ܢܦܫܐ ܒܫܘܦܐ ܕܥܠܘܟ ܗܘܝܢ.

ܚܕܐ ܐܝܬ ܠܝ or ܚܕܐ ܒܥܝܢ *hear what I have to say* (used to call attention to a subject about to be introduced).

ܦܝܫ ܐܝܟ ܗܘܝܐ *to remain as he is.*

ܦܐܬܐ ܩܕܡ ܦܐܬܐ *face to face.*

ܦܐܬܘܗܝ ܟܡܝܫ ܠܗ *his face fell.*

ܦܐܬܪܘܦܘܗܝ ܝܬܝܒܐ ܝܠܗ *he is fidgeting.*

ܦܘܡܐ ܕܣܝܦܐ *the edge of the sword* (Gk. *στόμα μαχαίρας*).

ܦܘܫ ܒܫܝܢܐ *goodbye* (said by a person leaving, see ܙܠܘܐ ܡܫܝܢܘܟ).

ܦܠܛ ܙܟܝ *to be acquitted.*

ܦܠܛ ܠܐܘܪܥܐ ܕ (or ܩܕܡ) *to go to meet* one arriving.

ܦܠܛ ܠܒܗܪܐ *to be brought to light.*

ܦܠܛ ܡܢ ܗܘܫܘܗܝ *to go out of one's mind.*

ܦܠܛ ܡܣܟܢܐ (or ܡܣܟܢ) *to become bankrupt.*

ܦܪܝܚܐ ܠܗ ܓܪܡܗ *he made himself angry.*

ܦܪܩ ܡܢ ܐܝܕܐ ܕ § 71, *to have done with* (a person).

ܦܬܚ ܦܠ *to tell a fortune.*

ܦܬܝܚ ܠܗ ܠܒܘܗܝ *he wore his heart on his sleeve.*

ܙܠܝܟ ܡܘܬܐ = ܥܠܝܟ ܡܘܬܐ.

ܥܠܐ ܕܠܒܘܟ (= ܢܚܬܐ ܠܠܒܘܟ) *May it descend to your heart!*

ܩܵܐܹܡ ܠܹܗ ܦܵܐܹܡ ܕ *to oppose.*

ܩܘܼܪܒܵܐ ܠܒܝܕܹܗ *at hand (of place).*

ܩܘܼܪܒܵܐ ܠܡܵܘܬܵܐ *near to death.*

ܩܸܛܡܵܐ ܒܪܹܫܝ *Ashes on my head!* (said by a man on hearing bad news).

ܩܲܝܸܕ ܚܘܼܠܵܐ *to settle or arrange a matter.*

ܩܲܝܕܵܡܵܘܟ݂ ܒܛܵܒ݂ܬܵܐ or ܩܵܐ ܨܲܦܪܵܐ *good morning.*

ܩܲܡܨܹܐ ܒܸܡܚܵܝܵܐ ܝܠܹܗ *there is a plague of locusts.*

ܩܵܪܹܐ ܒܫܸܡܵܐ ܕ *to appeal to* (a higher court)—not colloquial.

ܩܸܕܵܡܘܼܗܝ ܒܕܲܒ݂ܝܼܚܵܐ ܝܠܹܗ (pronounce ܚ = ܥ) *he is dead.*

(ܩܵܐ ܩܸܕܵܐ ܠܒܝ or) ܩܸܕܵܚܵܐ ܒܸܣܝܵܩܵܐ *I have caught cold.*

ܩܸܛܠܵܐ ܕܩܵܐ ܡܲܩܛܘܼܠܹܐ ܠܕܵܘܹܗ (or ܝܠܹܗ) *there was great bloodshed.*

ܩܸܕ݇ܠܝܼ ܠܒܝܼ ܕܝܵܗܘܼܗܝ (or ܝܠܹܗ ܒܕܸܠܝܼ or ܝܠܹܗ) *I have found out about it* (a plot), *I see it now* (a difficult problem).

ܩܪܝܼܫܵܐ ܒܪܹܚܵܢܵܐ ܝܠܹܗ *it smells bad* (meat, etc.).

ܩܪܲܡܫܵܘܟ݂ ܒܛܵܒ݂ܬܵܐ *good night, good evening* (said by one leaving).

ܟ݂ܘܼܠ ܚܲܕ = ܕܸܟ ܚܲܕ.

ܦܵܐܘܼܚ Z. ܟܠܹܗ or ܟ݂ܘܼܠ or ܕܸܟ ܚܲܕܟܵܕ ܕܸܟ ܚܲܕ or ܕܸܟ ܚܲܕܟܵܕ ܒܝܼܵܩܸܕܝܘܼܬܵܐ ܟܠܹܗ Z. *Welcome!*

ܪܹܫܵܐ ܕܝܲܪܚܵܐ *the first day of the month.*

ܪܹܫܵܘܗܝ ܒܩܵܠܸܒ݂ܬܵܐ ܝܠܹܗ ܡܸܢ ܚܘܼܠܵܐ *he understands the business.*

ܪܹܫܵܘܟ݂ ܗܵܘܹܐ ܒܸܣܲܡܵܐ *May your head be healed!* (condolence after a death).

ܫܵܒ݂ܸܩ ܒܫܲܠܵܡܵܐ *to say goodbye to one remaining behind.*

ܫܠܵܡܵܐ ܠܘܿܟ݂ *Peace to you!* (= *how do you do?, good morning,* etc. The answer is ܒ̇ܣܝܼܡܵܐ q. v.)

ܒܨܸܪ ܕܒܨܸܪ K. *a very little* [e.g. *a very little water* ܕܡܝܼܵܐ].

ܡܚܸܕ ܠܸܒܵܐ ܕ *to break the heart of.*

ܒܕܡܟ݂ܝ ܒܝܵܢܵܐ ܠܵܗܿ *I am sleepy.*

ܚܬ ܘܚܬ݂ܵܐ *bluff, outspoken.*

ܡܚܸܐ ܠܸܒܵܐ ܕ *to annoy greatly.*

ܡܚܸܐ ܕܦܘܫܘܼܚܬܵܐ *to say goodbye* (used of one departing).

ܡܚܸܐ ܠܸܒܵܐ *to take heart, be encouraged.*

ܡܚܸܐ ܡܼܢ ܟܬܵܒ݂ܵܐ ܕ (= ܚܓ݂ܒ) *to copy from a book.*

ܡܚܸܐ ܦܲܟܗܵܐ *to be a hypocrite* [so Al. ܡܲܚܝܵܢܵܐ ܕܦܲܟܗܵܐ *a hypocrite*, or ܡܚܸܐ ܦܲܟܗܵܐ id.; ܡܚܵܝܬܵܐ ܕܦܲܟܗܵܐ *hypocrisy,* see § 16].

ܡܚܸܐ ܕܪܝܼܚܵܐ *to smell* tr.

ܟܠܝܼܡ ܠܵܗܿ ܡܼܠܘܿܗܝ (or ܠܹܗ) *he was dazed, he lost his head, he lost the thread of the subject.*

ܡܚܕܝܼܬ ܠܘܿܪܗܹܐ *he died.*

For particular meanings of verbs see the author's Vocabulary of Verbs of Vernacular Syriac with English translations.

DERIVATION.

§ 76. Vernacular Syriac lends itself very much to the regular formation of derivatives. From all verbs nouns may be formed denoting an action or an agent.

NOUNS OF ACTION. (1) First Conjugation verbs form a noun of action as noted above in the sections on verbs, §§ 31—44 incl.

The second and third radicals take Zqapa, and ܐ is added. Thus we have ܦܪܵܩܵܐ *the act of finishing,* from ܦܪܵܩ *to finish.* Nouns thus formed (which are all masculines) are used also as pure substantives, and not only in the formation of tenses, but the plural is rare in most of them. For variations due to weak letters in the root see §§ 38—44 incl. This is a common O.S. formation.

These nouns are often used to denote the thing done rather than the action; thus ܥܒܵܕܵܐ *a deed,* (a noun not much used in U.), from ܥܒܵܕ *to do;* ܦܠܵܫܵܐ *a fight,* from ܦܠܵܫ *to fight* (the form ܦܠܵܫܬܵܐ, for which see below, is not much used in this verb); ܣܦܵܩܵܐ, from ܣܦܵܩ *to be empty,* in Al. = *a dish* or *jar* (= ܡܵܥܢܵܐ U. O.S. ܐܵܥܢܵܐ K.); ܦܪܵܣܵܐ, from ܦܪܵܣ *to spread,* in K. = *a tablecloth* (= ܣܘܼܦܪܵܐ U. Tkh.).

(2) Second Conjugation verbs form a noun of action by giving the first radical the same vowel that it has in the present participle, and by giving the second, or in quadriliterals the third, either Rwaṣa or Rwakha:—Rwaṣa if the first has Pthakha, and Rwakha if the first has Zqapa; the termination being ܹܐ. Thus ܡܲܚܘܼܒܹܐ *loving,* from ܡܲܚܸܒ *to love;* ܡܦܲܩܘܿܕܹܐ *commanding,* from ܡܦܲܩܸܕ *to command;* ܡܩܲܛܘܼܠܹܐ *causing to be killed,* from ܡܩܲܛܸܠ *to cause to be killed.* For variations see as above.

(3) More commonly used, apart from the formation of tenses, are the nouns of action in ܬܵܐ, except in the Alqosh dialect, where in the case of first conjugation verbs the first formation is more common; e.g. ܗܘܵܝܵܐ is more usual in Al. than ܗܘܵܝܬܵܐ *birth, being.*

These nouns are thus formed. First Conjugation verbs give the second radical Zqapa, and add the termination; but second conjugation verbs give the first radical the same vowel as the present participle, and the second radical, or in quadriliterals the third, Pthakha. Thus we have ܦܠܵܛܬܵܐ *the act of going out,* from ܦܠܵܛ *to go out* (first conjugation); but ܡܲܦܠܲܛܬܵܐ *the act of putting out,* from ܡܲܦܠܸܕ to put out (second conjugation); so ܡܲܚܒܸܬܼܵܐ the act of loving, from ܡܚܒ to love. These nouns are feminine and take the sixth form of plural. In Sal. etc. those derived from conj. 2 have Zlama on the first radical.

The Mim preformative, if vowelless, is silent in U. Sal. etc., and sometimes in K., usually in Al. Z. In K. and Al. there is sometimes a difference in meaning according as the Mim is sounded or not: thus ܡܚܲܕܬܵܐ is *the act of patching*, ܡܚܲܕܬܵܐ *a cloth* K.; ܡܲܚܒܼܝܵܐ is *the act of telling*, ܡܲܚܒܼܝܵܐ *a word*, Al. These nouns sometimes denote rather the thing done than the action, as above; thus ܡܲܫܬܝܵܐ = *a drink*, from ܫܬܐ *to drink* (= ܡܲܫܬܝܵܐ Al., O.S.). They are often used where we should use a finite verb; thus, *as I think* = ܒܲܣܒܵܪܝ ܕܝܠܝ. We may notice ܡܓܲܕܕܵܢܵܐ *a razor*, from ܓܲܕܸܕ *to cause to be shaved*. Note also that in Ṭiari there is a difference between ܠܥܵܣܵܐ or ܠܥܵܣܵܐ *a snack in the early morning*, from ܠܥܸܣ *to taste*, and ܠܥܲܣܬܵܐ *breakfast*, which is also the common word in U.; both also denote *the act of tasting*. ܡܲܬܩܵܠܵܐ *balance* U. (= ܡܲܬܩܵܠܵܐ K., O.S.; root ܬܩܠ) is not of this class.

Variations. (*a*) Verbs ܦܐ or ܦܘ when they interchange the first and second radicals in the formation of the tenses, § 38, interchange them also in making these nouns of action; e.g. ܝܘܠܦܵܢܵܐ *learning*, from ܝܠܦ *to learn*. So ܐܣܪ *to bind*, makes ܡܲܣܪܵܐ U. Q. Sal. Gaw., but ܡܣܪܬܵܐ Ti. MB. Sh. Al. Ash.

(*b*) Verbs ܠܐ change ܐ into ܝ; as ܦܫܝܵܐ *remaining* or *remainder*, from ܦܫܐ *to remain*; for verbs with medial ܝ see § 40.

(*c*) Verbs ܠܥ add ܥ after ܠ, which is silent, as ܡܲܫܡܲܥܬܵܐ *hearing*, from ܫܡܥ *to hear*. It is then customary to write Zqapa on the second radical of second conjugation verbs (the third in quadriliterals).

(d) Verbs ܠ change ܐ to ܘ, as ܓܠܵܝܬܵܐ *revealing*, from ܓܠܝ *to reveal*. Here also it is usual to write Zqapa in the second conjugation, as ܡܕܲܒܩܵܢܹܐ *delivering*, from ܡܕܒܩ *to deliver*.

We must distinguish ܠܒܝܼܫܵܐ *clothing*, and ܠܒܵܫܵܐ *the act of clothing*; ܒܝܼܫܵܐ *shame*, and ܒܵܫܵܐ *the act of being ashamed*.

(4) Nouns of action are occasionally formed by giving the first radical Rwaṣa, and by adding ܬܵܐ ܝ, as in O.S. Words marked with an asterisk are ecclesiastical or literary only.

Words of the form ܩܘܼܛܵܠܬܵܐ.

ܕܘܼܟܪܵܢܵܐ O.S.* *a saint's day*, lit. *memorial* (ܕܟܪ *to remember*, O.S.); the ܪ sound remains in the substantive.

ܒܘܼܪܟܵܢܵܐ O.S. *blessed*, (ܒܪܟ § 46).

ܝܘܼܠܦܵܢܵܐ O.S. *learning* (ܝܠܦ *to learn*, O.S.).

ܝܘܼܩܕܵܢܵܐ K. *fuel*, see below (ܝܩܕ *to burn*, O.S.).

ܟܘܼܪܗܵܢܵܐ O.S., Al. *illness* = ܟܘܪܗܢܐ U. K. (ܟܪܗ Al. *to be ill*, as O.S. Ethpᶜel).

ܣܘܼܢܩܵܢܵܐ O.S.* *need* [Lord's prayer only], (ܣܢܩ *to need*, O.S.).

ܥܘܼܒܵܕܵܢܵܐ (ܥܒܕ) O.S.* *a noun of action* (O.S. ܥܒܕ *to act*).

ܥܘܼܕܪܵܢܵܐ O.S.* *help* (O.S. ܥܕܪ *to help*). Certain collects at the daily services are so called.

ܥܘܼܗܕܵܢܵܐ O.S.* *commemoration* (O.S. ܥܗܕ *to remember*).

ܥܘܼܡܚܵܢܵܐ Ti. see below.

ܦܘܼܠܚܵܢܵܐ O.S. *work* (rare), see below (ܦܠܚ *to work*, O.S.).

ܦܘܩܕܢܐ O.S. *a command;* in U. the ܩ often becomes ܟ, in Al. ܟ̰, §§ 119, 120 (ܦܩܕ K. *to command,* O.S. = ܡܦܩܕ U.).

ܦܘܪܥܢܐ O.S., K. *a reward* (ܦܪܥ *to pay,* O.S.).

ܦܘܪܩܢܐ O.S. *salvation* (O.S. ܦܪܩ *to save* = N.S. ܡܦܪܩ).

ܡܘܦܩܢܐ Al. J. Baz, see below.

ܩܘܪܒܢܐ O.S. *an offering, Holy Communion* (O.S. ܩܪܒ *to offer* = N.S. ܡܩܪܒ).

ܫܘܒܩܢܐ O.S. *forgiveness* (ܫܒܩ *to forgive,* O.S.).

ܫܘܠܛܢܐ O.S.* *authority, jurisdiction* (O.S. ܫܠܛ *to rule*).

ܬܘܟܠܢܐ O.S. Al. *hope, confidence* (ܬܟܠ Al. *to trust,* O.S.).

These are masculines and take the first plural.

With these compare: ܐܒܕܢܐ O.S. m. *destruction;* ܒܘܚܪܢܐ m. (O.S. ʹܒܘܚܢܐ) *examination,* § 77; ܝܩܕܢܐ O.S. m. *fuel;* ܥܘܩܢܐ Al. m. *affliction* = ܥܩܘܬ f. U. p. 27; ܥܡܛܢܐ Tkh. O.S. (ʹܥܡܘ Ti.) *fog* [O.S. *darkness*] = ܥܡܛ U.; ܡܛܠܢܐ Tkh. (ʹܡܘܛܠ Al. J. Baz) *a booth.*

Also the following masculines: ܚܘܒܠܢܐ O.S., Ti. *destruction* [O.S. *ease*]; ܒܢܝܢܐ O.S. *a building;* ܓܠܝܢܐ O.S. *revelation, the Transfiguration, the Apocalypse,* also a man's name (especially given to those born on August 6); ܚܡܝܢܐ *father-in-law,* = O.S. ܚܡܐ; ܡܢܝܢܐ O.S. *number;* ܚܣܝܢܐ *a sign of omission* in writing; ܦܠܚܢܐ *work* (O.S. ʹܦܘܠܚܢ); ܩܢܝܢܐ O.S. *cattle* (lit. *a possession*); ܩܪܝܢܐ O.S.* *a lection, lesson* (in the Liturgy).

(5) Nouns of action formed by giving the first radical Rwaṣa, and the last two Zqapa, are much more common. This is a favourite Pa'el formation in O.S., and the second radical in triliterals, with one

exception, is hard. These nouns are masculine and take the first plural. They do not take a preformative Mim.

Nouns of the forms ܦܘܼܩܵܕܵܐ, ܬܘܼܦܵܩܵܐ *etc.*

Those marked with an asterisk are ecclesiastical or literary only.

ܒܘܼܠܒܵܠܵܐ O.S. *babbling, confusion,* (ܡܒܲܠܒܸܠ *to babble,* O.S.).

ܒܘܼܣܵܡܵܐ O.S. *pleasure* (ܡܒܲܣܸܡ *to please,* O.S. Pa.).

ܒܘܼܪܵܟ݂ܵܐ O.S.* *marriage, marriage service-book* (ܡܒܲܪܸܟ݂ *to bless, marry* tr. O.S. Pa.).

ܒܘܼܫܵܠܵܐ O.S. *a cooked dish* (ܡܒܲܫܸܠ *to cook,* O.S. Pa.).

ܓܘܼܪܵܒܵܐ *temptation* (ܡܓܲܪܸܒ *to tempt,* Arab.).

ܕܘܼܒܵܪܵܐ O.S.* *deed* (ܡܕܲܒܸܪ *to rule,* O.S. Pa.).

ܕܘܼܗܘܿܢܵܐ K. see § 108.

ܗܘܼܓܵܝܵܐ O.S. *a spelling-book* [also in O.S. *meditation*] (ܡܗܲܓܹܐ *to spell,* and *to meditate,* both as O.S. Pa.).

ܗܘܼܠܵܠܵܐ O.S.* *a division of the Psalter* (O.S. ܗܲܠܸܠ *to praise*).

ܙܘܼܘܵܓ݂ܵܐ O.S.* *joining together, marriage* (ܡܙܲܘܸܓ݂ = O.S. Pa. ܙܲܘܸܓ݂ *to join, marry*).

ܙܘܼܝܵܚܵܐ O.S.* *a hymn, a church procession* (O.S. ܙܝܲܚ *to make a procession*).

ܙܘܼܡܵܪܵܐ O.S.* *a Gradual* (ܙܡܲܪ *to sing,* O.S. P'al and Pa.).

ܚܘܼܕܵܬ݂ܵܐ O.S.* *renewal,* esp. of the Holy Leaven (ܡܚܲܕܸܬ݂ *to renew,* O.S. Pa.).

ܚܘܼܘܪܵܓ݂ܵܐ (ܓ݂) *hurt, injury* (ܡܚܘܼܪܸܓ݂ *to injure,* § 83 A. 7[a]).

ܚܘܼܣܵܝܵܐ O.S.* *absolution* (ܡܚܲܣܹܐ K. Al. *to absolve,* O.S. Pa.).

ܚܘܼܫܵܒ݂ܵܐ O.S. *thought,* also ܚܘܼܫܵܒ݂, (ܚܫܝܼܒ݂ *to think,* O.S.).

ܚܘܼܬܵܡܵܐ O.S.* (ܛ also in O.S) *the Benediction,* in church (ܚܲܬܸܡ *to give the blessing,* O.S.).

ܦܘܼܢܵܩܵܐ *spoiling* of a child (ܡܦܲܢܸܩ *to spoil* tr.).

ܝܘܼܪܵܩܵܐ K., O.S. *green* = ܝܘܼܪܒܵܩܵܐ U. (ܝܪܸܩ § 45 *b*).

ܟܘܼܠܵܠܵܐ O.S.* *crown, crowning,* a marriage ceremony (O.S. ܟܲܠܸܠ *to crown*).

ܟܘܼܦܵܦܵܐ *a hem* (ܡܟܲܦܸܦ *to hem,* § 83 A. 12).

ܟܘܼܪܵܟܵܐ O.S. *shroud* (ܡܟܲܪܸܟ݂ *to shroud,* O.S. Pʿal, Pa. Aph.).

ܟܘܼܪܵܣܵܐ O.S. *a large sheet of paper* folded into several pages (O.S. ܟܪܲܣ *to shut*).

ܟܘܼܫܵܦܵܐ O.S.* name of some of the long prayers in the Liturgy (O.S. ܐܸܬ݂ܟܲܫܲܦ *to beseech*).

ܠܘܼܩܵܛܵܐ O.S.* *a lexicon,* esp. K. (O.S. ܠܲܩܸܛ, ܠܩܸܛ *to collect*).

ܡܘܼܟܵܟܵܐ O.S. *humiliation* (ܡܟܸܟ݂ *to be meek,* § 81).

ܢܘܼܗܵܪܵܐ O.S.* *commentary* (ܢܲܗܸܪ *to comment,* O.S.).

ܢܘܼܚܵܠܵܐ *sifted flour* (ܢܚܸܠ *to sift*).

ܢܘܼܚܵܡܵܐ O.S. *resurrection* (ܡܢܲܚܸܡ *to raise,* O.S. Pa.).

ܢܘܼܣܵܟܵܐ O.S.* *libation, the mixed chalice* (ܢܲܣܸܟ *to make a libation,* O.S. Pa.).

ܣܘܼܒܵܪܵܐ O.S.* *Advent,* the season (O.S. ܣܲܒܲܪ *to expect* [= ܣܲܟܸܪ N.S.], *to announce*).

ܣܘܼܠܵܩܵܐ O.S. *the Ascension* (O.S. ܣܠܸܩ *to ascend* = ܐܣܸܩ N.S.). Also called in U. ܟܠܵܬ݂ ܣܘܼܠܵܩܵܐ because little girls on that day make a procession dressed as brides.

ܦܘܼܪܵܥܵܐ O.S.* *conjugation* (ܡܦܲܪܸܥ *to conjugate,* O.S.; lit. *to bud*).

ܬܘܥܓܒܐ *wonder* = ܬܥܓܘܒܐ Al. (ܡܬܥܓܒ *to wonder*, Arab.).

ܬܘܟܦܢܐ O.S.* *burial* (O.S. ܟܦܢ *to shroud*, hence *to bury*).

ܬܘܥܪܩܠܐ O.S. *delay* (ܡܥܪܩܠ *to delay;* O.S. *to supplant*).

ܦܘܫܩܠܐ *forgiveness* (ܡܦܫܩܠ *to forgive*).

ܦܘܠܓܐ O.S.* *division, doubt*, § 98 (ܦܠܓ § 42).

ܦܘܪܟܐ (for ܦܘܪܟܢܐ) *ruin* (ܡܦܪܟ *to ruin*, Chald. Pa.).

ܦܘܩܕܢܐ O.S.* *command* (ܦܩܕ, ܡܦܩܕ *to command*, O.S. P'al and Pa.).

ܦܘܫܩܐ O.S. *translation, meaning* (ܡܦܫܩ *to translate*, O.S. Pa.).

ܩܘܕܫܐ O.S.* *consecration, Liturgy* (ܡܩܕܫ *to sanctify*, O.S. Pa.).

ܩܘܠܣܐ O.S.* *the interjections of the deacon* in the Liturgy (O.S. ܩܠܣ *to praise*).

ܩܘܫܝܐ O.S.* *hardening, non-aspiration* (ܩܫܐ *to be hard;* O.S. Pa. *to harden*), § 3.

ܪܘܟܟܐ O.S.* *softening, aspiration* (ܪܟܟ *to be soft*, § 81), § 3.

ܫܘܒܗܪܐ O.S. *pride* (ܡܫܒܗܪ Ti. *to be proud*, O.S. = ܡܫܬܒܗܪ U. § 30).

ܫܘܚܠܦܐ O.S. *change* (ܡܫܚܠܦ *to change*, O.S.).

ܫܘܠܡܐ O.S.* *end* (O.S. ܫܠܡ *to end* tr.).

ܫܘܡܠܝܐ O.S.* *confirmation* of a bishop's consecration by the Catholicos (O.S. ܫܡܠܝ *to confirm*).

ܫܘܒܩܢܐ *unfaithfulness* (ܡܫܒܩ K. *to forsake;* O.S. Pa. *to dismiss*).

ܫܘܪܝܐ O.S. *beginning;* also (*) *a short psalm* in the daily services (ܡܫܪܐ *to begin*, O.S. Pa.).

ܬܘܠܡܕܐ O.S. *education, discipline* (O.S. ܬܠܡܕ *to teach*).

ܗܘܕܳܥܳܐ O.S.* *commentary* (ܡܘܕܰܥ *to interpret*, O.S.).

ܗܘܕܳܥܳܐ *translation* (ܡܘܕܰܥ *to interpret*, Arab.).

ܗܘܕܳܗܳܐ O.S. *provision* (ܡܘܕܰܗ *to provide*, O.S.).

ܗܘܕܳܝܳܐ O.S. *mending* (ܡܘܕܺܝ *to mend*, O.S. Pa.; also ܡܚܰܝ N.S.).

Several nouns, chiefly foreign, are of this form but are not verbal nouns; as ܐܘܪܳܪܳܐ O.S.* m. *stole*, ὠράριον, *orarium*; ܘܙܳܢܳܐ O.S.* m. *girdle*, ζωνάριον; ܣܘܡܳܟܳܐ K. Al. Z. m. *male servant*, cf. ܒܠܚܳܡܳܐ § 114 *b*; ܓܘܓܰܝ m. *flower*, Turk.: ܓܘܓܰܝ m. *magpie*; ܓܘܟܳܐ f. *frock-coat*; ܡܘܬܳܪܳܐ *advantage*; ܟܘܡܳܬ *poor*; ܥܘܗܳܕܳܐ m. *strap for a cap*; and others.

§ 77. NOUNS DENOTING THE AGENT are formed from verbs as follows:

(1) The first radical has Zqapa in the first conjugation, Pthakha in the second, and ܳܢܳܐ is added; as ܩܳܠܶܢܳܐ *a fighter*, from ܩܠܰܒ *to fight*; ܡܦܰܫܩܳܢܳܐ *a translator*, from ܡܦܰܫܶܩ *to translate* (not ܡܰܦܫܩܳܢܳܐ as St.). These nouns are masculine and take the first plural. But they may also be used adjectivally: thus ܩܳܠܶܢܳܐ may mean *fighting* (as an epithet). A feminine in ܳܢܺܝܬܳܐ with the sixth plural may also be formed, as ܩܳܠܶܢܺܝܬܳܐ *a fighting woman*; but the fem. plural is uncommon. If used adjectivally the first plural will be used in the feminine, not the sixth; see under Adjectives, § 22. In Q. Sal. Gaw. the first syllable takes Zlama for Zqapa or Pthakha in second conjugation verbs.

These agents from the first conjugation are not used in O.S., Al. Ash.; those of the form ܡܰܩܠܳܢ being substituted; see below (3).

We must distinguish from these nouns words of the form ܐܶܓܪܳܢܳܐ, ܝܰܕܥܳܢܳܐ, ܢܳܨܚܳܢܳܐ (§ 76) which are not agents.

Note that ܡܛܪܢܐ *rain*, from ܡܛܪܐ *to rain*, is an inanimate agent. We must also distinguish between ܒܨܝܐ *examination*, and the agent ܒܨܝܢܐ *examiner*; between ܛܥܡܢܐ *palatable* (from ܛܥܡܐ *a taste*) and ܛܥܡܢܢܐ *a taster*; between ܫܡܥܢܐ *hearer* (pron. ܫ̇ in U.) and ܫܡܥܢܢܐ *made of wax*. ܬܒܪܢܐ means both *brittle* and *one who breaks*. Some Alqosh agents are noticeable: ܡܣܩܢܐ *the East* (lit. *causing to ascend*); ܡܥܪܒܢܐ (ܓ̰) *the West* (lit. *causing to set*); ܡܚܝܬܢܐ *descent of a hill* (lit. *causing to descend*: = U. ܡܚܝܬܐ). Note also ܡܨܦܝܢܐ U. K. *a cullender* (lit. *a strainer*), and ܫܠܡܘܬܐ (no Mim) *tradition*, from ܫܠܡܐ *to deliver*.

Variations. (*a*) In verbs of the second conjugation, second and third divisions, Zlama under the second (third) radical is retained in U. Sal. &c., as ܡܚܒܢܐ U. *lover*, from ܡܚܒܒ *to love*; ܡܗܡܙܡܢܐ U. *speaker*, from ܡܗܡܙܡ *to speak*; but not in K. Al. except in quadriliterals where there would be a difficulty of pronunciation, in which case an euphonic vowel is retained, as ܡܩܛܠܢܐ K. Al. *one who causes to be killed*, ܡܘܕܝܢܐ Al. *one who confesses*.

(*b*) In verbs ܠܐ or ܝܐ the ܐ is changed into ܝ, as ܦܝܫܢܐ from ܦܝܫܐ *to remain*; ܓܠܝܢܐ from ܓܠܐ *to reveal*.

(*c*) In ܝܐ verbs of the second conjugation, second and third divisions, the ܝ takes Khwaṣa in U.; thus ܡܦܪܡܝܢܐ from ܡܦܪܡܐ *to understand*. But in K. we have ܡܦܪܡܢܐ.

(*d*) Generally, in verbs ܠܥ, ܝ is added in K., not in U., as ܫܡܥܝܢܐ K., ܫܡܥܢܐ U. from ܫܡܥ *to hear*.

(*e*) In verbs medial ܥ, ܝ is sometimes added after ܥ, sometimes not. In the former case ܠ is silent. Thus from ܛܥܸܢ *to bear, carry*, we have ܛܵܥܢܵܢܵܐ or ܛܲܥܢܵܢܵܐ.

(*f*) For variations in irregular verbs see §§ 46, 47. Those which have in U. Pthakha for the present participle retain it for the agent. In U. the agents of ܛܵܠܸܒ, ܡܕܲܒܸܪ are ܛܲܠܒܵܢܵܐ, ܡܲܕܒܪܵܢܵܐ.

(2) *An habitual agent* is denoted in a limited number of words by giving the first radical Zqapa, the second Rwakha, and by adding ـܵܐ. These nouns are masculine and take the first plural; they are derived from the first conjugation (P'al). Note that ܦܵܠܚܵܢܵܐ = *one who at the moment is fighting*; ܦܵܠܘܿܚܵܐ = *one who is in the habit of fighting.* A few verbs also form a feminine in ܬܵܐ, with the sixth plural. Verbs ܠܐ often change ܐ into ܘ, verbs ܠܝ often add ܘ. Some of these words denote inanimate agents, or have acquired a secondary meaning; those marked with an asterisk are ecclesiastical or literary only.

Words of the forms ܩܵܛܘܿܠܵܐ, ܩܵܛܘܿܠܬܵܐ.

ܐܵܟ݂ܘܿܠܵܐ *a glutton* (ܐܸܟ݂ܲܠ *to eat*, O.S.).

ܕܵܒܘܿܒܝܼܬܵܐ *ant*, § 100 *f*. (No first conj. verb, but ܡܕܲܒܕܸܒ *to creep.*)

ܒܵܗܘܿܪܵܐ, f. ـܪܬܵܐ, Al. *bright* (ܒܗܸܪ K. Al. *to illumine*, O.S., cf. ܒܗܵܪܵܐ *light*).

ܚܵܫܘܿܠܵܐ O.S. and ܚܵܫܘܿܠܬܵܐ *a wooden spoon* (ܚܫܸܠ K., O.S. *to stir* = ܡܚܲܪܸܫ U.).

ܒܵܟ݂ܘܿܘܵܐ (for ܒܵܟ݂ܘܿܝܵܐ) *a crying child* (ܒܟ݂ܵܐ *to weep*, O.S.).

ܒܵܠܘܿܥܘܵܐ, rarely ܒܵܠܘܿܥܵܐ [which in O.S. = *a swallower*] and ܒܵܠܘܿܥܬܵܐ *throat* (ܒܠܸܥ *to swallow*, O.S.). Hence ܒܵܠܘܿܥܘܵܢܵܐ *a glutton*.

ܒܵܪܘܿܙܵܐ, f. ـܪܘܿܙܬܵܐ, U. *dry*, also metaph. *stubborn* (ܒܪܸܙ *to dry*, intr.).

ܒܵܪܘܿܝܵܐ O.S. *creator* (ܒܪܵܐ *to create*, O.S.).

ܒܪܘܩܬܐ *a sore on the neck*, = O.S. ܒܪܩܬܐ (ܒܪܸܩ *to flash as lightning*, as O.S., hence also metaph. *to have a sudden pain*).

ܟܕܝܘܬܐ K. *a beggar* (ܟܕܐ *to beg*, in O.S. *to collect*). In U. ܟܕܝܐ.

ܓܚܘܟܐ (hard Kap) *a gull*, also *a dimple* (ܓܚܟ *to laugh*, § 95 *e*); O.S. ܓܚܘܟܐ *a laugher*.

ܓܫܘܫܐ *a spy* (ܓܫܫ K. *to spy*, Arab. = ܡܓܫܫ K. U.).

ܓܪܘܕܐ *pumice stone* [O.S. *a locust*] (ܓܪܕ *to scrape*, O.S.).

ܓܪܘܡܐ *an axle* [O.S. *rolling-pin*] (ܓܪܡ K. *to roll* dough, also *to be silent*, in O.S. *to cut off*).

ܓܪܘܣܬܐ *a hand-mill* (ܓܪܣ *to grind in a hand-mill*, as O.S. Pa., cf. ܡܓܪܓܫ K. *to grind coarse*, ܓܪܓܫܐ *coarse split peas*). See ܓܪܘܣܬܐ in the next list.

ܓܪܘܦܐ *wooden shovel* for taking ashes out of earth-ovens [O.S. *one who sweeps away*], (ܓܪܦ *to shovel*, in O.S. *to sweep away*).

ܓܪܘܦܬܐ *the bank of a hill* (ܓܪܦ *to slide*).

ܓܪܘܪܐ *shaft* of a cart (ܓܪܪ *to draw*, O.S.).

ܕܠܘܦܐ, f. ܦܬܐ *dripping, leaky* as a roof (ܕܠܦ *to leak*, O.S.).

ܕܩܘܩܐ O.S. *a stone pestle* (ܕܩܩ, root ܕܩܩ, *to grind to powder*, O.S., cf. ܡܕܩܕܩ).

ܕܪܘܫܐ O.S. *disputer* (ܕܪܫ *to dispute*, O.S.).

ܙܒܘܬܐ O.S. (also ܙܒ in O.S.) *a bowl* (no verb).

ܙܕܘܚܐ K. or ܙܕܘܚܬܐ U. *a coward* (ܙܕܥ *to fear*, § 83 D. *c*). Hence ܙܕܘܚܬܐܝܬ *cowardly*.

ܙܠܘܡܐ *an oppressor* (ܙܠܡ U. K., Arab. = ܛܠܡ Al., O.S. *to oppress*. Cf. O.S. ܙܘܠܡ *to distort*).

ܚܕܘܪܐ O.S. *a vagabond* (ܚܕܪ *to wander about*, O.S.).

ܚܙܘܝܐ K., O.S. or ܚܙܘܘܐ U. *a sharp-sighted person* (ܚܙܐ *to see*, O.S.).

ܚܛܘܪܐ O.S. *a pounder* (ܚܛܪ *to pound*, O.S.).

ܚܣܘܟܐ *a currycomb* (ܚܝܟ *to curry*, § 95 *e*, O.S. ܚܟ), [both hard Kap in N.S.].

ܚܫܘܒܐ O.S. *a thinker* (ܚܫܒ *to think*, O.S.).

ܚܫܘܠܐ *a pestle* [in O.S. *a goldsmith*] and ܚܫܘܠܬܐ *a mortar* (ܚܫܠ *to pound* = חָשַׁל Chald.; in O.S. *to fuse metal*).

ܚܫܘܫܐ, f. ܫܬܐ, O.S.* *passive* in grammar (O.S. ܚܫ *to suffer*).

ܛܠܘܒܐ *a suitor*, also *a beggar* (ܛܠܒ *to ask*, Arab.). Hence perhaps ܛܠܝܒܘܬܐ (for ´ܛܠܘܒ) *spousals.*

ܝܕܘܥܐ K., O.S., or ܝܕܘܥܬܐ U. (pron. ܕ = ܥ), and ܝܕܘܥܬܐ *an acquaintance* (ܝܕܥ *to know*, O.S.). Cf. ܝܕܘܥܬܐ in the next list.

ܝܠܘܦܐ O.S. *a learner* (ܝܠܦ *to learn*, O.S.). Cf. ܝܠܘܦܐ in the next list.

ܝܩܘܪܐ, f. ‒ܪܬܐ, O.S. *heavy* (ܝܩܪ K., O.S. *to make heavy*).

ܟܡܘܪܐ *a sulky man* (ܟܡܪ *to be angry*, § 113 *d*).

ܟܠܘܒܐ *a seizer* (ܟܠܒ *to seize*, Arab.).

ܟܢܘܫܬܐ *a broom* (ܟܢܫ *to sweep*, O.S.).

ܟܣܘܚܬܐ *a pruning knife, a chisel* (ܟܣܚ *to prune*, O.S.).

ܟܦܘܪܐ O.S., and ܟܦܘܪܬܐ *apostate, infidel* (ܟܦܪ *to deny*, O.S.).

ܩܗܘܪܐ *choleric* (ܩܗܪ *to be angry*, Arab.).

ܟܪܘܙܐ O.S.* *preacher* (very rare), cf. ܡܟܪܙܘ § 45 *g*. But ܟܪܘܙܘܬܐ *a litany* or *a sermon*, is commonly used.

ܟܪܘܝܐ *sad* (ܟܪܐ K. Al. *to be sad*, O.S.).

ܠܝܘܡܐ, f. ܡܬܐ, O.S. *fitting* (ܠܝܡ *to suit*, O.S.).

ܠܥܘܣܐ or ܠܥܘܘܣܐ *jaw* (ܠܥܣ *to chew*, O.S.).

ܡܝܘܬܐ O.S. *a mortal* (ܡܝܬ *to die*, O.S.).

ܡܪܘܥܢܐ (for ܡܪܘܥܐ), f. ܥܬܐ ?, *sickly* (ܡܪܥ *to be ill*, O.S.).

ܢܒܘܚܐ, f. ܚܬܐ *barking* (ܢܒܚ *to bark*, O.S.).

ܢܒܘܙܐ, f. ܙܬܐ *shying* (ܢܒܙ *to shy*, in O.S. *to leap*).

ܢܟܘܬܐ Ti. *a biter* (ܢܟܬ Ti. *to bite*).

ܢܛܘܦܐ (or ܕ) *a drop* (ܢܛܦ *to drip*, O.S.).

ܢܟܘܦܐ, f. ܦܬܐ, soft Kap, *shy, modest* (ܢܟܦ *to be shy*, O.S.) = O.S. ܢܟܦܐ, Pthakha form, hard Kap.

ܢܥܘܨܐ, f. ܨܬܐ *biting, stinging*, for ܢܥܘ (ܢܥܨ *to bite, sting*, Chald. נְעַץ *to perforate*).

ܢܦܘܨܐ *a cotton beater* [a forked stick] (ܢܦܨ *to beat, shake*, O.S.).

ܢܩܘܫܐ O.S. *a semantron*, a wooden board and mallet beaten together to call people to church (ܢܩܫ Tkh. Al., O.S. [Shin silent U.], *to hit, strike*).

ܣܟܘܪܐ K. [ܕܥܝܢܐ is usually added], *a sty in the eye* (ܣܟܪ K. *to shut, fill up*, § 95).

ܣܥܘܪܐ *a sacristan, churchwarden* [in O.S. *an overseer*, esp. a chorepiscopus, because his duty was to visit], (ܣܥܪ K., O.S. *to visit*). Colloquial in U.

ܥܵܒ݂ܘܿܕܵܐ, f. ‒ܕܬܵܐ, O.S.* *active*, in grammar (ܥܒ݂ܸܕ *to do*, O.S.).

ܥܵܒ݂ܘܿܪܵܐ, f. ‒ܪܬܵܐ O.S. *transitory* (ܥܒ݂ܸܪ *to pass*, O.S.).

ܥܵܕ݂ܘܿܒ݂ܵܐ Al. *a torturer* (ܥܕ݂ܸܒ݂ Al. *to torture*, § 95 *c*).

ܥܵܕ݂ܘܿܠܵܐ, f. ‒ܠܬܵܐ, Al. *straight* (ܥܕ݂ܸܠ Al. *to be straight*, Arab.).

ܥܵܠܘܿܠܵܐ *a street* [in O.S. *one who enters*], and ܥܲܠܘܿܠܬܵܐ *a lane, a passage* in a house or outside (O.S. ܥܲܠ *to enter*).

ܥܵܡܘܿܪܵܐ O.S. *an inhabitant* (ܥܡܸܪ *to inhabit*, O.S.).

ܥܵܪܘܿܩܵܐ, f. ‒ܩܬܵܐ, K. *swift* (ܥܪܸܩ K. Al. *to run*, in U., O.S. *to run away*).

ܦܵܠܘܿܫܵܐ *a flat cake of dried manure fuel* (ܦܠܸܣ *to be flat*, Arab.).

ܦܵܝܘܿܫܵܐ, f. ‒ܫܬܵܐ, K. *cool*, § 21 (10) (ܦܝܸܫ *to be cool*, O.S.).

ܦܵܠܘܿܚܵܐ *a fighter* (ܦܠܸܚ *to fight*, § 97).

ܦܵܣܘܿܥܵܐ K. or ܦܵܣܘܿܥܬܵܐ U. *a step* (ܦܣܸܥ *to step*, O.S.; whence also the derived verb ܡܦܲܣܸܥ, pron. ܡܦ̈).

ܦܵܣܘܿܩܵܐ O.S.* *a paragraph* (ܦܣܸܩ K. *to cut, abbreviate*, O.S.).

ܦܵܩܘܿܕ݂ܵܐ O.S.* *the imperative mood* (ܦܩܸܕ݂ *to command*, O.S.; usually ܡܲܦܩܸܕ݂ U.).

ܦܵܪܘܿܓ݂ܵܐ *a skin eruption* (ܦܪܸܓ݂ *to chafe*, O.S.).

ܦܵܪܘܿܡܵܐ, f. ‒ܡܬܵܐ *sharp* (ܦܪܸܡ *to cut*, O.S.).

ܦܵܪܘܿܩܵܐ O.S. *a Saviour*, also (in N.S.) *the tail of a final letter* (ܦܪܸܩ *to finish* intr., in O.S. *to save*, as N.S. ܡܦܲܪܸܩ).

ܦܵܪܘܿܫܵܐ *book marker* [in O.S. *separater*], and ܦܵܪܘܿܫܬܵܐ *tablet, table of the law* (ܦܪܸܫ *to separate*, O.S.).

ܦܲܚܘܼܕܓ݂ܵܐ *hand's breadth* (O.S. [?] ܦܚܓ݂ *to measure with the hand*).

ܦܲܚܕܘܼܕܵܐ, f. ܕܬܵܐ_?, *tepid* (ܦܚܸܕ, pron. ܦ in U., *to be tepid*).

ܩܵܛܘܼܠܵܐ O.S. *a murderer* (ܩܛܸܠ *to kill*, O.S.).

ܩܲܠܘܼܠܵܐ, f. ܠܬܵܐ_, O.S. *light* (not heavy), in K. *quick* (O.S. ܩܸܠ *to be light*, whence N.S. ܡܨܲܠܝܼܠ § 83 A. 2).

ܩܲܕܘܼܨܵܐ *a biter* (ܩܕܸܨ *to bite*, p. 115). [Distinguish ܩܲܕܘܼܨܵܐ or ܩܲܕܘܼܪܵܐ *cartilage, tendon*.]

ܩܵܕܘܿܝܵܐ O.S.* *a reader*, and ܩܵܕܘܿܕܵܐ *a cock* (ܩܕܸܐ *to crow, call read*, O.S.).

ܩܲܕܘܼܝܵܐ *a wooden rake* (ܩܕܹܐ *to sweep*, p. 116).

ܕܵܟ݂ܘܿܠܵܐ K. or ܕܵܟ݂ܘܿܘܼܠܵܐ U. *a valley*, in Ti. *a torrent* (= O.S. ܕܵܚ݂ܘܿܠܵܐ *a torrent*) and ܕܵܟ݂ܘܿܠܬܵܐ K. or ܕܵܟ݂ܘܿܘܼܠܬܵܐ U. *id.*, root-meaning *to go* (?) *to explore*, as Heb. Pi.

ܕܲܗܘܼܒ݂ܵܐ, f. ܒ݂ܬܵܐ_, *quick* (ܕܗܸܒ݂ *to run*, O.S. ܕܗܵܒ݂).

ܕܲܚܘܼܒ݂ܵܐ O.S. and ܕܲܚܘܼܒ݂ܬܵܐ *a paramour* (ܕܚܸܒ݂ K. *to love*, O.S.).

ܚܓ݂ܘܼܒ݂ܵܐ O.S.* *a period of seven weeks* (no verb).

ܬܲܒܘܼܪܵܐ, f. ܪܬܵܐ_, *fragile* (ܬܒܸܪ *to break*, O.S.), cf. p. 224.

ܨܲܒܘܼܬܵܐ *a pair of tongs*, or *a large bone* (ܨܒܸܬ *to take*, O.S.).

ܩܲܕܘܼܣܬܵܐ *a button* (ܩܕܸܣ *to button*).

We may add ܙܵܟ݂ܘܼܬ݂ܵܐ U. ('ܗ K.) *victory*, for ܙܵܟ݂ܘܿܬ݂ܵܐ, from ܙܟ݂ܹܐ ('ܗ K.) *to conquer*, though ܙܵܟ݂ܘܿܐ is not found. Cf. ܙܵܟ݂ܘܼܬ݂ܵܐ above.

Several other words (mostly foreign) of this form are found, which are not derived from verbs; as ܐܓ݂ܘܿܢܵܐ O.S.* (West Syr. ܐܓ݂ܘܿܢܵܐ) *contest, of the martyrs*, = ἀγών, ἀγωνία; ܐܣܘܿܛܵܐ O.S. *the prodigal son*,

= ἄσωτος; ܓܓܘܠܬܐ O.S. *Golgotha*; ܚܠܘܒܬܐ and ܚܠܘܒܬܐ *milking vessel*; ܟܘܡܚܬܐ *dysentery*, ܕܠܘܥܬܐ *doorway*, ܚܠܦܬܐ U. *maternal uncle* (= ܚܠܐ K., O.S.); ܚܕܘܠܬܐ *tuft of hair on the top of the head* (for ܚܠܚܘܠܬܐ, root ܚܠܠ *to crown*?); ܚܟܦܬܐ *a slap*; ܚܦܢܬܐ *a loose shoe*, and ܚܕܘܣܬܐ *a sandal*; ܢܡܘܣܬܐ O.S. *the law* (of Moses) = νόμος; ܚܨܦܬܐ U. *paternal uncle* (= ܚܨܐ K.); ܟܘܚܬܐ *a small cake*; ܩܡܨܬܐ *a beetle*; ܦܬܘܪܬܐ O.S., Tkh. *table or tablecloth*; ܩܢܘܬܐ O.S. *rule, canon* = κανών, ܓܕܘܕܬܐ or ܓܕܘܕܐ *sinew, tendon* (see above), and some others. Compare also the following list.

Pthakha forms ܦܕܘܠܐ, ܦܕܘܠܬܐ.

The following words are added here to distinguish them from those in the above list; they are not agents, and many of them belong to the O.S. Pa'el formation of which ܒܟܘܪܐ *a son*, lit. *one begotten*, is an example, (distinguish O.S. ܒܟܘܪܬܐ *a father*, lit. *one who begets*). In U. most of these are usually pronounced with Zqapa on the first; but the Pthakha usually remains in K. Al. In Q. Sal. J. Gaw. they often have Zlama, with the second sound. In some cases there is room for hesitation in placing them in this class.

ܐܬܘܢܐ O.S.* *furnace*, root ܬܢܢ, cf. N.S. ܬܢܢ K. *to be smoked*.

ܒܠܘܛܐ O.S. *oak*.

ܒܨܘܪܐ, f. ܒܨܝܪ *less, inferior*, O.S. ܒܨܝܪ.

ܚܕܘܪܐ K. Sh. *sunny side of a hill* (= ܡܚܣܢܬܐ or ܡܚܣܐ U.).

ܓܕܘܫܐ, f. ܓܘܫ *large*, perh. from ܓܕܫ *to grind coarse* [hence is formed ܡܓܕܘܫ *to grow* = ܡܓܠܕܫ U.], see ܟܘܡܚܬܐ above.

ܒܬܘܠܐ, f. ܒܬܠ *cold* (of persons), cf. ܡܫܬܬܠ *to be cold*, p. 120.

ܒܬܘܚܐ O.S. *apple*.

ܒܲܣܘܼܡܵܐ, f. ‑ܣܘܼܡܬܵܐ, Al. *sweet* = ܒܲܣܝܼܡܵܐ U. K.

ܚܲܡܘܼܨܵܐ, f. ‑ܨܬܵܐ, O.S. *sour;* also in Al. ܚܲܡܘܼܨܝܵܬܵܐ *a sour dish* dressed with vinegar, etc.

ܚܲܪܘܼܦܵܐ K. and ܚܲܪܘܼܦܵܐ U. (Pthakha sound), f. ‑ܦܬܵܐ ?, *clever* = ܚܲܪܝܼܦܵܐ O.S. Cf. ܚܪܝܼܦܵܐ above.

ܛܲܠܘܼܝܵܐ K., O.S. *a boy, a child.*

ܚܲܠܘܼܦܵܐ, f. ‑ܦܬܵܐ, O.S. *clever;* usually ܚܲܠܝܼܦܵܐ in O.S.

ܝܲܬܘܼܡܵܐ *an orphan* = ܝܲܬܡܵܐ O.S.

ܟܲܡܘܼܢܵܐ O.S.* *cummin.*

ܡܲܒܘܼܥܵܐ as O.S. or ܢܲܒܘܼܥܵܐ K. or ܢܲܒܘܼܥܵܐ U. *fountain.* The first form is for ܡܲܒܒܘܼܥ', but in U. is pron. (as most of the others in this list) with Zqapa.

ܡܲܠܘܼܚܵܐ, f. ‑ܚܬܵܐ *salt,* adj. In O.S. subst., and so N.S. in fem.

ܥܲܡܘܼܩܵܐ, f. ‑ܩܬܵܐ *deep* = O.S. ܥܲܡܝܼܩܵܐ.

ܥܲܡܘܼܪܵܐ, f. ‑ܪܬܵܐ *dense* (as trees). In O.S. ܥܲܡܝܼܪܵܐ = (1) *inhabited,* (2) *green grass.*

ܦܲܛܘܼܪܬܵܐ (O.S. ܦ') *mushroom.*

ܦܲܩܘܼܥܵܐ O.S. *fig* (rare).

ܦܲܫܘܼܩܵܐ, f. ‑ܩܬܵܐ *easy* = O.S. ܦܲܫܝܼܩܵܐ.

ܬܲܢܘܼܪܵܐ O.S. *oven* (in the ground), § 92.

[Akin to these are several with Zlama or Khwaṣa, cf. § 85 (5); as ܓܸܪܘܼܕܵܐ m. *a scratch,* from ܓܪܵܕ (or ܓܪܵܕ) *to scratch;* ܕܸܒܘܼܪܵܐ m. O.S. and ܕܸܒܘܼܪܬܵܐ f. O.S. *horsefly;* ܘܸܪܘܼܡܵܐ m. *swelling,* from ܘܪܵܡ U. *to swell;* ܚܝܘܼܛܵܐ m. *a stitch* = O.S. ܚܝܵܛܵܐ; ܝܸܣܘܼܪܵܐ U. m. or ܐܸܣܘܼܪܵܐ K. m. *a bond, fetter* = ܐܸܣܵܪܬܵܐ Al. = ܐܸܣܘܼܪܵܐ O.S.; ܟܝܘܼܠܵܐ m. *measure* = O.S. ܟܲܝܠܵܐ; ܕܸܩܘܼܪܵܐ m. *a prick,* from ܕܩܵܪ *to prick;* and some others.]

We may notice here a very common rule with regard to Rwasa and Rwakha when they fall in the middle of a word, which has been usually followed in printed books. If the first radical has Zqapa, the second has Rwakha; if the first has Pthakha, the second has Rwasa. But this rule is quite arbitrary and does not appear to be desirable; it does not apply to abstracts in ܘܿܫܐ܀ or to diminutives in ܘܿܫܐ܀, ܘܿܫܐ܀, which have Rwasa and Rwakha respectively.

(3) *An habitual agent* is also denoted by giving the first radical Pthakha, and the second and third Zqapa, adding Alap. These are masculines and take the first plural; they are almost all derived from first conjugation verbs. In Al. Ash. where agents of the first form (p. 223) are not used, all first conjugation verbs thus form agents; elsewhere only a few do so, as in the list given below. In U. Pthakha has the sound of Zqapa in these words; in Sal. Q. Gaw. J. of second Zlama.

Words of the form ܦܲܥܵܠܵܐ.

ܐܵܣܵܪܵܐ O.S.* [West Syr. 'ܐܵܣܵܪܐ] *conjunction* (ܐܣܲܪ *to bind*, O.S.).

ܒܲܢܵܝܵܐ *a cook* U. K., *a builder* Al., O.S. (ܒܢܵܐ *to build*, as O.S.; also *to cook*).

ܕܲܒܵܫܵܐ *bee* (ܕܒܸܩ K. *to stick*, § 95 d).

ܕܲܓܵܠܵܐ O.S. *a liar* (ܡܕܲܓܸܠ *to lie*, O.S. Pa.; no first conj. verb).

ܕܲܝܵܢܵܐ O.S. (*déyâna*) *a judge* (ܕܵܢ *to judge*, O.S.).

ܙܲܝܵܪܵܐ (*zéyâra*) *proud* (ܙܵܐܹܪ U. *to swell, to be proud*).

ܙܲܡܵܪܵܐ O.S. *a singer* (ܙܡܲܪ *to sing*, O.S.).

ܙܲܢܵܝܵܐ O.S. *fornicator* (ܙܢܵܐ *to commit fornication*, O.S.).

ܙܲܩܵܪܵܐ O.S. *weaver, knitter* (ܙܩܲܪ *to weave, knit*, O.S.).

ܚܲܙܵܝܵܐ O.S. *a seer* (ܚܙܵܐ *to see*, O.S.).

ܚܲܛܵܝܵܐ O.S. *a sinner* (ܚܛܵܐ *to sin*, O.S.).

ܚܲܝܵܛܵܐ O.S. (*khéyâṭa*) *a tailor* (ܚܵܝܹܛ *to sew*, O.S.).

ܚܲܦܵܪܵܐ *digger* (ܚܵܦܹܪ *to dig*, O.S.).

ܚܲܨܵܕܵܐ *a reaper* (ܚܵܨܹܕ *to reap*, O.S.).

ܚܲܪܵܛܵܐ *a turner, joiner* (ܚܵܪܹܛ *to turn, scoop out*, O.S.). Also ܚܲܪܵܛ.

ܚܲܪܵܫܵܐ O.S. *a wizard* (ܡܚܲܪܹܫ *to bewitch*, as O.S. Ethpa. No first conj. verb).

ܛܲܚܵܢܵܐ O.S. *a miller* (ܛܵܚܹܢ *to grind*, O.S.).

ܟܲܢܵܫܵܐ *a sweeper* (ܟܵܢܹܫ *to sweep, collect*, O.S.).

ܟܲܣܵܚܵܐ O.S. *a pruner* (ܟܵܣܹܚ *to prune*, O.S.).

ܟܲܪܵܟܵܐ *an enshrouder* (ܡܟܲܪܟܹܐ *to shroud*, O.S. P'al and Aph.).

ܟܲܬܵܒܵܐ O.S. *a scribe* (ܟܵܬܹܒ *to write*, O.S.).

ܟܲܛܵܪܵܐ *testy; knotty*, as trees (ܟܵܛܹܪ U. = ܩ K. *to tie in a knot*, O.S. ܩܛܲܪ).

ܣܲܚܵܝܵܐ O.S. *a swimmer* (ܣܵܚܹܐ *to swim*, O.S.).

ܥܲܘܵܠܵܐ O.S. (Zqapa before Wau) *a transgressor* (O.S. ܥܵܘܸܠ *to transgress*).

ܦܲܠܵܚܵܐ O.S. *a worker, labourer* (ܦܵܠܹܚ *to work, serve*, O.S.).

ܦܲܠܵܫܵܐ *a fighter* (ܦܵܠܹܫ *to fight*, § 97).

ܦܲܪܵܚܵܐ [in O.S. *a prodigal*] *bird* = ܦܲܪܲܚܬܵܐ O.S., N.S. (ܦܵܪܹܚ *to fly*, O.S.).

ܨܲܝܵܕܵܐ O.S. *huntsman, fisherman* (ܨܵܝܹܕ *to hunt, fish*, O.S.). Cf. ܒܹܝܬ ܨܲܝܕܵܐ *Bethsaida*.

ܨܲܠܵܒܵܐ *tether* (ܨܵܠܹܒ K. Al. *to tie to a post*, and as O.S. *to crucify*).

§ 77 (3)] AGENTS. 235

ܡܨܲܠܝܵܢܵܐ *one who prays* (ܡܨܲܠܹܐ *to pray*, O.S. No first conj. verb).

ܩܵܛܘܿܦܵܐ *a plucker of grapes* (ܩܛܦ *to pluck*, O.S.).

ܚܵܡܝܵܢܵܐ *a sweeper*; also *obstinate, quarrelsome* (ܚܵܡܹܐ *to be angry, to sweep*; and in K. *to squeeze*, as Arab., pp. 116, 230).

ܪܵܘܝܵܐ O.S. (Zqapa before Wau) *a drunkard* (ܪܘܹܐ *to be drunk*, O.S.).

ܪܵܗܛܵܢܵܐ = O.S. ܪܵܗܘܿܛܵܐ *a runner* (ܪܵܗܹܛ *to run*, O.S. ܪܗܛ).

ܪܵܟ݂ܒܵܐ *rider* (ܪܟ݂ܒ *to ride*, O.S., § 46).

ܪܵܩܕܵܐ *a dancer* (ܪܩܕ *to dance*, O.S.).

ܢܵܩܕܵܐ *a cotton cleaner* (ܢܵܩܹܕ Tkh. = ܘܕ Ti. *to clean cotton*).

ܡܫܲܡܫܵܐ O.S. *a deacon* (ܡܫܲܡܫ *to serve as a deacon*, O.S. Pa.; no first conj. verb).

All the above form feminines in ܬܐ with the sixth plural.

Several are of similar form, but are not agents; as ܐܲܟ݂ܠܵܐ O.S. *trough*; ܐܲܠܵܗܵܐ O.S. *God*; ܐܲܠܵܗܬ݂ܵܐ *goddess* (p. 37); ܓܵܘܵܐ O.S. *inner* (Zqapa before Wau); ܓܲܢܵܒܵܐ O.S. (*géyâsa*) [*the penitent*] *thief*; ܗܲܕܵܡܵܐ O.S. *member, limb*; ܘܲܪܩܵܐ *paper*, Arab.; ܙܕܩܐ K. Al. *alms*, pron. ܙ = ܣ (= ܙܕܩܵܐ U.); ܝܚܝܕܵܐ *only begotten*; ܚܡܨܵܐ f. *green fruit*; ܟܵܘܝܵܐ *thin, lean*; ܚܫܵܡܵܐ Al. *supper*, Arab.; ܩܕܵܠܵܐ Al. *neck* (= ܨܵܘܪܵܐ U. K.), cf. O.S. ܩܨܵܐ *joints of the body*; ܩܕܪܵܐ *earthen pot*; ܩܝܡܬܐ *backbone*; ܩܢܦܐ O.S. *Caiaphas*; ܟܕܟܐ f. *a net*, Al. K. (= ܓܕܘܿܦܵܐ U.), also in K. *a window* (= ܦܢܓ݂ܪܐ U.) Arab.; ܩܨܵܐ *a bowl*; ܩܠܵܐ f. *a piece of board in a spinning-wheel*; ܗܕܝܐ Ti. Sh. *a joke* (conn. with ܗܕܝ, § 46 ?).

Somewhat similar are ܟܬ݂ܵܐ U. Q. Sh. *a beggar* = ܟܝܵܢܵܐ K.; ܢܵܕܵܐ or ܢܵܕܚܵܐ *potsherd*, § 88; ܠܢܵܢܵܐ *thief*. So ܦܕܵܢܵܐ *plough* = O.S. ܦܕܵܢܵܐ, § 85.

§ 78. (1) ABSTRACT NOUNS are formed, generally from substantives and adjectives, by changing the termination to ܘܬܐ, or in Sal. Q. etc. to ܘܬܐ, (ܘܬܐ Az. ?); if there is no termination, these endings are added on. Thus ܫܪܝܪܘܬܐ *truth*, from ܫܪܝܪܐ *true*; ܡܠܚܘܬܐ *the calling of a sailor*, from ܡܠܚܐ *sailor*, § 82 (1), cf. ܡܠܚܐ *a ship* (Turk.). These abstracts are feminine and take the sixth and ninth plurals, § 18.

Words ending in ܝܐ, § 67, p. 168, drop the point under the second Yudh in forming abstracts, and the Yudh becomes consonantal; as ܛܒܐ *good*, ܛܒܝܘܬܐ *goodness*.

A few of these abstracts are formed from particles; as ܐܝܟܢܝܘܬܐ *quality*, from ܐܝܟܢ *how?* (not very common), cf. ܐܝܟܢܐ *how?* § 67; ܕܠܩܘܒܠܘܬܐ *opposition*, from ܕܠܩܘܒܠܐ *against* (see also p. 237); and the irregular ܩܘܪܒܘܬܐ U. *proximity*, from ܩܘܪܒܐ *near*, § 21 (7). For other instances see below. These abstracts are often formed from compounds, as ܓܠܝܙܘܬܐ *carelessness*, from ܓܠܝܙ *careless* (ܓܠܙ *care*).

Some nouns of this form are not abstracts in sense, as ܢܘܠܘܬܐ *loom* (O.S. *a shop, inn*); ܒܝܬܘܬܐ *furniture*, from ܒܝܬܐ *a house*, O.S.; ܐܘܚܫܢܘܬܐ *banquet*, from ܐܘܚܫܢܐ *guest*, O.S., also ܐ U.; ܐܫܢܘܬܐ Ti. Al. *dinner, noon* (lit. *breakfast*), § 28 (13); ܫܡܫܢܘܬܐ *book of the deacon's part in the Liturgy* (also *diaconate*), from ܫܡܫܢܐ *deacon*, O.S.

Note that ܨܠܘܬܐ *prayer* (ܨܠܝ *to pray*), and ܡܚܘܬܐ *plague* (ܡܚܐ *to strike*), are not of this form, and have Rwakha, § 18 (9).

In some cases the abstract has the same meaning as the original; as ܦܟܘܬܐ = ܦܟ *doubt* (hard Kap); ܛܥܝܘܬܐ = ܛܥܝܢܐ *error*; ܪܒܝܘܬܐ = ܪܒܝܢܐ *increase, interest*.

§ 78] ABSTRACT NOUNS.

From ܫܒܪܬܐ *girl* (p. 48), we have ܫܒܪܘܬܐ *girlhood*.

Several of these abstracts are formed in ܘܬܐ ¨, as:—

ܐܝܟܢܘܬܐ *whereabouts*, from ܐܝܟܐ *where?*

ܐܝܢܢܘܬܐ O.S.* *case* (in grammar), from O.S. ܐܝܢܐ = N.S. ܐܝܡܢ *who?*

ܐܒܗܘܬܐ *fatherhood*, from ܐܒܐ *father*.

ܪܚܡܘܬܐ *friendship*, from ܪܚܡܐ *friendly*, cf. ܪܚܡܐ *friend*.

ܠܩܘܒܠܘܬܐ *opposite situation*, from ܠܩܘܒܠܐ *opposite*. Also regular. So ܕܕܐ *opposition*.

ܒܥܠܕܒܒܘܬܐ (U. ܕ) *enmity*, from ܒܥܠܕܒܒ *enemy*, regular in K.

ܗܕܡܘܬܐ *membership*, from ܗܕܡܐ *member*, O.S.

ܚܕܝܘܬܐ O.S. *unity*, from O.S. ܚܕ *one* = N.S. ܚܕ.

ܝܘܒܠܘܬܐ *relationship*, from ܝܘܒܠܐ *a relation*.

ܒܝܫܘܬܐ *badness*, from ܒܝܫܐ *bad*, § 21 (7). Also regular.

ܪܒܘܬܐ *largeness*, from ܪܒܐ *large*, § 21 (7).

ܐܡܗܘܬܐ *motherhood*, from ܐܡܐ *mother*. Also regular.

ܓܝܣܘܪܘܬܐ K. *richness*.

ܟܡܝܘܬܐ O.S. *quantity*, from ܟܡܐ *how much?* O.S.

ܣܦܪܘܬܐ *clerkship*, from ܣܦܪܐ *a clerk*. Also regular.

ܥܘܕܪܢܘܬܐ *obstinacy*, from ܥܘܕܪܢܐ *obstinate*.

ܪܚܝܩܘܬܐ *distance*, from ܪܚܝܩܐ *far*, § 21 (7).

ܒܗܬܘܬܐ *shame*, from ܒܗܬܐ *ashamed*.

Note also ܟܘܬܪܘܬܐ K. f. or ܟܘܬܪܐ Q. Sal. and also U. m. *multitude, excess*, from ܟܘܬܪ *excessive*.

We also have, like the above, the irregular ܐܝܬܘܬܐ (also ܐܝܬܘܬܐ) *being, essence*, from ܐܝܬ *there is*, O.S.; and ܚܒܪܘܬܐ *companionship* (also regular in K. as O.S.), from ܚܒܪܐ *companion*, O.S. And almost all adjectives in ܐܢܐ form abstracts in ܐܘܬܐ which in their case is the regular termination. In U. this termination is often in quick speech shortened to *ei'ta*.

Several abstracts have no original, as ܙܢܝܘܬܐ O.S. *fornication*; ܟܬܒܬܐ Tkh. Al. *a writing*, = ܟܬܒܐ U. K.; ܓܘܚܟܐ K. Sh. *joke*, cf. ܓܚܟ § 46; ܡܓܚܟܢܐ U. *joke*, cf. ܡܓܚܟܢܐ *joker*; ܓܝܕܘܬܐ Tkh. *joke*, cf. ܓܝܕܒ U. or ܓܝܕܒ U. *id.*, Turk.; ܡܘܕܥܬܐ J. *joke*; ܡܪܕܘܬܐ O.S. *education*, § 21 (5); ܫܬܝܕܘܬܐ *earnestness*, cf. ܡܫܬܝܕ *to be diligent*; ܗܝܡܢܘܬܐ O.S. *faith*; ܒܥܘܬܐ O.S. *a Rogation*; § 18 (9); ܚܕܘܬܐ O.S. *joy*; ܐܬܘܬܐ O.S. *letter of the alphabet*, cf. O.S. ܐܬܐ *a sign*; ܐܣܝܘܬܐ *cure*; ܡܡܝܩܢܘܬܐ *mocking*.

(2) The abstract of a noun denoting an agent (§ 77. 1) will generally be the noun of action (§ 76). Thus ܡܡܠܠܢܐ *speaker*, ܡܡܠܠܘܬܐ *speech*; but both forms are sometimes used, as ܚܣܡܢܘܬܐ and ܚܣܡܢܐ *envy*, from ܚܣܡ *to envy*. ܪܒܪܒܢܘܬܐ (O.S. ܡ) *pride*, is used in preference to ܪܒܪܒܘܬܐ. ܡܫܠܡܢܘܬܐ is used for *tradition*, ܡܫܠܡܢܐ for *the act of handing down*.

(3) A very few abstracts are formed by giving Rwasa to the second radical of a verb and adding ܐ, as ܚܡܘܣܐ *heat*, from ܚܡ *to be warm*, O.S.; ܕܠܘܚܐ O.S. *disturbance*, from ܕܠܚ *to disturb*, O.S.; ܟܦܘܪܐ O.S. *apostasy*, from ܟܦܪ *to deny*, O.S.; ܟܢܘܫܐ O.S. *an assembly*, from ܟܢܫ *to sweep, collect*, O.S.; cf. ܢܘܗܪܐ K. *light*, from ܢܗܪ K. *to dawn*, Arab.

We may notice that abstracts are more used by the Syrians than by Europeans. Thus they will often say ܒܪܢܫܘܬܐ *human nature,* where we should use the concrete *men.* For *the plural of nouns* they say ܣܓܝܐܘܬܐ ܕܫܡܗܐ, and so on.

§ 79. (1) DIMINUTIVES are formed by substituting ܘܢܐ m. (with first pl.) or ܘܢܬܐ f. (sixth pl.) for the termination of the original; or by adding on these if there is no termination. Thus ܛܠܝܘܢܐ *a little boy,* from ܛܠܝܐ *a boy;* ܒܟܬܘܢܬܐ *a little wife,* from ܒܟܬܐ *a wife, woman* [root O.S. ܒܟܬ *to spin, weave,* cf. O.S. ܒܝܟܬܐ *a hired spinster*]; ܚܬܘܢܬܐ *a little sister,* from ܚܬܐ *a sister.* According to Bar Zu'bi all these nouns have Rwakha.

These nouns are also used to denote endearment. Thus a family name for *father* is ܒܒܘܢܐ. (The original is not used.) So ܒܪܘܢܐ *a son* (from O.S. ܒܪܐ *id.*), ܐܚܘܢܐ *a brother* (from O.S. ܐܚܐ *id.*), ܣܒܘܢܐ U. *a grandfather* (from ܣܒܐ *an old man,* as O.S.; in K. *a grandfather*), ܢܢܘܢܬܐ *a grandmother,* U. (from ܢܢܐ *a mother* or *grandmother,* = ܣܒܬܐ K.) have now no diminutive force. So ܡܡܘܢܐ *paternal uncle,* from ܡܡܐ K. *id.,* ܚܠܘܢܐ *maternal uncle,* from O.S. K. ܚܠܐ *id.* p. 38.

Diminutives rarely denote contempt; as ܩܫܘܢܐ *priestling,* ܐܢܫܘܢܐ *mannikin.*

This termination is in some words shortened to ܘ for vocatives and titles prefixed to names. Thus ܒܒܘ or ܒܒܘ *father;* ܡܡܘ lit. *uncle,* a term of respect used in addressing bishops and old men, especially in U., and also when speaking of bishops. It is also prefixed to the names of old men, as ܡܡܘ ܝܥܩܘܒ lit. *Uncle James.*

The corresponding feminine is ܫܠܬܐ (lit. *maternal aunt*, from O.S. and N.S. ܫܠܬܝ), which may be used vocatively as a term of respect, or prefixed to a name as ܫܠܬܐ ܡܪܝܡ lit. *Aunt Mary*. When prefixed to names these may be used either vocatively or in speaking of the persons designated. Other instances of these nouns used vocatively are ܐܡܐ K. *mother*, dim. of ܐܡܝ U. or ܐܡܝ K. *mother*; ܣܒܗ *grandfather*; ܒܒܐ K. *father* (in U. only as a proper name); ܢܢܐ *grandmother*; ܕܕܬܐ or ܕܕ *paternal aunt*; ܫܠܬܐ *maternal aunt*.

Of the same form are ܟܠܬܐ *bride*, from ܟܠܠ *id.*; also ܡܬܢܬܐ U. *bladder*, ܥܠܩܐ *leech*, and ܡܨܥܬܐ U. *platform*, § 19. So ܫܘܢܪܐ f. *cat*, from ܫܘܢܪܐ m. *tom cat* (but ܫܘܢܪܬܐ *kitten*), ܡܫܡܫܬܐ U. *sunny side of a hill* = ܡܫܡܫܢܝܬܐ (from ܡܫܡܫ *to warm*) p. 231.

We may notice the curious diminutives ܒܣܝܘܣܝܬܐ U. K. Sp. *a very little*, and ܒܣܝܘܣܝܬ Sal., from ܒܣܝܘܣ *a little*, which is itself a diminutive, see § 82 (13), [in this word there is usually a very strong accent on the penultimate], ܚܡܝܨܝܬܐ K. *a very little*, from ܚܡ *any one*, (cf. ܘܚܕܕܘܢܝܬܐ *very little*, from ܘܚܕܕ *little*, ܨܥܝܪܝܬ U. *very small*, from ܨܥܝܪ *small*); ܚܡܝܣܝܬܐ *very gently*, from ܚܡܝܣ *gently*; ܐܣܝܓܝܬܐ which in Sal. = *only just* (a variant is ܐܣܝܓ) from ܐܣܝܓ *only*, in K. = *so many*, from ܬܘܣܓ § 67; ܒܣܝܘܣܘܣܝܬܐ Ti. *a very little*, from ܒܣܝܘܣ *a little*, see § 28 (9); ܡܠܠܬܢܝܬܐ Ti. (or ܬܠ MB. etc.) *morning twilight*, from ܡܠܠ § 67; ܐܢܓܘܢܝܬܐ Tkh. *here*, from ܐܢ K. Q. *id.*

(2) Diminutives are also formed by using a feminine form; as ܟܟܐ *a tooth*, ܟܟܬܐ *a little tooth* (of a cog-wheel). In Ṭiari these feminines are very common and often have no diminutive force. Thus Ṭiari men will say ܒܓܕܬܐ where other Syrians say ܒܓܕܐ

a bridge, ܓܹܫܪܵܐ for ܓܹܫܪܹܐ *a stone*, ܟܸܦܵܐ (with ܒ) for ܓܸܒܵܐ *a side* (ܕ)¹.

§ 80. NEGATIVES are formed by prefixing ܠܵܐ both to Syriac words and also to most imported words. But Persian words often prefer ܢܵܐ, the Persian equivalent to ܠܵܐ (*not*): as ܢܵܡܘܡܟܸܢ *impossible*.

The ܠܵܐ is written as a separate word, but it really forms one word with that which follows it and which it negatives; thus, ܥܲܠ ܠܵܐ ܐܬܝܵܘܟ݂ *about your not coming*.

ܠܵܐ can also be prefixed to adjectives and adverbs. This gives a more emphatic negative than if ܠܵܐ or ܠܹܐ were put with the verb. Thus ܠܵܐ ܛܵܒ݂ܐ ܗܘܵܐ *it was not-good (bad)* is stronger than ܠܹܐ ܗܘܵܐ ܛܵܒ݂ܐ *it was not good*.

ܠܵܐ is also used similarly with the infinitive, as ܠܵܐ ܠܦܲܠܵܚܵܐ *to refrain from working*, 1 Cor. ix. 6.

§ 81. (1) ADJECTIVES are freely formed from substantives by changing their termination to, or by adding on (*a*) ܵܢܵܐ ; (*b*) ܵܝܵܐ ; (*c*) ܢܵܝܵܐ ; (*d*) ܢܵܝܵܐ. The last three especially denote dwellers in a particular place. These Syriac terminations are very frequently added to foreign words.

Examples. (*a*) ܡܲܝܵܢܵܐ *watery*, from ܡܲܝܵܐ *water* (O.S., Al. ܡܝܵܐ).

(*b*) ܛܝܵܪܢܵܝܵܐ *a Tiari man*, from ܛܝܵܪܹܐ *Tiari* (lit. *the sheep-folds*), one of the Ashiret districts of Kurdistan.

---

¹ Several in Al. which end in ܘܢܵܐ are not diminutives; as ܬܸܡܗܘܢܵܐ *wonder, miracle* (= ܬܸܕܡܘܪܬܵܐ U. K.), ܚܸܪܝܘܢܵܐ *contention* (= ܚܸܪܝܵܢܵܐ U. K.), ܕܸܟ݂ܪܘܢܵܐ *remembrance* (= ܕܘܟ݂ܪܵܢܵܐ U. K.).

(*c*) ܬܟܘܡܢܝܐ *a Tkhuma man*, from ܬܟܘܡܐ *Tkhuma* (another Ashiret district). ܨܝܕܢܝܐ K. Al. *a hunter*, or *fisherman*, from ܨܝܕܐ *game*. (In U. ܨܝܕܐ is used, p. 234.)

(*d*) ܦܓܪܢܝܐ *bodily* (rarely ܦܓܪܢܐ), from ܦܓܪܐ *a body*; ܟ̰ܘܡܒܢܝܐ *a man of Chumba*, from ܟ̰ܘܡܒܐ *Chumba* (a village of Ṭiari).

Notice ܙܒܢܢܝܐ *timely*, from ܙܒܢܐ *time*; ܡܕܝܢܢܝܐ *citizen*, from ܡܕܝܢܬܐ *city*; ܥܠܡܝܢܝܐ, ܐܕܝܢܝܐ both *eternal* (the latter more colloquial), from old plural forms in ܝܢ, but the latter is not O.S.; see § 16. i. *e*.

Words in ܝܐ, ܝܐ, ܝ, may form adjectives in ܝܝܐ: as ܐܣܛܪܘܠܘܓܝܝܐ *astrologer*, from ܐܣܛܪܘܠܘܓܝܐ *astrology*.

The local adjectives are much more common in Kurdistan than in the Urmi plain, where the same idea is usually expressed by ܒܪ *son of* (a plural noun used as singular, § 16. ii. *c*) or ܒܢܝ *sons of*, as ܒܪ ܐܘܪܡܝ *an inhabitant of Urmi*.

Several of the local adjectives are irregular. Thus from ܐܘܪܡܝ *Urmi*, ܐܘܪܡܢܝܐ or ܐܘܪܡܝܢܝܐ Ti. (in Ashitha ܐܘܪܡܝ and ܐܘܪܡܝܢܝܐ respectively); from ܓ̰ܝܠܘ *Jilu*, ܓ̰ܝܠܘܝܐ; from ܕܝܙ or ܕܝܙ *Diz* (or *Dizin*) ܕܝܙܢܝܐ; from ܕܝܙܐ *Diza*, ܕܝܙܝܐ; from ܗܢܕ *India* (an earlier form of which is ܗܢܕܘ), ܗܢܕܘܝܐ *an Indian*, ܗܢܕܝܐ *a product of India*; from ܘܠܛܘ *Waltu*, ܘܠܛܘܝܐ or ܘܠܛܢܝܐ; from ܡܪܝ ܒܝܫܘ *Mar Bishu*, ܡܪܝ ܒܝܫܢܝܐ; from ܥܡܕܝܐ *Amadia*, ܥܡܕܝܢܝܐ; from ܨܝܕܢ *Sidon*, ܨܝܕܢܝܐ = O.S. ܨܝܕܢܝܐ; from ܩܘܕܫܢܣ *Qudshanis* (*Kochanis*), ܩܘܕܫܢܣܝܐ or ܩܘܕܫܢܝܐ; from ܛܘ *Tu*, ܛܘܝܐ or ܛܘܝܐ.

The termination ـܵܢܵܐ (see above) often denotes the same as the English adjectival termination *-ish*, as ܟܘܼܡܬܵܢܵܐ *blackish*, from ܟܘܼܡܬܵܐ *black*; ܣܘܼܡܩܵܢܵܐ *reddish*, from ܣܘܼܡܩܵܐ *red*; so ܝܲܪܝܼܟ݂ܵܢܵܐ *oblong*, from ܝܲܪܝܼܟ݂ܵܐ *long*. But ܟܘܼܪܵܢܵܐ = *grayish*, from ܟܘܼܪܵܐ *gray*.

ܚܕܵܢܵܝܵܐ O.S. *singular* (in grammar), from O.S. ܚܲܕ *one*, is irregular. The word for *plural* is ܣܓܝܼܐܵܢܵܝܵܐ O.S., from O.S. ܣܲܓܝܼܐܵܐ *many*.

From ܡܵܘܬܵܐ *death*, we have ܡܵܘܬܵܢܵܐ *deadly*, but this is also a masc. substantive = *a plague*. So ܕܪܵܥܵܐ *arm*, for ܕܪܵܥܵܢܵܐ; ܦܲܪܨܘܼܦܵܢܵܐ *a bully*, from ܦܲܪܨܘܼܦܵܐ *face*. Note also ܟܘܼܠܵܢܵܝܵܐ = *universal*, as O.S., from O.S. ܟܘܼܠܵܐ *the whole*.

(2) Adjectives are very much more common in Syriac than in Hebrew; but they are much less common than in European languages. The word ܡܵܪܵܐ *lord of*, § 16. ii. *f*, can be prefixed to almost any substantive to make an adjective. Adjectives thus formed are of either gender or number.

(3) Adjectives may be rarely formed by prefixing ܕ *of*, to the corresponding substantive, cf. ܪܘܼܚܵܐ ܕܩܘܼܕܫܵܐ *Spirit of holiness* = *Holy Ghost*. So ܘܲܪܕܵܐ ܕܕܲܫܬܵܐ *a rose of the plain* (i.e. the fields) = *a wild rose*.

(4) For the English terminations *-able, -ible*, the O.S. passive verbal noun in ـܵܢܵܐ is sometimes used, but not colloquially. Thus ܡܸܬܟܲܝܠܵܢܵܐ *measurable*, from ܟܵܐܸܠ. But see § 34 for a common method of paraphrasing these expressions.

(5) Adjectives are also formed directly from verbal roots. For those of the forms ܦܲܥܘܿܠܵܐ, ܦܥܘܼܠܵܐ see § 77 (2). More common are those of the old participial form ܦܥܝܼܠܵܐ, which we must distinguish from

the newer participial form ܩܛܝܼܠܵܐ. Some of these have become substantives. The Pthakha is usually sounded like Zqapa in U., not in K. Al. Z. In Q. Sal. etc. these usually have long Zlama on the first radical.

Words of the form ܩܛܝܼܠܵܐ.

(*a*) *Adjectives*.

ܟܚܝܼܕܵܐ O.S. *lean* (ܟܚܕ *to be lean*, O.S. Ethp'el).

ܚܣܝܼܕܵܐ *envious* (ܚܣܝܕ *to envy*, Arab.).

ܒܛܝܼܠܵܐ O.S. *idle, unemployed* (ܒܛܠ *to cease*, O.S.).

ܒܣܝܼܡܵܐ O.S. *pleasant* (ܒܣܡ *to be pleased*, § 76. 5).

ܕܠܝܼܠܵܐ K., O.S. *thinned out* (as trees) = ܕܠܝܠ U., p. 247 (ܡܕܠܠ *to thin out*, as O.S. Aph.).

ܕܩܝܼܩܵܐ O.S., K. *minute*, adj. = ܕܩܝܩ U. (ܕܩܩ *to make fine*, O.S.), see below, *b*, and p. 247.

ܙܕܝܼܩܵܐ O.S. *righteous* (O.S. ܙܕܩ *to be just*).

ܙܪܝܼܩܵܐ Sal. = O.S. ܙܪܝܩ *clever* (Chald. זרק *to cut*).

ܚܟܝܼܡܵܐ O.S., Al. *wise* = ܚܟܝܡܐ U. = ܚܟܝܡ Tkh. (ܚܟܡ K. *to be perfect*, in O.S. *to be wise*).

ܚܡܝܼܡܵܐ O.S., K. *warm* = ܚܡܝܡ U., p. 247 (ܚܡܡ *to be warm*, O.S.).

ܚܪܝܼܦܵܐ O.S. *sharp* (ܚܪܦ *to be sharp*, O.S.).

ܝܩܝܼܪܵܐ O.S., K. *honourable* = ܡܘܩܪܐ U. (ܝܩܪ K. Al. *to make heavy*, O.S.).

ܡܟܝܼܟܵܐ O.S. *gentle, humble*, p. 247 (ܡܟܟ *to be gentle*, O.S. ܡܟ).

ܡܪܝܼܪܵܐ O.S., K. *bitter* = ܡܪܝܪ U., p. 247 (ܡܪܪ K., ܡܪܪ U. *to be bitter*, O.S. ܡܪ).

ܢܶܩܕܳܐ Al. *clean* = ܚܣܺܝܘ U. = ܕܳܟܶܐ Ti. (ܕܰܟܺܝ Al. *to cleanse*, Arab.; *to drip*, U. as O.S. Pa.).

ܩܛܺܝܢܳܐ Tkh. *thin* = ܒܰܣܺܝܡܳܐ Ti. = ܢܳܘܺܟ U. (ܢܚܶܒ *to be thin*).

ܦܳܪܽܘܡܬܳܢܳܐ Al. *intelligent* (ܦܪܰܚ Al. *to understand*, § 39).

ܐܳܙܺܝܠܳܐ O.S.* *departed* (O.S. ܐܙܠ *to depart, die*), see below, *b*.

ܥܰܬܺܝܩܳܐ O.S. *ancient* (ܥܬܶܩ K. *to be old*, O.S.).

ܥܰܬܺܝܪܳܐ O.S., Al. *rich*; used everywhere for *Dives* in the parable (O.S. ܥܬܰܪ *to be rich*).

ܨܠܺܝܠܳܐ *sober*, p. 247 (ܨܠܝܠ *to become sober*; also in K. of water, *to become clear*; O.S. Pa. *to strain out*).

ܩܰܕܺܝܫܳܐ O.S. *holy* (ܩܕܶܫ *to be holy*, O.S.), see below, *b*.

ܩܰܪܺܝܪܳܐ O.S., K. *cold* = ܩܰܪܳܐ U., p. 247 (ܩܪܰܪ *to be cold*, O.S.).

ܪܰܚܺܝܩܳܐ *far* (ܪܚܶܩ *to be far*, as O.S. Ethpa.).

ܪܰܟܺܝܟܳܐ O.S. *soft* (ܪܟܶܟ *to be soft*, O.S. ܪܰܟ).

ܪܰܩܺܝܩܳܐ O.S. *fine* (O.S. ܪܩܶܩ *to make thin*; cf. N.S. ܡܪܰܕܩܶܩ *to hammer out metal*), p. 247.

ܫܰܚܺܝܢܳܐ O.S. *warm* (ܫܚܶܢ *to be warm*, O.S.).

ܫܰܡܺܝܢܳܐ O.S. *fat* (O.S. ܫܡܶܢ *to be fat or ripe*).

ܫܰܦܺܝܪܳܐ O.S. *beautiful* (ܫܦܰܪ *to please*, O.S.).

ܫܰܪܺܝܪܳܐ O.S. *true*, p. 247 (ܫܪܰܪ K. *to be strong*, O.S. ܫܰܪ; also in O.S. *to be true*).

ܬܠܺܝܠܳܐ O.S., K. *wet* = ܬܰܠܳܐ U. (O.S. ܐܶܬܬܠܺܝܠ *to be wet*).

All these form feminines in ܬܳܐ.

(*b*) *Substantives.*

ܒܫܝܠܬܐ f. *musk melon*, so called because it ripens by being buried in the sand while still growing. (ܒܫܠ *to ripen, be cooked*, O.S.)

ܓܕܝܫܐ m. (O.S. ܓ') *stack* (ܓܕܫ *to stack*, U. K.; in Al. *to happen*, both as O.S.).

ܓܪܝܡܬܐ f. *a fine* (ܓܪܝܡ *to fine*, Arab.).

ܕܩܝܩܐ m. *a minute* (of time), see above, *a*.

ܘܪܝܕܐ O.S. m. *vein* (no verb).

ܢܓܝܪܬܐ O.S. f. *axe* (no verb: connected with O.S. ܢܓܪ *to split* ?).

ܝܡܝܢܬܐ O.S. f. *right hand; a cubit* (no verb). In the former sense also ܝܡܝܢܐ.

ܢܗܝܪܐ O.S. m. *a light* [sun, moon, etc.] (O.S. ܢܗܪ *to shine*).

ܢܚܝܪܐ (O.S. ܢܚ') m. *nose* (O.S. ܢܚܪ *to snore*: ܢܚܪ K. Al. *to kill*; U. *to saw*).

ܢܦܝܪܐ f. *trumpet* (O.S. ܢܦܪ *to snort*).

ܣܪܝܕܐ m. *large sieve*, for earth (ܣܪܕ *to sift*, as Chald.).

ܥܢܝܕܐ O.S. m. *book of the burial service* for laymen, see above, *a*.

ܦܛܝܪܐ O.S. m. *unleavened cake* (O.S. ܦܛܪ *to be unleavened*).

ܩܕܝܫܐ O.S. m. *a saint*, see above, *a*.

ܩܪܝܒܐ O.S. m. *godfather*, lit. *a neighbour;* and ܩܪܝܒܬܐ O.S. f. *godmother* (ܩܪܒ K. *to be near*, O.S.).

ܩܫܝܫܐ O.S. m. *priest*, usually ܩܫܐ in N.S. (O.S. ܩܫ *to be old*).

ܫܚܝܦܬܐ O.S. f. *incense boat* (no verb).

ܫܠܝܛܐ O.S. m. a man's name, lit. *a ruler* (O.S. ܫܠܛ *to rule*).

ܓܕܝܕܐ m., ܚܕܐ f., *partaker* (ܓܕܝ *to partake*, hard Kap, Arab.).

ܐܦܝܢܐ O.S. m. *dragon* (no verb).

Of the same form are the foreign words ܐܘܝܢܟ *slack*, ܒܘܝܢܐ f. *treasure*, Turk. (also ܒܘܢܐ), ܓܬܒܬܐ f. *flute*, ܓܠܝܠܐ f. *peach*, ܓܕܝܒܕܐ m. *snare*. So ܣܟܝܢܐ f. *knife* = O.S. ܣܟܝܢܐ.

Note that words like ܕܠܝܠܐ come from ܕܠܠ roots, as ܕܠܠ, of which the P'al pres. part. is ܕܐܠ. Hence in N.S. the verbs appear with a medial Alap, while the adjectives have the doubled consonant. Yet under influence of the adjectives we get in N.S. ܕܓܝ, ܕܓܕ K. or ܕܓܕ U., ܕܓܝ, ܕܓܕ K. So ܫܘܟ Ti. *to bathe* = ܫܘܟ U. Tkh. § 39, and perhaps ܚܝ *to burn*, in cooking, from O.S. ܚܢܢ *smell of meat*, etc. The O.S. Pa'el of these verbs has the double consonant, and therefore in N.S. we have as second conjugation triliterals ܡܕܠܠ K. *to thin out trees*, ܡܨܝܠܠ *to become sober*, ܡܚܝܠܠ K. *to make light*; perhaps also ܡܫܝܠܠ *to be quiet* (akin to ܫܠܠ *id*.), and ܡܚܢܢ *to tame* (akin to O.S. ܚܢܢ *id*.).

§ 82. FOREIGN TERMINATIONS.

A large number of nouns and some verbs are taken from foreign languages, especially Persian, Turkish, Kurdish and Arabic. The nouns take the terminations ܐܝ (esp. K.), ܐܗ, ܐܘܐ very freely. The verbs are conjugated exactly like those which are from Syriac roots and regularly form verbal nouns, etc.

Most of the words imported into O.S. from the Greek are now obsolete; though scientific terms have in many cases been lately imported into the language from the Greek, sometimes through English, as ܓܝܘܓܪܦܝܐ for 'ܓܝܐ *geography*.

The commonest of the foreign terminations are as follows:

(1) ܓ݂ܝ from the Turkish, meaning one who performs the business indicated by the word (all masc.), as ܟ݂ܕܘܿܢܓ݂ܝ *a caravan driver*, from ܟ݂ܕܘܿ *a caravan*, f. When ܬܳܐ is added on to a foreign word (as above) it is usually dropped before this termination is added, as ܟ݂ܕ݂ܵܬ݂ܓ݂ܝ *a driver*, from ܟ݂ܕ݂ܵܬ݂ܐ *a waggon, cart*, f. This termination is sometimes added on to Syriac words, as ܐܘܪܚܓ݂ܝ *a traveller*, from ܐܘܪܚܳܐ *a road*, f., ܬܪܥܓ݂ܝ *doorkeeper*, from ܬܪܥܳܐ *a door*, m., ܟ݂ܫܓ݂ܝ = ܟ݂ܫܬܳܐ § 77 (3), *miller*. All these words take the first plural (ܓ݂ܝ̈) and make abstract nouns in ܓ݂ܘܬ݂ܐ. These nouns are very common. ܟ݂ܕ݂ܘܓ݂ܝ *petitioner*, from ܟ݂ܕ݂ܘ *petition*, f. is irregular.

(2) ܕܵܪ Pers. Kurd. (masculines), e.g. ܐܟ݂ܕ݂ܘܿܕܵܪ *tenant (of land)*, ܕܒ݂ܝܪܕܵܪ 2 K. *orator* (Kurd.), ܐܟ݂ܘܿܕܵܪ *husbandman* (O.S. ܐܟ݂ܘܿܕܵܪ), ܡܚܘܼܡܕܵܪ *wounded*, ܠܡܥܡܕܘܿܕܵܪ *journeyman*, ܕܘܵܓ݂ܕܵܪ *pitchfork*, ܓ݂ܢܸܕܵܪ *debtor*, ܡܡܘܚܡܕܵܪ *capable of speech*, ܝܘܿܢܓ݂ܕܵܪ *treasurer*, ܟ݂ܘܿܕܵܪ *caravan driver*, ܟ݂ܙܡܕܵܪ *merciful*, ܒܠܨܓ݂ܕܵܪ *sorcerer*, ܟ݂ܝܠܓ݂ܕܵܪ *wise*, ܫܕ݂ܘܕܵܪ *promise*, ܙܓ݂ܠܕܵܪ *sorcerer*, ܒܓ݂ܕܘܕܵܪ *grateful*, ܟ݂ܕܢܓ݂ܕܵܪ Al. *lawyer*, ܐܕܒܣܕܵܪ *historian*, ܐܕܡܛܕܵܪ *superstitious*, and many others.

(3) ܟ݂ܕ Pers. (masculines), as ܐܘܣܡܐܟ݂ܕ *artificer* (= ܨܵܡܘܿܐ § 19), ܟ݂ܡܓ݂ܕܟ݂ܕ *guilty*, ܐܘܕܘܐܟ݂ܕ *meddler*, ܣܠܐܒܐܟ݂ܕ *attendant*, *avaricious*, ܡܒܣܡܟ݂ܕ *coppersmith*, ܓ݂ܓ݂ܐܟ݂ܕ *grateful*, ܒܨܪܟ݂ܕ *painter*, ܟ݂ܕܨܐܟ݂ܕ ܗܝܡܐܟ݂ܕ *carpenter*, ܒܬܟ݂ܓ݂ܪܟ݂ܕ *pious*, ܝܥܓ݂ܐܟ݂ܕ *artisan*, ܟ݂ܕܟ݂ܟ݂ܕ *litigious*, ܟ݂ܕܒܓ݂ܟ݂ܕ *lawyer*, ܐܘܬܟ݂ܕ *repentant*, and some others.

(4) ܠܸܕ or ܠܵܕ Pers. (masc.), as ܕܘܢܝܠܵܕ *worldly* (ܕܘܢܝܐ *the world*, f.), ܕܝܢܝܠܵܕ *litigious* (ܕܝܢܳܐ *judgement*), ܡܒܪܐܠܵܕ *inheritor*,

(ܡܓ̈ܕܐ an unclaimed inheritance), ܬܘܓܪܐ merchant (ܬܘܓܪܬܐ trade), ܟܘܦܠܕ glassblower (ܟܦܐ glass, m.).

(5) ܗܡ Pers. (masc.), as ܓܝܬܚܡ calico maker (ܓܝܬܐ calico, m.), ܚܡܚܚܡ flint and steel maker (ܚܡܚܐ flint and steel, m.), ܒܙܠܚܡ cotton dresser (ܒܙܕ coloured cotton cloth, m.), ܫܥܬܚܡ watchmaker (ܫܥܬܐ f. a watch), ܦܠܢܓܚܡ saddler (ܦܠܢܐ m. a saddletree).

(6) ܕܢ Pers., as ܩܠܡܕܢ pencase, f. (ܩܠܡܐ pen, f.), ܚܝܕܢ tea-kettle, f. (ܚܝ tea, m.), ܚܨܕܢ travelling bag, f., ܗܕܠܕܢ vagabond, m., ܚܡܕܢ candlestick, m. (ܚܡܐ wax, f.).

(7) ܠܝܓ Turk., properly an abstract termination, ܐܘܪܠܝܓ middle, f., see p. 158, ܬܥܠܝܓ hood, f., ܘܠܟܠܝܓ a snug corner, f. (ܘܠܟܠܝܓ a protection, f.), ܡܘܫܓܘܠܝܓ expenditure, f. (also ܡܚܕܝܓ), ܡܘܫܓܘܠܝܓ first tidings (or present for tidings), f., ܬܘܚܘܕܠܝܓ first fruits, f., ܬܘܡܫܠܝܓ feast, f. (this word has become concrete exactly like the O.S. equivalent ܡܚܡܘܗܐ, cf. ܐܘܫܡܐ § 78), ܩܕܠܝܓ K. noise.

(8) ܠܝ, ܠܘ, ܠܘܝ Turk., usually denoting of or belonging to a place; as ܐܘܠܝ a native, m., ܒܘܡܨܠܘ or ܒܘܡܨܠܘ an Osmanli, ܒܕܠܘ a native, m., ܓܠܘ U. a bush, f. The names of many villages in the Urmi plain have this termination.

(9) ܡܐ Turk., as ܕܘܠܡܐ a button, ܕܘܠܡܐ a stuffed eatable, f., ܓܝܕܘܕܡܐ an ice (the sweetmeat) f., ܗܘܕܡܐ bar, bolt, m., ܗܘܡܣܡܐ K. kind, sort, m. (= ܐܘܢ U. m.), ܚܘܚܡܐ cast iron.

(10) ܓܕ Pers. (used by itself = a band, f.), ܬܘܓܕ amulet, f. (Turk. bazu, a calf), ܗܘܢܕܓܕ skilful (ܗܘܢܕ skill, f.), ܒܕܠܓܕ

furrier, m. (ܢܥܠܒܢܕ̈ *a horse shoe*, m.), ܢܣܒܠܢܓ̰ܝ̈ *story teller*, m. (ܢܣܒܝܕ *story*, f.), ܡܠܚܓ̰ܝ̈ *besieged* (ܡܠܚܕ̈ *castle*, f.), ܡܝܩܒܠܓ̰ܝ̈ *dovetailed* (ܡܝܩܒܝܕ̈ *padlock*).

(11) ܣܬܐܢ Pers. and Turk., denoting a place: ܐܦܓܐܢܣܬܐܢ *Afghanistan*, ܗܝܢܕܘܣܬܐܢ *Hindustan*, ܟܘܪܕܣܬܐܢ *Kurdistan* (with Kap, § 119), ܐܠܡܢܝܣܬܐܢ *Germany*, ܦܪܢܓܝܣܬܐܢ *Europe*, and many others.

(12) ܟܝ Turk., denoting *of or belonging to a person* (K. only), as ܩܠܡܐ ܝܘܢܟܝ *the pen of Jonah* (ܝܘܢܢ).

(13) ܓ̰ܐ Turk., a diminutive, ܒܐܓ̰ܐ *garden*, f. (Turk. *bagh*, *id.*; so N.S. ܒܐܓ̰ܝ *gardener*, m.), ܕܣܡܐܓ̰ܐ *handkerchief*, ܕܘܠܟ̰ܐ U. *bucket*, f. (ܕܘܠܐ K. *large bucket*:—so O.S.; Pers. *dol*), ܕܘܠܐܦܓ̰ܐ (or ܕ) *cupboard*, f. (Turk. and Mod. Gk. *dulapi*), ܒܝܕ̰ܓ̰ܐ *a little*, dim. of ܒܝܕ̰ §§ 28 (9), 79, ܣܗܢܓ̰ܐ *jar*, f., also *a small wooden tray*, from ܣܗܢ *a large tray*, m., ܫܟܠܓ̰ܐ *small carpet*, f. § 120, ܟܡܓ̰ܐ *fiddle*, f., ܬܘܓ̰ܐ *saucepan*, f. (ܬܘ *cauldron*, f.), ܐܣܓ̰ܐ *recess in a wall, or seat at a door*, f. (but ܟܘܐ f. is the usual word), ܗܒܓ̰ܐ *kettle*, f. (ܗܒ *id.*).

(14) ܢܫܐ *a house*, Pers. (all fem.), ܓ̰ܡܢܫܐ *printing office* (ܓ̰ܡܢܐ *printing press*), ܕܘܦܣܐ (*sic*) *prison*, from ܕܘܦܣ *prisoner*, m. (which is also ܕܘܦܣܓ̰ܝ), ܕܝܘܐܢܫܐ *judgement hall or sitting room*, from ܕܝܘܐ *judgement*, f., ܨܪܒܫܐ *ante-room* (because *coffee* [ܩܗܘܐ m.] is made there), and many others.

(15) ܒܘ Pers. as ܒܟܕܟ̰ܘ *litigious*, ܟܗܡܟ̰ܘ *conjurer*, m., ܗܙܕܟ̰ܘ *gambler*, m., ܡܝܟܕܟ̰ܘ *mummer*, m., ܟܡܕܟ̰ܘ *a dome*, f., *soldier*, m., ܕܘܡܒܟ̰ܘ *rope dancer*, m.

(16) ܩܘ as ܐܫܦܘ ܩܘ *cook* (male) U. (in K. ܐܫܦܓ̰ܝ); ܓ̰ܐܩܘ *tea-pot*.

(17) ܙܵܕܵܐ Pers. (masc.) meaning *son of*, as ܫܵܗܙܵܕܵܐ *prince* (lit. *son of the Shah*), which makes fem. ܫܵܗܙܵܕܬܵܐ *princess*, ܒܲܓܙܵܕܵܐ *nobleman* (son of a Bey).

(18) ܟܵܪ or ܟܵܐܪ, as ܚܲܣܵܕܬܟܵܪ or ܚܲܣܵܕܬܟܵܐܪ *zealous* (ܚܲܣܵܕܬ *zeal*, f.), ܒܝܼܓܵܪܟܵܪ *labourer* (forced), (ܒܝܼܓܵܪܵܐ *forced labour*), ܦܸܫܟܲܫ *a present*, f.

(19) ܝܼܬ a common abstract ending in Arabic words, as ܢܸܥܡܝܼܬ *grace*. Also used for concrete nouns, as ܡܲܟܢܝܼܬ *a dwelling*. These are feminine.

(20) We also have ܕܘܼܙ in ܦܵܠܵܢܕܘܼܙ *a pack-saddle maker*, from ܦܵܠܵܢ *a pack-saddle*, m.; ܡܲܢܕ in ܕܵܘܠܲܬܡܲܢܕ *rich* (cf. ܕܵܘܠܲܬ *wealth*); ܘܵܢ in ܕܲܪܓܘܵܢ *doorkeeper*, Al., from ܕܲܪܓܵܐ *a door*, and ܒܵܓܘܵܢ *gardener*, cf. (13); ܟܵܐ and ܟܵܐ in ܠܘܼܠܟܵܐ = ܠܘܼܠܵܐ m. *tube*, ܢܝܼܫܵܢܟܵܐ U. *sign*, m. = ܢܝܼܫܵܢܵܐ Al. m., ܩܲܠܝܲܢܟܵܐ Z. = ܩܲܠܝܵܢܵܐ K. = ܩܲܠܝܵܢ U. f. *water pipe*. We may here add the Persian prefix ܒܲܕ = *bad*; as ܒܲܕܢܵܡ *infamous*, ܒܲܕܦܘܼܡ *gluttonous*, ܒܲܕܪܲܢܓ *faded*, ܒܲܕܟܲܠܵܡ *sensual*, ܒܲܕܙܵܬ *scoundrel*.

§ 83. Derivation of Verbs.

The great majority of N.S. triliterals are found in O.S.; some which are not found in O.S. are found in Chaldee. Others are taken from the Arabic, and a few from other languages. In several cases where the form of the verbs is the same as in O.S., the meaning is different; sometimes it has altered under influence of the Arabic. But in many such cases the O.S. meaning is found in some one of the dialects though it is not in general use; thus ܛܥܵܝܵܐ is *to seek* usually in N.S., in O.S. and Al. *to err* (ܛܥܵܝܵܐ ܒܵܬܪܹܗ *to wander after* a person, so *to seek* him).

For ܠ, ܪܓ introduced into N.S. verbs to replace other letters in corresponding O.S. verbs, see §§ 100, 113.

The manner in which N.S. conjugations are derived from the old forms has been explained in §§ 30 sqq. Verbs derived from foreign languages follow the Syriac model in the formation of their tenses.

(A) *Quadriliterals.*

Quadriliterals in N.S. shew a great developement; the following are the principal classes of them[1].

(1) Causatives, corresponding to O.S. Aph'el, § 45.

(2) Palpel verbs, derived from ܥܥ roots (usually O.S.); but some are formed from other roots on the same analogy. Such are :—

ܡܕܒܕܒܠ *to creep*, cf. ܫܘܫܡܠܐ *ant*, § 77 (2).

ܡܟܦܘܟܘ Sp. (pron. ܟ = ܦ) *to squirt milk* from the cow, cf. ܟܘܟܐ *breast*, O.S., N.S. § 18 (5).

ܡܒܠܒܠ O.S. *to babble*, (cf. O.S. ܒܠ *to confuse*). Also *to grow, blossom*, K. = ܡܒܪܒܪ (5).

ܡܒܠܒܝ *to twinkle, be beautiful*, for ܡܒܝܒܝ Arab.

ܡܒܠܡܠ *to be confused* or *untidy*, for ܡܒܠܒܠ.

ܡܒܪܒܪ (pronounced thin) *to speak idly* in K.; *to bleat*, for ܡܒܠܒܠ see (3).

ܡܓܠܓܠ O.S. *to make round*; O.S. ܓܠ *to revolve*.

ܡܓܪܓܪ = ܡܓܪܓܪ below (10), Kurd.

ܡܕܠܕܠ *to thin out* trees = ܡܕܠܠ K. § 81 (p. 247).

ܡܕܡܕܡ O.S. *to bleed*. Cf. O.S. ܕܡܐ = N.S. ܕܡܐ *blood*. Also ܡܕܕܡ U. see (15).

[1] Many of those to which intransitive meanings are here attached are also transitive or causative; and *vice versa*.

ܡܚܲܓܸܓ݂ *to turn over* as cattle, Arab.

ܡܚܲܕܡܸܕ O.S. *to make small* = ܕܲܩܸܩ N.S., O.S. (ܕܲܩ).

ܡܚܲܗܕܸܗ *to incite, mortify* (flesh). In O.S. *to remove*, from ܗܵܕ݂ *thither*, but Aph. ܗܵܕܸܗ *to mock*, from root ܗܕ݂ܕ݂.

ܡܚܲܗܕܸܕ *to crash, burst into laughter.* In O.S. Palpel *to injure, fight;* but P'al *to yelp*.

ܡܚܲܘܲܚ *to prod,* K. or *to be pale,* the latter from Arab.; cf. Chald. זְךְ *to be clean,* so Heb.

ܡܚܲܙܡܸܙ *to ring* as a hollow vessel, O.S. ܙܲܡ and ܙܲܡ; also ܡܚܲܙܘܸܙ in N.S., see (5) below.

ܡܚܲܛܘܸܛ *to sound as wine in a skin,* K., *to be shaken up,* U., *to burst into laughter.* In Chald. P'al *to bind.* Cf. O.S. ܘܚܛܒܐ *a wine skin.* Perhaps onomatopoetic.

ܡܚܲܢܕܸܕ *to bray.* Cf. O.S. ܘܲܢܕܐ *clamour.*

ܡܚܲܢܓ̰ܸܓ̰ *to search, pick out* with a knife, *pick* the teeth; O.S. ܢܒܲܫ *to dig,* § 113 e, or ܢܓ̰ *to scratch, rub.*

ܡܚܲܢܓܸܓ݂ O.S. *to wash away* as a flood, from ܡܓܲܠܓܸܠ *to wash,* as O.S.

ܡܚܲܡܣܸܣ K. *to snuff about* as a dog (no second Mim), O.S. ܡܵܣ *to smell.*

ܡܚܲܢܕܸܒ݂ O.S. *to have fever;* or in K. *to get warm,* from ܢܒ݂ܲܙ (O.S. ܢܒ݂ܲܙ) *to be hot.*

ܡܚܲܢܟܸܟ݂ *to feel faint,* Arab.

ܡܚܲܢܣܸܣ *to rustle, rattle,* Arab.

ܡܚܲܢܟܸܣ *to crush.* O.S. ܢܟܲܣ *to disturb,* with passive ܐܬܢܟܸܣ or perh. from ܢܟ݂ܘܿܣ K. *to crush,* as O.S.?

ܡܓܲܠܓܸܠ *to adorn oneself*, perh. O.S. ܓܲܠܸܠ *to cover*, see below (4).

ܡܦܲܩܦܸܩ *to flicker* (as O.S.), *wink*, *flutter* K., *clap* K.

ܡܦܲܘܦܸܘ or ܡܦܲܘܦܸܘ *to sputter* (the former in K. *to whine*), cf. ܡܦܲܘܦܸܘ K. or ܡܦܲܦܸܘ *to sputter*.

ܡܦܲܣܦܸܣ *to shiver in pieces*, *crash*, for ܡܦܲܣܸܣ § 113 *e*.

ܡܦܲܚܡܸܡ *to blacken*, *char*, *smoke* (for preserving), *parboil*; also passive of these, N.S. ܦܵܚܸܡ *to be black*; see also below (15) and § 92.

ܡܟܲܦܟܸܦ *to clap*, *to beat water with the hand* as children at play, *to roll in a ball*, as ants, perh. for ܡܟܲܦܟܸܦ, O.S. ܟܦ *to be curved*, O.S. ܟܲܦܵܐ *palm of the hand*.

ܡܟܲܪܟܸܪ *to deafen*; N.S. ܟܲܪܵܐ *deaf*, Arab. See also below (15).

ܡܟܲܬ݂ܟܸܬ݂ *to sob*, U. or *be dry*, *crack* as a dry kettle.

ܡܠܲܠܠܸܠ *to glisten*, from N.S. ܠܘܿܠܵܐ *splendour*, Kurd. *rozh* ?

ܡܲܠܗܠܸܗ U. *to pant* (sound ܗ), cf. O.S. ܠܗܵܬ݂ܵܐ *panting*; Heb. and Chald. root, *to be tired*, O.S. ܐܸܬ݂ܠܲܗܠܲܗ *to wonder*.

ܡܲܠܘܸܠ U. *to annoy*, *disturb*; O.S. ܢܟܐ *to injure*.

ܡܠܲܚܠܸܚ *to snuff about* as dogs, perh. = ܡܠܲܗܠܸܗ.

ܡܠܲܟ݂ܠܸܟ݂ *to prod*, from Arab. لك *to beat*.

ܡܠܲܡܠܸܡ O.S. *to mumble* = ܡܢܲܡܢܸܡ K. (16); root ܡܠܠ.

ܡܠܲܩܠܸܩ *to make loose*, *rumble*, Arab.; or *to glitter* = ܡܒܲܩܒܸܩ see (5).

ܡܠܲܬ݂ܠܸܬ݂ *to tread down*, Arab. So ܠܵܬ݂ K.

ܡܢܲܘܢܸܘ *to sob*, *whine* as a child, root ܢܘ; cf. N.S. ܢܘܿܪܕܵܐ *a spoilt child*, Pers.

§ 83 A]   DERIVATION OF QUADRILITERAL VERBS.   255

ܡܢܒܝܣ K. *to pant*, Arab.

ܡܢܒܚܝ *to groan* = O.S. ܢܶܓ݁ܙܰܬ݂?

ܡܢܓܕܓ *to tear, worry* as an animal = ܢܓܕ K., O.S.

ܡܢܡܝܕ *to be damp*, Pers. نم, cf. ܡܨܰܢ N.S. *damp*.

ܡܢܬܬܝܣ *to stammer, sob, hesitate*, from Arab. root *to croak*.

ܡܚܦܣܝ K. *to be loosed*, O.S. ܢܶܦܢܰܣ *to be weak*, or *languid*, see (3).

ܡܚܕܘܠ *to beseech*, for ܡܚܠܘܝ = Heb. הִתְפַּלֵל.

ܡܚܦܟܓ *to dissolve, mortify* (as flesh), O.S. ܢܶܩܦܰܓ, see also (15).

ܡܚܦܘܓ *to tear, pull* (wool); cf. O.S. فجوج *to make small*; see (15).

ܡܚܝܚܝ *to be hushed*, Arab. مصمص; no Mim prefixed.

ܡܚܝܕܝܕ *to chirp*, cf. O.S. and N.S. ܨܝܓܐ *a cricket*.

ܡܚܓܕܓ *to cut into logs*, O.S. ܓܕ, cf. N.S. ܓܶܕ *a log*.

ܡܚܦܠܦܠ *to lighten*, U., *hasten*, Al., *get less*, K., *fight*, K.; O.S. ܦܠ.

ܡܚܦܟܦܟ *to cluck*, O.S. ܦܟܦܟ. Cf. N.S. ܦܟ f. *clucking hen*.

ܡܚܝܚܝ or ܡܚܡܚܡܚ *to break in pieces*, N.S. ܨܚ *to break, cut*, cf. Chald. and Heb. קרץ, and Heb. קוֹסֵם *to cut*.

ܡܕܠܕܠ *to tremble, shiver*, also in K. ܡܕܣܕܣ = ܕܰܠܓ N.S. (Arab.).

ܡܕܠܕܠ K., or ܡܚܣܕܣ *to desire*, O.S. ܕܠ.

ܡܕܠܕܠ *to crawl*, O.S. ܕܒܟ.

ܡܕܚܕܘ K. (hard final Kap) *to boil food*, O.S. ܕܚܝ *to soften*, p. 247.

ܡܕܚܡܕ *to growl, purr*: in K. *to be angry* (in O.S. *make angry*); no second Mim.

ܡܪܲܡܪܸܣ *to be* or *make stiff*, as mud = Arab. رس.

ܡܪܲܦܪܸܦ *to flap the wings, brood, beat hard* as the heart, *pity, dangle*, O.S. ܪܦ.

ܡܪܲܥܪܸܥ *to shiver* intr. K., *bruise; have an abscess*, K.; O.S. ܪܥ.

ܡܪܲܩܪܸܩ *to hammer out* (O.S. Pa. *to make thin*), also in K. *to shiver*, p. 245 and above.

ܡܪܲܬܪܸܬ *to tremble, shiver*, O.S. ܪܬ.

ܡܚܲܫܚܸܫ K. *to feel faint*, O.S. ܚܫ. Also in N.S. *to crush*, = O.S. ܚܫܫ.

ܡܚܲܟܚܸܟ *to shake*, U., as Arab. Also in K. *to weave loosely;* ܡܚܲܟܠܸܟ *to sew loosely*, is perhaps the same word (both hard final Kap).

ܡܲܫܡܸܫ *to grope*. No Mim prefixed. Chald. מַשְׁמֵשׁ.

ܡܫܲܡܫܸܡ *to feel faint; to throw down*, K. Heb. Qal, and Chald. Ethp'el *to be* or *make desolate*.

ܡܫܲܠܫܸܠ *to dangle, drawl, be languid* = Chald. שַׁלְשֵׁל *to let down*.

ܡܫܲܦܫܸܦ *to glide*, O.S. ܫܦ. So ܫܲܦܫܲܦ N.S. *glidingly*.

ܡܫܲܩܫܸܩ *to clatter, rattle*, O.S. ܫܩ *to break*.

ܡܬܲܢܬܸܢ *to smoke, cense*, O.S. ܬܢ.

See also the onomatopoetic verbs below (15) which are of the same form.

(3) A few correspond to O.S. ܥܘ verbs, as:

ܡܕܲܫܕܸܫ *to tread down*, O.S. ܕܫ, but Chald. also דִּישׁ.

ܡܦܲܚܦܸܚ *to breathe hard*, O.S. ܦܚ *to blow*, see also (2).

ܡܫܲܪܫܸܪ *to fall* or *spout* as water, perhaps O.S. ܫܘܪ *to leap*. Cf. N.S. ܫܲܪܫܘܪܐ *a waterfall*, ܫܲܪܫܲܪ *noise of falling water*.

The verbs (all pronounced broad) ܡܓ̇ܰܓ̈ܕ to *roar* as an animal, or a fire, = O.S. ܓܰܕ (see 2), ܡܰܠܰܡܠܶܡ to *chew*, in K. to *gnash the teeth*, from ܠܰܡ to *chew*, N.S., O.S., and ܡܓ̇ܰܓ̈ܕ to *low* as buffaloes or camels, from O.S. ܓܰܕ *id.*, are similar.

(4) Some of these reduplicated verbs correspond to verbs ܠ or ܠܠ. Those which have ܠ are pronounced very broad: thus ܡܓ̇ܡܓ̇ܡܕ and ܡܓ̇ܡܓ̇ܪ are quite distinct in sound.

a. ܡܰܟܬܰܟܬ to *foam* = ܟܬܶܡ N.S. *id.*, cf. N.S. ܟܬܡ f. *foam*.

ܡܰܪܘܰܪܘ to *please* = ܪܳܘܝ N.S., O.S.

ܡܰܫܠܫܶܠ U. to *spoil* a child, perhaps connected with ܫܰܒܪܐ *a boy* (see 2) [or from ܡܰܫܒܪ § 47].

ܡܰܢܘܳܢܘ to *sob, whine*, נוה Chald. to *chide, low* (oxen), *bleat*.

ܡܰܨܠܨܶܠ K. to *hang*, perh. for ܡܰܚܠܚܶܠ = O.S. ܗܠܟ. Another form is ܡܰܕܢܕܶܠ = O.S. ܚܕܢܕܠ *id.*

b. ܡܰܚܘܚܶܕ to *make a hole* = ܚܘܕ, N.S., O.S.

ܡܰܕ̇ܡܕ̇ܡܕ to *weep*, = O.S. ܕܡܕ, = ܡܰܕܡܶܕ K.

ܡܰܢܒܘܠ to *tear* clothes (also in K. to *weep*), perh. for ܡܢܒܠ, from ܘܠܕ to *split* (Arab.). Also ܡܰܘܢܬܶܕ.

ܡܰܠܒܠܒܶܕ K. to *lap* = N.S. ܠܒܶܕ Arab.

ܡܰܦܨܦܨܶܕ to *crack*, = ܦܨܕ, N.S., O.S.

ܡܳܨܗܶܨܗܶܕ or ܡܰܚܓ̇ܓܳܐ or ܡܰܓ̇ܓ̇ܓܳܐ to *cut up*, ܨܗܶܕ, N.S., O.S.

ܡܰܕܩܕܶܩ to *knock* = Chald. תְּקַפ.

(5) Many quadriliterals are formed by repeating one or more letters of the root; as—ܡܓܠܕܓ *to grow*, see also (2), and ܡܓܕܓ݂ *id.* (the latter also *to hang* in K.), = דְגַ Al., O.S.

ܡܓܠܕܓ *to dig*, דְגַל *to wear out*, N.S., O.S.

ܡܓܕܓܘ *to scatter* = Chald. בּוּר by metath. Cf. ܡܓܕܓܘܣ below.

ܡܓܠܓܘ *to abhor*, also ܡܓܠܘܓܘ = ܡܓܠܓܝ K. (which in Arab. is *to deride*) = O.S. ܠܓܝ.

ܡܓܠܓܕܣ *to grind coarse*, K. = ܓܕܓܣ N.S., as O.S. Pa. In U. *to grow*, from ܓܕܘܣܐ *large*, § 77 (2).

ܡܓܠܓܕ *to drag*, ܓܕܓ *to draw*, N.S., O.S.

ܡܓܕܓܠ *to scatter, squander* = Chald. הרק.

ܡܓܕܓܣ *to pine away*, O.S. ܕܓܣ *to rub, wear*.

ܡܘܚܠܚܕ, also ܚܝ *to stare* = וְחַל N.S. *id.*

ܡܘܚܕܘܚܕ U. *to fill* = N.S. וְחַדּ.

ܡܘܚܠܚܣ *to dazzle*, Chald. זְלַק *to shine*, as O.S. Aph. In N.S. וְחܠܣ = *to stare*.

ܡܚܘܕܘܙ *to be moved* by news, *to start* with fear, O.S. ܐܗܕܘܙ.

ܡܚܘܕܘܣ *to break out* as sores or leaves, O.S. וְחܕܣ *to burst forth* as the sun (Castell). In Heb. also of leprosy, Qal.

ܡܚܘܕܘܚܕ or ܡܚܘܕܘܚ *to scratch* = N.S. ܘܚܕ or ܘܚܕ, O.S. ܘܚܕ.

ܡܚܘܕܘܙ *to fall from a height*, as water, root ܘܚܕ; in Heb. זרם *to inundate*. See also (2).

ܡܚܢܠܚܓ *to undermine* by water, O.S. ܠܚܓ *to burrow*, cf. ܡܚܢܠܟܓ (6).

ܡܚܢܕܢܚܕ *to gnaw*, from ܢܚܕ *to scrape*, as O.S., p. 234.

ܡܒܢܕܒܢ *to gnash* the teeth, O.S. ܒܢܕ.

ܡܚܕܝܕ *to delay*, O.S. ܐܗܢܕܕ *to hesitate*.

ܡܚܕܘܚܕ *to move*, from ܚܕܕ *to beat up* (eggs), *to strike*, as O.S. Also in K. *to wink* = ܡܚܕܩܕ. See (2).

ܡܚܢܕܚ *to knock about, shake*, hence *to bestir oneself*; root ܢܕܚ, as Chald. Hiph.

ܡܚܢܓܚ *to drag*, ܚܢܓ *to sweep, collect*, N.S., O.S.

ܡܚܦܢܦ U. *to swell* = O.S. ܐܗܢܦܦ, (ܢܦܚ *to blow*, N.S., O.S.; in K. metaph. *to tell a lie*).

ܡܚܦܢܚ *to crumble*, for ܡܚܦܕܚ, = O.S. ܚܕܚ and ܦܕܚ; see p. 269.

ܡܚܦܢܕ or ܡܚܦܢܕ *to stagger*, ܢܦܕ *to fall*, N.S., O.S.

ܡܚܦܕܚ *to wear out, tear* tr. = N.S. ܦܕܚ, O.S. ܐܗܦܕܚ *to be torn*.

ܡܚܦܕܣ *to scatter, take to pieces*, = ܦܕܣ N.S., O.S. (but cf. O.S. ܦܡܕܣ *to scatter*). In K. ܡܚܦܕܚ perhaps from ܦܕܚ N.S., O.S. *to separate*.

ܡܚܢܝܣ *to have spasms*, perhaps ܢܝܣ *to chop*, K., O.S.

ܡܚܢܝܣܐ *to examine*, perh. ܢܘܣ *to see*, N.S., O.S.

ܡܚܢܝܕ *to flow*, O.S. ܢܝܕ *to ooze*, § 45 g.

ܡܚܢܝܩ *to smart*, O.S. ܢܝܩ *to beat*, whence also ܡܚܢܦܩ or ܡܚܢܕܩ *to sob, beseech*, perh. from *beating the breast*.

ܡܚܦܕܒ *to shake, mix up*, K. (in U. *to pick raisins, to crack walnuts*), from Arab. قرش *to collect*. Hence also perhaps ܡܚܦܕܒܘ *to pack, gather up, economise*, in K. *to peel walnuts*.

ܡܚܣܒܢ *to become weak*, in K. *to fear*, = O.S. ܚܣܐ.

ܡܓܡܨܡ *to burn, be scalded, fine heavily,* = ܓܡܨ N.S., O.S.

ܡܓܡܨܬ K. *to eat the inside* (of an egg, etc.). So N.S. ܓܡܨ.

ܡܓܕܓܪ *to be languid, droop,* ܓܕܓ *to loose,* N.S., O.S.

ܡܓܕܓܕ *id.* = N.S. ܓܕܓ. Both also mean *to look downwards:* the latter also *to slip out of place;* and in K. *to fall from the hand,* and *to put out the eyes* (origin ?).

ܡܓܡܛܬ K. *to make neatly,* O.S. ܓܡܛ.

(6) Many are formed by the addition of an extraneous letter: as ܠ, e.g. ܡܓܙܠܓ K. or ܡܓܙܠܓ U. *to be numbed* with cold or pain, perh. from O.S. ܓܠܙ *to feel,* cf. N.S. ܓܠܙ *to be numb,* for ܓܠܙ, § 100.

ܡܓܕܘܩ *to fall over, die,* as a dying bird, perh. for ܡܓܕܘܩ, from ܓܦܠ *to fall,* [or for ܡܓܕܘܩ ? cf. N.S. ܓܘܕܩܬ f. *thick darkness,* O.S. ܐܓܕܘܩ *to become dark*].

ܡܓܠܓܪ *to remove ruins, clear out,* root ܓܠܓ (Chald. אתגלגל *to be stripped off*).

ܡܓܙܡ *to starve* = ܓܙܡ N.S.

ܡܓܘܙܓ *to be late,* N.S. ܓܘܙܓ *late,* Persian (quinqueliteral).

ܡܓܢܠܓ *to dig* as a mole = O.S. ܓܠܓ. Cf. ܡܓܢܠܝܓ (5) and ܓܠܓ N.S. m. *a mole.*

ܡܓܢܕܓ *to surround,* by metath. from ܓܕܘܙ N.S. *to go round,* as O.S.

ܡܓܠܓܪ (rare) *to carry* = N.S. ܓܠܓ?, § 46.

ܡܓܢܘܐ *to beseech* (in K. also *to mew*). Same root as N.S. ܓܢܘܝ *mediator,* Kurd. ?

ܡܓܕܪ (no Mim prefixed) *to prosper, tr. to thank,* N.S. ܓܕܪ f. *thanks,* Arab. منت *benefit.*

ܡܚܰܓ݂ܕܶܡ *to cut to pieces, crumble* = Arab. فرز, cf. N.S. ܦܳܕ݂ܽܘܿ Al. *a crumb*.

ܡܚܰܓ݂ܕܶܡ *to understand*, from ܦܳܕ݂ܶܡ N.S., O.S. *to cut*, cf. ܚܶܣܽܘܣܶܗ ܟܠ ܦܳܕ݂ܶܡ, § 75, p. 200.

ܡܚܰܝܡܺܝ *to howl, yelp, whine*, and metaph. *to beseech*, O.S. Pa. ܝܳܡܺܝ *to chatter* as birds, Chald. *to cry*.

ܡܚܰܩܡܶܩ *to howl*, in K. *to coo*; cf. Chald. קוּק *pelican*, קוּקִי *croaking*.

ܡܚܰܓ݂ܠܶܓ݂ Ti. or ܡܚܰܓ݂ܠܺܓ݂ܘ *to roll over*, cf. ܓ݂ܠܳܬ݂ *to turn, turn aside*?

ܡܚܰܓ݂ܒܶܓ݂ or ܡܚܰܓ݂ܠܶܓ݂ K. *to bring ewes to be milked*, O.S. ܥܳܓ݂ܶܕ *to call*? or cf. O.S. ܓ݂ܰܒ݂ܓ݂ܳܐ *a shepherd's crook, a rod*.

ܡܚܰܓ݂ܠܶܓ݂ U. *to run mad* (also *to starve*), perh. Chald. שָׁלַט *to make an onslaught* (or O.S. ܓ݂ܰܒ݂ *to be foolish*).

(7) ܒ, as ܡܚܰܓ݂ܠܶܒ݂ *to drink too much*, or in U. *to drink quickly*, perh. O.S. ܓ݂ܰܠܒ݂ *to purge*.

ܡܚܰܓ݂ܠܺܓ݂ܡ *to chew* = ܓ݂ܺܝܡ N.S., O.S.

ܡܚܰܓ݂ܡܶܓ݂ K. *to nail*, § 110 c, Chald. סָמַר.

ܡܚܰܘܒܺܓ݂ U. *to tear* (clothes) = ܡܚܰܘܒܳܒ݂ above (4).

(7ᵃ) ܓ݂, as ܡܚܰܒ݂ܘܳܓ݂ *to injure*, perhaps from O.S. ܒܶܗܶܓ݂ (pron. ܒܺܝܘܓ݂) *shame, injury*?

(7ᵇ) ܗ, as ܡܚܰܕ݂ܳܗܓ݂ K. *to feel slightly ill*, O.S. ܕ݂ܳܓ݂ *to feel*?

(8) ܘ, as ܡܚܰܓ݂ܕܽܘܓ݂ K. *to glean*, = ܡܚܰܓ݂ܓ݂ܶܕ N.S. as O.S. P'al, Pa.

ܡܚܰܓ݂ܠܽܘܓ݂ *to hiccough, eructate*, O.S. ܓ݂ܰܐܒ݂ *to be in pain*, Aph. *to vomit*.

ܡܚܰܓ݂ܕ݂ܽܘ Q. *to roll dough* = ܓ݂ܳܕ݂ܶܕ݂ U., cf. N.S. ܓ݂ܽܘܕ݂ܽܕܳܐ m. *a roller*.

ܡܚܘܕܘܕ (pron. ܘ = ܗ) *to make small*, see ܘܕܘܕ § 46; cf. § 110.

ܡܚܟܕܡ U., § 47, *to seek* = ܟܚܕ, § 46.

ܡܚܟܣܣ Al. *to whisper* = ܡܚܒܣ K., perh. ܟܣܐ *to hide*, N.S., O.S. Cf. ܚܘܡܣܢܐ N.S. *suspicion*.

ܡܚܦܕܡ U. *to gape* = ܦܚܕ N.S., as O.S. P'al.

ܡܚܨܕܘܕ U., § 47, *to revile* = ܡܚܨܕ N.S., as O.S. Pa.

(8ᵃ) ܣ, as ܡܚܣܡܓܕ K. Al. as O.S. *to be patient*, cf. O.S. ܡܓܕ *to expect*.

(9) ܠ, as ܡܚܕܢܠܡ *to sew coarsely*, perh. O.S. ܕܢܡ *to join*. ܡܚܕܓܠ K. *to intertwine*, from N.S. ܚܓܕ U. *to tie a knot* (by metathesis) = O.S. ܣܓܕ = ܓܚܕ K. Same as ܡܚܓܠܝ, see (10).

ܡܚܠܒܠܒ = ܠܒܠܒ (10) *to be lame*.

ܡܚܦܠܡ *to grope*, from N.S. ܦܚܐ Al., which also appears in ܡܚܐܦܡ, see (14).

ܡܚܦܡܠ = N.S. ܦܚܡ *to step*, as O.S.

ܡܚܓܕܓܠ *to tangle*, see ܡܚܓܕܓܠ above.

ܡܚܠܬܠ *to beat* = O.S. ܒܚܠ. Also ܡܚܓܕܢܠ in N.S., see (12).

ܡܚܓܠܡ, see above (6).

ܡܚܣܣܓܠ Al., see ܡܚܣܣܡ (10).

ܡܚܠܓܡܣ U. *to have a sore eye* = N.S. ܡܣܡܚ K. or ܓܡܣ K.

To these we may add from the first conjugation: ܝܗܒܠ *to give* = O.S. ܝܗܒ; and ܢܓܠ for ܢܓܠ *to snatch* = O.S. ܓܕܫ; and perhaps ܘܕܒܠ, § 46.

(9ª) ܒ. ܡܓܙܕܝܒ *to wallow* = N.S. ܡܓܙܕܙ (cf. ܒܠܒ O.S.) § 114, and above (2).

ܡܓܙܕܡܝ *to roll up* = ܓܙܕ N.S., O.S.

(10) ܡ. These are very numerous, especially in Urmi.

ܡܓܙܗܙ U. = ܓܙܗ K. Al. *to shine*, O.S.

ܡܓܗܕܙ *to fatten*, cf. ܓܗܕ *well fed*, N.S. Arab.

ܡܓܗܡܝ *to print*, cf. N.S. ܓܗܡܬ f. *a printing press*; also ܛܒ. ܓܗܡܬ p. 205.

ܡܓܙܕܝ *to bud*, cf. N.S. ܓܙܕܐ *a flower*.

ܡܠܝܛܝ K. (= ܡܠܛܝ U.) *to be dizzy* = ܡܠܝܛܝ (2).

ܡܠܝܢܝܣ = N.S. ܠܝܢܣ (ܒ) *to fall in* as a roof, Kurd.

ܡܠܝܒܝ *to rust*, cf. N.S. ܠܝܒ U. or ܠܒ K. m. *rust*, Kurd.

ܡܠܙܕܝ = O.S. ܠܙܕ *to have leprosy*.

ܡܠܙܕܝ K. *to be discoloured*, from ܠܙܕ N.S. *to be dirty*?

ܡܠܥܡܝ *to solidify* = ܒܝ ܠܥܡ O.S.

ܡܙܒܗ *to be mad*, cf. O.S. and N.S. ܙܒܗ m. *a devil*.

ܡܙܠܕ *to protect*, cf. N.S. ܙܠܕ f. *a protection, shield*, § 82 (7).

ܡܙܡܝ *to weep* = ܡܙܡܝܕ K., as O.S. P'al, Pa., see (4) b.

ܡܙܕܢܝ *to wound*, cf. N.S. ܙܕܬ f. *a wound*, U. (Arab.).

ܡܙܕܢܝܒ *to be late*, see (6) above.

ܡܘܬܒܝ U. *to subdue*, cf. N.S. ܘܬܒ *subject*.

ܡܘܬܒܝ *to litter*, also *to dung a garden* (ܘ = ܗ Tkh.) = K. ܡܘܬܒܝ as O.S. Pa.

مْحَوْسَمِي U. = مْحَوْسَم K. *to put milk* or *butter in food* during a fast, §§ 39, 108 c (O.S. وَسَم *to defile*, as Chald.).

مْحَوْسِجِي U. *to make brave* (rare). Cf. N.S. بِسَم *to be bold*, K. Al., and وَسَخْد *bold*, or in Al. = *difficult*.

مْحَوْدْزْ *to cast the evil eye*, and in K. *to wonder*, perh. O.S. وَزْد *to watch carefully*.

مْحَوْبْدِجِي U. (و = س) *to lessen*. See مْحَوْحِمْز (8).

مْحَوْفِز K. *to put meat in food* during a fast, cf. O.S. وِفْد *to be foul, to smell bad as meat*.

مْحَوْدْجِي *to be strong*, from N.S. وَدْج m. *strength* (Turk.).

مْحَوْدْجِي *to be yellow, have jaundice*, from N.S. وَدْد *yellow*.

مْحَنْجِلِي U. *to be cold* = مْحَنْجِل N.S. U. But in Al. = *to spoil* tr., as O.S.

مْحَنْبْجِي U. *to become dark* = نْجِب N.S. (Chald. *to be hid*), by metathesis. Cf. O.S. and N.S. سْوِجْنِا m. *darkness*.

مْحَنْبْدْجِي *to bewitch* = مْحَنْبْدْز N.S., as O.S. Pa.

مْحَنْبْعِتِي *to reckon* = نْجِب as O.S. For the ث cf. سْوْمْحْتْنا O.S. *account*.

مْحَجْدِي *to be dirty* as the eyes = مْحَنْبْك K. as O.S. P'al.

مْحَجْدِي *to be leafy*, cf. O.S. and N.S. جْدْفا m. *a leaf*.

مْحَنْبْج U. *to be* or *make heavy* = نْجِد K. Al. as O.S.

مْحَجْجْد U. *to veil*, cf. N.S. جِجْد m. *a Mussulman woman's overall*, also *a tent*, Turk.

مْحَجْنْكِي *to jingle, clank*, cf. N.S. جِنْك m. *a cymbal*.

مْحَجْفِلِي *to defile*, cf. N.S. جْفْد *unclean*, Turk.

§ 83 A] DERIVATION OF QUADRILITERAL VERBS. 265

مجَدِّر or مجَدِّر *to make a hedge*, cf. N.S. جَفْد *a hedge*, Kurd. also *to be leafy, to be crowded*, for مجَدِّر.

مجَدِّم *to pity*, cf. N.S. خَدِر *pitiful*.

مجَدِّل *to tangle*, N.S. خَدِ *to tie*, see مجَدِّهل above (9).

مجَلَّع *to be lame*, Pers., cf. لِنْك Tkh. *lame, maimed*.

مُوجِدِر *to be a stranger* = O.S. جُدَر. Cf. O.S. and N.S. مُوجَدَّر *a stranger*.

مُحَمِّدَ U. *to saddle* = مِحْمَد N.S. Cf. O.S. and N.S. هُدَكَ *a saddle*.

مجَبِّج *to cloud over*, cf. O.S. and N.S. جُبَج *a cloud*.

مُحَمِّل U. *to be* or *make wise*, cf. N.S. نِهِل K. = ذِملُدَّر U. *wise*, Pers.

مجَدِّم *to be old* = نجوس K. as O.S.

محَفِجِج *to go bad* as gum, perh. O.S. فَجِ *to be doubtful, tepid*.

مَفْدِي U. = محَفِّد K. *to make a floor*, N.S. فَدَ *a floor*, Arab.

مَفْعِم U. *to grieve*, tr., فَعِ N.S. *to be sorry*, Turk.

مَنِيسو *to clear up*, from N.S. عِسفه *fine weather*, Arab.

مَنِيلس K. *to chop* = نَلَس K., as O.S.

مَحْفَجَد *to be hunchbacked*, and in U. *to arch*, = N.S. نَجَد *to arch*, (cf. N.S. عِجَدَه *an arch*, مُوجَدَّه *hunchbacked*, p. 58), O.S. مُجَد *to tie in a knot*.

محَصِجَد *to tie* K. = N.S. نَجَد K., = O.S. مَجَد as above. In U. *to bend, stretch oneself, to push back*, perhaps O.S. مَجَد *to delay*.

محَنِدِي U. *to approach* = نَدِ N.S. as O.S., cf. موذَن *near*.

S. GR.

ܡܚܲܡܕ݂ܝ݂ to sting (nettles), shrink back, perh. N.S. ܚܡܝ to be angry.

ܡܚܲܡܕܸܪ to make bold (no Mim prefixed), cf. N.S. ܚܲܡܕ݂ܵܐ bold, Pers.

ܡܚܲܡܒܸܟ U. to colour, tr., cf. N.S. ܨܸܒܓܵܐ colour, Turk.

ܡܚܲܡܓܸܠ U. to entice = ܓܲܢܕܸܠ N.S. as O.S. Pa.

ܡܚܲܡܣܸܕ݂ to blacken = O.S. ܚܲܫܸܟ.

ܡܚܲܡܣܸܝ to make dirty, blight, also in U. metaph. to reject food, cf. N.S. ܚܣܵܐ blight, ܚܸܣܝܵܐ dirty, O.S. ܚܲܣܝܼܒ to rust, rare in P'al.

ܡܚܲܡܣܸܕ݂ K. to madden, cf. O.S. and N.S. ܫܹܐܕ݂ܵܐ a devil. In U. ܡܫܲܐܕ݂.

ܡܚܲܡܬܸܢ to blacken with smoke = ܡܚܲܢܬܸܢ K., cf. O.S. ܬܸܢܵܢܵܐ smoke.

ܡܚܲܡܟܸܦ to be beautiful, cf. O.S. and N.S. ܫܲܦܝܼܪܵܐ beautiful.

ܡܚܲܡܣܸܡ (ܐܲܠ.) to consider, O.S. ܚܫܲܒ to define.

ܡܚܲܡܕܸܢ U. to smear with fat, O.S. and N.S. ܚܘܼܕܢܵܐ fat.

ܡܚܲܡܕܸܒ to be pale or lean from illness = Chald. חָשׁ.

(11) ܣ. A few verbs forming what may be called the Saph'el conjugation.

ܡܣܲܡܒܸܕ݂ U. to visit, O.S. ܣܲܓܸܕ݂ to associate with.

ܡܣܲܡܕܸܡܝ to wander about, search for food, scent, Arab. مسك to wander.

ܡܣܲܡܕܸܠܸܓ to shiver, totter = ܓܵܠܸܓ N.S. from Arab. Also to make a kalendar, K., from O.S. and N.S. ܣܵܡܘܼܕܠܵܐ a kalendar.

ܡܣܲܡܗܸܒ Al. to hasten, as O.S.

ܡܣܲܡܕܸܟ to conjugate, decline (nouns), as O.S., lit. to branch out.

[§ 83 A]   DERIVATION OF QUADRILITERAL VERBS.

(12) ܕ.—ܡܓܕܝܕ *to stir* = N.S. ܓܝܕ K., cf. ܬܣܦܩܬ *a spoon* O.S. and N.S.

ܡܓܕܡܕ *to take in the hand, crunch* = ܟܡܕ N.S. (Chald. *to bend, curve*).

ܡܓܕܘܕ *to rock*, O.S. Pa'el דּוּד *to shake*.

ܡܙܘܕܓ U. for ܡܒܕܓܐ below.

ܡܙܘܕܘܟ K. *to throw down* = Chald. הֲדַף as Heb. Qal.

ܡܙܘܕܓܠ *to joke, play boisterously, beat up eggs*: root הדם, in Arab. *to break*.

ܡܕܢܟܕ, also ܡܕܘܢܕ K. and ܡܓܢܟܕ K. *to ring, clink, tick*, cf. O.S. וܢܓܠ *ringing*, ܦܢܓܠ *bell*.

ܡܕܘܡܝܕ K. *to swell*, perh. from N.S. ܘܡܝܕ *to fill full*.

ܡܒܕܓܐ *to clasp, button* = N.S. ܫܒܓܐ (in which pron. ܓ as ق) *to hug*, Chald. חֲבַק as Heb., cf. O.S. ܣܚܦܐ *a hug*.

ܡܒܕܓܝ U. *to search*, see ܡܒܕܘܟ below; also *to mix up* (cf. N.S. ܫܓܝ *to enclose, include*, as O.S.).

ܡܒܕܘܟ *to push*, or by metathesis ܡܒܕܓܗ, cf. N.S. ܫܘܟ *to be overturned* as a house, perh. O.S. ܗܒܟ *to invert*.

ܡܒܕܡܝܕ U. *to hug* = ܡܓܕܡܝܕ nearly. See also (16).

ܡܒܕܓܝ K. *to search carelessly* (in U. ܓܝ). [Qy. Heb. חָפַשׂ *to search*, ש = ܓ? In Chald. *to dig*.] Also ܡܓܕܓܘ K.

ܡܓܕܢܝܣ *to knock down, die, fall suddenly*, O.S. ܚܓܣ *to kill, wound, bruise*.

ܡܓܢܠܕ = ܡܓܢܠܟ (10). See also (16).

ܡܓܕܡܝܕ *to wither* = N.S. ܕܡܝܓ = ܕܡܝ O.S.

ܡܓܕܘܦ *to gather up, carry off* (as floods). So ܡܚܕܘܦ (which is also *to hem*). [In K. ܚܕܘܦ, first conj., is used of stray cattle, *to return of their own accord.*] Qy. Heb. הִכְפִּישׁ *to overthrow, immerse,* or O.S. ܚܕܦ (so N.S. ܚܕܦ) *to thrust in, compress?* In K. ܡܓܕܘܦ, ܡܩܕܦ § 119.

ܡܓܕܘܕ K. *to crack* = N.S. ܩܕܕ as O.S.

ܡܓܕܓܠ *to twist, wind* = N.S. ܩܕܠ as O.S. Pa.

ܡܓܕܓܘ K., see ܡܦܠܓܘ above (9).

ܡܓܕܘܣ K. *to make a clatter,* O.S. ܡܓܢܣ *noise of flint and steel struck together.* Also in K. *to be old,* (perhaps O.S. ܡܓܣ *to make bald*); in U. *to be an orphan,* and *to trample.*

ܡܓܕܠܓ *to roll up,* perhaps O.S. ܡܓܠ *to go round.*

ܡܓܕܘܣ *to smash, crumple,* cf. N.S. ܩܡܣ *to crush,* O.S. and N.S. ܩܡܚܐ *flour.*

ܡܓܕܡܓܕ *to have colic (to have an internal strain),* and ܡܓܕܡܓܕ or ܡܓܕܓܕ or ܡܓܕܘܓܕ *to wrinkle, crumple,* O.S. ܡܓܕ *to be wrinkled or strained.* So N.S., O.S. ܩܡܕ *to squeeze, twist, strain* (O.S. Ethp'el *to be wrinkled*), ܩܡܕ *to pinch.*

ܡܓܕܘ *to crouch.* So N.S. ܩܦܘ or ܟܦܘ or ܢܦܘ § 120.

ܡܓܕܘܦ Tkh. *to gather up, gather (a dress),* O.S. ܓܗܡܦ *to be gathered.*

ܡܓܕܘܣ *to buffet,* O.S. ܩܦܣ.

ܡܓܕܙܕ *to beat,* O.S. ܓܙܕ. Also ܡܓܠܬܙܕ in N.S., see (9).

ܡܓܕܢܛ or ܡܓܕܢܛ *to crack,* perhaps O.S. ܓܢܛ *to break.*

ܡܓܕܦܟ K. or ܡܓܕܘܦ U. *to break,* O.S. ܚܦܟ.

ܡܬܦܪܨ U. *to be crowded;* cf. N.S. ܬܦܝܨ *crowded*, adj.

ܡ.ܬܪܒܨ *to trim* a candle; perhaps O.S. ܬܒܨ *to repress.*

ܡܬܪܩܠ *to stumble*, O.S. ܐܬܬܩܠ.

(13) ܫ. The old Shaph'el conjugation.

ܡܫܒܗܪ Ti. or ܡܫܬܒܗܪ Ti. or ܡܫܬܒܗܪ U. *to be proud*, from Shaph'el and Eshtaph'al; root ܒܗܪ, O.S. ܫܒܗܪ and ܐܫܬܒܗܪ.

ܡܫܚܠܦ O.S. *to change;* root ܚܠܦ. Also by metathesis ܡܫܚܪ.

ܡܫܥܒܕ *to oppress, strike;* O.S. ܫܥܒܕ *to subdue*, root ܥܒܕ.

ܡܫܛܪܚ *to sprawl*, root ܛܪܚ (Chald. טְרַח *to be tired;* Arab. *to prostrate*).

ܡܫܬܡܠܐ Al. *to be fulfilled.* So O.S.; root ܡܠܐ.

We may perhaps add ܡܫܪܒܟ K. *to plane*, from N.S. ܪܒܟܐ *a plane*, § 75, p. 207.

(14) ܬ. ܬܠܗܬ or ܬܠܗܪ *to pant*, see ܡܠܗܠܗ above (2).

ܡܬܦܪܟ *to crumble*, so Az. O.S. ܦܪܟ *to rub*, N.S. ܦܪܬܘܟܐ *a crumb* (also ܦܪܬܟܐ, and in Al. ܦܪܬܘܟܐ), see p. 259. In O.S. ܐܬܦܪܟ is *to doubt, to be anxious.*

Also what may be called the Taph'el conjugation.

ܡܬܓܒܪ for ܡܬܕܒܪ *to govern*, or *provide for* (esp. with food), O.S. ܕܒܪ. Cf. N.S. ܬܓܒܪܬܐ or ܬܕܒܪܬܐ f. *counsel, guidance.*

ܡܬܢܓܣ *to be unclean*, root ܢܓܣ, Arab.

ܡܬܠܡܕ O.S. *to make disciples;* in K. *to torment.* O.S. ܠܡܕ *to teach.*

ܡܓ̈ܢܕܓܕ *to shake the head*, U., *tug at*, K.; N.S. ܢܓܕ *to take by force, shake the head, fall as leaves.* So O.S. ܓܕ, ܢܓܕ.

ܡܓ̈ܢܓܫ K. *to snatch, gnaw* = ܢܓܫ, N.S., O.S.

ܡܓ̈ܕܠ *to educate, punish*, Arab.; O.S. has ܓܕܠ *to be a young man, grow up*, § 37.

ܡܓ̈ܦܓܕ Al. *to think* = N.S. ܡܦܓܕ. The N.S. ܦܓܕ K. Al. *to stop, hinder*, is O.S. ܦܓܕ *to constrain*.

ܡܓ̈ܦܘܫ *to search*, Arab., = N.S. ܦܓܫ Al. *id.* So ܡܓ̈ܦܠܓܫ, ܡܦܕܓܫ.

ܡܓ̈ܕܒܝ or ܡܓ̈ܠܒܝ U. *to pant;* perh. לָחַץ Heb. *to compress.*

ܡܓ̈ܕܚܫ K. *to be boiled to rags, be angry.* O.S. ܕܚܫ *to boil* (often metaphorically, with love, anger, etc.).

ܡܓ̈ܢܕܗܕ *to tear,* for ܡܓ̈ܢܕܗܕ, from N.S. ܢܓܕ *to snatch.*

(15) Many verbs are onomatopoetic: as—

ܡܓ̈ܒܓܒ O.S. *to bubble.*

ܡܠܠܠܠ or ܡܠܠܠܠ *to crawl.*

ܡܕܡܕܡ *to hum, moan.*

ܡܓܪܓܪ *to growl, roar, thunder,* and in K. *to coo,* see ܡܓܪܓܡ.

ܡܓܪܓܪ *to rattle, creak;* in K. *to crackle, growl.*

ܡܓܕܓܕ *to trot,* cf. N.S. ܓܕܓܕ *trotting.*

ܡܓ̈ܕܒܪ or ܡܓ̈ܕܒܪ K. *to stutter;* the latter in U. *to bleed* (2).

ܡܘܘܘ *to buzz.*

ܡܘܠܘܠ *to wail,* cf. O.S. ܘܠܘܠܬܐ *a howling.*

ܡܘܙܝ *to whiz* as an arrow, *rattle.*

ܡܣܘܣܘܣ *to squeak* as a mouse.

ܡܘܝܙܘܝܙ *to whine.*

ܡܘܛܘܛ *to whine.*

ܡܘܪܘܪ *to whirr.*

ܡܘܦܘܦ *to whip, beat,* in U. *to swell.*

ܡܢܣܢܣ *to breathe hard.* So N.S. ܢܣܢܣ *one who breathes hard.*

ܡܢܪܢܪ *to snore, gargle, purl, flow* as tears, Arab.

ܡܙܢܙܢ *to twang, buzz, hum, croon.*

ܡܟܘܟܐ *to chirp, squeak.*

ܡܟܟܟܟ *to tick, click, creak.*

ܡܟܡܟܡ *to call* as a goat to its kids. See (2) above.

ܡܟܢܟܢ *to tingle.*

ܡܟܣܟܣ K. *to squeak* as a mouse.

ܡܟܦܟܦ *to hiss, breathe hard,* rare in U.

ܡܟܦܟܦ or ܡܦܟܦܟ *to chirp.* See also (2).

ܡܟܛܟܛ *to knock stones together, crackle,* K., *chatter* (teeth) U., *flicker,* Al., *to quack, quarrel, talk idly.*

ܡܟܪܟܬ *to tickle.*

ܡܟܪܟܪ *to giggle, to purl.* See also (2).

ܡܟܪܟܪ *to chirp, cry out, creak, scream;* also *to clean cotton,* cf. N.S. ܟܪܟܪܬܐ f. *cotton cleaner.*

ܡܟܫܟܫ (so O.S. ܢܟܫ Gen. xv. 11) *to cry 'kish'* (to scare away birds or set dogs on to fight).

ܡܠܦܠܦ *to munch, mumble,* cf. N.S. ܠܦܠܦ m. *a mumbler.*

ܡܚܡܕܡܕ *to hiss, scream.*

ܡܚܩܡܩ or ܡܚܩܡܩ *to bleat, moo.*

ܡܚܦܝܦ U. or ܡܚܦܝܦ or ܡܚܘܚܘ or ܡܚܦܦ *to whisper;* cf. ܦܚܦܝ *whispering.* See also (2).

ܡܚܦܝܣ *to hiss* U., *snore* U., *whistle* K.

ܡܚܕܚܕ (pron. thin) *to spin a top, brandish, bleat;* (pron. full) *to snort.*

ܡܚܣܝܣ *to cackle;* and in U. *to shake in singing.*

ܡܚܕܡܕ *to thunder*, and ܡܚܡܕܡܕ K. *to rumble, crash* (the latter in U. *to be downhearted*), cf. ܡܚܕܟ.

ܡܚܩܕܩ *to caw, croak, bubble* as a water pipe; in K. *to crack, quarrel.*

ܡܚܬܚܬ *to pelt* as rain; in U. *to bubble.* Cf. ܚܬܚܬ *raining heavily.*

ܡܚܡܚܡ *to speak through the nose;* cf. ܚܡܚܡ *speaking nasally.*

ܡܚܦܚܦ *to spit*, as rain.

ܡܚܦܩܦ *to stamp, patter, beat.*

ܡܚܛܡܛ (pron. thin) *to tick, click.* See (4) b.

ܡܚܕܚܕ *to be hoarse.* See (14).

(16) Some verbs are taken direct from foreign languages or from some other N.S. word of foreign origin, and cannot be classified as above, as:—

ܡܚܙܚܙ *to be shy,* N.S. ܚܙܟ *denial* (Turk.).

ܡܚܠܚܠ K. *to be dazzled,* N.S. ܚܠܚܠ m. *spark.* (Also ܡܚܠܚܠ *to be dazzled, to break* as clouds.)

§ 83 A]   DERIVATION OF QUADRILITERAL VERBS.   273

مجذيقذ *to crown*, N.S. جِنقُذ m. *a crown*.

مجّمعذا *to be bold, not to stand on ceremony*, N.S. جَمْعَى *familiar, friendly*.

مجذخيذ *to be double-minded*, in U.; hence metaph. *to be much patched*, Pers.

مجمدوك *to peck*, N.S. جِمدوك m. *a beak*.

مجذدمي *to apply medicines, to poison*, N.S. دُدْمَذ m. *medicine*, Pers. (also borrowed in O.S.).

مذهمومر *to speak*, rare in K., N.S. همومت f. *word* [Kurd. *ham* (together), *zeman* (tongue), Nöld. App. I.].

محوّسحم K. *to trouble*, N.S. وسعذى f. *trouble*, Turk.

محونيذ *to be sulky, swagger*, Arab. زنغل. Hence also perh. مجليغذ *to boast*.

مجَّحتم *to arm*, Kurd., cf. N.S. جُحذ m. *armour*.

مجلتس, also مجلتح *to beat, birch, have weals*, N.S. جلدومنه f. *a weal*.

مجمجذ *to have a bad smell*, N.S. جمجوذ f. *stench*. So perhaps مجّمجا *to soil*, otherwise مجلحا and مجذدجا.

مجبكلذ U. *to be curved, bent*, N.S. جبكلذ m. *fork, fish-hook*, Turk.

مجبكذ *to tear* with the claws, N.S. جبكذا m. *rag*, Kurd. Hence also perh. مجبجذ, and مجبتجذ *to tear*. See also (12).

مجبكد *to swing*, N.S. جبكمد f. *a swing*.

مجذديه U. *to veil*, N.S. جذده m. *a veil*, Kurd. [or حذرها].

مجبكذ *to rake* (no Mim prefixed), N.S. جبكذ m. *a rake*.

S. GR.   35

ܡܚܘܝܿܕ *to reconcile, be reconciled*, N.S. ܡܘܝܿܕ and ܡܘܝܿܕܐ *reconciled*.

ܡܚܢܼܒܼܠ *to descend from father to son*, N.S. ܡܢܼܒܼܠ m. *a descendant*.

ܡܗܕܗܡܹܙ *to stun*, N.S. ܗܕܗܡܝ and ܗܕܗܡܕܐ *stunned*, Turk.

ܡܚܘܨܘ K. *to fast*, Kurd.

ܡܚܠܓ݂ܝ (hard Kap) *to stammer*, N.S. ܠܓ݂ܝ *stammering*, adj., Turk. Perhaps ܡܚܕ݂ܝ (hard Kap) *to shrink back, to slip from the hand*, is connected with it.

ܡܚܦܸܕܸܙ U., ܡܚܦܸܢܕܸܙ K. with Pthakha sound, *to dam*, N.S. ܦܸܕܸܙ f. *a dam*, Turk.

ܡܚܦܸܕ݂ܝ U., ܡܚܦܕ݂ܓ݂ܝܙ K., or by metath. ܡܚܓ݂ܕ݂ܝܙ K. *to wedge in*, N.S. ܦܕ݂ܝ m. *a wedge*.

ܡܚܢܝܕܠ *to make to stand up, to stand firm, to hang the head*, N.S. ܢܝܕܠ m. *a chair*, rare; Turk.

ܡܚܛܥܕ݂ܐ (or ܣ U.) *to dare*, Kurd.

ܡܚܕ݂ܝܕ݂, no Mim prefixed, *to defile, to die a natural death as cattle*, N.S. ܡܚܕ݂ܘܕ݂ *unclean*, Turk.

ܡܚܓ݂ܘܗܐ *to covet* (= ܡܚܓ݂ܢܝ Al.) Pers. Kurd. Arab.

ܡܚܓ݂ܿܕ݂ܘ K. Pthakha sound, *to acquaint, know*, N.S. ܓ݂ܿܕ݂ܘ K. *acquainted*, Kurd.

ܡܚܢܥܒܼܕ Tkh. *to be a sojourner*, N.S. ܡܚܢܥܒܼ m. *a sojourner*, Arab.

ܡܚܒܢܬܠ U. *to be lazy*, N.S. ܚܢܬܠ *lazy*, Turk.

ܡܚܓ݂ܕ݂ܠܙ *to interpret*, cf. N.S. ܓ݂ܕ݂ܠܡܢ m. *dragoman*, Arab.

(17) The following from O.S. and Chald. words or roots cannot be classified with the above list:

ܡܙܕܘܝ *to be cheap*, N.S. ܙܕܘܝ *cheap*, O.S. ܙܕܘ *cheapness of corn*.

ܡܙܕܡܠ O.S. *to be or make a widow or widower*.

ܡܟܠܟܠ *to coo, prattle, crow*, O.S. ܟܠܟܠܘ *prattling*.

ܡܓܕܕ (pron. ܠ = ܚ) Chald. נִגְדֵּר *to roll*; also in K. *to tilt up*. Cf. O.S. ܟܕܘܕܐ *ball*.

ܡܙܕܒܠ K. *to oppose* = O.S. ܕܠܩܒܠ, N.S. ܕܙܡܘܠ *against* (hybrid word ?), see § 69.

ܡܕܪܡܢ O.S. *to believe*, § 83 D. *a*.

ܡܘܠܗܝ *to disturb, annoy*, O.S. ܘܠܗܝ *to shorten*; cf. O.S. ܘܠܗܝܐ *disturbance*.

ܡܒܕܩܕ U. *to eat quickly*, possibly from ܐܟܠܬܡܕ *supper*, § 16, ii. *g*. See also (12).

ܡܓܕܓܕ O.S. *to murmur*.

ܡܣܟܢ O.S., no Mim prefixed, *to be poor, to impoverish*, cf. ܡܣܟܢܐ O.S., N.S. *poor*. [Also caus. of ܫܬܩ, and = *to hush*.]

ܡܓܕܠܠ *to delay*, O.S. *to involve, twist*; cf. O.S., N.S. ܠܙܘܕܠܐ *delay*, § 76.

ܡܩܕܩܝ O.S. *to rinse*.

ܡܓܕܝܡ K. *to butt, to be old*; both perh. from ܕܩܕܩܐ *skull*, O.S., N.S.

ܡܠܘܠܕ *to have worms*, see § 47.

ܡܓܕܠܥ O.S. = ܠܥܓܕܡ (16).

ܡܓܕܗܡ O.S. *to supply*.

(18) The following are of uncertain derivation: ܡܓܕܒܙ *to hang*

(see 5); ܡܟܲܒܸܕ to *torment*, cf. ܠܡܲܒܸܕ, § 76; ܡܟܲܕܸܟ to *die*, of dogs and bad men; ܡܲܕܸܕܸܐ to *hesitate*; ܡܲܕܸܗܸܪ to *neigh*; (Sp. ܟܲܙ) to *be muddy or broken*; ܡܲܣܡܸܚܝ to *be damp*; ܡܲܣܒܘܕ to *swagger, to raise the feathers*, as a bird; ܡܲܓܠܸܛ to *baste*; to *beat gently* (see 16); ܡܓܲܠܓܸܡ K. or ܡܲܓܠܸܓ to *sob, pant*; ܡܲܕܡܸܓ to *throw, expel*; ܡܲܓܢܸܛ to *hang*, tr.; ܡܓܲܕܸܨ Al. to *roar*; ܡܲܓܕܸܡ to *roar*, as a fire; ܡܲܟܠܸܕܐ U. to *deceive*; ܡܲܓܕܸܢ to *toss in bed*, as a sick man; ܡܲܚܦܸܕܪ K. to *graft, vaccinate*; ܡܲܚܕܸܦܠ to *hit out right and left, to lay waste*; ܡܲܚܦܸܕ to *smile*, K., to *be crisp*, as snow, U.; ܡܓܲܚܕܸܪ K. to *clatter*; ܡܲܓܡܸܨ to *be dirty* or *musty*; ܡܲܓܕܸܝ to *gather* flowers; ܡܲܓܕܸܗܠ K. to *roll*; ܡܲܓܗܸܐ U. to *sob*; ܡܲܓܢܸܓ to *whine*; ܡܲܓܕܸܒ to *tingle*; ܡܲܓܕܸܗܬ to *tack, sew loosely, to be pitted with smallpox.*

(B) *First Conjugation quadriliterals.*

A few verbs of the first Conjugation are quadriliteral; in most cases ܘ or ܗ has been inserted owing to the second radical being weak. Such are ܟܵܘܸܓ to *wish*, ܠܵܚܸܒ to *bleat*, ܝܵܠܸܒ to *be tired*, ܕܘܩܸܢ to *cement*, ܝܵܗܸܒܠ to *give*, and the rest; see § 46. In the last case the ܠ is perhaps due to the frequency with which the preposition ܠ *to*, follows this verb.

(C) *Quinqueliterals.*

These are conjugated like the second conjugation quadriliterals. Such are ܡܓܲܕܸܢܟ K. or ܡܲܓܕܸܢܟ K. to *be late*, ܡܲܓܕܸܝܟܠ K. to *oppose*, ܡܲܚܘܸܕܸܐ U. to *lessen* (ܘ like ܗ as in ܘܸܕܘܕܐ *little*). For ܡܸܓܲܡܨܸܠ, ܡܸܟܲܗܓܸܠ, see § 30.

(D) *Triliterals.*

Some triliterals are formed by the omission or addition of a letter. Thus :

a. By omitting ܗ from quadriliterals; as ܡܲܕܠܸܚ U. *to be dizzy, to interrupt,* from ܡܲܕܠܗܸܚ K. (Kurdish) = ܡܲܕܠܲܗܸܚ; ܡܲܗܸܡܸܢ U. *to believe* (ܡܲܗܘܡܸܢ Sal.), from ܡܲܕܗܸܡܸܢ K., O.S. [root ܗܡܢ, the O.S. Aph. being irregularly ܗܡܸܢ. We have also in N.S. ܡܲܕܡܸܚ *to be peaceful or tame* K., *to entrust* Al.]; ܡܲܫܓܸܕ U. *to madden,* from ܡܲܫܓܗܸܕ K. [cf. O.S. and N.S. ܫܹܐܕܵܐ *a devil*]; ܡܲܕܓܸܢ *to tame,* from ܓܢܵܐ *peace,* O.S., N.S. Cf. the noun ܓܘܼܕܵܐ U. *a chimney or vent,* also ܓܘܼܕܹܬܵܐ or ܓܘܼܕܝܼܬܵܐ U. K., lit. *a little eye.*

b. By adding ܠ, as ܕܠܸܟ *to be numb,* perhaps for ܕܟܹܐ, from O.S. ܕܟܸܐ *to feel,* cf. ܡܲܕܕܟܸܚ U. or ܡܲܕܕܠܸܟ K. *to be numb;* and several in the second conjugation as ܡܲܕܠܸܚ (above), ܡܲܕܗܸܢ U. *to air before the fire* = ܡܲܕܗܘܼܢܵܐ K., cf. N.S. ܗܹܘܿܐܐ *steam, vapour;* ܡܫܲܝܸܕ *to strengthen,* O.S. ܫܲܝܸܕ, cf. N.S. and O.S. ܫܲܝܸܠܕܵܐ *strength;* ܡܲܠܟܸܒ *to encourage* = O.S. ܠܲܒܸܒ, cf. N.S. and O.S. ܠܹܒܵܐ *heart;* ܢܲܓܸܠ *to stain, blot,* Chald. ܠܟ, cf. N.S. ܠܸܟܵܐ *a stain* (Turk.). For see above A (9).

c. From O.S. passives by taking in ܐ or ܒ of the passive prefix. We thus perhaps have ܘܲܕܸܕ *to fear,* O.S. root ܘܲܕ *to be moved or agitated* (so Al. ܘܲܕܸܕ); ܓܸܕܸܒ *to be numb,* qy. from ܐܲܒܢܵܐ formed from ܐܲܒܢܵܐ *a stone;* ܓܲܕܸܒ *to come to oneself* (after a faint), *to awake* = ܐܸܬܬܲܥܝܼܕ.

Hence also perhaps the reason why ܒ of ܓ݂ܰܕ݂ is pronounced ܐ, the influence of O.S. ܠܰܒ݂ܓ݂ܕ݂ being felt. [Nöld. § 96.]

d. Several causatives are triliteral, owing to one of the letters of the root being weak and having dropped out. See § 45 *b, c.*

VOWELS AND CONSONANTS.

§ 84. *Rules for Aspiration in Syriac words.* ܓܘܕܓ݂ ܘܩܘܫܝܐ

These are taken from Bar Zu'bi's grammar; but those only are given which affect N.S. and they do not apply to foreign words.

1. At the beginning of a word the letters ܒܓܕܟ are hard.

2. Standing second after a vowelless letter, soft, as ܟ݂ܒܕ݂ܐ *marrying*. Except the first radical, in N.S., of 2. conj. verbs preceded by ܡ.ܕ.

3. After a silent or fallen letter, hard, as ܡܕܝܢܬܐ (ܬ) *city*; ܟܦܪܐ (ܟ) *vine*, for ܓܘܦܢܐ O.S. ܓܦܢܐ; ܐܢܬ *thou*.

4. A final letter is soft, except as above and unless it follows a vowelless consonant. [Thus most words which transgress this rule are foreign. For numerous exceptions see § 95.]

5. *Nouns.* If the first has Pthakha, the second Khwaṣa, Rwaṣa or Zqapa, the second is hard, as ܐܰܟܳܪ *husbandman*, ܥܰܬܝܩܐ *ancient*. But if the second is vowelless, it is soft, as ܓܰܒ݂ܪܐ *husband*.

6. After Khwaṣa these letters are soft, as ܒܪܝܬܐ *creation*.

7. If the first radical has a vowel, and the second none, the third radical is hard; as ܣܗܕܐ *m. witness.* But there are many excep-

§ 84] RULES FOR ASPIRATION IN SYRIAC WORDS. 279

tions, both in O.S. and N.S., as ܕܲܗܒ݂ܵܐ m. *gold*, ܦܝܼܢܟ݂ܵܐ *a dish*, O.S. (πίναξ), ܚܲܠܒ݂ܵܐ m. *milk* U., *curdled milk* K. [In K. *sweet milk* is ܚܲܠܝܵܐ lit. *sweet*.]

8. After Rwaṣa a vowelless letter is soft, as ܬܸܫܒܘܿܚܬܵܐ *glory*. But if it has a vowel, it is hard; as ܬܸܫܒܘܿܚܬܵܐ *anthem*.

9. If all the letters have vowels, the third is soft, as ܚܲܝܵܒ݂ܵܐ m. *debtor*, ܘܵܩܘܿܦ݂ܵܐ m. *joining*, ܚܲܦ݂ܝܼܛܵܐ *active*, ܩܲܕ݂ܝܼܫܵܐ m. *sponsor* (in O.S. also *a neighbour*).

10. Verbal nouns of all sorts follow the verb in the matter of aspiration, as ܟܵܬ݂ܘܿܒ݂ܵܐ m. *writer*, ܟܬ݂ܵܒ݂ܵܐ m. *book*; ܡܙܲܒܢܵܢܵܐ *seller*, ܙܵܒ݂ܘܿܢܵܐ *buyer*. So in nouns from N.S. causatives, which differ from O.S. (§ 94), as ܡܲܙܕܲܒ݂ܕܵܢܵܐ (ܒ) *one who gives in marriage*. But in O.S. words like ܡܸܬ݂ܟܲܬ݂ܒ݂ܵܢܵܐ (ܬ) *writeable*, have the third radical hard. These are occasionally used in N.S. by the learned, § 81, 4.

11. Feminines in ܬܵܐ have ܬ hard in the case of agents of the form ܟܵܬ݂ܘܿܒ݂ܬܵܐ, and past participles like ܟܬ݂ܝܼܒ݂ܬܵܐ, the preceding vowelless letter remaining soft (ܒ).

12. But other nouns vary, as ܓܲܢܬܵܐ (ܬ) *garden*; but ܚܸܣܢܵܐ (ܬ) *a fort*.

13. Plurals in ܬܐ (K. Al.) have ܬ soft.

14. Nouns ending in ܘܼܬ݂ܵܐ have ܬ hard in O.S., but soft in N.S. (K. Al.). ܬ in the termination ܝܵܐ is soft.

15. *Verbs.* The second radical of the first conjugation is soft; of second conjugation triliterals hard.

Quadriliterals in O.S. have the second and fourth radicals soft, the third hard. For exceptions in N.S. to these rules see §§ 94, 95.

16. In the present participle the last radical is soft, as above, rule 4. In N.S. it remains soft throughout, in feminine and plural. In O.S. it is hardened. Thus:

ܓܢܒ m. { O.S. ܓܢܒܐ f. ܓܢܒܝܢ Pl. / N.S. ܓܢܒܐ f. ܓܢܒܝ Pl. } *to steal.*

§ 85. Vowels and Consonants. Relation of Vernacular Syriac words to those of Classical Syriac, and of the dialects to one another.

Vowels.

Words in N.S. which have a vowel less than in O.S.

ܐܓܪܐ m., O.S. ܐܸܓܪܐ *a roof*, (ܓܠ), but ܒܪ ܐܓܪܐ Ti. = ܒܪ ܐܸܓܪܐ (also ܒܪܒܪ') O.S. *a lunatic.*

ܐܝܪ U., also ܐܝܪ K., as O.S. m. *May.*

ܐܢܝ *they* = O.S. ܗܢܘܢ, ܗܢܝܢ. So several pronouns §§ 10—12.

ܐܣܛܘܢܐ m., O.S. ܐܸ', *pillar*, rarely with ܛ in N.S. = στῦλος.

ܐܣܦܪܐ f., O.S. ܐܸ' *omelette* = σφαῖρα.

ܐܫܬܐ K., Al. = O.S. ܐܸܫܬܐ f. *fever*, = ܡܫܚܫܚܢܐ U.

ܚܘܪܐ, O.S. ܚܸ' *white.*

ܛܠܠܐ K. = O.S. ܛܸܠ' *shadow* (ܛܠܝܠܐ U. etc.).

ܟܘܡܐ, O.S. ܐܘܟܡܐ *black.*

ܠܥܙܪ also ܠܥܙܪ as O.S. *Lazarus.*

ܡܫܬܒܗܪ U. (Ti. ܡܸ') = O.S. ܡܫܬܒܗܪ *to be proud.*

ܢܥܡܐ m., O.S. ܢܥܡܐ *an ostrich.*

ܣܟܝܢܐ f., O.S. ܣܸ' *knife.* So ܣܟܝܢܬܐ *id.*

ܣܩܘܦܬܐ, O.S. ܐܸܣܩܘܦܬܐ *threshold*, § 119.

ܥܕܵܢܵܐ f., O.S. and Al. ܥܸܕ' [m. in O.S.] *time*, (ܕ݂)

ܥܸܩܵܪܵܐ m., O.S. ܥܸܩܵܪܵܐ *root.*

ܦܕܵܢܵܐ f. (ܕ like ܬ), O.S. ܦܕ' *plough*, §§ 97, 104.

ܩܕܵܡ, O.S. ܩܕܸܡ, sign of past tense.

ܣܘܦܵܐ m., O.S. ܣܘܦܢܵܐ *large basket.*

ܥܪܣܵܐ, O.S. ܬܥܪܣܵܐ *bed.*

ܥܢܝܵܐ, O.S. ܥܢܝܬܵܐ *a quarter of a garlic.*

ܬܢܵܢܵܐ m., O.S. ܬܸܢܵܢܵܐ or ܬܘܢܵܢܵܐ *smoke.*

ܬܩܘܠܬܵܐ, O.S. 'ܬܩ *weight.*

Note also ܢܒܘܥܵܐ Al. *fountain* = 'ܢܒ K., p. 232.

§ 86. *Words in N.S. which have a vowel more than in O.S.*

a. All which have ܐ prosthetic in N.S., but not in O.S. See below, § 96.

b. Many feminines formed from masculines; a half vowel in O.S. corresponding to a whole vowel in N.S., as ܡܲܠܟܬܵܐ *queen*, also more rarely ܡܲܠܟܬܵܐ as in O.S., from ܡܲܠܟܵܐ *king*; ܕܸܡܥܬܵܐ *tear*, O.S. ܕܸܡܥܬܵܐ (masc. sing. not used). Hence in reading O.S. the Syrians often convert a half vowel into a whole one and even accent it; they pronounce ܐܸܬܥܒܸܕ *he was made*, as if ܐܸܬܥܲܒܸܕ *ithîwidh*, with the accent on ܥ; so they read ܐܸܬܪܲܚܲܡܥܠܲܝܢ *have pity on us* (usually written as one word in the service books), as if ܥ had Zqapa, *ithrakhamâlén*, with the accent on the penult.

c. In U. verbal nouns of second conjugation Pthakha triliterals, all quadriliterals (unless one letter is virtually silent as in ܡܫܲܢܩܸܡ *to punish*, pron. ܡܫܲܩܸܡ), and all second conjugation ܠܐ verbs; as

ܡܲܗܠܸܦܵܢܵܐ U. *teacher* = ܡܗܲܠܦܵܢܵܐ K., O.S.; ܡܨܲܠܝܵܢܵܐ U. *one who prays* = ܡܨܲܠܝܵܢܵܐ K., O.S.

d. Plurals of nouns in ܝܵܐ in U., as ܩܲܪ̈ܝܵܬ݂ܵܐ U. *beams* = ܩܲܪ̈ܝܵܬ݂ܵܐ K., O.S.

e. ܐܸܚܪܵܝܵܐ, O.S. ܐܚܪ' *last.* [Sal. ܐܚܪ', first Zlama.]

ܓܕܝܫܵܐ, O.S. ܓ' *stack*, Chald. גְּדִישָׁא, p. 246.

ܓܘܡܪܵܐ, O.S. ܓ' *coal.*

ܕܝܵܬ݂ܹܩ f., also as Eastern O.S. ܕܝ' *Testament* (Old, New).

ܕܸܡܵܐ m., O.S. ܕ' *blood.*

ܟ݂ܵܓ݂ܲܕ m., O.S. ܟ݂' *paper* (also Arabic).

ܚܕܥܣܲܪ, O.S. ܚܕܲܥܣܲܪ *eleven.*

ܚܘܼܘܝܵܐ (in U. pron. ܚܘܼܘ'), O.S. ܚܘܼܘܝܵܐ *serpent*, f. So ܚܘܵܐ (or ܚܘܘܵܐ) m. for ܚܘܵܐ (O.S. ܚܸܘܝܵܐ); pl. ܚܘܼ̈ܘܵܬ݂ܵܐ (ܚܘܘ'), O.S. ܚܘܼ̈ܘܵܬ݂ܵܐ.

ܡܚܝܠܬܵܐ, O.S. ܡܚܘܼܠܬܵܐ *sieve* (root ܚܠܠ).

ܢܚܝܪܵܐ m., O.S. ܢ' *nose, promontory.*

ܣܸܡܵܠܵܐ, in O.S. and Al. also ܣ' *the left.*

ܥܪܘܒܬܵܐ Al. = ܥܪ' U. K., O.S. *Friday.*

ܥܣܲܪ K. *ten* (f.), O.S. ܥܣܲܪ.

ܦܠܵܢ or ܦܠܵܢܝܘܿܢ, O.S. ܦܠܵܢ [f. ܦܠܵܢܝܬܵܐ, O.S. ܦ'] *so and so.*

ܩܘܡܬܵܐ Al. = ܩܘܼܡܬܵܐ U. = O.S. ܩܘܼܡܬܵܐ *stature.*

ܫܸܡܵܐ m., O.S. ܫ' *name.*

ܫܸܩܘܿܠܵܐ m., O.S. ܫ' *skirt* of a garment, *front flap* of a coat tail. Also ܫܩܘܿܠܵܐ N.S.

[§§ 86, 87]   CHANGE OF VOWELS.   283

ܗܘܠܟܐ U. = O.S., K. ܕܘܠܟܐ *worm*, § 88 *g*.

ܬܠܬ K. ܬܠܬ Q. *three*, f., O.S. ܬܠܬ.

ܬܡܠ K. *yesterday*, O.S. ܬܡܠ (also O.S. ܬܘܡܠ).

§ 87. *Pthakha and Zqapa.* There is a very common tendency in N.S., especially in Urmi, to turn Pthakha into Zqapa. This is perhaps partly for compensation[1] and is due to the dislike of the Syrians to the doubling of a consonant, unless it is written double, when they pronounce both consonants distinctly, see § 4 (7).

a. Before ܘ where the Western Syrians write Pthakha, the Eastern Syrians write Zqapa (§ 7). In N.S. (esp. U.) there are a few exceptions, like ܡܟܘܒ *to answer* (in K. ܡܟܘܒ).

b. In accordance with the rule in § 6 (1) all Pthakhas before a silent letter and ܗ are pronounced Zqapa, except in a few verbs, as ܡܕܚܕܚ *to oppress, strike,* ܡܕܗܩܝ Ti. Al. *to vomit,* (lit. *to overturn*), ܡܚܘܚܡ U. (= ܡܚܘܡܕ K.) *to put milk or butter in food during a fast,* ܡܚܕܟܕܪ K. *to dam,* ܡܕܗܩܕܘ K. *to acquaint, know;* in some compounds of ܝܕܥ, § 28 (9), but ܝܕܥ itself is pronounced usually with Zqapa (see § 91); and in the numerals 13 to 19 in K., § 26.

c. Many second conjugation triliteral verbs have Zqapa for Pthakha on the first radical, perhaps to compensate for not doubling the second radical. A few differ according to district:—

ܡܟܘܒ U. ܡܟܘܒ K. *to answer*.

ܡܟܡܕ U. ܡܟܡܕ K. *to assemble,* tr.

ܡܚܘܡ U. ܡܚܘܡ K. *to join,* tr.

ܡܣܢܓܕ U. *to be cold* (of persons), ܡܣܢܓܕ Al. *to spoil* tr., p. 120.

---

[1] So in Al., in cases where ܠ is omitted, short *i* sound often becomes *é*; ܐܡܕܒ
I said is *méri* or *mIri*; ܕܓܕܒ *he remembers me* is *takhéri*.

ܡܲܛܒܸܥ U. ܡܛܲܒܸܥ K. *to sink*, tr.

ܡܲܥܓ̰ܸܙ U. *to annoy*, ܡܥܲܓ̰ܸܙ K. *to be tired of.*

ܡܲܦܠܸܓ U. ܡܦܲܠܸܓ K. ܡܦܲܠܸܓ̰ Al. *to divide.*

ܡܨܲܪܸܦ U. ܡܨܲܪܸܦ K. *to refine metals.*

ܡܲܫܘܸܕ U. ܡܫܲܘܸܕ K. *to promise.*

ܡܲܫܘܸܡ U. ܡܫܲܘܸܡ K. *to happen.*

ܡܲܕܪܸܐ U. ܡܕܲܪܸܐ K. *to throw.*

ܡܫܲܬܸܦ or ܡܫܵܬܸܦ *to partake.*

ܡܲܬܘܸܒ U. ܡܬܘܸܒ K. *to repent*, also ܬܵܐܸܒ K. Al. ܡܬܵܐܸܒ Al.

Traditionally the O.S. ܢܒܲܪܸܟ *he will bless*, is read as if with Zqapa, and so all Pa'els with ܪ.

d. For those causatives of verbs ܦܐ, ܦܝ, ܥܐ, ܥܝ which vary between Pthakha and Zqapa, see § 45 *b*, *c*.

e. Several first conjugation verbs in U. Ash. have Pthakha on the first radical[1]. These in K. as in O.S. have Zqapa; see § 46.

f. Many words which etymologically, or on the analogy of O.S. would have Pthakha, are in many districts, especially in Urmi, pronounced with Zqapa. In other districts, especially in K. Al., they vary between Zqapa and Pthakha. It seems better to write these with Pthakha on the O.S. analogy or according to the etymology. Such are the feminines of the form ܡܲܠܝܼܟܬܵܐ *queen*, from ܡܲܠܟܵܐ, § 86 *b*.

g. So also words of the form ܦܲܥܘܼܠܵܐ § 77 (2), p. 231.

h. And those of the form ܦܲܥܵܠܵܐ § 77 (3), p. 233.

i. And those of the form ܦܲܥܝܼܠܵܐ § 81 (5), p. 244.

[1] ܝܵܕܥܸܢ *I know*, in Al. is *yădin* or *yédin*; ܟܹܐܕܥܸܢ is *kidin* or *kēdin*.

j. In Ṭi. Al. MB. the names of the first four days of the week are pronounced with a Zqapa on ܒ, as ܚܕܒܫܒܐ = O.S. ܚܕ ܒܫܒܐ *Sunday*, p. 287. [But in Al. also with second Zlama, as *ṭloshéba*.]

k. Also the following sometimes have Zqapa, esp. in U.

ܐܒܘܢܐ m. *bishop*, Arab.; lit. *our father*, cf. O.S. ܐܒܘܢ.

ܐܚܘܢܐ m. = O.S. ܐܚܐ *brother*, § 79.

ܐܝܟ *as*, O.S.; usually pron. *âkh* (p. 169). So ܕܐܝܟ.

ܒܪܝܡܬܐ etc., § 16 (2) *b*.

ܥܝܦܐ Tkh. = ܥܝܦܐ U. m. *labour, trouble*.

ܒܐܪ (p. 160) in Al. has Pthakha, but ܒܐܪܒ always Zqapa.

ܗܩܬܐ U. = ܗܩܬܐ K. m. *reward, pay* (= ܐܓܪ Al.).

ܙܓܐ O.S. = ܙܓܐ Ti. = ܙܓܐ U. Ti. *bell*, m., p. 288.

ܚܕܘܬܐ *joy*, O.S.

ܠܟܝܢ Al. also ܠܟ *but*, p. 188.

ܡܠܐܟܐ *angel*, m. O.S. (both with Zqapa sound).

ܡܫܟܢܐ m. (O.S. ܡܫܟܢܐ) *tabernacle, goats' hair tent.*

ܡܘܙܢܐ U. or ܡܘܙܢܝܬܐ K., O.S. (for ܡܘܙ) *balance.*

ܣܡܡܐ (ܣ Ti.) m. *poison* (= ܙܗܪ Tkh.). In O.S. *medicine.*

ܐܡܪܐ O.S. = ܐ Ti. = ܐ U. *a male lamb.*

ܩܫܐ, O.S. ܩ *priest* [for ܩܫܝܫܐ, p. 246].

ܪܩܐ *Raca* O.S.

l. Some words with Pthakha in O.S. have Zqapa almost if not quite universally in N.S. and are therefore so written.

ܚܠܐ *vinegar*, m., O.S. ܚ.

ܡܚܛܐ f. U. = ܡܚܛܐ f. Ti. = ܡܚܛܐ O.S. m. *a needle.*

ܡܫܝ m. *back, girdle, loins*, O.S. ܡܨ, for ܡܕܢܝ.

ܟܦܬܐ f. *metal bowl*, O.S. ܟܦ; usually in N.S. ܟ.

ܝܠܕܐ m. *boy*, O.S. ܝܠܕܐ.

ܝܡܐ f. *sea*, O.S. ܝܡܐ m., Heb. יָם, Chald. יַמָּא.

ܡܢܘ *who* = O.S. ܡܢ (ܡܢܘ). The Azerbaijan Jews have Pthakha here.

ܣܠܐ m. *basket*, O.S. ܣܠ.

ܕܕܐ *very*, so Az. (in K. Al. ܕܕܐ is used as an adjective = *great*).

ܪܒܝ m. *teacher*, § 20 (14), O.S. ܪܒ.

ܬܡܐ (in Ti. Pthakha) *there* = O.S. ܬܡܢ, p. 167.

m. Zqapa is pronounced Pthakha in ܩܛܠܠܝ *he killed me* (f.), and so the other persons, § 50.

§ 88. *Zlama for Pthakha or Zqapa.*

There is a great tendency to use Zlama in N.S. for O.S. Pthakha or more rarely for Zqapa. This is especially the case in Salamas, Qudshanis, etc. Also in foreign words Zlama in one district corresponds to Pthakha or Zqapa in another. We thus have:—

a. The present, the imperative etc. in second conjugation verbs in Sal. Q. etc. See §§ 35 sqq. and 91.

b. Also in the same districts many words of the form ܫܡܫܐ *deacon* (pronounced ܫܡܫܐ), etc., § 77 and see below § 91.

c. Universally in verbs etc. where under the influence of the letters ܐܗܚܥ O.S. writes Pthakha, N.S. writes Zlama; as ܝܬܒ N.S. = ܝܬܒ O.S. *he dwells*.

d. So the 2nd pers. singular masculine of the first present of verbs, and of the preterite where the object is expressed synthetically

§ 88] CHANGE OF VOWELS. 287

(§ 50), as ܩܛܝܠܟ ܐܢܬ N.S. = ܩܛܝܠܟ (ܐܢܬ ܩܛܠ) O.S. *thou killest*,

ܩܛܝܠܐ ܠܗ N.S. = ܩܛܝܠܐ ܠܗ (ܐܢܬ ܩܛܠ) O.S. *he killed thee* (m.), and so if the subject is of the first person sing. masc.

e. The first five days of the week in most districts, § 28 (5) and p. 285; as ܒܚܕܒܫܒܐ m. = ܒܚܕܒܫܒܐ O.S. *Sunday*.

f. The past participle of verbs ܓܠܐ, first conjugation, as ܓܠܝܐ for ܓܠܝܐ O.S. *revealed*.

g. Also the following:—

ܐܓܪ (*égar*) Al. = 'ܐ *if*, p. 185.

ܐܟܠܐ m., O.S. 'ܐ or 'ܐ *moth, book-worm*, § 89.

ܠܓܡܣܐ, or ܠܓܡܣܐ Al. = O.S. *below*.

ܐܪܒܥ K. = ܐܪܒܥ O.S. *four*, f.

ܐܪܚܐ U. m. or 'ܐ U. K., O.S. *guest*.

ܐܪܚܝܐ U. f. or 'ܐ K. *mill*, § 96.

ܐܪܡܠܬܐ, O.S. 'ܐܪܡܠܐ, *widow*.

ܐܫܒܥ Tkh., ܐ Ti. = ܫܒܥ O.S. *seven*, f. (ܐ), p. 64.

ܒܗܪܐ Al., 'ܐ U. K. *light*, m. But in K. they generally say ܟܘܕܪܐ.

ܚܡܒܕܒ Ti. Sh., ܚܡܒܐ U., ܚܡܒܕܒ Tkh. or ܓܣܘܕܒ MB. *stove*, f., [usually ܓܘܕ (ܐ) in K.].

ܬܘܓܒܐ, ܬܘܓܒܐ, cf. § 67.

ܒܣܐ (*bésa*) Al., 'ܐ U. K. *enough*.

ܒܩܪܐ, O.S. 'ܐ *herd*, m.

ܒܪܢܫܐ, also 'ܐ as O.S. *son of man*.

ܒܪܩܐ or 'ܐ as O.S. *lightning*.

ܓܒܐ U. Q. Sal. m. (ܓ), or ܓܒܐ K. f. = O.S. ܓܒܐ (for ܓܒܐ) *side*, p. 225.

ܓܒܝܐ U. *beggar* = 'ܓܒܐ O.S. (*collector*), p. 235.

ܓܒܪܐ Ash., 'ܐ Z. = 'ܐ U. K., O.S. *man* (in U. *husband*). So in U. ܓܒܪܝܐ *husbands*, p. 50.

ܓܕܝܐ = O.S. 'ܐ *kid*, m.

ܓܠܗܘܬܐ Tkh. = 'ܐ Al. *labour, trouble*.

ܓܢܒܐ = 'ܐ O.S., Al. *thief*, m.

ܓܢܬܐ Tkh. = 'ܐ Ti., O.S. *garden*.

ܓܪܒܐ U. = O.S. ܓ' *leprosy*, f.

ܓܪܟ (*gérek*) Al. = ܓ' U. *must.*

ܓܫܪܐ *bridge*, see p. 42.

ܕܗܒܐ Al. (second Zlama) = ܕ' O.S., U. *gold*, m.

ܕܝܡܐ = ܕܝܡ U. *rain-watered land.*

ܕܝܢܐ Sal. = ܕ' U. *debt*, Pers. m.

ܕܝܥܬܐ Tkh. *resin, sweat*, p. 42.

ܕܦܢܐ = O.S. ܕ' *side*, f.

ܕܝܩܢܐ = O.S. and Al. ܕ' *beard*, m.

ܕܫܬܐ U. K. = ܕ' Al. Z. *plain.*

ܗܕܟ K. = ܗܫܐ O.S. *now.*

ܙܓܐ (U. first, Ti. second Zlama) = O.S. ܙ' *bell*, m. Also ܙ' Ti. (ܓ : cf. ܙܓܠܐ N.S. *cliff*, m.).

ܙܠܐ = O.S. ܙ' *reed*, m.

ܚܒܪܐ K. Al. = ܚ' O.S., U. *companion*, m.

ܚܝܠܐ Sal. = ܚ' U. K., O.S. *strength, host*, m.

ܚܠܒܢܬ Sal. = ܚ' U. *a present*, (ܚܠܒܢܬܐ Tkh., eighth pl.).

ܚܫܐ Sal., U., sometimes K. = ܚ' K., O.S. *suffering*, m.

ܚܬܢܐ = O.S. ܚ' *bridegroom*, m.

ܛܢܦܐ rare = O.S. ܛ' *unclean* (usually ܛܡܐ).

ܝܘܡܐ = O.S. ܝ', § 112, m.

ܟܟܐ U. K. = ܟ' Ti. = ܟ' Az. = O.S. ܟ' *tooth*, m. So ܟܟܬܐ U. K. = ܟ' Ti. *a tooth of a cogwheel.*

ܟܦܢܐ = O.S. ܟ' *famine, hunger*, m.

ܟܪܒܐ *furrow*, O.S. ܟܪ', p. 206.

ܟܬܘܬܐ, see § 121.

ܠܚܡܐ MB. = ܠ' O.S., U. K. *bread*, m.

ܠܒܐ Sal. (first Zlama) = ܠ' U. K. f. § 18 (2).

ܡܝܐ (i.e. ܡܝܐ) U. K. = ܡܝܐ O.S., Al. Z. *water.*

ܡܢܝ Sal. = ܡ' U. K. *who*, § 13.

ܡܬܠܬܐ *maxim*, from ܡܬܠܐ O.S. and N.S. *parable.*

ܢܗܪܐ (Sal. first, Z. second Zlama) = ܢ' U., O.S. *river*, m.

ܢܦܛܐ U. = ܢ' K., O.S. *naphtha, paraffin*, m.

ܣܗܪܐ Tkh. Ash. = ܣ' U. Ti., O.S. *moon*, m.

ܣܘܪܝܬ and ܣܘܪܝܝܬ Al. *Syriac.*

ܣܚܘܐ = ܣ' O.S. *swimming.*

ܣܬܘܐ Q. = ܣ' U. K., O.S., p. 285.

ܣܬܘܐ = O.S. ′ܣ *winter*, m.

ܫܝܩܬܐ = O.S. ′ܫ *thigh*, f.

ܫܝܘܦܐ K. = ′ܫܘ U., O.S. *signet.*

ܥܩܪܬܐ or ܥܩܪܬܐ U. *a barren woman* = ܥܩܝܪܬܐ K. Sal. The O.S. has ܥܩܪܐ m. ܥܩܪܬܐ f.

ܥܝܢܬܐ, ܥܝܢ etc., see p. 64.

ܦܚܪܐ = O.S. ′ܦ *potsherd*, m. Also ܦܚܪܬܐ § 77 (3).

ܦܠܟܐ Al. = ′ܦ Tkh. (U. ܠܦܩܐ) *wave.*

ܦܩܚܐ, O.S. also ′ܦ *blossom*, m.

ܦܦܘ Ti. = ′ܦ Sh., ܦܘܦܘ U. Tkh. *hoopoe* (otherwise ܦܦܘܦܘܩܐ Tkh. m. ܦܦܘܦܘܩܬܐ m. Ti., ܦܘܦܘܩܐ Ti., ܫܘܠܝܡܢ ܬܪܢܓ Ti., ܪܢܓܐ ܕܫܠܝܡܘܢ U. K. m.).

ܦܩܥܐ or ܦܩܥܬܐ = O.S. ܦܩܥܐ *crack*, also in N.S. *blossom*, m.

ܦܪܐ U. = ′ܦ O.S. = ′ܦ K. *lamb*, m.

ܦܪܕܝܣܐ U. = ′ܦ K., O.S. *Paradise*, f.

ܦܪܙܠܐ = O.S. ′ܦ *iron*, m., p. 293.

ܦܪܨܬܐ U. f. = ܦܪܨܬܐ Al. *opportunity.* (In K. ܡܘܚܠܬܐ.)

ܦܪܬܘܟܐ m. = O.S. ܦܪܬܘܟܐ or ܦܪܬܘܬܐ *crumb*, cf. ܡܦܪܬܟ § 83 (14) and ܦܪܬܐ m. § 18 (5). Also ܦܪܬܘܬܐ.

ܨܦܘܢ Sal. = ′ܨ U. *soap*, m.

ܨܚܘܐ = O.S. ′ܨ *fine weather.*

ܩܘܪܕܝ or ′ܩ (also ܐ) Al. *Kurdish.*

ܩܩܒܢܐ = O.S. ′ܩ *partridge.*

ܩܪܛܠܐ = O.S. ′ܩ *basket.* So N.S. ܩܪܛܠܬܐ *a smaller basket.*

ܩܪܩܦܬܐ, rarely as O.S. ܩܪܩܦܬܐ *skull.*

ܪܒܐ Q. Sal. = ′ܪ U. K. *many, very,* (O.S. ܪܒܐ *great*), § 25 (7).

ܪܚܫܐ *going*, § 46, = O.S. ′ܪ *an insect, or creeping.*

ܫܫܠܬܐ = O.S. ܫܫܠܬܐ or ′ܫ *chain.*

ܫܢܬܐ (*î* U., *é* Al.) = O.S. ′ܫ *year.*

ܫܥܬܐ (*é*) Al. or ′ܫ as O.S. *hour.*

ܬܘܠܥܬܐ U. = O.S., K. ܬܘܠܥܬܐ *worm*, f. (Also N.S. ܬܘܠܥܐ or ܬܘܠܥܐ, ܬܘܠܥܢܐ Tkh.)

ܬܡܢܬܥܣܪ or ܬܡܢܬܥܣܪ Ti. = O.S. ܬܡܢܬܥܣܪ *eighteen.*

ܬܡܘܙ part of U., elsewhere ′ܬ as O.S. *July*, m.

ܬܪܝܢ see § 121 and p. 64.

h. On the other hand we have N.S. Pthakha or Zqapa for O.S. Zlama in the following:—

ܒܹܠܟܵܐ, also as O.S. 'ܒܹ *scabbard*, f.

ܡܸܕܲܪ, in O.S. also 'ܡܹ *entrail*, m.

ܓܸܕܼܳܕܵܐ U., also 'ܓܹ as O.S. = ܓܹܕܳܕܵܐ K. (ܓ) = ܓܘܼܕܳܕܵܐ (ܓ) Diz *sheep* (rarely singular, m.).

So also N.S. and Az. ܐܝܼܐ *I* = O.S. ܐܝܼܐ.

ܩܘܼܡܕܵܐ in O.S. also 'ܩ *mushroom*.

ܦܸܠܓܵܐ = O.S. and Al. 'ܦ *half*, m.

ܒܸܓܕܵܐ U. Ti. = 'ܒ Tkh. (cf. O.S. ܒܸܓܕܵܐ pl.) *almond*, m. [unless it should be ܒܸܓܕܵܐ = O.S. ܒܸܓܕܵܐ].

i. We have Zlama for Pthakha as an euphonic vowel in forms like ܡܲܟܼܘܼܡܘܲܬܵܐ U. Ti. = ܡܲܟܼܘܼܡܘܼܬܵܐ Tkh. = ܡܲܟܼܡܘܼܬܵܐ O.S. Also in Al. before a vowelless consonant with ܠ, ܬ, ܕ, and ܡܚ (ܡܹ). In U. these in speaking take, when necessary, a half Zlama; in O.S. Pthakha. But in forms like ܠܸܟܕܵܐ, ܕܸܟܕܵܐ a whole Zlama in N.S.

§ 89. (1) *Rwaṣa in N.S., not in O.S.*

a. The past participles of all second conjugation verbs, and hence the preterites, ܡܲܟܼܘܼܡܲܕܼ N.S. = ܡܲܟܼܡܲܕܼ O.S.

b. Also the following:—

ܓܲܡܘܼܠܵܐ, O.S. 'ܓ *camel*, m.

ܓܠܝܼܠܵܐ, O.S. ܓܠܝܼܠܵܐ *round*.

ܣܘܼܠܡܵܐ Sal. Sp. = 'ܣ U. K., O.S. *dream*, m.

ܣܘܼܟܵܐ Al. = O.S., U. 'ܣ *darkness*, m.

ܣܘܼܦܵܐ = O.S. ܣܘܼܦܵܐ *pig*, m.

ܛܲܠܘܼܠܵܐ = O.S. ܛܲܠܵܐ *dew*, m.

ܒܲܚܣܘܼܡܝܵܐ = O.S. ܒܲܚܣܘܼܡܝܵܐ *rhubarb*.

ܡܣܘܼܡܕܵܐ = O.S. ܡܣܝܼܡܵܐ *reverend*.

ܢܘܼܣܒܵܐ Al. = 'ܢ O.S., U. K. *hole*, m., p. 304.

ܓܘܼܡܚܵܢܵܐ or as O.S. 'ܓ *fog*, m., § 76.

ܓܘܼܦܪܵܐ or as O.S. 'ܓ *earth*, m.

ܓܘܼܕܓܵܐ Diz, *sheep*, § 88, *h*.

ܓܘܼܪܕܸܢ Al. = ܓܸܪܕܸܢ U. Tkh. f. = ܓܸܪܕܵܐ O.S. *finger*, § 95, *g*.

ܩܘܡܬܐ U. K. = ܩܘܡܬܐ Al. = ܩܘܡܬܐ O.S. *stature.*

ܥܘܩܒܬܐ *elbow* (also of a stove) = O.S. ܥܩܒܬܐ *heel, ankle.*

ܪܘܡܬܐ = O.S. ܪܡ' or ܪܡܬܐ *hill.*

ܪܘܦܫܐ *shoulder,* m. The O.S. ܪܦܫܐ is *a winnowing shovel* = N.S. ܪܘܦܫܐ, which also is *an oar* and *a shoulder blade.*

ܫܒܘܠܐ = (?) O.S. and N.S. ܫܒܠܐ *ears of corn.*

ܬܪܘܨܐ *true* = O.S. ܬܪܝܨܐ *upright* (whence ܛܪܝܨܐ N.S. *fat*). Cf. O.S. ܬܪܝܨ ܫܘܒܚܐ *orthodox.*

Similarly we have ܕܘܪܐ U. = ܕܪܐ K., O.S. *an age,* m.; ܝܘܡܐ U. Sal. Q. Gaw. Tkh. J. = ܝܘ' Ti. Al., O.S. *day,* m. For ܡܘܪܝ see § 13.

(2) *Rwaṣa in O.S., not in N.S.*

ܒܨܘܪܐ, O.S. ܒܘ', *examination,* m.

ܒܘܪܟܐ, O.S. ܒܘܪ', *knee,* f.

ܓܚܟܐ, O.S. ܓܘ' *laughter,* m.

ܕܚܢܐ, O.S. ܕܘ', *millet.*

ܕܝܠܐ, O.S. ܕܘ', *thread, weft,* m.

ܕܥܬܐ, O.S. ܕܘ', *sweat,* f., § 105.

ܚܠܕܐ, O.S. ܚܘ', *mole.*

ܚܪܒܐ *bad,* O.S. ܚܘ' or ܚ', *desolate.*

ܚܘܒܐ with affixes, § 25 (5).

ܟܚܠܐ, O.S. ܟܘ', *eye-paint.*

ܠܓܡܐ, O.S. ܠܘ', *bridle,* m.

ܡܚܠܐ = O.S. ܡܚܘܠܐ (O.S. pl. ܡܚܘܠܐ), *a sieve,* p. 282.

ܦܠܚܢܐ, O.S. ܦܘ', *work,* m.

ܦܡܐ Ti. = ܦܘܡܐ U. Tkh., O.S. *mouth, edge* (of a sword), m.

ܦܪܛܢܢܐ, O.S. ܦܘ' (ܛ like ܛ usually), *flea,* m.

ܪܚܩܐ, O.S. ܪܘ', *far,* (ܪܘܚܩܐ Al.).

ܫܡܫܡܐ, O.S. ܫܘ', *sesame,* f.

Similarly we have ܟܟܒܐ (or ܟ' Al.) often for ܟܘܟܒܐ [or ܟܘܟܒܐ O.S.] *a star,* m.; ܐܠܝܪܐ Ti. for ܐܘܠܝܪܐ O.S. *storeroom;* ܟܦܦܐ Ti. = ܟܘ' U. *low;* ܛܠܥܘܬܐ or ܛܠܥܝܬܐ m. *error;* ܥܘܪܒܢܐ or ܥܪ' (also

ܦܢܝܬܐ f.) *corner;* ܓܡܘܫܬܐ or ܓܡܘ' *handful.* Also in Al. some feminines in ܝܬܐ, ܝܬܐ are often pronounced with *u*, as ܛܠܝܒܬܐ *ṭlubta.*

§ 90. *Rwaṣa* in part of the Urmi plain is generally followed by a Yudh sound in speaking. Thus ܒܙܘܪܐ *bazaar* (so O.S.) becomes ܒܙܘܝܪܐ or even ܒܙܘܝܪܐ sometimes. In Sal. Sp. etc. an aspirated ܠ often follows Rwaṣa; as ܦܘܠܝܐ for ܦܘܠܐ *money.* And also either ܠ or ܝ follow similar sounds, such as ܝܒ or ܝܒ. Thus ܝܬܝܒܬܐ *having sat* (f.), ܠܒ ܫܒܒ *I was worth;* and even in words like ܓܢܒܬܐ *stealing* (ܓܢܝܒܬܐ).

§ 91. In Gaw. J. and to a somewhat smaller extent in Q. Sal., Pthakha and Zqapa very often have the second long-Zlama sound; as ܚܕ *one,* pron. *khé;* ܩܕܡܝܐ *first,* pron. *qémâya;* ܒܣܡ *he heals,* pron. *bésim,* § 35; ܚܠܐ, (O.S. ܚܠܐ), *vinegar,* m., pron. *khéla;* ܩܐ *for,* in Sal. pron. *qé;* ܓܢܐ *soul,* f., pron. *géna;* ܟܘܐ *recess in a wall,* f., in Sal. pron. *kéwi;* ܐܬܘܢܐ *furnace,* m., *étuna.* So some Al. words, § 88.

§ 92. *Metathesis* is very common in N.S.

a. *Vowels.*

ܐܪܡܠܐ U. = ܐܪܡܠܐ K. = ܐܪܡܠܐ O.S. *widower.*

ܒܪܬܩܠܐ *echo,* f., and similar words, § 16, *e,* for ܒܪܬ'.

ܒܪܬܐ, O.S. ܒܪܬܐ *daughter.*

ܓܦܬܐ, O.S. ܓܦܬܐ (ܬ) *vine,* f.

ܚܒܪܬܐ U. = O.S., K. ܚܒܪܬܐ *companion,* f., § 17.

ܚܕܬܐ U., ܚܕܬܐ (ܬ) K. = O.S. ܚܕܬܐ (ܬ) *new,* f. (root ܚܕܬ).

ܚܘܫܒܢܐ ('ܚܫ K.) = O.S. ܚܘܫܒܢܐ *account, reckoning,* m.

§ 92] METATHESIS.

ܕܘܗܪܐ (p. 73) f. = O.S. ܕܗܪܐ m. *midday meal, noon.*

ܡܟܢܐ K. = O.S. ܡܓܢܐ or ܡܓܢܬܐ *shield,* f.

ܣܥܪܐ, O.S. ܗܣܪܐ *barley,* pl. So ܗܣܕܢܐ = O.S. ܗܣܕܬܐ *barley-corn,* cf. § 45, *d, e.*

ܓܕܡܕܐ = ܓܡܕܐ O.S. *scorpion,* f.

ܦܪܙܠܐ, (for ܦܙܘܠܐ) = O.S. ܦܪܙܠܐ *iron,* m., § 88, *g.*

ܥܡܝܕܟܐ or ܟܡܘܕܟܐ (O.S. ܟܣܕܘܕܐ) *blackbird,* from ܟܡܝܕ *to be black.*

ܗܓܕܝ (ܓܕܝ) = O.S. ܗܓܕܝ *October, November,* m., § 28 (12).

b. *Consonants.*

Numerals like ܐܙܕܓܕܩܣܪ K., ܐܙܕܩܕܗܘܣ U., § 28 (1).

Most verbs ܩܕ and ܩܒ in forming the verbal noun, etc., § 38. So also in Sp. in the present of some verbs ܩܕ, as ܡܨܕܓܝ = ܡܓܨܕܓܝ *they are baptized,* ܕܘܠܒ = ܕܒܘܠ *they weave,* and sometimes in Al.

Also the following:—

ܐܡܓ MB. or ܡܓ U. or ܓܡ as O.S. *to swear.*

ܐܨܡ Z. Az. or ܐܡܨܬ Ti. = ܡܐܨܬ U., O.S. *a vessel, dish,* m.

ܐܘܕܗܝ Al. (*anhé* or *anhi;* fem. only) = ܘܗܝܡ *they,* § 10.

ܐܦܪ MB. as O.S. or ܦܪ U. K. or ܦܪ U. *to bake.*

ܐܝܕ or ܩܪܝܪ *to be cold,* p. 120.

ܐܘܕܨ or ܕܨܘ (as O.S.) *to spit.*

ܨܓܐ K. (as O.S.), ܨܓܝ U., ܝܓܨܕ Tkh. *to wish.* So Az. imperative ܓܨܝ *wish.*

ܠܓܝܕܐ for O.S. ܠܠܝܕܐ *ice,* m.

ܐܥܠܬܐ (rare) = ܥܠܬܐ U., ܥܠܬܐ Tkh. *cause, subject.*

ܠܘܡܨܐ U. or ܠܘܡܨܐ U. or ܠܗ ܐܦܨܐ Ti. *fist*, m., perh. from ܠܘܡܨܬܐ *handful*, which is also sometimes inverted to ܠܘܡܨܐ. In N.S. ܠܡܨ = *to hold in the hand*, § 113, m.

ܠܒܝܬܐ f. also as O.S. ܠܓܒܝܢܐ or ܠܓܒܢܐ ܓܒܝܢ *eyebrow*.

ܠܨܘܕܐ = O.S. ܠܨܘܕܐ = ܠܘܨܡܐ Tkh. = ܠܘܡܨܕܐ Ti. *coal*.

ܗܕ, some parts of, § 46.

ܢܘܟ K. *to tumble* or *push down*, perh. = ܢܗܟ K. *to invert* = O.S. ܗܦܟ.

ܣܠܩܦܐ or ܠܢܩܦܐ as Arab. or ܠܒܕ K. *quilt*, m.

ܣܩܒܬܐ or ܡܚܒܬܐ Ti. f. = ܡܚܒܬܐ O.S. m. *needle*.

ܢܗܟ see ܢܘܟ above.

ܚܨܕ as O.S. or ܚܝܨܕ in Baz, *to reap*.

ܣܘܐ or ܣܘܐ *to be worth*, p. 124.

ܟܦܟ *to fold* = O.S. ܟܦܟ (Pa'el).

ܛܥܡܕ a variant in U. for ܛܥܡ *to taste*.

ܡܓܕܠ U. K. = ܡܠܕ Al., O.S. *to bear, lay (eggs)*. So ܡܓܕܝܠ U. K. Az.

ܢܠܘ or ܟܪܘ *to hasten*, p. 107.

ܢܠܦ (as O.S.) and ܟܠܦ *to learn*.

ܩܗܘܕܐ U. ܩܘܕܐ K. *a bond*, see § 112, and p. 288.

ܢܓܝ or ܢܓܝ (the O.S. ܢܓܝ) *to be long*.

ܢܓܛ Al., O.S. or ܢܓܛ Tkh. *to be green* (in O.S. *to be pale*).

ܟܡܪ = O.S. ܟܡܪ or ܐܟܡܪ *to be black*.

ܟܡܪ or ܐܟܡܪ *to shut*, § 113, e.

ܟܕ݂ in K. = ܟܕ݁ܝ U. *to subside*, as a swelling, Heb. שָׁכַךְ.

ܟܣܦܐ Sal. = ܟܘܫܢܐ U. or ܟܘܫܢܐ U. *a kokha* (village officer).

ܠܟܣ, O.S. ܠܢܣ or ܠܚܣ *to lick*.

ܠܡܠܕ or ܡܠܡܠܕ *full to the brim*.

ܠܒܟܐ as Arab. or ܢܠܟܐ *curse*, f.

ܟܡܐ *to lap*, for ܟܪܡ, § 46, p. 118.

ܠܕ݂ or ܠܕܕ݂ܐ or ܕܠܟ all K. *a wood*, m.

ܡܚܠܠܕ or ܡܚܠܚܠܕ K. *to crawl*.

ܡܓܠܕ for ܡܓܠܕ O.S. *to freeze*, see ܠܓܝܕ above.

ܩܒܣܓ U. = N.S. ܚܫܟ *to become dark*, § 83 A. (10).

ܡܚܕܩ or ܡܚܕܚܐ *to push*. See ܫܘܩ above.

ܡܚܕܪܐ from O.S. ܚܕܪ *to go round*.

ܡܚܕܩܕ in the K. sense *to wink*, perhaps for ܡܚܕܩ. =
ܡܚܕܩܕ § 83 A. (2).

ܡܓܨܓܨ or ܡܓܨܓܨ *to clap, chirp*. The latter also *to whisper*.
See below, § 113, e.

ܡܓܕܓ or ܡܓܕܓ *to make a hedge*, p. 265 and § 113, e.

ܡܓܕܓܕ K. from N.S. ܓܕܕ, § 119, *to intertwine*, p. 262.

ܡܠܡܠܕ O.S. *to mumble*, perh. conn. with ܡܠܠ p. 254.

ܡܚܡܗܡ *to whine* = ܡܗܡܗܡ or ܡܚܝܡ, p. 271.

ܡܨܡܕܐ (ܗ often as ܘ) or ܡܨܡܕܐ as O.S. *fine flour*, m.

ܡܚܕܓ K. or ܡܚܓܕ݂ܓ K. or ܡܚܓܕ݂ܓ U. *to wedge in*, p. 274.

ܨܝܐ, some parts of, § 46.

ܡܚܨܕܨܓ or ܡܚܨܕܓ or ܡܚܨܕܡܨ *to wrinkle, crumple*, p. 268.

ܡܚܩܕܚܠ *to tangle*, from N.S. ܩܚܕ K. (O.S. ܣܚܕ) *to tie in a knot*, § 119, and p. 262.

ܡܕܦܪ U. *to throb, twitch*, = O.S. ܕܦ *to wink, flap the wings* (not the same word as ܡܕܦܪ K. or ܡܕܦܪ U. *to throw*).

ܡܓܣܝܕ or ܡܓܣܠܟ *to change*, p. 269.

ܡܓܕܚܣ *to sprawl*, Chald. מָרַח, p. 269.

ܡܓܕܢܟ K. or ܡܓܕܩܣ U. *to break*, O.S. ܚܒܟ, p. 268.

ܢܚܗ K. Al. (as O.S.) or ܢܚܣ K. Al. *to descend*.

ܢܚܟ U. = ܢܚܒ Al., O.S. = ܢܚܨ K. *to attack, hit*.

ܣܚܒ or ܣܚܒ *to be old*, § 46.

ܡܗܟܢܝ or ܡܗܕܝ or ܡܗܕܢܐ Sal. (with ܒ sound) = ܓܗܕܢܐ O.S. *pillow*.

ܡܣܘܩܝ or ܡܣܘܢܝ = O.S. ܡܣܟܘܩܢܐ *threshold*.

ܟܘܗܕܐ or ܟܘܣܕܐ = O.S. ܕܘܣܚܕܐ (whence ܕ in N.S.) *rat, mouse*, m.

ܟܕܪ U. K. or ܕܟܪ U. *to rain, snow*. The former also is *to curdle* (but pron. ܟܕܪ), and in Al. *to hold, hold together*, as O.S. Perhaps the sense of rain or snow is that of drops of water holding together.

ܓܚܬܐ U. Tkh. Sal. = ܒܚܕܐ Ti. = ܓܚܕܐ Al., O.S. *nine*, m.

ܓܚܓܐ Tkh. = ܒܚܓܐ Sh. = ܓܚܒܕ Ti. = ܓܚܒܕ Al. = ܗܒܕ O.S. *nine*, f.

ܦܓ U. = ܣܦܓ K. (O.S. ܣܦܓ) *to lose taste*, also in K. *to be disliked*.

ܦܕܢܐ U. or ܦܕܢܐ K. = ܟܘܦܐ O.S. *branch*, m. (in Al. ܕܘܡܣܐ).

ܦܣܢܐ U. K. = ܦܣܢܐ Tkh. *flower*, m., p. 289.

§ 92] METATHESIS. 297

ܨܵܦܹܐ K. = ܨܵܦܹܐ U. *to be strained* (liquids), Chald. צף *to be pressed*, [the first also *to leak, to dry up*, the second *to be pure or clear*].

ܡܨܲܡܓܸܕ = ܡܚܓܸܕ = ܓܲܡܓܸܕ Tergawar, *to crouch, die,* used of dogs and non-Christians.

ܡܲܓܕܹܠܐ Tkh. *raven,* for ܢܲܡܓܕܵܐ = ܢܲܡܓܸܕ p. 289 ?

ܩܠܝܼܕܵܐ U. K. = ܩܠܝܼܕܵܐ O.S. Al. Bo. = κλεῖδα, *key,* f. [Greek words are constantly taken into Syriac from the accusative, as now in Greece the accusative remains in common speech to the exclusion of the nominative.] In Kurd. *qlîl*.

ܩܘܕܫܢܝܐ or ܗܿܘ *a Qudshanis man.*

ܩܝܼܪ Al. = ܩܝܪܐ p. 107. Distinguish ܩܝܪ *to be cold,* p. 109.

ܩܲܠܡܵܐ as O.S. m. f. = Arab. ܩܡܠܗ *louse.*

ܩܝܘ U. Tkh. or ܩܝܘ or ܩܝܒ K. *to gather* (clothes).

ܪܕܵܐ = ܪܕܐ Sp. *to be tired,* p. 118.

ܪܥܐ K., also ܪܥܐ K. (O.S. ܪ) *to think,* p. 303.

ܪܟܸܒ often in U. for ܪܟܒ *I ride,* p. 130.

ܪܘܣܝܹܐ or ܪܘܣܝܐ *permission,* f., Arab.

ܪܟܕ or ܪܟܕ K. *to find out about* (so N.S. ܪܟܕ p. 98), *receive news.* O.S. ܪܟܕ ?

ܪܚܡ U. as Arab. = ܪܚܡ Al. also as Arab. *to be in love,* p. 109.

ܪܚܛ *to run about or away,* also in K. *to wrench,* for ܪܨܚ. Cf. O.S. ܪܚܨ *to break,* Heb. רצץ *to run about.* Cf. O.S. and N.S. ܫܘܩܐ *a bazaar, street.*

ܪܩܕ ܓܪܩܐ or ܓܪܩܐ *a lizard,* p. 34.

ܬܢܘܪܐ, usually ܬܢܘܪܐ as O.S., *an oven in the ground,* p. 232.

S. GR.   38

§ 93. A noun is often repeated for emphasis, or to express a collective substantive, or for some such reason, and the first letter is then changed to Mim. The second time the noun is sometimes shortened. Thus ܙܘܿܙܹܐ ܡܘܿܙܹܐ *all sorts of money*; ܢܵܫܵܐ ܡܵܫܵܐ *a kind of man*; ܟܬܵܒ݂ܵܐ ܡܬܵܒ݂ܵܐ or ܟܬܵܒ݂ܵܐ ܡܟܬܵܒ݂ܵܐ *some sort of a book*; ܠܒ݂ܘܿܫܹܐ ܡܒ݂ܘܿܫܹܐ *passenger's luggage* (clothes and things of a similar nature) etc. This is only colloquial, and we may compare the English nursery language, 'Georgey-porgey' and the like. The same sense is rarely obtained by adding ܓܕܓܒ § 25 (3).

§ 94. *Irregular aspiration in N.S.*

In the following cases letters are aspirated in N.S., where according to the analogy of O.S. they should be hard.

a. When the ground form has an aspirate, or the reverse, all the inflections and almost always all the derivatives have the same in N.S.; thus we have for the present of the verb *to steal* ܓܵܢܹܒ݂, ܓܵܢܒ݂ܵܐ: not ܓܵܢܒܵܐ (ܒ) as in O.S. § 84; so causatives follow the primitives and not the rule in O.S. that 'the radical following the Aph'el preformative is soft, the next hard, the next soft'. Thus ܡܓ݂ܲܟ݂ܸܒ݂ (ܒ) not ܡܓ݂ܲܟ݂ܒ݂ (ܟ) as O.S. *to give in marriage*; and so several causatives or virtual causatives which have no primitive, as ܡܓ݂ܲܕܓ݂ܸܡ, not ܡܓ݂ܲܕܓܸܡ, *to rebuke, scold*; so also verbs derived from nouns, or other verbs, as ܡܓ݂ܲܕ݂ܓ݂ܸܒ݂ *to have leprosy*, from ܓܲܕ݂ܒ݂ܵܐ O.S. and N.S. (ܓ U.) *leprosy*, m. f.; ܟܵܒܹܣ U. *to become dark*, same as ܫܓ݂ܲܡ (both ܓ); ܡܓ݂ܲܕܓܸܒ݂ *to cloud over*, from ܟܒ݂ܒ݂ܵܐ O.S. and N.S. *cloud*, p. 45, from which we must distinguish ܟܲܕ݂ܒ݂ܵܐ (ܒ) *shame*, pronounced respectively *éwa, oiba*. But we have ܡܲܣܬܘܵܒ݂ܵܐ *old age*, and ܛܲܝܒ݂ܘܵܬ݂ܵܐ *grace*, as O.S. (the latter not colloquial) from ܬܳܐܒ, ܬܘܳܒ. We have ܗܶܢܓܘܳܓܐ U. K. Al., O.S. *repentance*, against ܬܝܳܒܘܬ: but ܬܘܳܒ K. Al. We find ܪܳܟܒ U. (foreign) and ܪܟܳܒ U. both = *rider* (the former in Al. is *a nobleman*); ܓܶܢܙܢܐ (foreign) *library*, f., against ܟܬܒ *to write*, ܟܬܳܒܐ *book*, m.; ܒܥܶܬܓܢܬܐ = ܒܥܶܬܓܢܐ *female*; and so some others.

b. The ܟܝ in the pronominal affixes of the second person is soft, as against the forms which probably correspond to them in O.S. See § 11.

c. In Tkhuma, Ṭiari, Alqosh and neighbouring districts the terminations ܬܐ܆, ܐܘܬܐ܆, have ܬ soft, as against O.S. Thus ܣܘܪܰܝܬܐ *a Syrian woman* (O.S. ܬ); ܡܰܘܬܐ *death* (O.S. ܬ). So ܒܰܝܬܐ *house* (O.S. ܬ). This of course only applies to the districts where ܬ and ܦ are at any time aspirated. In Upper Ṭiari the endings ܬܐ܆, ܬܐ܆, are always pronounced *ésha*, see below, § 124.

d. In Tkhuma the ܬ in the second person personal pronouns and endings of verbs is soft. Thus ܐܰܢܬ *thou*, m.; ܝܬܘܢ *you are*, pl. But ܐܢܬܘܢ *you*, has ܬ hard.

e. The first radical of verbs in either conjugation should by the usual N.S. rule be hard, but there are the following exceptions:—

ܟܐܒ Al. *to be sorry.*	ܦܗܘܡ (ܦ) Al. Bo. Z. *to understand, remember.*
ܟܒܫ U. *to conquer.* In K. 'ܟ.	
ܟܒܫ Al. *to subdue.*	ܡܫܰܓܪ or ܡܫܓܪ Al. *to dine.*

Also in Al. Bo. Z. a few other foreign verbs beginning with Pe.

f. The following are exceptions to the rule that the second radical of second conjugation triliterals should be hard:

ܡܟܰܢܒ *to clean, prune,* in K. *to cauterize* (under influence of ܕܟܐ *to be clean*).

ܡܕܝܕ *to inform*, in Ashitha, elsewhere with hard Dalath.

The verb ܡܗܝܡܠ or ܡܗܝܢܠ is sometimes spelt with medial ܒ, but this seems to be inaccurate, see § 47.

g. The names of the first five days in the week in N.S. universally have ܒ for O.S. ܒ̇, as ܚܘܒܫܒܐ for ܚܕܒܫܒܐ. In N.S. the ܒ makes a diphthong with the Pthakha: as *kho-shiba*.

h. Also the following:

ܐܬܐ : ܐܬܘ MB. Sh. *come* (Imp.), ܐܬܝܡܐ : ܐܬܝܡܘܢ Tkh. *id.* = O.S. ܬܐ : ܬܘ § 46.

ܟܝܒܢܐ U. = ܟܒܝܢܐ O.S. (ܒ̇) *beggar*, § 88, *g.*

ܡܘܪܟܐ = O.S. ܐܘܪܟܐ *length*, m.

ܠܝܬ in K. *lath* or *lĭth*, Al. *léth*, U. *lĭt*, *there is not*, O.S. ܠܝܬ. But ܠܝܬ ܠܝ in Al. is *lăti*.

ܟܘܒܒܐ see p. 291.

ܥܪܒܐ J. K. = ܥܪܒܐ U., O.S. = ܥܪܒܐ Diz *sheep*, § 88, *h.*

§ 95. *Irregular hardening in N.S.*

In the following cases the O.S. rule is not followed.

a. ܬ and ܦ are always hard in U. J. Sal. Q. Gawar, etc. Also see below, p. 303.

b. In the second conjugation the preformative ܡܲ does not soften the following letter, whether the ܡܲ have a vowel or not, e.g. ܡܕܩܠܠ (ܕ) = O.S. ܡܕܩܠܠ (ܕ̣) *to thin out*; ܡܕܒܚ = O.S. ܡܕܒܚ (ܕ̇) *to cause to be sacrificed*. And so with virtual causatives such as ܡܟܪܙ *to preach*, O.S. ܡܟܪܙ; ܡܟܣܠ *to be lazy*, Arab.; ܡܟܣܦ K. *to give* or *take interest*, cf. O.S. ܟܣܦܐ *money*; ܡܙܕܩ *to justify*, § 119.

c. The prepositions ܒ, ܠ, ܕ, and the conjunction ܘ do not aspirate the following consonant as in O.S., nor do they take a vowel, unless perhaps a half Zlama (see page 290); thus ܕܒܟܬܒܐ N.S. = ܕܒܟܬܒܐ (ܒ) O.S. *which is in the book.*

d. Contrary to O.S. analogy the second radical in the first conjugation is hard in N.S. in the following verbs, mostly of foreign origin:

ܟܦܦ *to foam,* cf. N.S. ܟܦܘ or ܟܦܘܟ *foam,* f.

ܟܦܢ Al. *to grieve,* p. 299.

ܕܒܚ K. *to cut up* (sheep, etc.), cf. N.S. ܕܒܚ as O.S. *to sacrifice.*

ܕܒܠ Al. = ܙܒܠ K., § 123, *to subdue.*

ܕܒܪ K. *to eat one's fill.*

ܕܒܫ K. *to be sticky,* cf. N.S. and O.S. ܕܒܫܐ *honey,* m.

ܕܟܪ *to strike* with the hand or fist. Distinguish ܕܟܪ *to remember.*

ܙܕܠ *to fear,* § 83, D, *c.*

ܚܒܩ for ܚܒܩ *to hug,* cf. O.S. ܚܘܒܩܐ *an embrace,* Chald. חֲבַק *to hug;* so Heb.

ܚܒܪ *to find out,* cf. N.S. ܚܒܪܐ *word, news,* m., Arab.

ܟܡܠ K. *to grow perfect,* cf. ܡܟܡܠܐ § 81 (5), Arab.

ܛܒܥ *to sink,* U. K. *print,* Al. (ܛ from Arab.) O.S. ܛܒܥ, cf. O.S. and N.S. ܛܒܥܐ *a die,* m., and ܛܒܥ Al. *to sink into sleep.*

ܝܬܒ (ܬ) U. K., 'ܐ Al., *to sit,* O.S. ܝܬܒ (ܬ).

ܪܡܙ *to beckon.*

ܠܚܟ *to lick,* p. 295, (hardening so as to distinguish Kap and Khéith).

ܡܟܟ *to be gentle,* O.S. ܡܟ, cf. O.S. and N.S. participial adjective ܡܟܝܟܐ *gentle,* whence is derived ܟ in the N.S. verb.

ܢܟܬ Ti. *to bite*, § 120, *c*.

ܣܒܪ *to trust, venture, talk, not to be homesick;* and with a ܦ sound *to expect*, cf. O.S. ܣܒܪ *to hope, think*, ܣܲܒܲܪ *to expect, announce*, and O.S. ܣܒܪܐ *hope*, N.S. ܣܒܪܐ *contentment* (sense from Arab.).

ܣܟܬ *to be hushed*, Arab.

ܣܟܪ Tkh. (ܟ J.) *to dam up, fill* = O.S. ܣܟܪ *to shut*, § 77 (2).

ܥܬܩ K. *to be old;* O.S. ܥ, N.S. ܐ under influence of ܥܬܝܩܐ *ancient*, § 81 (5).

ܦܟܗ K.; O.S. ܦܟܗ, § 92, *b*, p. 296.

ܩܘܐ K. (ܒ U., O.S.) *to collect as water in a reservoir*, also (K.) *to be angry;* ܩܘܐ is *to bail water.* Cf. O.S. ܩܘܐ or ܩܘܒܬܐ *a reservoir;* N.S. ܩܘܐ *a mug*, m.

ܩܒܠ K. Al. *to receive* = O.S. ܩܒܠ, and U. ܡܩܒܠ; hence ܒ. ܩܒܠ is *to complain:* also in K. *to prosecute*, as O.S.

ܪܦܐ *to be tired*, pp. 118, 297.

ܪܟܒ, in U. Z. Al. *to ride*, p. 130, O.S. ܪܟܒ or ܪܟܸܒ, cf. N.S. and O.S. ܪܲܟܵܒܵܐ *rider* (whence ܘ in the N.S. verb).

ܪܟܟ *to be soft*, cf. O.S. ܪܟ and ܪܲܟܸܟ *to make soft*, and cf. O.S., N.S. ܪܲܟܝܼܟܵܐ *soft* (whence ܘ in the N.S. verb).

ܫܒܗ K. *to be like*, Arabic, cf. ܡܫܲܒܸܗ Al. = O.S. ܫܲܒܸܗ *to liken*.

ܫܟܣ K. *to be innocent, guileless.*

ܫܟܐ Al. *to accuse*, Arab.

ܬܒܥ *to adhere to, to be a follower of*, Arabic, cf. O.S. ܬܒܥ *to follow for vengeance.*

ܐܓܰܪ to remain firm, K. to stay, Al., Arab.

ܐܓܶܣ K. to thrust, prod, O.S. ܐܓܶܣ. See ܢܓܶܣ § 104.

e. In the following verbs the last letter is hard.

All verbs ending in ܠ and ܒ make those letters hard in the preterite except in Al., e.g. ܚܓܶܒܽܘܟ I did, ܐܶܡܪܶܒ Ti. I said (= ܐܶܡܪܶܒ).

First Conjugation—

ܒܠܰܕ to be busy.

ܒܪܰܟ to kneel, O.S. ܒܪܰܟ and ܒܪܰܟ. The hard ܟ from N.S. ܒܶܪܟܳܐ (O.S. ܕܟ) a knee.

ܓܚܶܟ (but ܓܚܶܟ Ti.) to laugh, O.S. ܓܚܶܟ or ܓܚܶܟ. The hard ܟ from N.S. ܓܶܚܟܳܐ (O.S. ܕܟ) laughter.

ܕܠܶܒ U. or ܫܠܶܒ K. to conquer, Arab. غلب, O.S. ܢܟܶܒ, p. 299.

ܕܪܰܟ to fill up (ܕܪܰܟ K. is to trample, strike = Chald. דְּרַךְ to tread).

ܕܘܶܒ to sweat, O.S. ܠ, cf. ܕܶܘܒܳܐ (O.S. ܕܟ) sweat.

ܕܪܰܟ K. to beat down (earth), O.S. ܕܪܰܟ, hard ܟ from O.S. ܕܘܪܟܬܐ a footstep?

ܗܘܶܓ K. or ܕܗܓ K. to think, see § 92, perh. ܠ from O.S. ܗܘܶܓܳܠ meditation.

ܘܠܶܒ to put out (the eyes).

ܘܓܶܡ to be sullen, Arab.

ܫܘܶܙ to curry (horses), O.S. ܫܘܶܙ and ܒܚܶܙ; Arab. and Chald. root ܣܚܫ, the hard ܟ in N.S. from Arab.

ܫܚܶܡ to be dark, O.S. ܟ, cf. ܚܶܫܟܳܐ darkness, m., p. 290.

ܛܠܒ *to ask for*, Arab.

ܢܬܠ U. *to pluck*, O.S. ܬܠ.

ܢܗܒ Al. *to rob, take captive*, Arab.

ܢܩܒ K. (ܒ from Arab.) *to make a hole, make hollow*, O.S. ܒ, cf. O.S. and N.S. ܢܩܒܐ *eye of a needle*, m. (ܒ N.S., ܒ O.S.) and ܢܩܒܬܐ *female*, f., which has ܒ in both languages. Cf. ܢܘܩܒܬܐ p. 47.

ܣܠܒ *to rob, take captive*, Arab.

ܪܓܒ K. Al. *to be pleased, will* (usually impersonally), cf. ܪܓܒܘܬܐ Al. *will*, Arab.

ܪܥܒ Al. *to torment*, Arab.

ܦܪܟ U. = ܦܪܟܗ for which see above (*d*).

ܦܪܟ *to stab, burst* (so Chald. Pa'el, but ܟ). The hard ܟ to distinguish it from ܦܪܟ as O.S. *to chafe*, and ܦܪܚ as O.S. *to fly*.

ܣܠܟ *to turn aside*, Arab.

ܕܪܠ, see ܕܪܠܐ above (*d*).

ܕܘܠ K. *to finish, be ready*.

ܕܥܠ or ܕܥܣ Tkh., see § 92.

ܫܟܟ U. (or ܫܟܥ K.) *to subside* as a swelling, or *escape* as wind from a bladder, § 92, (root ܫܟܟ in Heb. *to subside*, whence hard ܟ).

ܫܠܠ *to pluck*, O.S. ܫܠܚ? (also in Al. Ti. ܫܠܦ is *to pluck*, in O.S. *to extract*).

ܫܪܟ *to partake*, as Arab. So N.S. ܫܪܝܟܐ *partaker*, m. Distinguish O.S. and N.S. ܫܪܟܐ *remainder*, O.S. ܫܪܟ *to remain*.

ܥܪܟ *to fasten the eyes* K., *be dirty* K., *get a bad name* K., *plant* U.

ܥܕܠ *to give up* (a bad habit) Kurd., Arab.

Second Conjugation triliterals:

ܡܲܓ̰ܘܸܒ U. or ܡܓ̰ܘܸܒ K. *to answer*, Arab. etc. = O.S. ܓ̰ܵܘܸܒ.

ܡܓ̰ܲܪܸܒ *to tempt, try*, Arab.

ܡܗܲܘܸܠ K. *to air before the fire*, cf. N.S. ܗܘܿܠܵܐ *steam*, m.

ܡܲܙܘܸܓ U. ܡܙܘܸܓ K. *to join, marry*, O.S. ܙܲܘܸܓ Pa'el. For ܓ cf. N.S. and O.S. ܙܘܿܓܵܐ *a pair*, m., ζεῦγος.

ܚܒܸܒ *to love*, O.S. ܚܲܒܸܒ and ܐܲܚܸܒ. For ܒ cf. O.S. and N.S. ܚܘܼܒܵܐ *love*, m.

ܡܫܲܠܸܠ *to be* or *make lame*, Kurd. So N.S. ܫܲܠܵܐ or ܫܲܠܸܠ *lame*.

ܡܣܲܪܸܓ *to saddle*, O.S. Pa'el. For ܓ cf. O.S. and N.S. ܣܲܪܓܵܐ *a saddle*, m.

ܡܥܲܓ̰ܸܒ *to wonder*. See ܥܲܓ̰ܸܒ above.

ܡܥܲܕܸܒ K. Al. *to torment*. See ܥܲܕܸܒ above.

ܡܲܟܸܪܸܟ or ܡܟܲܪܸܟ. Same as ܟܲܪܸܟ above (all hard Kap).

ܡܲܬܘܸܒ U. *to repent*, Arabic. In K. Al. ܬܵܝܸܒ, also Al. ܡܬܲܝܸܒ, O.S. ܬܵܒ.

ܡܬܲܘܸܟ K. (or ܡܬܲܘܸܟ) *to uphold*.

ܡܬܲܪܸܓ U. Same as ܬܲܪܸܓ above.

f. In the following quadriliterals the second or fourth radical is hard:

ܡܓܲܒܓܸܒ (or ܡܓܲܒܓܸܒ) *to foam, scum*. See ܓܒܵܐ above (*d*).

ܡܲܓܲܠܓܸܠ or ܡܓܲܠܓܸܠ K. *to crawl*.

ܡܕܲܪܕܸܒ *to be doubleminded*, U., *to be much patched*, K.

ܡܕܓ݂ܕܸܓ݂ *to trot,* tr., or ܡܕܓ݂ܕܸܓ݂.

ܡܕܲܡܕܸܪ *to peck.*

ܡܕܘܕܹܐ (in Tkh. ܘ is like ܣ) *to litter, dung* = ܡܕܘܙܸܠ K. as O.S. Pa. See ܘܬܸܠ *below* (g).

ܡܕܘܕܹܐ U. = ܡܘܕܹܐ Al. See § 123.

ܡܕܘܚܘܹܐ *to be pale.* In K. *to prod, prick,* § 83 (2).

ܡܢܲܕܹܐ U. *to be or take cold* = ܡܢܲܬܸܠ U. In Al. ܡܢܲܬܸܠ = *to spoil,* tr., as O.S.

ܡܢܒܘܕܸܓ݂ *to injure.*

ܡܕܲܚܸܢ *to arm oneself,* Kurdish.

ܡܕܲܓ݂ܕܸܓ݂ *to be dry or thirsty, crackle as a dry kettle.* In U. *to sob.*

ܡܕܲܟܗܸܕ *to pant,* § 45, g.

ܡܕܲܟܕܸܠ *to prod,* § 83 (2).

ܡܕܲܢܚܸܢ *to groan,* perh. O.S. ܐܸܬܐܲܢܲܚ.

ܡܕܲܗܡܸܗ *to wander about.*

ܡܕܲܩܠܸܩ *to stammer.*

ܡܕܲܟܕܸܟ *to shrink, slip from the hand.*

ܡܕܲܢܟܘܸܢ *to pull wool, tear.* In K. *to whisper,* §§ 113, e, 123.

ܡܕܲܓ݂ܕܸܓ݂ K. *to boil food,* under influence of O.S. ܕܲܟܹܐ *to soften.*

ܡܕܲܟܕܸܟ *to tremble, shiver,* O.S. ܕܵܟ = ܡܕܲܟܕܹܟ K. and ܡܕܲܨܕܸܨ K.

ܡܕܲܟܕܸܠ *to sew loosely, tuck.*

ܡܕܲܓ݂ܟܸܢ *to weave loosely,* K., *shake,* U.

ܡܕܲܠܸܕ *to guide, govern.* See § 83 (14).

[§ 95]   HARDENING.

ܡܕܲܟܕܸܟ to tack, stitch, be pitted with small pox.

g. Also the following have irregularly hard letters:

ܐܝܼܬ there is, before ܠ, as ܐܝܼܬܠܝܼ I have.

ܐܸܫܬܵܐ six (f.), K., O.S. ܐܸܫܬܵܐ.

ܒܝܲܕ by means of, O.S. ܒܝܲܕ.

ܟܣܘܿܦܵܐ a gull, m., O.S. ܓܵܟ ' one who laughs, cf. ܓܵܚܸܟ above (e).

ܕܘܿܓܠܵܐ lie, m. Should by rule be ܠ, § 84 (8) and so it is in Al. and O.S. For ܠ cf. ܡܕܲܓܸܠ to lie.

ܘܸܓܠܵܐ litter, dung, m., O.S. ܘܸܓܠܵܐ. See ܡܕܘܿܟܸܐ above (f). ܕ under Arabic influence.

ܚܕܸܥܣܲܪ eleven, O.S. ܣܲܓ (ܕ).

ܫܸܣܦܵܐ a currycomb, m., as the verb ܫܲܣܸܦ to curry. See above (e).

ܣܲܟܝܼܢܵܐ f. and ܣܲܟܝܼܢܬܵܐ knife, in spite of § 84 (2) because of O.S. ܣܲܟܝܼܢܵܐ id., which has hard Kap in accordance with § 84 (5).

ܥܕܵܢܵܐ time, f., O.S. ܥܕܵܢܵܐ (hence ܕ).

ܥܸܩܒܵܐ heel, f., O.S. ܥܸܩܒܵܐ.

ܦܲܕܵܢܵܐ plough, f., in spite of § 84 (2), because of O.S. ܦܲܕܵܢܵܐ.

ܐܸܨܒܲܥ (ܛ like ܩ) finger, f., O.S. ܐܸܨܒܲܥ. So Al. ܨܘܿܕܬܵܐ § 89, b (ܕ through Arabic).

ܐܸܬܡܸܠ yesterday, O.S. commonly ܐܸܬܡܵܠܝ, but ܐܸܬܡܸܠ is also found, § 86.

ܕܘܿܟܵܐ f. and ܕܘܿܟܬܵܐ place, have ܕ against § 84 (8), and so in O.S.

h. Generally when words have their last letter hard, especially if other than verbs, they may be presumed to be foreign words: such as ܦܝܘܿܬ answer, m., ܕܲܩ steep, ܚܲܓܸܓ indeed, ܣܲܒܸܬ because.

Interchange of the Consonants, etc.

§ 96. ܐ prosthetic is very common in N.S. as also in O.S. We thus have many Greek words beginning with στ (ܣܛ'), σχ (ܣܟ'), etc., as ܐܣܟܘܠܝܐ *a scholar* [ܐܣܟܘܠܐ *school*, is rare, ܡܕܪܫܬܐ being used instead], ܐܣܛܦܢܘܣ *Stephen*, ܐܣܛܘܟܣܐ *elements* (στοιχεῖα). So:—

ܐܚܢܢ or ܐܚܢܝ or ܐܚܢܢܝ *we*, O.S. ܚܢܢ (old form ܐܢܚܢܢ).

ܐܚܛܝܬܐ Sal. or ܚܛ' Sal., = ܚܛܝܬܐ O.S., U. K. Al. *sin*.

ܐܚܪܐ *dung*, for ܚܪܐ, = O.S. ܚܪܐ.

ܐܠܬܚܬ *below*, O.S. ܠܬܚܬ, Al. ܠܬܚܬ § 67.

ܐܟܡܐ Al. = ܟܡܐ *how much?* § 67.

ܐܡܐ *hundred*, O.S. ܡܐܐ (also N.S., § 26).

ܐܩܠܐ f. *foot*, perh. for ܐܪܓܠܐ = O.S. ܪܓܠܐ.

ܐܪܚܝܐ U. 'ܐ K. *a mill*, f., for ܪܚܝܐ : O.S. ܪܚܝܐ.

ܐܪܡܘܢܐ or 'ܪ or ܪܡܘܢܐ K. or ܐܪܡܘܢܐ Ti. m., = O.S. ܪܘܡܢܐ *pomegranate*.

ܐܫܒܥ Tkh. Q. (ܫ Ti. Ash. Sh. Al.) *seven*, f., O.S. ܫܒܥ.

ܐܫܒܥܣܪ K. *seventeen*, O.S. ܫܒܥܣܪ etc.

ܐܫܒܛ (ܫ) *February*, m., or in K. as O.S. ܫܒܛ.

ܐܫܬܐ *six*, m. (so also O.S. sometimes), and so all derivatives.

ܐܬܫܥܐ *nine*, K., and so derivatives, see §§ 26—28.

So sometimes in Al. with ܠ, ܒ; e.g. ܠܒܝܬܝ, pron. *ĕlbéthi*. On the other hand ܣܦܪܓܠܐ = O.S. ܐܣܦܪܓܠܐ m. *quince*; and see p. 280.

§ 97. ܓ has the sound of ܟ in ܓܲܦܠܵܐ *in the midst.*

So ܬܲܚܡܸܙܬܵܐ Sal. *pillow,* § 92.

ܚܓܸܪ *to wish,* in MB. and so ܒܓܸܪ in Tkh., § 46.

ܫܲܓܸܦ *to hug,* § 95, *d.*

ܡܓܲܘܸܓ Sp. *to squirt milk from an udder.*

ܡܲܟܓܸܟ *to foam,* § 95, *f.*

ܡܓܲܡܸܓ, in U., but ܟ in K., *to say grace,* O.S. ܗܲܡܢܸܟ = *grace after meat,* also *compline,* because said in the monasteries after the only full meal of the day (ܣܓܸܕ *to be satisfied,* O.S. ܣܒܸܥ).

ܡܲܓܡܸܓ K. (sometimes) *to look closely* Ti., *make firm,* Tkh. *punish,* Tkh.

ܣܲܓܸܕ *to expect,* § 95, *d.*

ܓܸܪܵܐ *finger,* f., O.S. ܥܸܒܥܵܐ.

ܟ has the sound of ܓ in ܐܲܠܦܹܐ *Alaps:* pl. of ܐܲܠܦ f. (not in sing.).

So ܡܲܫܓܸܕ *to incite, be industrious,* O.S. ܢܫܸܕ.

ܡܒܲܓܸܟ *to search,* (but ܟ sound in K.), § 83 (12). There is also ܡܒܲܓܸܕ *to mix up:* O.S. ܣܓܲܟ *to enclose, include.*

ܦܲܕܵܢܵܐ *a plough,* f., in the district of Narwa, where ܦ retains its sound, §§ 85, 104.

ܦܲܓܸܕ (in Baz) *to be warm or thirsty, to fear greatly.* Elsewhere Pe. In U. ܦܲܓܸܥ.

ܦܓܸܕ (in Tkh.) *to be crooked,* § 113, *j.* Elsewhere Pe.

So ܕܲܓܸܙ *bastard* = Turk. پیج; ܕܓܸܕ *brass* = Turk. پرنج; perh. ܓܘܦܬܵܐ *cheese* = O.S. ܓܒܸܬܵܐ (root ܚܠܒ). For ܘܲܩܦܵܐ see § 107.

Probably also ܡܒܼܢܕܝܚ = ܡܒܼܢܕܘܟ, both *to push*; and ܡܓܼܣܓܕ = ܡܓܼܣܓܠ both *to change*. See above, § 92.

ܒܥܫܩ *plate*, has ܦ sound in sing., ܒ sound in pl.

ܒ is silent after, or coalesces with Rwaṣa, as ܩܘܼܒܠ *against*. ܒ is silent in ܗܘܼܒܠ *give* (imperative) = O.S. ܗܲܒ, and its plural. So in ܡܗܘܼܒܠܬܐ Tkh. *the act of giving*, § 46. Perhaps ܠܗܒܐ *a flame*, m. = לַהַב Chald. and Heb., cf. O.S. ܫܲܠܗܸܒ *to flame*. ܒ is often silent in the imp. of verbs ܥܒܒ, see § 41, as ܫܘܼܒܘܩ *leave alone*, pronounced *shuq* or *shwuq*.

§ 98. ܠ is silent in many words, chiefly in those which have ܠ̣ in O.S. The transition from ܠ̣ to ܠ is a very natural one. So ܦܠܓ K. (rare in U.) or ܡܦܠܓ U. Al. or ܡܦܠܓ K. *to divide*, in Al. sometimes ܡܦܠܓ ܦܠܓ = O.S. ܦܠܓ *to divide into two parts*, ܦܠܓ *to divide into several parts*, also *to doubt*. Cf. ܦܠܓܘ, ܦܠܓܐ p. 103. The ܠ remains in ܦܠܓܐ *half*, m. (O.S. ܦ̈) and in the O.S. phrase retained still and always now prefixed to the Nicene Creed: ܒܫܪܪܐ ܠܒܪ ܕܠܐ ܦܘܠܓܐ *in truth and without doubt*. So:—

ܕܓܠ *to look intently*, O.S. ܕܓܠ p. 98.

ܐܦ U., ܐܦ K. Z. = ܐܦ Z. *also*, p. 161.

ܠܓܡܐ *a bridle, bit*, m., O.S. ܠܓܡܐ § 89; in K. Sh. *a jaw*.

ܐܓܪ Al. *to hire*, O.S. ܐܓܪ. Hence Al. ܐܓܝܪܐ *a hired servant*.

ܡܓܢܐ K. *a shield*, f., O.S. ܡܓܢܐ.

ܡܙܓ or ܡܙܓ as O.S. *to mix liquids*: esp. *hot and cold water*.

ܢܓܗ K. *to dawn*, O.S. ܢܓܗ.

ܢܓܗܐ K. *the dawn*, m., O.S. ܢܓܗܐ or ܢܘܓܗܐ.

ܢܪܓܐ *small axe, chopper*, m., O.S. ܢܪܓܐ. Pronounced in N.S. *nar'a*, as if with ܥ for ܓ.

ܣܝܓ K. *to make a hedge*, O.S. ܣܓ.

ܣܝܓܐ Al. *avenue* (= ܣܒܚܒܝ U.), O.S. ܣܝܓܐ *a hedge* or *loose wall*.

ܪܓܘܠܐ m. and ܪܓܘܠܬܐ, see p. 230.

ܪܓܫ *to feel, to wake*, O.S. ܪܓܫ.

ܫܓܕܐ *almond*, m., § 88, *h*.

ܫܓܪ *to kindle*, O.S. ܫܓܪ.

ܫܓܫ *to shake*, O.S. ܫܓܫ (we have also N.S. ܫܓܝܫ *to disturb*).

ܫܘܓܠܐ m. *business, affair* = Kurd., Turk. *shughul*.

ܫܪܓܐ and ܫܪܓܬܐ *a native lamp*, f. = O.S. ܫܪܓܐ m.

The ܓ falls in all parts of these verbs, and in their causatives.

§ 99. ܓ and ܓ̰ are frequently interchanged, the former being more used in U., the latter in Ṭiari, as ܓ̰ܝܢܐ or ܓܝܢܐ *soul, self*; ܒܕ ܓ̰ܝܒܝ or ܒܕ ܓܝܒܝ *instead of me*.

For ܓ and ܨ see below, § 113, *m*.

§ 100. There is no ܓ̰ in O.S. In N.S. it comes in various ways.

a. It represents ج or چ in words from Arabic, Persian, Turkish, etc., as ܓ̰ܘܢܣ U. *nice*, ܓ̰ܡܥ *sum total*.

b. In some cases it corresponds with ܓ of O.S. as ܓ̰ܠܓ̰ܠ *to split open* (a vessel or skin), *to be talkative*, perh. O.S. ܓܠܓܠ *to uncover*, ܓ̰ܪܕ *to scrape*, = N.S., O.S. ܓܪܕ: also in N.S. *to strip leaves* (as in

Arab.), ܠܵܚܹܕ݂ in K. *to rake mud*, as O.S. ܠܚܕ݂, also *to slide* (Jamal from Arab.), ܪܵܓ݂ܹܡ *to stone* (a person), as O.S. ܪܓ݂ܡ (Jamal from Arab.), ܡܚܲܩܹܓ݂ K. *to look on at a show*, perh. O.S. ܚܕ݂ܝ *to amuse oneself*, ܡܚܲܕ݂ܹܓ݂ also, as O.S. ܡܚܲܕ݂ܹܓ݂ *to interpret* (Jamal from Arab.). For ܓܠܸܒ cf. *h*, below.

c. Perhaps ܓ = ܚ in ܪܵܓܹܕ݂ *to be numb*, for ܪܵܚܹܕ݂ from O.S. ܪܚܕ݂ *to feel*, see ܡܚܲܕ݂ܹܓ݂ or ܡܚܲܕ݂ܹܓ݂ below (*h*).

d. ܓ = ܘ in ܓܵܘܹܫ *to move*, intr., probably = Chald. ܢܘܫ *id.*; ܢܵܓܹܙ U. = ܢܵܘܹܙ K. *to rebuke*; ܢܵܓܹܒ K. = ܢܵܘܹܒ U. *to shoot with a gun, peck*, perhaps connected with O.S. and N.S. ܢܘܩܵܒ݂ܐ *a dot*, m. and ܢܵܟ݂ܘ Ti. *to bite*, § 120, *c.*

e. ܓ = ܐ in ܐܘܪܡܸܓ݂ܢܵܝܐ or ܐܘܪܡܸܐܢܵܝܐ *an Urmi man*, § 81 (1).

f. ܓ = ܚ in ܡܚܲܕ݂ܹܓ݂ *to crawl, creep* = O.S. ܕܚܠ. Perhaps this is connected with ܕܸܚܕ݂ܵܐ *insect*, m. (O.S. ܪܚܫܵܐ) and ܡܚܲܕ݂ܓܸܕ݂ *to creep*, ܢܸܓ݂ܠܵܐ *ant*, m. ܓ = ܚ in ܚܘܓܵܐ m. *calf* = O.S. ܡܘܚܫܢܵܐ (μόσχος).

g. ܓ = ܩ in ܡܓܸܨܒ U. also ܡܩܸܨܒ *to sprout* (also ܡܓܝܼܕ K.)— same root as N.S. ܨܲܥ *to be green*, O.S. ܝܘܩܢܵܐ *green*.

h. ܓ = ܒ in ܓܠܸܒ K. *to snatch*, for ܒܠܸܒ § 95; cf. ܕܘܢܵܒ݂ܵܐ Ti. = 's ܒܸܓ݂ U. § 16; ܓܠܸܒ *to strip off* (bark, or the skin) = ܒܠܸܒ *to strip*, O.S. ܓܠܸܒ; ܡܓܝܼܒ U. *to rust*, from N.S. ܓܝܼܒ U. or ܒܝܼܓ K. *rust*, m., Kurd.; ܡܚܲܕ݂ܹܓ݂ U. also ܡܚܲܕ݂ܹܓ݂ K. *to be numb*, perhaps from ܪܚܕ݂ O.S. *to feel*. Cf. ܪܵܓܹܕ݂ above, *c.*

i. ܓ and ܓ̰ are sometimes interchanged, as in ܓܠܝܼܕ *to be tired*, in Ti. ܓ̰ܝܼܕ (elsewhere ܓ̰ܝܼܕ or ܓ̰ܝܼܕ is *to be smooth*); ܡܓܝܼܕ

§§ 100—103]   CHANGE OF CONSONANTS.   313

K. = مجْلِي U. *to sprout* (see above, *g*). فَجِيِي K. = فَجِي U. = ثَجِي Baz *to be warm* or *thirsty, to fear greatly;* حَوْمِلَى or حَوْجَى f. *lane, quarter* of a city; and so some other foreign words where N.S. ܠ = ج, as ܟܝܼܢܛܵܐ f. *wallet* = Turk. جانطه; ܠܝܼܦܵܠܕ f. *sack* = Turk. چوال.

§ 101. ܠ in many parts of Kurdistan, especially in MB. and Ti., has often the sound of ܣ as ܦܓ݂ܕܵܐ *body*, pronounced ܦܣܕܵܐ; this is very common.

In other districts also we have ܠ and ܣ interchanged, as ܟ݂ܵܠܸܬ U. = ܫܵܠܸܬ K. *to conquer;* ܡܚܵܠܓ݂ܵܐ or ܡܚܵܫܓ݂ܵܐ Al. *to dine* (at midday), ܡܚܵܡܠܓ݂ܠ K. or ܡܚܵܡܣܓ݂ܣ U. K. *to covet, long for.* ܠ = ܣ in ܠܒ݂ܵܐ Al. = ܣܒ݂ܵܐ U. *care, trouble,* f.

For the interchange of ܠ and ܚ and ܒ see below, §§ 113, 120.

§ 102. ܠ and ܘ are interchanged in ܟ݂ܵܕܓܵܐ or ܘܵܕܓܵܐ *to scratch* (= ܘܕܵܓ݂ܠ, N.S. and O.S.); also *to be squeezed out*, as juice. So N.S. ܟ݂ܵܕܘܓ݂ܵܐ *a scratch*. ܡܚܵܘܒܵܕ = ܡܚܵܘܒܵܕ K. *to ring* as metals, *clink*, also ܡܚܵܡܒܵܕ K. See § 110, *e*.

ܠ stands for ܦ in ܐܵܕܝܘܡ Tkh. *today*, § 67.

§ 103. ܦ often falls in N.S., as in the following words:

ܐܘܡܵܢܵܐ ('ܘܗ K. MB.) *master workman*; cf. ܐܘܡܵܢܕܵܐ § 19, where the ܦ reappears.

ܚܵܕ *one* (O.S. ܚܕ), and in any compounds, but not in ܣܚܕܵܐ § 111.

ܚܕܟ݂ܵܐ Q. *eleven*, see § 26.

ܚܵܕܬܵܐ *new* (m.) § 21 (9) = ܚܸܕܬܵܐ or ܚܸܕܬܵܐ Q. [The Q. fem. is ܚܸܕܬܵܐ *khéta*, but also ܚܕܵܬܵܐ as U.]

ܡܕܝܕ, several parts of, in Gaw. Sal. § 46.

ܢܕܥܘܬܐ Sal. = ܢܕܥܘܬܐ knowledge.

ܒܠܕܐ boy. O.S. ܝܠܕܐ.

ܒܠܕܬܐ girl, for ܝܠܕܬܐ.

ܚܘܕܢܐ J. mule. In U. pronounce ܒ § 17, p. 38.

ܡܕܨܠ or ܡܕܨܚ Al. = ܡܕܝ ܡܕ ܡܕܝ how much, p. 163, cf. ܡܕܝ ܗܘ so much.

ܡܘܕܝܢܐ how can I tell? = ܡܘܕܝ ܡܕܝ § 73.

ܡܕܡܪ, O.S. ܡܕܡܪ. In N.S. sign of the past tense.

ܡܕܡ before. O.S. ܡܕܡ.

ܡܕܡܝܐ, O.S. ܡܕܡ, first.

ܓܕܐܝ Al., final Nun for ܢ? See § 67 s. v. ܚܘܕܢܐ.

Perhaps also ܢܕ (ܢܕܢܟܐ Q. Sal.) ear is for ܐܕܢܐ from O.S. ܐܕܢܐ or for the pl. ܐܕܢܐ; and ܕܝܢ for ܕܝܢ § 70 (3).

§ 104. ܕ has the sound of ܬ in several words.

a. At the end of many foreign words, such as (ܡܓ) ܓܕ besides, ܡܔܝܕ mosque, ܓܝܓܕ indeed, ܩܓܕ trick, ܐܙܘܕ free, etc. But the ܕ sound is also used, and reappears if a termination is added; e.g. ܐܙܘܕܘܬܐ freedom.

b. Also the following:

ܐܕܠܠܝ U. to-night, § 67.

ܒܝܓ by means of, § 68.

ܕܝܗܫ to thrust, in U.; in K. the sound is between ܕ and ܬ. Chald. דחם.

ܕܓܕ to remember, under influence of O.S. ܐܗܓܕ id. (Az. ܠ).

ܕܘܟܕܢܐ Al. *remembrance*, m.

ܕܡܝ Al. = ܛܒ Ti. *to sink*.

ܗܕܟܐ *thus*, § 67.

ܡܕܠܕܠ = ܡܕܠܕܠ K. *to hang*, p. 257.

ܦܪܕ K. = ܦܪܐ Al. *to pass* (Arab. with Tc).

ܦܕܢܐ *plough*, §§ 85, 97.

ܕ ܩܕ *in order that* (qăt: also qû-d).

ܩܘܦܕܐ O.S. *an owl*, f. (pl. ܩܘܦܕܐ).

But ܛ has the sound of ܕ in ܕܚܣ *to boil, ferment*, (in U., but in K. the ܛ sound remains, as in O.S. ܕܚܣ. Cf. N.S. ܡܕܪܕܚܣ K. *to be boiled to rags*).

In Al. ܕܕܬܐ, the pl. of ܥܕܬܐ *Church*, is pronounced *étátha*.

Compare also ܦܕܝܐ U. and ܦܕܝܬ Al. *opportunity*, p. 289.

ܕ = ܛ in ܢܕܝܕ Sh. (see §§ 103, 105).

§ 105. ܕ has the sound of ܛ in the following words:

ܕܪ *to return, be converted*, in MB. only (elsewhere the ܕ sound) § 46.

ܕܥܟ (also with ܕ) *to extinguish*. So O.S. Pa'el.

ܕܩܪ *to prick, indent*, O.S.

ܕܥܐ *to sweat*, O.S. (ܛ in U. but ܕ in K.).

ܕܘܥܬܐ *sweat*, O.S. 'op. But ܕ in K., and also in U. in the sense of *resin, sap*.

ܢܕܥ *to know* (in present only), in U. In other places the ܕ sound, but see §§ 103, 104. So ܢܕܘܚܐ, ܢܕܘܕܗܐ.

The Jews of Azerbaijan pronounce ܕܓܕ with a ܛ sound. See § 104.

§ 106. ܒ = ܬ or ܘ.

a. ܒ apparently = ܬ in ܒܝܬ ܓܒܪܐ *a husband's brother* and ܒܝܬ ܓܒܪܬܐ *a husband's sister* = O.S. ܒܝܬ ܓܒܪܐ, ܒܝܬ ܓܒܪܬܐ.

So ܡܓܕܕ Al. = ܡܓܕܕ *again*, § 67.

b. ܒ and ܘ are interchanged in foreign words, especially in the Alqosh dialect which is most influenced by the Arabic. Thus ܘܚܒ K. = ܕܒܚ Al. *to subdue*, (U. ܡܟܘܒܫ) cf. ܘܚܒ *subject*. So compare ܝܘܡܬܐ K. *service* (U. ܒܠܡܬܐ) with ܫܡܫ K. Al. *to serve* (§ 114), ܫܡܫܐ Al. *a male servant*, ܫܡܫܢܬܐ K. or ܫܡܫܬܐ Sh. *maid servant*, and ܗܘܕ U. Tkh. with ܗܒܕ Al. *ready*. In Zakho this change is frequent in Syriac words, § 124.

ܫܡܟܡܬܐ *some*, is in Al. sometimes pronounced *khădma*.

§ 107. ܗ is much interchanged with ܚ, especially in words from the Arabic. As in the N.S. dialects, except only that of the Plain of Mosul (Alqosh), where the people hear Arabic spoken on all sides of them and so have learnt its sounds, there are only the two sounds ܗ and ܚ (or ܓ݆ܝ) to represent the Arabic ه, ح and خ, there is much confusion. In the Alqosh vernacular MSS. referred to in the Introduction we find ܓ݆ܝ = خ (even at the beginning of a word), ح = ܚ, ه = ܗ. But this assumes a difference between ܚ and ܓ݆ܝ which does not exist in the other N.S. dialects; and to represent words with an aspirated initial letter is against all Syriac usage, see § 94, *e*.

When Arabic words are taken into Syriac ه almost always becomes ܗ; خ becomes ܚ; and the intermediate ح becomes either ܗ or ܚ, usually the former, especially in U., but ܘܣܡ *bold* (in Al. *difficult*) is always pronounced with ܚ, and so its derivatives ܘܒܝܕ K. Al. *to be brave*, ܡܟܘܒܝܕ U. (ܡܟܘܒܝܕ K.) *to embolden*: cf. ܘܗܡܬܐ *trouble* (f.), in K. *difficult*. ܬܘܣܡܐ *slander*, f. = Arab. بهتان.

ܗ and ܚ are interchanged in N.S. in the following words:—

ܒܗܣ U. K. = ܒܚܣ Al. *report*, f., Turk. بحث.

ܥܝܗܟܐ U., 'ܚ Al. K. *foal of an ass*, m. (in Tkh. ܟܘܕܢܬܐ).

ܗܘܡܬܐ U. Al., 'ܚ K. *power*, m.

ܗܟܡ U., 'ܚ K., *governor*, m., but ܗܟܝܡ *doctor*, always has ܗ.

ܗܦܣܐ K. or ܗܒܣܐ K. = ܚܒܣ Al. *prison*, f. (in U. ܕܘܒܫܢܩܐ f.).

ܗܩ U., ܚܩ Al. Tkh. *right, just, true;* also *justice.* Cf. ܗܩܬܐ p. 285.

ܡܗܟܡ U., 'ܡܚ K., *to govern* (but ܚܟܡ, ܡܚܟܡ have ܚ only, § 45, *h*).

ܡܗܟܐ or ܡܚܟܐ Al. *to say*, Arab., conn. with ܡܗܘܕܐ *to tell*, § 119?

ܡܗܦܘܪ or ܐܪ' Tkh. Sh. = 'ܡܚ Ti. *carpet* (= ܫܠܒ U.).

ܡܗܘܝܠ U., 'ܡܚ Al. (not used in K.), *to beget, bear.* So ܡܗܝܘܠ U. Tkh. = ܗܝܒܠ U. f. = ܡܚܝܘܠ Al. *produce, fruit* [= ܢܒܠܬܐ Tkh. = ܐܢܓܐ Tkh. = ܝܠܒܐ Al. = ܚܘܒܢܐ U. Tkh. = ܦܪܝܐ Al. = ܒܪ ܗܡܥ Al.].

ܡܗܘܕܡ U., 'ܡܚ K., *to clasp*, p. 267, cf. ܚܕܡ § 95, *d.*

ܡܚܠܚܠ *to snuff about as a dog* = ܡܗܠܗܠ U. *to pant* (sound ܗ).

ܡܝܠܗܬ U. *counsel*, cf. ܡܝܠܚ K. *to take counsel*, in Al. *to reconcile* (from Arab.); also *to chop*, K. = O.S. ܝܠܚ.

ܦܗܡ K., O.S., ܦܗܡ Al. *to remember, understand*, in O.S. Pa. *to compare.* Often ܦ in Al. Bo., § 94, *e.* The ܗ is from Arab. See p. 98.

ܪܚܛ *to run*, O.S. and Al. ܪܗܛ.

§ 108. ܗ is frequently silent.

a. Always at the end of a word (except ܡܗܠܗܠ U. *to pant*, § 107), though not marked with *talqana.*

b. In many parts of verbs of the form ܩܛܗܐ and their causatives, § 46.

c. In the following words:—

ܐܳܕܺܝ *this* = ܗܳܕܶܐ § 12, and many derived adverbs, § 67.

ܐܰܠܳܗܳܐ *God*, in the adverbs on p. 159.

ܐܶܫܬܶܗܘ *appetite*, f., Arab. Turk. اشتها.

ܚܰܒܗܰܪ U. K. *report*, f., § 107.

ܒܪܚܡܘܗܐ usually ܒܪܚܡܘܬܐ, § 16, *wife's brother*.

ܓܳܗܐ *time*, has ܗ frequently: and the plural is often pron. *gâ-î*.

ܟܘܼܗܐ Sal., ܗ̇ U., *fault*, f. (so ܟܘܼܗܢ Sal. *our fault*).

ܕܗܘܢ *to cement*, see ܡܕܗܢ below.

ܕܘܗܘܢܐ K. = ܕܗܘܢܐ U. = ܕܘܗܢܐ O.S. *cement*, § 76 (5).

ܗܘ, ܗܝ and several other pronouns, §§ 10—12.

ܗܘܐ, ܗܘܘ *was, were;* and various parts of ܗܘܐ *to be*, § 46.

ܗܢܐ *to please*, some parts of, § 46.

ܙܗܢ f. *intellect*, Arab. Turk. ذهن.

ܙܘܗܡܐ *a summer pasture* (the encampment), see p. 98.

ܝܗܒ *to give*, some parts of, § 46.

ܝܗܘܕܝܐ also ܝܗܘܕ' as O.S., *a Jew*, also ܝܗܘܕܝܐ, Yudh silent.

ܟܗܝܗ *to go out* (as a candle), *to die*, all parts of, O.S. ܟܡܗ *to be darkened.*

ܡܕܗܢ K. *to pour in oil* or *grease*, O.S. ܕܗܢ *to be greasy*, § 39.

ܡܒܗܝܥ Ti. Al. *to vomit*, §§ 45, *g*; 87, *b*.

ܡܣܘܗܡ K. = ܡܣܘܗܡܝ U. *to defile.* See p. 98.

ܡܙܘܠܗܦ *to disturb*, cf. O.S. ܙܘܠܗܦܐ *disturbance*, p. 275.

ܡܒܝܗܕ Tkh. *to light a candle*, § 45, *g*.

ܡܦܪܗܙ K. *to fast*, from Kurd. Turk. پرهيز *a fast*.

ܘܡܘܕܲܥ K. *to acquaint, to know*, § 87, *b*.

ܢܟ݂ܗ *to dawn*, several parts of, § 46.

ܣܗܼܕ K. *to bear witness*, sometimes in all tenses.

ܦܗܘܿܪ Al. Bo. (فى), § 107, has often ܗ.

ܩ݁ܗ݁ܝ *dried manure* (for stable litter).

ܦܗܓܿ U., all tenses, § 92.

ܕܗ *free, rid*, contracted from ܕܗܐ *ease*, Arab., Nöld. p. 59 ?

ܪܗܘܿܡܐ *Rome*, and its adjective.

ܒܗܫܝ *sha-i*, *a halfpenny*, s. and pl. (lit. *Shah's money*).

d. Also the following words are found both with and without ܗ :—ܗܘܿܣܼܕ݁ܐ K. MB. = ܐܘܿܣܼܕ݁ܐ U. *master workman*, Arab., pp. 49, 313; ܗܘܐܕ݁ܟܝ or ܐܕ݁ܝ *of course*, p. 161; ܗܗܿܡܼܝ U. = ܗܿܡܼܝ K. Al. *easy*; ܗܘܿܕ݁ܗܒܣ or ܟܘܿܕ݁ܗܒܣ (as Turk.) *shameless*; ܗܟܼܝܕ݁ U. K. = ܟܼܝܕ݁ Al. *cautious, prudent* (Arab.); ܗܘܿܟܟ݁ܕ݁ Sal. = ܐܘܿܟܟ݁ܕ݁ U. K. *clear, evident* (Arab.). So ܗܢܿܗ *in vain* = Arab. عبث ; ܗܘܿܗ *air, tune,* f. = Pers. اواز ; ܗܘܿܓ݁ܕ (rare) *help*, f. = Turk. امداد ; ܗܘܿܩ݁ *lantern*, f. = Arab. فنار.

§ 109. *Insertion of* ܘ, *and interchange of* ܘ *and* ܒ.

a. Wau is inserted in all verbal nouns of the second conjugation of verbs ܣ and ܣ in U. Sal. Q. Gaw., §§ 42, 44.

b. In the verbs of § 83 (8).

c. Also in the following :—

ܗܘܿܠܐ Al. (ܠ Tkh.) *labour* (= ܠܠܝ U. p. 285).

ܕܗܘܢ and ܕܗܘܿܢܼܐ K., § 108, *c*.

ܡܣܝܼܓ݂ Al. as Arab. = O.S. ܡܣܝܼܓ݂ܘܿܕ݂ only begotten (= ܝܼܚܝܼܕ݂ U. Tkh.).

ܥܸܪܒܹܐ ewe, f., cf. O.S. ܥܸܪܒܵܐ sheep (Chald. often inserts ܐ).

ܘܸܕ݂ܘܿܕ݂ܵܐ cowardly, § 77 (2).

ܘܝܵܢܹܐ tares = O.S. ܘܝܼܢܘܿܢ = ζιζάνια, Pers. word. The Wau is from Arab.

ܚܕ݂ܝܼܪܘܿܬ݂ܵܐ around, from ܚܕ݂ܝܼܪ (ܒ݂) § 69 (2).

ܚܙܘܵܐ vision, m., as O.S., from ܚܙܹܐ to see.

ܚܙܘܿܘܵܐ keen-sighted, § 77 (2).

ܚܵܠܘܿܘܵܐ maternal uncle, p. 231.

ܚܸܪܡܵܐ = O.S. ܚܸܪܡܵܐ or ܛܫܹܐ secret.

ܚܵܒ݂ܘܿܕ݂ܵܐ U. an acquaintance, § 77 (2).

ܠܵܘܛܬ݂ܵܐ as O.S. curse, f., from ܠܵܛ to curse.

ܠܵܘܡܵܐ as Arab. لوم blame, m. from ܠܵܡ to blame.

ܠܵܥܘܿܥܵܐ jaw, § 77 (2).

ܡܵܚܘܿܠܵܐ sickly, ib.

ܚܵܠܘܿܘܵܐ U. paternal uncle, ib.

ܩܸܢܛܵܐ U. branch, § 92.

ܦܵܬ݂ܘܿܟ݂ܵܐ tepid, ib.

ܨܵܗܹܐ = O.S., Al. ܨܵܗܘܹܐ thirst; O.S. has both ܨܵܗܹܐ and ܨܵܗܘܹܐ for thirsty.

ܬܵܪܢܵܓ݂ܵܐ cock, § 77 (2).

ܬܵܪܥܘܿܣ U. = ܬܵܪܥܘܿܣ K. guard, m. Turk. قراغول.

ܕ݂ܟ݂ܘܿܢܵܐ valley, § 77 (2).

ܗܵܠܘܿܢܵܐ grape (hung on a string for winter use, from ܗܵܠܵܐ to hang).

§§ 109, 110]   CHANGE OF CONSONANTS.   321

d. ܫܒܓܐ *seven*, in U. etc. (not Ti.) is pron. *sho-wa*. So its derivatives, §§ 26, 28.

e. For Rwaṣa inserted, see § 89; see also the demonstrative pronouns of § 12.

f. Some foreign words are pronounced either with Rwaṣa or Zlama, as ܓܡܠܦܐ or ܗܓܡܠܦܐ *attack*, f.; ܛܒܗܩ or ܛܒܗܩܘ *tobacco*, f.

§ 110. The sounds ܘ, ܣ, ܥ are interchanged in some words.

a. ܘ is often like ܣ or ܥ in the following words:

ܚܘܣܦܐ *pool*, m., Arab. حوض.

ܠܐ ܬܕܘܠ Ti. *do not fear*, § 46.

ܘܚܕܐ O.S. *little* (usually pron. *sura*, in Ti. *sura* or *sʿura*. In Al. Z. *zura*). So the derivatives ܘܚܕܗ *to grow small*, ܡܚܘܕܗ or ܡܚܘܕܢܝ *to make small*, pp. 262, 264.

ܘܟ : ܘܟܕ : ܘܟܗ : ܘܟܡܗ *go*, § 46 (often).

ܘܙܩܦܐ O.S. *Zqapa*, m. (but ܘ is also common).

ܘܨܝܒܐ O.S. *cross*, m. (sometimes).

ܘܙܕ O.S. *to weave* (sometimes).

ܘܙܕ and ܣܙܕ *to scratch*, are parallel forms both in O.S. and N.S.

ܡܘܚܠܝ *to litter, dung*, has ܘ = ܣ in Tkh., p. 263.

ܡܘܠܝܠܝܕ *to stare*, also ܡܝܠܝܠܝܕ. Qu. = ܘܟܕ *to stare?*, p. 258.

ܡܘܗܪܐ *hair*, O.S. ܡܘܥܪܐ (so the K. Al. pl.; in U. pl. ܡܥܘܗܪܝ). The Al. sing. is ܡܥܘܗܪܐ with a ܘ sound.

ܣܕܘܬ or ܣܕܗܕ K. *to uphold*.

ܒܘܥܨܐ U. or ܒܘܥܨܐ K. *a ring* (sometimes), but not in ܒܥܘܨܐ Al.

S. GR.   41

b. ܨ has the sound of ܙ in ܚܨܸܕ *to reap*, and ܚܨܵܕܵܐ *harvest*, usually, but not in the Baz form ܚܵܨܸܕ.

So ܡܵܨܝܵܘܬܵܐ U. *a lizard*, § 16.

ܡܲܡܨܸܐ (in U., ܨ in K.) *to suckle* or *suck up*. In the primitive ܡܵܨܸܐ *to suck*, ܨ remains.

ܫܵܪܸܨ *to burst forth*, Hebr. שָׁרַץ, and ܫܪܵܨܵܐ (in Ti.; elsewhere ܨ) *creeping thing*, as O.S. Cf. N.S. ܫܪܘܿܨܵܐ m., *young of locust*.

Also ܙܲܕܦܵܐ K. *ivory, mother of pearl*, m. (p. 31) = Turk. صدف, and ܙܘܒܵܢ *sling*, f. = Turk. صپان.

c. ܣ has the sound of ܙ in the following words:—

ܡܲܣܡܵܪܵܐ K. *a nail*, or *the pole star*, m., Chald. מַסְמְרָא, [= ܡܸܣܡܵܪ U. *nail*]. So ܡܣܲܡܸܪ K. *to nail*, § 83, 7.

ܥܣ Z. *to* (sometimes).

ܡܣܲܒܸܬ U. or ܡܣܲܒܸܬ K. *to prove*, but not in ܣܒܵܬ *proof*, or ܣܒܵܬܘܼܬܵܐ *id.* (Turk. ثابت).

ܡܲܣܓ݂ܸܕܵܐ K. *a mosque*, § 113, *g*.

ܣܡܝܕܵܐ or ܣܡܝܕܵܐ *fine flour*, § 92, *b.* (sometimes).

d. ܙ = ܫ̃ in ܙܕܵܐ Ti. = ܫ̃ܕܵܐ Tkh. *to throw, cause to rebound, clean cotton* (O.S. ܫܕܵܐ *to throw*).

e. ܙ = ܓ̰ in ܡܓ̰ܪܓ̰ܸܪ = ܡܙܪܓ̰ܸܪ K. *to ring* or *clink* as metals. The latter also *to tick* as a clock, § 102.

f. ܙ = ܕ. ܡܙܲܪܙܸܠ U. = ܡܙܲܪܕܸܠ U. *to tear*. The former in K. is *to weep loud*.

§ 111. ܚ is often silent in K. in the word ܚܕܵܐ *one*, f., and

sometimes in J. For ܣ = ܗ or ܗ̇ see pp. 316, 317; for ܣ = ܓ݂ or ܓ
see p. 313.

ܣ = ܓ݂ in ܡܣܢܕ݂ܶܩ K. (in U. ܡܣܢܕܶܓ݂) = ܡܓ݂ܢܕܶܩ to search, see
p. 267.

§ 112. *Interchange of* ܣ *and* ܙ. This is very common both in
O.S. and N.S.

    a. Regularly in verbs ܩ̣ܘ, ܢܣܰܒ, ܐܙܰܠ, §§ 38, 39, 42.

    b. Also in the following words:—

ܐܶܪܣ U. = ܐܶܪܙ K. Sh. *course*.

ܣܳܘܓ݂ܳܐ = ܙܳܘܓ݂ܐ O.S. *length*, m.

ܝܰܠܶܣ U. Sal., = O.S. ܝܰܠܶܙ *to wail*, § 46.

ܝܣܳܡܶܐ U. K., O.S. or ܐܘܡܶܐ MB. Sh. or ܚܡܰܐ U. *to swear*, § 46.

ܢܣܰܕ or ܐܣܰܪ as O.S. *to bind*.

ܐܣܘܳܪܐ U. *a bond*, m. = Al. ܐܶܣܕ݂ܳܐ = ܐܣܘܕ݂ܳܐ K.; O.S. ܐܶܣܘܪܳܐ or
ܐܣܘܕ݂ܳܐ.

ܢܦܶܐ U. K. or ܐܘܦܶܐ MB., O.S. or ܦܳܐ U. *to bake*, § 46.

ܢܓ݂ܶܕ *to be long*, O.S. ܢܓ݂ܶܕ.

ܝܺܬܶܒ U. K. or ܐܘܬܶܒ MB. *to sit*, O.S. ܒܗܶܒ (ܐ), p. 301.

ܡܰܬܩܠܳܐ U. = ܡܰܬܩܳܠܳܐ K., O.S. = ܡܰܬܩܳܠܳܐ Ti. *a balance*, p. 217.

    c. *Insertion of Yudh*. In the present of verbs of the form
ܬܕܶܝܪ or ܨܳܗܶܐ, § 46. Also in ܐܢܺܝ m., ܐܢܺܝ f., Al. sometimes for ܐܢܶܬ,
ܐܢܺܬ *thou* (p. 16); ܢܰܦܫ Al. or ܢܦܫ as U. K. *soul*, f.; ܕܺܕ݂ܟܳܐ U. Tkh.
a yard (the measure), m. = O.S. ܕܕ݂ܟܳܐ (in Al. ܕܕ݂ܟܳܐ lit. *an arrow*, m.):
ܕܕ݂ܟܳܐ in K. also is *an arm* = ܕܺܕ݂ܟܳܐ U. m. = ܕܕ݂ܟܳܐ O.S., Al. and

sometimes in Ti. [in Sh. ܕܘܿܟܬܵܐ m., p. 291]; ܝܚܘܣܒܹܗ Al. *ring*, p. 321; ܡܵܘܕܕܵܢܵܐ m. *arable land* = Turk. مزرعه; ܐܕܵܟܢܵܐ or ܐܕܵܟܵܐ f. = ܐܕܵܐ O.S. m. *a native lamp*.

d. *Omission of Yudh.* In some Gawar forms in ܠܐ verbs, § 42; in Urmi verbs of the form ܡܕܲܢܡܸܓ = ܡܕܲܝܡܸܓ *to believe*, § 83 D; and in ܒܚܵܢܬܵܐ U. *a chimney, a vent of an earth oven* = ܒܚܵܢܬܵܐ K. = ܒܚܝܼܢܬܵܐ Sh. (feminine of ܒܚܵܢܵܐ *an eye*); also in ܩܠܝܘܼܢܐ *a water pipe* (*hubble-bubble*) U. = ܩܠܝܘܼܢܵܐ ܕܚܲܢܬܵܐ K. In K. ܩܠܝܘܼܢܵܐ f. is an ordinary pipe for tobacco (or ܩܠܝܘܼܢܬܵܐ), the Urmi ܓܹܚܘܼܣ f. Also in several causatives, § 45; in U. feminines of the form ܓܲܕܕܵܐ, p. 59; and so ܘܲܕܕܵܐ, fem. of ܘܲܕܵܐ U. K. or ܘܲܠܕܵܐ Al. *young of an animal* (root ܘܠܕ p. 335?).

§ 113. ܓܹܐ is not found in O.S. In N.S. it is much used for ܕܹܐ in Tiari and sometimes elsewhere; as ܓܚܵܐ Ti. = ܓܚܵܐ U. *butter*, m.; ܓܸܕܗܵܐ Ti. = ܓܸܕܗܵܐ O.S. = ܓܸܚܗܵܐ U. = ܓܸܚܗܵܐ Al. Z. *belly*, f.; ܓܚܵܐ Ti. = ܓܚܵܐ U. = ܕܚܵܐ, Az. = O.S. ܓܚܵܐ *tooth*, m., and the like.

The sound in N.S. seems to come in various ways:—

a. It represents چ in foreign words, as ܓܘܼܓܟܵܐ U. *a flower*, m., Turk. چیچك; ܓܘܿܓܹܐ *a magpie*, m., Pers. چوچه.

b. It corresponds to O.S. ܕܹܐ, as in Tiari words above; also in ܓܡܝܼܚ *to be extinguished*, O.S. ܕܡܝܼܚ; ܓܸܦܵܐ m. *a clap of the hands* (usually pl.), O.S. ܕܦܵܐ, ܕܦܵܐ *the palm of the hand*; ܓܲܕܹܐ *to climb*, perh. O.S. ܚܕܹܐ *to surround* [as N.S. ܚܕܹܐ (K.) *to go round*, and ܡܚܲܓܹܐ *to envelop in a shroud*]; ܡܚܲܓܸܣ or ܡܲܕܲܓܸܣ K. *to rebuke*, perh. from O.S. ܐܓܸܣ *id*.

§ 113]   CHANGE OF CONSONANTS.   325

c. ܓܕ: as ܣܘܓܕܡ = (in the manuscripts) ܣܘܓܕܡ Qudshanis, the village of Mar Shimun, the Catholicos.

d. ܓܦ = ܘ: ܡܓܓܘ = ܡܓܓܘ K. to sputter, ܓܢܕ to be angry, to be alienated, perhaps = Heb. זר id.

e. ܓܦ = ܠ:

ܓܕܡ or ܓܢܡ to shut, Heb. אטם (so Chald.).

ܘܓܪܐ or ܓܕܪܐ to scratch = ܘܓܢܕ N.S., O.S. see p. 313. Cf. N.S. ܓܕܘܓܠܐ a scratch, p. 232.

ܓܠܟ to split = Chald. טלד (or O.S. ܟܠܟ to break?).

ܓܦܝ to thrust, prick = ܓܦܝ in which ܦ is pron. ܠ, § 105.

ܘܓܢܕ = ܡܓܘܕܠ = ܡܓܘܕܘܐ as above, p. 258.

ܡܓܒܓܝܗ to search, pick the teeth, pick out with a knife, O.S. ܢܒܕ to dig, or Chald. חק id., p. 253.

ܡܓܒܓܣ to break in pieces, crash = ܡܓܒܣܠ to crush, pp. 253, 254.

ܡܓܓܓܗ or ܡܓܓܓܗ to cut, perhaps = O.S. ܢܓܕ to cut, p. 257.

ܡܓܓܕܝ in the sense to be leafy or crowded = ܡܓܢܕܝ, cf. O.S. and N.S. ܓܕܦܐ a leaf, m., pp. 264, 265.

ܡܓܓܘܗ = ܡܓܦܕܝܗ U. = ܡܓܦܟܟ = ܡܓܘܓܗ K. to whisper.

ܡܓܕܡܗ or ܡܓܓܕܡܕ or ܡܓܓܕܡܗ to wrinkle, crumple = ܣܓܕ O.S., see p. 268 and below.

ܦܓܟ K. to wring the neck, pluck = N.S., O.S. ܦܓܟ to cut off, twist, pluck (grapes).

ܦܓܝܗ to pinch = ܦܓܕ N.S. to twist, distort, squeeze. See above.

ܦܕܘܓܠܐ or ܦܕܘܓܠܐ tendon, m., § 77 (2), p. 231.

f. ܓܦ = ܣ: ܓܠܝܗ or ܓܠܣܗ to bruise, crush.

g. ܡܣܓܕ K. Sh. = ܡܣܓܕܐ K. Q. = ܡܣܓܕ U. = ܡܣܓܕ : ܡܣܓܕ = ܡܣܓ *g.*
(§ 110, *c*) = Arab. مسجد *a mosque.* The root is ܣܓܕ *to worship*, Heb. Chald. O.S. Arab.

h. ܣ = ܓ (see also § 119) : ܡܨܕܐ U. in the sense *to glitter* (as snow) = ܡܨܕܐ K., see § 45, *h*. Perhaps also ܡܣܒܓܐ, see above, *e*.

i. ܓ = ܟ :

ܥܩܒܐ or ܥܩܒܐ f. *heel*, Turk. اوكچه.

ܟܘܡܨܐ *fist*, m., see § 92, *b*.

ܣܘܟܬܢܐ O.S. = ܒܓܬܘܢܐ U. = ܒܓܬܘܢܐ K. *an account, reckoning*, m.

ܓܕܠ U. = ܓܕܠ K. *to toss up*; also, in K. *to get ready for battle* [but ܡܓܝܕ K. = ܡܓܝܕ p. 328].

ܟܬܢܐ U. = ܒܟܬܢܐ Al. Tkh. = Turk. چوبان *a shepherd*, m. (also ܕܚܢܐ U. Tkh. as O.S.).

ܓܕܝܪ *to be smooth*, and so ܡܓܘܓܕ *smooth*, or ܓܘܚܢܐ, O.S. ܓܕ *to smooth*.

ܓܡܓܐ *to fade slightly: have a sore eye: collapse, as a football.* O.S. ܓܡܕ *to fade*, O.S. ܓܚܓܝܣ *to be squeezed dry*. Cf. also N.S. ܡܓܕܡܣ *to fade*, p. 267.

ܓܕܘ = ܓܕܘ = ܓܝܠܘ *to pierce, put out the eyes*; in K. *to fade slightly*.

ܡܓܓܝ = ܡܓܓܝ *to blister, prick up the ears*. The latter also is *to give a pledge, flood*, § 45, *g*.

ܡܓܓܕ *to plaister*, O.S. ܓܕܕ *to slip*, ܓܕܘܓܡܐ *viscosity*.

ܡܓܕܦܠ = ܡܓܕܦܠ *to crack, snap*, p. 268.

ܡܚܓܓܝ *to go bad*, as gum; perh. O.S. ܕܓܝ, see p. 265.

ܡܚܓܓܝ = ܡܚܓܓܝܣ *to whisper*, see above, *e*, and p. 272.

§§ 113, 114] CHANGE OF CONSONANTS. 327

j. ܓܹܐ = ܟܹܐ : ܡܒ݂ܲܓܹܫ *to find,* is pronounced ܡܒ݂ܲܟܹܫ in U. ܡܒ݂ܲܓܹܣ in K., (also rarely 1st Conj., but with Mim).

ܦܓܲܠ *to twist,* perhaps O.S. ܦܓ݂ܲܠ *to twist,* or O.S. ܦܟܲܠ *id.*

k. ܡܲܓ݂ܠܹܡ U. = ܓܲܡܹܐ = ܓܲܡܹܐ K. = ܓ݂ܲܡܹܐ K. = ܓܹܡܹܐ = ܓܝܼܠܹܡ *to have a sore eye,* see *i,* above. For ܦܓܲܠ see *j,* above.

l. ܓܹܐ = ܟܐ : ܓܕܹܒ or ܐܓ݂ܕܹܒ = ܐܓܕܹܡ O.S. *October or November,* m. (in pl. *autumn,* ܐܓ݂ܕܲܝܹ̈ܐ N.S.), ܢܓ݂ܲܠ *to pluck, cut* (K.), perh. [p. 262] = O.S. ܓܕܲܥ *to cut or root out;* or possibly Heb. נָשַׁל *to extract* (so Arab.), *shake down* (fruit). In N.S. ܢܓ݂ܲܠ = *to gnaw, snatch.* From this root probably comes ܡܓܲܓܹܐ *to tear or worry* as an animal, p. 255. For ܒܓ݂ܸܠ = ܒܕ݂ܸܠ and its variants, see §§ 26—28, 96.

m. We have ܟ and ܠ interchanged in ܕܝܼܟ݂ܠ K. = ܕܝܼܟ݂ܠ Al., Arab. = ܕܝܼܟܠܟ݂ Tkh. *a cock,* [in U. ܩܕ݂ܘܿܩܬܐ lit. *the crower*]; ܠܟ݂ܕ *to take in the hand* (cf. ܠܘܼܡܚܲܠ p. 294), cf. O.S. ܐܚܲܕ݂ܟ, and Chald. גָּמַשׁ *to curve* (as the hand?); ܡܓܲܕ݂ܕ݂ *to roll,* see p. 275. For ܠܟ݂ܢܹܐ = ܕ ܠܓ݂ܢܹܐ see § 68. Also at the end of foreign words ܟ and ܠ are constantly interchanged, ܟܝܼ and ܠܝ. In Al. ܓܝܼܟ *to laugh,* sometimes has initial Kap.

n. ܟ is silent in J. in the affix ܘܿܟ݂ *thy.*

§ 114. *Interchange of liquids, etc.*

a. ܠ, ܡܚ, ܢ, ܪ are interchanged in the following words:—

ܒܝܼܠܘܼܠ as O.S., but usually ܒܝܼܢܘܼܠ *September,* m., p. 73.

ܐܸܢܡܲܪ Al. = ܐܸܡܲܪ *who,* § 13, O.S. ܐܸܡܲܪ.

ܐܸܣܛܘܼܡܢܐ (O.S. ?) Gk. στῦλος, *pillar,* m.

ܒܲܝܛܲܪ m. *horse doctor* = Turk. بيطار.

ܓ̰ܹܠܵܦ݂ܕܵܪ U. or ܓ̰ܹܠܵܦ݂ܕ U. = ܓ̰ܹܠܵܦ݂ܕܵܐ Q. = ܓ̰ܹܠܵܦ݂ܕܵܬ݂ K. = ܓ̰ܹܠܵܦ݂ܕ U. Tkh. (all ܐ) *deserted, ownerless.*

ܓ̰ܝܼܠܵܗ̈ܢܹܐ *white cherry* (p. 53) = Turk. كراز or كراس.

ܓ̰ܸܕ݂ܝܼ *to be ruined by water, to be shipwrecked,* perh. = ܓ̰ܝܼܕ݂ as O.S. *to choke, drown.* Also ܓ̰ܸܕ݂ܝܼ in K. = *to nick with a knife,* O.S. ܓ̰ܕ݂ܝܼ *to cut.*

ܓ̰ܝܼܓ̰ܗ = ܓ̰ܝܼܓ̰ܗ § 113, *k.*

ܓ̰ܝܼܘ = ܓ̰ܝܼܘ = ܓ̰ܕ̰ܘ § 113, *i.*

ܓ̰ܕ̰ܟ Ti. *to play,* perh. = O.S. ܚܕ̰ܕ *to be prosperous, happy.*

ܠܬ̰ܝܼܟ = ܢܬ̰ܝܼܟ = ܡܬ̰ܝܼܟ = ܢܘܬ̰ܝܼܟ *to carry,* §§ 45, 46.

ܡܓ̰ܕ݂ܘܼܟ *to fall over, die,* perh. from ܢܘܼܟ *to fall,* p. 260.

ܡܓ̰ܠܬ̰ܝܼܟ = ܡܓ̰ܕ݂ܢܸܟ K. *to babble,* p. 252.

ܡܓ̰ܠܬ̰ܝܼܟ also = ܡܓ̰ܕ݂ܢܸܟ *to grow* = ܕ̰ܵܓ̰ Al., O.S. p. 258.

ܡܓ̰ܠܸܢܝܼܟ *to roll, roll over, stagger,* perhaps = ܡܓ̰ܠܬ̰ܝܼܟ from ܓܠܠ *to be round;* or from ܢܵܦܸܠ *to fall.* So ܡܓ̰ܟܸܕ݂ p. 263.

ܥܕ̰ܘܡܓ̰ܕ݂ܢܸܐ, also as O.S. ܢܘܡܓ̰ܕ݂ܢܸܐ *Festival of the Twelve Apostles.*

ܡܓ̰ܝܼܓ̰ K. = ܡܓ̰ܠܸܒ K. *to blossom,* § 45, *g,* and p. 312.

ܡܓ̰ܠܵܓ̰ܸܪ = ܡܓ̰ܕ݂ܵ = ܡܓ̰ܕ݂́ = ܡܓ̰ܕ݂́ *to soil.* The first also *to beat gently* = ܡܓ̰ܠܸܬ̰ܢܵ or ܡܓ̰ܠܬ̰ܢܸܣ p. 273.

ܡܓ̰ܡܸܗܠ and ܡܓ̰ܕ݂ܢܗܠ from ܓ̰ܵܗܕ, pp. 262, 265.

ܡܓ̰ܕ݂ܡܸܪ and ܡܓ̰ܕ݂ܢܗܪ f. *ointment* = Turk. ملهم.

ܡܓ̰ܡܓ̰ܸܕ U., O.S. = ܡܓ̰ܢܸܕ݂ K. *to mumble,* p. 254.

ܡܓ̰ܠܸܢܸܟ or ܡܓ̰ܠܸܢܟ *to lame or be lame,* pp. 262, 265.

§ 114]   CHANGE OF CONSONANTS.   329

ܠܲܡܨܵܐ or ܒܿ or ܒܿܬܸܦ m. *the pulse* (Turk. لمس ?).

ܠܲܡܕܵܐ m. *felt*, Turk. نمد.

ܠܲܡܨܵܢܵܐ *German*, Turk. نمسه or لمسه *Germany*.

ܡܒܝܼܪ *to leak*, O.S. ܢܒܥ *to ooze*, p. 111.

ܡܓܕܓܝ = ܡܓܠܓܝ K. *to grope*, pp. 262, 268.

ܡܓܕܩܝ *to crumble*, p. 259.

ܡܓܕܩܝ U. = ܡܓܕܓܝ K. = ܡܓܓܓܪ K. *to wedge in*, p. 274.

ܡܓܕܘܠ *to beseech*, Heb. הִתְפַּלֵל, p. 255.

ܡܓܡܓܡ *to rumble or crash*, K. = ܡܓܕܡ or ܡܓܕܟܡ *to thunder*. In U. ܡܓܡܓܡ = *to be downhearted*, perh. for ܡܓܡܓܠ, O.S. ܡܓܠ *to be musty*.

ܡܓܠ U. = ܡܪܪ K. *to be bitter*. See § 81 (5).

ܡܓܒܣܕ for ܡܓܒܠܟ *to alter*, § 92, b.

ܡܓܕܠܓܝ or ܡܓܕܠܓܝ *to switch, beat*.

ܡܓܚܫܒ Al. = ܡܚܫܒ U. K. *to consider*, p. 266.

ܡܓܕܠܝ or ܡܓܠܣܝ U. *to pant*, p. 270.

ܡܓܕܓܕ *to tear*, from N.S. ܢܓܕ *to snatch*, p. 270.

ܡܢܣܒܠ m. *descendant*, Arab. Turk. سلسله, p. 274.

ܦܠܦܠ *black pepper*, f., Tkh. Sh. = O.S. ܦܠܦܠ = πέπερι (in U. ܐܗܡܘܐ f., in K. ܟܬܘܟܫܡ or in Tkh. ܟܣܦܓ). So ܦܠܦܠܟ K. *red pepper* (= Sh. U. ܣܓܕ f.).

ܦܕܦܕ U. Sh. = ܦܠܟܠܡܢ Sh. = ܦܕܦܕܘܓܢ Tkh. = ܦܕܦܕܘܢܟ Ti. (= ܓܢܘܕܢܟ Tkh.) *a top*.

ܩܢܘܢ m. = ܩܢܘܢܐ p. 231, *rule, canon*.

S. GR.   42

ܫܠܵܬܹܠܝܼܕ K. = ܫܠܵܬܹܠܝܼܕ K. *noise* [also ܩܵܠܵܐ K., ܫܲܠܫܠܬܵܐ
U. ܩܵܠܘܿܗ Sh. ܩܵܠܘܿܢܝܟܵܐ Tkh. ܩܲܕ݂ܚܝܼܡܹܕ Tkh.].

ܕܘܘܢܵܡܹܐ or ܕܘܘܟܡܵܐ U. *newspaper*, m. Pers., (in K. ܠܘܿܚܵܐ f.).

ܓܕܝܼܓ݂ (ܒ) or ܓܸܕܸܢܟܵܐ or ܓܲܠܓ݂ܕܵܐ *trousers tied at the ankle*, m.

ܓܲܕ ܟܸܡܬܵܐ *turnip* (p. 54), Turk. شلغم.

ܕܠܲܕ݂ܗܹܕ = ܗܘܕܲܕ݂ܗܹܕ Q. *twelve*, § 26.

b. Liquids are interchanged with other letters:—

ܐܸܡܓ݂ܝ *when* = O.S. ܐܸܡܓ݂ܝ (in Ti. ܐܸܡܸܕ݂).

ܚܒܸܠ U., also ܚܒܸܠ as O.S. *to number*.

ܚܕ݂ܸܕ݂, also ܚܲܕ݂ܸܕ݂ *to rub*.

ܕܪܵܙ Ti. Al. = ܕܪܵܟ Tkh. *to push*.

ܒܝܼܠܸܚܡܹܗ U. Ti. Sh. = ܝܘܡܹܚܵܐ K. *service*, f., p. 316.

ܟܠ *all*, sometimes pron. ܚܘܸܡ before a noun, esp. in Al. Z.

ܡܸܣܘܕܸܒ MB. = ܬܸܢܕܸܒ *stove*, § 88, *g*.

ܚܸܫܵܐ f. *a wood*, Turk. بيشه, Kurd. ميشه.

ܡܸܓ݂ܠܬܵܐ *ladder*, O.S. ܡܸܚܠܬܵܐ, Arab. سلم.

ܒܝܼܙܩܵܐ *earring*, O.S. ܩܸܕ݂ܫܵܐ.

ܩܲܕ݂ܡܸܕ݂ܬܵܐ Al. *skull* = ܩܸܕ݂ܡܸܟ݂ܬܵܐ U. K., p. 289.

ܡܓ݂ܒܓ݂ܠܹܕ݂ K. = ܡܓ݂ܠܹܒܕ݂ K. *to bring ewes to be milked*, p. 261.

ܠ is silent in some parts of ܐܘܿܠ, § 46, and in ܚܠܸܓ݂ܡܹܕ݂ܐ *supper*
(lit. *evening meal*); sometimes in ܟܠ *all*, in Al. K. and in the preposition ܠ with affixes, § 32 (4) etc.; in the preterite of verbs ending in
ܠ, ܡ, ܢ, p. 85; and sometimes in that of verbs ܠܠ, ܠܠ in Al.;

thus ܟܡܥܒܕ ܠܗܘܢ is in Al. often pron. *jmé'ûn* (as if ܠܐ). So ܕܝܦܐ K. = ܕܦܠܐ U. *the left hand* (also ܣܡܠܐ as O.S.; in Al. ܕܘܡܠܐ).

§ 115. ܡܢ falls in ܐܕܝܘܡ *to-day*, § 67; so ܝܘܡ ܡܘ ܝܘܡ Al. *daily*.

Also ܒܪܡܫܐ U. *in the evening*, § 67.

ܡܢܕܥܡ see p. 30.

ܡܕܡ Ti. = ܡܕܡ O.S. = ܡܢܕܝ U. *thing*.

ܩܘܡ m. ܩܘܡܝ f. *get up* (imperative). But ܡܢ often remains in Al.; and everywhere in the plural ܩܘܡܘܢ.

Also as a preformative in all second conjugation verbs in U. Sal. Sup. J. Q. Gaw. etc., and elsewhere in those beginning with Mim, § 35; also usually in Al. in the second conjugation infinitive.

§ 116. ܢ often falls, especially at the end of a word:—

a. In the plural of the present participle: ܦܬܚܝ = O.S. ܦܬܚܝܢ, ܟܠܝ = O.S. ܟܠܝܢ.

b. In the past participle in ܩܛܝܠܝ ܠܗܘܢ K. = O.S. ܩܛܝܠܝܢ ܠܗܘܢ *he killed them* (they were killed by him).

c. In K. Al. often (in Ti. almost always) at the end of the second pers. plural of verbs and pronouns, e.g. ܐܚܬܘ = ܐܚܬܘܢ *you*, pl.

d. ܐܚܢܝ or ܐܚܢܢ, O.S. ܚܢܢ *we*.

ܐܝܟܢܐ etc. § 121.

ܐܢܝ or ܐܢܝ (Zlama with either sound) Al. or ܐܢܘܢ = ܗܢܘܢ O.S. *they*, §§ 10, 12.

ܐܢܬ m. ܐܢܬܝ f. *thou*, so O.S.

ܒܬܘ or ܒܬܘܢ *entire, a whole number*[1], Turk. بتون.

[1] This word is much used in counting; where we should say *five* a Syrian would often say ܚܡܫܐ ܒܬܘܢ.

ܓܢܒܪܐ *giant*, m., so O.S.; not colloquial in N.S.

ܢܘܿܛܦܬܵܐ K. *drop* = ܢܘܿܛܦܬܵܐ p. 228.

ܡܕܝܼܢܬܵܐ *city*, so O.S. The ܢ reappears in the plural ܡܕܝܼܢܵܬܼܵܐ.

ܡܬܼܡܠ U. = ܡܬܼܡܠ K. *for instance*.

ܡܢ *from*. The Nun often falls before a noun etc., esp. in K. Al.

ܡܣܝܠܬܐ *a sieve*, from ܢܣܠ to *sift*, pp. 282, 291.

ܡܢܕܪܟܼ U. or ܡܢܕܪܟܼ K. = O.S. ܕܟܼ ܡܢ *again*, p. 316.

ܡܬܼܩܠܐ *balance*, root ܬܩܠ, pp. 217, 323.

ܡܕܢܕܪ K. = ܡܕܢܕܪ U. *to dam*, cf. N.S. ܣܟܪܐ *a dam*, p. 274.

ܡܙܕܓܪ U. = ܡܙܕܓܪ K. *prohibited*.

ܫܢܬܐ (O.S. 'ܫ') *a year*. The Nun reappears in the plural ܫܢܹܐ. Nun is inserted in ܣܓܘܠܬܐ m. *cluster of grapes*, cf. ܣܓܠ *to pluck*.

§ 117. ܡ final in Salámas is often like ܠ or ܓܝ; as ܩܘܡ or ܩܘܡ *save*, pl. ܠ ܣܡܣܡܠܝ *heal me*. See § 90.

ܡ before ܬ or ܒ is pron. like ܡܒ, as ܐܢܒܪ (*ǎmbar*) *store-room*.

§ 118. ܥ, which gives a semi-guttural sound to the accompanying vowel in U. and part of K. (especially Ti.) has usually only the force of ܐ in Tkh. Al. Ash. Hence they make in Tkhuma a causative, ܡܥܩܪ (*mé-qǐr*) *to take root*, from ܥܩܪ *to dig*. But in some words even in these districts ܥ modifies the sound, especially at the beginning of a word.

The break due to ܥ [§ 4] is especially marked in Ti. Thus they will say *b'éli* for ܒܥܠܝ *I wished*. In most districts, even where

ܒ does often make a break, this would be *béli* or *bíli*. So ܒܹܝܬܵܐ *act of desiring*, which in most districts cannot be distinguished from ܒܲܝܬܵܐ *a house*, in Ṭiari has a marked break.

§ 119. *Interchange of* ܒ *and* ܓ (*or* ܔ *in Baz*).

ܓ݁ = קָא Chald. (γε) = קָא or קִי Mand. (Nöld. § 20, 146).

ܟܘܣܐ (or ܟܘܣܝ ?) *hair*, m. perh. = O.S. ܟܘܡܨܐ *id.*

ܟܘܪܕܡܗܐ *Kurdistan*, but ܟܘܪܕܢܐ or ܟܘܪܕܢܐ *a Kurd*.

ܟܘܕ U. = ܩܛܪ K. *to tie a knot*, pp. 262, 265.

ܓܗܕܐ U. = ܩܛܪܐ K. = ܩܛܪܐ O.S. *a knot*, m.

ܡܓܙܓ Al. and ܡܓܙܓ Al. *to speak* = ܡܚܟܐ U. K. *to tell*?

ܡܓܚܒ U. or ܡܚܒ K. or ܡܓܒܘܒ or ܡܓܒܙܒ or ܡܚܒ K. *to gather up, carry off*, esp. as floods, p. 268.

ܡܓܒܕ *to justify*; cf. Heb. קשט = O.S. ܩܘܫܬܐ *truth*, and N.S. ܟܐܢܐ *upright*, and Al. ܟܒܝܢܐ *fat*: same connexion as between ܟܕܝܢܐ *fat*, and ܗܕܝܢܐ *true*; both of which mean literally *well made*, § 123.

ܡܓܚܢ *to groan*, O.S. ܐܬܐܢܚ p. 255.

ܡܚܡܓܕ Tergawar = ܚܒܕ § 92, *b*, p. 297.

ܗܣܘܦܐ, O.S. ܗܓܘܦܐ, Heb. סַקְפְּתָא *threshold*, p. 280.

ܡܓܕܡ = ܡܘܡܕ Sal. = ܓܕ Al. sign of the past tense, p. 82.

ܟܡܢܐ as O.S. = ܟܡܢܐ Baz *flour*, m. [See further, § 113, *h*.]

ܓܘܕ K. *to hug* = ܟܘܕ K. *to wrap*, Chald. קָפַל.

ܦܓܕ O.S. *caper berry* = Arab. كبر.

ܒ is silent in ܟܘܡܕܢܐ *command*, in part of U. § 76 (4); § 120, *c*.

§ 120. *Interchange of* ܒ *and* ܓ *or* ܟ.

a. ܒ = ܓ or ܟ in many foreign words; خ and ق of Pers. Turk. etc. often become ܒ and ܓ or ܟ in N.S., or if the softer sound is taken in the singular, the harder is used in the plural, § 18 (13); or both forms are found in N.S., as ܚܛܒ or ܚܠܒ *in arrears*, Arab. باقى; ܚܠܒ or ܚܒ *garden*, § 82 (13). So ܐܘܟܣܢܐ U. *small fire-place* = Turk. اوجاق; ܒܠܟܡ f. *shield* = Turk. قالقان; ܕܘܣܟܐ m. *mallet* = Turk. طوقمق; ܒܟܠܐ f. *hood* = Turk. باشلق; ܟܘܡܒܪܐ f. *bomb* = Turk. خمبره, etc. So also ܐܢܗ̈ܐ = ܕܟܗ ܐܢܗ̈ܐ § 73.

b. ܒ = ܓ, see § 100, *g.*

c. ܒ = ܓ in a few words:—

ܚܛܒ K., ܓ U. *certainly*, § 67, Arab. يقين.

ܡܓܪܓܪ = ܡܓܪܓܪ *to thunder*, cf. ܡܓܡܓܪ § 114, *a.*

ܒܟܪܐ also ܒܩܪܐ *eye of a needle*, p. 304.

ܢܟܘ Ti. *to bite* = ܢܩܘ *to peck*? See p. 312.

ܩܘܡܨܢܐ *command*, m., in Al. has ܓ, § 119.

ܛܝܘ or ܨ.ܝ.ܘ U. Tkh. = ܓܝܘ K. *to gather* (clothes), *to crouch*, p. 297.

ܨܓܕ Ti. = ܓܕܐ *to bleat, cry out*, § 46.

ܕܓܨ Tkh. = ܕܓܒ p. 297.

§ 121. ܕ in Ti. is often pronounced ܓ, as ܐܡܓܒܝ = ܐܡܕܒܝ *I said*.

ܕ falls in some words:—

ܐ ܐܝܕܟܐ, ܐܝܕܐ etc. *other*, p. 57.

ܐܩܪ *to be cold*, from O.S. ܩܕܪ, p. 120?

ܒܰܪܬܳܐ Al. (sometimes) *son*, § 19.

ܒܰܪܬܳܐ Al. *daughter*, § 19.

ܟܰܪܣܳܐ U. = ܟܶܐ Ti. = ܟܶܐ Al. Z. = ܟܰܪܣܳܐ O.S. *belly*, f.

ܡܳܪܬܳܢ Al. = ܡܳܪܬܝ U. K., O.S. lit. *My Lady* (title of St Mary).

ܥܰܪܣܳܐ *bier*, f.; O.S. ܥܰܪܣܳܐ *bed*.

ܩܰܪܢܳܐ *horn*, f. O.S. ܩܰܪ.

ܕܺܝܟ, *some parts of*; see ܐܘܠ § 46.

ܓܰܪܕܳܐ *almond* (?), §§ 88, *h*, 98.

ܬܪܶܝܢ Al. = ܬܪܶܝܢ K. Al. = ܬܪܶܝܢ O.S. *two*, f. § 26.

Nöldeke (§ 24) suggests ܘܰܪܢܳܐ *young of an animal* = ܘܰܪܢܳܐ from ܘܓܕ *to be small*. See p. 324.

§ 122. ܓ is silent in a few words, as ܡܶܓܕܪܳܟ *again*; in U. both ܓ and ܕ silent, in K. ܕ silent, § 116, *d*. ܢܓܶܒ U. = ܢܒܶܕ K. = ܢܓܶܒ Al. Tkh. *to hit, attack*, O.S. ܢܓܶܒ; see ܢܬܶܩܒܶܠ § 77 (2). ܟܶܕܓܰܪ *ears of corn*, p. 291. ܟܓܰܕ Al. *except* (p. 179), often has ܓ.

Compare also ܡܶܓܕܶܓ K. *to plane*, p. 269 (in U. ܓܶܕܓܶܕ ܟܒܰܪ).

§ 123. Interchange of ܢ and ܠ.

ܐܶܗܬܢ f. *fear*, awe, Turk. احتياط.

ܠܰܗܕܶܝܢ N.S. = ܠܰܗܕܶܝܢ O.S. *then* = εἶτα.

ܐܶܣܛܽܘܢܳܐ, or with ܢ, *pillar*, m., § 85, Arab. ستون.

ܙܥܽܘܦܳܐ, or with ܠ, *appetite*, f., p. 318.

ܛܰܥܢܳܐ *obedience*, f., Arab. اطاعت.

ܛܪܵܐ (p. 122) in Al. becomes ܛܪܝܼܬ before ܬ.

ܛܘܼܒܬ f. *leg* (of mutton) = Turk. بوت.

ܛܵܦܸܠ see p. 328.

ܛܝܼܢܵܐ see p. 313.

ܚܵܛܸܪ, rarely ܚܵܛܝܼܪ f. *sake*, Arab. خاطر.

ܛܲܒܲܩܵܐ, or 'ܬ, *storey*, m., Turk. Arab. طباقه.

ܛܘܼܦ K. = ܬܘܿܦ U. *cannon*, f., Turk. طوپ and طوب.

ܛܸܠܦܵܐ *eyelash*, m. (O.S. ܬܸܠܦܵܐ), § 18 (5).

ܛܠܲܡ, or 'ܬ, the latter chiefly in U. (O.S. ܛܠܲܡ), *to be lost* or *destroyed, to lose its sound*, as a letter; in Al. *to throw*, as Chald.

ܛܵܠܵܐ and ܛܵܐ *for* (ܡܛܠ O.S.), have ܬ usually in J. Al. Z.

ܛܵܣܵܐ (O.S. 'ܛ), usually pron. 'ܬ in U., *metal bowl*, f., § 87, *l*.

ܛܦܵܐ K., 'ܬ U., *to stick* intr., *be lighted*. In K. also *to wrestle, catch up*. So also ܡܛܲܦܸܐ *to stick, light*, tr., O.S. ܛܦܵܐ *to shut, join*.

ܛܦܲܪ, or 'ܬ, *to stick to*; so ܡܛܲܦܸܪ K. *to incite, stick*. ܛܦܲܪ is also *to put the claws into, cope with, attack*. Cf. ܛܦܵܪܵܐ, p. 50.

ܛܪܲܕ U. K., 'ܬ Al., *to persecute, drive out*, O.S. ܛܪܲܕ [ܬܪܲܕ in U. K. is *to crumble*, as Arab.].

ܛܪܝܼ *to be fat*, ܛܪܝܼܵܐ *fat*. Same root as ܬܪܝܼ *to be mended, get well* (O.S. ܬܲܪܝܼ *to make well*); 'fat' = 'well made,' cf. ܡܛܲܪܝܵܐ Al. § 119. So ܬܪܘܿܨܵܐ or ܛܪܘܿܨܵܐ *true*.

ܛܘܼܦܚܲܛ f. *tally, nick-stick*, Pers. چوب خط.

ܛܘܼܪ, ܛܘܿܪ, ܛܝܼܪ and derivatives, § 119, and pp. 262, 265.

ܠܘܼܛܝ *vagabond*, m., Pers. لوطی.

ܡܛܘܿܪܵܐ Al. = ܡܛܘܿܪܸܝܬ U. = ܛܪܝܼܬ K. = ܛܪܝܼܬ Al. *to subdue*.

ܡܲܛܠܵܒ, or with ܬ, *contents, design, purpose*, f., Arab. مطلب.

ܡܟܲܕܟܸܕ or ܟ́ or ܬ́ *to tickle*, p. 271.

ܡܥܲܛܸܠ Ti. or ܬ U. *at a loss, at a standstill.* Arab. معطل.

[Also ܗܒܲܕܵܐ K. ܠܒܸܕܘ Sh.]

ܡܦܲܬܦܸܬ K. = ܡܦܲܛܦܸܛ U. *to whisper*, § 113, *e*.

ܡܣܲܒܸܛ K., with ܬ U., *to prove, affirm*, § 110, *c*.

ܢܘܼܩܛܵܐ f. *dot, point*, Turk. نقطه.

ܣܘܼܠܛܵܢ, rarely with ܬ, *captain*, m., Arab. سلطان.

ܣܲܩܲܬ, or with ܛ, U. Tkh. *maimed, lame*, Arab. سقط, p. 305.

ܫܲܪܵܣܬ *true*, and ܫܲܪܵܣܬܘܼܬܵܐ *truth*, often with ܛ.

ܥܲܬܵܪ, or with ܛ, *grocer*, m., O.S. ܥܛܵܪܵܐ, Arab. عطار.

ܦܘܼܬܲܬܵܐ f. *apron*, Arab. Turk. فوطه, Pers. فوته.

ܦܲܪܬܲܥܢܵܐ *a flea*, usually with ܛ, § 89 (2).

ܩܘܼܚܬ *scarce*, Turk. قحط.

ܩܘܼܬܝ f. *small box*, Turk. قوطى, Kurd. قوتى.

ܩܵܬܝܼܪ m. *mule*, Turk. قاطر.

ܫܲܪܬ f. *condition, covenant*, Arab. شرط.

ܫܵܬܝܼܪ m. *runner, footman*, Turk. شاطر.

ܫܵܬܸܚ U., or with ܛ, *to air clothes* (O.S. ܫܛܲܚ *to spread*). With ܛ also in N.S. *to stretch oneself, spread open.*

ܬܲܒܥ *temper*, f., Arab. طبع.

ܬܵܘܵܐ m. *fryingpan*, Turk. طاوه and تابه.

ܬܘܼܩܡܵܩ m. *mallet*, see p. 334.

ܬܘܼܩܵܐ *necklace*, m., Turk. طوق.

ܬܘܼܬܝ ܩܘܼܫܝ *parrot*, m., Turk. طوطى قوشى.

ܬܠܵܬ݂ܵܐ, or ܬܠܵܬܵܐ, *three*, and cognate numerals, § 26, very often have ܛ initial. In ܬܠܵܬ݂ܵܝܗܘܢ *all three of them*, both Taus often = ܛ, and so in ܬܠܵܬ݂ܡܵܐܐ U. In ܬܠܵܬ݂ܝܢ Tau usually remains.

ܬܲܡܲܥܟܵܪ, or with ܛ, *avaricious*, Pers. طمعكار.

ܬܸܢܟܹܐ U., in K. with ܛ, *tin* (in sheets), Turk. تنكه.

ܬܸܦܠ *infant*, m., rarely with ܛ, Arab. طفل.

ܬܲܣܡܵܐ f. *strap* (p. 46), Turk. تصمه or طاصمه.

ܬܵܩ *layer*, Turk. طاق.

§ 124. *Interchange of* ܬ *and* ܫ.

In O.S. a ܬ frequently corresponds to a Hebrew ש: e.g. ܬܲܠܓܵܐ O.S. Chald. and N.S. *snow* = שֶׁלֶג Heb. So also in N.S. ܬ and ܫ are sometimes interchanged. Thus N.S. ܬܦܵܟ݂ *to be spilt* or *upset* = N.S. ܫܦܵܟ݂ *to overflow, be poured out*, O.S. ܫܦܲܟ݂ *to pour out*, cf. ܡܬܦܸܟ݂ and ܡܫܦܸܟ݂ N.S. both *to pour out* or *spill*.

In Upper Ṭiari ܬ very frequently has the sound of ܫ. Thus ܒܲܝܬܵܐ *house*, ܐܵܬܹܐ *come*, ܐܸܬܹܐ ܠܝܼ *I came* (but not ܐܵܬܹܐ the present participle and tense), ܟܬܵܝܬܵܐ *hen*, ܡܘܼܬܝܼܬܵܐ *brought*, f., are pronounced respectively *bésha, shâ, shélî, kshésha, mûshésha;* and so all endings in ܝܼܬܵܐ, and many others. For the aspirate, see p. 299.

In Zakhu aspirated Tau frequently becomes Simkath: thus ܒܲܝܣܵܐ, ܐܵܣܹܐ, ܣܸܦܪܵܐ, ܣܹܝܒ, ܡܣܲܣܣܵܐ, ܐܝܼܣ, ܠܲܝܣ (*las*); but ܐܝܼܬ݂ܠܹܗ etc. The same words also are used with ܬ in Z., though less frequently. So ܦ = ܘ, as ܟܲܦܘܵܐ, ܡܘܼܠܒ, for ܟܲܦܦܵܐ ܡܦܲܠܒ etc.

§ 125. ܬ in the Qudshanis dialect often has a sound between ܗ and ܟ݂, as ܡܝܼܬܵܐ *dead*, pronounced *mikha* (nearly). For this sound cf. § 107. So many parts of the verb ܐܵܬܹܐ *to come*, § 46.

§ 126. ܐ frequently falls, especially in U. Sal. Q. Gaw.:—

a. In plurals in U.: ܣܘ̈ܣܰܘܳܬܐ *horses*, frequently pronounced *sûsâwâ-î*, ܡܰܘܳܬܐ *villages*, frequently *mâwâ-î*, p. 67.

b. In Sal., Gaw., J., and Q. plurals. The ܐ disappears (but see p. 40), and the accent thus comes to be on the last syllable remaining. ܕܷܦܢܐ *side*, and ܕܷܦ̈ܢܐ (= ܕܷܦܢܳܬܐ) *sides*, are only distinguished by accent, *dípna* and *dipná*. So ܕܷܦ̈ܢܰܢ *our sides*.

c. In Sal. Gaw. J. Q. the ܐ falls in singulars in ܢܐ, as ܟܘܣܝܬܐ *a hat*, for ܟܘܣܝܬܐ; ܛܶܠܳܠܝܬܐ *shade*, for ܛܶܠܳܠܝܬܐ. So also ܦܳܬܐ *face* = ܦܳܬܐ; ܡܳܬܐ *village* = ܡܳܬܐ p. 67; ܒܝܬ *house* = ܒܝܬܐ.

d. In the same districts ܘ replaces ܐ in the abstract termination ܘܬܐ § 78, as ܙܰܕܝܩܘܬܐ *righteousness* = ܙܰܕܝܩܘܬܐ. So even in U. ܝܰܬܝܪܘܬܐ m. *excess* = ܝܰܬܝܪܘܬܐ K. f.

e. In all districts in compound nouns of the form ܦܰܪܚܢܰܝܟܰܠܒ *a butterfly* (sic); and the fem. pres. part. in K. as on p. 34.

f. In ܚܕܐ, ܚܕܐ and words derived from them, § 16 (2).

g. ܐܝܬ ܒܝ Ti. Al. *I can* = ܒܝ ܐܝܬ; so ܐܝܬ often when alone in Q., and elsewhere also when = ܒ § 67; so often ܠܟ Al. *lé.*

ܠܓܷܣܐ ܠ *below* = ܠܓܷܣܐ § 67.

ܐܬܐ *to come*, and its causative, many parts of, §§ 46, 47.

ܒܳܬܰܪ U. = ܒܳܬܰܪ K., O.S. (ܐ) *after.*

ܕܷܣܡܰܠ U. Tkh. *a napkin, handkerchief*, f. (usually), Pers. دستمال (also ܢܷܫܝܦܐ U. ܡܷܚܝܟܐ K. ܩܶܢܒܐ Al.).

ܚܰܕܬܐ Q. = ܚܰܕܬܐ *new*, and similar forms, § 21 (9) and p. 313.

ܬܠܳܬܐ U. *three*, m., and cognate numerals, p. 65.

APPENDIX.

I. Vernacular of the Jews of Azerbaijan.

The Jews of North-west Persia speak a dialect which bears a close resemblance to that of the Urmi Syrians. The following specimen, to which a literal translation in Urmi Syriac is added, is from a leaf* printed at Odessa by an Azerbaijan Jew as an example of a proposed translation of the Old Testament into his native tongue. It is given exactly as written, except that Syriac letters are used instead of Hebrew to shew more clearly the relation to the vernacular Syriac. The Jewish writer has not inserted Dagesh forte.

Psalm ii.

Azerbaijan Jews. | *Urmi Syrians.*

(Syriac text in two columns, verses 6 and 7)

---

¹ ܗ for ܚ.—² Cf. O.S. ܚܘܠܟܢܐ *power*. Heb. and Chald. שִׁלְטוֹן. ܐ for ܠ.
—³ The adjective comes before the noun, contrary to the Syriac usage.—⁴ ܐ. for ܠ.—
⁵ The future without ܒܕ as in Ṭiari.—⁶ Apparently the final syllable has the second long Zlama sound, the first the short Zlama sound as U., as against the K. sound, which is Khwaṣa.—⁷ This method of taking affixes is unlike O.S. or N.S. The ܠ corresponds to the first ܘ in ܟܝܒܝ.—⁸ The substantive verb, formed on the same prin-

---

* The author is indebted for this leaf to the Rev. Dr Labaree of the American Presbyterian Mission at Urmi.

APP.] VERNACULAR OF THE AZERBAIJAN JEWS. 341

[Syriac text in two columns, with numbered notes (8)–(11) and (8)–(11)]

ciple as the 3 sing. of N.S., and 3 pl. in K. etc. But the pronoun is not in the affix form as we should expect. The forms given in this extract are, 2 s. m. ܒܠܟ, 3 s. f. ܒܠܗ, 3 pl. ܒܠܗ.—⁹ The same metathesis as in N.S., see § 92, b. ܡܓܝܕ from ܡܓܝܕ or ܢܓܝܕ.—¹⁰ For the metathesis cf. ܢܬܠ Tkh. = ܬܠ § 46.—¹¹ For the form of the verb cf. ܠܒ K., ܐܠܝ Al.—¹² ܒ for ܠ as above. So sometimes in K. ܒ takes the place of ܠ as the sign of the direct object.—¹³ The preformative ܡܨܕ omitted as in U. The Rwaṣa (Kibbuts under ה in the original) stands for ܠܗܘܢ. The ܗ is omitted as in N.S.; the ܠ as occasionally in N.S.; the ܢ as in Ṭiari.—¹⁴ Turk. دمور.—¹⁵ Construct state. For the metathesis cf. ܐܡܕܬ K. = ܡܕܬ O.S., U.—¹⁶ The writer represents the ܓܿ sound by ܝ.—¹⁷ For this word cf. § 83 (14).—¹⁸ Heb. עתה.—¹⁹ The כ of ܕܓܕ has a ܠ sound, as it has a ܠ sound in N.S., cf. §§ 104, 105.—²⁰ For the ending of N.S. ܡܒܝܬܡܗ.—²¹ Pthakha for N.S. Zqapa.—²² The verb ܫܡܫ to serve, is used in K., Al.—²³ This word seems to show a verb

Psalm iii.

ܟܠ ܘܕܚܠܬ ܠܘܗܝ U. Ti., *Do not be afraid*, see § 46, or ܘܕܝܠ, cf. N.S. ܘܕܝܕ, under ܘܕܝܕ.—[24] The verb ܕܚܒ *to love*, as O.S. is used in K.—[25] The abstract termination seems to be ܠ܍ = ܐܘܬܐ.—[26] This second conjugation form, unlike anything in O.S., is common to this language and N.S. The verb ܐܓܕ (1st Conj.) is used in Al., as O.S., *to trust*.—[27] ܠ in this language seems to have no other force than א and to make no break in the middle of a word, unlike N.S. Thus ארא = ܝܕܚܠ. So here ܠܕ is changed into ܠ. Cf. N.S. verbs ܠܠ.—[28] ܡܢ for ܡܚܒ.—[29] The pronoun affix for 3 s. m. is given in the original variously ܗ֊ and ܗ֊, unlike N.S. Cf. O.S. forms like ܡ.ܩܛܠܬܝܗܝ *thou (f.) didst kill him*; and the Heb. 3 s. m. affixes וֹ‎יה‎, וֹיה‎, ֹיה‎.—[30] So the ܒ is often omitted in N.S. in the second present tense before a labial.—[31] See ܬܘܡܐ § 68.—[32] In U. the ܡܢ is very rarely dropped before a vowel, § 68.—[33] Cf. O.S. ܪܚܡܬܐ mercy.—[34] The verb ܩܪܐ to call, is used in K., not in O.S., but so Hebrew קרא.—[35] So in N.S. they say ܡܓܕܪ ܦܘܢܝܐ to answer.—[36] Cf. ܟܠ ܠܗ, one of the past forms of ܐܙܠ § 46.—[37] ܕ for ܠ of N.S. ܓܢܐ in O.S. = delirium.—[38] Perhaps = ܓܕܕ to be strong, K. Also O.S. to become true.—[39] ? O.S. ܚܕܘܬܐ joy, y = ܝ.—[40] ܟܠ for ܟܠ as in Tiari.—[41] ܒ for ك.—[42] See § 69.—[43] Apparently = ܕܟܕܘܣ U. or ܕܟܕ K. See § 50.—[44] So O.S. P'al. In N.S. in this sense it is 2 Conj.—[45] = ܕܚܨܢܐ K. Cf. Turk. يان side.—[46] See p. 331.—[47] Cf.

ܕܝܼܟܼܝܼܬܵܐ : ܓܵܪܵܐ ܕܟܬܵܒܼܵܐ ܐܲܓܼܒܲܝܬܼܘܿܢ | ܗܘܿܕܟܼܣ [48] (8) [49] ܦܿܕܿܥܒܿ [50] ܙܝܼܕ

ܠܘܿܗܝ * ܗܿ (8) ܩܘܿܕܡܵܢܼܐ : ܗܿ | ܣܘܿܘܿܗ [8] ܙܿܟܼ : ܗܿܡܓܼܕܵܐ ܣܚܵܘܿܕ

ܕܡܿܕܵܢܼܐ ܠܟܼܗ : ܗܿܡܸܕܵܐ ܓܲܣܚܵܘܿܕ | ܣܘܿܕܟܼ [41] ܐܲܢܝܼܟܼܣ : ܗܸܠܵܗ *

ܠܒܼܥܘܿܕ ܠܵܗ ܓܼܠܝܼܩܘܿܝܼ : ܗܸܠܵܗ *

O.S. ܕܿܥܒܼܕܵܐ *wicked.*—[48] See § 50.—[49] This seems to be feminine, unlike the Syriac equivalent ܩܘܿܕܡܵܢܼܐ.—[50] Perhaps = N.S. ܐܵܝܼ or ܐܵܝܼ *this* (f.).

II. PROVERBS[1].

1. ܡܢ ܪܘܒܗ ܡܚܐܕܗܝ ܠܚܡ ܣܡܢܗ Of his spittle he is making bread and butter. 'He will skin a flint to make soup.'

2. ܦܠܘ ܕܡܠܝܢܗ ܕܦܘܡܕܗ ܠܐ ܗܘܐ : ܐܒܠ ܡܫܚܐ ܘܪܙܐ ܟܘܕ ܒܥܐ U. Pillau is not for filling the mouth, but oil and rice are necessary. Said when a man is not careful in his eating, and does not know the pleasures of the table.

3. ܣܒ ܡܣܩܠܬܗ ܠܓܘܗ ܡܓܗܕ ܟܣܗ ܕܢܩܝܒܗ Let him put his reels by themselves. Said by a man when told that another is angry: Never mind, I do not care; I have nothing to do with him.

4. ܟܘܠܚܗ ܕܡܝܐ ܕܬܘܕܢܐ ܕܦܩܪ ܕܐ ܦܝܓܕ A pitcher of water breaks on the way to the well, cf. Eccles. xii. 6. 'A sailor dies on the sea.'

5. ܪܒܐ ܠܝܗ ܡܝܓ : ܣܩܦܐ ܟܘܠܘܝ ܠܐ ܡܛܝ ܠܝܗ. Aliter: ܕܒܐ ... ܕܣܓܠܐ The rope was short and did not reach you. Said when a man comes in too late for a thing, or if he does not listen to the beginning of a story and then wishes to have it repeated. 'A day too late for the fair.'

6. ܢܩܡܘܬܕܐ ܕܓܘܒܐ ܠܐ ܚܓܝܕ ܘܗ : ܘܓܕܙܠܡܩܐ ܒܐ ܡܩܘܡܕܝܠܐ ܠܝܗ ܬܚܓܘܩܕܘܗ The rat could not get in at the hole, and now he has hung a turnip on to its tail. Said when a man after failing to do a thing tries to do something more difficult.

[1] The explanations added here are those given by the Syrians from whom the proverbs were collected.

7. ܢܫܐ ܒܢܫܐ: ܘܛܝܪܐ ܒܦܪܐ *A man among men, and a bird among feathers.* A man cannot stand alone.

8. ܟܠ ܥܪܒܐ ܒܐܩܠܐ ܕܝܗ ܒܢ ܬܠܝ ܠܗ *They hang every sheep by its own leg.* A man pays the penalty for his own misdeeds.

9. ܐܢ ܠܐ ܝܕܥܬ: ܚܙܝ (K. ܚܘܪ) ܠܫܒܒܘܟ *If you do not know look at your neighbour.* Do not be content to remain ignorant.

10. ܠܐ ܡܢ ܥܘܒܕܗ ܕܐܠܗܐ: ܘܠܐ ܡܢ ܒܬܐ ܕܢܫܐ K. *Not from the affairs of God and not from the houses of men.* Do not pry.

11. ܐܢ ܒܡܦܩܬܐ ܕܫܡܫܐ ܠܐ ܫܚܝܢܬ: ܒܡܥܪܒܘܗܝ ܠܐ ܫܚܝܢܬ *If you do not get warm at sunrise you will not get warm when it sets.* If the beginning is wrong, the end cannot be right.

12. ܡܢܕܝ ܕܠܐ ܕܡܐ ܠܡܪܗ: ܟܒܝܬܐ ܝܠܗ K. *That which does not resemble its master is spurious.* 'Like father, like son.'

13. ܠܐ ܚܙܝܬ ܣܛܢܐ: ܘܠܐ ܥܒܕܬ ܨܠܝܒܐ K. *If you do not see Satan you need not make the sign of the cross.* You would not have gone wrong had you not fallen among bad companions.

14. ܗܘ ܕܠܐ ܫܡܥ ܒܐܕܢܗ: ܡܫܡܥܝ ܩܕܠܗ ܒܬ ܡܫܡܥܝ ܠܗ K. *If a man will not listen with his ear they will make him listen at the back of his neck,* i.e. beat him.

15. ܗܘ ܕܓܝܪ ܘܠܐ ܡܫܐܠ: ܡܒܪܒܠ ܘܠܝ ܕܟܝܪ ܒܗ K. *The man who marries without asking (advice) may lose his wife and no one will take any notice of him.* No one should act without advice.

16. ܠܐ ܝܕܥܬ ܛܝܒܘܬܝ: ܗܕܟ ܕܡܢܣܝܬ ܚܕ ܐܚܪܢܐ K. *You will not know the benefit you get from me till you try another.* No one knows when he is well off.

17. ܐܢ ܠܐ ܐܬܐ ܗܘ ܐܚܪܝܐ: ܠܐ ܝܕܥܚ ܡܫܘܚܬܐ ܕܗܘ ܩܕܡܝܐ U. *If the last does not come we shall not know the measure of the first.* [The same.]

18. ܗܘ ܕܢܝܡ ܩܕܡ ܒܥܠܕܒܒܗ : ܒܝܫܬܐ ܡܥܝܪܝܢ ܠܗ ܀ K. *If a man sleeps in the presence of his enemy, calamities will wake him up.*

19. ܡܝܐ ܪܫ ܩܪܐ : ܓܘܙܐ ܪܫ ܩܘܒܬܐ ܀ *Water on the top of a gourd, walnuts on the top of a dome.* One can get nothing into a fool's head.

20. ܗܘ ܕܠܐ ܫܡܥ ܠܩܘܠ ܡܪܗ : ܩܪܐ ܡܕܢܗ ܛܒ ܡܢܗ ܀ K. *A gourd's head is better than a man who will not obey his superior.* A fool is better than a disobedient man.

21. ܐܢ ܣܒܬܐ ܨܒܝܐ ܠܨܘܡܐ : ܥܪܘܒܬܐ ܘܐܪܒܥܒܫܒܐ ܣܓܝ ܐܢܘܢ ܀ K. *If an old woman wants to fast, Fridays and Wednesdays are plenty.* Said to a man to dissuade him from doing a thing he is fond of: Do not do it now, there is plenty of time to do it in.

22. ܐܢ ܓܢܒܐ ܗܘܐ : ܠܠܘܬܐ ܣܓܝ ܐܢܘܢ ܀ U. *If you are a thief there are plenty of nights.* [The same.]

23. ܐܢ ܠܐ ܐܙܠ ܒܪܝܫܗ : ܠܐ ܝܕܥ ܠܗ ܡܫܘܚܬܐ ܕܪܓܠܗ ܀ K. *If (a man) does not walk on his head he will not know the measure of his foot.* Great men ought to consider their inferiors.

24. ܒܝܬܗ ܕܕܓܠܐ ܝܩܕ ܠܗ : ܘܐܢܫ ܠܐ ܗܝܡܢܗ ܀ (aliter ܕܫܢܝܐ) *The liar's (madman's) house was burnt and no one believed him.* 'He cried Wolf so often that no one believed him when the wolf came.'

25. ܚܠܒܐ ܡܓܒܢܐ ܕܒܐܝܕܐ ܛܒ ܡܢ ܡܐܐ ܕܠܐ ܡܝܟܘܬܐ ܀ K. *Sour milk which has been tried is better than untried curds.* 'A bird in the hand is worth two in the bush.' In K. ܚܠܒܐ is sour, not sweet, milk.

26. ܡܕܝܢ ܒܚܕ ܐܕܢܗ ܘܡܦܩ ܒܐܚܪܢܐ (sic) : ܘܡܦܩ ܠܗ ܒܐܚܪܬܐ ܀ *He takes it in at one ear and lets it out at the other.*

27. ܪܫܐ ܕܛܝܢܐ ܗܘ ܝܗܒܠܗ ܙܚܡܬܐ ܠ ܐܩܠܗ U. *A mud head gives trouble to its foot.* A foolish governor is the bane of the people.

28. ܐܢ ܒܩܠܐ ܪܡܐ ܦܝܫ ܗܘܐ ܒܢܝܐ ܒܝܬܐ : ܚܡܪܐ ܬܪܝܢ ܩܠܥܐ ܒܚܕ ܝܘܡܐ ܒܢܐ ܗܘܐ ܒܚܕ ܝܘܡܐ K. *If a house could be built by loud talking, an ass could build two castles in one day.* 'Much cry, little wool.'

29. ܡܪܝ ܠ ܚܡܪܐ ܡܚܘܝ ܬܪܒܝܬܘܟ : ܡܫܩܠܠܗ ܕܘܢܒܗ. ܗܘ ܡܘܒܠܐ ܚܡܪܐ ܠܗ *They said to the ass, Shew your good breeding, and he lifted up his tail.* Said when a man plays the fool, when he ought to be serious.

30. ܡܦܢܝܐ ܡܝܬܐ ܡܢ ܒܝܬ ܩܒܘܪܐ ܠܗ ? *Do they turn away a dead man from a graveyard?* Said by a man who is turned out of his lodging after nightfall.

31. ܢܦܠܐ ܟܣܐ ܠ ܩܠܗ : ܝܐ ܩܠܗ ܝܐ ܥܢܝܬܗ *The bowl has fallen: either (I heard) the sound of its (fall) or the echo.* 'If you throw mud some is sure to stick.'

32. ܐܬܐ ܠܗ ܚܡܪܐ : ܡܫܘܬܩܠܗ ܙܡܪܐ *The ass has come and stopped the singing.* Said of an interruption.

33. ܩܪܩܢܐ ܩܪܐ ܩܪܩܢܐ ܠ ܩܕܡ *A cock crows in the presence of another.* Said when an accusation is made secretly.—Confront the parties.

34. ܕܠܐ ܬܦܪܘܩ ܠܐ ܙܠ : ܟܐܦܐ ܠܗܠܘܗ *Do not (go) far behind, (put) a stone on it.* Restrain yourself.

35. ܗܘ ܕܡܝܬܝܘܗ ܒܠܠܝܐ : ܡܝܬܝ ܠܗ ܒܝܘܡܐ U. *Let him who brings it by night, bring it by day.* I do not care whether he does it secretly or openly.

36. ܗܘ ܕܡܘܒܠܐ ܠܗ ܠܗ ܒܝܬܐ ܫܢܬܐ ܩܕܡܝܬܐ : ܐܗ ܫܢܬܐ ܠܐ ܡܝܬܝ ܠܗ K. *Let not him who brought it to the house last year bring it this year.* Said of an incorrigibly idle person.

37. ܀܀܀܀܀܀܀ U. *Hereafter we will not light the lamp.* Said sarcastically of an ugly bride or the like. [Cf. no. 125.]

38. ܀܀܀܀܀܀܀ *He is an unwashed spoon.* Said of one who interferes.

39. ܀܀܀܀܀܀܀ U. *A slender turnip has a thick root.* 'Quality is better than quantity.'

40. ܀܀܀܀܀܀܀ *They had not left a man in the house, and he said, Take my armour to the chief man's house.* [Same as no. 6.]

41. ܀܀܀܀܀܀܀ *A herb grows according to its root.* 'Like father, like son.'

42. ܀܀܀܀܀܀܀ *No man calls his own dowi sour* [dowi is a drink made from curdled milk, water, and herbs]. 'Every man thinks his own chickens are the best.'

43. ܀܀܀܀܀܀܀ *A good name: a deserted village.* Said of a famous man or place that is poor.

44. ܀܀܀܀܀܀܀ *The floods have swept away the mill and he is asking for the hoppers* (loose pieces of wood used to bring the wheat down on the millstone). Said when a man expects to find something valuable in a house which has been cleared out by robbers. Cf. no. 127.

45. ܀܀܀܀܀܀܀ *If the master of the house is an accomplice with the thieves, they can take the bull out by the skylight.* 'A man's foes are they of his own household.'

46. ܀܀܀܀܀܀܀ U. [in K. substitute ܀܀܀

ܕܡܝܬܐ for ܢܝܪܕܝܢ ܡܘܠܠܐ] *The Mollah Nasir Din said: If Nasir Din had not been dead the wolves would not have carried off his ass.* If the heads of the nation were not asleep, no one could injure it.

47. ܐܢ ܗܪܝܣܐ ܠܐ ܝܘܬ ܐܟܝܠܐ: ܠܟܡܐ ܗܘ ܡܘ ܒܛܢܘܢܬܐ ܝܠܗ؟ *If you have not eaten the cooked wheat, why have you the stomach ache?* If you have nothing to do with the matter, why do you interfere?

48. ܬܪܥܘܗ ܕܕܐܒܐ: ܕܐܒܐ ܒܬܪܥܐ *At the report about the wolf, the wolf is at the door.* 'Talk of the Devil and he is sure to appear.'

49. ܪܫܐ ܕܟܘܣܝܬ ܙܘܢܐ ܝܠܗ *The top of the hat is a hole.* Said of a man who cannot keep a secret.

50. ܡܝܬܘܢ ܕܟܣܒܪܐ ܝܠܗ: ܚܝܐ ܚܠܘܐ ܒܐ ܐܟܠܝ *A dead man thinks the living are (always) eating sweetmeats.* Said of a man who thinks a rich man's lot altogether enviable. Halwa is a sort of 'Turkish delight.'

51. ܦܝܕܐ ܠܐ ܡܚܝܟ ܒܪܟܒܐ: ܝܘܡܘܗܝ ܠܐ ܥܒܪ *Let not the foot traveller mock at the rider: his day will not pass.* Said if a poor man rails at the rich.

52. ܟܪܒܘܠܐ ܒܟܝܐ ܝܠܗ ܥܠ ܟܐܦܐ *The clod is weeping for (the fate of) the stone.* Cf. 'Daughters of Jerusalem, etc.'

53. ܛܥܢܐ ܢܦܝܠܐ ܝܠܗ: ܠܩܘܛܝ ܡܫܩܘܠܐ ܝܠܗ *The load has gone and he is asking for the box.* Same as no. 44. When a horse's load has fallen down it is unreasonable to expect the box which was placed on the top of the load to be still in its place.

54. ܗܦܬܐ ܗܦܬܐ: ܡܠܥܣܬܗ ܒܝܫ ܝܬܝܪܐ *Hafta for hafta: yet it requires more munching* [1 hafta = 4 lbs. avoirdupois]. The Urmi people tell a story against the mountaineers that one of them brought down honey to sell and exchanged it for carrots, hafta for hafta. He complained that the carrots were harder to munch than the honey, in the above words.

55. ܒܶܙ ܡܶܢܕܶܘܣ ܕܝܩܶܐ ܒܐܦܰܘܗܝ ܘܐܡܶܪ. ܡܶܛܪܰܐ ܕܓܶܕܝܳܢܳܐ ܠܶܗ One of them spat in his face, and he said, It is spring rain. Said if a man pays no attention to reproof, but takes it as a matter of course.

56. ܘܗܰܒ ܟܶܣܦܳܟ: ܘܐܰܟܽܘܠ ܚܰܠܒܳܐ Pay (your) money and eat the halwa (see no. 50). 'Money down.'

57. ܟܰܠܒܳܐ ܒܶܐ ܢܳܒܰܚ: ܩܰܛܳܪܳܐ ܒܶܐ ܥܳܒܰܕܳܐ The dog barks, but the caravan enters. Said when a man pays no attention to an insult.

58. ܟܽܘܕܢܳܐ ܐܰܗܐ ܠܐܳܗܶܐ ܡܰܣܡܽܘܗܝ ܒܢܰܥܠܳܐ. ܘܩܰܛ ܘܳܙ ܡܰܟܽܘܡܰܓܳܐ ܟܶܠܐ ܕܥܽܘܠܳܗ They came to shoe the mule and the frog put out her foot too (to be shod). If one man gets a present everyone else expects one too.

59. ܐܰܕܢܳܐ ܕܐܳܬܶܐ ܒܕܝܠܽܘܗܝ ܐܰܗܐ: ܒܶܐ ܥܶܕܰܕܳܐ ܗܽܘܡ A guest who comes of his own accord (lit. foot) is without honour.

60. ܣܳܟܰܕܳܐ ܡܺܝܬܳܐ ܟܽܘܕܢܳܐ ܒܶܐ ܗܽܘܡ A dead donkey becomes a mule. Said when a man exaggerates his losses.

61. ܠܐܳ ܩܶܥܡܶܕ ܣܳܟܶܕܝ. ܩܰܝܛܳܐ ܒܶܐ ܐܳܬܐ: ܡܰܢܓܠܳܐ ܒܶܐ ܣܳܘܓ Do not be sorry, my donkey. The summer is coming and I will reap some clover. Said in order to put off an importunate beggar.

62. ܐܶܣܩܰܢ ܕܣܰܒܰܕ ܠܶܗ ܕܶܣܢܳܐ ܨܽܘܦܰܕܡܶܕ ܚܰܓܰܕܳܐ: ܘܐܶܢܐ ܗܳܘܝ ܡܶܚܶܬܳܒܠܰܓܕܳܐ ܣܳܘܦܳܢܰܢ ܠܶܗ ܒܚܰܕܰܢ We went to get something out of our beards, but we had to add our moustaches to them. Said when a man gives a bribe to get an office, and he not only fails but is fleeced further.

63. ܓܰܢܳܒܳܐ ܠܓܰܢܳܒܳܐ ܫܰܘܰܐ: ܚܽܘܡܶܓܶܗܳܘܣ ܒܶܐ ܡܰܢܟܶܕ ܠܶܗ When a thief meets a thief he hides his club. 'Turk fears Turk.'

64. ܘܡܰܕܺܝܗܽܘܢ ܠܟܽܠ ܐܳܕܺܝܬܳܐ: ܩܕܳܢܺܝܗܽܘܢ ܠܟܽܠ ܒܓܰܕܽܘܬܳܐ Their pride is out of doors (lit. in the door), but their pounded wheat is in a gourd: i.e. they keep up appearances, but they are poor. Gourds, dried and

hollow, are used by the poor as jars. This is said of a man who boasts without having anything to boast of.

65. ܡܚܐܦܐ ܕܘܟܝܐ ܠܡܝܐ ܚܓܢܐ *Under pretence of chickens the hen pecks.* Said of a man who takes more than his share under some pretence.

66. U. ܕܣܒܬ ܠܒ ܕܓܘܫܐ ܕܓܘܦܐ̈ܐ . ܠܐܠܐ ܡܚܕܐ ܚܕܘܡܐ ܕܐ *I went after the smell of the chops, but (they were only) branding donkeys.* Said when a man is disappointed.

67. ܡܢ ܚܠ ܕܟܠ ܣܗܕܐ ܣܘܩܐ : ܕܐ ܗܘܐ ܢܒܝܕ ܕܝܩܢܐ (*If you take) a hair from every beard, you will make a beard.* Said when asking subscriptions for a charitable object. 'Every little makes a mickle.'

68. ܕܐܒܐ ܕܩܢܙܒ : ܡܓܚܟܢܐ ܕܓܠܒܐ ܟܕ ܗܘܐ *A wolf when it gets old is the laughingstock of the dogs.* A rich man who loves his money is thought nothing of.

69. ܙܕܟܐ ܡܚܒܝܒܢܐ ܡܬܐ ܕܝܢܐ ܟܕ ܓܗܠܐ *Soft earth drinks in water easily.* Said in praise of gentleness (ܡܚܒܝܒ) means both *soft* and *gentle*).

70. ܙܘܕܩܐ ܦܠܚܐ ܡܠܗ : ܕܓܢܐ ܒܢܐ ܠܟܐ *The husband* (lit. *male*) *is a labourer, the wife a mason.* Said when a wife is a good manager though her husband's earnings are small.

71. ܗܕܒ ܦܝܕܩܢܐ ܗܘܝ ܚܕ : ܢܒܝܕ ܠܗܘܢܐ ܕܐ ܦܠܟܟ ܠܗ *If two chestnuts become one they (can) crack a walnut.* 'Union is strength.'

72. U. ܡܢ ܠܚܕ ܕܓܢܠܐ ܡܓܢܕܓܕܒ : ܠܕܘܗ ܡܓܢܕܓܘܗܕ ܠܟܐ *Instead of the buffaloes crying out, the cart cries out.* Said if the man who inflicts an injury complains instead of the injured person.

73. ܘܩܘܝ ܗܟܕ : ܡܘܠܠܐ ܡܢ ܡܓܕ ܦܠܝܕ ܠܗ *Give money and bring the mollah out of the mosque.* Money can do anything.

74. ܗܘܢܢܐ ܗܕ ܕܓܠܐ ܗܘܣܘܗܘܦܣܘܗ ܕܕܐ ܠܟܐ : ܚܙܕܦܢܐ ܚܛܝܒܢܐ. ܗܘܕܗ ܕܐ *While the wise man is turning it over in his mind* (lit.

pouring it on his wisdom) *the fool jumps over the brook.* 'Fools rush in where angels fear to tread.'

75. ܬܚܶܝܬ ܓܶܠܳܐ ܡܰܝܳܐ *Water beneath straw.* 'Still waters run deep.'

76. ܣܘܣܝܐ ܕܰܟܝܳܒܐ: ܢܒܛܢ ܣܘܡܗ ܒܚܝܠܐ *A gentle horse kicks hard.* [The same.]

77. ܐ݇ܢܳܫܳܐ ܙܥܘܪܐ: ܒܝܬܠܗ ܣܘܡܗ ܓܘܪܐ *A little man has big dreams*, i.e. talks big.

78. ܚܰܕ ܡܢܝܗܘܢ ܡܨܒܝܪܗ: ܐܢܐ ܗܘܝܢ ܡܣܘܟܪܐ: ܗܘ ܐ݇ܚܪܢܐ ܡܨܘܒܝܪܗ: ܚܕܟܡܐ ܒܢܝܐ ܐܝܬ ܠܗ؟ *One of them said I am a eunuch. The other asked how many children he had.* Said if a man asks an unnecessary question.

79. ܒܣܪܐ ܐܶܢ ܙܳܘ: ܡܪܕܘܗܝ ܠܐ ܗܘܐ ܐܟܠܐ *If the meat be cheap the soup will be uneatable.* 'Cheap and nasty.'

80. ܣܘܣܝܐ ܐܦܝ ܕܕ.ܓܒܠܐ ܐܘܪܚ: ܐܝܢܐ ܥܠ ܓܘܗ ܕܟܣܣܗ ܕܘܡ ܓܢ ܐܙܠ *Though a snake go crooked, yet he goes straight into his own hole.* However wicked a man is, he ought not to injure his own family. 'It is an ill bird that fouls its own nest.'

81. ܓܠܕܐ ܡܢ ܒܝܬܚܢܘܬܐ ܣܝܕ ܐܣܩܠ ܓܢ ܟܠܒܐ: ܐܝܢܐ ܐܩܠܗ ܕܟܣܣܗ ܓܢ ܥܒܝܕ *A dog steals a leg (of mutton) from the butcher's shop, but he cuts off his own leg*; i.e. they will not let him go there again. Almost 'A burnt child dreads the fire.'

82. ܡܢܕܝ ܕܡܣܟܝܢܐ ܕܣܝܩ ܠܗ: ܥܠ ܕܥܬܝܪܐ ܡܚܙܝ ܗܘܐ ܠܗ *If a poor man's things are stolen (lit. go) the rich man is warned (to look out).* Thieves begin with small things.

83. ܪܫܗ ܠܐ ܝܠܗ ܕܟܣܣܗ *His head is not his own.* Said of a man who can refuse nothing to those who beg of him.

84. ܚܕܵܒ݂ ܦ݁ܓ݂ܘܼܓ݂ܒ݂ ܟܲܠܬܝܼ ܐܲܢܬܝ ܫܡܲܥܝ ܒ݁ܪܵܬܝ ܐܵܡܪܸܢܘܵܟ݂ܝ *My daughter, I am talking to you; my daughter-in-law, listen.* Said when a man speaks to another in order that a third person may hear. It is not the custom for a man to speak to his daughter-in-law, and therefore when he wishes to scold her, he scolds his own daughter instead.

85. ܬܲܥܠܵܐ ܒ݁ܪܸܓ݂ܠܵܗ ܡܸܬܦ݂ܪܸܣ *The sly fox is caught by* (lit. *knocks against*) *his own foot.* Said when a guilty man is convicted by his own words.

86. ܟ̰ܡܵܐ ܕ݁ܡܵܚܹܝܬ ܠܩܲܛܘܼܣܵܐ ܗܲܕ݁ܟ݂ܵܐ ܕ݂ܘܲܕ݁ܪܵܐ ܒ݁ܐܲܦܵܟ݂ *The more you scratch a cat the more it will fly* (lit. *return*) *in your face.* If you injure a man he will injure you.

87. ܚܸܘܝܵܐ ܠܹܐ ܒ݁ܥܵܐ ܠܢܲܥܢܵܥܵܐ ܐܝܼܢܵܐ ܗܘ̤ ܒ݁ܐܝܼܕܹܗ ܕ݁ܬܲܪܥܹܗ ܓ̰ܘܼܕ݂ܘܵܢܹܗ *A snake dislikes mint, but it grows at his door* (*hole*). If you do not like a thing it is sure to be always meeting you.

88. ܐܝܼܕ݂ܵܟ݂ ܠܟ݂ܫܘܼܚܵܐ ܕ݁ܓ݂ܘܼܠܵܟ݂ ܦ݁ܫܘܿܛ ܠܵܗ̇ *Stretch out your foot according to the measure of your carpet.* 'Cut your coat according to your cloth.'

89. ܗܘܼܢܬܵܐ ܚܕ݂ܵܐ ܕ݁ܡܓ݂ܠܬܸܬ݁ ܠܵܗ̇ ܒ݁ܣܝܼܢܵܐ ܒ݁ܪܹܝܚܵܐ *If you rake up a dunghill, it will smell.* Said to pacify two men, generally to dissuade them from calling one another names.

90. ܢܵܫܵܐ ܙܥܘܿܪܵܐ ܒ݁ܥܵܒ݂ܝܼܪ ܒ݁ܬܲܪܥܵܐ ܡܲܢܟ݂ܸܦ݂ ܩܕܵܠܹܗ *When a small man enters a gateway he bows his head.* Said if a man takes unnecessary precautions.

91. ܐܘܼܟ݂ܠܲܢܘܼܟ݂ ܠܓ݂ܝܼܠܵܐ ܘܗܘ̤ܝܹܬ ܣܢܵܕ݂ܵܐ ܕ݁ܚܡܵܪܵܐ *You have eaten the halwa* (no. 50) *and are riding the donkey.* You have it all your own way.

92. ܡܸܢ ܣܘܼܣܝܵܐ ܣܠܝܼܩ ܠܹܗ ܘܕ݂ܟ݂ܝܼܒ݂ ܠܹܗ ܠܚܡܵܪܵܐ *He has got down from the horse and is riding the ass.* He has had a fall.

93. ܚܕ݂ܘܡܝ ܥܡ ܚܕܝ: ܒܕܘܝ ܕܟܠܢܐ ܡܘܕܝ ܒܟܐ؟ *Your portion with my portion* (i.e. we are eating together), *what are you staring at?* 'Share and share alike.'

94. ܚܘܪܐ ܥܡ ܓܡܠܐ ܓܐ ܦܠܚ: ܐܝܢܐ ܠܐ ܡܨܐ ܕܐܟܠ The *ox can work with the buffalo, but* (then) *he cannot eat* (he is too tired). Said when a poor man tries to spend like a rich companion and becomes bankrupt.

95. ܣܘܣܐ ܓܕܕܐ ܡܘܚܝ ܠܐ ܡܩܒܠ *Let not the brave horse receive the whip.* 'Do not beat a willing horse.'

96. ܣܘܣܐ ܘܓܕ ܚܘܕܢܐ ܓܐ ܦܠܚܝ: ܕܐܘܠܟܝ ܣܡܕܐ ܓܐ ܡܝܬ *The horse and the mule will fight, and between them the ass will get killed.* Those who interfere between two combatants get the worst of it.

97. ܐܠܗܐ ܓܐ ܡܚܝܛ ܠܛܘܪܕܢܐ ܪܡܐ: ܓܐ ܝܗܒܕ ܓܠܐܕ ܗܬܐ *God looks at the high mountains and gives* (them) *perpetual snows.* God recompenses each man as is right. Said especially of bad men.

98. ܠܓܡܠܐ ܟܐ ܚܢܐ ܕܟܠܘܢܐ ܡܝܚܗܘܡܗ ܟܒ. *He is giving the camel to drink out of a walnut husk* (not the shell). Said when a man gives a ridiculously small gift to one in need.

99. ܒܕܝܢܐ ܡܕܘܝܐ ܓܐ ܫܕܝ: ܐܕܟܝ ܐܪܒܥܝ ܠܐ ܝܗܝ ܡܝܨܝ ܗܘܗ ܠܡܩܠܘܗܝܕ *The fool threw a stone down the well, but forty wise men could not get it out.* Aliter (Socin) ܒܕ ܒܕܝܢܐ ܓܐ ܡܕܘܝܐ ܒܕ ܓܪܩܐ ܐܪܒܥܝ ܐܗܘܝ ܠܐ ܡܝܨܝ ܠܐܚܕܝ. ܘܡܩܠܘܗܝ ܟܐ.

100. ܟܠܐ ܚܝܕܢܐ ܓܐ ܫܕܝ: ܒܕܝܢܐ ܘܡܚܓܐ ܠܢܦܫܝ ܓܐ ܩܛܠܝ *The bride and bridegroom are happy, but the fools of the village kill themselves.* A fool gets no enjoyment out of life.

101. ܓܡܠܐ ܓܐ ܦܠܚ: ܓܡܠܐ ܓܐ ܐܟܠ؟ *The buffalo works; does the buffalo eat* (sc. *alone*)? A man ought to share with his family.

102. ܬ݂ܥܠܐ ܣܘܢܝܓܠܦ ܕܝܢܬܢ ܓܕ ܡܚܕ ܠܗ. ܠܥܢܒܐ: ܚܡܘܥ ܗ̈ܘܘ ܒܣܡܩܝܗܝ The fox could not reach the bunch of grapes, and said, How sour they were!

103. ܠܓܘܕܐ ܡܨܝܐ ܢܐ݂ܬܗܐ ܓܒ ܗ̈ܘܐ A wall has ears.

104. ܡܚܐܐ ܗܘܠܓܕ ܠܐ ܡܬܠܢ ܙܪܕܐ The river will not always bring down vine stocks. 'Lay by for a rainy day.'

105. ܐܗܢ ܡܝܐ ܣܬܝܢܬ ܩܒܢܐ ܚܣܕܐ: ܒܝܕ ܣܘܒ ܒܝܬܕܘܕܐ ܐܗܢ If water comes once in a channel, one may hope it will come again. Said when a man loses his money.

106. ܓܕܝܐ ܣܥܘܗ ܒܕܪܓܠܕ ܠܐ ܩܐܙ The kid will not always stay under the basket. Everyone may hope to get rich.

107. ܚܒܠܐ ܩܛܝܕ ܠܗ: ܚܕܓܐ ܡܕܘܕܘܗ ܠܗ The rope is cut, and the burden is scattered. Said, e.g., when a wife dies: the relationship made by her marriage is weakened by her death.

108. ܡܗ ܠܐܪܒܐ ܐܥܢܕܗܘܗ: ܘܟ ܡܕܐܒܝ ܒܕܒܐ. ܐܥܠܗ ܒܝܗܢܗ ܐܝܬ They said to the wolf, Go and tend the sheep; he said, My feet are bare. Said if a man is bidden to do something for his own advantage and he refuses.

109. ܗܘ ܕܚܙܕܪ ܓܐܙܐ: ܓܐ ܗ̈ܘܐ ܚܟܝܡܐܕ ܡܢ ܗܘ ܓܢܫܝܐ ܕܐܢܐ ܥܠܐ He who travels much is wiser than he who lives to a great age. Said of a traveller.

110.¹ ܣܪܐ ܕܘܣܟ ܙܘܢ ܠܐܪܥܐ. ܐܢܐ ܓܐ ܐܥܢ ܠܟܠܕܝ ܗܘܠ ܕܚܕܘܪ Spit on the ground; I will come back soon before it dries.

111. ܚܡܘܨܝ ܒܕܝܟܐ ܓܐ ܩܕܡܐ ܠܟܐܦܐ A sharp word cuts a stone. The opposite of 'Hard words break no bones.' The Syrians consider an insult worse than a blow.

¹ These to no. 123 inclusive are from Socin.

112. ܟܡܐ ܕܡܝ̈ܐ ܕܪܐ ܦܝܫܝ ܒܚܕܐ ܕܘܟܐ: ܒܣ ܡܣܪܚܝ *Whenever water remains long in one place it stinks.* 'Familiarity breeds contempt'?

113. ܡܬܠܐ ܟܪܝܐ ܚܠܝܐ *A short proverb is sweet.* 'Short and sweet.'

114. ܟܠ ܐܝܟܐ ܕܐܚܕܬ ܠܗ ܒܐܝܕܘܟ: ܐܗܐ ܕܘܢܝܐ ܒܬ ܥܒܪܐ: ܕܘܙ ܝܠܗ ܒܬ ܐܙܠܐ *However you may hold it in your hand, this world will pass away; certainly it will go.*

115. ܬܪ̈ܥܐ ܕܐܚܝܕ̈ܐ: ܒܠ̈ܝܐ ܥܒܝܪ̈ܐ *Doors locked, misfortunes past.* 'Ignorance is bliss.'

116. ܐܝܟ ܟܡܐ ܕܕܡܟ ܐܪܢܒܐ: ܗܕܟ ܗܘܝܐ ܒܬ ܪܗܛܐ *The more a hare sleeps the more she runs.* Said by a lazy man to excuse himself.

117. ܡܐܝܟܐ ܙܒܢܘܟ ܐܗܐ ܗܘܢܐ *Whence did you buy this wisdom?* Said ironically to a foolish person.

118. ܟܕ ܡܪܝܐ ܐܠܗܐ ܡܦܠܓܠܗ ܗܘܐ ܗܘܢܐ: ܐܢܐ ܠܐ ܝܘܢ ܗܘܐ ܬܡܐ *When God was dividing intellect, I was not there.*

119. ܓܒܪܐ ܚܕܐ ܢܘܪܐ: ܒܟܬܐ ܬܫܥ ܢܘܪ̈ܐ *A man is one fire, a woman nine.* (Said of love.)

120. ܐܢ ܐܢܐ ܒܬ ܡܢܫܝܢܘܟ: ܒܬ ܡܢܫܝܢܗ ܝܡܝܢܝ *If I forget you I will forget my right hand.* Cf. Ps. cxxxvii. 5.

121. ܓܘܠܐ ܐܟܠܠܗ ܝܘܢ: ܦܝܫܐ ܠܗ ܡܘܚܕܐ *I have eaten the sack and the little bag remains.* Said by an old man.

122. ܟܐܦܐ ܝܩܘܪܬܐ ܒܕܘܟܬܐ ܕܓܢܘܗ *A heavy stone remains in its place.* Qy., the converse of 'A rolling stone gathers no moss'?

123. ܟܠܗ ܕܘܢܝܐ ܕܣܝܪܬ ܠܝ: ܐܬܪܐ ܕܝܝ ܚܠܝܐ ܝܘܢ ܠܝ *Though I have travelled over the whole world, I found my own country the sweetest.* 'There is no place like home.'

124. ܣܡܨ̈ܪܐ *We have stripped the ass, his tail remains.* We have broken the neck of the task.

125. ܘܕܝܚ ܠܗ ܝܡܚܐ K. *The sun has risen.* [Same as no. 37.]

126. ܝܡܚܐ ܚܡܡܕܐ ܠܗ ܪܫܐ ܕܚܓ̈ܐ *The heat is burning the bald men's heads.* Said sarcastically of a very cold place.

127. ܪܚܝܐ ܚܪܒܐ ܐܝܬ ܒܗ ܬܪܝܢ ܚܛܛ̈ܐ U. *A deserted mill has two hoppers* [see no. 44]. Said of a poor room which yet has some one good thing in it.

128. ܟܝܣܗ ܕܘܝܕܝ ܢܩܒܐ *His pocket has a hole in it.* Said of a spendthrift.

129. ܕܘܢܝܐ ܕܬܪܢܓܠܐ ܙܒܠܬܐ *The cock's world is the dung-hill.* Said of a narrow-minded person.

130. ܓܒܪܐ ܙܩܢܐ ܕܩܢܐ ܬܪܬܝܢ ܐܢܬ̈ܐ ܚܢܐ ܘܡܢܐ ܚܢܐ ܣܒܬܐ ܘܡܢܐ ܛܠܝܬܐ ܚܢܐ ܡܢܛܦܐ ܡܢ ܕܩܢܗ ܣܥܪܐ ܐܘܟܡܐ ܘܡܢܐ ܚܘܪܐ ܥܕ ܕܩܢܐ ܕܦܢܐ K. *A man married two wives, Khana and Mana. Khana was old and Mana young. Khana plucked the black hairs out of his beard, and Mana the white hairs, till his beard was finished.* Said of a man who tries to please everybody and pleases none.

ADDITIONS AND CORRECTIONS.

P. 6, l. 2, *add* (also ܒܚܕ).

l. 21, 22, *for* make, *read* makes; *for* Jamel, Jamal.

p. 7, l. 7, *after* sounded, *add* unless final.

p. 10, par. (7), *add* There are no half vowels for Shva; thus ܒܢܝ is *bné* not *běné*.

The conjunction ܘ *and* is sometimes pronounced *wĕ* in Al.

l. 23, *for* § 37 *b*, *read* § 87 *b*.

p. 16, *sub fine*, *add* In writing O.S. the Eastern Syrians use the following :—ܘܗ or ܘܿܗ, both pronounced *how*, used before a relative and when = *ille*; ܘܗ or ܘܼܗ, both pronounced *ŭ*, used as a copula, the ܗ being often omitted, as ܟܐܒ for ܘܗ ܟܐܒ or ܘܼܗ ܟܐܒ *he is good*; ܘܗ, pronounced *hŭ*, = *iste*. Also ܗܘܝܘ, pronounced *hŭyŭ*, = *he is*. The feminine usage is similar.

p. 27, l. 8, *add* ܠܝܠܝ m. f. *night* = O.S. ܠܠܝܐ m. (for ܠܝܠܝܐ); ܥܠܡ *eternity*, used both as abs. and constr. state; perhaps also ܕܥܣܒ f. *ease, relief*, lit. *wideness*, and ܡܢܫܠܝ *suddenly*, ܡܢܕܪܫ Ti. *again*, pp. 165, 166, for ܣܓܕܐ ܣܝܓ see p. 308. See also Proverb 20 (p. 347).

p. 31, l. 9, *after* genders, *add* and numbers; rarely a superfluous Dalath follows.

l. 22, *add* ܢܘܡܚ ܠܦ Al. *the west*; so ܢܘܡܚ ܘܕܫ Al. *the east*.

l. 24, *for* ܘܕܦ *read* ܘܕܩ.

p. 32, l. 6, *for* ܕܗܟܐ *read* ܕܗܘܗ.

p. 34, l. 1, *add* also ܟܣܬܐ U.; *after* head, *add* and temples.

l. 6, *for* (a bird), *read* a lizard.

sub fine, *add* to masculines ܚܒܛ *calico*, ܕܟܐ *braid*, ܡܚܡܨ *fist*.

pp. 35, 36, *add* ܓܲܕܵܐ is sometimes fem. in N.S. *Add also* ܐܬܪܵܐ *country*, m., rarely f. N.S.: m. O.S.; ܟܲܐܣܵܐ *metal bowl*, f. N.S. = ܟܣܵܐ m. O.S.; ܚܘܼܕܪܵܐ *kiln*, m. O.S., f. N.S.; ܚܘܼܕܵܗܝ *seat*, f. N.S. = O.S.; ܡܸܛܪܵܐ m.; ܡܸܛܪܵܐ *rain*, f. U.K., m. Q., O.S.; ܥܲܕܵܠܵܐ *lamp*, is m. in Baz, f. in Q. The following are m. in Q.:— ܛܲܗܪܵܐ, ܒܓܲܕܵܐ, ܬܲܘܕܵܐ, ܡܕܝܼܢܬܵܐ, ܠܲܒܵܐ, ܓܝܼܢܵܬܵܐ.

p. 37, l. 15, ܕܸܟܵܐ is m. and f. in Q.

l. 18, ܡܲܠܕܲܓܼܵܐ is also found. *Add to fem.* ܓܕܝܼܢܬܵܐ from ܓܲܕܵܐ *kid*.

p. 38, *add* ܩܘܿܦܵܐ f. *frog*, ܩܲܣܝܼܢܵܐ *tadpole*; ܓܕܵܢܵܐ f. and ܓܸܕܢܝܼܬܵܐ or ܣܘܼܕܢܝܼܬܵܐ *all = corner*; the fem. of ܟܲܠܕܵܐ is also ܟܲܠܕܬܵܐ.

p. 41, l. 18, *add also* ܨܵܦܲܢܟܵܐ ; cf. p. 334.

pp. 41, sqq., *add to regular plurals* :—

(1) ܓܲܟܹܢܹܐ m. *braid*; ܚܝܼܢܹܐ m. *calico*; ܓܲܕܵܓܹܐ O.S., also ܓ K., a herb found in K., Numb. xi. 5; ܚܲܩܹܐ *loins*. ܬܘܼܓܹܐ *mulberry*, makes ܬܘܵܗܹܐ in Q.

(2) ܕܸܕܹܐ Al. *breast*; ܗܲܡܕܹܐ Al. m. *master* (also 3, see § 19); ܚܵܝܹܐ U. Tkh. *breast*; ܣܲܠܵܐ m. *basket* (with handle), in Al.: elsewhere 1. [ܒܸܚܕܹܐ is rarely 1, and in Al. 3; ܓܲܕܵܐ is also 1 in Q. etc.] ܕܹܟܹܐ *head*, ܟܘܼܡܹܐ *mouth*, in Al. take 2. [ܠܲܓܹܐ is also 1].

(2a) ܓܕܵܡܸܓ m. (U. form) *evening*, sometimes; ܓܕܵܡܸܓ K. m. also takes 3.

(3) ܓܕܲܠܵܐ f. *watch of the night*, also 1; ܕܘܼܡܵܐ K. O.S., or ܕܲܟܵܗ K. *owl* f.; ܟܹܠܵܐ f. *time*, in Tkh. Al. p. 70; ܚܘܼܠܬܵܐ f. *fruitstone*, also 1; ܠܸܩܢܵܐ f. *kneading tray*; ܕܘܿܕܵܐ f. *pearl*; ܘܸܕܵܐ f. *marsh*; ܣܘܿܕܵܐ f. *treasure*, also 1 [also ܣܘܿܝܼܵܐ f. 1]; ܛܵܘܵܐ (a large bird); ܚܵܘܕܵܐ f. *flour bin*; ܚܸܓܵܐ f. *wooden disc* used in the game of 'touch,' also *the holder of the disc*; ܓܲܕܵܐ f. *garden bed*; ܓܲܕܵܐ m. f. *sledge*, also 1; ܡܘܼܓܕܵܐ f. *leather bag*, also 1; ܡܸܛܪܵܐ m. f. *rain*; [ܡܸܥܢܬܵܐ f. *grindstone*, also takes 1]; ܓܸܣܬܵܐ (N.S. ܬ, O.S. ܒ) *heel*, also 1; ܟܘܼܡܕܵܐ m. *candle*, in Ti., elsewhere 1; ܗܘܼܦܟܵܐ

m. *table cloth, table set for meals*, in Al., elsewhere 1; ܡܘܕܐ f. *arch*; ܕܚܓܐ Al. *ship* (= ܠܒܐ U.).

(4) [ܓܕܐ Q. *husband* (= ܒܐ U.) takes 1]; ܓܘܐ m. *walnut tree* (with 1, *walnut*); ܓܠܐ (p. 44) in Q., in the sense *stacked hay*; ܓܕܢܐ Al. Ti. m. *arm* (= ܓܕܢܐ p. 46); so Q. but with pl. as U.; ܘܡܨܡܐ m. K. *summer pasturage* (the camp), also 1; ܒܘܢܐ m. *kinsman*, also 1; ܣܠܘܟܐ m. *wedding feast*, also 1; ܣܒܕܐ m. *leaven*, also 1; [ܓܕܐ m. *mountain*, O.S., also takes 1]; ܒܠܥܐ m. *herb*, also 1; ܕܗܪܐ f. *noon, midday meal*, also 1; ܓܕܐ m. *pocket hole*; ܓܠܐ m. U. *buffalo bull*, also 1 (= ܠܒܕ K.); ܓܘܐ m. *cotton plant*, O.S.; ܒܣܐ m. *dough*, also 1; ܣܦܬܐ f. *edge of a roof*; ܩܘܡܐ *nostril*, in Al. (also 5); ܦܕܐ m. *hamstring*; ܚܘܦ K. m. *porch*; ܨܒܐ m. *summer*, O.S., also 1; ܒܠܐ f. *nest*, O.S., also 3; [ܕܐ also takes 4 in the sense of *head*]; ܥܒܐ m. *door post*, in U.; also 1 in Q.; ܥܕܟܐ (p. 46) in Q. makes ܥܕܟܒܐ; ܓܕܐ m. *he goat*, also 1, Turk. (= O.S. ܗܒܟܐ).

(5) ܓܠܐ (or ܓܠܠܐ) K. *shadow*, = O.S. ܓܠܠܐ; ܦܕܕܐ m. *curtain*, usually 1; ܥܬܘܟܐ *wisp of hair* (with 1, *head of grain*); [ܓܦܐ, ܘܘܟܐ and ܡܣܬܐ Al. also take 1].

(8) ܗܒܢܐ Tkh. f. *present* = ܒܠܟܐ § 45 f.; [ܚܕܘܓܐ also takes 6]; ܣܠܕܐ f. *grandmother*, in Al.

(9) ܒܘܒܐ f. *shrub*, also *sleeve*; ܒܘܓܐ f. *ewe lamb* (one year old); ܒܓܕܐ f. Al. *female companion*, § 17; ܒܣܐ K. f. *midwife* (= ܡܚܨܕܐ U.); ܓܚܕܐ Al. f. *round cake* (= ܓܕܦܐ U.); [in Q. the sing. of ܒܘܕܕܐ is also ܒܘܓܕܐ and ܒܘܓܘܕܐ].

S. GR. 46

p. 42, l. 2, *for* 8 lbs., *read* 4 lbs.

p. 45, ܟܘܦܐ also f.; *for* ܟܕܐ f. *thigh*, *read* ܟܕܐ f. *rump* (half); so p. 47; *for* ܠܟܬܘܕܐ *read* ܠܟܬܘܕܐ (singular rare); ܗܡܨܐ is fem.

p. 46, ܗܘܦܐ in Q. is *an axle; for* ܓܝܡܨܐ *read* ܓܝܡܨܐ (p. 338); for ܕܘܕܐ, ܕܘܕܝܠ is used in Q.; ܕܟܢܐ is fem.

p. 50, *add* ܟܣܐ f. *knife*, pl. ܟܣܬܬܐ (Turk.); *for* ܓܠܟܐ in Q. they say ܓܠܐ (first Zlama).

p. 51, ܡܘܟܐ in Q. makes also ܡܘܘܠ.

p. 52, l. 1, *add* Singular in Q. also ܒܩܐ *kernel*.

ܠܩܢܐ K. f. *fever*, and ܢܕܟܐ f. *end*, have no pl.; the latter borrows that of ܢܫܕܘܡܗܐ.

p. 53, *add* In Q. K. the masculine forms ܠܝܒܟܡܐ, ܢܓܙܡܚܢܐ (also ܓܝ ?), ܓܢܓܐ, ܗܡܓܡܐ, ܡܝܥܡܝܓܐ, ܡܓܐ, ܠܟܠܟܬܘܡܐ are also used; in Q. ܩܝܘܓܐ is *a hazel nut*.

l. 7, *for* ܕܝܕܟܢܐ *read* ܕܝܕܟܢܐ.

sub fine, add ܩܘܠܟܢܐ *pea*, pl. ܩܘܠܟܐ and 6.

p. 54, l. 10, ܗܘܡܕܟܢܐ is used in Q. for *a little girl's trousers*.

p. 55, l. 20, *for* (O.S. ܒ) *read* (O.S. دِبْ).

p. 56, par. (12), *for* Bas, *read* Baz; *add* ܡܠܓܢܘܒ is also used.

p. 58, par. (5), *add* ܟܝܕܐ *high spirited* (as a horse), ܓܠܟܐ *speckled*, ܚܘܠܟܐ Al. *lame*, make fem. in ܐ.

par. (7), ܡܒܟܐ in Al. makes fem. ܡܒܟܐ.

par. (8), *add* ܢܓܦܐ *heathen*, and ܓܢܦܐ *unclean*, do not take the euphonic vowel in the feminine.

sub fine, *for* absolute, *read* limited.

p. 59, l. 8, *for* ܩܢܣܐ, ܩܢܣܢܐ *read* ܩܢܣܐ, ܩܢܣܢܐ.

ADDITIONS AND CORRECTIONS.

p. 64, In Al. the K. feminines are used, except for *nine*. But ܒܰܓ is used before ܐܰܠܳܗܳܐ.

p. 69, *add* ܕܟܰܗܘܳܕܰܝܣܽܘ ܕܟܰܗܘܳܕܰܟ Al. or ܕܟܰܗܘܳܕܰܘܢ Al.

p. 70, l. 13, *add to the list* ܓܰܗܕܳܐ Tkh. f. *time*, ܓܰܕ Tkh. f. *id.*

p. 74, Sachau gives for Al. ܗܘܳܕܳܐ m., ܡܠܟܬܳܐ f. *(ilei)* ; ܡܕܳܐ m. ܗܳܘܳܘܣܳܐ f.

p. 75, *sub fine, add* But in Al. ܚܰܕ ܡܠܳܐ is *kmélé*.

p. 79, l. 9, *for* ܕܺܡܣܳܢܳܐ, ܕܺܡܣܺܢܳܐ *read* ܕܺܡܺܢܳܐ, ܕܺܡܺܢܳܐ.

p. 83, Also ܕܳܗܳܐ ܩܕܺܡܬܳܐ Al. (paradigm form).

p. 96, ܐܶܗܕܐ is used alone for the infin. in Al., but also ܠܳܐ.

p. 99, ܓܕܳܓ. Imperat. also ܣܰܓܶܓ in Al. as O.S.

p. 100, Sachau gives for Al. *gále* for 3 sing., but *gálitûn* 2 pl., *gáli* 3 m. pl., *gálei* 3 f. pl.; *glélé* for 3 sing. pret.

p. 104, In Al. ܟܰܠ verbs in first present and pret. are often treated as if ܠܳܐ ; as for ܟܰܪܝܺܕܳܗܝ , *shmélé*. The pl. imperat. is also ܟܰܗܶܟܳܗܶܟ Al.

p. 112, l. 1, 2, *for* ܥ *read* ܣܘ *throughout* (cf. p. 322).

p. 119, ܘܰܕܙ. In Al., imperative also ܘܰܕ.

p. 120, ܙܳܗܰܐ. Past part. ܙܳܗܺܐ Al.

p. 126, ܗܶܓܳܐ. In Al. pret. *also* ܡܶܓܺܗܰܗܘ (first Zlama) ; with fem. object ܡܰܣܓܒܺܗܰܪ ; the verbal noun ܗܰܓܠܳܐ is much used by itself as a noun of action.

p. 131, ܓܡܰܚܡ, ܡܚܰܡܳܐ also used in Al. The verbal noun in Al. is ܡܚܰܕܗܳܐ.

p. 134, In Al. for ܟܰܠܕܺܬܳܗܝ *I shew her*, we have also ܟܰܠܕܶܬܳܗܝ, second Zlama (p. 81, note).

p. 137, So in Al. ܠܺܝ ܥܓܶܒ is *he left me* as well as *I left*.

p. 156, l. 5, *for* ܗܳܕܺܝ *read* ܗܳܕܶܝ. Add to Alqosh adverbs : 2ܡܣܓܕܳܐ (both ܓ) together, ܕܟܰܕܟܶܒܶܗ *apart*, ܕܺܕܳܗܶܕ *immediately*, ܚܰܓܕܰܢܳܐ *perhaps* (p. 203, l. 4), ܓܶܬܺܒܳܐ and ܚܰܓܒܳܐ *very*, ܠܶܟܕܳܐ (*lékun*) and ܟܳܘܗܳܐ *perhaps*,

ܒܵܬ݂ܵܪ ܕܵܢܵܗ ܟܠܗ ‎ thereafter, ܡܚܣܘܼܒܵܐ ‎ early (p. 290), ܩܵܡܝ ‎ why, ܒܿܓ݂ܵܐ ‎
or ܒܿܓ݂ܵܐ ܒܸܓ݂ ‎ somewhat, ܒܿܕܝܼܒܵܐ ‎ near.

p. 193, l. 7, for ἐγω, read ἐγώ.

p. 201, l. 16, for ܒܿܚܸܕ݂ܟ݂ܵܐ ‎ read ܒܿܚܝܼܕ݂ܟ݂ܵܐ ‎ or ܒܿܚܝܼܕ݂ ‎ (Arab.).

p. 209, l. 4, for ܗܘܵܩܕܵܐ ‎ read ܗܘܿܩܕܵܐ ‎.

     l. 12, for ܒܚܿܘܡܝ ‎ read ܒܐܘܿܡܝ ‎.

p. 225, l. 5, add The U. agent of ܚܿܡܹܐ ‎ to be extinguished, to die (p. 103), is ܒܿܚܸܡܘܿܝܵܐ ‎.

p. 232, add ܒܿܕ݂ܘܿܩܵܐ ‎ green, Al.

p. 235, l. 16, for ܘܿܕܲܩܵܐ ‎ read ܒܿܕܲܩܵܐ ‎.

p. 249, sub fine, for a calf, read an arm; for amulet, read armlet.

p. 250, l. 22, for ܒܿܚܘܿܡܹܬܘܿ ‎ read ܒܐܘܿܡܹܬܘܿ ‎.

p. 258, l. 6, for ܡܲܚܿܕܝܼ ‎ read ܡܲܚܿܕܝܼ ‎ (Arab. كنص).

www.ingramcontent.com/pod-product-compliance
Lightning Source LLC
Chambersburg PA
CBHW030344230426
43664CB00007BB/532